# THE TRAGIC ERA
*The Revolution after Lincoln*

ANDREW JOHNSON

# THE TRAGIC ERA

## The Revolution after Lincoln

BY

## CLAUDE G. BOWERS

THE LITERARY GUILD OF AMERICA

Incorporated

1929

The Riverside Press
CAMBRIDGE · MASSACHUSETTS
PRINTED IN THE U.S.A.

# PREFACE

IF Hilaire Belloc is right in his opinion that 'readable history is melodrama,' the true story of the twelve tragic years that followed the death of Lincoln should be entertaining. They were years of revolutionary turmoil, with the elemental passions predominant, and with broken bones and bloody noses among the fighting factionalists. The prevailing note was one of tragedy, though, as we shall see, there was an abundance of comedy, and not a little of farce. Never have American public men in responsible positions, directing the destiny of the Nation, been so brutal, hypocritical, and corrupt. The Constitution was treated as a doormat on which politicians and army officers wiped their feet after wading in the muck. Never has the Supreme Court been treated with such ineffable contempt, and never has that tribunal so often cringed before the clamor of the mob.

So appalling is the picture of these revolutionary years that even historians have preferred to overlook many essential things. Thus, Andrew Johnson, who fought the bravest battle for constitutional liberty and for the preservation of our institutions ever waged by an Executive, until recently was left in the pillory to which unscrupulous gamblers for power consigned him, because the unvarnished truth that vindicates him makes so many statues in public squares and parks seem a bit grotesque. That Johnson was maligned by his enemies because he was seeking honestly to carry out the conciliatory and wise policy of Lincoln is now generally understood, but even now few realize how intensely Lincoln was hated by the Radicals at the time of his death.

A complete understanding of this period calls for a reappraisal of many public men. Some statesmen we have been taught to reverence will appear in these pages in sorry rôles. Others, who played conspicuous parts, but have been denied the historical recognition due them, are introduced and shown in action. Thus the able leaders of the minority in Congress are given fuller treatment than has been fashionable, since they represented more Americans, North

and South, than the leaders of the Radical majority, and were
nearer right on the issues of reconstruction. Thus, too, the brilliant
and colorful leaders and spokesmen of the South are given their
proper place in the dramatic struggle for the preservation of
Southern civilization and the redemption of their people. I have
sought to re-create the black and bloody drama of these years, to
show the leaders of the fighting factions at close range, to picture
the moving masses, both whites and blacks, in North and South,
surging crazily under the influence of the poisonous propaganda on
which they were fed.

That the Southern people literally were put to the torture is
vaguely understood, but even historians have shrunk from the unhappy task of showing us the torture chambers. It is impossible to
grasp the real significance of the revolutionary proceedings of the
rugged conspirators working out the policies of Thaddeus Stevens
without making many journeys among the Southern people, and
seeing with our own eyes the indignities to which they were subjected. Through many unpublished contemporary family letters
and diaries, I have tried to show the psychological effect upon
them of the despotic policies of which they were the victims.
Brutal men, inspired by personal ambition or party motives, assumed the pose of philanthropists and patriots, and thus deceived
and misguided vast numbers of well-meaning people in the North.

In the effort to re-create the atmosphere and temper of the
times, I have made free use of the newspapers of those times. Invaluable for this purpose has been my access to the unpublished
diary of George W. Julian, which covers the entire period. Through
him we are able to sit in at important conferences that hitherto
have been closed to the historians.

Much attention has been given to the amusements and the social background because of the unprecedented prominence of
women throughout these struggles. Gay ribbons and furbelows
and flirting fans were not far distant from the fighting. The women ranged in culture and character from the incomparable Kate
Chase Sprague to the dusky sisters of the mixed salon in Columbia,
South Carolina. Never had women lobbyists used their sex in
securing legislative favors for selfish groups so brazenly — or so
cleverly. The tragedy of Mrs. Belknap is as significant of the

spirit of the times as the impeachment proceedings against Johnson.

The story of this Revolution is one of desperate enterprises, by daring and unscrupulous men, some of whom had genius of a high order. In these no Americans can take pride. The evil that they did lives after them. They changed the course of history, and whether for ultimate good or bad is still on the lap of the gods. The story carries lessons that are well worth pondering.

CLAUDE G. BOWERS

# CONTENTS

## VIII. THE REVOLUTION HURRIES ON

# CONTENTS

# CONTENTS

# CONTENTS

Visiting statesmen sent South — The claim in Louisiana — Notorious corruption of Returning Board — No Democratic member — How the Board worked — Criminals tabulate in secret — Garfield's part — The case of Amy Mitchell — Of Eliza Pinkston — Board for sale — Grant's 'visiting statesmen' charmed by nobility and integrity of Board — Proceedings in Florida — Situation in South Carolina — Returning Boards do their work — Threat of civil war — Sentiment of conservatives — Tilden's timidity and weakness — Conkling's attitude — The Democratic surrender — Hayes flirts with Southern members — Progress of negotiations with Southern Democrats — Schurz proposes Southerner in Cabinet — The bargain at Wormley's Hotel — Conkling again — Kate Chase Sprague — Hayes counted in — Reactions — Charles Francis Adams to Tilden — Conspirators rewarded — W. E. Chandler neglected — Blaine's appeal for him — A new policy — No further need of old — Final scenes in Columbia.

# ILLUSTRATIONS

# THE TRAGIC ERA
*The Revolution after Lincoln*

# THE TRAGIC ERA

•.•

## CHAPTER I

### 'THE KING IS DEAD; LONG LIVE THE KING'

#### I

A DISMAL drizzle of rain was falling as the dawn came to Washington after a night of terror. In the streets men stood in groups discussing the tragic drama on which the curtain had not yet fallen. The city was 'in a blaze of excitement and rage.'[1] Then, at seven-thirty, the tolling of all the church bells in the town, and a hush in the streets. Lincoln was dead.

At the Kirkwood Hotel[2] soldiers stood guard within and without, and before the door of a suite on the third floor an armed sentinel was stationed. The night before, Andrew Johnson, occupant of these rooms, had been awakened from a deep slumber and told of the tragedy at Ford's Theater. Shaken with emotion, he had clung momentarily to the fateful messenger, unable to speak. Then, disregarding the protests of his friends, he had turned up his coat collar, drawn his hat down over his face, and walked through the crowded streets to the deathbed of the stricken chief. There he had stood a brief moment, looking down with grief-corrugated face upon the dying man.[3] Thence he had hurried back to his closely guarded rooms.

With the tolling of the bells, he had been formally notified by the Lincoln Cabinet that the chief magistracy had passed to him; and at ten o'clock, in the presence of the members of the Cabinet, Senators, and a few intimate friends, he stood before Chief Justice Chase, with uplifted hand, and took the oath of office. He 'seemed to be oppressed by the suddenness of the call upon him,'[4] and yet, withal, 'calm and self-possessed.' The sobering ef-

---

[1] Julian, MS. Diary, April 15, 1865.    [2] On the site of the present Raleigh.
[3] Sumner to Bright, Pierce, IV, 241.    [4] *Men and Measures*, 376.

fect of power and responsibility accentuated his natural dignity of mien. Kissing the Bible, his lips pressed the twenty-first verse of the eleventh chapter of Ezekiel.[1]

'You are President,' said Chase. 'May God support, guide, and bless you in your arduous duties.'

The witnesses pressed forward to take his hand, and he spoke briefly, pledging that his policies would be those of his predecessor 'in all essentials.' [2] Then, requesting the Cabinet to remain, as the others filed out, he instructed them to proceed with their duties,[3] and 'in the language of entreaty' asked them to 'stand by him in his difficult and responsible position.' [4] That very night Charles Sumner, bitterly hostile to the reconstruction plans of Lincoln, intruded upon the new President with indecent haste to discuss 'public business,' [5] and that very day one of the Radical leaders was complaining that Johnson 'has been already in the hands of Chase, the Blairs, Halleck, Grant & Co.' [6]

## II

Nowhere did the murder fall so like a pall as in the South. 'A canard!' cried Clay, of Alabama, in concealment with other Confederate leaders in the country home of Ben Hill in Georgia, when the news reached him; and when the verification came he exclaimed in tones of anguish, 'Then God help us! If that is true, it is the worst blow that has yet been struck the South.' [7] Even the young Southern girls were horrified and instantly sensed the significance of the deed.[8] Vallandigham, the 'copperhead,' thought it the 'beginning of evils,' since even those who had opposed Lincoln's policy had come 'to turn to him for deliverance,' because 'his course in the last three months has been most liberal and conciliatory.' [9]

It was this very policy of conciliation that so easily reconciled the party leaders in Washington to Lincoln's death. They had launched their fight against it long before; had sought to prevent

[1] Chase's story, Warden, 640.
[2] Welles, II, 289.
[3] Ibid.
[4] Men and Measures, 376.
[5] Sumner to Bright, Pierce, IV, 241.
[6] Julian, MS. Diary, April 15, 1865.
[7] Belle of the Fifties, 245.
[8] Confederate Girl's Diary, 436; Mrs. Brooks, MS. Diary, April 21, 1865.
[9] Life of Vallandigham, 406.

his nomination in 1864; and it was just a little while before that the Wade-Davis Manifesto had shaken and shocked the Nation with its brutal denunciation of Lincoln's reconstruction plan. At the moment of his death there was no lonelier man in public life than Lincoln.

This Manifesto was an accurate expression of the spirit of the congressional leadership of his party. It referred contemptuously to 'the dictation of his political ambition'; denounced his action on the Wade-Davis reconstruction plan as 'a stupid outrage on the legislative authority of the people'; warned that Lincoln had 'presumed on the forbearance which the supporters of his Administration had so long practiced'; and demanded that he 'confine himself to his executive duties.' A more outrageous castigation of a President had never been written. The exigencies of a presidential campaign had forced a semblance of harmony, but the feeling of hostility which bristles in this document was beating fiercely beneath the surface when the assassin's bullet removed this conciliatory figure from the pathway of the leaders. 'Its expression never found its way to the people,' wrote Julian, though in both branches of Congress there were probably not ten Republicans who really favored the renomination of Lincoln in 1864.[1] Thus, among the Radicals, 'while everybody was shocked at his murder, the feeling was nearly universal that the accession of Johnson would prove a Godsend to our cause.' [2]

With a strange insensibility, these men, soon to dominate, left the Nation to bury its dead, while they turned instantly to devices definitely to end the Lincoln policies through his successor. That Johnson would fall in with their plans they had no doubt. Had any one surpassed the violence of his denunciations of the Southerners in 1864? Had he not talked of confiscation and punishment for treason? Thus, they reasoned, he would readily agree to a reconstruction imposed upon the South by the 'Loyalists' there and the Radicals of the North.[3] Besides, they thought, Johnson's previous association with the Committee on the Conduct of the War would put him 'onto the right track.' [4] They thought, too, that Grant's was a descending star, because 'his terms with Lee

---

[1] Julian, *Recollections*, 244.    [2] *Ibid.*, 255.    [3] Sherman, *Recollections*, I, 359.
[4] Julian, MS. Diary, April 16, 1865.

were too easy,[1] and Thad Stevens, speaking at Lancaster three days before Lincoln's death, had denounced the terms with the declaration that he would dispossess those participating in the rebellion of 'every foot of ground they pretend to own.' [2]

Scarcely had the body of the murdered President turned cold when, on the very morning of his death, members of the war committee that had been so obnoxious to Lincoln hastened to Johnson, but they found him in no mood to discuss anything but the apprehension of the assassins.[3] This rebuff, however, did not deter Charles Sumner. That night, as we have seen, less than twenty-four hours after the murder, found him seated in the Kirkwood House urging negro suffrage upon Johnson.

That afternoon, within eight hours of Lincoln's death, a caucus of the Radicals was conferring on plans to rid the Government of the Lincoln influence. One of the participants, who 'liked the radical tone,' was 'intolerably disgusted' with the 'profanity and obscenity.' There, among others, sat Ben Wade, Zack Chandler, and Wilkeson, correspondent of the 'New York Tribune,' who proposed 'to put Greeley on the war path.' In the discussion as reported, 'the hostility for Lincoln's policy of conciliation and contempt for his weakness' was 'undisguised,' and 'the universal sentiment among radical men' was that 'his death is a Godsend to our cause.' Moving with revolutionary celerity, these practical men had agreed to urge on Johnson the reconstruction of his Cabinet 'to get rid of the last vestige of Lincolnism,' and Ben Butler was chosen for Secretary of State! [4]

Sunday was a wearisome day for the new President. Lincoln's body was resting in the East Room of the White House. The city was silent and sad, with crape everywhere fluttering in a chilly breeze. Temporary offices had been provided Johnson in the Treasury, and there, in the morning, he met his Cabinet in a general discussion of reconstruction plans, in which Johnson's attitude was one of severity.[5]

The members of the Cabinet filed out, the Radical Republican leaders filed in. 'Johnson, we have faith in you,' exclaimed Ben

---

[1] Julian, MS. Diary, April 16, 1865.  [2] *Lancaster Intelligencer*, March 21, 1867.
[3] *Life of Chandler*, 279.
[4] Julian, MS. Diary, April 15, 1865.  [5] Welles, II, 291.

Wade, explosively. 'By the gods, there will be no trouble running the government.' The presidential reply was such that the visitors 'applauded his declarations and parted after a very pleasant interview.'[1]

Leaving the Treasury, the conspirators hurried to the Willard to meet Ben Butler, who had hastened to the city. He, too, had other fish to fry than to bow at the bier of Lincoln. Had he not been slated for Secretary of State? He was 'in fine spirits,' and that night he, too, had a conference with Johnson. No doubt in Butler's mind about the necessity for a new Cabinet. 'The President must not administer on the estate of Lincoln,' he said with his squint.[2]

Sunday night found the conspirators nervously active. Sumner and a few Radicals were in conference with Stanton on the reconstruction plan for Virginia, and Sumner, listening, interrupted to inquire what provision was made for the negroes to vote.[3]

Clearly, Stanton was no stranger to this Radical group.

Thus, with events seemingly moving satisfactorily for the Radicals, nothing was being taken for granted, for there were skeptics. Grim old Thad Stevens, the genius of the group, was grinding his teeth impatiently in the red-brick house in Lancaster; and Professor Goldwin Smith, describing Johnson's accession as 'an appalling event,' was calling for impeachment before he had been three days in office. Nor was Ben Butler taking any chances. Just three days after Lincoln's death, he was declaiming within hearing distance of the White House that as for Virginia 'the time has not come for holding any relations with her but that of the conqueror to the conquered.'[4] This denunciation 'of the noblest acts of the late President' and 'inflaming excited crowds into senseless cheers for the policy which that Magistrate ever refused to approve,' by 'an unscrupulous general whose cowardice and incapacity always left his enemies unharmed upon the field,' was attacked by the 'New York World.'[5] The very day Butler was speaking, Johnson, a stenographer beside him, was addressing an Illinois delegation, and at the conclusion a copy of his remarks was handed to him. Glancing over the copy, and noting his pledge to continue the Lincoln policies, he asked if his meaning had not been slightly

---

[1] Julian, MS. Diary, April 16, 1865.    [2] *Ibid.*    [3] Welles, II, 291.
[4] *New York World*, April 21, 1865.    [5] April 22, 1865.

changed. Preston King, intimate friend and adviser, suggested that all reference to Lincoln be omitted, and Johnson nodded assent. This incident encouraged the Radicals still more.[1]

Thus, with the body of the martyr still in the capital, the politicians, and, for a time, the President with them, were engaged in the speedy burial of the programme of conciliation and concession. Thus the burial of Lincoln was left to the people, for the politicians were too busy with their plans to be diverted by a dead President, who, to them, was well out of the way.

### III

Four days after the death of Lincoln, his funeral was held in the East Room. During this period the city was in mourning; no smiles on the faces of the plain people in the streets. While the politicians were drinking, smoking, joking, boasting. planning, indulging in profanity and obscenity in many conferences behind closed doors, the men and women of no importance were filing by the casket of the dead. No martial music now. Everything was swathed in black. Ben Wade, soon to become an idol of his Radical associates, was decent enough to remain away.[2] The day before, crowds began pouring into the city, and all day long the ordinary people had been struggling for admission to the White House.[3]

Two days more, and all that was left of the War President was removed from the capital, and we shall find that, for at least three years, Lincoln was dead indeed at the scene of his greatness.

### IV

With the black-draped funeral train of Lincoln speeding westward, the enemies of his policy turned with increased determination to the management of his successor. From nine in the morning until five in the evening, he could be found at the Treasury, and hither hurried the Radical leaders to cultivate him, and here delegations marched in processions. Johnson saw them all. The doors were all but thrown wide open to the world. The luncheon hour found him with a cup of tea and a cracker. In the six weeks of his incumbency of his temporary quarters, there was certainly no

---

[1] Blaine, II, 9–11.   [2] *Life of Wade*, 13.   [3] Julian, MS. Diary, April 18, 1865.

whiskey in the room; and yet, so bitter were some of his speeches toward the Southern aristocrats and leaders that Secretary McCulloch 'should have attributed them to the use of stimulants if he had not known them to be the speeches of a sober man.'[1]

Every evening he might have been seen, a little weary, driving to the comfortable home of Representative Samuel Hooper at H and Fifteenth Streets, which had been placed at his disposal until Mrs. Lincoln could conveniently leave the White House. There he lived in close communion with Preston King.[2]

Any one familiar with the Washington of the previous decade, with its lordly leisure and aristocratic elegance, would scarcely have recognized, in the city of the summer of 1865, the town he had known before. Society was dull, the doors of the finer houses closed. The long rows of grinning negro slaves had disappeared from the streets, and the pompously dignified and unctuous gentlemen who had lolled in the large armchairs of the lobbies and parlors of hotels were no longer to be seen. A correspondent observed that 'a crowd of bristling short-haired Puritans had pushed them from their stools.'[3] Droves of strange negroes, flocking in from the South, laughing uproariously, and a bit too conscious of their freedom, jostled the pedestrians on the streets. The martial tread of army officers resounded on the pavements, and sharp-faced, furtive-eyed speculators and gamblers were seen everywhere, and women of indifferent morality, soon to become so familiar to the capital, had already begun their march upon the town with much swishing of skirts.[4]

It was in this atmosphere and environment that the Radicals intrigued and fought to mould the policy of Johnson. Their earlier talks with him indicated a sympathy so complete that they were a little concerned lest he go too far in the way of punishing the Southern leaders. Some gloomily foresaw a 'bloody assizes.'[5] Julian vacillated awhile from one view to the other. Accompanying the Indiana delegation on a visit to Johnson, and hearing Oliver P. Morton read 'a carefully prepared essay' to the effect that 'there is no power to punish rebels collectively by reducing a

---

[1] *Men and Measures*, 374.   [2] *New York Herald*, June 2, 1865.
[3] *New York World*, June 6, 1865.   [4] *Destruction and Reconstruction*, 241.
[5] Blaine, II, 13; Schurz, *Reminiscences*, II, 150.

State to a territorial condition,'[1] Julian was puzzled by Johnson's apparent acquiescence. It was discouraging to hear him declaring himself opposed 'to consolidation, or to the centralization of power in the hands of a few.'[2] Not so assuring, certainly, as the Illinois address, a few days before, to the effect that 'the American people must be taught . . . that treason is a crime and must be punished.'[3] And yet, a week later, following a conference with Johnson, Julian recorded that the President 'talks like a man on the subject of confiscation and treason.'[4] Sumner, who lingered far into May to influence the presidential mind on the negroes and suffrage, was convinced of Johnson's sympathy. 'He accepted this idea completely,' wrote Sumner to John Bright.[5] 'Our new President accepts the principle and the application of negro suffrage,' he wrote another.[6] 'I am charmed with his sympathy, which is entirely different from his predecessor's,' he wrote another.[7] In his numerous contacts, Sumner found 'his manner excellent and even sympathetic' and on negro suffrage 'well disposed'; and after conferring with him on the subject, Sumner and Chief Justice Chase had 'left him light-hearted.'

However, Carl Schurz was not so certain, thinking Johnson's statements on negro suffrage 'betrayed rather an unsettled state of mind.'[8] Telling themselves over and over that Johnson was with them, the Radicals were becoming uneasy by the middle of May. It was disconcerting, maddening, to note the sympathetic tone of the Democratic press toward him,[9] and its suggestion that he would play a great rôle in history 'by strictly adhering to the letter and the spirit of the Constitution and by a wise and conciliatory course toward the masses of the Southern people.'[10] It was manifestly dangerous to permit this to proceed unchallenged. Stanton, always Master of the Back Stairs, bethought him of Johnson's admiration for Senator Fessenden, and implored him to use his influence.[11] A conference was called to devise ways and means of saving the Administration from conservative influence

[1] Foulkes, I, 440.　　　　[2] Moore, Johnson, 484.　　　　[3] Ibid., 470.
[4] Julian, MS. Diary, May 4, 1865.　　　　[5] Pierce, IV, 241.
[6] To Scheiden, Pierce, IV, 242.　　　　[7] To Lieber, Pierce, IV, 242.
[8] Schurz, Reminiscences, II, 150.　　　　[9] New York World, April 17, 1865.
[10] Ibid., April 19, 1865.　　　　[11] Life of Fessenden, II, 12.

and control. There sat Wade, Sumner, Chandler, Julian, and others, but 'nothing was done,' wrote Julian in his diary.[1] Both Sumner and Wade scouted the idea that Johnson was unfavorable to negro suffrage, and Julian and Chandler left, a little reassured.

But not so all the old-line Abolitionists; and the very night the politicians were conferring in Washington, Wendell Phillips was declaring to a cheering crowd at Cooper Union, in New York, that the ballot for the negro was imperative. He was not opposed to State rights within limits. 'If we are ever to be saved from the corruption of power, it will be by these break-waters.' A strange mood possessed the orator that night — he spoke even against a policy of vengeance. The audience sat sullen. But not for long. Up sprang a young man with long black hair and a poet's face, to declare that 'the punishment of treason is death and not vengeance,' and the crowd stormed its approval of Theodore Tilton. Davis? — he should hang! And, he added, the negroes are better entitled to the vote than white Irishmen. Cheers again. We shall hear such sentiments increasingly from now on.[2]

Thus the fight to determine the reconstruction policy shifted from the capital to the country. The leaders, thoroughly alarmed, hastened to their homes to take the field. Soon all over the country could be heard the voice of orators and the shouts of multitudes, for with his North Carolina Proclamation Andrew Johnson definitely accepted the Lincoln policy and the fight was on. All the hate against Lincoln, half concealed, was now turned, by the politicians, against his successor.

V

In considering North Carolina with his Cabinet, Johnson had before him the plan approved by Lincoln, and after some divergent views as to suffrage had been expressed, the Lincoln plan was adopted.[3] Johnson had determined to hew as closely to the line laid down by his predecessor as possible. 'I know he went to the White House with that determination,' wrote Thurlow Weed.[4] The bitter quarrel between Lincoln and the leaders of his party had prevented the enactment of a law for Johnson's guidance.

[1] May 13, 1865.          [2] *New York World*, May 13, 1865.
[3] Welles, II, 301.          [4] Weed, *Memoir*, II, 450.

Years later, John Sherman was to assert that 'he did substantially adopt the plan proposed and acted upon by Mr. Lincoln.' [1]

Naturally enough, the North Carolina Proclamation opened the floodgates of abuse. When Sumner heard of it in his Beacon Street home, in Boston, he was inexpressibly shocked. To think that the negroes had not been given the franchise, 'thus excluding them as Mr. Lincoln had done.' Manifestly this new man was no better than Lincoln after all.[2] This exclusion of the negroes was 'madness,' he wrote Bright.[3] The change was due to 'Southern influence' and 'the ascendancy of the Blairs.' [4] Quite as disturbed was Carl Schurz, who wrote Johnson of his misgivings, and was invited to call; and thus he went forth at Johnson's suggestion on an inspection tour of the South.[5] This tour was not made without a consultation with Chase, Sumner, and Stanton, and he went forth to justify their position. It was a serious tactical blunder on Johnson's part.

Having taken the bit in his teeth, Johnson proceeded vigorously along the line of his North Carolina Proclamation, and soon, under Provisional Governors of his selection, the work of presidential reconstruction was in progress. In every instance, with one exception, he appointed Governors who had been consistent Union men, and not one appointment was unworthy. In Tennessee, Virginia, Arkansas, and Louisiana, where Unionist Governments previously had been organized, the sitting Executives were recognized. Soon these men were calling Conventions to take the steps stipulated for the restoration of the States to the Union; and this was irritating to the Radical leaders in the North. It was an assumption of the power of the President to reconstruct; and it offered no hope for immediate negro suffrage.

### VI

Instantly the fight was on. The congressional 'smelling committee' on the conduct of the war, by constantly encroaching on the powers of the Presidency, had been a source of constant annoyance to Lincoln. Never has the Presidency meant less than during the years with which we are concerned. The contempt for the

---

[1] Sherman, *Recollections*, 361.    [2] Pierce, II, 249.    [3] *Ibid.*, IV, 254.
[4] To Scheiden, Pierce, IV, 254.    [5] Schurz, *Reminiscences*, II, 157.

Presidency disclosed itself during the summer in outrageous insults to the three former Presidents living in retirement. Buchanan, an old man in the beautiful country home of Wheatland at Lancaster, was the object of constant assaults, and the publication of his 'Vindication' overwhelmed him with abuse. When, on Lincoln's death, Fillmore, hovering about the sick-bed of his wife, and, ignorant of the request that private houses be draped, hung no crape, he awoke one morning to find his house smeared with ink.[1] At the same time the venerable Franklin Pierce, speaking at a memorial meeting, was interrupted with a yell, 'Where is your flag?' and with scorn the old man flung back his answer, 'It is not necessary for me to show my devotion to the stars and stripes by any special exhibition, or upon the demand of any man or set of men.'[2] The revolutionary era had begun. The terror had not long to wait.

But the burning topic of agitation through the summer was immediate, unconditional negro suffrage. The supporters of Johnson were first in the field to anticipate attacks, though the Custom-House crowd in New York planned to use the Cooper Union meeting to repudiate his policy. Having no doubt of its success, it wished to dignify the meeting with the presence of Grant, who, caring nothing for politics then, refused to see its committee. The committee then had recourse to Johnson, who, absorbed in work and not suspecting the design, gave them a letter to Grant. Thereupon he received them and accepted the invitation. In the confusion, the conspirators rushed their resolutions through, but their triumph was short. John A. Logan spoke in vigorous support of the President's policy.

'I disagree with those who think these States are but territories,' he said. 'We fought . . . upon the theory that a State cannot secede.' As for negro suffrage, the President had no right to declare negroes may vote: 'If he does, he does it in the teeth of the Constitution.' The States alone have the power, 'and until they make such a decision in their sovereign capacity as a State, no President has the right to decide for them.'

A few of the politicians hissed, but the hisses were drowned in a hurricane of cheers. And this, despite the distribution of circulars

[1] *New York World*, April 22, 1865.    [2] *Ibid.*, April 27, 1865.

attacking Johnson and advocating immediate negro suffrage. Thus the President emerged with an endorsement, but we shall very soon find the orator of the occasion responding to the party lash and joining in the hue and cry against him. It is well to bear Logan in mind as a type, for we shall meet him again as one of the managers to impeach the President because of the very policies he so vigorously espoused that night at Cooper Union.[1] In truth, the politicians moved at first against a strong current of opposition to negro suffrage in the North. Even Lyman Trumbull for a time was not prepared to doubt the wisdom of the President's policy.[2] This was two months after the bristling-bearded Secretary of the Navy had convinced himself that Johnson was 'gathering to himself the good wishes of the country.'[3]

Meanwhile, disturbing antipathies to the negroes were disclosing themselves in the North, and even in the Nation's capital. Two hundred rioting soldiers in Washington had smashed the furniture of saloons and disreputable houses frequented by the two races with especial severity to the negro transgressors.[4] The slapping of a white woman by a negress in Salem, New Jersey, precipitated a race riot in which negroes fared badly.[5]

Nor was this opposition to negro suffrage confined to the mobs. It was about the time John Sherman was poring with perplexity over some letters from his brother, the General. 'My belief is that to force the enfranchised negroes as "loyal" voters on the South will produce new riot and war,' he was reading, 'and I fear Sumner, Wilson and men of that school will force it on the Government or prolong the war *ad infinitum*. . . . My army will not fight in that war. The slaves are free, but not yet voters.'[6] Momentarily impressed, the politician replied that 'the negroes are not intelligent enough to vote,' albeit we shall soon find him bowing to the party lash.[7] Not afraid to speak out publicly, the General in a banquet speech in Indianapolis denounced negro suffrage and 'indiscriminate intercourse with the whites.'[8] This aroused the fury of those

---

1 *New York Herald*, June 7, 8, 9, 1865; *New York World*, June 8, 1865.
2 Welles, II, 322.        3 *Ibid.*, II, 300.
4 *New York World*, June 12, 1865; *New York Herald*, June 11, 1865.
5 *Salem Standard*; quoted, *New York World*, June 24, 1865.
6 Sherman, *Letters*, 248.        7 *Ibid.*, 249.        8 *New York World*, July 28, 1865.

soon to become masters in the art of abuse and bulldozing. 'Never since he led the great army on the immortal march,' said the 'New York World,' 'has there been so good an opportunity for casting foul words at the most brilliant soldier of modern times.' [1]

And 'the casting of foul words' had begun. Ben Butler had been the first in the field. The Union League Club of New York demanded negro suffrage 'in the late rebellious States,' [2] and soon this powerful club was sending organizers among the Southern negroes to incite their distrust of their former masters and bind them together as a race in secret societies. Charles Sumner was beside himself, talking suffrage incessantly in the streets, in clubs, at dinner-tables, and writing the wife of Commodore Eames imploring her to have her husband coax Welles into camp. [3] Boutwell joined Sumner in making speeches, and the agitation culminated in a mass meeting in Boston demanding suffrage as the price of peace. [4] All over the land the extremists were on the march. Ben Wade, haunting the White House, was bitterly pronouncing the Government a failure and complaining of executive power. [5] Sumner was writing the negroes of North Carolina to demand suffrage, and the 'New York Herald' was saying he had 'just as much right to counsel the negroes of this State on that point as he has those of North Carolina.' [6] And Ashley of Ohio, Stanton's friend, and destined to some infamy, was telling his Ohio neighbors that the Radicals 'intend under God to crush any party or any man who stands up against universal suffrage.' [7] It was soon evident to Welles that 'prominent men are trying to establish a party on the basis of equality of races in the Rebel States for which the people are not prepared.' [8]

In Indiana the suffrage question was threatening the solidarity of the Republican Party. George W. Julian, with the fervor of his abolition days, was crusading over the State for negro suffrage and against the reconstruction policy of Johnson, and making some impression. [9] Soon Oliver P. Morton was forced to the platform to combat his views, and the 'Indianapolis Journal,' the party organ,

[1] *New York World*, July 27, 1865.   [2] Bellows, 87.   [3] Welles, August 18, 1865.
[4] *New York World*, July 10, 1865.   [5] Welles, II, 325.   [6] June 1, 1865.
[7] *New York Herald*, June 17, 1865.   [8] Welles, II, 369.
[9] Julian, MS. Diary, September 3, 1865.

was denouncing Julian in a long tirade.[1] It was under these conditions, with politicians conservative, the people confused, that Morton defiantly defended Johnson and attacked negro suffrage at Richmond, and Julian replied at the State House in Indianapolis.

## VII

The power of Morton was at this time supreme. He was the idol of his party and of returning soldiers, whom he assiduously cultivated. A consummate politician, dictatorial and domineering, he brooked no rivals. He was on the threshold of his national career, and it is interesting to note that he signalized his entrance by denouncing the position he was almost immediately afterward to assume.

Negro suffrage! he exclaimed, and without 'a period of probation and preparation'! Why, perhaps 'not one in a thousand could read.' How 'impossible to conceive of instantly admitting this mass of ignorance to the ballot'! And how dare Indiana propose it? — Indiana with twenty-five thousand negroes who can read and write, and who are refused the ballot or the right to testify in court — whose children are excluded from the schools. 'With what face,' he asked, 'can Indiana go to Congress and insist upon the right of suffrage to the negroes of the South?' And enfranchise them in the South, where through their numerical strength they would elect negro senators, governors, and judges? Preposterous! No, 'colored State governments are not desirable . . . they will bring about a war of races.' [2] This speech attracted wide attention and the 'New York World' thought that the speaker 'will in a short time make a tolerable Democrat.' [3] Two months later, when he called on Johnson, he was complimented on the speech as the strongest presentation of the Presidential policies thus far made. In less than three years he was to wear the mantle of Thad Stevens!

In exuberant spirits Julian replied in a rabble-rousing speech to a delighted throng of Radicals. Jeff Davis? 'I would indict him . . . I would convict him — and hang him in the name of God.' And what an outrage that Lee was unmolested, running

[1] Julian, MS. Diary, November 4, 1865.    [2] Foulke. I, 444–50.    [3] October 3, 1865.

'up and down the hills and valleys of Virginia,' and taking over the presidency of a college 'to teach the young idea how to shoot'! Hang him, too! And stop there? Not at all. 'I would hang liberally, while I had my hand in.' And confiscate Southern aristocrats' property, too. Take a rebel with forty thousand acres — enough to make farms for many loyal men. 'I would give the land to them and not leave enough to bury his carcass in.' And negro suffrage? Why not? 'When the Government decided that the negro was fit to carry a gun to shoot rebels down, it thereby pledged itself irrevocably to give him the ballot to vote rebels down.' [1] It was a slashing attack on the Republican machine under Morton and the party conservatives winced. Julian, said the 'Indianapolis Journal,' 'has the temper of a hedgehog, the adhesiveness of a barnacle, the vanity of a peacock, the vindictiveness of a Corsican, and the duplicity of the devil.' [2] Julian was riding with the current and was content.

But the authoritative voice of Republieanism was heard about this time, and from the moment Thaddeus Stevens spoke at the court-house in Lancaster one autumn day, the wise ones knew where the victory would lie. When Jere S. Black said 'the utterances of Mr. Stevens are the deliverances of his party,' he spoke with historical accuracy.[3]

Here we must pause to listen to the prophet and the master.

VIII

Through the spring and summer of 1865, Stevens had been unhappy. He had never been entirely happy over Lincoln's activities and views. We have seen that he had been chagrined because of the liberality of Grant's terms of surrender. During the greater part of the summer he had remained in the red-brick house in Lancaster, and there, in July, an emissary from the wife of an imprisoned Confederate leader had sought him 'on account of his independence of character and official leadership in the house of Congress and of his party.' The grim old warrior had declared in the conversation that not even Davis could be tried for treason because 'the belligerent character of the Southern

[1] Julian, *Speeches*, 262–90.    [2] Julian, MS. Diary, November 22, 1865.
[3] *Lancaster Intelligencer*, October 11, 1865.

States was recognized by the United States.' He hinted of 'profound questions of statesmanship and party' and requested that he be not quoted.[1] A month before had found him inclined to a sarcasm 'without much sting.' [2]

It was a large and curious crowd that gathered at the courthouse in Lancaster to hear the law laid down. That the speech was carefully meditated and prepared is evident in its almost immediate publication in pamphlet form for circulation among party leaders throughout the country. Strangely enough, it contained no reference to negro suffrage, but it expressed other views so extreme that an unfriendly reporter insisted that the meeting was 'sadly lacking in enthusiasm' and that 'all present seemed bewildered and amazed at the troubles that were so plainly seen to environ their party.' [3] The purport of the speech was that the Southerners should be treated as a conquered, alien enemy, the property of their leaders seized and appropriated to the payment of the national debt. This could be done without 'violence to established principles' only on the theory that the Southern States had been 'severed from the Union' and had been 'an independent government de facto, and an alien enemy to be dealt with according to the laws of war.' Absurd, he said, to think of trying the leaders for treason. That would be acting under the Constitution; and that would mean trials in Southern States where no jury would convict unless deliberately packed, and that would be 'judicial murder.'

Getting to close grips with Johnson, he scouted the idea that either he or Congress could direct the holding of conventions to amend the constitutions. That would be 'meddling with the domestic institutions of a State . . . rank, dangerous, deplorable usurpation.' Hence 'no reform can be effected in the Southern States if they have never left the Union; and yet the very foundations of their institutions must be broken up and relaid, or all our blood and treasure have been spent in vain. But by treating them as an outside, conquered people, they can be refused admission to the Union unless they voluntarily do what we demand.'

Warming to his task, the bitter old man demanded punishment

---

[1] Mrs. Clay, 291.    [2] Welles, II, 325.
[3] *Lancaster Intelligencer*, September 13, 1865.

for the most guilty — but how? If the States had not been out of the Union, only through trials for treason that would miscarry; if a conquered people, a court-martial would do the work. Property must be seized — but how? Only on the theory of a conquered people and under the rule laid down by Vattel that the conqueror 'may indemnify himself for the expenses and damages he has sustained.' And what vast prospects presented by confiscation! Every estate worth ten thousand dollars and containing two hundred acres should be taken. Consult the figures: 465,000,000 acres in the conquered territory, of which 394,000,000 acres would be subject to confiscation. This would dispossess only 70,000 people, and nine tenths would be untouched. And the 394,000,000 acres? Give forty acres to every adult negro, which would dispose of 40,000,000 acres. Divide the remaining 354,-000,000 acres into suitable farms and sell it at an average of ten dollars an acre, and thus secure $3,540,000,000. And how use that? 'Invest $200,000,000 in six per cent government bonds and add the interest semi-annually to pension those who have become disabled by this villainous war; appropriate $200,000,000 to pay damages done loyal men, both North and South, and pay the residue of $3,040,000,000 on the national debt.'

And 'what loyal man can object to that'? he demanded triumphantly. Did some one object to the punishment of innocent women and children? 'That is the result of the necessary laws of war.' Revolutionary? 'It is intended to revolutionize the principles and feelings of these people.' Of course it 'may startle feeble minds and shake weak nerves,' but 'it requires a heavy impetus to drive forward a sluggish people.' This policy would mean equality in the South, impossible 'where a few thousand men monopolize the whole landed property.' Would not New York without its independent yeomanry 'be overwhelmed by Jews and Milesians and vagabonds of licentious cities'? More: this would provide homes for the negroes. 'Far easier and more beneficial to exile 70,000 proud bloated and defiant rebels than to expatriate four million laborers, native to the soil and loyal to the government.' Away with the colonization scheme of the Blairs with which they had 'inoculated our late sainted President.' 'Let all who approve of these principles tarry with us.' he concluded, thus assuming the power of the dictator. 'Let all others go with copperheads and rebels. Those will be the opposing parties.' [1]

Easy to imagine the confusion, the fear, the awe of the followers of the stern old revolutionist, as they slowly broke up and returned to their homes. Even the 'New York Tribune' and the 'Philadelphia Press' were a little nonplussed. The Democratic 'New York World' had an interpretation of its own based on the conviction that 'Mr. Stevens is no fool and knows better than to believe this stuff,' which is 'a shabby mask to real purposes he wishes to conceal from the general public.' One of these was the mobilization of the Republican politicians against the policies of Johnson, who would be pounced down upon in a furious onslaught when Congress met. 'The real leaders . . . see that unless the South can be trodden down and kept under foot for long years, or unless they can give the negroes the ballot, and control it in their hands, their present political supremacy is gone forever.' The other purpose was to 'protect himself and fellow plunderers in their scheme for buying up the richest Southern land for a nominal price.' Thus 'confiscation in his mouth means plunder for his purse.' [2]

While Stevens was burnishing his arms for the conflict, another, who had been a thorn in the side of Lincoln and had insulted him with his Manifesto, was nursing his rising wrath in a sick-room in Maryland, and just before the pen fell from the lifeless fingers of Henry Winter Davis, he sounded another call to battle in a letter against Johnson in 'The Nation.' A demand for the immediate enfranchisement of the newly liberated slaves, it was a vicious attack on Johnson. 'We remember his declaration that traitors should be punished,' he wrote, 'yet none are punished; that only loyal men should control the States, yet he has delivered them to the disloyal; that the aristocracy should be pulled down, yet he has put it in power again; that its possessions should be divided among Northern laborers of all colors, yet the negroes are still a landless homeless class.' [3] Within a few days Davis was dead.

Thus, long before Johnson made his attack on the congressional leaders, these, without personal provocation, were bombarding

---

[1] From original pamphlet printed in Lancaster in 1865.
[2] September 11, 1865.
[3] *The Nation,* November 30, 1865.

him with abuse — because he was carrying out the policies of Lincoln.

## IX

Meanwhile Johnson, now in the White House after a long wait, was busy day and night with the solution of his problems. Southerners seeking pardons, petty politicians in pursuit of place, Union soldier deserters trying to escape punishment, and the merely curious wishing to shake his hand, pressed in upon him. Even departmental matters, passed upon adversely by the Cabinet heads, were carried to him. The anterooms and staircases were crowded with coarsely dressed men, bronzed with the sun of the battle-fields and smelling of tobacco. From nine in the morning until three, Johnson received the suppliants courteously, but not without impatience with the sluggish-minded. At three the doorkeeper, his hand full of unpresented cards, threw the door open, and with a wild scrambling for place, the motley crowd rushed into the room. Rising to facilitate the reception of each, Johnson hurried them by. Beside him at a table stood a secretary. In the center of the room was usually a pile of pardons, guarded by a young major in uniform.[1] It was observed that in these hurried conversations the President displayed tact and a marked capacity for the disposal of business.[2] Sometimes it was a woman appealing for a father, brother, sweetheart, and it was noticed that his cold dignity softened to gentleness.

By June this torture called for the protests of the press. The 'New York Herald' correspondent thought 'if the pressure of the last few weeks is kept up it is doubtful whether he will be able to stand it.'[3] Members of the Cabinet thought it would 'break any man down,' and Welles wrote that 'if some means are not devised of protecting him from personal interviews by . . . busybodies of both sexes, they will make an end of him.'[4] With the enervating heat wave and humidity of July, it was whispered that Johnson, still sick, was threatened with a stroke.[5] He had grown pale and languid, not having left the White House in a month. He was persuaded to take a river excursion on the Don, and though it

[1] Reid, 304–05.    [2] *The Ruffin Papers*, Swain to Ruffin, 37–39.
[3] June 27, 1865.    [4] July 6, 1865.    [5] Welles, II, 327.

was a cool, cloudy day he was wracked with headache. After that, he took occasionally to the river, but the pressure was unabated. Warned that he should exercise, he took no heed.[1] 'It is quite a marvel,' wrote a correspondent, 'the President's health is not permanently impaired,'[2] and the assurance of a Tennesseean that 'Andy is as hard as a knot and you can't kill him' did not convince. At length he succumbed, and asked if something could be done to protect him, and Seward drew up some orders which the Cabinet adopted.[3] After that he was enticed from the stuffy rooms for an occasional drive to Rock Creek and Pierce's Mill, and out on the Georgetown road, over which Jackson and Van Buren were wont to ride on horseback.[4]

But he was never free from care, for the favor-seekers were the least of his worries. Ben Butler had pushed his way to the very door of the sick-room to insist on the execution of Davis and Lee, and to urge severity.[5] The party bosses annoyed him by assessing Government employees for political purposes. The process of reconstruction in the South presented ever-recurring problems, and he was not unmindful of the conspiracy in incubation against him, and suspected the loyalty of Stanton, not without cause. Johnson had taken the position that suffrage was a matter for the States, and everywhere he was being attacked and misrepresented.

By early autumn the passion for negro equality had reached such a heat that the President of Vassar College was saying that 'God is gathering on this continent . . . the elements of a new and glorious nationality, meaning out of many races to mould one new one; and among the rest he has brought the negro.' He was convinced that 'in a new land you ought to have no advantage of a negro, civil, political or social, simply because your skins are of a different complexion.' The 'New York World' protested against having 'the peculiarities of that doctrine taught to young girls and budding women.'[6] From the South came disheartening reports of the extravagant expectations of the freedmen and their refusal to work. Thus, when in October colored soldiers appeared at the White House, Johnson sought to give them friendly advice, warning them against idleness, assuring them that liberty did not

---

[1] Welles, II, 340, 347.    [2] *New York World*, August 2, 1865.
[3] Welles, II, 354.    [4] *Ibid.*, II, 367.    [5] *Ibid.*, II, 348–49.    [6] September 6, 1865.

mean lawlessness, and urging them to adopt systems of morality
and to abstain from licentiousness. He impressed upon them the
solemnity of the marriage contract, advised them to control their
passions, develop their intellect, and apply their physical powers
to the industrial interests of the country.[1] This advice aroused the
ire of the Radicals, and the answer was not long in coming. Even
the scholarly 'Nation,' conceding the excellence of the admoni-
tions, waxed sarcastic without apparent cause.[2] Not so mild the
criticism of Wendell Phillips, stirring up sectional hate in Boston.
He, like Stevens, was mourning over the 'loss of the war.' Under
the Johnson policies the South was victorious. But it was the
advice to the freedmen that called forth his sardonic mirth.
'Well,' he said, 'he [Johnson] goes on in this speech and says,
"work, work, work"; be very industrious; be very economical;
stick to your families, reverence your wives [here the audience
burst into scornful laughter] ; teach them to be chaste; be chaste
yourselves; remember the great duty resting upon you; perform
the great husband and wifely duties.' Here there were roars of
laughter and rounds of applause. 'That speech a hundred years
hence,' continued Phillips, 'the historian will hold in his hand as
a miraculous exhibition of what America could set at the head of
her political forces to lead her in this great hour. Oh, God grant
that no Swift, no Rabelais with his immortal pen hold up that
speech to the indignation and scorn of the world.'[3]

Such was the spirit of the element soon to bludgeon its way to
the control of the race problem at its most critical juncture, and
Johnson understood its meaning. And yet John Sherman, writing
to the General, observed that 'he seems kind and patient with all
his terrible responsibility.'[4]

Here we must pause in the recital of events to become more
intimately acquainted with the man who was to become the storm-
center of almost four tragic years of revolutionary hate and terror.

[1] McPherson, 49–51.        [2] October 19, 1865.
[3] New York World, October 17, 1865.        [4] Letters, 259.

# CHAPTER II

## ANDREW JOHNSON: A PORTRAIT

### I

NO one could have approached Andrew Johnson without a feeling of respect. Henry Adams, who had seen, first and last, a dozen Presidents at the White House, recalled this one many years afterward as 'the old-fashioned Southern. Senator and statesman at his desk,' and concluded that he was 'perhaps the strongest he was ever to see.' [1] About the same time a courtly and cultivated man of the world was writing that 'he looks every inch the President.' [2] When Charles Dickens was presented, and the two men 'looked at each other very hard,' the novelist, who was not given to the flattery of American politicians, thought him 'a man with a remarkable face' and 'would have picked him out anywhere as a character of mark.' [3] And Charles Francis Adams, diplomat, familiar with the manners of courts and of statesmen to the manner born, was 'impressed with his dignity,' his 'quiet composure,' and the neatness of his clothes.[4] Still another, who attached much importance to manners, thought that 'nobody could have been more courteous or punctilious or have borne himself with more dignity or decorum.' [5] Even Carl Schurz, who was to join so lustily in the hue and cry against him, reluctantly admitted that 'his contact with the world has taught him certain things as to decent and correct appearance.' [6] These references to his neatness are important as measuring in a minor detail the enormity of the misrepresentations on which prejudice against him has been fed; for no less a writer than Rhodes, the historian, has given currency to the utterly indefensible story that he was slovenly in attire. The very opposite was true, as Mr. Rhodes, who met him, must have known. He always dressed in broadcloth, in perfect taste, and with meticulous care. In truth he was distinguished for exceptional neatness in person and

[1] Henry Adams, 245.  [2] *Old Days at Chapel Hill*, letter of Governor Swain, 117.
[3] Forster, III, 423.  [4] Winston, 173.  [5] Wise, 110.  [6] Schurz, II, 96.

dress.[1] In outer appearance, at least, he was a gentleman, lacking nothing that Sumner had, except the spats.

A stranger, meeting him standing expectantly at his desk, would have thought him a little below medium height because of the compactness of his build, but he measured five feet nine, and stood erect. The first impression would have been of unusual powers of physical endurance and sinewy strength. Interest would have been immediately awakened by his face, which Dickens found 'remarkable . . . indicating courage, watchfulness, and certainly strength of purpose.'[2] The large, shapely head with black hair, the dark eyes, deep-set and piercing, the mouth with lines of grim determination extending downward from the corners, which some associated with strength and others with cynicism,[3] the strong nose, and the square cleft chin, all contributed to the powerful impression made upon the English novelist. The complexion, described as of 'Indian like' swarthiness,[4] did not serve to brighten the face which one, not friendly, thought dull and stolid,[5] and another, also hostile, thought 'sullen . . . betokening a strong will inspired by bitter feelings.'[6] And yet a lady of fine culture who visited him was impressed with the smallness and softness of his hands, and 'cheeks as red as June apples.'[7] We may well believe, at any rate, that it was a face with 'no genial sunlight in it.'[8] If it lacked sunshine and denoted grim determination and even some bitterness, it was not without reason in the hard and bitter battles he had fought, and the long-drawn torture of his pride, which was not least among his qualities.

## II

Like Lincoln, and Thad Stevens, who was to be his most inveterate foe, he was born of lowly parentage and in poverty, in the little log shack now carefully preserved in Raleigh. Long after he had attained national prominence, it was whispered about that he was the illegitimate son of a gentleman of some distinction, and the gossips were able to name the man without being able to

[1] *Morse Henry*, i, 152–54; 'Defence and Vindication,' by W. P. Brownlow, *Taylor-Trotwood Magazine*, September, 1908.

[2] Forster, iii, 423.    [3] Wise, 110.    [4] Crook, 81.    [5] Wise, 110.

[6] Schurz, ii, 95.    [7] Mrs. Clay, 311.    [8] Schurz, ii, 95.

agree on his identity.[1] When, in the second year of his Presidency, he attended the ceremonies at the dedication of his father's monument, he was reported to have referred to him doubtfully as 'the man who is said to be my father,' and that story persists to this day. Standing uncovered at the grave, he really said: 'I have come to participate in the ceremonies of dedicating a monument to a man you respected, though poor and of humble condition. He was my father, and of him I am proud. He was an honest and faithful friend — a character I prize higher than all the worldly fortunes that could have been left me.' [2] And there was justification for this pride, for this father — porter, sexton, janitor — was respected by all the people, chosen city constable, and made captain of a militia company. An accommodating man, he was always in demand at barbecues and banquets for the basting of young pigs, and he was an excellent caterer. A passion for companionship held him to the town when he could have bettered himself in the country, and he was lacking in ambition. Plunging into an icy stream to save two lives, he contracted an illness from which he died, and during his illness 'he was visited by the principal inhabitants of the city, by all of whom he was esteemed for his honesty, industry, and humane and friendly disposition.' [3]

Thus, at the age of four he was left a penniless orphan, bound out as soon as possible as an apprentice to a tailor, to be fed and clothed for his services until he attained his majority. This period is naturally shrouded in obscurity. We have a momentary glimpse of him holding the horse of the elegant John Branch, while the latter was having a fitting in the shop, and refusing pay for the service.[4] Sensitive, imaginative, strangely proud, he may have brooded over the comparison of his lot with that of other children more happily placed. It is of record that in a childish prank he broke a window, ran away in fear of arrest, and was advertised as a runaway apprentice; that he lingered awhile in a near-by town, which memorializes the sojourn with a monument; and pushed on to South Carolina, where, at Laurens Court-House, he worked at his trade for a year; that he returned to work out

[1] *Marse Henry*, I, 155.     [2] *New York World*, June 5, 1867.

[3] *Raleigh Star*, January 12, 1812; quoted, Jones, *Life*, 13.

[4] Haywood, *John Branch*, pamphlet.

his apprenticeship, to find the tailor gone; and, finding himself under a cloud as a result of his flight, determined to test his fortune in Tennessee. Thus one autumn day an eighteen-year-old boy, accompanied by a woman and a man, entered Greeneville, after days of hardship in crossing the mountains in a cart drawn by a blind pony.

That he was sensitive and proud is evident in his determination never again to wear the collar of an employer. Soon married to a woman of character and some attainments, plain but of good family,[1] he became the proprietor of a small shop; and by honest work and assiduous application prospered so well that he had attained a competent fortune before he was thirty-four. It was in this mountain town that his political character was moulded.

### III

Soon able to read and write, through the tutelage of his wife, the printed page opened to his eager mind a world of wonders he was keen to explore. During the day he employed men to read to him at fifty cents a day; and, plying his needle often far into the night, he listened to the reading of his wife. His partiality ran to books on politics and government; he pored with delight over a collection of orations, and after that followed the speeches of contemporary statesmen through the newspapers, for which he had a fondness similar to Lincoln's. Soon the little tailor shop became the clubhouse of laborers of the aspiring sort who had ambitions of their own. Born with a genius for controversy and an impulse toward expression, he was soon participating in the town debates, manifesting more than ordinary resourcefulness in verbal combat. To cultivate his natural gift, he walked time and again, regardless of the weather, to the college, four miles distant, to match his wits against those of the more favored students.

By this time he had developed a belligerent class consciousness, inevitable in one of his pride, and under the social organization of the community. First in the scale came the aristocrats, who owned slaves; then the merchants, who had money; and then the poor, who were the laborers. Excluded from the first two, he made a virtue of belonging to the last. Thus it was the carpenters, brick-

[1] *Marse Henry*, I, 155–56.

layers, plasterers, shoemakers, and small farmers with whom he
associated; and it was these who frequented his shop to discuss
politics and the grievances of the submerged. Thus the shop
became a small Jacobin club, fired with the revolutionary spirit
of democracy. Among the members were a few robust souls who
fanned the flames of his discontent. A little while, and these
determined upon a minor revolution in the governing forces of
the community. The aristocrats, in the minority, had dominated
the city government; it was time for the plebeians, in the majority,
to assert themselves. Thus, with the issue clear-cut between the
plebeians and the patricians, he was pushed forward as the former's candidate for alderman, and won. That was the spring
Andrew Jackson entered the White House. In his twenty-seventh
year, Johnson's followers proposed him for the legislature, and,
running against a Whig aristocrat noted as an excellent speaker,
he prevailed, and amazed even his friends by his prowess on the
platform.

Holding aloof from party organizations, he was, at this juncture,
a Jeffersonian — outspoken in his attacks on centralization.
Soon he was numbered among the most ardent of the Jacksonians. While not binding himself by partisanship, he hated the
Whigs, representing the slave-owning aristocracy, who looked
down upon the workingmen with indifferent scorn. Soon he had
won the favorable notice of Jackson and Polk, and in 1840, in
his thirty-second year, and after eleven years in politics, he became a regular Democrat for the first time and canvassed the
State as an elector at large for the Van Buren ticket.

Thus, while all his instincts were fundamentally Jeffersonian,
he had been accorded position in the Democratic Party primarily
because he had made himself the idol of the working classes and
of the mountaineers. It was to these that he appealed when he
made his race for Congress. His platform was personal — a pledge
to reduce tariff taxes on necessities and shift them to the luxuries
of the rich, to fight the battle for the homeless. Were there not
vast stretches of unoccupied lands in the West? He already had
a vision of his homestead law. Taken at his word, he was elected
and served ten years.

If his career in the House was not scintillating, it was serious and useful. Living simply in a boarding-house on Capitol Hill, any visitor would have found upon his table the writings of Jefferson, Plutarch's 'Lives,' works on the Constitution and political subjects. No one made a more intelligent use of the Congressional Library; no one was more pathetically eager for self-improvement.[1] Frequently he might have been seen haunting the little Senate Chamber listening to the eloquence of Webster, Clay, Calhoun, and Benton.

It was then that he began his fight for his Homestead Act, which, after many vicissitudes, was to be written into law.

When, after a term as Governor, he reached the Senate, the Nation was heading for war, and no one displayed a saner statesmanship. Thenceforth his was a struggle for the Constitution and the Union, in the Senate, on the platform, in the caucus. When war came, he imperiled his life at the instance of Lincoln and left the politicians to the safety of the Senate house, to undertake the desperate duties of the Military Governor of Tennessee. In the unrolling of the story before us, we must keep this in mind always: no leader, civil or military, was subjected to such hardships and deadly dangers, and it was in recognition of his services that he was nominated on the ticket with Lincoln in 1864. Such, rapidly sketched, was the previous career of the new President.

IV

Since we shall find him constantly assailed as a traitor to 'the Party that elected him,' we must get an accurate impression of his politics. There is no possible palliation for this misrepresentation. A Democrat all his life, he was not nominated by the Republican Party nor as a Republican. He was chosen in a Union Party Convention, as a Southern Democrat, and expressly because he was a Democrat. 'He was always a Democrat,' wrote Greeley at the time of his nomination; 'he was a Senator from a slave State; he supported Breckinridge for President; but he never wavered or faltered in his devotion to the national cause; and he has carried his life in his hand from the outset.' Years after the hysteria of reconstruction days had passed, one of the leaders of the movement to impeach him wrote that 'Mr. Johnson never identified himself

[1] Winston, 41.

with the Republican Party'; that 'neither in June, 1864, nor at any other period of his life had the Republican Party a right to treat him as an associate member'; and that 'he was . . . what he often proclaimed himself to be — a Jacksonian Democrat.' [1] Indeed, four months before his nomination with Lincoln, while he was fighting the Union's battles in the fiery furnace of Tennessee, he told a political acquaintance that 'if the country is ever to be saved it will be done through the old Democratic Party.' [2] He held through life to the Jeffersonian doctrine that 'stands firmly by the combined and recorded judgment of the people until changed or modified by them,' and had faith 'in the integrity and capacity of the people to govern themselves.' [3] This declaration of fundamental faith, expressed in his inaugural address as Governor of Tennessee, was fiercely denounced by the reactionary forces of the State. 'Instead of the voice of the people being the voice of a demon,' he said on another occasion, 'I go back to the old idea, and I favor the policy of popularizing all our free institutions . . . and bringing them nearer to the people.' [4] Indeed, his attitude toward two tendencies that were to be pronounced in the years immediately following the war would have made impossible his affiliation with the politicians who were soon to call for his crucifixion. He was an uncompromising enemy of centralization — as much so as Jefferson. 'Your States,' he said, '. . . are sinking into mere petty corporations . . . mere satellites of an inferior character, revolving around the great central power here in Washington. There is where your danger is. It is not in centrifugal power being too great, but in the centripetal influence all drawing here.'

And he was as bitterly hostile to privilege and monopoly as Jackson. 'The tendency of the legislation of this country is to build up monopolies,' he said, '. . . to build up the money power . . . to concentrate power in the hands of the few. The tendency is for classes and against the great mass of the people.' Throughout his life we find him constantly giving utterance to expressions that might have flowed from the pen of Jefferson. 'I believe that governments are made for men and not men for governments.' [5]

---

[1] Boutwell, ii, 97.
[2] Evidence of Stanley Matthews in Impeachment Trial.
[3] Moore, *Life and Speeches*, 77.      [4] *Ibid.*, 55.      [5] *Ibid.*, 471.

'I am opposed to consolidation or to the concentration of power in the hands of the few.' [1]

Thus his proposed constitutional amendments further to democratize the Government through the voting of presidential electors by districts instead of by States, for the popular election of Senators, and for definite long-time terms for Justices of the Supreme Court. Thus, a radical in his democracy, he had nothing in common with the forces soon to take possession of the Government. Nor was this devotion to the masses a demagogic simulation. One who knew him well and spared not his faults has recorded that 'his sympathies were easily stirred by rags in distress.' [2] Nor, despite the popular clamor raised against him, did he ever lose faith in the people. 'Cherish always the support of the common people,' he advised young Benton McMillin, just entering public life. 'I have found them a never-failing or faltering element of strength.' [3]

### V

It was in keeping with this feeling for the plain people that he fought his long-drawn stubborn battle for his homestead law providing one hundred and sixty acres to every head of a family who would migrate to the public domain and cultivate the soil. To this, despite discouragement and defeat, he clung with a passionate tenacity because he knew the misery of the homeless wanderer and something of the longing for one's own vine and fig-tree. The moment he accumulated a little money, he bought a hundred acres of farm land.

There was something of the social revolutionist in this man's temper. He bitterly resented the enormous landholdings of the aristocracy while thousands of industrious men were unable to own the roof above their heads. 'I am no agrarian,' he once said, 'but if through an iniquitous system a vast amount of land has been accumulated in the hands of one man . . . then that result is wrong.' [4] Blaine thought his resentment against land monopoly amounted to hatred. He denounced the landed aristocracy as 'in-

[1] Moore, *Life and Speeches*, 484.          [2] *Marse Henry*, I, 152.
[3] Told the author by Governor McMillin.
[4] Address at Nashville, October 24, 1864.

flated and heartless,' and warned of such agrarian struggles as in
Ireland.[1] His congressional speeches, however, were sane and
forceful. Did some one say it was impossible to give public land
away? 'If you can grant your public lands as gratuities,' he replied, 'to men who go out and fight the battles of the country . . .
is it not passing strange that you cannot grant land to those who
till the soil and make provision to sustain your army?'[2] More:
'Do you want cities to take control of the government?' Are not
the 'rural population, the mechanics . . . the very salt of it?'
Yes, 'they constitute the mud sills.'[3] This fight for free lands in
the unpopulated territories of the West was strongly opposed by
the pro-slavery element as tending to the ultimate loss of congressional power, and from this time on Johnson was looked upon
as a renegade to the South. And yet there is no evidence on which
to justify the bizarre theory that he was aiming at slavery. Dis-
liking it, not on moral but on economic grounds, ever and anon
in the bitterness of debate this hostility would flash forth in a biting
phrase; but we shall see that he was not interested in the emancipation of slaves. He accepted the institution as established.

### VI

There was no justification for the Southern theory that Johnson
would interfere with slavery through congressional action. 'My
position,' he declared in the Senate,[4] 'is that Congress has no power
to interfere with . . . slavery; that it is an institution local in its
character and peculiar to the States where it exists, and no other
power has the right to control it.' He had no sympathy with the
programme or methods of the abolitionists. 'He always scouted
the idea that slavery was the cause of our trouble [the war] or
that emancipation could ever be tolerated without immediate
colonization,' wrote Julian, the abolitionist. 'At heart a hater
of abolitionism.'[5] Speaking in the Senate at the time of the
John Brown raid, he excoriated those who stirred up sectional
strife, to the peril of the Union, on the slave question. 'John
Brown stands before the country as a murderer,' he said. 'The
time has arrived when these things ought to be stopped; when

---

[1] Blaine, II, 5.          [2] Moore, *Life and Speeches*, 24.          [3] *Ibid.*, 35.
[4] June 5, 1860.          [5] *Recollections*, 243.

encroachments on the institutions of the South ought to cease; . . .
when the Southern States and their institutions should be let
alone; . . . when you must either preserve the Constitution or
you must destroy this Union.' [1] John Brown compared to Christ?
What blasphemy! 'I once heard it said that fanaticism always
ends in heaven or in hell . . . I believe it true.' John Brown a god?
'Those may make him a god who will, and worship him who can
— he is not my god and I shall not worship at his shrine.' [2]

Fighting desperately as the war clouds lowered for the Union
he loved and the Constitution he revered, he was not concerned
with slavery. 'The constitutional guarantees must be carried out!'
he thundered. And then, turning to agitators of the slavery question, he continued: 'We do not intend that you shall drive us out
of this house that was reared by the hands of our fathers. It is our
house . . . the constitutional house.' Having thus defied the disunionists of the North, he turned to those of the South. 'Are we
going to desert that noble and patriotic band who have stood by
us in the North?' he asked. Lincoln elected? Ah, 'a minority
President by nearly a million votes; but had the election taken
place upon the plan proposed in my amendment to the Constitution by districts, he would have been this day defeated.'
Run away because Lincoln enters? 'I voted against him; I spoke
against him; I spent my money to defeat him; but still I love my
country; I love the Constitution: I intend to insist upon its
guarantees. There and there alone I intend to plant myself, with
the confident hope and belief that if the Union remains together,
in less than four years the now triumphant party will be over-
thrown.' [3]

With the war clouds thickening a month before Lincoln's inauguration, Johnson still stood in the Senate passionately fighting
for the Union and against the radicals on both sides the line.
'There are politicians,' he said, 'who want to break up the Union
to promote their personal aggrandizement; some desire the
Union destroyed that slavery may be extinguished.' He, instead,
would 'wrest it from the Philistines, save the country, and hand
it down to our children as it has been handed down to us.' And

---

[1] *Congressional Globe*, December 12, 1859.    [2] *Ibid.*
[3] *Ibid.*, December 18, 19, 1860.

then, an impassioned denunciation of the abolitionists. 'Thank God I am not in alliance with Giddings, with Phillips, with Garrison, and the long list of those who are engaged in the work of destruction, and in violating the Constitution of the United States.' [1] Never to the hour of the Emancipation Proclamation had Johnson sanctioned any interference with slavery. His plan to throw the Western country open to settlement would have strengthened the congressional forces against slavery — but he was thinking of the benefits to the poor whites. When he favored the admission of California with slavery he was not seeking to serve that institution — but to open more opportunities to the homeless whites.[2] Thus he voted against Southern sentiment for the admission of Oregon — but he was thinking of homesteads and not of slavery.

Yet he disliked the institution, and, like Lincoln, hoped for its extinction through colonization. Thus he spoke in favor of the admission of Texas. To increase the slave dominion? No; because Texas would 'prove to be the gateway out of which the sable sons of Africa are to pass from bondage to freedom.' [3] He disliked slavery because of its degrading effect on white labor — always he was thinking of that. Thus, speaking of Lincoln's Emancipation Proclamation, he declared that 'the emancipation of the slaves will break down an odious and dangerous aristocracy,' and 'free more whites than blacks in Tennessee.'

Nor can it be charged that he changed his views as to the purpose of the war when he took issue with the Radicals on the spirit of reconstruction. Scarcely had the war begun, when Johnson, in the Senate, proposed resolutions setting forth the spirit and purpose as he saw it. The war should be prosecuted in no spirit of oppression, 'nor for any purpose of conquest or subjugation, nor purpose of overthrowing or interfering with the rights or established institutions of those States, but to defend and maintain the supremacy of the Constitution and all laws made in pursuance thereof.' And there was another clause which foreshadowed his own policy of restoration — the purpose was to 'preserve the

---

[1] *Congressional Globe*, February 5, 6, 1861.
[2] *Ibid.*, House, June 5, 1850.
[3] *Ibid.*, House, January 21, 1845.

Union with all the dignity, equality, and rights of the several States unimpaired.' [1]

Thus, like Lincoln, he did not like slavery; like Lincoln, he recognized the constitutional rights of slavery; like Lincoln, he did not care for the abolitionists; like Lincoln, he was more interested in the preservation of the Union, with or without slavery; and like Lincoln, he thought the war was waged for the preservation of the Union and for no other purpose.

## VII

In the misrepresentation of Johnson during the contests of his life, he was accused of being a Catholic in some quarters, an atheist in others, and he was neither. He affiliated with no church, but he put his belief on record: 'So far as the doctrines of the Bible are concerned, or the great scheme of salvation, as founded and taught and practiced by Jesus Christ, I never did entertain a solitary doubt.' [2] It is probable that in his earlier life he was restrained from affiliating with a church because of the discriminations he found there between the rich and the poor. He was temperamentally incapable of submitting to such discrimination in the house of God. At times he disclosed a certain partiality to Catholicism, and this has been ascribed to his admiration of its policy of recognizing no distinctions in worship. Not only did he occasionally attend Catholic services in Washington, but he entered one of his sons in a Catholic school.

This contributed less, however, to the charge that he was, in spirit, a Catholic than his robust battles against Know-Nothingism and the religious intolerance of his times. He had been attacked on the false ground that he had put his daughter in a Catholic school in Georgetown. She had really attended Mrs. English's Seminary for Young Ladies, which was non-sectarian. But Johnson was intolerant of intolerance. He was as firmly convinced as Jefferson of the injustice and tyranny of any sort of interference with the freedom of conscience. On one occasion in the House, when a speaker had given utterance to a proscriptive thought, Johnson had flamed with wrath. 'Are the bloodhounds of proscription and persecution to be let loose on the Irish? Is the

[1] *Congressional Globe*, Senate, July 26, 1861.          [2] Winston, 40.

guillotine to be set up in a republican form of government?' It was his devastating crusade of defiance against this spirit that first established his leadership, by right, of the Tennessee Democracy in 1854. 'Show me a Know-Nothing,' he shouted to bigots, pale with fury, and to the sound of the cocking of pistols, 'and I will show you a loathsome reptile on whose neck every honest man should set his heel.' [1] In replying to an attack on Catholics charged with responsibility for the defeat of Clay in 1844, he left no doubt of the liberality of his views. 'The Catholics had the right secured to them by the Constitution of worshipping the God of their fathers in the manner dictated by their consciences. . . . This country is not prepared to establish an inquisition to try and punish men for their religious beliefs.'

To measure the depth of his feeling on religious liberty and against proscription, it must be remembered that he represented a district containing but few Catholics and permeated with a prejudice against them. Nothing could better illustrate the courageous intellectual honesty of Andrew Johnson.

VIII

'But Andrew Johnson was a drunkard' — and he was nothing of the sort. This slander grew out of his unfortunate condition at the time of his inauguration as Vice-President. There were extenuating circumstances to the incident that reduce a scandal to a misfortune.

Previous to the inauguration, he had been so ill that he determined to take the oath at Nashville, but Lincoln, wishing the psychological advantage in the North of a Southern man being sworn in at the capital, urged him to reconsider. Under these conditions he reached Washington one or two days before the ceremonies.[2] The night before, he attended a party given by Colonel Forney, where there must have been some drinking.[3] A short time before the hour for the inaugural ceremonies the next day, he entered the office of Vice-President Hamlin, complaining of feeling faint and asking for a stimulant. A messenger was

---

[1] Winston, 72.

[2] 'Defence and Vindication,' *Taylor-Trotwood Magazine*, September, 1908.

[3] B. C. Truman, *Century Magazine*, January, 1913.

dispatched for some brandy, and Johnson drank a glass, and, in the course of conversation while waiting, two more. When he rose to enter the Senate Chamber, he was perfectly sober, but the heat of the crowded room had its effect, and when, after much delay, he was sworn in, he was in a befuddled state of mind.[1] One witness writes that Lincoln sat facing Johnson with an expression of 'unutterable sorrow,' but that he did not join in the condemnation of others. We have it on reliable authority that he had sent an emissary to Nashville to report on Johnson's habits.[2] 'It has been a severe lesson for Andy,' he said, 'but I do not think he will do it again.'[3] Another talked with Lincoln about the incident. 'I have known Andy Johnson for many years,' he said. 'He made a bad slip the other day, but you need not be scared. Andy ain't a drunkard.'[4] While it was an age of hard drinking among public men, and a drunken Senator on the floor of the Senate was not unusual, there was a simulation of outraged dignity among Senators, and Sumner even suggested impeachment.

Such was the unhappy incident, and out of this was created the myth of Johnson's habitual drunkenness. A penniless and obscure youth, without family prestige or influential friends, who, within a few years, accumulated a modest fortune, and through sheer ability rose to a position of authority, could not have been a drunkard. However, his enemies made the most of the 'slip,' and within two weeks of his accession to the Presidency a London paper was referring to him as 'a drunken mechanic.' This impelled the 'London News' to publish the result of its investigation. 'We are assured,' it said, 'by those who cannot but know the facts . . . that that incident cannot without injustice . . . be taken to represent Mr. Johnson's character. Those who know him well describe him as a man of real capacity and temperate habits.'[5] From Benjamin C. Truman, who sat with him at the same table in Nashville at least once a day for eighteen months, we have it that he never took wine or liquor with a meal, 'never drank a

---

[1] *Life of Hamlin*, 497; Sherman, *Recollections*, I, 351.
[2] Truman, *Century*, January, 1913.      [3] Forney, I, 177.
[4] *Men and Measures*, 373.
[5] *London News*, April 27, 1865: quoted, *New York Herald*, May 11, 1865.

cocktail in his life, never was in a barroom, and did not care for
champagne.' He did, however, 'take two or three or four glasses
of Robertson County whiskey some days; some days less, and
some days and weeks no liquor at all.' [1] A White House attaché
who served through five administrations testifies that, while
the cellars were always stocked with fine wines and liquors
which were served to guests, Johnson 'never drank to excess.' [2]
'Except in the time of his absence in the fall of 1865,' continues
this dependable witness, 'I saw him probably every day . . . and
I never saw him once under the influence of liquor.' [2] In reply to
a direct question by Chief Justice Chase concerning Johnson's
reputation for sobriety in Tennessee, Parson Brownlow, his
most vituperative foe, replied that, while he was not a total abstainer from liquors, 'nobody in Tennessee ever regarded him as
addicted to their excessive use'; and that while the speaker had
denounced him for everything of which he was guilty he 'had
never charged him with being a drunkard because he had no
grounds for doing so.' [4] To this the Chief Justice replied that with
the one exception he had never seen Johnson intoxicated. 'I
knew him in the Senate before the war,' Chase continued, 'and
then I knew he was not a dissipated man. While he was President
I saw him very often, frequently late at night, and sometimes on
Sunday, but I never saw him under the influence of spirits in the
slightest degree.' [5] To the testimony of his foes we may properly
add that of a member of his Cabinet. 'For nearly four years I had
daily intercourse with him,' said Secretary McCulloch, 'frequently
at night, and I never saw him when under the influence of
liquor.' [6] The fact that he was habitually described in the press
and from the platform through the bitter struggles of his régime
as a 'drunkard' measures the appalling turpitude and reckless
dishonesty of his enemies.

Thus we have brushed aside a few favorite falsehoods used
against him in his time and preserved by some historians since.
He was not a traitor to the Republican Party, for he never belonged to it; he was not slovenly in his dress, but the direct

---

[1] *Century*, January, 1913.          [2] Crook, 83.          [3] *Ibid*.
[4] 'Defence and Vindication,' *Taylor-Trotwood Magazine*, September, 1908.
[5] *Ibid*.          [6] *Men and Measures*, 374.

opposite; he did not change his view of the purpose of the war, but held to it; and he was not a drunkard.

IX

The oratory of Johnson was that of the frontier, elemental, without finesse, graceless, void of humor, overcharged with intensity, but often overpowering in its sincerity, and persuasive in its downright honesty. Only his finely modulated voice suggested art, and it was natural. No man spoke at critical moments with more tremendous power. In youth he had read over and over the orations of Fox, Pitt, and Chatham, and no one knew the qualities of a great oration better. If he failed to attain the highest standards, it was due, in a measure, to the limitations of his education. Thus he fell into occasional grammatical errors, but, when not overwrought by feeling, he was a master of forceful rhetoric. To read his early congressional speeches is to marvel that one unable to read well at the time of his marriage could have spoken with such flowing fluency or have mastered such an extensive vocabulary.

The weakness of his speeches, the lack of humor and the lighter tones, was, in a sense, his strength in most of his tremendous struggles on the stump and in Congress. No audience ever heard him, to doubt the depth of his convictions or the sincerity and absolute candor of his utterance. Throughout his life it was his destiny to speak generally on subjects that fired human passions and involved profound fundamental principles that were, to him, as sacred as the Gospel. Fighting his early battles in a section where men took their politics in deadly earnest and carried them to the limits of personalities, he was forced to master the art of the rough-and-tumble repartee. Time and again he was to speak at the peril of his life, and he never faltered or moderated his tone. More than once his speaking was interrupted by the cocking of pistols. Speaking once under such sinister conditions, he was warned that the repetition of his speech would injure his party. 'I will make that same speech to-morrow,' he replied, 'if it blows the Democratic Party to hell.' A difficult orator, if you please, but an honest one. Told that he would be assassinated if he spoke in one community that teemed with enemies, he appeared upon the

platform with the comment that he understood shooting was to be
one of the preliminaries, and that decency and order dictated that
these be dispensed with first. Drawing a pistol from his pocket, he
paused expectantly. There was a dead silence. 'Gentlemen, it
appears I have been misinformed,' he said, quietly returning the
pistol to his pocket, and launching forthwith into an uncompromising speech.

He was familiar with mobs long before he made his 'swing
around the circle.' He met them when thundering against the
Ordinance of Secession in his canvass of Tennessee in the midst
of frenzied crowds mustering into the service of the Confederacy.
It was his fighting speeches that captivated the North until he
turned them against the disunionists of that section. Speaking
often in Indiana during the war, he was greeted by enormous
throngs of wildly enthusiastic men.[1] This, however, should be kept
in mind — he was never a demagogue. This breed does not bare
its breast to bullets. Nor were his speeches frothy and unsub-
stantial things — they were packed with substance. Laborious
and exhaustive research preceded his public appearances. In
Congress he haunted the Congressional Library in search of facts.
He had a passion for evidence. When preparing for the stump, his
office had the appearance of a factory at the close of day. It was
filled with pamphlets, works on economics, speeches, histories, and
always at hand a copy of the Constitution. A huge scrapbook
preserved newspaper clippings that might prove useful. His
method strangely resembled Lincoln's.

The height of his eloquence was reached in the impassioned
appeals for the Union and the Constitution in the Senate on the
verge of war. No one then approached him in sheer eloquence, for
there was a heart-throb in every word. Strong words and hard,
biting phrases and harsh, and yet through all something very like
a sob.

Thus, with his insight into the heart of the masses, his great
personal magnetism, his musical voice and fighting presence, his
rapidly marching sentences a little undisciplined and undecorated
like the citizens' army of the French that marched to the protection of the frontier against the embattled world, he was im-

[1] *Men and Measures,* 372.

pressive and effective. The critical sneered at his grammatical errors and jeered at his stinging sentences, but there never was a time that his enemies did not fear their effect upon a crowd. That is the reason, as we shall see, that they organized mobs to howl him down on his memorable journey to Douglas's tomb.

### X

He was unfashionable among public men of the period of his Presidency because of his meticulous honesty. His declination of a fine equipage with a span of horses proffered by a New York City group, on the ground that he had always made it a practice to refuse gifts while in public station,[1] was criticized as not without vulgarity. Handling millions as Military Governor of Tennessee, he was poorer on leaving than on taking office, and this was intolerable stupidity to not a few patriots of the time.[2] His absolute integrity made an impression on Benjamin R. Curtis, who came to know him intimately in the days of the impeachment.[3] A member of the Cabinet, of notable personal integrity, found that 'in appointments money was not potent, offices were not merchandise,' and that he 'never permitted himself to be placed under personal obligations.' His enemies were to subject his character and career to a microscopic examination for three years, without finding a single incident on which so much as to hang an insinuation. Scarcely one among his traducers could have stood the test, and this itself made him impossible.[4] Nothing depressed and alarmed him more than the moral laxity in public life; and he foresaw that the railroad grants would mean 'nothing but a series of endless corrupting legislation.' Thus he was thought vulgar in the house of Cooke. It were bad enough to be a plebeian and champion of labor; it were intolerable that he should be an enemy of favor-seeking capital.

By instinct he was the soul of candor, but, surrounded all his life with enemies, he had acquired a touch of craftiness. One of his most trusted friends found that 'he gave his confidence reluctantly,'[5] Dickens thought his manner 'suppressed, guarded,

---

[1] *New York Herald*, May 25, 1865.   [2] Winston, 239.
[3] Quoted by Woodburn, 330.   [4] *Men and Measures*, 377.
[5] *Ibid.*, 405.

anxious,'[1] and a famous journalist found him 'crafty to a degree.'[2] Thus, while assuming a haughty indifference to personal criticism, he was, at heart, supersensitive to abuse or snubs. At times in utter depression he wished that 'we [himself and family] were all blotted out of existence and even the remembrance of things that were.' Then he could unbosom himself to an intimate with appalling bitterness and strike back at his enemies in Greeneville as 'the God-forsaken and hell-deserving, money-loving, hypocritical, backbiting, Sunday-praying scoundrels of the town.'[3] And yet he seldom whined; he was too combative for that, and he fought with a ferocity and zest which never failed to inflict wounds. He gave no love-taps in battle, but used the battle-axe. One of his most inveterate foes conceded that 'his courage passed far beyond the line of obstinacy.'[4] He would side-step neither man nor devil; and yet he nursed no resentments and could grasp the proffered hand of Ben Butler after the impeachment fiasco, offer his hand to Morton, who had deserted his standard to become one of the most ferocious of his foes, and speak kindly of Parson Brownlow, who had called him 'the dead dog in the White House.'[5] He flared in a fight, but his momentary bitterness died with the occasion; and this was to be denounced as a vice by his enemies when his bitterness toward the men of the Confederacy turned to sympathy when they fell.

Nor was he merely a creature of prejudices and emotions. We have seen his method of preparing speeches. One of the soundest historical scholars of the period found that, 'in the formation of his opinions on great questions of public policy,' he was 'as diligent as any man in seeking and weighing the views of all who were competent to aid him.'[6] A tireless worker all his life, the attachés of the White House were to be amazed at the industry of a man who kept six secretaries busy, and 'except for an hour or so in the afternoon and at meal times rarely left his desk until midnight.'[7] On his tremendous tasks he brought to bear an intellect far beyond the average. His worst enemies reluctantly conceded that 'he was not deficient in intellectual ability,'[8] and, as an old man,

[1] Forster, III, 424.     [2] *Marse Henry*, I, 152.
[3] To Blackstone McDaniel, Winston, 65, 66.     [4] Boutwell, II, 106.
[5] Crook, 97.     [6] Dunning, 19.     [7] Crook, 84, 85.     [8] Boutwell, II, 104.

Henry Adams, who was a super-intellectual with a background of intellectual snobbery, recalling his youthful prejudices, was 'surprised to realize how strong the Executive was in 1868 — perhaps the strongest he was ever to see.' [1] One of the financiers of the war, a member of the Cabinet in position to judge, was convinced that 'in intellectual force he had few superiors.' [2] It was not lack of ability, but an incurable deficiency in tact that was to curse him through life; and on this there is a general agreement. Secretary McCulloch found him utterly tactless, and one of the great lawyers and jurists who defended him in the impeachment was impressed with the fact that 'he has no tact and even lacks discretion and forecast.' [3] Tactless with men, he was the heart of tenderness with his family and toward women and dependents. His daughter, recalling his relations with a slave, his bodyguard in Greeneville, thought her father more the slave than the master of the negro. Toward the invalid wife he was ineffably tender, and in his moments of excitement a soft 'Andrew, Andrew,' from her calmed him instantly. With his daughters he was ever indulgent, proud of them and their attainments. He loved children, and these understood him intuitively. An attaché at the White House found his grandchildren 'an important interest in the President's life.' [4]

There was to come a time when the immeasurable meanness of his enemies was to charge him with unfaithfulness to his wife, but this slander failed to convince. He appears to have inspired confidence in women, even in the highest circles of society prone to feel that nothing but vulgarity could emanate from a man of the people. The wives and daughters of the stricken South were to make their innumerable appeals to him and to be received with the deepest sympathy. Most of these had worthy causes; some women sought him on less meritorious missions, and observers felt that 'he found it hard to believe that anything but merit and need could lurk behind a pair of beseeching woman's eyes.' Indeed, he had 'an amiable weakness for women, particularly for pretty women.' [5] When the fashionable Mrs. Clay sought him in behalf of her imprisoned and threatened husband, and met the charming widow of Stephen A. Douglas in the corridor, the latter

[1] Henry Adams, 24–25.    [2] *Men and Measures*, 406.
[3] Woodburn, 330.    [4] Crook, 87.    [5] *Ibid.*, 92.

volunteered to accompany her to see 'the good President.' The haughty Southern belle at first was doubtful of his goodness, for he was coldly composed in his civility, but she was quick to note him 'softening under the ardent appeals of Mrs. Douglas.'[1] Beset with enemies seeking an opening against him, he was forced to move with circumspection in granting favors to Confederate leaders, and Mrs. Clay was clearly unable to understand. But when, weeping, she begged him to promise not to turn Jefferson Davis and Clay over to a military commission, he earnestly replied, 'I promise you, Mrs. Clay; trust me.' And when, thoughtless of the implied reflection upon his word, she asked him to take an oath, he solemnly raised his hand and repeated the promise. He kept his word.[2]

One day a woman, daughter of a former member of the Senate and of Jackson's Cabinet, entered to beg him for the restoration of her home, in possession of military officers. He told her with some emotion that as a boy in Raleigh he had often held her father's horse and been kindly treated, and that he had not forgotten. Her property was ordered restored. Where suffering and sorrow were concerned, he was as tender as Lincoln.

This delicacy of the man who had emerged from the depths was manifest in his conversation. A courtly gentleman was impressed by the care and exactitude of his diction in familiar talk, and by the fact that he never used an oath nor told a risqué story. He was clean-minded.[3] He was not a polished conversationalist, and his range of interest was deep rather than wide, but on subjects that interested him, he talked with fluency and force. He has been described as 'a man of few ideas,' which were 'right and true,' for which 'he would suffer death sooner than yield up or violate one of them.'[4]

Such was the vivid character and personality of the man who was to fight a memorable battle for constitutional rights and liberties and to suffer contumely for generations because of the slanders of his enemies. Honest, inflexible, tender, able, forceful, and tactless, his was a complex nature. But it was fortunate for the Republic that he had two passions — the Constitution and the Union.

[1] Mrs. Clay, 311.                    [2] *Ibid.*, 328–29.
[3] *Marse Henry*, i, 154–55.          [4] B. R. Curtis, Woodburn, 330.

# CHAPTER III

## WITH CHASE AMONG THE RUINS

### I

THE smoke had scarcely ceased to curl above the smouldering ruins of the South, and Lincoln had not yet been buried, when Chief Justice Salmon P. Chase set forth into the stricken region, accompanied by journalists, on a political mission. Before following him on his journey, let us take a hasty survey of the country through which he will pass.

For some time now a straggling procession of emaciated, crippled men in ragged gray had been sadly making their way through the wreckage to homes that in too many instances were found to be but piles of ashes. These men had fought to exhaustion. For weeks they would be found passing wearily over the country roads and into the towns, on foot and on horseback. It was observed that 'they are so worn out that they fall down on the sidewalks and sleep.'[1] The countryside through which they passed presented the appearance of an utter waste, the fences gone, the fields neglected, the animals and herds driven away, and only lone chimneys marking spots where once had stood merry homes. A proud patrician lady riding between Chester and Camden in South Carolina scarcely saw a living thing, and 'nothing but tall blackened chimneys to show that any man had ever trod this road before'; and she was moved to tears at the funereal aspect of the gardens where roses were already hiding the ruins.[2] The long thin line of gray-garbed men, staggering from weakness into towns, found them often gutted with the flames of incendiaries or soldiers. Penniless, sick at heart and in body, and humiliated by defeat, they found their families in poverty and despair. 'A degree of destitution that would draw pity from a stone,' wrote a Northern correspondent.[3] Entering the homes for a crust or cup of water, they found the furniture marred and broken, dishes cemented 'in various styles' and with 'corn cobs substituting for spindles in

---

[1] Mrs. Brooks, MS. Diary.  [2] *Diary from Dixie*, 384.
[3] *Annual Encylcopædia, 1865*, 392.

the looms.' [1] The houses of the most prosperous planters were found denuded of almost every article of furniture,[2] and in some sections women and children accustomed to luxury begged from door to door.[3]

In the larger towns the weary soldier found business prostrate except with the sutlers, in full possession now that the merchants were ruined, and these were amassing fortunes through profiteering without shame. In Charleston the shops were closed, the shutters drawn. There was no shipping in the harbor, where the piers were rapidly decaying. Cows were feeding on the vacant lots and grass was growing between paving-stones in the principal streets. Warehouses were deserted, and the burnt district looked 'like a vast graveyard with broken walls and tall blackened chimneys.' [4] The once aristocratic clubs were closed, along with the restaurants, and it was noted that 'no battle blood' mantled 'the face of the haggard and listless Charlestonians one meets.' [5] One, who momentarily rejoiced in what he saw, found that 'luxury, refinement, happiness have fled from Charleston and poverty is enthroned there.' [6] Columbia was one mass of ruins, and only the majestic columns of what had once been Wade Hampton's hall of hospitality remained. There, the prostration complete, intellectuals of the college faculty in rags were supplied with underclothing by a benevolent society of women.[7] Thus it was in towns and cities generally. Everywhere destitution, desolation, utter hopelessness. In some of the cities brave attempts were being made to restore something of business prosperity, but this rested almost wholly on the speculators from the North. The natives were literally without money, their Confederate paper and bonds now worthless. The banks had closed their doors — ruined. The insurance companies had failed. The one hope for the restoration of the cities was the resumption of normal activities in the country, the cultivation of the plantations as of old.

But in the country the situation was desperate, for the herds — cattle, sheep, and horses — had been driven away. The master of one of the best plantations in Mississippi had returned to find only a

[1] Reid, 224.               [2] Mrs. Smedes, 228.          [3] *Annual Encyclopædia, 1865*, 29.
[4] Schurz ii, 164.          [5] Reid, 66.                  [6] Welles, ii, 315.
[7] LeConte, 230.

few mules and one cow left.[1] Houses, fences, and barns, destroyed, had to be rebuilt — and there was no money. Farming implements were needed — and there was no credit. But the gravest problem of all was that of labor, for the slaves were free and were demanding payment in currency that their old masters no longer possessed. The one hope of staving off starvation the coming winter was to persuade the freedmen to work on the share, or wait until the crops were marketed for their pay. Many old broken planters called their former slaves about them and explained, and at first many agreed to wait for their compensation on the harvest. Many of them went on about their work, 'very quiet and serious and more obedient and kind than they had ever been known to be.' [2] It was observed that with the pleasure of knowing they had their freedom there was a touch of sadness.[3] Some Northerners, who had taken Mrs. Stowe's novel too literally, were amazed at the numerous 'instances of the most touching attachment to their old masters and mistresses.' [4] One of these was touched one Sunday morning when the negroes appeared in mass at the mansion house to pay their respects. 'I must have shaken hands with four hundred,' she wrote.[5] Something of the beautiful loyalty in them which guarded the women and children with such zeal while husbands and fathers were fighting far away persisted in the early days of their freedom. Old slaves, with fruit and gobblers and game, would sneak into the house with an instinctive sense of delicacy and leave them in the depleted larder surreptitiously.[6] Occasionally some of these loyal creatures, momentarily intoxicated with the breath of liberty, would roam down the road toward the towns, only to return with childlike faith to the old plantation. But for the suggestions of soldiers and agitators, the former masters and slaves might easily have effected a social readjustment to their mutual benefit, but this was not the game intended. The negroes must be turned against their former masters; it was destiny perhaps that the carpetbagger should be served. Quite soon an extravagant notion of proper compensa-

---

[1] Mrs. Smedes, 229.          [2] *Ibid.*, 228.
[3] *Whites and Blacks under the Old Régime*, 152.
[4] Schurz, Rpt., Ex. Doc. 2, 39th Cong., 1st Sess.          [5] Mrs. Leigh, 21.
[6] Mrs. Smedes, 246.

tion for services was to turn the freedmen adrift.[1] Soon they were drunk with a sense of their power and importance.

## II

One day a South Carolina woman wrote in her diary that 'negroes are seen in the fields plowing and hoeing corn,' and a month later that 'the negroes have flocked to the Yankee squad.' The revolution had been wrought.[2] The first evidence that outside influences had been at work upon the freedmen was furnished in their bizarre notions of labor, that under freedom all system ceased. At all hours of the day they could be seen laying down their implements and sauntering singing from the fields. If freedom did not mean surcease from labor, where was the boon?[3] And since they had changed their condition, why not their names? Former owners, meeting negroes born on their plantations and addressing them in the familiar way, were sharply rebuked with the assurance that they no longer responded to that name. 'If you want anything, call for Sambo,' said a patronizing old freedman. 'I mean call me Mr. Samuel, dat my name now.'[4] Had the intoxication of the new freedom worked no more serious changes in the negro's character, all would have been well, but he was to meet with influences designed to separate him in spirit from those who understood him best.

Very soon they were eschewing labor and flocking to army camps to be fed, and here they were told, with cruel malice, that the land they had formerly cultivated as slaves was to be given them. Accepting it seriously, some had actually taken possession and planted corn and cotton.[5] The assurance was given them solemnly that when Congress met, the division would be made.[6] Quite soon they would have it on the authority of Thaddeus Stevens.[7] Convinced of the ultimate division, they could see no sense in settling down to toil for the meager wages the impoverished planters could afford to pay. There was pathos in their faith in the blue coat, and their congestion about the army posts soon tested the patience of the commanders. Even the negro women

[1] Worth, to Whittlesby, I, 451.   [2] Mrs. Chestnut, 384, 394.
[3] Mrs. Leigh, 26.   [4] Mrs. Chestnut, 389.   [5] Mrs. Leigh, 27.
[6] Doc. Hist., quoted, Ala. Hist. Soc., Letters of Samford, IV.   [7] Lancaster speech.

were wont to array themselves in cheap, gaudy finery, and carry bouquets to soldiers in festive mood.[1] When military orders drove them from the camps, they flocked to villages, towns, and cities, where, in the summer of 1865, they lived in idleness and squalor, huddled together in shacks, and collecting in gangs at street corners and crossroads.[2] So sinister was the tendency that he who was to become their political leader in North Carolina on their enfranchisement warned them against 'crowding into towns and villages, subsisting on Government rations, contracting diseases, and incurring fearful risks to their morals and habits of industry.'[3] But warnings and pleas were of no avail to turn them back to the fields. They were to become the owners of the land, their former masters dispossessed, and while waiting for the possession of their property they could depend on Government rations, and their wits. Hearken to the advice of their former masters and mistresses? Had not their new friends from the North been at pains to teach them these were enemies? Freedom — it meant idleness, and gathering in noisy groups in the streets. Soon they were living like rats in ruined houses, in miserable shacks under bridges built with refuse lumber, in the shelter of ravines and in caves in the banks of rivers.[4] Freedom meant throwing aside all marital obligations, deserting wives and taking new ones, and in an indulgence in sexual promiscuity that soon took its toll in the victims of consumption and venereal disease. Jubilant, and happy, the negro who had his dog and a gun for hunting, a few rags to cover his nakedness, and a dilapidated hovel in which to sleep, was in no mood to discuss work.[5]

All over the South that summer the negroes held their jubilee. A weird wave of religious fervor swept them into a crazy frenzy, and day after day they gathered in groves where imported preachers worked on their emotions. Shouting, praying, howling, they turned their backs on the old plantation preachers, who disapproved of the methods of the visiting evangelists, who in many instances turned out to be unscrupulous organizers for the Northern Radicals. At night the vicinity of the revivals was pillaged of poultry and vegetables on the theory that the Lord should pro-

---
[1] Mrs. Chestnut, 394.    [2] Fleming, 271; *Memoirs of Holden*, 35.
[3] Holden in the *Raleigh Standard*, April 24, 1865.    [4] Fleming, 273.    [5] *Ibid.*

vide.[1] Great black multitudes stood shouting on the banks of streams as preachers converted and immersed. 'Freed from slavery,' shouted an old woman emerging, dripping, 'freed from sin. Bless God and General Grant.' [2]

And with it all went the feeling that the topsy-turvy world had just been righted, and that they, as God's chosen children, were to be the proprietors of the land and the favored of paradise. Thus groves rang with song:

> 'We'se nearer to de Lord
> Dan to de white folks an da knows it,
> See de glory gates unbarred.
> Walk in, darkies, past de guard.
> Bets yer dollah he won't close it.

> 'Walk in, darkies, troo de gate.
> Hark de cullid angels holler,
> Go way, white folks, you're too late.
> We'se de winnin' culler.' [3]

Soon celebrations of a more threatening sort were being held, demanding suffrage — a forerunner of much that was to come. For under the patronage of the new friends from the North, the negro had already become the equal of the white in blue and the potential master of the man in gray. Even their vocabulary had expanded in the light of freedom. 'Where are you going?' asked a white man of a neighbor's former slave as he was striding militantly down the road. 'Perusin' my way to Columbia,' he replied, for 'peruse' had a royal sound.[4] Everywhere they were on the march. 'My sister-in-law is in tears of rage and despair,' wrote a lady in her diary. 'Her servants have all gone to a big meeting at Mulberry though she made every appeal against their going.' [5]

They were free — waiting for the master's land, assured of heaven.

### III

If the negroes caused some uneasiness, many of the army of occupation were more disturbing. When the soldiers marched into

[1] Fleming, 273; *Doc. Hist.*, i, 92, 93.    [2] Fleming, 273.
[3] *New York World*, August 2, 1865.    [4] Mrs. Chestnut, 394.    [5] *Ibid.*, 402.

a community, visions of rapine and rape terrorized the women.[1] Unfounded as were these fears, there were instances where soldiers, unworthily officered, maliciously frightened women and children by pushing into houses and jeering at the faithful negroes who stood by to protect them.[2] But the meanest offenses of soldiers were committed against the blacks who gathered about them in childish faith, to be worse maltreated than by former masters, who, in numerous instances, interfered to protect them from the cruelty of their 'deliverers.'[3] Even more cruel was the persistent effort of soldiers to instill into the negro's mind a hatred of the men with whom he would have to live after the army should march away. The correspondent of 'The Nation' ascribed the labor and race troubles to the bad influence of the negro's Northern friends, 'particularly soldiers.'[4] Emissaries of radicalism were constantly inflaming the freedmen with a false sense of their importance, turning them against the native whites, encouraging their indolence with wild tales of the inevitable division of the plantation lands among them.[5] Young colored women, gayly making their way to camps to 'enjoy mah freedom,' were frequently used for immoral purposes. 'The negro girls for miles around are gathered to the camps and debauched,' wrote an indignant citizen to General Sherman, in protest. 'It surely is not the aim of those persons who aim at the equality of colors to begin the experiment with a whole race of whores.'[6] Officers, waiting to be mustered out, regaled themselves with women, cards, and whiskey, for there was an enormous sale of liquor in the vicinity of the camps.[7] In Charleston, where only the taverns thrived, 'flushed and spendthrift Yankee officers' were found by Whitelaw Reid 'willing to pay seventy-five cents for a cobbler.'[8] Abandoned white women trailed the camps, and disreputable houses sprang up in the vicinity of the posts.[9]

Other irritating features of the occupation there were in abundance — such as the requisition of the finest private houses for the use of officers.[10] And to this was added an unnecessary offen-

[1] Mrs. Brooks, A School Girl's Diary, MS.     [2] Mrs. Chestnut, 385–86.
[3] Wallace, 37.     [4] Vol. I, 107.
[5] The Negro in South Carolina under Reconstruction, 26–27.     [6] Thompson, 138.
[7] Fleming, 263.     [8] Reid, 66.     [9] Fleming, 263.     [10] Reid, 46–47.

siveness toward the Southern whites taking the amnesty oath. An editor who wrote a harmlessly amusing editorial about it was pompously denounced by the commander of the post as 'necessarily a bad man, incendiary in his character' and guilty of 'a high crime,' and he was arrested, his office seized, his paper suppressed.[1] Thus the Southerner who was sober was meditating treason, and he who smiled was guilty of its commission. When, in taking the oath, one man laughingly asked if the dog that accompanied him should take it, too, he was arrested and thrown into jail.[2]

Inevitably, under such conditions, conflicts between civil and military authorities were not rare. From every quarter protests poured into Washington against the high-handed tyranny of some of the military commanders. Ordinary thieves were wrested from the civil authorities, to be tried, or released, by military tribunals. Such incredible stupidity or tyranny as the release of a grafting treasury agent arrested for various crimes, on the ground that State courts had no authority over these petty officials, aroused the wrath of thousands.[3]

It only remained for the Federal Government to drive the disarmed people to the verge of a new rebellion by stationing negro troops in the midst of their homes. Nothing short of stupendous ignorance, or brutal malignity, can explain the arming and uniforming of former slaves and setting them as guardians over the white men and their families. Even the patient Wade Hampton was moved to fury; and he wrote hotly to Johnson denouncing 'your brutal negro troops under their no less brutal and more degraded Yankee officers' by whom 'the grossest outrages were committed . . . with impunity.'[4] This is not an exaggerated picture. Even Northerners, not prone to sympathize with the prostrate foe, were shocked and humiliated by the scenes they saw. In streets and highways they took no pride in the spectacle of thousands of blacks with muskets and shimmering bayonets swaggering in jeering fashion before their former masters and mistresses. These colored soldiers were not so culpable as the whites who used them to torture a fallen enemy. These were children, acting as children would under the circumstances. March-

---

[1] Avery, 345. The case of A. P. Burr, of the *Macon Journal*.        [2] *Ibid.*, 346.
[3] Ramsdell, 82; Garner, 98–100.        [4] *Doc. Hist.*, I, 47.

ing four abreast in the streets, they jostled the whites from the pavements. In rough and sullen tones the sentries challenged old crippled and emaciated men in tattered gray. So insolent did their conduct become in some communities that women no longer dared venture from their doors, and citizens in the country no longer felt it safe to go to town.[1] Noisy — often, when intoxicated, dangerous — they gave the freedmen refusing to work a sense of racial grandeur, and encouraged the dream of the distribution of the white man's land.

Worse than the men were the degraded white officers who commanded them.[2] From every quarter appeals reached Washington for their removal, for the fears of the whites were not of the imagination. Thus, at Chester they clubbed and bayoneted an old man; at Abbeville white men were ordered from the sidewalks; in Charleston they forced their way into a house, ordered food, and, after partaking, felled the mistress of the household. In retaliation for the blow of a white man entrusted with the guardianship of a young woman who had been insulted, negro soldiers dragged him to camp, murdered him in cold blood, and danced upon his grave.[3] These are not carefully selected cases to make the picture black — the evidence is overwhelming that they do not exaggerate the peril thus placed at the doorsteps of the whites. Here and there were colored troops, under the discipline of decent white officers, who conducted themselves with propriety and without offense. There was such a regiment in Florida.[4] But always, with these newly freed negroes armed and in easy reach of liquor, the shadow of an awful fear rested upon the women of the communities where they were stationed.

## IV

Nothing could have been finer than the spirit and courage with which the women faced defeat and misfortune, and yet, despite their simulated smiles in that spring that came unusually early in 1865, there was bitterness and sorrow in their hearts.[5] Not only had they lost husbands, sons, brothers, and sweethearts, but they were impoverished and their cause had failed. Even so there was

[1] Reid, I, 48.  [2] Garner, 105.  [3] Reynolds, 5–6.
[4] Wallace, 19.  [5] Schurz, II, 181.

no bending of their pride. A correspondent traveling in South Carolina noted their 'superior presence' and a 'certain air of vehemence or pertness.' [1] Disaster and poverty could not rob them of their charm. For the sake of the returning warriors, humiliated by defeat, they made merry over the makeshifts imposed upon them in matters of dress, wearing their homespun and their calico with a regal grace. And though it was observed that 'hardly any one at church is out of mourning,' by one who thought 'it piteous to see so many mere girls' faces shaded by deep crape veils and widow's caps,' [2] they turned bravely to the soothing of the wounded spirits of their men. Within two weeks of the surrender, a traveler was amazed to see the young people at Winnsboro gayly celebrating May Day amid the still smoking ruins.[3] In midsummer a young girl was writing in her diary that 'we are trying to help our soldiers forget, and are having picnics and parties all the time.' [4] Popular were the 'starvation parties,' where no refreshments were served, and picnics where young folks danced to the music of fiddles.[5] Soon they were turning to tournaments where riders, armed with hickory lances, rode past posts collecting rings suspended to them on the end of the lance for the glory of their ladies. There was billing and cooing, even among the graves.

But toward the conquerors they were implacable. The rumor, false, no doubt, that General Sherman had boasted he would bring every Southern woman to the washtub, intensified their hatred of the army of occupation.[6] Sometimes soldiers would amuse themselves by sitting on back fences to jeer the former mistress of slaves as she washed the family linen. Thus the attempts of the younger subordinate officers to enter the social circles of the communities where they were stationed were rebuked. The Southern men treated the soldiers and Northerners, flocking into the South to profit on the necessities of a stricken people, with courtesy in business, but the women were the rulers of the homes. Many of the soldiers were undeserving of social courtesies. When women crossed the street to evade them, or swept their skirts aside in passing, they were met with insulting comments on their clothes

---

[1] *New York World*, June 28, 1865.      [2] Mrs. Leigh, 12.
[3] Mrs. Chestnut, 384–85.      [4] Mrs. Brooks, MS. Diary.
[5] Dr. J. N. White, MS. Reminiscences.      [6] Mrs. Smedes, 234.

and ankles.[1] And woe to the woman who succumbed to a Northern officer in romance. When the daughter of a former Governor of North Carolina married a dashing Yankee officer who had entered her village at the head of cavalry, the wedding invitations were generally ignored, and when the bride departed for her Northern home, it was said that a daughter of the South had gone away loaded with jewelry and finery that had been stolen from women in States farther south.[2]

With the women moved by emotions, memories of the dead, pity for the living, the Southern men, facing realities, had accepted defeat as final, and asked nothing better than a speedy removal of the soldiers and the restoration of normal conditions. Here and there could be heard the defiant cry of an irreconcilable; ever and anon the thoughtless gave utterance to a foolish thought; but among men of sobriety and judgment there was a general acquiescence in the verdict of the battle-field. Carl Schurz, eager to justify the policy of the Radicals, treasured up every idle gesture and foolish word of irresponsible and unimportant men as proof that the mailed hand could not be withdrawn with safety. But Grant, with a better understanding of the people, was 'satisfied that the mass of thinking men . . . accept the present situation in good faith'; and Watterson found 'unmistakable evidence of a determination to renew in good faith their former relations.' [3] More impressive and conclusive to the President and posterity was the report of Benjamin F. Truman, which was a sharp contradiction of the extravagant partisan findings of Schurz. In truth, nothing was more remote than politics from the minds of men threatened with economic ruin. 'Politics are never mentioned and they know less of what is going on in Washington than in London,' wrote Mrs. Leigh.[4]

v

And it was into this section, with the smoke still curling from the ruins, that Salmon P. Chase sallied forth on a mission of politics. His purpose was not unknown to the Radical politicians, and not unguessed by the people generally. 'The chief justice started

[1] Fleming, 320.    [2] Old Days at Chapel Hill, 94–99.
[3] Doc. Hist., I, 51.    [4] Mrs. Leigh, 13.

yesterday on a visit,' wrote Sumner to Bright, '. . . and will on his way touch the necessary strings, so far as he can. I anticipate much from this journey.'[1] A clever young journalist was with him to chronicle the story of his progress.[2]

The party entered the black belt obsessed with the primary importance of negro suffrage, and the amazement of the Southern whites imparted the zest of amusement to the visitors.[3] Chase heard of the refusal of the negroes to work, and saw them living in idleness and squalor and lolling in the sunny streets, but this did not impress him unfavorably. Everywhere he was received with the courtesy and reverence due his rank, but this did not touch him. Local leaders called upon him with flowers and strawberries and sought information as to their probable fate. They were reconciled, and not bitter — and they were threatened with negro suffrage.[4] At Wilmington, where Chase delivered a 'lost speech' from the spacious home of an evicted family, he found it necessary to sow a little seed. Already the negroes, loitering in the streets and about saloons, were talking politics. The Union League Clubs of New York and Philadelphia had been busy with their emissaries in the organization of political negro clubs, and delegations of these filed into the presence of the Chief Justice, made their bow, and had their hopes encouraged. With judicious solemnity he listened to the spokesman: 'I tell you sah we ain't noways safe 'long as dem people makes de laws. We's got to hab a voice in the pinting ob de law makers. Den we knows our frens and whose hans we's safe in.'[5] The visitors heard that the freedmen were refusing to work, but if the Chief Justice, in giving copious advice, ever suggested the necessity for industry, it was not recorded by the Boswell at his elbow.

Passing on to Charleston, the Chase party picked its way among the ruins and witnessed the terrible depression and poverty of the people, but the Chief Justice was not there to study ruins. A great negro mass meeting was organized in his honor. There he faced 'certainly the blackest faces, with the flattest noses and the wooliest heads — the mouths now and then broadening into a grin or breaking out into that low oily chuckling gobble of a laugh no

[1] Pierce, iv, 242.      [2] Whitelaw Reid.      [3] Reid, 26–27.
[4] Ibid., 32–33.      [5] Ibid., 51–52.

white man can ever imitate.' The negro women, gaudily dressed, and wearing kid gloves, were even more enthusiastic than the men. And Chase was in fine fettle. His judicial robes had been thrown aside, and it was a politician and partisan, eager for presidential honors, that faced the black swaying crowd. As he poured forth his promise of the vote, the black faces beamed and glowed. 'Dat's true foh shore!' shouted an old woman. The younger women enjoyed the entertainment less vocally, contenting themselves by giggling, slapping their hands, and peering over at the men to see how they were acting.[1] 'If all the people feel as I do,' said the Chief Justice, 'you will not have to wait long for equal rights at the ballot box; no longer than it would take to pass the necessary law.' [2] This Charleston speech, delivered five weeks after the surrender, did not meet with unalloyed delight in the North. The 'New York Herald,' which had charged, on his departure, that Chase was on an electioneering tour,[3] denounced the Charleston speech as 'an incendiary talk' and found 'the whole tenor of the speech that of a firebrand thrown into a complicated and difficult situation.' It thought him 'prompted solely by an inordinate ambition to set himself up in opposition to the Government and to promulgate theories and dogmas which, if followed up in the same spirit, will plunge the whole Southern country into a social war more dreadful in its results than the rebellion.' [4] The 'New York World' failed 'to perceive how it either comports with the dignity, or is consistent with the proprieties of that great position [the Chief-Justiceship] to be perambulating a disquieted portion of the country making harangues on a disturbing question which the authorities have not yet decided.' [5] But Chase was undisturbed, and was making progress.

Thus, while lingering in Charleston, he passed over to the Sea Islands, inhabited by the most primitive and ignorant of field workers in cotton and rice. Here again a meeting was arranged in his honor; and here, too, he found potential voters entitled to the ballot. Reid the Boswell was a little shocked at the abysmal ignorance of this audience and thought perhaps too much was being said by some of the Chief Justice's platform companions of the

[1] Reid, 80–82.　　　[2] Ibid., 81–86.　　　[3] New York Herald, May 20, 1865.
[4] Ibid., June 1, 1865.　　　[5] New York World, May 22, 1865.

escape from the tyranny of wicked masters. But there was no re-buke from Chase. A strange spectacle he presented that hot day, facing this Congo crowd chanting in his honor:

'Me-is-ta-ah Che-a-ase a-sittin' on de tree ob life,
Me-is-ta-ah Che-a-ase a-sittin' on de tree ob life,
Roll, Jordan, roll;
Me-is-ta-ah Che-a-ase a-sittin' on de tree ob life,
Roll, Jordan, roll;
Me-is-ta-ah Che-a-ase a-sittin' on de tree ob life,
Roll, Jordan, roll.
Roll, Jordan, roll.
Ro-o-oll, Jordan, ro-o-oll.'

Thereupon the Chief Justice descended from 'de tree ob life,' to ad-dress those whom he would introduce into the body of American citizenship without delay. 'A few words of calm advice,' recorded Boswell. Among other things he advised study.[1] Sitting in his room at Charleston, he wrote at length to Johnson. He had found the largest classes of the whites eager for the restoration of the old order, without slavery. But there were the 'progressives' who be-lieved 'that the black man made free must be allowed to vote,' and the 'progressives' were 'men of sagacity and activity,' though few had been in conspicuous positions.[2] It is significant that he did not indicate whether these 'progressives' were natives or immigrants from the North from whom the carpetbaggers were to be recruited.

On to Savannah. People in the streets in the rags of poverty. The famous shell road was gone, and Chase's carriage wheels sank deep in sand. There he found eighty-five hundred negroes unwilling to work, but eager for the ballot, and a committee of these filed into his room to make their plea. 'Suppose you were permitted to vote,' asked Chase the politician, 'what guarantee would the Government have that you would know how to vote, or that your influence would not be cast on the side of bad morals and bad politics?' The negroes grinned in toleration. 'Oh, Judge, we know who our frens are.' And that was promising.[3]

More discouraging was the committee of leading white citizens who called to protest against mixed schools. This shocked the Chase party, albeit no mixed schools were tolerated in the North.

[1] Reid, 105–08.     [2] Schuckers, 521–23.     [3] Reid, 143.

Quite as shocking, to hear these men who had seen cherished relatives perish on battle-fields speaking in kindly fashion of Lee and Stonewall Jackson, and the men in faded gray.[1] And yet the chronicler, thus shocked, observed that 'the bearing of the rebel soldiers was unexceptionable,'[2] and he was disgusted when a drunken Northern sergeant 'insisted on cutting the buttons from the uniform of an elegant gray-headed Brigadier who had just come in from Johnston's army.'[3]

On, now, to Jacksonville. A negro guard pacing along the wharf — negroes in uniforms sauntering through the streets — a West-Pointer in charge of the army post established in the finest house in town, while his staff loafed about the billiard rooms. And there, at night, an old colleague of the Senate, Yulee, called for a chat, to be saddened and astonished at Chase's reference to immediate suffrage. While polite, the Chief Justice apparently enjoyed the discomfiture of his guest.[4]

Thence on to Mobile. Here, business in a state of torpor — soldiers everywhere — shops and warehouses along the levee closed. Chase drove out the old shell road and found unchanged in the villages the hedges of the Cherokee rose, and the arbors of scuppernong grapes, and orange trees, and the glossy leaves of the magnolia. It was in Mobile that the military forces staged a review in his honor, and negro troops marching under his approving eye 'brought curses to the mouths of nearly all on-lookers.'[5] A stubborn people, these Mobilians! They were insisting they would not tolerate negro suffrage. No doubt it was Johnson's North Carolina Proclamation, thought the visitors.[6]

And then on to New Orleans, happy hunting ground of Northern speculators, and home of Radicals whose language the Chief Justice could understand. A tall, thin, sallow man, with a cadaverous, saturnine face, called at once — Durant, Republican leader, brilliant speaker, untamed fanatic.[7] He shared Chase's obsession on the ballot for the blacks. And it was in New Orleans that Chase had what seemed to him a beautiful experience. In the once elegant home of Pierre Soule, he attended a fair given by the negroes.

[1] Reid, 152–53.    [2] Ibid., 155.    [3] Ibid., 156.
[4] Reid, 164; Schuckers, Chase to Sumner, 523.    [5] Reid, 213.
[6] Ibid.    [7] Reid, 232–33; T. J. Durant.

Negroes selling ice-cream from Soule's tables; raffling articles of finery in Soule's parlors — the tables had turned. Not unnoticed by Chase's party were the negro women. 'Beautiful,' thought Boswell. And how they pounded on Soule's piano, and shook the books of Soule's library with their songs! The charms of the evening went to the head of at least one member of the party, who found the negro women 'as handsome, as elegantly dressed, and in many respects almost as brilliant' as any white women Soule himself had ever entertained.[1]

With pleasing memories of the Soule house party, Chase passed on into Mississippi and Tennessee, where, at Memphis, he was shocked on reading the President's Mississippi Proclamation. 'It disappoints me greatly,' he wrote Kate Chase Sprague. 'I shall be glad if it does not do a great deal of harm.' To which he added in righteous mood, 'I shall stick by my principles.' That these principles and this campaign tour in the South could do infinitely more harm to whites and blacks alike than any or all the proclamations of Johnson, never occurred to Chase.

### VI

Meanwhile the Southern people were fighting for the preservation of their civilization. The negroes would not work, the plantations could not produce. The freedmen clung to the illusion planted in their minds by demagogues that the economic status of the races was to be reversed through the distribution of the land among them.[2] This cruelly false hope was being fed by private soldiers, Bureau agents, and low Northern whites circulating among the negroes on terms of social equality in the cultivation of their prospective votes. 'Nothing but want will bring them to their senses,' wrote one Carolinian to another.[3] At the time, however, the negroes were warding off want by prowling the highways and byways in the night for purposes of pillage. In one week, in one town in Georgia, one hundred and fifty were arrested for theft.

More serious than this annoying petty stealing was the wholesale pillaging by Treasury agents, who swarmed over the land like the locusts of Egypt following the order confiscating all cotton that had

---

[1] Reid, 245.        [2] Doc. Hist., I, 353–54.
[3] Ruffin Papers, Cameron to Ruffin, 35.

been contracted to the fallen Confederacy.[1] It mattered not whether the cotton had been contracted for or not; these petty officials rumbled over the roads day and night in Government wagons with soldiers, taking whatever they could find. One agent in Alabama stole eighty thousand dollars' worth of cotton in a month.[2] The burden of proof was put upon the owner, and the agent in Arkansas enforced rules of evidence no planter could circumvent.[3] When, in Texas, agents caught red-handed were indicted, the army released them.[4] When, as in Alabama, the stealing was so flagrant that prosecutions were forced, proceedings were suddenly stopped as the trail of crime led toward politicians of importance.[5]

This, then, was the combination against the peace of a fallen people — the soldiers inciting the blacks against their former masters, the Bureau agents preaching political and social equality, the white scum of the North fraternizing with the blacks in their shacks, and the thieves of the Treasury stealing cotton under the protection of Federal bayonets. And in the North, demagogic politicians and fanatics were demanding immediate negro suffrage and clamoring for the blood of Southern leaders. Why was not Jeff Davis hanged; and why was not Lee shot?

The gallant figure of the latter had ridden quietly out of the public view. No word of bitterness escaped his lips, and he sought to 'promote harmony and good feeling.'[6] His own future was dark enough, the fine old mansion at Arlington gone, and he had no home. Sometimes, astride old Traveller, he cantered along country roads looking for a small farm.[7] 'Some quiet little home in the woods,' he wrote, declining the offer of an estate in England.[8] June found him settled in a four-room house in a grove of oaks near Cartersville, with his wife and daughters.[9] Then came the offer of the presidency of Washington College. Should he accept? Was he competent? Would it injure the institution? He would like to 'set the young an example of submission to authority.'[10] One September day, his decision made, found him mounted on old Traveller riding toward Lexington. The ladies of the town helped furnish his little office, and admirers sent articles of furniture for his house and

[1] LeConte, 230.   [2] *Doc. Hist.*, I, 25–27.   [3] Staples, 89.
[4] Ramsdell, 44.   [5] Fleming, 299.   [6] *Recollections and Letters of Lee*, 162–63.
[7] *Ibid.*, 166–67.   [8] *Ibid.*, 170.   [9] *Ibid.*, 174.   [10] *Ibid.*, 181.

the family took possession. In old letters we have a vision of Lee, the sinister conspirator pictured in the Northern papers, proudly displaying to his wife and daughters the pickles, preserves, and brandied peaches the neighbors had sent in, and the bags of walnuts, potatoes, and game the mountaineers had given.[1] But the patriots of the North were not to be deceived by appearances. 'We protest,' said 'The Nation,' 'against the notion that he is fit to be put at the head of a college in a country situated as Virginia is.'[2] And Wendell Phillips was exclaiming to a cheering crowd at Cooper Union that 'if Lee is fit to be president of a college, then for Heaven's sake pardon Wirtz and make him professor of what the Scots call "the humanities."'[3]

## VII

Such was the spirit of the North when the Southern Conventions and Legislatures began to meet. Mississippi led off with a hundred delegates, all but two of whom were able to qualify, since ninety-eight had opposed secession. Seven had been members of the Secession Convention and six had voted against the ordinance. Having nothing to conceal, it was decided to report the debates in full to satisfy the North that the results of the war had been accepted in good faith. But when a few, discussing abolition, proposed some form of compensation, the skeptics above the Ohio cried 'Aha!'[4] The proposal was thereupon abandoned.[5] Moving with the utmost circumspection, the action of the Convention was a challenge to the fairness of the foe, but Charles Sumner denounced it as 'a rebel conspiracy to obtain political power.'[6]

Then came the election, with the legislative candidates called upon in the canvass to define their position on negro testimony in the courts. 'Aha!' exclaimed the Radicals, their eyes glued upon the scene. 'Negroes as a class must be excluded from the witness stand,' declared the 'Jackson News.' 'If the privilege is ever granted, it will lead to greater demands, and at last end in the admission of the negro to the jury box and ballot box.'[7] 'Aha!' screamed the Radicals, advocating suffrage. True, the 'Jackson

---

[1] *Recollections and Letters of Lee*, 202–04.        [2] September 14, 1865.
[3] *The Nation*, November 2, 1865.        [4] Garner, 87.        [5] *Ibid.*, 88–89.
[6] *Ibid.*, 94.        [7] *Ibid.*, 94.

Clarion' favored negro testimony, but it was only the adverse attitude that interested Thad Stevens and Sumner. And when a Confederate Brigadier who had voted against secession was elected Governor, and the opponents of negro testimony carried the Legislature, a howl of derision came down on the winds from the North.

Came then the Legislature, and the attempt to find laws to meet the new conditions born of emancipation. Negroes were forbidden the use of cars set apart for the whites, and the Stevenses and the Sumners ground their teeth. When the races intermarried, they could be imprisoned for life. It was made a crime to give or lend deadly weapons, ammunition, or intoxicating liquors to the freedmen, and this was denounced as discrimination. Negro orphans could be apprenticed, under rigid court regulations, and the abolitionists pricked up their ears and heard the rattle of chains. If the apprentice ran away, could he not be apprehended and restored — just like a slave? More: when a freedman broke a contract to labor, could he not be arrested and taken back? If he could no longer wander whistling at noonday from the field, and leave his work to witness an immersion, what a mockery would be his freedom! Laws against vagrancy, against adultery, the latter bearing harder on the whites than on the blacks, 'tis true, but still aimed at freedom — all bad.[1]

Instantly the Northern politicians, bent on the exclusion of the Southern States until negro suffrage could fortify their power, were up in arms. 'The men of the North will convert . . . Mississippi into a frog pond before they will allow any such laws to disgrace one foot of soil,' thundered the 'Chicago Tribune.'[2]

During the fall and winter, the Southern Legislatures proceeded with similar enactments to meet a similar social and economic crisis. The vagrancy laws, so desperately needed and so bitterly denounced, were little different from those of Northern States.[3] Nor were they so severe as those enforced by the military authorities seeking the same end — the ending of idleness and crime and the return of the freedmen to the fields. A Southern writer has described these military orders as 'tyrannical as ukases of a czar.'[4]

[1] *Doc. Hist.*, I, 282–89.          [2] December 1, 1865; Garner, 115.
[3] Such as those of Massachusetts, Connecticut, Wisconsin, and Indiana.
[4] Avery.

These provided severe punishment for negroes using disrespectful language to a former master, forbade them going from one plantation to another without a pass, and ordered daily inspections of negro cabins to discourage stealing. At Milledgeville, all who could, and would not, work were set to compulsory labor in the street without pay. At Atlanta, a curfew law was put into operation.[1] In Texas the negroes were told that unless they returned to work on the old plantation, they would be forced to work without wages, and they were denied the right to travel the highways without the permission of their employers.[2] Thus the higher army officers on the ground, familiar with conditions, sought to serve both races through the rehabilitation of industry. This, too, was the intent of the Black Codes of the South. An eminent historian has pronounced these laws for the most part 'a conscientious and straightforward attempt to bring some sort of order out of the social and economic chaos,' and in principle and detail 'faithful on the whole to the actual conditions with which they had to deal.'[3]

But there was nothing judicious in the attitude of the Radical politicians. Sitting in his little office in Lancaster, grim Thad Stevens, meditating a plan of reconstruction of his own, and girding his loins for a death struggle with Johnson, chortled in sardonic glee. These hated men of the South were stocking his arsenal. And he was whetting his knife.

Let us journey down to Lancaster and meet him.

[1] Avery, 343; Thompson, 49.      [2] Ramsdell, 48.      [3] Dunning, 57–58.

# CHAPTER IV

## THADDEUS STEVENS: A PORTRAIT

### I

MORE than one stranger to Lancaster appeared that summer, to find his way up a narrow, tree-lined street in the old section to a three-and-a-half-story red-brick house with two front doors, one opening into the home and the other into the office of Thad Stevens. In the same block was an old hotel, and at the corner was a beer saloon. For a generation, politicians had frequented the office day and night, and in the home the master had spent many years with his books. On summer evenings he might have been seen frequently sitting on the steps, which were directly on the street, or walking along leisurely under the trees, or examining the fruit trees in the back yard. Perhaps a comely mulatto woman would respond to the knocker and usher the visitor into the presence of the grim old man in an easy-chair.

If the visitor had seen the portrait of Stevens by Eicholtz, painted when the old man was in his thirty-eighth year, he would have been shocked at the face and figure before him in the room. He would have expected a handsome and patrician face, with bright, beaming eyes denoting some softness and sentiment, and some elegance of apparel, with ruffled shirt-front and black stock, and would have been disappointed. The charm of those earlier years had long since fled. The softness, suggesting sentiment, was gone. The old man in the chair was much thinner of face, his lips no longer full, but hard and set, the cheeks pale rather than of a healthy glow, and albeit the hair was black, it was but a wig imitation.[1] If he rose to meet the guest, it would have been observed that his movements were stiff and angular, for this was an old man of seventy-three. He now availed himself of the privilege of old age to be less careful of his appearance, and he was clearly not concerned with the concealment of his defects. When an old abolitionist woman impulsively requested a lock of his hair, the

[1] Callender, 144.

old man handed her his wig with a sardonic grin.[1] An illness had left him bald as a plate, but it was a luxurious mass of black hair that covered his nakedness.

Despite a crippled foot, he had, in earlier years, been an impressive figure, almost six feet in height, and with the fine muscular development of an athlete. In truth, he had been a famous horseman in his time, and he abandoned the saddle and the pleasures of the canter only when old age decreed. As a young man at Gettysburg, he kept his own hunters and rode to hounds, and long afterward old mountain men loved to tell of his daring in the chase.[2] And he had been a lusty swimmer, too, boasting in his prime that he could have swum the Bosphorus as easily as Byron, who also had a club foot. But the canter, the chase, the swim were no longer for the bitter old man who sat that summer in his house in Lancaster meditating war. His mouth was large and expressive of his biting tongue and sarcastic nature. The upper lip was thin. A prominent aquiline nose gave him the look of an angry eagle — a dominating, if not a domineering aspect. His head was large and well-formed. 'His countenance had more the stony features of authority than sweetness,' said a friend.[3]

After an hour's conversation, the visitor would have left with an unsatisfied curiosity as to the character of this amazing man. Despite the debilitated body, he would have been impressed with the tremendous force that flowed from it, and with the bitterness of its spirit. And, in a sense, it was the most disturbing bitterness imaginable, for there was something of a wild gayety about it. Here, surely, was an untamed eagle, or an old man strangely unsoftened by the years. Had he not said with a chuckle that he intended to die 'like Nicanor, in harness,' and 'die hurrahing'? [4] And such candor! Cunning this old man might possess, but it was not the cunning of concealment. His worst enemies were to admire and respect him for his frankness; and however offensive to reason some of his convictions, he had the courage to express them without a qualm. He had, said a journalist who often disagreed with him, 'opinions of his own, and a will of his own, and he

[1] Hensel, *Stevens, the Country Lawyer*, 26.
[2] Dickey, *Congressional Globe*, December 17, 1868.
[3] Morrill, *Congressional Globe*, December 18, 1868.       [4] McCall, 350.

THADDEUS STEVENS
At the Age of Seventy-Five

never flinched from the duty of asserting them.'[1] This man in his den was as much a revolutionist as Marat in his tub. Had he lived in France in the days of the Terror, he would have pushed one of the triumvirate desperately for his place, have risen rapidly to the top through his genius and audacity and will, and probably have died by the guillotine with a sardonic smile upon his face. Living in America when he did, he was to become the most powerful dictatorial party and congressional leader with one possible exception in American history, and to impose his revolutionary theories upon the country by sheer determination.

## II

His had been a bitter and an abnormal life. Born in poverty in a Vermont village seventy-three years before Andrew Johnson succeeded to the Presidency, he had but a slight remembrance of his father, who was also a mysterious character. A village shoe-maker who seems to have taught his young son how to make the family shoes, he enjoyed a local notoriety as a wrestler. Then he passes out of the picture. Some say that he was killed in the War of 1812; others that he just tired of the chains of domesticity and wandered away never to be heard of any more. Just as gossip has explained Lincoln's genius by giving him various fathers among the great, and accounted for Andrew Johnson's power in the same graceful manner, it was sometimes said that Talleyrand, meandering about America in 1791, was Stevens's father. Whoever the father, the mother evidently was a woman of strong character, for she appears to have been the one love of Stevens's life. We get glimpses of her flitting about from one sick-room to another ministering to her neighbors and dragging the child along.

It has been suggested by Professor Woodburn it was at these sick-beds that he learned to sympathize with suffering, though tenderness was never to be an obtrusive part of his character where his prejudices were touched. Living remote from wealth and fashion, he early formed an incurable contempt for aristocracy, and this was to determine his political views to a considerable extent. Even at Dartmouth College, where he was an assiduous student, his class consciousness was awakened. 'The democracy rule in

[1] *The Nation*, August 20, 1868.

the fraternities,' he wrote a benefactor after leaving college. 'The aristocracy make threatening grimaces, but it is only sport for us poor plebeians.' [1] It was about this time that Andrew Johnson was making a virtue of his plebeian blood.

Beginning the practice of law at Gettysburg in Pennsylvania, he concentrated on his profession until his forty-first year. It was a delightful region, broken enough to be beautiful and yet with fertile fields, with farms and forests alternating, and with the distant hills and mountains clothed with woods from base to summit. Scattered about near by were quaint little villages, and along the streams were a number of mills. Life in such a community made him familiar with the hopes, fears, and prejudices, and the hearts of ordinary men.[2] He was in the full flower of his maturity when he entered the Legislature, to take rank instantly as a leader through his genius in debate and his intense hatred of Jackson and the Jacksonians. This enemy of aristocracy fairly frothed with rage against the Jacksonian Democracy, and fought with fervor for the moneyed aristocracy represented by Nicholas Biddle and the Bank. In his earlier years he had been as fervent in the support of the Hamiltonian aristocracy. It is these marked contradictions in his character that make him so difficult of analysis.[3] It was at this time that he became the field marshal of the Anti-Masonic Party of his State, denouncing the Masonic order as 'a secret, oath-bound, murderous institution that endangers the continuance of Republican government.' [4] In the national convention of this proscriptive party in 1832, he loomed large, and in a bitter speech declared that members of the order had most of the political positions through intrigue. In the characteristic extravagance of his partisanship, he sought the passage in the Legislature of a resolution of inquiry into the desirability of making membership in the order cause for peremptory challenge in court, when one and not both principals in a suit were Masons. He would have excluded all Masons from the jury in criminal trials where the defendant was one, and have made it unlawful for a judge belonging to the order to sit in such a case. So stubbornly did he fight for this resolution that it was

---

[1] Woodburn, 7.      [2] Buckalew, *Congressional Globe*, December 18, 1868.
[3] McCall, 31, 47.      [4] Woodburn, 14.

barely defeated.[1] In his forty-second year, he sponsored a measure
for the suppression of Masonry; and the next year, following the
trail like a bloodhound, he succeeded in securing a legislative
inquiry into the 'evils' of the order. The resolution was adopted,
but, because of the failure to provide for contempt proceedings
against witnesses refusing to answer, it was futile. Nevertheless
he filed a report painting a gloomy picture of the subversive and
sinister purpose of the lodge. Carrying his fight to the finish,
he spoke in Hagerstown, Maryland, on the proposition that
'wherever the genius of liberty has set a people free, the first
object of their solicitude should be the destruction of Free Masonry.'[2] Thus he rose rapidly to the unquestioned leadership of
the proscriptive party; and, effecting a coalition between his
party and the Whigs, he succeeded in electing an Anti-Mason
Governor and became the most potent member of his board of
advisers. Through the pressure of patronage and the pull of
power, he forced another investigation of Masonry under his
chairmanship, and witnesses were arrested for contempt and imprisoned until the Legislature tired of the farce.[3]

By this time his hatred of Masonry had become an obsession.
When the stage was set for the nomination of Harrison in 1836,
Stevens rejected him because of his toleration of Masonry and
supported Webster; and when the State Convention endorsed
Harrison, he and his followers withdrew in high dudgeon, and
he issued a bitter address in support of another convention to
name another candidate. The people were cold, the project
failed; and Stevens's hate of Jackson literally lashed him into the
support of Harrison. This Masonic madness has been ascribed by
some of his biographers to a hate of privilege; and, drolly enough,
this 'hate of privilege' could not interest him in Jackson, who was
then fighting the most bitter battle against privilege in American
history — only another of the inexplicable twists in this strange,
strong man.

It was in this period, too, that he became the leader in the famous Buckshot War which grew out of an election dispute in
Philadelphia. With his usual ferocity of expression, he denounced
the Democrats of that city as roughs and toughs. The result was

---

[1] Woodburn, 16.   [2] *Ibid.*, 19.   [3] *Ibid.*, 23.

two Legislatures and the threat of civil war. A hair-trigger situation was thus created and bloodshed was imminent when the Stevens faction was forced to capitulate. This was a foreshadowing of the extremes to which he would go in a party struggle.

### III

When, disappointed and embittered by the failure of Harrison to accord him official recognition, he retired from the Legislature, he was both admired and feared by friend and foe alike. Even among his political associates, he was thought erratic and unreliable as a leader; and, disgusted with politics, and impelled to recoup his fortunes, he moved to Lancaster, where the professional field was more fertile. Here for six years he engaged in a lucrative practice, ever and anon making sallies into the political field, but with little encouragement. His own party felt him unsafe. The local organization set its face sternly against him. When, a year after his change of residence, he attempted to revive the anti-Masonry issue, and, by electing Democrats, force the Whigs to take him into their inner counsels, and failed, he found himself more than ever ostracized.[1] Then he retired to his tent in sullen mood to await an invitation. The most effective orator of his party in the State, this promised better, and he did not have long to nurse his grievance in solitude. In the Clay campaign of 1844, he was desperately needed, and he lingered in his tent. All local appeals were ignored, and it was only when Clay himself made personal appeal that he put on the armor. We have a picture of him speaking with Webster in Philadelphia and drawing the latter's crowd to his stand.[2] Thus, forcing his party in Lancaster to come to him, he was elected to Congress in 1848, as a Free-Soil Whig of the extreme sort. And thus he began his congressional career at the age of fifty-seven, albeit not with the obscurity of the average new member. His fame was nation-wide among the Radicals, and when he found that the extreme Whigs and Free-Soilers held the balance of power, he was put forth by his group as a candidate for Speaker in the prolonged contest which finally ended in the election of a pro-slavery Southern Democrat.

He soon qualified as the most bitter and vituperative enemy of

[1] McCall, 61.     [2] *Ibid.*, 63.

slavery in the House. His speeches were philippics. But when the Compromise of 1850 temporarily closed the door on slavery discussions, he soon tired of the protective tariff, which he discussed in his second term with more picturesqueness than economic intelligence, and retired in 1852.

He was now in his sixtieth year. He turned again to his profession, taking little interest in politics until the Kansas-Nebraska Act drew him from his retirement, and he entered upon the last phase of his career. He was the moving spirit in the meeting of twenty at Lancaster which launched the Republican Party locally in 1855; was a delegate to the Convention of 1856, when he supported Justice McLean, with whom he had flirted in Anti-Masonic days, and in 1858, he returned to Congress. He was now sixty-six years old.

IV

Here in the very beginning we encounter another of the mysteries of his motivation — he supported a North Carolina slave-owner for the speakership. His biographer explains this inconsistency on the ground that the slave-owner was also a high-protectionist.[1] Stevens was personally interested in iron. Thereafter, however, he threw himself with youthful energy and with the bitterness of an old man into the struggle against slavery. In 1860, he supported Simon Cameron, whom he despised, as a State obligation, albeit he really favored McLean, and certainly was not impressed with Lincoln.

Then came the war, and this old man of sixty-nine, a realist to the core, sat back and smiled pityingly and contemptuously on those who predicted a speedy victory. He knew that it would be long and bloody, and he sounded the warning.[2] When Crittenden offered his resolution defining the purpose of the war as the preservation of the Union without emancipation or the subjugation of the South, he voted against it. Henceforth we shall find him brutally consistent. To him the war was an opportunity to free the slaves, to punish the South, to crush its aristocracy. 'I do not say that this war was made for that purpose,' he said.[3] 'Ask those who made the war what its purpose is.'

[1] Woodburn, 138.   [2] Reply to Colfax, *Congressional Globe*, July 24, 1861.
[3] Conscription speech, *Congressional Globe*, August 2, 1861.

When in the early days men measured their steps by the Constitution, he scouted the idea that the Constitution was operative. 'The laws of war, not the Constitution,' he growled; and we are to hear this growl from him until the end. 'Who pleads the Constitution?' he demanded with a scowl. 'It is the advocates of rebels.' [1] When men drew back before the proposition to arm the slaves and turn them against their masters, he jeered at their sensibilities. 'I for one shall be ready to go for it — arming the blacks — horrifying to gentlemen as it may appear.'

A little longer, and we find him formulating a resolution for emancipation. Idle talk, thought the 'New York Times.' [2] No one knew better than he that the proposition was premature — he was sowing seed, he could await the harvest. In the mean while he could fertilize and tend the field with the propaganda of sectional hate. In and out of season this old man fulminated against the South and its leaders. Hang the leaders — crush the South — arm the negroes — confiscate the land. And the radicals everywhere thrilled to the impassioned voice of the revolutionist. The Abolitionists had cared nothing for the Constitution, little for the Union, and they responded with a cheer. What a weak and cowardly waging of war! said Stevens. 'No sound of universal liberty has gone forth from the capital. Our generals have a sword in one hand and shackles in the other.' [3] Thus, recognizing the atmosphere as revolutionary, he pushed to the fore and seized the banner of the Radical Republicans to hold it until it fell from his lifeless hands.

Whatever may be said in criticism, he was the vitalizing force in the House, and he energized the whole country. Like Danton thundering from the tribune — 'audacity, audacity, audacity' — he was the perfect leader to ride on the whirlwind and direct the storm. Toward Lincoln, sitting patiently and lonesomely in the White House, he cast scornful glances. What a Cabinet! he thought — 'an assortment of rivals whom the President has appointed from courtesy, a stump speaker from Indiana, and two representatives of the Blair family.' When the elections in 1862 showed Republican losses, he thundered, 'Without a new Cabi-

[1] Callender, 111.   [2] January 25, 1862.
[3] Congressional Globe, January 22, 1862.

net there is no hope.' The repudiation of Frémont's amazing military emancipation only confirmed Stevens's opinion of Lincoln's impossible weakness.[1] Then came the President's plan of compensation. 'The most diluted milk and water proposition ever given to the American nation,' he snorted. And so on for months, with criticisms of Lincoln's policies and methods. Just a momentary flare of enthusiasm for the patient, weary man in the White House when he issued the Emancipation Proclamation. But after the fashion of revolutionists, Stevens was pushing ahead. Emancipation was not enough. The South must be punished under the rules of war, its land confiscated, the slaves made equals of the whites — nothing less. These offending States were out of the Union and in the rôle of a belligerent nation to be dealt with by the laws of war and conquest.[2] Yes, and Congress, not the Executive, must deal with them. Thus, in 1864, Stevens was forcing the fighting against Lincoln, culminating in the Wade-Davis Bill, its passage, and the pocket veto and the President's proclamation of explanation. 'What an infamous proclamation!' wrote Stevens to a friend.

At the moment the bullet of Booth closed the career of Lincoln, he was less the leader of his party than Thad Stevens.

V

Such the background of the old man meditating, in Lancaster in the summer of 1865, a war on Johnson. This was his career: what of his character? Like all human beings, he was not all white nor black.

His political character was that of a misanthrope, and he could have smiled indifferently upon the parliamentary methods of Walpole. He once replied to a fellow partisan who said his conscience would not permit him to take a certain course: 'Conscience, indeed! Throw conscience to the devil and stand by your party.'[3] Having little faith in his fellow men, he was convinced that all were governed by their baser and more selfish instincts. He was the perfect cynic. Reproached for a parliamentary trick denounced as a 'most outrageous thing,' he was so much the cynic

---

[1] Woodburn, 183.    [2] *Congressional Globe*, January 8, 1863.
[3] *Philadelphia Ledger*; quoted, *Lancaster Intelligencer*, January 17, 1866.

that he was not in the least annoyed. 'You rascal,' he replied with his dry grin, shaking his fist playfully under the nose of his accuser, 'if you had allowed me to have my rights, I would not have been compelled to make a corrupt bargain in order to get them.'[1] It was characteristic of him not to deny the trickery. He despised hypocrisy. His worst faults were not concealed.

This frank indifference to the morals of his strategy made him a dangerous foe in political and congressional struggles. His tremendous power as a party leader lay in the biting bitterness of his tongue and the dominating arrogance of his manner, before which weaker men shriveled. When a colleague dared question the wisdom of his policy, he replied with studied contempt that he did not 'propose either to take his counsel, recognize his authority, or believe a word he says.'[2] His flings were consuming flame, his invective terrible to withstand. 'The Almighty makes few mistakes,' he once said in court, inviting attention to the countenance of the defendant. 'Look at that face! What did he ever fashion it for save to be nailed to the masthead of a pirate ship to ride down unfortunate debtors sailing on the high seas of commerce.'[3] One who observed him well thought that 'the intensity of his hatred was almost next to infernal.'[4] There were no neutral tones in his vocabulary. 'I could cut his damn heart out,' he once exclaimed, referring to Webster, after his 7th of March speech. When a friend, conveying the news of John Brown's raid, lamented that he would probably be hanged, Stevens replied, 'Damn him, he ought to hang.'[5] He had no sympathy with failure. Thus there was a hardness about him that made men dread him. Time and again he was to enter a party caucus with sentiment against him to tongue-lash his followers into line. It was easier to follow than to cross him. He had all the domineering arrogance of the traditional boss. He brooked no opposition. Schurz noted even in his conversation, 'carried on with a hollow voice devoid of music . . . a certain absolutism of opinion with contemptuous scorn for adverse argument.' He was a dictator who handed down his decrees, and woe to the rebel who would reject them.[6]

[1] Boutwell, II, 9.    [2] Reply to Bingham, *Congressional Globe*, January 28, 1867.
[3] Hensel, 224.    [4] Cox, *Three Decades*, 365.    [5] Hensel, 23.    [6] Schurz, II, 214.

On his feet, speaking, there was much about him to awe the spectator. A master of robust Anglo-Saxon speech, he spoke with pith and point, but as a stern master laying down the law. Despite his lame foot, he stood straight as an arrow until extreme old age, and firmly poised. There were few purple patches in his speeches, and yet at times there were flashes of supreme eloquence. The general impression, however, was rather that of force and fire. The coldly stern face, the beetling brows, his underlip protruding with an intimidating defiance, he was neither graceful nor appealing to the sympathies. His power on the platform or in the House was in his awe-inspiring earnestness — that and the impression he conveyed of dignity and authority. He spoke, too, always for a purpose, and went directly to the point. Here a bolt of wit, there of irony, and then a glow of humor — but these were flashes, and he was deep again in his argument or invective. There was a suggestion of cruelty in his wit and something clammy in his humor — like a surgeon joking at his job. Something like the jollity of Marat, it was. 'It smacked of Voltaire.' [1] Gestures he had but few, and these were angular, graceless, jerky, but when he accentuated the intensity of his passion by clasping his long bony hands together in front of him, the effect was dramatic. Thus, unconscious though it may have been, he had art in his delivery — he dramatized himself and his subject. His was distinctly the eloquence of a revolutionary period. An orator who served with him in the House said that 'in the great French struggle, his oratory would have outblazed Mirabeau.' [2] Charles Sumner, with whom oratory was an art, hesitated whether to describe him as an orator or as a debater of the school of Charles James Fox. There was nothing in the Stevens of debate that remotely resembled Fox, and his oratory was so individualistic as to puzzle the imitator of Cicero and Burke.[3]

Staggering on the verge of the grave in the last years of his life, he remained the reigning wit to the end. Even on his death-bed he replied to a visitor's observation on his appearance with the

---

[1] Cox, 365.

[2] Schurz, II, 214; Julian, *Recollections*, 309; *Congressional Globe*, Donnelly, December 17, 1868; *ibid.*, Senator Morrill, December 18, 1868.

[3] *Congressional Globe*, December 18, 1868.

comment that 'it is not my appearance but my disappearance that troubles me.' [1] Unlike Lincoln, he was not a story-teller. His wit and humor were inspired by occurrences about him. He scattered them with a reckless prodigality. Many of his best *mots* were spoken in running undertones in the course of debate, as the old man moved about the floor, and audible chuckles followed him in his meanderings, to the annoyance of the speaker. 'He daily wasted, in this private and semi-grotesque distribution of mirth, sense, and satire, a capital sufficient, could it have been preserved, to rival almost any of the acknowledged masters among the colloquial wits of this or any other age,' thought Senator Morrill. [2] There was a bitter Voltairian flavor to his fun. 'They ask us to go it blind,' a speaker in the House was saying, when Stevens convulsed the members with the interpolation, 'It means following Raymond' — one of his pet aversions. [3] Dodging an ink bottle thrown at him in Lancaster in a tavern brawl, he dryly said, 'You don't seem competent to put ink to better use.' [4] A perambulating speaker in the House pacing the aisles arrested his attention. 'Do you expect to get mileage for that speech?' he asked, and, turning his back, walked away. Yielding reluctantly to a tiresome member, he fired a Parthian shot: 'I now yield to Mr. B., who will make a few feeble remarks.'

The best and most pointed illustration of his humor is found in his apology to Lincoln for an unkind observation on a trait in Cameron. 'You don't mean to say you think Cameron would steal?' asked Lincoln. 'No, I don't think he would steal a red-hot stove.' Finding the reply too good to keep, Lincoln repeated it to Cameron, who indignantly demanded a retraction. Stevens went forthwith to the White House. 'Mr. Lincoln, why did you tell Cameron what I said to you?' he asked. 'I thought it was a good joke and didn't think it would make him mad.' 'Well, he is very mad and made me promise to retract. I will now do so. I believe I told you he would not steal a red-hot stove. I now take that back.'

Thus, in his wit and humor there was always something of a sting. He was amusing with his bow, but his arrows hurt. The

[1] Forney, I, 37.      [2] *Congressional Globe*, December 18, 1868.
[3] Henry J. Raymond, Boutwell, II, 10.      [4] Hensel, 15.

waggery, however, contributed not a little to his prestige in the House. He was picturesque and colorful, able, eloquent, and resourceful, dominating and domineering.

### VI

In his daily life he was essentially a man's man, with a sprinkling of the masculine vices and virtues. In his home at Lancaster, he was conspicuously absent from the social affairs of the community. Engrossed in his profession and in politics, he found other means of recreation. Though not given to the vice of quotation, some of his speeches disclosed a mind in contact with the literary classics. He read history and the classics, but little poetry or contemporary fiction.[1] It was said that 'he loved Pope's "Essay on Man" more than Siderfin's Reports.'[2] In his sleeping-room, on a table by the bed in which he was wont to read, were usually found copies of Shakespeare, Dante, Homer, Milton, and the Bible.[3] But it is easier to imagine him in the midst of his cronies in his office in the evening, chatting with neighbors in the tree-lined street, or gathered about a table in a smoke-filled room, with cards. Very old men remember that he never visited the homes of the city. His friends knew where to find him. The son of one of his warmest admirers and political lieutenants recalls that his father 'never admired his tastes and companionships,' and that he 'was a gambler and had no social side.'[4] Whenever it was necessary for him to entertain visiting celebrities, he would summon the wife of his close friend Dr. Carpenter, across the street, to receive for him.[5]

His biographer, while conceding that he gambled, playing poker and other games for money, denies the popular impression that he was an inveterate gambler. There was, nevertheless, long a tradition around Gettysburg that the gambling proclivities of the young there were due to the example Stevens set while living in the community. An unmarried man, with no social life or inclinations, with few if any close associations with women, and living in a town where there was little entertainment outside the

---

[1] Hensel, 25.       [2] *Globe*, December 17, 1868, Woodward.
[3] *Ibid*., Dickey.       [4] Author's notes at Lancaster.
[5] Author's Lancaster notes — recollections of Carpenter's daughter.

homes he did not visit, it would have been remarkable had he not toyed with the vixen of chance. There are too many stories of his gambling floating about Lancaster to this day to leave any doubt about it. No one knew better the value of money, for poverty had taught him. But he had the spirit of the gambler which was to manifest itself in his political life. He played and often played high and recklessly, but he played fairly, and when he lost, he paid without grumbling.[1] The story is still told of one of his all-night sessions at a faro table in the basement of a hotel in Lancaster. In the early morning a farmer from whom he had ordered hay called down the stairs to him. 'Well, what do you want?' thundered the weary Stevens. 'I have a load of hay here; what shall I do with it.' 'Go back and put it on the ace of spades,' rumbled the voice down the stairs.[2] This gambling propensity did not pass with old age or the period of his heaviest political responsibilities in Washington, which was thickly studded with gambling-houses. He was wont to invite congressional associates to his house on New Jersey Avenue, where a cold lunch would be served in prolonged sessions with the cards.[3] One morning Blaine met him coming down the steps of a fashionable gambling-house, where he had spent the night. As the two men paused to exchange greetings, a negro preacher approached with a request for a contribution toward the building of a church. Reaching into his pocket, Stevens drew out fifty dollars in bills and gave them to the suppliant; then, as the latter bowed himself away, Stevens turned wryly to Blaine with the comment that 'God moves in a mysterious way his wonders to perform.' Thus he played for money to add spice to the game, and not from motives of gain; he played like a gentleman; lost like one; and with his earnings he was often generous as a prince.

Whatever his views upon religion may have been, he kept them to himself. His tolerance of all religions might have been due to his divorcement from all creeds. He attended no church, which, within itself, would have colored the general impression of his character in the community in which he lived. For the Baptists he had a certain sentimental regard due to the fact that it was the church of his mother, but he was probably a free-thinker. The

---

[1] Hensel, 12.   [2] Author's Lancaster notes.   [3] Stewart, *Reminiscences*, 205.

'Lancaster Intelligencer,' commenting on a statement in the 'Lancaster Express' that Stevens 'never made any special profession of religion,' said that it might 'have said with truth that he had been all his life a scoffer at religion and a reviler of sacred things.'[1] That 'his mind was a howling wilderness, so far as his sense of his obligation to God was concerned,'[2] was the opinion of Jeremiah S. Black; and Senator Grimes disliked him as 'a debauchee in morals.'[3] Even so, one of his best friends was a Catholic priest in Lancaster, with whom he liked to talk and walk; and he was tenderly fond of children, and extremely sensitive to the appeals of the poor, to whom he was unvaryingly generous.[4]

As a business man, he was both a success and a failure. His professional income, large for the time and place, the absence of a family, and his gambler's instinct made him more or less of a plunger in investments. As Canal Commissioner of Pennsylvania, a position calling for business judgment and methods, he was so unsuccessful that he never outlived the charge of using public money to advance the interest of his party. All his undertakings here were failures, owing, according to Simon Cameron, to his 'impatience of details operating against him in everything of a business nature outside his profession.'[5] In the iron and other industries in which he invested he amassed a fortune, only to lose everything and find himself two hundred thousand dollars in debt through the failure of a partner. Appalling though the debt then was, he sternly set himself to the task of discharging every penny through his professional earnings, and within six years he had wiped out all but thirty thousand dollars of the obligation.[6] It was with this incubus still resting upon him that he entered Congress in 1848; and before he returned to Congress for his second service, ten years later, he had liquidated it all and accumulated another fortune, which was wiped out through the destruction of his foundry by the Confederate troops on their dash into the State. When he died, he left a comfortable but comparatively small fortune. He sought money in the spirit of the gambler for

---

[1] July 6, 1867.      [2] Hensel, 27.      [3] Welles, II, 447.
[4] *Congressional Globe*, December 17, 1868, Woodward; *ibid.*, Morrill, December 18, 1868.
[5] *Congressional Globe*, December 18, 1868.
[6] McCall, 58.

the love of the game of making it, but it does not appear that his various losses greatly depressed him.

## VII

Because of his obsession on negro rights to absolute equality, and his inveterate hatred of the Southern whites, his relation for many years to Lydia Smith, a mulatto, and until his death his housekeeper, cannot be ignored. It was the fashion of his enemies in his time openly to charge that there was an intimacy between them much more personal than that of employer and employee. The charge was made publicly in the newspapers of the country and of Lancaster, and Stevens never entered a denial. Indifferent and contemptuous as he was of public opinion, none but one with the most callous sensibilities could have remained silent under the attack. That she was his housekeeper, devoted to his interests, there can be no doubt; that she was his mistress is not susceptible of legal proof. This much is undisputed: In the rear of his house in Lancaster, among the fruit trees, stood a little house, occupied by Lydia Smith and her husband, a very black negro barber, with their two children, likewise black. Mrs. Smith was a mulatto, and was engaged as housekeeper for the bachelor lawyer. After a time the husband died, and the widow moved into the master's house, and there she lived for many years. When Stevens went to Washington, she accompanied him there. Wherever he was, there she was also. There are old people in Lancaster to-day, who, as children, remember her as one who was liked and respected by the white people of the community. She was neat and comely, accommodating and kindly, and the best white women of the neighborhood frequently invited her assistance in preparing for parties. That she was devoted to Stevens was evident to all. In time, as he grew feeble, she became indispensable, acting as a buffer between him and those who would unnecessarily sap his strength. When, in the house on New Jersey Avenue near the Capitol in Washington, he entertained his friends among public men at cards or conversation, it was she who met them at the door, and prepared and served the lunch.[1] One of those who was a frequent guest concluded from his host's manner that he 'seemed quite fond' of her,

---

[1] Stewart, *Reminiscences*, 205.

and was convinced that his regard for her was 'not entirely platonic.' [1] It would not have been discreditable to Stevens to be 'quite fond of her' in view of her maternal kindness in ministering to his comfort in the home and nursing him in sickness. However, this visitor, a member of the Senate, says that the relationship of the statesman and the mulatto 'created some scandal' in Washington.

This assumption that she was Stevens's mistress was not confined, however, to undertone gossip, which is never impressive. It was current in the press, and in no instance was the publisher rebuked or threatened with a libel suit. In the summer of 1867 the editor of a Southern paper, the 'Union Springs Times,' called at Stevens's house in Lancaster to inquire as to his seriousness in proposing the confiscation of the great Southern estates. In writing of his visit, he said bluntly that Stevens 'lived in open adultery with a mulatto woman whom he seduced from her husband.' This 'seduction' was manifestly untrue. The housekeeper lived with her husband until his death, and many years later was buried by his side in the Catholic cemetery in Lancaster. 'The mulatto manages his household both in Lancaster and Washington,' the editor continued, and this was true. 'She receives or rejects visitors at will,' he went on, 'speaks of Mr. Stevens and herself as "we," and in all things comports herself as if she enjoyed the rights of a lawful wife.' The editor had 'no word of unkindness or abuse of her,' describing her as 'a neat, tidy housekeeper who appears to be as polite as well-trained negroes generally are.' This article was republished in full in the 'New York World,' [2] and was never challenged by Mr. Stevens; nor did he cease to treat the Washington correspondent of the 'World' with courtesy.

A more impressive illustration of his indifference to, or acquiescence in, these published stories of his intimacy with Lydia Smith is found in an editorial in the 'Lancaster Intelligencer.' This grew out of an interesting incident showing his absolute fidelity to the idea of equality between the races. He had purchased a lot in a new cemetery, and later, on reading the deed, and noting that the burial of negroes was forbidden, he returned the deed on the ground that he preferred to be buried in a cemetery

[1] Stewart, *Reminiscences*, 205.          [2] June 20, 1867.

where no such discrimination was made. The 'Lancaster Express,' Republican, commenting on his action, thought it conclusive evidence of his sincere belief in absolute equality. To this the 'Intelligencer' replied editorially:[1] 'Nobody doubts that Thaddeus Stevens has always been in favor of negro equality, and here, where his domestic arrangements are so well known, his practical recognition of his pet theory is perfectly well understood. . . . There are few men who have given to the world such open and notorious evidence of a belief in negro equality as Thaddeus Stevens. A personage, not of his race, a female of dusky hue, daily walks the streets of Lancaster when Mr. Stevens is at home. She has presided over his house for years. Even by his own party friends, she is constantly spoken of as Mrs. Stevens, though we fancy that no rite of Mother Church ever gave her a right to it. It is natural for men to desire to sleep their last with those they loved in life. If Thaddeus Stevens insists on being buried side by side with the woman he is supposed to have taken to his bosom, it is entirely a matter of taste. But why did he not purchase a lot in an African burying ground at once? There no white man's bones would have jostled his own, and she who has so long been his most intimate associate might have been gathered to his side without exciting public scandal.' This was published in the leading paper of the small city in which Mr. Stevens lived and at a time when he was in town. There was no demand for a retraction, no suit for libel. The editorial was afterwards copied in papers throughout the country. Lydia Smith continued to live with him in the rôle of housekeeper and was to stand weeping at his bedside when he died, and to be a beneficiary of his will. These are the facts, and from these the reader must draw his own conclusions.

There is not the scintilla of a doubt that he pushed to the utmost limit his ideas of absolute equality, socially and politically, between the races. In the summer of 1867, subscriptions were being solicited for the support of the Home for Friendless Children in Lancaster, and Mr. Stevens was approached for a contribution. He refused a penny without a guarantee that colored children should be received on equal terms with the white — a proposition shocking enough at the time. No such assurance could be given,

[1] July 6, 1867.

THE HOUSE OF THADDEUS STEVENS

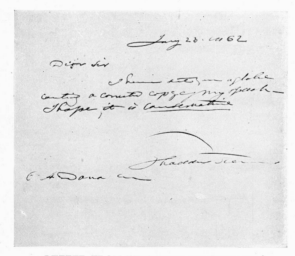

LETTER FROM THADDEUS STEVENS TO
CHARLES A. DANA

and Stevens, the most generous of men, a lover of children, particularly of children in distress, refused to contribute. 'There is boldness and consistency in this act of Old Thad,' said the 'Lancaster Intelligencer,' publishing the story.[1] The 'Harrisburg Telegraph' applauded Stevens's position.[2] That one holding such extreme views should have demanded the immediate enfranchisement of the freedmen, an absolute equality of civil rights, and the confiscation of the land of the Southern aristocrats and its division among the negroes in forty-acre tracts, is not surprising. Many ascribed his deep-seated hatred for the Southern whites to the influence of Lydia Smith.[3] His fondness for her is shown in the fact that there is in Lancaster to-day a portrait of this comely mulatto from the brush of Eicholtz, a prominent painter who also did a portrait of Stevens.

## VIII

The mind of Stevens was not formed for constructive work. He achieved no distinction in the Constitutional Convention of Pennsylvania because of the lack of constructive capacity.[4] Godkin, in a dispassionate survey of his career, could not find that he had so 'associated himself with any public measure or series of measures as to make it a memorial of him personally.'[5] That distinguished journalist apparently failed to realize that Stevens was the father of reconstruction measures, albeit time was soon to show that these were more destructive than constructive.

Perhaps the most distinguished and useful work of his career was his brilliant fight in the Legislature for the preservation and extension of the public school system. Because of the cost of maintenance, there was a popular clamor against the schools. That this would have prevailed but for the remarkable speech of Stevens, all contemporary authorities agree. It was a superb piece of lofty eloquence, and his peroration, expressing the hope that 'the blessings of education shall be conferred on every son of Pennsylvania, shall be carried home to the poorest child of the poorest inhabitant of the meanest hut of your mountains,' literally saved the schools. He himself thought this his greatest service,

[1] June 6, 1867.    [2] June 8, 1867.    [3] Stewart, *Reminiscences*, 205.
[4] Hensel, 11.    [5] *The Nation*, August 20, 1868.

and he once said that he would feel abundantly rewarded 'if a single child, educated by the Commonwealth, shall drop a tear of gratitude on my grave.' [1] He spoke effectively in favor of the establishment of an art school in Philadelphia, and for the endowment of the academies and colleges of the State.[2] This, however, was the work of the advocate. Success in that capacity achieved, he stepped aside and took no part in the creative work. He could defend, he could attack; he could not construct.

And he could not compromise — that was at once his strength and weakness. It made him a leader while he lived, and a failure in the perspective of the years. He held no council, heeded no advice, hearkened to no warning, and with an iron will he pushed forward as his instinct bade, defying, if need be, the opinion of his time, and turning it by sheer force to his purpose.

A striking figure on the canvas of history — stern, arrogant, intense, with a threatening light in his eye, and something between a sneer and a Voltairian smile upon his thin, hard lips. Such was the greatest party and congressional leader of his time.

We shall follow him now into the fight and note his character in his actions. The summer of 1865 has passed, his plans are made, and he takes the train for Washington to cross swords with Andrew Johnson.

[1] Woodburn, 51.          [2] *Ibid.*, 53.

# CHAPTER V

## 'THE WAR GOES ON'

### I

WE have seen that during the summer of 1865 the Radical group under Stevens and Sumner had been mobilizing their forces for a mass movement against all the policies of Johnson. A few days before the opening of Congress, the members began to pour into the capital, and before the gavel fell the enemies of the President had struck the first blow. Among the earliest arrivals was Schuyler Colfax, Speaker of the House, whose advent was not unheralded. Of statecraft he had partaken daintily, but a fluency of expression, added to a pleasing personality and a perpetual smile, had made him a popular figure on the platform. In debate the nimbleness of his tongue stood him in good stead. In speech he was the master of the obvious.

This was the man who entered the capital to the roll of drums, sent on ahead to sound the keynote of opposition to Johnson in anticipation of the latter's Message. The crowd that assembled before his lodgings on the night of his arrival was not a spontaneous tribute to the great; the audience had been provided in advance. And when the 'Smiler' appeared, to acknowledge the homage, it was not an extemporaneous, but a carefully premeditated speech that was delivered. It was a pro-negro speech, a declaration of the invalidity of presidential reconstruction, a call for the political proscription of the natural leaders of the South; and by its tone and manner it served notice that Congress, and not the President, would determine the future of the conquered territory. That night the speech was flashed over the country, to be read the next morning at the breakfast tables.

This was the first gun fired by the Radical group, and there was no misapprehension as to its meaning. It meant war. The 'National Intelligencer' thought the speech in bad taste;[1] a member of the Cabinet recognized it instantly as 'the offspring of an in-

[1] Hollister, 372.

trigue, and one that is pretty extensive'; [1] but the Radical group
hailed it with jubilation. Blaine thanked the orator 'for having
given a good keynote for the rallying of our party,' and Sumner
wrote delightedly that he had 'hit between wind and water' and
that 'the public has been longing to find some way of escape from
the Presidential experiment.' [2] A Methodist Bishop, representing
the political preacher destined to some notoriety, wrote him to
'stand by the sentiment expressed and depend upon it the country will stand by you.' [3] Long afterward, Colfax was to exult in
the feeling that his speech was 'the initiation of the Congressional
policy.' [4]

Busy as swarming bees were the conspirators in the few days
preceding the falling of the gavel. Hardly had Boutwell of Massachusetts reached the city when he was slyly summoned to a private
room by Secretary Stanton, to be warned against the latter's
chief. Orders had been given the army without Stanton's knowledge. He was afraid that Johnson would attempt to reorganize
Congress and give control to the Southerners and the Northern
Democrats. There ought to be a law to deprive the President of his
constitutional rights as Commander-in-Chief; and the one promised was afterwards passed.[5] Thus, in the beginning, the mystery drops from Stanton, revealing him as a spy in the President's household.

Sumner, having insulted Johnson during the summer, with that
strange insensibility born of inordinate vanity, hastened to the
White House to remonstrate against the President's policy, and to
pour forth a recital of 'Southern crimes.' When Johnson called
the roll of Massachusetts murders and Boston assaults, the Senator
was pained by his 'prejudices, ignorance, and perversity.' The
two-and-a-half-hour conference convinced Sumner that the President was 'changed.' [6]

The very night Sumner was quarreling with the President, the
Republicans met in caucus with Thad Stevens in control. The determined old man had the advantage of having a definite programme to propose. He demanded a joint committee of fifteen to
whom the question of the admission of Representatives from the

[1] Welles, ii, 385.              [2] Hollister, 274.              [3] Bishop E. R. Ames, *ibid.*, 273.
[4] *Ibid.*, 272.                 [5] Boutwell, ii, 107–08.        [6] Pierce, iv, 286; 289.

States recently in rebellion should be referred — without debate. There was some dissent, a little grumbling, and then a rumbling in the throat of the infuriated Stevens, before which weaker men recoiled timidly. When he threatened to leave the caucus, the opposition collapsed. He had won the vital point without a fight! Henry J. Raymond, champion of the presidential policy, was a sentinel asleep on duty. The constitutional provision that each house should be the judge of the eligibility of its members had been scrapped. And when the caucus designated Stevens as the spokesman of its purpose, it placed the scepter in his hands.[1] The man in the White House heard the news and chuckled in expectation of the discomfiture of his foes. Wait until Tennessee should be reached on the roll-call, and Maynard, a loyal member of the House since the war, and a Radical himself, should present himself — they would not dare deny him![2]

Long before the hour of meeting, the galleries were packed to capacity. The city then, and for some years thereafter, teemed with men with no ostensible means of support who used the Capitol for entertainment, shuffling through the corridors, and taking possession of the privileged seats in the galleries in violation of rules. These were to cheer and hiss; if Dantons and Marats on the floor, why not *sans-culottes* in the galleries? Thus, when the gavel fell on that opening day, the diplomatic gallery was filled with the riff-raff, and correspondents found their seats in the press section occupied by lolling loafers from the streets. Moving about familiarly on the floor, office-holders and petitioners for patronage shuffled over the bright new carpet. The buzz of conversation, the chuckle and the laugh, in an atmosphere charged with expectancy.[3]

II

Let us look down for a moment from the crowded galleries and get a glimpse of the leaders of the drama. In the Senate we shall want first of all to see Sumner, for he has been an object of curiosity ever since an irate South Carolinian struck him down with a cane. There he sits, soberly, senatorially, a rather handsome man with a conceited countenance, sartorially impeccable, and among

[1] *Life of Hayes*, I, 278; Welles, II, 388.       [2] Welles, II, 388.       [3] Barnes, 16.

his colleagues something of an exotic — for does he not affect the English style and wear spats? He is busy with some papers, for he has many resolutions to offer. Not far away, quite the opposite type, and yet as radical as Sumner — a rough, domineering man of evident vulgarity, with crudely carved features, and an insolent expression — Ben Wade, possessing all of Sumner's vices and none of his virtues.

On the same side, two men conversing. The one with sparse gray hair and side whiskers, of slight figure and thin, academic face, who seems so self-effacing, is attracting attention because his power, if not apparent at a glance, has long been felt. His face denotes suffering and weariness. A remarkable man, this Fessenden, whose mind moves with the precision of logic, and whose speeches, packed with solidity, captivate without eloquence, though spoken in the conversational tone. There was cold science in his analysis of sophistry. The Democratic leader across the aisle (Hendricks) thought him the greatest debater he had ever heard.[1] He has the pride of Sumner without his pomp. He is talking with a serious man whose manner suggests something cold and unsympathetic, his countenance everything of intellect and high-mindedness. He possesses Fessenden's qualities in debate — no humor, no ornament, machine-like logic, the self-possession of innate dignity. This is Lyman Trumbull, who, with Fessenden, had felt bitterly on slavery and rebellion, but hopes to reconcile the factions, unite the party, and thwart the extreme views of Stevens.[2]

Let us mark well the handsome man of commanding presence with the suave expression at the head of the little group of Democrats, for during the next three years he is to speak the verdict of history in debate, to be strangely slighted by historians. Thomas A. Hendricks was the moral and intellectual equal of any man on the floor. His fine ability and rare political sagacity had marked him for the highest honor years before, when William Maxwell Evarts first met him in the Supreme Court.[3] It is in the years with which we are now dealing that Evarts thought that 'among the eminent men who took part in debate no man appeared better in his composure of spirit, in his calmness of judgment, in the cir-

---

[1] Schurz, II, 217.    [2] White, Trumbull.    [3] Evarts, Arguments, III, 213.

cumspect and careful deliberation with which, avoiding extreme extravagances, he drew the line which should mark out fidelity to the Constitution as distinguished from addition to the supremacy of party interests and party passions.'[1] Another statesman of fine discrimination and intellectual attainments was later to recall the fact that during the Johnson Administration he was 'the acknowledged champion of that great conservative sentiment . . . that brought about the return of the people of the seceded States.'[2] Others were to recall the purity of his character, the courtesy of his manner, his fidelity to duty.[3] Able in debate, meticulously cautious as to the accuracy of his statements, logical in his methods, at times eloquent, and always impressive, he saw from the beginning what Trumbull and Fessenden discovered too late, and, unlike Reverdy Johnson, was never to compromise with the foe. 'Certainly his eloquence was persuasive and effective,' said Evarts. 'Certainly his method of forensic address was quite admirably free of all superfluity.'[4]

But since the real drama is in the opening of the House, let us hurry there and locate the leaders before the gavel falls. About halfway back from the Speaker's rostrum, and near the center aisle, where he can easily catch the Speaker's eye, sits Stevens, grim, and with the fire of battle in his eye. Not far away is the Democratic floor leader, James Brooks, courteous, suave, plausible, editor of the 'New York Express,' long prominent in the councils of the Whigs, who through some strange twist in war days was sent to Congress by Tammany as a Democrat. A good parliamentarian, he was not an orator; but close at hand, awaiting the summons to oratorial combat, we see one of the most imposing figures in the House, of commanding stature, and with the eye, head, and manner of the natural orator, Daniel Wolsey Voorhees. Famous for his speeches in defense of John Cook, one of John Brown's men, and of Mary Harris, there surely never was a voice more musical or more finely modulated to every feeling, never an eye more eloquent than those hazel orbs that changed colors with varying emotions. For thirty years he never was to lose the power to fascinate the blasé galleries of House and Senate.[5]

[1] Evarts, *Arguments*, III, 214.   [2] Turpie, *Sketches*, 235.   [3] *Men and Measures*, 73.
[4] Evarts, *Arguments*, III, 216.   [5] Turpie, *Sketches*, 334–40; *Men and Measures*, 74.

Second only in interest to Stevens on the Republican side is the fashionably dressed, thick-set, bearded man, who, though nearly fifty, seems scarcely forty, and who exudes geniality as he moves about the floor. This is Henry J. Raymond, Republican Chairman, founder and editor of the 'New York Times,' champion of Johnsonian policies. With a brilliant mind, sparkling social graces, great capacity, and tireless industry, with a rare mastery of both the written and spoken word, he was soon to find that there was no place for such as he in the new order of things. There was an easy-going complacency about him that did not harmonize with revolutionary days. He loved society, liked to drive his span of bays in the parks, enjoyed good company, especially if composed of good listeners. But he had two qualities that disqualified him for political leadership — he saw both sides of every question and was incapable of hate. 'If those of my friends who call me a waverer could only know how impossible it is for me to see but one aspect of a question, to espouse but one side of a cause, they would pity rather than condemn me,' he once said.[1] With his eyeglass and small gold-headed cane, he could fit in with a company of cultured gentlemen in one of their drawing-rooms, but in a revolutionary age he was as a cork bobbing on the angry waves.[2]

### III

The gavel falls. The clerk, born in Gettysburg, where Stevens began the practice of the law, editor for a while of a paper in Lancaster where Stevens lived, had his orders from the caucus through Stevens himself, and began to call the roll. When Tennessee was passed, Maynard sprang to his feet, waving his certificate of election. 'The clerk cannot be interrupted while ascertaining whether a quorum is present,' said the clerk severely, and Maynard resumed his seat. At the conclusion, Brooks rose to protest and to demand the authority for ignoring Tennessee.

'I can give my reason if necessary,' said the clerk.

And then, from the seat halfway back, the contemptuous tones of Stevens: 'It is not necessary. We know all.'

Yes, retorted Brooks, the resolution of a party caucus. And

[1] *Life of Raymond,* 225.
[2] *Life of Raymond,* 215–18; *Sunshine and Shadow in New York,* 638–39.

could the gentleman from Pennsylvania inform him when he intended to press this resolution?

Stevens seemed bored. 'I propose to present it at the proper time,' he drawled. The galleries chuckled loudly and clapped hands. The revolution had begun.

Proceeding to the election of officers, Stevens rose to nominate for chaplain a minister described as 'the most eloquent man in the United States since the fall of Henry Ward Beecher.' Again the galleries chortled at this thrust at the clergyman who had espoused the cause of Johnson. It was the beginning of Beecher's troubles, from which he was to extricate himself by crying 'mea culpa, mea culpa,' to the revolutionists.[1]

That day, after Sumner in the Senate had introduced a series of impossibly extreme resolutions on reconstruction, the two Houses adjourned without the customary naming of a committee to inform the President that they were ready for his communication. 'I am most thoroughly convinced that there was design in this . . . to let the President know that he must wait the motion of Congress,' wrote Gideon Welles. For henceforth, through the revolution, Congress was to assume supremacy in the affairs of government.'

## IV

The Committee of Fifteen, the Committee of Public Safety of this revolution, was named on the motion of Stevens. The Message of Johnson, a powerful, dignified, and sound State paper, which Welles thought Seward had touched up, but which was in fact written by Bancroft, the historian, was read.[3] The reaction of the country to this forceful Message chilled the hearts of the extremists. 'Full of wisdom,' said the 'New York Times.' 'Force and dignity' was noted by 'The Nation,' which thought it 'certainly clearer' than Lincoln's, and assuredly 'the style of an honest man who knows what he means and means what he says.'[4] Sumner was hysterical. 'The greatest and most criminal error ever committed by a government,' he declared. What is a republican government? he demanded of Welles. Sumner knew, for he 'had

[1] *Congressional Globe*, December 5, 1865.      [2] Welles, ii, 392.
[3] *Ibid*.                     [4] December 14, 1865.

read everything on the subject from Plato to the last French pamphlet.' And here negroes were being excluded from the State Governments — outrageous! Had not a general officer from Georgia just informed him that 'the negroes . . . were better qualified to establish and maintain a republican government than the whites?' And how could Welles, a New England man, support the President? Had he read Sumner's Worcester speech? 'Yes,' the Connecticut Yankee replied, but 'I did not endorse it.' 'Stanton does,' said Sumner. He had thought it 'none too strong' and 'approved every sentiment, every opinion and word of it.' [1] Thus Stanton's treachery unfolds.

Meanwhile Stevens, infinitely stronger and more practical than Sumner, was planning to force the issue. In the interval, one bitterly cold day, Grant stood before Johnson reporting on his observations in the South. Sumner had been deluged with letters from strangers in that section, charging butchery and outrages against the blacks; and Grant reported conditions satisfactory, the people loyal, and was asked to make a written report.[2] This intensified Sumner's annoyance, and he fumed and fretted.

In the White House, Johnson, calm, busy with conferences, not unmindful of the treachery about him, moved with caution and awaited events. He had begun to suspect Stanton, but when that official returned after an absence to speak sneeringly of Sumner, the mystery deepened. 'Some one is cheated,' wrote the Cabinet diarist.[3]

But there was nothing cowardly or underhand about Thad Stevens. The old man, shut up in his house, was forging his thunderbolt, and on December 18, with galleries packed, with a sprinkling of negroes, the floor crowded, he rose to challenge the Administration. An historical moment. Here spoke a man who was determining the immediate destiny of a people, and he spoke with the decision and force of an absolute monarch laying the law down to a cringing parliament.

Who could reconstruct? he demanded. Not the President, he said, for Congress alone had power. 'The future condition of the conquered power depends on the will of the conqueror,' he continued. 'They must come in as new States or come in as con-

[1] Welles, ii, 394.        [2] Ibid., ii, 397.        [3] Ibid., ii, 406.

quered provinces.' Thereafter he referred to them as provinces —
'provinces that would not be prepared to participate in constitutional government for some years.' Then what? 'No arrangement so proper for them as territorial governments,' where they
'can learn the principles of freedom and eat the fruit of foul rebellion.' And when consider their restoration? Only when the
Constitution had been so amended 'as to secure perpetual ascendancy to the party of the Union' — meaning the Republican Party.

That was the persuasive feature of Stevens's amazing programme that was intended to overcome the momentary scruples
of the more conservative of his fellow partisans. Negro domination — before it the conservatives drew back shocked. But such
domination in the South, or the loss of the loaves and fishes —
that was different. The old man was a good psychologist. He was
really thinking primarily of the negroes, for whom most of his
party associates cared not a tinker's dam; but they were interested
in power, and how so certainly perpetuate that power as by denying these States a vote in the Electoral College until they agreed to
grant suffrage to the freedman.

Yes, negro domination in the South or the loss of power. 'They
[Southerners and Democrats] will at the very first election take
possession of the White House and of the halls of Congress.' And
then, ruin! But there were no pious poses in the bitter old man
now speaking. Make the South enfranchise the negroes, and 'I
think there would always be Union men enough in the South,
aided by the blacks, to divide the representation and thus continue
Republican ascendancy.' This a white man's government? 'Sir,
this doctrine of a white man's government is as atrocious as the
infamous sentiment that damned the late Chief Justice [Taney] to
everlasting fame and I fear everlasting fire.'

When Stevens sank wearily into his seat, he had planted the
most attractive of ideas in the minds of his fellow partisans who
had held back. He had conducted them to the mountain-top
and offered them the indefinite power they sought. 'The Nation'
found his reference to Taney in hell something 'we can hardly
trust ourselves to commend,' and concluded that 'many people
will be ready to believe that a person who uses such language in
debate is hardly in a fit state of mind to legislate for . . . any State

or Territory.'[1] But the politicians in the cloak-rooms, the hotels, and bar-rooms were deeply interested in the suggestion.

Three days later the galleries again were packed when the elegant Raymond replied in defense of the President's policies. To a conservative audience of judicious men the speech of Raymond, finely phrased, sanely tempered, and logical, would have appealed, but not to the crowd in the galleries. Restating the theory on which the war was fought, that the Southern States had not been out of the Union and certainly not a separate power, he said: 'They were once States of the Union — that every one concedes — bound to the Union and made members of the Union by the Constitution of the United States. . . . They did not secede. They failed to maintain their ground by force of arms — in other words, they failed to secede.'

And talk of 'loyal men in the South'? Loyal to what? 'Loyal to a foreign independent power, as the United States would become under those circumstances?' Certainly not. Simply disloyal to their own government and 'deserters from that to which they owe allegiance.' More: if an independent power, they had the authority to contract debts, 'and we would become the successors and inheritors of its debts and assets, and we must pay them.' And why, having fought for the Union, now forbid reunion? 'I am here,' he concluded, 'to act with those who seek to complete the restoration of the Union. . . . I shall say no word and do no act and give no vote to recognize its division, or to postpone or disturb its rapidly approaching harmony and power.'

Raymond had courageously and handsomely discharged a patriotic duty, but he had signed his political death-warrant. He had joined the Gironde when the Mountain, backed by the mob, was in the ascendant.

## V

There was a third party to this debate whom it is the fashion to ignore, albeit he spoke for more white men in the country than either, though representing a party with a meager representation in the House. He spoke for the 1,835,985 men who had voted the Democratic ticket in the election of 1864, and for all the whites of

[1] December 28, 1865.

the South, and these men are entitled to their word in this debate.
Daniel W. Voorhees spoke on the proposition embodied in resolutions he had previously offered in behalf of the Democracy that
'no State or number of States . . . can in any manner sunder their
connection with the Federal Union except by a total subversion of
our present system of government.'

When Voorhees, a favorite orator, rose, the galleries were
crowded. The little group of Democrats gathered about him.
Thad Stevens had business outside, but Raymond found a seat
close by.[1] If he was embarrassed by the support of the brilliant
orator, he made no sign. This was easily the oratorical masterpiece of the three; and, read to-day, seems as the voice of prophecy. Beginning with a reference to the Radical pose of friendship for Johnson during the summer, he described it as 'the conspiracy to assail him with the masked face of friendship and the
treacherous sword of Joab.' He analyzed the purpose of the Colfax speech as intended to pave the way for the select committee
'created by the magic wand of the conscience-keeper of the majority [Stevens] . . . that potent wand which has evoked from the
vasty deep more spirits of evil and malignant mischief than generations will be able to exorcise and put down.' Seizing on Stevens's
reference to the States as dead carcasses, he continued: 'He knows
that dead carcasses are more easily carved to pieces, torn limb from
limb and devoured by the hungry maw of confiscation, than living
States.' Yes, 'it is safer and less troublesome to rob a corpse than
to pick the pockets of the living.' Hurrying on to the painting of a
picture of the carpetbaggers in the offing, he paid tribute to the
Provisional Governors, and said: 'But then what a military governor of South Carolina, for instance, that idol of the Radicals,
Ben Butler, would have made! Aye, there is the rub. What fat,
unctuous, juicy pickings have been lost to the faithful by this cruel
policy of the President. . . . All the wolves and jackals that wait
till the battle is over to mangle the dead and wounded snarled
their disappointment and rage at the President, but will now open
in full chorus over the delightful vision which arises before them
from the formation of the committee of fifteen.' Rebel debt?
'Every one knows, of course, that it will never be paid. All history

[1] *New York World*, January 12, 1866.

tells us that the debt of a defeated revolution is always lost.' And what did Stevens's theory mean? 'It is a notice that the war to restore the Union was an utter failure — that the war is over and yet the Union is rent in twain.'

Pleading for a speedy restoration of the Union, he passed on to the wrongs of Government thriving unnoticed behind the smoke screen of sectional prejudice and hate. 'How long,' he asked, 'can the inequalities of our revenue system be borne? . . . We have two great interests in this country, one of which has prostrated the other. . . . The agricultural labor of the land is driven to the counters of the most gigantic monopoly ever before sanctioned by the law.' Then on he hurried, to favors to the bondholders, through their immunity from taxation. 'The Nation's gratitude takes a strange turn,' he said. 'It lavishes its gifts, its garlands, and its favors on the money-changers of the temple, and causes the defenders of the Government at the cannon's mouth to pay tribute to their monstrous greed.'

This speech foreshadowed the policies and effects of the next ten years with marvelous prescience.[1] The merciless lashing so picturesquely given the extremists goaded them to fury, and Bingham of Ohio replied with personal abuse.[2] 'One of the most brilliant and polished efforts ever delivered by the gentleman . . . a masterly effort,' said the 'New York World' of Voorhees's speech.[3] Many years later, Blaine recalled it as a 'powerful speech.' [4] The Republican press was unanimous in abuse, the Radical papers because they had been stung, the conservatives because they had been embarrassed at the outset of their contest with the Radicals by the approval of the Democrats. The Voorhees resolutions were voted down by a strict party vote, but the Democrats had defined their position and taken their stand. And the Radical group had served notice on the conservatives in the Republican Party that no quarter would be given. The war was on.

[1] *Congressional Globe*, January 9, 1866.
[2] *New York World*, January 12, 1866; Blaine, *Twenty Years in Congress*.
[3] January 10, 1866.    [4] *Twenty Years in Congress*.

VI

Society immediately felt the effect of the tightening political lines. It was not notably brilliant that winter, albeit the war was over, and, with it, much anxiety. None of the old houses that had flourished and sparkled before the war were thrown open to entertainment. It was the boast of Mrs. Ogle Tayloe, dwelling in the fine old mansion on Lafayette Square, that she had not crossed the threshold of the White House since Harriet Lane went out.[1] Old friends calling informally that winter found the pictures covered, the chandeliers wound with protective wrappings. The palatial home of Mrs. A. S. Parker at Four and a Half and C Streets which, with its fine conservatories, spacious parlors, and glistening dancing-floor, had been a favorite rendezvous in the days of Pierce and Buchanan, was quiet now. The old aristocracy, partial to the social leadership of the South, resented the new pushing crowd and gave it a wide berth. True, Kate Chase Sprague, unsurpassed in beauty, elegance, or charm by the haughtiest of the ante-bellum belles, was reigning now, but this winter she had laid aside the crown. The President's receptions were crowded, and throngs shoved and jostled in the drawing-rooms of Cabinet members, but entertaining on a large scale was confined to those whose official positions prescribed parties.

It was not long until political differences, bordering even then on hatreds, divided society into groups. Even the French Minister's party was under suspicion. 'On Friday night went to the party at the French Minister's,' wrote Julian,[2] 'which was the grandest display I ever saw. I never knew before how much wealth could do in dazzling the eye and charming the senses. . . . French all over . . . dancing and waltzing perfectly charming . . . music superlative. . . . About half-past eleven a lunch was served consisting of choice fruits of all kinds, dainties and drinks, and when I left at midnight a regular supper was being prepared.' Merely a diplomatic function? Old Gideon Welles, scanning the horizon eagerly for signs of storm, was not so sure. 'Last night at . . . a large party given by Marquis Montholon, the French Minister,' he wrote. 'Am inclined to believe there was something political as well as social in the demonstration.'[3] It was just a

---

[1] Mrs. Clay.    [2] MS. Diary, February 11, 1866.    [3] Welles, II, 430.

little before that Welles had been impressed by the large number of fashionable folk who had been former playmates of the Southerners who were frequenting his wife's receptions. 'So many who have been distant and reserved were present as to excite suspicion,' he wrote. No doubt, he thought, they took this method of manifesting sympathy with the Johnson policies. Indeed, he had noticed quite a sprinkling of these people at the last White House reception. And why not? 'If professed friends prove false and attack him, he will not be likely to repel such friends as sustain him,' he said. 'I certainly will not.'[1] Thus society was dividing into the camps of the red and the white in the war of the roses, and with hostesses a bit timid, statesmen turned to such entertainment as they could find. Ristori was playing, and the playhouse was neutral ground where all could gather in safety.[2] And there was Handel's 'Messiah' with a chorus of a hundred voices, 'and the celebrated Miss Houston of Boston.'[3] And there were the parlor readings at the home of Julia Ward Howe, where one might meet Chase, Guroski, and some Radical Senators and a few ladies.[4] Or one could find gayety enough at the official receptions and see 'the new style of wearing the hair — turning it loose.'[5] But when it was possible to meet congenial political company at a séance, the entertainment was at its best. At the moment, spiritualism was fascinating the country, and some nervous editors were denouncing it as a free-love movement, but what would you have when the town was dull? Thus quite a gathering of Radical statesmen assemble now and then at 27 Four and a Half Street 'to hear the spirit of Theodore Parker through Mrs. Cora V. Daniels as medium.' The lady drifts into a trance, and 'after a very pretty prayer' invites the Nation's rulers to ask questions about 'the state of the country.' Serious? Listen to the lady conveying the message of Parker: In less than eight weeks Johnson will arrest the leading Republicans . . . convoke a Congress of Southerners and copperheads . . . and the 'patriots.' like Stevens, will hold another Congress, probably in Ohio . . . and a bloody conflict will follow, 'extending this time into the Northern States,' but in the end the Radicals will prevail. Thus Cora was less medium than mind

[1] Welles, II, 421–22.      [2] Grimes, 308.      [3] Ibid., 322.
[4] Julian, MS. Diary, February 24, 1866.      [5] Ibid., January 26, 1866.

reader. Of course these statesmen knew that Parker was not present and had sent no silly message, but it was the kind of message for the audience — and so the statesmen hurry out into the night.' [1]

## VII

And now began the great push for negro suffrage — with the District of Columbia for the first experiment. In the referendum election on the pending suffrage bills, Washington and Georgetown had cast 7369 votes against them and 36 for them, but no matter. The party whip began to swish in the air and cut the shoulders of the skeptics. General Sherman was writing his embarrassed brother that to place the ballot in the hands of an illiterate majority of blacks fresh from slavery would 'produce more convulsions.' [2] The Northern intellectuals and *literati*, along with the politicians with an eye on votes, were earnest in the cause. William Cullen Bryant thought it would be setting a noble example to the Nation to force suffrage on the helpless District. [3]

Thus, one January day, the galleries of the House were packed to suffocation with whites and blacks. The debate was long and fervent. The opposition fought for time, but all motions for postponement were promptly voted down. Voorhees, from the Democratic side, moved a recommitment with instructions for the framing of a bill admitting all to the vote who could read the Constitution, or who were assessed for, and paid, taxes in the District, or who had served in, and been honorably discharged from the military or naval service. One or two Republicans proposed changes in these instructions. Thad Stevens turned and glowered.

'I hope we will not make these instructions any better than they are,' he rumbled; 'they are bad enough at best.'

The recommittal motion failed; the roll was called. When Henry Raymond's name was reached and he voted for suffrage, 'a benignant smile seemed to pass at that moment over old Thad Stevens's face' [4] — he was dragging Raymond into camp by his whiskers. With the announcement of the result to a House and

---

[1] Julian, MS. Diary, March 6, 1866.          [2] *Letters*, 261–62.
[3] Godwin, *Life*, Letter to Mrs. Watterson, II, 241.
[4] *New York World*, January 19, 1866.

galleries tense with suppressed excitement, the chamber fairly rocked with cheers and shouts from floor and gallery. Radical members, in high glee, moved about the floor grasping each other's hands, and whites and blacks in the galleries and in the corridors later fraternized as brothers, and in the eyes of many were tears of joy.[1] The pounding of the Speaker's gavel made no impression on the galleries, and Colfax, in resentful tones, shouted his inability to maintain order in the galleries if members would not on the floor.[2]

Thus the bill passed to the Senate, to be lost in the congestion of the closing hours, but notice had been served upon the South, and that was marking progress.

### VIII

A very little while, and Frederick Douglass, mulatto orator, leading a delegation of blacks, filed into the White House. Sumner had just made one of his extravagant speeches in the Senate, and it was not a humble orator who approached the President, to be courteously received, and stepped forward to make his demands for suffrage in the South. Johnson stood at respectful attention through the speech, and then made reply. He had opposed slavery as a monopoly with the slave-owners in a minority controlling political power. During the days he was opposed to slavery, the negroes had looked with contempt upon the working white man. 'Where such is the case,' he said, 'we know there is enmity, we know there is hate.' The poor white was opposed both to the slave and the master, for the two combined to hold him in economic bondage. 'Now,' said Johnson earnestly, 'the query comes up whether these two races, situated as they were before, without preparation, without time for passion and excitement to be appeased, and without time for the slightest improvement, whether the one should be turned loose upon the other at the ballot box with this enmity and hate existing between them. The question comes up right here whether we do not commence a war of races.' This was a prophecy, almost immediately to be fulfilled. Johnson concluded by saying that the franchise was a matter for the States.

While he was talking, the attitude of Douglass, smiling con-

[1] Julian, MS. Diary, January 19, 1866.    [2] *Congressional Globe*, January 18, 1866.

descendingly, had been one of studied insolence, considering the station of the speaker. As the negro turned to leave at the head of his delegation, he uttered a threat:

'The President sends us to the people, and we go to the people.'

'Yes,' said Johnson, keeping his temper, 'I have great faith in the people. I believe they will do what is right.' [1]

This frank exposition of his views invited a deluge, and it descended. The 'Chicago Tribune' hysterically insisted that the negro had more ability, logic, and eloquence than the President; and Phillips, addressing a bitter crowd at the Brooklyn Academy of Music, denounced Johnson as a traitor and demanded his impeachment. Julian thought that 'his late speech to the colored people dooms him,' and was sure he was 'a very small man, and . . . a slave of the bottle.' [2]

Meanwhile the Senate was brilliantly debating Trumbull's bill continuing the Freedmen's Bureau indefinitely, extending its operations to freedmen everywhere, authorizing the allotment of forty-acre tracts of the unoccupied lands of the South to negroes, and arming the Bureau with judicial powers to be exercised at will. Trumbull and Fessenden bore the brunt of the defense, and Hendricks, leading the attack, assailed the judicial feature, the extension of the Bureau's power throughout the country, and the creation of an army of petty officials. 'Let the friends of the negroes be satisfied to treat them as they are treated in Pennsylvania . . . in Ohio . . . everywhere where people have maintained their sanity upon the question,' said Cowan of Pennsylvania.

With some moved by a sincere interest in the freedmen's welfare, the average politician was thinking of the tremendous engine for party in the multitude of paid petty officials swarming over the South, for its possibilities had been tested.[3] It was a party measure, and as such it was passed.

While still pending in Congress, the bill had been carefully studied in Administration circles and found 'a terrific engine . . . a governmental monstrosity.' [4] Such was the opinion of Johnson, who calmly prepared to meet it with a veto.[5] Thus one day he sat three hours with the Cabinet discussing his Message and taking

[1] McPherson, 53–55.          [2] MS. Diary, February 11, 1866.
[3] Pierce, *Freedmen's Bureau*, 161.          [4] Welles, II, 433.          [5] *Ibid.*, II, 433.

its opinion. There was a clear division of sentiment. 'Speed was disturbed,' Harlan 'apprehensive,' Stanton 'disappointed.' The insurgents must have squirmed under Johnson's discussion of the conspiracy against him, though it could not have been news to Stanton.

In tense excitement, and a little dazed, the Senate sat listening to the Message. Merciless in its reasoning, simply phrased, there was no misunderstanding its meaning. The Bureau's life had not expired; why pass the bill at all? it asked. And no juries in times of peace! No indictment required! No penalty stipulated beyond the will of members of the court-martial! No appeal! No writ of error in any court! 'I cannot reconcile a system of military jurisdiction of this kind with the Constitution,' said the President. Where in the Constitution is authority to expend public funds to aid indigent people? Where the right to take the white man's land and give it to others without 'due process of law'? More: the granting of so much power over so many people through so many agents would enable the President, 'if so disposed, to control the action of this numerous class and use them for the attainment of his own political ends.' The Message closed with the Johnsonian proposition that with eleven States excluded from Congress, the bill involved 'taxation without representation.'

The next day Trumbull replied, the vote was taken, and the veto sustained. A prolonged hissing in the colored galleries, some cheers in the others, and the visitors were expelled. When Voorhees in the House sought to announce the action of the Senate, his voice was drowned with cries of 'order.' [1] But great crowds with a band of music celebrated in front of the Willard, listening to orators praising Johnson, and the 'New York Tribune' declared that 'the copperheads at their homes were firing guns in honor of the presidential veto.' [2]

'The President stands squarely against Congress and the people,' wrote the indignant Julian.[3] 'Neither Jefferson nor Jackson ... ever asserted with such fearless fidelity and ringing emphasis the fundamental principles of civil liberty,' said the 'New York World.' [4] 'I confess,' said Henry Ward Beecher lecturing in Brook-

[1] New York World, February 21, 1866.     [2] February 21, 1866.
[3] MS. Diary, February 20, 1866.     [4] February 20, 1866.

lyn, 'that reading his message has left a profound impression upon my mind that he urges most serious and weighty reasons why . . . it [the bill] should not at present become the law of the land.' [1] But Theodore Tilton was assuring Julian that 'three fourths of Beecher's congregation are against him' — which was serious enough for the highest paid minister in the land; [2] and the Reverend Doctor Cheever of New York was piously praying that the Lord would take Johnson 'out of the way,' matching Phillips's reference to him as 'an obstacle to be removed.' [3] And the New Jersey Legislature adopted a resolution denouncing the veto, offered by Thad Stevens's friend Scovel, who said Johnson had 'made the worst investment of his life.' [4]

But many were delighted, and laughing scoffers went about Washington describing the Senate scene — Sumner, dark but dignified, busy with 'the arrangement of his hair and his papers'; Ben Wade, 'bloated with bottled wrath'; Henry Wilson, nervously running through his scrapbook 'to see if he could find another "Southern outrage."' [5] In the midst of the gloom, John Sherman sat reading annoying letters from the General. 'I am a peace man,' he read. 'I go with Johnson and the veto.' [6] And a great crowd made merry at Cooper Union in New York, where Seward and Raymond spoke aggressively in defense of Johnson's policies. 'Any section with men in it fit to live,' said Raymond, 'would become exasperated and goaded into rebellion within one year after such a policy [as the Radicals'] had been inaugurated.' [7] It seemed for a moment that Johnson was on the top of the world, but the watchful Welles was dreading 'the dark revolutionary intrigues of Stevens.' [8]

IX

The drama of factional hate was now hastening to a climax. On Washington's Birthday, the Radicals had arranged ceremonies at the Capitol in memory of Henry Winter Davis, who had insulted Lincoln with his Manifesto and Johnson in his letter to 'The

[1] New York World, February 21, 1866.    [2] MS. Diary, March 19, 1866.
[3] New York World, February 26, 1866.    [4] Ibid., February 23, 1866.
[5] Ibid., February 24, 1866.    [6] Letters, 263.
[7] Life of Raymond, 175–84.    [8] Welles, II, 435.

Nation.' Some thought it was 'intended to belittle the memory of Lincoln and his policy as much as to exalt Davis, who opposed it.' [1] It was a charming, sun-flooded day, and the Avenue was crowded with promenaders such as had not been seen since the days when the sutlers and contractors had swarmed over the thoroughfare during the war. The wires hummed with messages, commendatory and condemnatory, of the veto.[2] After the mass meeting at Grover's Theater, addressed by Hendricks, 'Sunset' Cox, and Montgomery Blair, in approval of Johnson's action, a serenade for the President was proposed and the procession marched.

Emerging from the north door, Johnson faced a surging crowd of wildly excited partisans — a fighting crowd, and Johnson caught the spirit. Provocation enough he had had. Sumner had been denouncing him with fierce invective, and Stevens had said that for one of his actions he would have lost his head a few centuries before.[3] There was no longer any doubt as to the character of the Committee of Fifteen — a revolutionary body as dictatorial as the Directory of the French Revolution.

As Johnson passed to the portico, he had no thought of an extended speech, having half promised Secretary McCulloch merely to make acknowledgments, but he was flushed with victory and he threw discretion to the winds. He attacked the Committee as 'an irresponsible central directory' — a true description — and said it had assumed all the powers of Congress, as it had. He declared that the war was fought on the theory that the States were not out of the Union — and this was true. And then, falling into the frontier oratory which had been so popular with the Radicals until now, he went on:

'I am opposed to the Davises, the Toombs, the Slidells . . . but when I perceive on the other hand men still opposed to the Union . . . I am still for the preservation of these States.'

At this, the crowd, having tasted blood, called for names.

'I look upon as being opposed to the fundamental principles of this Government and as now laboring to destroy them, Thaddeus Stevens, Charles Sumner, and Wendell Phillips.'

'Forney,' cried a voice, referring to the editor.

---

[1] Welles, ii, 438.          [2] *New York World*, February 24, 1866.
[3] *Congressional Globe*, January 31, 1866.

'I do not waste my time on dead ducks,' he continued.

The Radical press was beside itself with fury, the 'New York Tribune' describing the crowd as such as is found at the prize ring and in 'drunken ward meetings,' and Johnson as having spoken 'in loud, excited tones, gritting his teeth, and accompanying his words with violent gesticulation.' [1] Forney's paper was scandalously abusive, and Johnson's enemies were busy as usual circulating the story that he was drunk. The rather boorish Count Gurowski was reported around 'repeating the dirty scandal,' [2] and Julian in his diary referred to the speech as a 'drunken speech to the copperhead mob.' [3] 'The Tribune,' however, exonerated Johnson of intoxication. 'The accounts given by the most trustworthy witnesses,' it said, 'are that he was entirely sober.' [4]

But Johnson was quite as vigorously approved. 'The Union is restored and the country safe,' wired Seward from New York to some one in Washington. 'The President's speech is triumphant and the country will be happy.' [5] Raymond in 'The Times' thought the speech 'strong, direct, and manly,' and 'The Herald' observed that Johnson had taken 'plain issue with Stevens & Co. in honest and homely words.' But Garrison, speaking in Brooklyn, denounced Seward's commendation. 'It would have been far better,' he said, 'for thee to have died beneath the knife of the assassin.' [6] The 'New York World' recalled that 'we have had a Tennessee President before whose intrepid openness made the nincompoops and red tapists of his day stare and gasp.' [7] The 'Chicago Times' proposed that Johnson have Stevens, Sumner, and Phillips arrested, and forcibly dissolve Congress.[8]

Thus Johnson had forced the fighting into the open, and the scandal mill was working on him. A Senator was whispering that he was often drunk and kept mistresses in the White House, and Beecher was warning a Cabinet member of the tale.[9]

And Thad Stevens? He rather respected a two-fisted fighting man, and it was some time before he took notice, and then in the lighter vein.

[1] February 26, 1866.          [2] Welles, II, 439.          [3] February 24, 1866.
[4] February 24, 1866.          [5] New York Tribune, February 26, 1866.
[6] Ibid., February 28, 1866.          [7] February 24, 1866.
[8] Quoted, The Nation, March 8. 1866.          [9] Welles, II, 454.

'Why does the gentleman suppose for a single moment,' he asked in the House, 'that the speech was a fact? (Laughter.) . . . What I say now I do not wish to have reported. It is a confidential communication and I suppose none will violate the confidence I repose in them. (Laughter.) Sir, that speech was one of the grandest hoaxes ever perpetrated, and has been more successful than any except the moon hoax, which I am told deceived many astute astronomers. (Laughter.) It is part of a cunning contrivance of the copperhead party who have been persecuting our President since the 4th of last March. Why, sir, taking advantage of an unfortunate incident that happened on that occasion (Laughter) they have been constantly denouncing him as addicted to low and degrading vices.' [1]

But Thad Stevens was not through, as we shall see. It was in that speech that he declared for a reapportionment intended to deprive the South of members, to put a tax on cotton, to treat the Southern States as conquered territory. He was moving forward — pushing his party with him.

[1] *Congressional Globe*, March 10, 1866.

# CHAPTER VI

## THE FINAL BREAK

### I

THE day after the serenade speech, Thad Stevens and the revolutionists put all compunctions behind them in their determination to pass their Radical measures over presidential vetoes with a two-thirds vote. Some time before, the Committee on Elections in the House, sitting on the contested seat of the eloquent Voorhees, had voted unanimously, with the exception of Dawes, the chairman, that the orator was entitled to his seat. When the news reached the floor, there was much scurrying about among the Radicals and no little storming on the part of Stevens. The committee had acted? No matter, it could act again; and in the second action all the Republican members voted, under the lash, to unseat the supporter of Johnson.

When the report was submitted, Voorhees took the floor, stated the facts, and on Dawes's bold denial, asked him directly if the committee had not on a specified date voted unanimously in his favor. Dawes sanctimoniously pleaded the secrecy of the committee room amidst general merriment, and Ingersoll, Republican, demanded the truth before the putting of the question. Banks solemnly dwelt on the awfulness of a disclosure of committee deliberations, and after Ingersoll had vainly asked for the minutes of the meeting, Voorhees rose to quote Stevens's comment that 'one vote may prove of great value here,' and to charge that in disregard of the evidence he was to be denied his seat in the interest of a two-thirds vote to deal with Johnson's vetoes.

A bit perturbed, Dawes again rose to explain what had happened in a statement violative of the truth, when Marshall, a member of the committee, disgusted at the mockery, declared that Voorhees had stated the original action of the committee with absolute accuracy. The roll was called, and, with Ingersoll excepted, the Republicans voted to unseat the premier orator of the Democrats.[1] It was the first of many crimes to be committed. Meeting Stevens on the floor, Voorhees took him to task, half in jest, half in earnest. 'Oh, no,' said Stevens, shaking his head waggishly, 'your case was good enough, but it was that two-thirds vote that killed you — that fatal two-thirds' — and, with a peculiar chuckle, he turned and hobbled off.[2] Whatever his faults, there was no pious pretense in Thaddeus Stevens.

II

A little before, Trumbull had introduced his Civil Rights Bill, providing against discrimination in civil rights or immunities on account of race, color, or previous condition of servitude, and the debate had turned upon the constitutional power of Congress to pass laws for the ordinary administration of justice in the States. Adopting the machinery of the Fugitive Slave Law, the last clause authorized the use of the land and naval forces in the enforcement of the act. Senator Hendricks, leading the attack, chided the Republicans for adopting the features of the Fugitive Slave Law, giving the marshals the right to summon whomever they saw fit to assist in its execution. Trumbull and others rather gloated over the turning of the tables. The Opposition was especially hostile to the use of the land and naval forces. 'This bill is a wasp,' said Hendricks, moving to strike out the last section with this provision. 'Its sting is in its tail.' In the House the frail, bearded statesman Michael Kerr, made the most powerful speech in opposition. Its passage was a foregone conclusion.

It was the claim of Trumbull that he had consulted Johnson in an effort to meet his views in the framing of the measure, and, in the absence of contradictory evidence, this must be accepted as the truth. But it was never the intention of Johnson to approve the bill. On the morning of the delivery of the veto, he laid his Message before the Cabinet. Stanton urged him to sign.[3] The next afternoon the veto was read in the Senate to a full chamber, with the galleries packed. 'Feeble as it was villainous, and we hope to override it,' wrote Julian in his diary.[4]

'In all our history,' ran the message, '. . . no such system as

---

[1] *Congressional Globe*, February 23, 1866.        [2] Callender, 155.
[3] Welles, ii, 464.        [4] MS. Diary, March 28, 1866.

that contemplated by the details of this bill has ever before been proposed or adopted. They establish for the security of the colored race safeguards which go infinitely beyond any that the General Government has ever provided for the white race. In fact, the distinction of race and color is, by the bill, made to operate in favor of the colored and against the white race. They interfere with the municipal regulations of the States, with the relations existing exclusively between a State and its citizens, or between inhabitants of the same State — an absorption and assumption of power by the General Government which, if acquiesced in, must sap and destroy our federative system of limited powers, and break down the barriers which preserve the rights of the States. It is another step, or rather stride, to centralization and the concentration of all legislative power in the National Government.'

In anticipation of such a veto, the Senate, after the passage of the bill, had unseated Senator Stockton, Democrat, of New Jersey, on a technicality of the most contemptible character. This crime was committed under the party lash. Trumbull had reported Stockton entitled to his seat, and the committee, with one exception, had been unanimous. But moral scruples had been conveniently shed, and when the vote on the report sustained it with a majority of one, Senator Morrill, who was paired with a sick Senator, promptly dishonored his pair and voted, to create a tie. At this, Stockton, who had not voted, cast a vote for the report. The next day, Charles Sumner, whose moral sense was never keen where his prejudices were concerned, moved a reconsideration because of Stockton's vote and the motion carried.

With a new vote impending, the sick Wright of New Jersey, whose pair with Morrill had been so shockingly dishonored, wired a request for a postponement until he could arrive on the morrow. The request was refused. Stewart of Nevada, who had voted for the report before, dodged, the Jersey Senator was thrown out, and a disgraceful act consummated. That it was a brazenly partisan performance was not doubted at the time. Julian referred to it as the 'gratifying vote ousting Senator Stockton';[1] and two days later, we find Thad Stevens wiring his Radical friend James

[1] MS. Diary, March 28, 1866.

M. Scovil in the New Jersey Legislature, 'By all means hurry up your election . . . give us no conservative . . . a Radical like yourself or nothing,' because 'a copperhead is better than a twaddler.' [1] Welles was disgusted with Sumner, Fessenden, and Morrill for their part in 'a high-handed, partisan proceeding.' [2]

The revolution was hurrying on.

III

Even after stooping thus, the Radicals were not at all certain they could override the veto. The death of the venerable Senator Foote offered an excuse to postpone the test of strength and thus give time to whip the scrupulous into line. 'It is very sad that we should be tried this way,' wrote Sumner in martyr mood to the Duchess of Argyll.[3] In the midst of the cracking of the whips, the funeral of Foote brought all the contestants together in the Senate Chamber, for Johnson joined in paying tribute.[4] In the interval the excitement in streets, lobbies, and hotels was electric. Wild talk was heard of overthrowing the Government, and Johnson concentrated all his energies and resources on the struggle. Mrs. Clay, calling repeatedly, was met with hastily scrawled cards from the President. 'It will be impossible for me to see you until too late. I am pressed to death.' 'There is a committee here in consultation; I cannot tell what time they will leave.' It was at that time that Mrs. Clay wrote her father that Johnson 'will fall, if fall he must, battling.' His fine fighting spirit had won her over, and she turned to diversions, visiting the studio of Vinnie Ream, then in vogue, with Voorhees.[5]

Even with the beginning of the debate, no one was ready for the test. Stevens was interesting himself in postponing action until Foote's successor, hurriedly named, could arrive. The next day postponement was pressed by Administration supporters because of the serious illness of Wright and Dixon. The day before, Dixon had ridden out to gather strength for the ordeal. When Hendricks pleaded for a postponement because Wright's physician had warned that it would be dangerous for him to appear, and Trumbull, with characteristic decency, had agreed, Ben Wade objected.

---

[1] *Lancaster Intelligencer*, April 13, 1866.        [2] Welles, ii, 464–65.

[3] Pierce, iv, 276.        [4] Welles, ii, 466.        [5] Mrs. Clay, 369.

'If God Almighty has stricken one member so that he cannot be here to uphold the dictation of a despot, I thank him for his interposition and I will take advantage of it if I can.' This elevating sentiment was lustily cheered by the galleries with their whites and blacks. That night Dixon was ready to be carried in. Infuriated by the brutality of Wade, the supporters of Johnson prepared to filibuster through the night, after the brilliant but dissipated McDougall of California had delivered an extraordinary rebuke. The Senate thereupon adjourned.

Meanwhile the whip was falling cuttingly on the weaklings, and the aspiring Stewart of Nevada decided his bread was buttered on the Radical side; so also, Morgan of New York. The next day, Wright, desperately ill, reached the Capitol, at the peril of his life, and was carried into the chamber — but Dixon could not attend. Had he been present, Johnson would have won; without him, the veto was overturned by one vote. The galleries exploded with enthusiasm, and jubilant Radicals, having tasted blood, swarmed into the streets, red-faced, vociferous, triumphant. It was the beginning of the end.

That night the Radicals marched in battalions to Grant's reception, to make him a part of their celebration and appropriate him to themselves. There were Stevens and Wade, grimly exultant, and there, too, the boyishly enthusiastic Theodore Tilton, over from New York, mingling excitedly in the group, and gloating over the accession of Morgan. And then, like a thunder clap ——

'The President of the United States.'

Johnson, smiling, his daughter on his arm, entered early, to be received cordially and to linger long. If his equanimity was disturbed, there was no outward evidence. But the poker face of Stevens reddened, Wade glowered, and Trumbull was manifestly astounded. And then came Montgomery Blair and some of his ladies, and Alexander H. Stephens, the man with puny body and robust mind, and the Radical plan for the monopolization of Grant was wrecked.[1]

A few days later the House overrode the veto without debate. Bingham, who had bitterly denounced the bill, crept to the storm cellar and dodged, and Stanton's friends had been notably active.

[1] Welles, ii, 477–78.

Henry Raymond voted to sustain the veto, but his influence had been frittered away.[1]

It was at this juncture that the friends of Johnson began urging upon him the dismissal of Stanton, but he was clearly annoyed. 'I am breasting this storm,' he replied. He would be ready to act at the proper time.[2]

IV

And Stevens was pushing forward. Within a few days he offered his Amendment, which was to be the nucleus of the Fourteenth. The crux of it was the third section, disfranchising all who had adhered to the Confederacy until July 4, 1870, which would have excluded the overwhelming majority of the Southern people. Apropos of Sumner's attack upon the Fourteenth Amendment as it originally went to the Senate, the unforgiving old man lunged at him savagely, in beginning. 'It was slaughtered,' he said, 'by a puerile and pedantic criticism, by a perversion of philological definition which, if, when I taught school, a lad who had studied Lindley Murray had assumed, I would have expelled him from the institution as unfit to waste education upon.'

The second section of the pending Amendment was not so good as that 'sent to death in the Senate,' providing for confiscation. 'Forty acres of land and a hut would be more valuable to him [the freedman] than the immediate right to vote.' Yes, failure to give it would invite 'the censure of mankind and the curse of heaven.'

Turning to his disfranchising section, and conceding a difference of opinion, he declared it 'the most popular of all.' Even so, it was 'too lenient.' Better far to extend the exclusion until 1876, 'and to include all State and municipal as well as national elections.'

Blaine reminded him of Lincoln's pledge of pardon and amnesty written into law. Stevens shook his head. Garfield asked if he were willing to make the South 'a vast camp for four years more.' Stevens was willing.[3] Raymond sought to argue with a prejudice and a fixed idea. Would not Stevens's section create the impression that the Republicans were seeking a method 'of influencing and controlling the presidential election of 1868?' Stevens smiled

---

[1] Welles, ii, 479.        [2] Ibid., ii, 482.        [3] Congressional Globe, May 8, 1866.

sardonically at the simplicity of his foe. Raymond thought Stevens's section designed to make impossible the South's adoption of the Amendment. Why, it would make the South another Ireland. This charge of a desire to prevent adoption was heard frequently in the debate.[1]

These academic moralists had irked the practical politician from Lancaster intolerably, and in closing the debate he shocked them with frank admissions. Adopt the third section, he said, or 'that side of the House will be filled with yelling secessionists and hissing copperheads.' This section or nothing! Party motive? 'I do not hesitate to say at once that section is there to save or destroy the Union [Republican] Party.' Better were it the year 18,070 instead of 1870, for until that remote future 'every rebel who shed the blood of loyal men should be prevented from exercising any power in this government.' Clawing with bony fingers among his papers, he found and held up a report — 'the screams and groans of the dying victims of Memphis.'

A colleague interrupted to ask if Stevens could build a penitentiary big enough to hold eight million people.

'Yes' — and Stevens's voice cut the air like a saw — 'a penitentiary which is built at the point of the bayonet down below, and if they undertake to come here we will shoot them down.'[2]

The roll was called, and Raymond, a bit shamefacedly, followed Stevens — his master — and the House smiled and cheered. With the announcement of the vote passing the measure, there came a pandemonium of jubilation in the galleries, white and black. 'I do not want our proceedings interrupted by the nigger heads in the gallery,' shouted a member[3] — and the galleries hissed, unrebuked by Colfax.[4]

But short shrift was made of Stevens's section in the Senate, and Howard's substitute was accepted, excluding all participants in the rebellion from national office, but with the provision that Congress, by a two-thirds vote, could remove the disability. A tragic blow to Stevens, who was stricken and confined to his house, feverish with disappointment and rage.[5]

---

[1] *Congressional Globe*, May 9, 1866.          [2] *Ibid.*, May 10, 1866.
[3] Eldredge of Wisconsin.                        [4] *Ibid.*
[5] *New York World*, June 4, 1866.

The Fourteenth Amendment was perfected in a party caucus in the Senate, and Senator Hendricks made the most of it. Here was a measure touching the Constitution itself actually withdrawn from open discussion in the Senate to be passed upon 'in the secret councils of a party.' Yes, 'for three days the Senate Chamber was silent . . . the discussions transferred to another room . . . with closed doors and darkened windows where party leaders might safely contend for a political and party purpose.' [1] Four days after Hendricks spoke, the measure passed.

And five days later, Thad Stevens, pale and feeble from his fever, made one of the most pathetic speeches of his career, worthy in eloquence of a better cause. In his 'youth, in manhood, and in old age' he had 'fondly dreamed' that when 'any fortunate chance broke up for a while the foundations of our institutions,' they would be so remodeled 'as to have freed them from every vestige of human oppression, of inequality of rights, of recognized degradation of the poor, and the superior caste of the rich.'

The old man's voice trembled, and, after a pause, he resumed: 'This bright dream has vanished "like the baseless fabric of a vision." I find that we shall be obliged to be content with patching up the worst portions of the ancient edifice, and leaving it in many of its parts to be swept through by the tempests, the frosts, and the storms of despotism.'

Why, then, did he accept the measure? 'Because I live among mortals and not among angels.' Too many men anxious 'to embrace the representatives of rebels.' Too many ambitious 'to display their dexterity in the use of the broad mantle of charity.' Too much of 'the unscrupulous use of patronage.' Too many 'oily orations of false prophets, famous for sixty day obligations and protested political promises.' [2]

Thus the Amendment passed; and Andrew Johnson, submitting it according to law, clearly indicated his dissent from amending the Constitution in the absence of eleven States. 'A noble proof of his strength of character, and his immovable fidelity to the Constitution,' commented the Democratic organ.[3]

[1] *Congressional Globe*, June 4, 1866.　　　　[2] *Ibid.*, June 13, 1866.
[3] *New York World*, June 23, 1866.

V

The day after the failure of the Freedmen's Bureau Bill, a new measure was introduced; and about that time Johnson sent J. B. Steedman and J. S. Fullerton, reliable men, into the South to investigate the operations and effect of the Bureau activities. After four months of intensive and conscientious investigation, they submitted a report, a separate one for each State, containing serious charges, few without substantial foundation.[1] Time was to prove that they had shown marked moderation.[2] The movements of the investigators were followed with sleuth-like vigilance by the Radicals, and the 'New York Tribune,' attacking Fullerton at New Orleans on the basis of a letter from that city, charged that he had been 'welcomed like a Rebel Brigadier General,' and had not been in town twenty-four hours 'before he was seen walking the streets arm in arm with a signer of the Louisiana Ordinance of Secession.'[3] The Radicals were not interested in facts — they were moving sternly forward to a purpose — the perpetuation of their power. The second Freedmen's Bureau Bill was pushed to passage, and Johnson returned it with a veto more powerful than the first. Many Republicans were sadly shaken, and it required a vigorous application of the party whip to force them into line, but they yielded, and the measure passed over the veto.[4]

The Revolution had gained momentum.

VI

Throughout this session, sinister figures were seen moving about, and behind the smoke screen of the sectional conflict, men of acquisitive passions, who knew precisely what they wanted, were busy sowing and reaping. The reconstruction of the North was not being overlooked. Agents of interests seeking special governmental favors were swarming lobbies and corridors, half concealed in the dust of the more dramatic struggle. A mania for

---

[1] Pierce, *Freedmen's Bureau*, 65.

[2] House Ex. Doc., 39th Cong. Session, No. 120.

[3] June 15, 1866.

[4] Professor Burgess (page 89) says on the merits of the question the veto could not have been overridden.

rapid accumulations of fortunes by fair means or foul was apparent to the observant, and, while the masses of the people were intoxicated with their hates and passions, a few statesmen understood the significance of the new day. 'The truth is,' wrote John Sherman to the General, 'the close of the war with our resources unimpaired gives an elevation, a scope to the ideas of leading capitalists, far higher than anything ever undertaken in this country before. They talk of millions as confidently as formerly of thousands.'[1] The house of Jay Cooke in Washington, presided over by his amiable brother, was a favorite resort of not a few statesmen; and Mr. Cooke was interested in railroads and in the speedy resumption of specie payments. It was common gossip that members of Congress were not above the persuasion of the dollar in the determination of their course. 'I am more and more disquieted by the signs of bribery I see,' wrote Julian in June.[2] The scrupulous Senator Grimes was expressing his disgust at the liberality with which the national domain was being doled out. 'Nearly all the grants of lands to railroads and wagon roads find their way into the hands of rich capitalists,' he declared in the Senate,[3] 'and in eighteen months or two years after this grant is made, the script will be in the hands of the wealthy of the country.' Voorhees in the House, and Hendricks in the Senate, had solemnly warned of the tendency, but their politics was unpopular and they were put down as 'demagogues.' Even 'The Nation' was concerned over the influence of the railroads, 'the most formidable in any community,' and thought they were tending to the poisoning of politics and to the domination of the State.[4] Very soon Andrew Johnson was to grieve the judicious with the open declaration that 'an aristocracy based on nearly two billion and a half of national securities has arisen in the Northern States to assume that political control which the consolidation of great financial and political interests formerly gave to the slave oligarchy,' and to predict that 'the war of finance is the next war we have to fight.'[5] And at that moment he added another corps to the army of enemies, recruited from the moneyed class.

[1] *Letters*, 258.          [2] MS. Diary, June 24, 1866.
[3] *Congressional Globe*, February 7, 1866.
[4] April 27, 1866.          [5] Interview with Halpine, McPherson, 141–42.

The 'New York World' was denouncing the lobby of the
Northern Pacific as a gang of 'plunderers,' and describing it in the
'galleries, looking down on the scene like beasts of prey.' [1]

The spirit of Hamiltonian centralization was dominant in the
councils of the ruling party. Johnson had called attention to it in
his first veto; Welles had commented on it in his diary; and the
'New York World' was saying that 'the bummers section are to-
day just what the Federalists were in 1797,' and insisting that it
'fight under its true colors, and without trickery.' [2] It had now
become easy to confuse the public mind as to the meaning of
State Rights — for had not the war shot that to death forever?

Out in the agricultural sections there was uneasiness and confusion. During the war a tremendous industrial development had
resulted from war conditions and high tariffs, and the industrialists were aggressively asserting themselves in Washington. The
log-rolling for higher tariff rates had been so impudent that Godkin in 'The Nation' denounced the lobby and the unscientific
method of fixing rates, 'secretly as Congress does,' as 'one of the
most fertile sources of corruption ever opened in any age or country.' [3] Many commercial organizations were hostile to the increase in rates, and the New York Chamber of Commerce protested that it 'would mar the prosperity of agriculture, by increasing the cost of its supplies without enhancing the price of its
products.' [4]

The penetrating could readily see the significance of it all —
the passing of influence in government from the agricultural to the
industrial element. One day an Iowa representative [5] warned
Thad Stevens 'of a great storm coming from the West.' [6] So
stubborn was the protest of the farmers that a gesture of conciliation was made to them by abandoning the plan to increase the
rate on pig iron six dollars a ton. This so disgusted Stevens, personally interested in iron, that he refused to vote. [7] But it was in the
Senate where the most bitter battle between the industrialists and
the agriculturists was staged, and there Senator Grimes of Iowa
led for the farmers, strongly supported by the Mid-Western

[1] April 27, 1866.          [2] June 4, 1866.          [3] July 5, 1866.
[4] Signed by A. A. Lowe, *Congressional Globe*, July 9, 1866.          [5] Wilson.
[6] *New York World*, June 30, 1866.          [7] *Ibid.*, July 11, 1866.

Republican press. When a tariff measure seemed certain of passage, the 'Chicago Tribune' said, 'If Andrew Johnson has a grain of political sagacity, he will veto the bill and set himself up as the champion of the people against extortion and robbery.'[1] With Hendricks interpolating, to encourage the rumpus, the Democrats sat back and watched the enemy clawing at one another. Henderson of Missouri ridiculed the argument that the tariff would help the farmers, who were then burning their corn because they could not find a market.[2] But it was Grimes of Iowa who bore the brunt of the battle. His insurgency enraged the protectionists, and scurrilous attacks on his personal integrity were made by the 'Iron Age.' British gold had bought him. 'The Tribune,' hysterical in its abuse, sent its weekly edition free to every man of consequence in Iowa and the Northwest in the hope of ruining him. So indecent did some of these attacks become that Fessenden rose in indignant protest, and the leaders, becoming alarmed, postponed action until the next session.

VII

All the while the bitter drama of deadly personalities was gradually unfolding. One night a Johnson club in Washington went forth on serenades to the President and members of the Cabinet, with the view to forcing the hands of the latter. Speed, the Attorney-General, speedily rushing into the arms of the Radicals, ran away, and Harlan refused to appear. Welles, who disliked speeches, amazed to find 'perhaps a thousand people . . . with a band of music' before his door, merely expressed his adherence to the Administration. Dennison 'acquitted himself with credit,' according to the friends of the President, but it was Stanton these serenaders were after.

Appearing at the door of his house, flanked on either side by a candle-bearer, he read a carefully prepared address. He was not yet ready to unmask — must move with caution, and with caution he moved.[3] He had instinctively favored negro suffrage enforced by national authority, but had yielded to adverse arguments; had advised the approval of the Freedmen's Bureau Bill,

[1] Quoted, *New York World*, July 9, 1866.
[2] *Congressional Globe*, July 12, 1866.          [3] Welles, ii, 512–13.

but that was past; so, too, with the Civil Rights Bill, but he dropped this instantly; but he was opposed to the exclusion from suffrage of all who had adhered to the Confederacy — Stevens's plan, which he knew would not be adopted.

Forney, in the 'Philadelphia Press,' sneered at McCulloch for supporting Johnson with vigor, and found Stanton the incorruptible patriot still.[1] Not so easily satisfied the fervent Theodore Tilton, of 'The Independent.' Stanton had disappointed this young-man-in-a-hurry. The speech 'did not express the true man, Edwin M. Stanton; it is without his soul, without his enthusiasm ... his earnestness ... his love of liberty.' Would that he had spoken more worthily!

'So good-bye, Mr. Stanton,' chirped the 'New York World' with glee. 'He is with reason disliked by the Democrats; conservative Republicans have no reason to love him; and now the Radicals regard him as a backslider.'[2]

But Tilton did not understand the flexibility of Stanton so well as the real Radical leaders, and they were satisfied.

Johnson went his way, reticent, lonely, grim, determined, but cautious. There was no chip on his shoulder. He merely stood on his rights and for his principles. But he forced no fighting — not yet. This irked the 'New York World,' which chided him gently because of 'his halting infirmity of purpose during a crisis of the most important conflict of opinion which has ever prevailed in this country.'[3]

And yet there was nothing of timidity in his attitude. When he spoke, it was with boldness, but he was being urged to speak not at all. Welles and Trumbull agreed that it was bad — the latter was emphatic.[4]

Then suddenly Johnson's hand struck out, when Forney became too abusive of his policies, and the country was reading a letter from the editor written four months before, fulsomely praising these policies — and soliciting a job for a friend![5] Forney, in the meanwhile, had weakened under the lash and gone over to the enemy. Logan had defended Johnson's policies at Cooper Union

---

[1] Quoted, *New York World*, May 23, 1866.   [2] May 31, 1866.
[3] June 16, 1866.   [4] Welles, April 19, 1866.
[5] *New York World*, July 2, 1866.

— and he was going; and Morton had made a sweeping defense — and he was going, too. Principle everywhere was yielding to expediency. Patriotism was bowing to party.

Watchful, but patient, Johnson went his way. One day, appearing at the national fair for the benefit of the home for soldiers and sailors, he had made a really beautiful speech. 'Yours is the work of peace, to pour the balm that healing may take place,' he said.[1] When Parson Brownlow, in a communication to Congress, described him as 'that dead dog in the White House,' he was silent. But 'The Nation' thought it a cowardly attack and said so. Probably Johnson 'looks on Brownlow now as Prince Hal, after his father's death, looked on Falstaff.' [2]

The crisis was coming on apace. Dennison, the Postmaster-General, had slowly cooled toward the President and went out quietly and decently in July, and a few days later, James Speed, Attorney-General, followed, with a strange fling of bitterness in view of his seemingly Conservative leanings before. It was good riddance for Johnson, who was enabled to replace them with friends and supporters of capacity.[3] But Stanton held on. He was not the sort that resigns; and he was too valuable as a spy in the camp.

That summer, tragedy came close to Johnson. Senator Lane of Kansas committed suicide, and Preston King drowned himself in the Hudson. The former had valiantly defended the President against Ben Wade's insults in the Senate; and the latter had been his most intimate adviser and personal friend. In the case of Lane, the suicide was due to miserable health; the secret of King's death died with him. But the Radicals instantly knew the reasons. Years later, with a smug hypocrisy that staggers credulity, Blaine explained that Lane had been 'profoundly attached to Lincoln' and that 'his strange course under President Johnson was never clearly disclosed.' Having been profoundly attached to Lincoln, it was a mystery to Blaine, who had not been similarly attached, why Lane should have supported the man who was fighting for Lincoln's policies.[4] In keeping with Blaine's version, we

[1] New York World, June 7, 1866.          [2] July 26, 1866.
[3] A. W. Randall for Postmaster-General, and Henry Stanbery for Attorney-General.
[4] Twenty Years in Congress, II, 186.

have the letter written to Colfax. 'It was his participation in this destructive policy [Johnson's],' he wrote with a touch of Uriah Heep. 'I sorrow for him, but I am not surprised.'[1] And so with King. It was because of Johnson's course, wrote Blaine.[2] God had touched the consciences of men so wicked as to have scorned the leadership of Thad Stevens and Ben Wade.

Often that summer, Johnson, with a carriage packed with his grandchildren, would drive out to Rock Creek and rest at Pierce's Mill, or in a near-by meadow, where he loved to walk alone. Before returning, he would pluck flowers for his invalid wife. Sometimes he went to the peace of Glenwood Cemetery, and wandered among the graves. On one of these occasions an attendant was startled to find him laughing — since he seldom laughed. The attaché hurried to him, to find him sober as usual.

## VIII

The announcement of Stevens's plan for military reconstruction convinced the President's friends that only an impressive appeal to the country could awaken it to the dangers. One morning in June at Welles's breakfast table, he and Senator Doolittle agreed on the necessity for action, and submitted their views to Johnson, who acquiesced and suggested a National Convention. Within a few hours both Doolittle and the venerable Frank P. Blair, at Silver Springs, were drafting the call. Even this task presented embarrassments calling for compromise and conciliation. The Blairs, knowing that the Democrats would have to be the backbone of the movement, were fearful of the influence of Seward in the framing of the document. The first draft admittedly was so couched as to satisfy Henry J. Raymond, to the disgust of Welles.[3] This was done for the effect of having his signature to the call as Republican National Chairman. The major objection to the draft was the omission of any reference to the constitutional changes, which might be interpreted as a capitulation on the part of the President,[4] but in a three-hour conference at the White House one fragrant June morning, the point was waived on Raymond's account. At least one of the conferees left 'desponding and un-

---

[1] *Life of Colfax*, 274.        [2] *Ibid.*, II, 186.        [3] Welles, II, 528.
[4] *Ibid.*, II, 533.

happy,' because 'the cause is in bad and over-cunning, if not treacherous hands.' [1] It was noted, too, that 'the Democrats, who in their way are the chief supporters of the President's measures, are snubbed.' [2] This, too, was out of deference to Raymond. A week later, however, despite the opposition of the 'New York World,' the Democrats in Congress agreed to swallow their pride and coöperate.[3]

Thus the call went out, and instantly the Republicans were out gunning for Raymond. On the night of July 11, a caucus was called, 'venomous, reckless, the worst yet,' [4] in which all the hellhounds of insane hate were let loose. Johnson was denounced. Most of the participants wanted to sit all summer to deal with any presidential appointments that might be made. A resolution was adopted depriving the President of the control of Government arms, and distributing these among the 'loyal States.' [5] In the midst of the clamor, a noise was heard in the gallery, and the members discovered one lone negro looking on. Pandemonium! A spy! Worse, perhaps a reporter!

'Damn him, bring him down here,' shouted the alarmed Stevens.

The poor trembling black was dragged before the grave and reverend seigniors of the State and asked how he entered.

'By de do',' he answered tremulously. He did not know it was a caucus, he said, but thought it was the Congress.[6]

The negro ejected, Stevens offered a fiercely worded resolution denouncing the proposed Convention and reading out of the party all Republicans who might give it countenance. This was the signal for the pack to open up on the offensive Raymond, and the next day both the 'New York Tribune' and the 'New York World' had it that he had expressed himself as in penitent mood, and had assumed that none but Republicans would be admitted as delegates to the Convention.[7] Whether he really went to the mourners' bench, we do not know. He always denied it; the members of the caucus insisted that he had; and the probability

[1] Welles, ii, 533–35.
[2] Ibid, ii, 538.          [3] Ibid., ii, 542.
[4] Raymond to Weed, Weed, Memoirs, ii, 452.          [5] Ibid.
[6] New York Tribune, July 12, 1866; New York World, July 13, 1866.
[7] Both of July 12, 1866.

is that he told the truth, since he was a prominent figure in the
Convention. He gave his own version in the 'New York Times,'
expressing contempt for the attack upon him,[1] and startling sane
conservative folk with a disclosure of the proceedings. The
Northern States called upon to organize, drill, equip the militia,
with two thirds of the arms, ammunition, and ordnance of the
National Government to be turned over to them! 'The first step
toward the preparation of another civil war,' said the 'New York
World.' [2] This version, borne out, too, in Raymond's letter to
Weed,[3] called forth a defiant editorial from the Democratic organ.
'Let them go on if they dare,' it said. 'The bullets and gibbets,
however costly, which in that case would assuredly rid us of the
inflamers of our first and the plotters of our second civil war may,
after all, be the only way to a calm world and a long peace.' [4]
Meanwhile, with the Democrats allotted half the delegates to the
Convention, to the annoyance of Raymond,[5] the Administration
forces pushed on with preparations for the Convention, and Stanton again momentarily showed his hand. At a meeting of the Cabinet, he volunteered that he had refused bunting asked, and sneeringly said that Welles might furnish it. 'I always show my colors,'
replied the Yankee, 'and it would be well that you showed yours.'
'You mean the Convention? I'm against it,' snapped Stanton.
Seward looked uneasy. 'We cannot get along this way,' said
Welles to Johnson. 'No, it will be pretty difficult,' replied the
long-suffering man.

Stanton was now beginning to feel strong enough to show his
hand. It was the hand of treachery.[6]

IX

The campaign of 1866 really began when nearly fifteen thousand
people assembled in a huge wigwam in Philadelphia, August 14,
in the National Union Convention for which the friends of the
Administration had been making elaborate preparations. The
spirit of sectional conciliation was dramatized when a Union and

---

[1] July 18, 1866.          [2] July 20, 1866.          [3] Weed, *Memoirs*, II, 452.
[4] *New York World*, July 20, 1866.
[5] To Weed, Weed, *Memoirs*, II, 452.
[6] Welles, II, 573-74.

a Confederate officer [1] marched down the center aisle arm in arm
to a thunder of applause. Men like Hendricks, Democrat, served
on the resolutions committee with men like Raymond, Republican.
Seldom has a finer set of substantial and patriotic men sat down
together in the interest of a cause. The opening speech of Senator
Doolittle was dignified and able; the Address to the American
People, prepared by Raymond, was a noble document, reiterating
the right of representation, the constitutional right of the States
to prescribe qualifications for the franchise, the traditional theory
that amendments to the Constitution could be made only through
the votes of two thirds of the States, and paying a tribute to
Johnson.[2] The resolutions declared slavery dead forever, and the
great crowd rose and cheered; and they repudiated the Confederate debt. Generous, too, the cheering of the declaration that the
negroes should have 'equal protection in every right of person and
property.'

Bubbling with enthusiasm, the delegates hurried to Washington
personally to present the resolutions with their respects. They
stood crowded in confusion in the East Room when Johnson and
his party, which included Grant, descended from the library by
the private stairway, and there was a wait for ten minutes until
the visitors could be properly placed.[3] Welles thought Johnson's
improvised speech 'happily' done, but, alas, he referred to Congress as the Congress of only a part of the States, and the gossips
had it on the wings of the wind that he meant by this to bring in
the Representatives of the South with the aid of the army. Stanton was conspicuously absent. The criticism of Grant's presence
by the Radical press was none the less bitter because the 'New
York World' suggested that 'its bearing on the politics of the
country was understood.' [4]

For a brief moment there was jubilation in the camp of the
President, and pressure was brought to bear upon him to dismiss
Stanton at once.[5] But with Raymond it was a sadder story.
From that hour he was the target of abuse from the Radicals, his
name was dropped from the list of Republican leaders, the Na-

---

[1] Governor James L. Orr of South Carolina and General Couch of Massachusetts.
[2] *Life of Raymond* has the address in full.        [3] Welles, II, 582.
[4] August 20, 1866.        [5] Welles, II, 581.

tional Committee met and removed him from the chairmanship, and the State Convention of New York endorsed its action. Thad Stevens had his party in his pocket and was the cock of the walk.

Meanwhile, the Radical group, with the connivance, if not through the initiative, of Stanton, arranged for a Loyal Union Convention at Philadelphia; [1] and thither a little later journeyed a nondescript crowd of men. James Speed, with the zeal that converts feel, attacked Johnson with ferocity in his opening address. In close touch, Stanton was given a momentary fright by the report that a resolution commendatory of his position would be adopted, and he hurried word to the leaders that such action 'would be prejudicial to any good influence I may be able to exert.' [2] From the South flocked the carpetbaggers, and Frederick Douglass, the negro orator, appeared upon the scene to the discomfiture of Oliver P. Morton, who begged Theodore Tilton to persuade the black leader to take the first train home. In truth, it was not a happy occasion for Morton, who labored earnestly with the Southern delegates not to insist on a negro suffrage declaration. [3] The speeches were uniformly abusive, and the 'bloody shirt' was waved with zest. Of the seven delegates from North Carolina, but two were natives, the others carpetbaggers. One of these was A. W. Tourgée, whose 'Bricks Without Straw' and other novels of reconstruction days had a long vogue; and there was a preacher from the North, a Freedmen's Bureau agent recently convicted of dishonesty by a military commission, and another minister, who began as a Confederate chaplain, and, being accused of treason, went over to the Union army and was later made a Bureau agent. [4] Stories the bloodiest created the keenest delight, and Tourgée solemnly declared no loyal man safe in North Carolina, and told of a recent discovery of fifteen murdered negroes in a pond, and of the migration from the State under threats to life and property of twelve hundred Union soldiers who had settled there. [5] 'A tissue of lies from the beginning to the end,' wrote Jonathan Worth, an honest man; and he wrote a North

[1] Flower, 309.    [2] *Ibid.*
[3] Told Julian by General Shaffer at Freeport, Illinois, November 4, 1866; MS. Diary.
[4] Hamilton, 179, note.    [5] Worth, ii, 774.

Carolinian who sat in the convention that sent Tourgée as a delegate, demanding the names of the twelve hundred men and the location of the pond where the fifteen murdered negroes had been found.[1] False or true, these stories served the purpose of the Radical propagandists, and scores of such fabrications floated out from the convention hall.

The Union League Club of Philadelphia entertained lavishly for the delegates and the Union League Club of New York, which had sent delegates, invited the delegates to a mass meeting in New York City, their expenses paid; and the tribe of carpetbaggers, always found where something could be had for nothing, hastened to the metropolis to be wined and dined.[2]

Followed then the Johnson Soldiers' and Sailors' Convention at Cleveland, where the most dashing and picturesque of the delegates was General Custer, ardent in the support of the President. His presence was deeply resented by the Radicals, and because of his letter to John W. Forney, setting forth his views on national affairs, 'The Nation' pronounced him as much misplaced in politics 'as the Viscount of Dundee would have been in the Archbishopric of Canterbury, or Murat on the Bench of the Court of Cassation.'[3] It was not that Custer was in politics — most of the generals were — but that he was in politics for Johnson. The most sensational incident of this convention was the able letter of Henry Ward Beecher bestowing his blessing, but his wealthy congregation, then a political machine, paying him an enormous salary, growled ominously, and wrote him a letter of rebuke which 'The Nation' thought 'grave and well written.' We shall soon find the eloquent minister recanting publicly from the pulpit.

There followed the anti-Johnson Soldiers' and Sailors' Convention at Pittsburgh, where it was not so absurd for generals to participate. This was personally conducted by Ben Butler, and the result was unmeasured abuse of the President.

Meanwhile, blood had been shed in the streets of New Orleans.

[1] Worth, ii, 772, 774.
[2] Bellows, 89.    [3] August 26, 1866.

# CHAPTER VII

## PATRIOTS MOB A PRESIDENT

### I

WITH both sides in savage mood, two bloody incidents in the South played into the hands of the Radicals. In Memphis a group of boisterous drunken negro soldiers, recently disbanded, interfered with the police in the discharge of a legitimate duty, shot an officer, and precipitated an indiscriminate slaughter of the blacks by the rowdy element in the community.[1] In New Orleans, the revolutionary plan of the Radicals to enfranchise the negroes for party purposes, by an illegal summoning of the delegates of an extinct Constitutional Convention of two years before, aroused the indignation of all and the murderous wrath of the lower classes, and culminated in a massacre. No one questions the conclusion of Professor Burgess[2] that 'common sense and common honesty would hold that the Convention [of 1864] had been finally dissolved.' No one honestly doubted it then; but it was not an age of common sense or common honesty. The purpose was to seize on power and hold it with the army, for the negroes and the carpetbaggers.[3] The president of the defunct Convention refused to act because of the manifest illegality of the proposed call; and even he who agreed to substitute hurried to Washington to secure the countenance of the Republican leaders. He conferred with Thad Stevens, 'Pig Iron' Kelley, and Boutwell, the Puritan; and immediately thereafter the 'New York Times' announced that he 'returned with the assurance that Congress will support the Convention.' Indeed, as the 'Times' report of a Republican caucus proves, Boutwell had urged a postponement of adjournment that Congress might immediately give validity to the new Constitution when adopted.[4] In the congressional investigation reference was made to letters in possession of a Mr. Flanders, signed by members of Stevens's committee, sanctioning the desperate enterprise, but

[1] Testimony of Dr. S. J. Quinvy, H. R. 39th Cong., 1st Sess., Report 101.
[2] *Constitution and Reconstruction*, 93.
[3] R. K. Cutler, H. R. 39th Cong., 2d Sess., Report 16, p. 33.          [4] *Ibid.*, 540.

Mr. Flanders was not summoned to the witness chair.[1] Stevens admitted he might have written him; and conceded that he had told the messenger from New Orleans that the Convention would be legal.[2] Had there been no convention, there would have been no massacre; and there would have been no convention without the encouragement of the Radical leaders in Washington.

The conservatives and whites of character and property, at first incredulous, sought to persuade the Radical leaders in Louisiana to abandon their mad revolutionary project — to be met with jeers. A judge who charged the grand jury on the illegality of the plan was arrested and charged with 'treason and endangering the liberty of citizens under the Civil Rights Bill.'[3] The Mayor and Lieutenant-Governor appealed to the military forces, to be informed, after a queer reticence, that the army would release the delegates if arrested on indictment in a court.[4] They appealed to Johnson and Stanton on that warning. Stanton did not reply; Johnson instructed that the military forces would be expected 'to sustain, not obstruct or interfere with the proceedings of the courts.'[5] This telegram was shown the general in command, and the Mayor and Lieutenant-Governor understood the day before the Convention was to meet that soldiers would be on hand to preserve order.

The night before the Convention was one of jubilee and defiance, two or three thousand negroes parading the streets with torches, shouting exultantly; and at a mass meeting they listened to Dr. Dostie, Radical leader, in an incendiary speech. The negro should have his vote — and would! Another meeting would be held. 'I want you to come in your power,' shouted the half-crazed orator. 'I want no cowards to come. . . . We have 300,000 black men with white hearts. Also 100,000 good true Union white men who will fight beside the black race against the hell-hound rebels. . . . We are 400,000 to 300,000 and can not only whip but exterminate the other party. . . . The streets of New Orleans will run with blood.'[6]

Thousands of white families did not sleep that night in New Orleans.

[1] R. K. Cutler, H. R. 39th Cong., 2d Sess., Report 16, p. 259.
[2] *Ibid.*, 489.        [3] Ficklen, 163–66.        [4] *Ibid.*, 165.
[5] *Ibid.*        [6] *Annual Encyclopædia, 1866*, 451–54.

Dawn came. A proclamation from the Mayor called on the people to preserve the peace. The police were mobilized at headquarters for emergencies. General Baird agreed to have troops within easy call — but fatally blundered in thinking the Convention would meet at six o'clock in the evening and not at noon. The troops were at Jackson Barracks far away. Governor Wells, who had gone over to the Radicals, had hidden himself at home.[1] Thus the Convention met without molestation, and adjourned to permit the sergeant at arms to bring in the absent members.

Then the rattle of a drum — and down the street the flying of a flag — and a procession of negroes, intoxicated with a feeling of triumph. On they marched until, at Canal Street, a white man jostled a marcher, who struck the white. On to Mechanics' Institute, where the Convention was to sit, and there they paused to hurrah. Some of the blacks were armed, and the first shot was fired by one of these at a policeman who had arrested a newsboy for stirring up trouble. The shot brought the police from headquarters on the run, and they charged the procession. The negroes threw bricks and retired into the hall. But all the fury of combat had been awakened, and some of the police fired into the blacks. Dostie, who would live by the sword, died from a sword-thrust in the stomach. In the massacre that followed but one member of the Convention was killed; but there were dead and wounded borne away on drays; and former Governor Hahn, attacked by the mob, was saved by the police fighting for his life. Not all the police turned beast by any means, and the Chief knocked down one of his own men engaged in brutal work. Whiskey played its part; race feeling did the rest; but the better element was not involved.[2]

When the son of President Taylor, alighting from a tram, heard pistol shots and saw a crowd of roughs and negroes running, he sought to learn the meaning. He met no one he knew — his kind were not abroad. He was impressed by the great number of boys from twelve to fifteen, and stopped one youth, who, pistol in hand, was pursuing a fleeing negro. The boy explained that a convention was being held to take away his vote; and when Taylor asked him how long he had enjoyed that inestimable privilege, the youth sheepishly put away his pistol.[3] Baird's troops came up after the

[1] Ficklen, 166.    [2] Ibid., 169.    [3] Destruction and Reconstruction, 248-49.

riot was over, and then patrolled the streets with negro troops further to exasperate the people.

General Phil Sheridan hastened back to his post from Texas, and hurried a report to the President, admitting the incendiary character of Dostie's bloody speech, conceding that one in ten of the marching negroes carried arms, pronouncing the instigators of the Convention 'political agitators and bad men'; and then denouncing the press for opposing the Convention, and furnishing the Radicals what they wished in the sentence, 'Northern men are not safe.' He was instructed by Johnson that pending an investigation he had full military power to maintain order.

The 'political agitators and bad men' petitioned Congress on 'the St. Bartholomew day of New Orleans,' and protested against being left to 'assassins.' General Baird, who had blundered, appointed some of his officers to investigate, and they reported that it was a conspiracy to crush the Convention.[1] Johnson thereupon summoned Colonel Richard Taylor to Washington to get his version, and, on his recommendation, placed General W. S. Hancock in charge, and order was restored.[2]

The Congressional investigation brought the inevitable partisan reports.[3] But an impetus had been given to the waving of the 'bloody shirt,' which had commenced, and thenceforth for years the North was to be told that the Southern whites devoted themselves mostly to the killing of inoffensive blacks.

II

Meanwhile, Andrew Johnson had set forth on his historic journey to the tomb of Stephen A. Douglas in Chicago. With him were Grant and Farragut; and, among members of his Cabinet, Seward, Welles, and Randall. In the party, too, were Mrs. Patterson, Mrs. Farragut, and Mrs. Welles. Arrangements were made to travel by day alone, and these were adhered to with the exception of the trip by steamer from Louisville to Cincinnati.[4] That Johnson proposed to advocate his policies en route there can be no doubt; it was

[1] Ficklen, 170.
[2] *Destruction and Reconstruction*, 251.
[3] H. R. 39th Cong., 2d Sess., Report 16.
[4] Welles, II, 588.

just such a tour as Roosevelt and Wilson were to make in later years. As President, he felt he had a right, without the consent of Congress, to carry his fight to the people.

Riding to the station in Washington through throngs of cheering people, with flags and bunting flying from the buildings, he was to receive ovations all through Maryland and Delaware, and appear on the rear platform introducing Farragut and Grant. It was not until Philadelphia was reached that the organized partisan mobbing of the President began. There the Radical city officials extended no official welcome, and attempts were made through trickery to prevent a demonstration by the people. False information as to the time of the train's arrival was broadcast, but the politicians failed in their conspiracy. Flags were everywhere, many factories were deserted, and when the train stopped at the station, the enthusiastic crowd broke the police lines to clamber upon the platform and to the top of the car. Laborers were straining their throats with cries for 'the tailor President' and the 'Savior of the Union.' When, with difficulty, a lane was forced through the multitude for the passage of the presidential party, and the carriages were reached, the police lines were again crashed as men rushed forward to grasp the President's hand. The procession passed through two miles of welcoming tumult, and it was noted that the Union League Club was not decorated in honor of the head of the Nation. Smug, sour-visaged men within looked out from the windows contemptuously upon the scene. In one of the two speeches Johnson made, he sounded the intended keynote of the journey: 'I trust that the day is far distant when the land we love shall again be drenched with brothers' blood. (Good.) I trust the country will return to peace and harmony and that reconciliation will be brought about, and we be enabled to stand together, one people and one Union.' [1]

The 'New York Tribune's' account was one of studied insult. When a confused driver of a cart turned his horse into the crowd, and Johnson sought to quiet the people and prevent a panic, the incident was so described as to make him appear cheap, absurd. The correspondent boasted that the city was 'perfectly bare and destitute of adornment.' The mobbing of the President had com-

[1] *New York World*, August 29, 1866.

menced.[1] The next day, receptions were held at Camden and Trenton; and at New Brunswick, Johnson spoke again.

'Now that the rebellion has been put down . . . there is an issue made that the States are still out of the Union, which is precisely what the rebels undertook to effect. . . . The States were never out of the Union. (Thunderous applause.) The Union is preserved, "one and inseparable." . . . Let us stand upon a common platform — the Union of these States — lifting ourselves above party and the shackles of party.'

At Newark he stood on the platform at Market Street before a sea of faces, while guns fired a salute and twenty locomotives screeched. Pressed for time, he had but a moment to talk. 'It has been my fate for the last five years,' he said, 'to fight those who have been opposed to the Union. . . . I intend to fight all opponents of the Constitution . . . to fight the enemies of this glorious Union forever and forever.' It was a happy party at this stage, with Grant and Farragut bantering like boys and trying to push each other to the platform.

Then came New York — a veritable triumph. The streets were packed; at noon all work suspended; and from the Battery to the City Hall the streets were jammed from curb to curb with barely room for the carriages to pass. Alexander T. Stewart, the leading merchant, voiced the welcome of the reception committee. 'I thank you for your welcome,' said Johnson simply; 'I appreciate it from the bottom of my heart, and' — with a graceful bow to Stewart — 'particularly appreciate the source from whence it comes.' When, in the Governor's Room at the City Hall, he received official greetings, it was noted that he seemed deeply moved. A moment on the balcony, bowing to the shouting multitude in the park, and he returned to the open barouche drawn by six horses, and the procession moved up Broadway to Twenty-Third Street, a file of cavalry marching on either side to protect the carriage from the crush. At all the windows, ladies leaning out and waving handkerchiefs. Even 'The Tribune' was nonplussed. 'So far as popular demonstration and enthusiasm is concerned,' it said, 'the ovation . . . forms a striking contrast to all other displays of the kind that have preceded it in this city.' [2] That night a civic

[1] *New York Tribune*, August 29, 1866.

[2] August 30, 1866. This description based on accounts of the *Tribune*, *Herald*, and *World*.

banquet was given in his honor at Delmonico's, where he stayed. It has not been fashionable to quote from the wise and patriotic speech he made there, but it is necessary in order to understand the later occurrences at Cleveland and St. Louis, of which we have probably heard too much.

'Let me ask you,' he said, 'are we prepared to renew the scenes through which we have passed? . . . Are we again prepared to see these fair fields . . . drenched in a brother's blood? Are we not rather prepared to bring from Gilead the balm that has relief and pour it into the wound? . . . They are our brethren . . . part of ourselves. . . . They have lived with us and been part of us from the establishment of the Government to the commencement of the rebellion. They are identified with our history, with all our prosperity.' Admitting an ambition to contribute to a real reunion, he closed in a moving peroration. 'Then I will be willing to exclaim as Simon did of old of Him who had been born in a manger, "I have seen the glory of the salvation, now let thy servant depart in peace." That being done, my ambition is completed. I would rather live in history in the affections of my countrymen as having consummated that great end than to be President forty times.'

At this point General Sandford sprang to his feet, calling for three cheers, and the diners rose in an ovation.[1]

That night, at midnight, crowds lingered before Delmonico's until Johnson appeared and bowed. The next morning in the early dawn found the presidential party driving through Central Park. Leonard Jerome, grandfather of Winston Churchill, the British statesman, had Grant behind a fine span of horses; and when the General, puffing his cigar, took the reins, some one suggested that the park police be summoned. Coming up behind Johnson's carriage drawn by four horses, Grant let his horses out in a spirited race until the Jerome team went thundering by, to the amusement of Johnson, who waved and laughed.[2] Leaving the city, the party stopped at West Point; thence on to Newburgh, Poughkeepsie, Peekskill, and to Albany, where, after a greeting from the Governor, a reception was held, and at night, in response to a serenade, Johnson spoke briefly. He here referred to the attempts of the Radical press to prejudice the people against him in

[1] *New York World*, August 30, 1866.          [2] *Ibid.*, August 31, 1866.

advance and expressed his contempt for enemies of the Constitution, 'North and South.' After a display of fireworks, Johnson retired, badly worn by the trip.

The next day, at Schenectady, the 'New York Tribune' noted that his voice was failing and he was showing the strain;[1] but after a generous reception he spoke briefly. 'I know no backward step,' he said. 'I intend to go forward in my path of duty because I know it is right.' At Rome he spoke again. 'By the Eternal, the Union and Constitution must be preserved.' At Auburn, where he rested at the home of Seward, he declared 'there is not enough power on earth to drive me from my purpose.' Thence on to Buffalo, where the venerable Fillmore, acting as chairman, endorsed Johnson's policy, and the latter, in reply, merely reviewed it in detail.[2]

The trip from Buffalo to Cleveland was wearisome, the train constantly crowded with committees, with scarcely standing room in the cars. Grant reclined on a trunk in the baggage car, using a carpetbag for a pillow. At every station crowds had assembled, and Johnson spoke a few words, though by this time he was sadly worn and not a little irritable. At Erie, an old woman boarded the train with flowers for Johnson and Grant; the former graciously received his, but the General did not appear.[3]

Thus, worn and weary, Johnson reached Cleveland. He had traveled many miles, spoken many times, and never in bad taste. His talks had been uniformly wise, just, patriotic, on one theme — the sanctity of the Constitution and the Union. The response of vast throngs had been enthusiastic. General John A. Rawlins, with the party, commented on it in letters to his wife.[4] As the Radical chiefs observed the triumphant progress, they were increasingly enraged and disturbed. Johnson was making headway. And it was just at this juncture in the home State of Ben Wade that ruffians engaged to set things right.

### III

On the afternoon of the day of the arrival of the presidential train, the streets of Cleveland were crowded beyond precedent. The skies, overcast during the day and threatening a rainy night,

---

[1] September 1, 1866.          [2] *New York World*, September 4, 1866.
[3] *New York Tribune*, September 4, 1866.          [4] *Life of Rawlins*.

cleared toward evening, and long before the arrival of the train the lake-front by the station was thronged and the depot crowded. Throughout the day every train increased the multitude.[1] So powerful was the pressure of the crowd that the police were barely able to maintain an open space for the alighting of the party, and when Johnson appeared, the shouts were like the thunder of artillery. Ovations for Johnson, for Farragut, for Custer, and considerable disappointment at the absence of Grant, who had gone directly to the Detroit boat, much indisposed.[2] The streets from the station to the Kennard Hotel on the public square was a solid mass of humanity. The hotel was lively with its Chinese lanterns, and flags flying from every window, and near-by residences were brilliantly illuminated. It was after an informal dinner that the party was escorted to the Bank Street balcony, where Johnson was formally welcomed by the President of the City Council.[3]

That there had been a determined effort to organize a mob to heckle the President there can be no doubt. The day before, the· 'Cleveland Herald,' a Radical paper, had distributed circulars bitterly attacking Johnson, accusing him of treason to Lincoln, to party, and country. While the vast majority of the mammoth crowd was decent and well disposed, it contained a sprinkling of the scum of the community, many of them drunk, and not a few there deliberately to insult the head of the Nation. A stone, thrown into the crowd, struck and disabled one of the spectators before the President appeared.

Fagged and irritated by the pulling and hauling, it was Johnson's intention to say but a few words and retire. Scarcely had he begun when the hecklers began shouting their insults, coarse and personal, and in his irritation, due to physical weariness, the fighting spirit of the man who had won the admiration of the North by facing and fighting mobs was aroused. That he was greatly excited is well established.[4] Surrounded by enemies, there is not one scintilla of evidence that he was under the influence of liquor. In his give-and-take debate with the mob he made some of the most

---

[1] *Cleveland Herald*, Republican, September 4, 1866.
[2] *Cleveland Plain Dealer*, September 4, 1866.          [3] *Ibid.*
[4] Testimony of D. C. McEwen, correspondent *New York World*, Impeachment Trial, *Congressional Globe*, 102.

telling points of his speech. Even the bitterly hostile 'Cleveland Herald,' commenting editorially, said that 'the crowd was indebted to these annoyances for some of the best points made. . . . Mr. Johnson was thoroughly aroused and showed that he could not only parry, but thrust, and he made some telling points that were enthusiastically enjoyed by the crowd, and gave some advice that sensible men can profit by.' [1] Thus, a typical illustration of his thrusts:

'You let the negroes vote in Ohio before you talk about negroes voting in Louisiana. (A voice, "Never.") Take the beam out of your own eye before you see the mote that is in your neighbor's. You are very much disturbed about New Orleans, but you won't let a negro go to the ballot box to vote in Ohio.'

Such retorts were considered in very bad taste, and the party papers joined in the mobbing of the President without a word of criticism of the mobs.

The next morning, great throngs in the streets wildly cheered Johnson as an atonement, but the Radicals now had their cue. Henceforth, mobs were part of the programme. At Norwalk, a rowdy gang was mobilized, and in the midst of Johnson's plea for a real restoration of the Union, one of the disturbers yelled 'New Orleans.' Johnson paused: 'I should like to see the fellow who cries "New Orleans."' The crowd pushed forward a disreputable-looking creature. 'I thought you would look just about so,' said Johnson, turning with a smile to accept a bouquet of flowers.

At Chicago there was no untoward incident; and the party pushed on to St. Louis, where a scene similar to that at Cleveland was staged by the Radicals. Aside from a few hot-tempered retorts to insults, Johnson's speech here seems absolutely sound to-day.

Homeward bound, a novel experience in the Mid-West awaited Johnson at Terre Haute, where he was received with the courtesy and hospitality due his station. Multitudes on horseback, in the rain, responded with shouts to his ringing defense of the constitutional liberties of the people. Not one insult; and not one sentence in bad taste from him. But this was only a gracious interlude, for at Indianapolis he was to meet the most shameless mob of the journey. Escorted to the Bates House by a torch-bearing pro-

[1] September 4, 1866.

cession, he appeared upon the balcony and before he could be introduced, the mob element began shouting for Grant. Before he had uttered a word, he had been greeted with groans. Ignoring the affront, the President of the United States began:

'Fellow citizens [cries for Grant]: It is not my intention [cries of 'Stop!' 'Go on!'] to make a long speech. If you will give me your attention for five minutes [cries of 'Go on!' 'Stop!' 'No, no, we want nothing to do with traitors!' 'Grant! Grant!' and groans]. I would like to say to this crowd here to-night [cries of 'Shut up!' 'We don't want to hear from you, Johnson'].

Johnson paused, and then retired from the balcony. Fighting followed in the streets and a man was killed.[1] So shocking was this outrage that the 'Indianapolis Journal,' Radical Republican organ, ran a hypocritical apology the next morning. 'Had such a scene been anticipated, the most strenuous efforts would have been made by Union citizens to prevent it,' it said. But the 'Indianapolis Herald' declared the scene carefully staged, 'rumors of a disturbance having been rife throughout the day.'[2] The atmosphere was just right for the mob. Governor Morton had hurried from the city on the approach of the President, and a short time before a Radical orator had made an inflammatory attack on Joseph E. McDonald, Democratic leader, pointing to his house while the mob cried, 'Hang him! hang him! let's hang him!'[3] Sobered by the shameful incident, decent citizens gathered at the Bates House on the morrow in atonement again, and Johnson spoke from the balcony.

Through Ohio, town after town turned out its ruffians. At New Market, Johnson was greeted with insulting placards and shouts for Grant and Custer. The latter responded. 'I was born two miles from here,' he said, 'and I am ashamed of you.'[4] At Steubenville, such hooting and groaning that Johnson did not respond. Custer, furious, hurled defiance at the mob, and Johnson in one sentence paid his compliments to the decent part of the crowd and 'in a cat-o'-nine tails paid his respects to the black-

[1] New York Tribune, September 11, 12, 1866.
[2] Quoted New York World, September 14, 1866.
[3] New York World July 31, 1866. The speaker was W. P. Fishback.
[4] New York Tribune, September 14, 1866.

guards,' and retired.[1] At Pittsburgh a hearing was denied, the mob groaning and shouting insults for an hour until Grant appeared and ordered the ruffians home.[2]

Never in history had a President gone forth on a greater mission — to appeal for constitutional government and the restoration of union through conciliation and common sense; and never had one been so scurvily treated. City officials in Baltimore, Philadelphia, Cincinnati, Indianapolis, and Pittsburgh had refused an official welcome; the Governors of Ohio, Indiana, Illinois, Michigan, Missouri, and Pennsylvania had not appeared; and in the more than forty congressional districts traversed, but one Radical Congressman had paid a call of courtesy.[3] Trouble had been expected in Philadelphia, but nowhere else.[4] Everywhere the mob was the aggressor; and nowhere was the President protected against its insults. Newspapers and magazines teemed with misrepresentations and falsehoods, and no one was more culpable than the cultured James Russell Lowell in the 'North American Review.' He reached a rather low level in his characterizations of Seward as 'a bear leader,' of Johnson as 'his Bruin,' and in describing the trip as 'this indecent orgy.' The notable snobbery of the poet asserted itself in his reference to Johnson's 'vulgar mind, and that mind a Southern one.'[5] The reference to 'this indecent orgy' was low and false. 'As a member of the party,' wrote B. C. Truman years later,[6] 'I can say that there was no drunkenness at all on the trip. Johnson, who had given up whiskey for sherry, indulged in but little of the latter, and Grant drank not at all.' But the Radicals had become such adepts at lying that even Rhodes was convinced of the 'orgy.' One of the most nauseous of the tribe, J. M. Ashley, Member of Congress, crony of Stanton, was writing the latter of his 'surprise and humiliation' because Grant was too drunk to appear at Cleveland and Johnson 'in such a condition that it would have been better if he had gone into seclusion'; and Stanton was accepting the slander with a sanctimonious sigh.[7] It was agreed by all the tribe that Johnson was undone; but what a

[1] New York Tribune, September 14, 1866.        [2] Ibid.        [3] Welles, II, 588–96.
[4] Ibid.        [5] North American Review, October, 1866.
[6] Century, January, 1913.
[7] Flower, Life of Stanton, Stanton to Ashley, September 14, 1866.

fright they had had until they hit upon that device at Cleveland!

At Lancaster, Thad Stevens was chuckling in his unpleasant way, and making the most of the mobs in a talk to his neighbors. The trip had been a 'circus.' Sometimes one 'clown' (Johnson) performed and sometimes another (Seward). 'I shall not describe to you,' he said, 'how sometimes . . . they entered into street brawls with common blackguards; how they fought at Cleveland and Indianapolis. . . . They told you he [Johnson] had been everything but one. He had been a tailor — I do not think he said drunken tailor — no, he had been a tailor. [Laughter.] He had been a city alderman. [Laughter.] He had been in the Legislature — God help that Legislature! [Great merriment.] He had been in Congress and now he was President. He had been everything but one — he had never been a hangman and he asked leave to hang Thad Stevens.'

But when Johnson returned to the White House, he showed no chagrin. 'His manner was absolutely as when he first took upon himself the cares of office.' He made no reference to the trip, and 'there was not an added line in his face.' [1]

### IV

Meanwhile, with an election approaching, what were the Southern people doing? Everywhere a feeling of utter depression and hopelessness. The mob groans from the North seemed curses on the South. With party politics few were concerned. Sympathy there was with Johnson, but few counted on his success. 'If the policy of Thad Stevens is to prevail,' wrote Jonathan Worth to a prospective immigrant, 'I could not conscientiously advise anybody to emigrate to North Carolina. That policy would degrade nine tenths of our adult population.' [2] Many were convinced of the settled purpose of the Radicals 'to subjugate the Southern people after the manner of Poland and Ireland under James I and Cromwell.' In carrying out such plans it was feared they 'would not scruple to call in the aid of the blacks.' [3] The rule of carpetbaggers was looming dark on the horizon. Even such men as Fessenden of Maine were demanding the right to appoint Govern-

[1] Crook, 112.          [2] Worth, i, 591.
[3] *Ruffin Papers*, Edw. Conigland to Ruffin, 76.

ment officials in the stricken States.[1] In North Carolina, W. W. Holden, embittered by his defeat for Governor, was turning to the extremists and foreshadowing the use of military forces to sustain the Radical rule.[2] Given half a chance, the average Southerner would have eschewed politics to devote his energies to the economic rehabilitation of the country.[3] But the fear of the domination of negroes and carpetbaggers could not be thrown off. The blacks were becoming intoxicated with the idea of acquiring political power — and soon. Had they not assembled in the Methodist Church at Tallahassee to choose a Congressman and make a collection to defray his expenses to Washington? And while there was some merriment when he made a pleasure jaunt to Savannah and returned to give an account of his stewardship, the incident was too suggestive for real enjoyment.[4]

Then there was the Fourteenth Amendment disfranchising the leaders of the people and demanding their degradation — that was intolerable. Everywhere that was agreed. 'If we are to be degraded,' wrote Worth,[5] 'we will retain some self-esteem by not making it self-abasement. . . . If we were voluntarily to adopt this amendment I think we should be the meanest and most despicable people on earth.' The brilliant editor of the 'Mobile Register,' John Forsyth, wrote that 'it is one thing to be oppressed, wronged, and outraged by overwhelming force; it is quite another to submit to voluntary abasement.' [6] In Mississippi the sentiment was bitterly against adoption.[7] In Texas the Governor denounced it. In Arkansas the Democrats were organized and fighting fiercely and effectively against 'Old Imbecility,' as they dubbed Governor Murphy, and the Radicals there were broadcasting to the North that 'Union men are being hunted down and shot by rebels.' [8] The Republican Party was being formed in all the States, and the Opposition had not yet merged because of the inveterate hatred of former Whigs and Democrats. In Georgia, where the Governor had attacked the Fourteenth Amendment, the picturesque Joe Brown, Confederate War Governor, was going over to the Stevens crowd

[1] Worth, I, 469.     [2] Hamilton, 171.
[3] Advice of Governor Jenkins, Thompson, 164.     [4] Wallace, 38–39.
[5] To W. D. Hedrick, Worth, II, 665.
[6] Fleming, 394.     [7] Lowry.     [8] Staples, 108–09.

with recommendations of acceptance on the theory of a conquered people. This desertion was soon to unify the Opposition and ere long there would be fine fighting in Georgia.[1] Meanwhile, to serve the purposes of radicalism, weird tales of 'outrages' against blacks and carpetbaggers were being hurried to the Northern press. The Tourgée fabrication of the fifteen murdered negroes in a pond was being used with fine effect. Northern press correspondents were in the South mingling with the lowest elements in bar-rooms, brothels, to pick up the meaningless mouthings of the vulgar for political consumption. Silly stories of 'outrages' were telegraphed without investigation. Even General Swayne protested frequently against these slanders, but without avail. Reports went out that no man's life was safe on the highways of North Carolina. 'A man may travel in North Carolina with as much security as in any State of the Union,' indignantly wrote Worth in reply to an inquiry. 'Cases of disturbance save in the chief towns are almost unheard of, and in the chief towns they are much less frequent than in your cities.'[2]

As part of the propaganda, petitions were sent the President complaining of an alleged persecution and indictment of Union men for acts committed in the Union cause, and these were featured in the Northern press; the fact that an investigation disclosed but two indictments out of the fifty-six mentioned, and one of these for illegally selling liquor, was not permitted to reach the Northern people.[3]

v

Such were the conditions under which the important campaign of 1866 was fought. The Johnsonians, and Democrats supporting them, sought through serious constitutional arguments to reach the minds of the voters; the Radicals were concerned solely with their passions. Soon circulars were secretly circulating among the Irish attacking Johnson because of the performance of his duty apropos of the Fenian move on Canada.[1] Then appeared the 'Philadelphia Ledger' canard, charging that Johnson had asked his Attorney-General for an opinion on his right to send a message to

---

[1] Fielder, *Life of Brown*, 421–22, 424.          [2] Worth, I, 498.
[3] Hamilton, 182.          [4] *New York World*, November 21, 1866.

'an illegal and unconstitutional assemblage pretending to be the Congress of the United States,' and as to whether his oath of office required him 'to enforce those provisions of the Constitution which give to each State an equal right of representation in Congress.' This was intended to create the impression that he planned a *coup d'état*. It was not a new bugaboo, for had not the Radicals in caucus discussed means of preventing it? Sumner was solemnly warning the Bostonians against the danger. 'You may judge him [Johnson] by the terrible massacre at New Orleans,' he wrote Bright. 'Stanton confessed to me that he [the President] was its author.' [1] Ah, these 'confessions' of Stanton! 'The Ledger' story was just a new eruption, denounced by the 'New York World' as instigated by speculators 'who wished to influence the gold market by playing on the fears of the country.' [2] A little skeptical itself, after having spread the story, 'The Public Ledger' investigated and apologized. Some one 'in office' had informed it that the paper had been seen on the Attorney-General's desk.[3] More treachery — some one 'in office.'

And what new banner is this fluttering from the hilltops where Radicals do congregate? Why, it is the 'bloody shirt,' new flag of our Union, to render mighty service for more than a generation. Oliver P. Morton was its Betsy Ross. He is discussing reconstruction and dare not stick to the text lest that Richmond speech rise to plague him. What can he say? Let us listen: 'Every unregenerate rebel . . . calls himself a Democrat. Every bounty jumper, every deserter, every sneak who ran away from the draft calls himself a Democrat. . . . Every man who murdered Union prisoners . . . who invented dangerous compounds to burn steamboats and Northern cities, who contrived hellish schemes to introduce into Northern cities . . . yellow fever, calls himself a Democrat. Every dishonest contractor . . . every dishonest paymaster . . . every officer in the army who was dismissed for cowardice calls himself a Democrat . . . In short, the Democratic Party may be described as a common sewer and loathsome receptacle.' [4] Thus the great man wandered on, while men actually cheered themselves hoarse over this '*exposé*' of the infamies of Johnson's policies. At the

[1] Pierce, IV, 298.          [2] October 11, 1866.          [3] October 15, 1866.
[4] Foulke, *Life of Morton*, I, 474–75.

same time, Zack Chandler was touring in the West. 'Every man who murdered and stole and poisoned was a Democrat'; and Johnson was a tool of the rebels. And Roscoe Conkling, histrionically, was holding forth as .well. 'The President . . . deceitful errand . . . imperial condescension . . . supercilious patronage which seems to ape Louis Napoleon . . . This angry man, dizzy with the elevation to which the assassination has raised him. . . .' Was any one in doubt of the meaning of a Johnson victory with the aid of the Democrats? It was to restore rebels to power, to pay for the slaves, to make the Nation pay for damages done the South in the war, to make the United States assume the rebel debt.

Thus Roscoe Conkling confirmed his right to the orator's crown, and men cheered such utterances to the echo.[1] Soothed by the sound, he warmed to his task. 'Women and children shot down for decorating Union soldiers' graves . . . Now the rich traitor is courted and caressed and the poor Unionist butchered with the connivance of Andrew Johnson.'[2] 'Are you ready to put your rights . . . property, and the honor of the nation to be raffled off by the murderers of your children?'[3]

Thus Wendell Phillips writes in the 'Anti-Slavery Standard' that Johnson must be impeached, and the Government turned over to some one selected by the House pending the impeachment.[4] Then, laying down his pen, he rushed to the platform of Cooper Union. 'This mobocrat of the White House,' he said to the frenzied patriots — impeach him! Remove him during the trial! Four years, too long for Presidents! Imagine — 'Andrew Jackson when once planted upon the Government lasted eight years.'[5]

Yes, echoed Ben Butler, not to be outdone. 'Impeach him and remove him now.' And how? Let the Senate sergeant at arms place him under arrest and tell him that unless he does as told 'the boys in blue will make him.' More: if Johnson dare call on the standing army, these 'boys in blue' will sweep it away 'like cobwebs before the sun.'[6] Thus Butler, squinting from the platform in Cleveland and Cincinnati. And while Butler was gasconading

---

[1] *Life of Conkling*, 370, 388.          [2] *Ibid.*, 278.          [3] *Ibid.*, 276.

[4] Quoted, *New York World*, September 27, 1866.

[5] *Ibid.*, October 26, 1866.

[6] *Ibid.*, October 9, 1866; *The Nation*, October 11, 1866.

against phantoms in the West, the scholarly Sumner, facing the Bostonians in Music Hall, was exclaiming: 'Witness Memphis, witness New Orleans, who can doubt that the President is the author of these tragedies?'

With such an onslaught of the political bravos and bullies, Republicans, keeping the company of their common sense, were either driven to silence or the mourners' bench. Henry Raymond refused another congressional nomination in a manly letter declaring his adherence still to Johnson's policies, and retiring because his opinions were not in harmony with the sentiment of those with whom he had been acting.[1] Henry Ward Beecher, who had been generously blackguarded for his support of Johnson, was not of the stuff of heroes. His congregation paid him handsomely, and it was against him. For once in his life he had failed to line up with the heavy artillery and he was unhappy. Thus one night he made his recantation before a crowded audience at the Academy of Music, Brooklyn. 'When in a matter of politics I am overruled, what shall I do?' he asked. 'Shall I sulk and refuse to work?' It was not in his nature to refuse to work, and, plunging headlong, he rehabilitated himself in the esteem of the pew-holders by making what 'The Nation'[2] described as 'a savage onslaught on the Democratic Party as the enemy of all good causes.' It was so violently contradictory of his letter to the Cincinnati Convention of a month before that the Democratic organ made merry over the manifest absurdity. 'This seems the most maliciously cruel attack ever made on the reputation of a public man,' said 'The World,' referring to the publication of the recantation speech. 'When Mr. Bennett whirls about, no one is surprised; when Mr. Raymond trims it is considered a matter of course; but Mr. Beecher is supposed to be governed by higher motives, and what would be venial in them would be infamous in him.'[3] There were a few unhappy days for the well-paid crusader of the Lord. 'Sunset' Cox spoke immediately afterward in Brooklyn in a merciless excoriation. Beecher's speech, he said, reeked of party, party, party. It was full of hate and venom and slander. It was the voice of a trimmer, the turn of a weather-cock.[4] It required men of

[1] *Life of Raymond*, 189–90.  [2] *The Nation*, October 18, 1866.
[3] *The World*, October 16, 1866.  [4] *Ibid.*, October 18, 1866.

stronger moral character than Beecher to withstand the fusillade of abuse turned on the supporters of Johnson.

It was at this time that Thomas Nast wheeled into the fight with cartoons in 'Harper's Weekly' of bitterness and brutality. The gentle and conservative George William Curtis, the editor, was a bit shocked, thinking it bad policy 'to break finally and openly with our own Administration,' and, in a letter to Nast, said the pictures suggested were such hard hits he hoped 'it may not be necessary to use them in these disputes';[1] but Fletcher Harper disagreed. 'It is not necessary that all should agree. Mr. Curtis and Mr. Nast are personally responsible — each for his own contribution'; and thus the pencil of Nast reënforced the tongues of Stevens, Butler, Phillips, Sumner, and Morton.[2] And just then Hannibal Hamlin, who had never forgiven Johnson for displacing him in the Vice-Presidency, although appointed Collector of Customs in Boston by his successor, resigned in a bloody-shirt letter,[3] and he was soon upon the stump demanding Johnson's impeachment, and accusing him of responsibility for the New Orleans massacre.[4]

Only from the women did the Radicals encounter opposition that really hurt. Elizabeth Cady Stanton had annoyed them persistently by asking why intelligent white women of property were not considered as much entitled to a vote as the semi-barbarous negroes of the islands off Charleston.[5] She made much of the claim that 'James Brooks was the only Congressman last winter who had the nerve and decency to present the Woman's Suffrage Memorial to Congress' — and he was the Democratic leader of the House.[6]

In the midst of the tumult and the shouting, the Democrats were trying to reason with people whose ears were attuned rather to abuse. Their efforts offered little hope of harvest. In a meeting at Cooper Union, Horatio Seymour was pleading for a policy of restoration — speaking with the voice of prophecy: 'There is danger from the growing corruption which festers when far-off States are put under the control of agents with unusual and

[1] Paine, Life of Nast, 123.       [2] Ibid.
[3] Hamlin, Life of Hamlin, 509–10.       [4] Ibid.
[5] New York World, October 13, 1866.           [6] Ibid., November 21, 1866.

undefined powers, meddling not only with public concerns, but with private business and family affairs. These agents, mostly adventurers and men unknown to the people, and beyond the reach of the eye of those who pay the cost of keeping them, are more tempted by love of power and lust for money to act corruptly. This form of government for the South, base and debasing, lives only by keeping up the passions and hates of the people of this country.' [1] Samuel J. Tilden was speaking powerfully, too, supporting Johnson as possessing 'the qualities which yesterday we were wont to applaud,' and declaring his policy 'the true constitutional doctrine.'

But this was crying against the wind. Beecher screamed 'copperhead'; Butler, 'rebel hounds'; Sumner, 'defenders of the New Orleans massacre'; and Morton's voice was reverberating still — 'every man who murdered Union soldiers was a Democrat.' The result was inevitable. The Radicals won easily, and the doom of the South was pronounced. 'We may read our destiny in the indications just at hand from the Northern elections,' wrote one Southerner to another — 'utter ruin and abject degradation are our portion.' [2]

But there was jubilation in quarters not concerned with the punishment of the South nor with negro suffrage as such. The 'Philadelphia North-American' rejoiced because 'the present Chief Magistrate is not a friend of domestic industry,' and the 'New York World' declared 'the Protectionists are hugely delighted. . . . It gives them at least two years more to plunder the country.' [3] In the branch bank of Jay Cooke & Company at Washington, presided over by the genial Henry Cooke, there was much festivity. 'Holding a regular levee,' he wrote his brother, 'Colfax, Washburne, Spaulding, Sherman, and others among the callers. . . . They all feel that as visitors they are masters of the situation and can, with their two thirds, run the machine of government themselves.' [4] The house of Cooke was wanting Government money for its private enterprises and the skies were as the skies of Italy.

In England the London 'Telegraph,' interpreting the election,

[1] *Life of Seymour*, 160–67.　　　　[2] *Ruffin Papers*, Edwards to Ruffin, 123.
[3] November 13, 1866　　　　[4] Oberholtzer, *Cooke*, II, 25.

thought the United States 'may remain a republic in name, but some eight million of the people are subjects, not citizens.' [1] It was in these elections that the old Republic of Jefferson went down and the agriculturists were definitely shunted aside to make way for the triumphant industrialists and capitalists.

[1] November 9; quoted, *New York World*, November 24, 1866.

# CHAPTER VIII

## THE REVOLUTION HURRIES ON

### I

EAGER under the leadership of Stevens to press their advantage from the election, the Republican leaders were deep in conferences before Congress convened. The feeble old man had heavy work before him, and Nature warned him that his time was short. Never had he been more domineering; and while some resented the shaking of the bony finger of the tottering man whose life was flickering, these bowed obeisance at a glance from his piercing eye. 'Genius and audacity without wisdom,' wrote one observer; 'imagination but not sagacity, cunning but not principle.' [1] No matter — he had power and he was prepared to use it without stint.

One idea was firmly fixed in Stevens's mind — that the revolution had concentrated governmental power in Congress. What more proper, then, than a civic reception to the members on their arrival, closing with a banquet? Instantly Colonel Forney was scurrying about, demanding the dismissal of Government clerks to lengthen the parade. Fifteen hundred marchers responded to the call — mostly negroes — and the spectator from the terrace beheld a dizzy scene, with freedmen in variegated costumes, negresses in bright turbans, blacks mounted on skinny cart-horses, politicians and placemen lolling in carriages. [2] Though Welles's negro servant thought the parade a fizzle, [3] the revolutionists were content. The story sent abroad would stir the party fever in far places.

The House met, and Stevens moved an adjournment without waiting for Johnson's Message. When Samuel J. Randall inquired if it were not customary to hear the Message, Colfax, with his fixed grin, refused to hear. The Message arrived, and some one moved a postponement of the reading, but this would have been too insolent, and the clerk began to read. A little while, and

---

[1] Welles, II, 626.      [2] *New York World*, December 4, 1866.      [3] Welles, II, 631.

Stevens interrupted. 'Our friends are now in the east portico expecting us,' he announced. It was enough, and statesmen festively filed out to smile upon the turbaned heads, negroes on cart-horses, political overseers in carriages.[1] That night, in a barn-like structure, the welcomers greeted the statesmen at a banquet — all but the negroes, who were denied admission. Little of grandeur in the scene, and yet had not other revolutionists met in a tennis court? The services of Fisk Mills, the sculptor, had been requisitioned even as were those of David in another age, and all about, as in the days of the French Revolution, were symbolical pictures and busts — the stern features of Stevens, the set smile of Colfax, the patriarchal benignity of Greeley, the cold dignity of Trumbull.[2] And then oratory — revolutionary too.

That day at the White House, Andrew Johnson was bowing over the hand of Madame Ristori, the actress, and his daughters were showing her over the grounds and conservatory in the rear.[3]

The revolution had advanced by leaps and bounds. The Republican caucus just before Congress met had been as tumultuous as a meeting of the Jacobins. Orators tongue-lashed the President; Stevens proposed to instruct the Senate on presidential appointments, and when a bold spirit suggested that the Senate needed no advice, up sprang Stevens 'like an acrobat,' his followers cheering. How dared any one question the power of the House 'fresh from the people'? He did not know what might be the selfish motive of the objector — this with a blasting look at the shrinking culprit. But there was more. Why not investigate Johnson? asked Boutwell. Splendid! said Stevens. When he returned home last summer he found the people complaining that he had been too conservative. 'They have got ahead of me,' he said; 'I have got to catch up.' [4]

And there sat poor Henry Raymond, stripped of honors, shunned and scorned, the circulation of 'The Times' slipping. Four days later in another caucus, Ashley, the vigilant patriot, observing him in the room, proposed that he withdraw. The deposed chairman of the party rose nervously to demand an explanation. He was a Union man — and the caucus laughed. He

[1] *New York World,* December 6, 1866.   [2] *New York Tribune,* December 6, 1866.
[3] *Ibid.*   [4] *Ibid.,* December 3, 1866.

had always been a Union man — and more laughter. One toler-
ant member, moved to pity, proposed that the determination of
his course be left with Raymond. Then up sprang Stevens, and the
caucus chuckled. A mere sardonic smile in Raymond's direction,
and the caucus was convulsed. The dictator would never consent
to a Johnson Republican sitting in, for there was no such species,
but if Raymond were penitent, he might be accepted on probation.

'Was not the Republican Convention an Andy Johnson Convention?' thundered the dictator. 'I did not think so when I
went in,' Raymond meekly replied. 'Do you still adhere to the
Address of that Convention?' persisted Stevens. 'According to
my interpretation of it,' was the response.

'Put him out,' shouted the extremists.

The vote was taken on the motion to leave the decision with
Raymond, and he escaped expulsion by a majority of two out of
seventy-four votes cast.[1]

Stevens was ruling with a rod of iron, his rooms crowded with
politicians, many from the South. To these he unfolded his plan to
rule the South ten years by the sword, with Territorial Governors
and Legislatures, and with the education of whites and blacks
under the control of Washington. Thus would the freedmen be
trained for citizenship. Otherwise — negro suffrage at once. 'In
my county,' he said, 'there are fifteen hundred escaped slaves.
If they are specimens of the negroes of the South, they are not
qualified to vote. Twelve months hence you will have reconstruction acts with negro suffrage.'[2] In the Senate the conservatives
were deprived of chairmanships and sent to the bottom.[3] The
upper chamber speedily passed the House bill of the preceding
session bestowing the ballot on the negroes of the District of
Columbia.

The day Johnson submitted his veto of the measure to his
Cabinet, Grant was sitting in, and thought it 'contemptible business for members of Congress whose States excluded the negro to
give them suffrage in the District.'[4] Johnson read his Message
refusing consent, because to give suffrage 'indiscriminately to a
new class, wholly unprepared by previous habits and opportunities

---

[1] *New York World* and *Tribune*, December 6, 1866.    [2] Holden, *Memoirs*, 85, 144.
[3] Welles, II, 637.    [4] *Ibid.*, III, 3–7.

to perform the trust which it is to demand, degrades it,' and tends finally 'to destroy its power.' The Cabinet approved — all but Stanton, who read a carefully prepared statement in favor of the measure.

The veto was promptly overridden, with frenzied enthusiasm in the House,[1] and soon the negroes, under the management of white demagogues, controlled the election.[2] The experiment had worked in the District — why not in the South?

## II

Before following the course of the revolution, let us pause to sense the atmosphere in which the drama was staged. Never had there been so many idle men in the streets of the capital, the termination of the war having flooded it with a dangerous floating population that fought for places. Of the thirty thousand negroes two thirds did not average a day's work in a week. No matter — they could furnish a gallery audience for the play. The poorhouse was so congested that only a fraction of the vagrants could be offered shelter.[3] The hotels were packed to capacity.

In society, politics cast a shadow between the bright lights and guests. Deep down was a feeling of uneasiness, and hostesses moved in an atmosphere of treachery which was felt. Danton would still visit the salon of Madame Roland, but Madame would speak her mind about him when he was gone. On New Year's Day, the enemies of the President would mingle with his friends at the White House, trudging on foot or driving through the slush and melting snow to shake the hand of him they had marked for slaughter. As the hatred deepened, the presidential levees were to lose none of their popularity, and that in February, 'brilliant beyond precedent,' was so crowded that women fainted and a detail of police had to be summoned from the station. 'The largest reception ever witnessed at the Executive Mansion' — and yet by this time the more rabid of the Radicals had the decency to remain away.[4] A restless impulse drove people to these receptions. Grant, living in the old home of Douglas, was receiving

---

[1] Welles, III, 8.          [2] *Ibid.*, III, 102.

[3] *Washington Star*, November 25; quoted, *New York World*, November 27, 1866.

[4] *Ibid.*, February 21, 1867.

multitudes, and 'it took from one to two hours to pass from the street . . . to the cloak-room upstairs.' [1]

That was the winter that Sumner, having taken unto himself a young wife, was moving a little more jauntily in the drawing-rooms. The autumn before his marriage to the beautiful Mrs. Hooper had been one of palpitations between satisfaction and misgivings. 'I tremble sometimes at the responsibility I assume,' he wrote George Bancroft.[2] Soon he was installed with his bride and her eight-year-old child in a home at 322 I Street, with a French tutor for the child, a family pew at the Epiphany, and the carriage and span of horses that had belonged to Lord Lyons. Despite the bitter battles at the Capitol, that winter found him more and more at dinners and balls.[3] Soon the gossips, noting the disparity in the ages of the two, were putting their bobbing heads together. A handsome young attaché of the Prussian Legation was found so attentive to the lady that even John Bigelow thought 'such an intimacy crowded rather close on the honeymoon.' [4] Soon the whispers would be busy with the story of an amber necklace; soon a blight fell on the budding romance, and ladies were smiling behind their fans, and statesmen were discussing the story over their cigars. Bryant, the poet, thought the tragedy that of 'a woman not content with a husband who is too exclusively occupied with himself and his own greatness.' [5] Others suggested more delicate reasons, but almost universally the blame was laid on Sumner. Thus the winter was sometimes chill for him, and he would return for the next alone, and more lonely than ever.

But drawing-rooms and ballrooms did not monopolize the interest of those engaged in the somber drama at the capital. A stream of fashionable ladies was pouring into the studio of little Vinnie Ream in the basement of the Capitol, where she was working on her Lincoln.[6] And at the theater, Ristori was appearing in her greatest rôles, Forrest in Shakespearean plays, and Joe Jefferson, playing 'Rip Van Winkle,' was coaxing laughter from the grimmest of the Radicals.[7] Thus life was not without its lure.

[1] Julian, MS. Diary, February 9, 1867.    [2] Pierce, IV, 304.    [3] *Ibid.*, 304–05.
[4] *Retrospections of an Active Life*, IV, 115–16.    [5] *Ibid.*, IV, 134.
[6] *New York World*, April 12, 1867.
[7] Julian, MS. Diary, December 23, 1866.

III

Then came the Supreme Court decision in the Milligan case denying the right of Congress to suspend trial by jury where a court was sitting, and the ringing opinion of Justice David Davis, startling as a fire-bell in the night, was hailed by Senator Hendricks as 'among the landmarks of human liberty.' [1] Instantly the Radical batteries were turned upon the Court, even 'Harper's Weekly' proposing that it be 'swamped by a thorough reorganization and increased number of judges.'

To Thad Stevens it was a golden opportunity. 'That decision,' he exclaimed, 'though in terms perhaps not so infamous as the Dred Scott decision, is yet far more dangerous in its operation upon the lives and liberties of loyal men. . . . That decision has unsheathed the dagger of the assassin and places the knife of the rebel at the breast of every man who dares proclaim himself . . . a Union man.' Now, surely, every one could see the necessity for drastic action.

That drastic action he now proposed — a bill dividing the South into military districts under a commander armed with arbitrary power, and with no date set for the termination of the military despotism. Never had Stevens seemed more vigorous or bitter. 'Every government is a despotism,' he said. 'Better for the black man if he were governed by one king than by twenty million.' Only the one king must not be Andrew Johnson. 'He and his minions shall learn that this is not a government of kings and satraps, but a government of the people, and that Congress is the people.' And why this bill? Because it 'would assure the ascendancy of the Union [Republican] party.' And then, with a look of defiance, 'Do you avow the party purpose? exclaims some horror-stricken demagogue. I do.' Courage determines great events. Ripe scholars and reformers like Melanchthon fell below Luther because they lacked his audacity. 'We may not aspire to fame,' he continued. 'But great events fix the eye of history on small objects and magnify their meanness. Let us at least escape that condition.' [2]

The drooping spirit of Raymond momentarily soared again in a brilliant protest against 'handing over the control of [the South]

[1] *Congressional Globe*, February 15, 1867.          [2] *Ibid.*, January 3, 1867.

to the absolute and sovereign will of a brigadier-general of the regular army.'[1] Nor were the Johnson Republicans the only ones to recoil — Blaine and Bingham urged a termination of the military despotism on the reconstruction of the States with negro suffrage and with little disfranchisement of the whites. But when the haggard old man, with ashen face and flashing eyes, applied the lash to the champions of 'universal amnesty and universal Andy Johnsonism,' and pointed his long finger at the moderates as 'hugging and caressing those whose hands are red and whose garments are dripping with the blood of our and their murdered kindred,' they cringed and crawled to camp. The Blaine-Bingham amendment was defeated, and the trembling old man, with exultant look and something of a leer, pulled himself to his feet.

'I wish to inquire, Mr. Speaker, if it is in order for me now to say that we endorse the language of the good old Laertes that Heaven rules as yet and there are gods above?'

Colfax smilingly replied, 'It will be in order for the gentleman to say it,' and the galleries laughed and cheered.[2]

In the Senate the fight was renewed for the Blaine-Bingham amendment, and as confusion came with the multiplicity of plans, the Republicans went into caucus to force an agreement. They adopted the amendment, authorized the President instead of the General of the Army (Grant) to name the military commanders, provided for Constitutional Conventions to be elected by both races, and the admission of the States on the adoption of Constitutions giving negroes the vote. All this relating to suffrage was done over the protests of Trumbull and Fessenden, and largely at the instance of Sumner. 'Without the colored vote,' wrote that intellectual to John Bright, 'the white unionists could not be organized. The colored vote was necessary. . . . It was on that ground, rather than principle, that I relied most.'[3]

Stevens was enraged. He had purposely made no provision for negro suffrage because in the more radical Fortieth Congress, soon to convene, he had planned further legislation. combining the enfranchisement of negroes, the disfranchisement of whites, and the confiscation of white men's property. In a bitter protest, he

---

[1] *Congressional Globe*, February 8, 1867.
[2] *Ibid.*, February 13, 1867.          [3] Pierce, IV, 319–20.

touched on the sore spot in the Senate's action. 'God helping me, and I live, there shall be a question propounded to this house ... whether a portion of the debt shall not be paid by the confiscated property of the rebels. But, sir, this prevents it.'

The House again bowed to its master, but the Senate insisted on its bill, and after adding two minor amendments the measure passed, and the way was opened for the pillaging of the South.

## IV

But there was more to do. The Tenure-of-Office Act, forbidding the President to remove officials named by him with the Senate's advice, without that body's consent, must be passed. There was nothing mysterious in the purpose, as Hendricks's reference to the Cabinet implied,[1] but Sherman thought 'no man of any sense of honor would hold a position as a Cabinet officer after his chief desired his removal.' [2] Within a year Sherman was to find the man with 'no sense of honor,' and to vote for the President's impeachment because of that man's removal.

On Washington's Birthday, Johnson laid the two bills before the Cabinet, and Stanton, making the most of Reverdy Johnson's support of the Military Bill, urged him to sign.[3] The clear treachery of this advice was as a knife-thrust to the President, who, for the first time, manifested excitement and indignation. With flashing eyes he discussed the incident with loyal members of the Cabinet. Could it be, he wondered, that Stanton imagined he was not understood? [4] Four days later, Stanton advised the veto of the Tenure-of-Office Act. Good, said Johnson, would Mr. Stanton write it? Alas, he was so busy! Ignoring the pretext, Johnson asked Seward to prepare it with Stanton's assistance, and Seward, crossing the room to his colleague, suggested that they enter upon their duty.[5]

Meanwhile, Jeremiah S. Black, great constitutional lawyer, was so engrossed in the preparation of the veto of the Military Bill that he did not even raise his head when any one entered the Cabinet room, where he worked at the President's table.[6] Soon the

---

[1] *Congressional Globe*, February 18, 1867.   [2] *Ibid.*   [3] Welles, III, 49.
[4] *Ibid.*   [5] *Ibid.*, III, 51.   [6] *Ibid.*

veto Messages were read — that of the Tenure-of-Office Act, the
work of Stanton himself.

The morning these Messages went to Congress, Johnson was
more than usually depressed, the conferences of the preceding
night having deprived him of his accustomed sleep, but he was
calm and determined.[1] The Messages were powerful in reasoning
and unanswerable in their objections. 'To the publicist and
historian of this day they are masterpieces of political logic, constitutional interpretation, and official style,' wrote Professor
Burgess, thirty-five years later.[2] But when they were read, no
Republican Senator pretended to listen, and John Bigelow,
looking on in amazement, was so 'shocked' that he 'began to
doubt whether the Constitution was in safer hands now than it had
been when the South was in the saddle.'[3] Reverdy Johnson attacked the veto, Hendricks defended, the roll was called, the veto
overridden, and the galleries rejoiced. There was but mild applause over the vote on the Tenure-of-Office Act.[4] 'It is now perfectly manifest,' wrote a Radical, 'that impeachment is to be our
only remedy.'[5] And the next day the 'New York World' published the names of the two thirds in borders of black, with the
comment: 'The time is coming when every man in the above list
will stand accurst in our history.'[6]

It was unquestionably a wicked day's work.

v

Obsessed with the idea of impeachment, the revolutionists
caucused for two hours on the night of January 6, 1867, on a pretext for such action, with Thad Stevens advising delay. 'Yes, sir,
I think he ought to be impeached,' he said, 'but I am not willing
to go into the matter hastily; when it is done, it ought to be done
thoroughly and certainly.'[7] Unimpressed, the morrow found Loan
of Missouri and Ashley of Ohio introducing resolutions charging Johnson with every imaginable crime. Absurd as these were,
Welles was fearful that 'infamous charges, infamous testimony,

[1] Wells, III, 56.        [2] Burgess, 126.          [3] *Retrospections*, IV, 45.
[4] *Congressional Globe*, March 2, 1867.           [5] Julian, MS. Diary, March 3, 1867.
[6] March 6, 1867.
[7] *New York World*, January 7, 1867.

and infamous proceedings could be produced as easily, honestly, and legally as Butler could get spoons in New Orleans.' [1]

And a week later, Loan gave a disgraceful exhibition — insinuating that Johnson had instigated the assassination of Lincoln! Next to Lincoln, he said, Johnson stood in direct line of succession, and 'by birth, education, and association' he was a Southern man. Worse — 'a lifelong pro-slavery Democrat,' and 'influenced by all the grosser animal instincts' and a 'towering ambition.' What more natural than that the 'Jesuitical leaders of the rebellion' should prefer such a man in the seat of power? And how easy! 'But one frail life stood between them and the chief magistracy.' Thus 'the crime was committed . . . an assassin's bullet directed by rebel hand and paid for by rebel gold made Andrew Johnson President.'

When an indignant member demanded that the words be taken down, Colfax, smiling as usual, as though such charges were customary, ruled the language unexceptionable. Thus encouraged, Loan pushed on, attacking the judiciary; and when a member asked if he did not feel his own self-respect and that of the House called for some particle of evidence 'on which that charge, so grave, is founded,' Loan refused to answer, and Colfax smilingly announced that 'the gentleman refused to answer further.' [2] There was an appeal from the decision, which was sustained by a strict party vote.

Meanwhile, in the Senate, Sumner's personal attacks on Johnson suggested to Welles 'a demagogue filled with whiskey,' [3] and the London 'Times' was commenting that 'it is the Constitution rather than Mr. Johnson that is in danger.' [4]

The investigation dragged along, with nothing found on which to base proceedings, and it was agreed to postpone action until the more radical Fortieth Congress should convene.[5] But the depraved Ashley, counseled by Colfax, and encouraged by Stevens and Ben Butler, was out to get the evidence through purchase or manufacture.

This delectable creature has been strangely slighted by histori-

[1] Welles, III, 12.          [2] *Congressional Globe*, January 14, 1867.          [3] Welles, III, 23.
[4] January 12, 1867; quoted, *New York World*, January 24, 1867.
[5] Julian, MS. Diary, January 27, 1867.

ans. He was a man of many points, with a political position more than good; and, low and corrupt as he was, he enjoyed the comradery of more circumspect leaders who loom large as respectable dignitaries on the page of history. He was an interesting creature in that he had skeletons in his closet. Only five years before, he had been caught soliciting a bribe for securing the appointment of F. M. Case as Surveyor-General of Colorado, and letters were found conclusively proving the charge. The price of his influence was to be the appointment of Ashley's brother as Case's chief clerk, and a share in all land speculations on town sites. A fortune in the job, wrote the itching fingers of the super-patriot.[1] Miraculously escaping damnation for this crime, Ashley persisted in his weird ways. Within a few days of Lincoln's assassination, he had domineeringly approached Johnson, demanding an appointment for the brother of a Congressman he claimed thus to have bought to vote for the amendment abolishing slavery. Enraged at Johnson's refusal to be a party to any such bargain, he turned with venomous hate on the President.[2]

Thus Ashley's leadership caused some misgivings among the conservatives, and Henry Cooke warned his brother, Jay, of the plan to impeach 'as a political measure, to put Ben Wade in the Presidency, and pack the Supreme Court with tools of the Radicals.'[3]

When the extra session merged with the regular, Ashley was still referring darkly to Johnson and assassination, and when Randall inquired if there were an insane asylum near, the members were still able to laugh. But Ben Butler was fervently declaring that 'if any man stands in the way of the great march of the country . . . he must be taken out of the way.'[4] Soon Butler, brother to Ashley under the skin, was pushing him hard for leadership in the impeachment, declaring against adjournment since 'Andrew Johnson is a bad man and this House and Senate should sit here to take care of his acts.' Blaine was skeptical as to the public demand for impeachment, insisting that out of 1700

[1] Ashley letters to Case, *New York World*, January 19, 1867, from *Rochester Union*; also, *World*, January 12, 1867.

[2] Interview with Johnson, *Cincinnati Commercial*; quoted, *New York Tribune*, July 30, 1867.

[3] Oberholtzer, *Cooke*, ii, 25–26.          [4] *Congressional Globe*, March 7, 1867.

or 1800 party papers, not twenty-five regarded the impeachment talk seriously. Nonsense! snorted Thad Stevens. Had not a meeting in Schuylkill County, Pennsylvania, within the last two weeks demanded it? 'Nobody outside of Congress is demanding it now,' Blaine replied. Whereupon, casting scruples to the wind, Stevens retorted by quoting a private conversation of Blaine that there would be no impeachment, since 'we would rather have the President than that scalawag Ben Wade.' [1]

With the revolutionists critical of the procrastination of the investigating committee, Butler was mysteriously promising them startling revelations soon; [2] for it was at this time that Butler and Ashley were hobnobbing with jail birds in an attempt to manufacture a case of murder against Andrew Johnson.

## VI

The Democratic victory in Connecticut did not sweeten the mood of the revolutionists, and Horace Greeley was complaining that had the negroes there been given the vote, two hundred would have turned the tide.[3] Worn by the worries of the session, Thad Stevens was resting uneasily at Lancaster, seeing friends and transacting business daily, despite rumors that he was dying.[4] Even at home, worries retarded his recuperation. There was Senator Henry Wilson making conciliatory gestures to the Virginians, and the old man seized his pen to write a sizzling rebuke to the meddling Yankee. 'Who authorized any orator to say there would be no confiscation?' he demanded. 'Who is authorized to travel the country and peddle out amnesty?' [5] Nothing was nearer his heart than confiscation. His pen was busy. 'We do not confiscate loyal men, nor rebels unless they are rich,' he wrote a Southerner. 'A few will suffer, not enough, I fear; some innocent men will, I fear.' [6]

Two days later, the editor of an Alabama paper called at Stevens's house to seek his real intentions as to confiscation. Ushered into the library, he found a frail old man 'very thin in flesh,'

---

[1] *Congressional Globe*, March 23, 1867.          [2] *Ibid.*, March 29, 1867.
[3] *New York Tribune*, April 3, 1867.          [4] *Ibid.*, April 11, 1867.
[5] *Lancaster Intelligencer*, April 30, 1867.
[6] To F. S. C. Summerkamp, May 21, 1867; quoted, *New York World*, June 10, 1867.

seated in an easy-chair. He smiled faintly for a moment, just a moment, and was grim again.

Asked if he pursued his policy on principle or for party, he snapped back: 'I do nothing merely for party purposes. I regard my proposed action as equitable and resting upon principles of law.'

'But the Constitution,' remonstrated the visitor.

'The Constitution . . . has nothing to do with it,' he said. 'I propose to deal with you entirely by the laws of war.'

'And be satisfied with nothing less than confiscation?' asked the visitor.

'No, sir, anything less would be unjust to those wronged by your crime.'

Here, wearied by his passion, Stevens complained of being tired.

But, persisted the Southerner, suppose Alabama enfranchised negroes, provided for their education, guaranteed their protection in courts and society, and sent good men to Congress who could take the test oath, would they be admitted?

The tired man paused a moment, looked his visitor in the eye, and, with a thundering 'No,' closed the interview.[1]

Meanwhile, in Washington, Johnson was struggling with his problems and against disease.[2] Grant, a bit more at ease, was worried over the presidential gossip. In his library lined with books presented by Boston admirers, John Bigelow found him and spent an evening with him. Did Grant like Washington? He would like it better if there were a half-mile road on which he could drive fast horses.[3]

It was the summer Johnson journeyed to Raleigh to assist in the dedication of the monument to his father. Here he spoke feelingly of his youth, his devotion to the Constitution, the Union. 'Let us repair the breaches made by the war and restore the Union,' he pleaded.[4] In the State House he greeted whites and blacks at a reception, and then rode to the cemetery and listened to tributes to his father.[5] Leading dignitaries of the State accompanied him from the State capital to the University at Chapel

[1] Editor Drake, *Union Springs Times*; quoted, *New York World*, June 20, 1867.
[2] *New York World*, June 11, 1867.          [3] *Retrospections*, IV, 58.
[4] *New York World*, June 4, 1867.          [4] *Ibid.*, June 5, 1867.

Hill, where he was to dine with the president of the university on Commencement day.[1] It was observed that he was 'sad and taciturn.' Addressing the students, he urged the study of 'the principles of the Constitution and free government.' [2] With some of his party he attended the students' ball, and seemed happiest with the young. Tired and depressed, it had made him none the happier to find that his host was a total abstainer. The day was hot. He was worn by the ceremonies. Finally breaking away from the dignitaries, he wandered over the beautiful campus with some of the students, and one of these suggested that there was a bottle of real Kentucky rye in the dormitory. Gladly enough, he trooped with the students upstairs in the Old South Building; there was a scurrying about for ice, sugar, and the 'makin's,' and he drained two generous glasses. One of the boys thought afterward that he was 'athirst, and the hospitality of the boys was uncritical.' [3]

Back in Washington, important matters were pending. Phil Sheridan was riding his high horse in New Orleans, and in the Cabinet there was a sharp division in the discussion of his removal.[4] After many Cabinet meetings, in which Johnson was 'nervous and apprehensive,' Attorney-General Stanbery issued an interpretation of the Military Bill, liberal as possible to the South, to the effect that an applicant for registration as a voter taking the prescribed oath was entitled to go upon the registry, and that the Board could not question the oath. 'If he is right, then Congress is criminally wrong,' wrote Greeley in 'The Tribune.' 'If right we can no more reconstruct the South under this bill than we could under . . . Mr. Swinburne's last poem.' [5] This editorial thrust was less intolerable to Johnson than the impertinent message of Sheridan to his superior that the Stanbery interpretation opened 'a broad and macadamized road for perjury and fraud to travel.' The 'New York Times' thought the insubordination without parallel in recent military history,[6] but Greeley could find no insubordination.[7] Johnson could see that Sheridan was rapidly becoming the Field Marshal of the Radicals.

[1] *Ruffin Papers*, Worth to Ruffin, 180.          [2] *New York World*, June 7, 1867.
[3] *Southern Exposure*, 37–38.          [4] Welles, III, 104; 151–52; 153–56.
[5] June 17, 1867.          [6] June 24, 1867.          [7] *New York Tribune*, June 25, 1867.

Instantly Thad Stevens wrote the 'Washington Chronicle' urging that a quorum be present in July to deal with the situation.[1]

## VII

In the mean time Johnson was off to Boston to the laying of the cornerstone of the new Masonic Temple, and, passing through Philadelphia, where hospitality had not been offered, he found himself in the midst of ovations. Great throngs waved greetings in all the towns passed. In New York City he rode in an open barouche drawn by four horses from the Battery to the Fifth Avenue Hotel, along Broadway, packed with men and women in festive mood. In Boston the reception was so warm, the much-abused man was deeply moved. Flowers were thrown into his carriage. Returning, the Connecticut ovations were generous, and at Hartford he made his most telling speech in a paragraph: 'The best efforts of my life have been exerted for the maintenance of the Constitution, the enforcement of the laws, and the preservation of the Union of the States.' The 'New York World' editorially complimented Boston and excoriated Philadelphia. 'A direct rebuke from Radical Boston to Radical Philadelphia.'[2] Johnson returned to the White House more confident of popular support than he had been in a year.

## VIII

Awaiting his return to the battle-field, Thad Stevens sat one day in his house in Lancaster giving a strange interview to the 'New York Herald.' He sat on a lounge, the correspondent in a chair, and there was a third party concealed in an adjoining room, unknown to the master of the house. This was a stenographer who had gone before to take the interview precisely.[3] Observing that the correspondent was taking few notes, the old man talked freely. The Military Bill had been botched by 'demoralized Republicans.' Sherman had interfered with his 'usual meddlesome folly.' In truth, Congress itself was demoralized. 'Some

[1] *New York World*, June 17, 1867.
[2] *New York World*, June 21, 22, 24, 25, 26; *New York Tribune*, June 27, 1867.
[3] *Lancaster Intelligencer*, July 15, 1867. Thomas B. Cochran, the stenographer.

members had their wives in Washington and their women at home, and others had their women in Washington and their wives at home, and it was impossible to keep them together.' Of course, no one but Congress had any power to interpret the Military Act. 'Neither had the conquered people any right to appeal to the courts to test the 'constitutionality of the law' for 'the Constitution had nothing to do with them nor they with it.' Stanbery's interpretation was mere usurpation. Impeachment? Certainly! Stevens would propose it as a matter of 'duty and conscience.' Evidence? None needed. Johnson's official acts were enough. Confiscation? Assuredly — and that not too mild. Blood-letting? Why not? Yes, he would have military commissions look into the cases of those responsible for prison miseries. But the confiscation measure would have to wait, for the patching-up of the Military Bill would require all the time. The trouble with men like Schenck and Bingham was 'they have no bone in their back and no blood in their veins.' Could impeachment carry now? No, thought the old man — 'on account of jealousy on the part of the opponents of Senator Wade.' The contest between Fessenden and Wade for President pro tem. had been bitter 'and personal motives and feelings will interfere to prevent Wade from occupying the Presidential chair.' And what did he think of New York Republicans? That State would be lost 'by the dish water which has been thrown around by Greeley and Gerrit Smith.' But Pennsylvania was worse. 'Cameron and his men with their hands full of greenbacks [in the senatorial election]' would 'certainly beat us here in the next election.' And what did Stevens think of Raymond? The worse failure he had seen in Congress. A pretty style, but sophomoric, and 'in the midst of his most perfumed harangues a few words of common sense would knock him flat.' And Ben Butler? A 'false alarm,' at once superficial, weak, and impracticable. Indeed, a 'humbug.'

The correspondent passed out of the house on South Queen Street, wondering if Stevens, even at his age, was not hungering for the Presidency.[1] This amazingly frank interview created a sensation without compromising Stevens's leadership.

[1] *New York Herald*, July 11, 1867, five columns.

IX

The July session convened with the picturesque old thunderer the cynosure of all eyes in the galleries, filled with women. The diplomatic corps was out in force. Down on the floor, Stevens, 'apparently in the last stages of debility,' was seen 'feeble and tottering on his cane or crawling from desk to desk.'[1] Julian thought him 'more feeble than . . . ever before.'[2] The Radicals were harmonious, and within five days Ben Butler had introduced his resolution to investigate Johnson's connection with the murder of Lincoln, and his committee was soon at work. 'The Herald' interview had not diminished Stevens's popularity with those he had charged with having their 'women,' and there was always a congestion of visitors before his door.[3] His weak denial of the personal portions of the interview had been accepted in the Pickwickian sense, and when a member asked if he had really said that 'The Herald' was 'the only true Union paper during the war,' the flicker of a smile crept over the haggard face as he replied that 'this cross-examining is very dangerous, for it might bring me into difficulty with my friend Horace Greeley.' The House laughed and the incident was closed.[4]

The bill to declare the 'true meaning and intent' of the Military Act, apparently written by Stanton, was speedily passed.[5] It struck down every vestige of home rule and civil liberty. The debate found Oliver P. Morton vigorously replying to his own Richmond speech, for he had undergone a speedy transformation since his denunciation of the radicalism of Julian. Because of his crippled condition, he spoke seated, and Hendricks was the first to congratulate him, though he later twitted him on his somersault.[6]

The night the bill passed, a large crowd with several bands marched to the home of Stevens, who, too exhausted to appear, was represented by a friend, and he was lauded as the supreme patriot.[7]

Johnson was prompt with a vigorous veto, and, as the House

[1] New York Herald, July 4, 1867.
[2] MS. Diary, July 4, 1867.
[3] New York Herald, July 8, 1867.
[4] Congressional Globe, July 10, 1867.
[5] Gorham, II, 373.
[6] Foulkes, II, 37–38.
[7] New York World, July 22, 1867.

clerk read it in strangely ringing tones, the silence was sepulchral. Boutwell spoke bitterly, hinting at impeachment, and Stevens said unseen forces were at work to prevent that consummation devoutly to be wished. This comment was on the tongues of the gossips that night. Did he mean the fight over the presidential succession or did he refer to the Masons?[1] But no matter — Stevens had the votes and the veto was answered.

X

Meanwhile, Sandford Conover, whose real name was Dunham, sojourning in the jail as a convicted perjurer, was receiving distinguished callers, for he who had sought the murder of Confederate leaders on his perjured testimony seemed promising to Butler and Ashley. Here was a man practiced in perjury, with the heart of an assassin, and Johnson's complicity in the murder of Lincoln must be established on manufactured evidence. Soon Ashley was sneaking to the jail to confer with the black-hearted scoundrel and his wife, explaining just what he and Butler required in the way of evidence. They wanted witnesses to prove that Booth had conferred with Johnson more than once; that they had corresponded — this to be shown by messengers who carried the notes; that Atzerodt had been sent armed to Johnson's hotel to disarm suspicion; and that Booth had told friends the murder was planned with Johnson's connivance. Soon the 'witnesses' were produced, and the testimony they were to give gone over carefully with Butler and Ashley. With lawyer-like caution, Butler amended, added to, subtracted from, the statements to make them more convincing. And the 'witnesses' were assured they would be 'splendidly rewarded.'[2]

This low conspiracy was to fail because of Dunham's refusal to proceed without a pardon, and soon, with the Republican press denouncing Ashley for his blunders, he was to write the 'Toledo Blade' denying he had publicly accused the President of murder, and defiantly defending his association with Dunham with the

[1] *New York Herald*, July 20, 1867.
[2] Dunham's letter to Johnson in the report of the Attorney-General on the former's petition for pardon, published in full with Ashley's notes to Dunham, *New York Herald*, August 10, 1867.

statement that he would have called on a murderer on the eve of
his execution to get evidence, if offered.[1]

Meanwhile, the impeachment plans dragged along, and Stevens
sat listening to excuses for the delay, with a sneer. Six months,
and nothing done, he grumbled. He knew the bad psychological
effect of these failures to find evidence. 'I should like to know,'
he said, 'if they have finished taking the testimony of my friend
Horace Greeley,' and the incident closed with a laugh.[2] Indeed,
by the end of the session the absurdity had become grotesque,
with the Democrats making sport of the proceedings. 'We have
seen the distinguished gentleman from Massachusetts shake his
head most seriously, saying that he hoped things might not be as
bad as they might be, but that if they were as bad as they might
be, he did not know what the consequences would be.'[3]

## XI

With the statesmen *en route* home on adjournment, Johnson
turned his attention to Stanton. With Chief Justice Chase he
discussed his plan to substitute Hancock for Sheridan, and to
displace Stanton with Grant. The wily politician of the Supreme
Court advised against the disciplining of Sheridan, and thought
Grant's appointment would satisfy the country but for the implication in the removal of Stanton.[4] That very day the Cabinet had
discussed the insubordination of Sheridan, with Welles and Randall favoring his removal and McCulloch warning of his popularity.
Johnson himself was in fighting mood. 'What have we to expect
from keeping quiet?' he demanded. Impeachment? 'If I am to
be impeached for this, I am prepared.'[5]

On the very day Chase was writing Greeley of his conversation
at the White House, Johnson demanded Stanton's resignation.
'It is impossible to get along with such a man in such a position,'
he told Welles, 'and I can stand it no longer.'[6] Stanton replied
with a curt refusal, and there was a momentary lull, during which
the press discussed the silent drama. Stanton was secluded in his
office with his favorites and with a Chesterfieldian officer at the

[1] *Toledo Blade*, December 19, 1867; quoted, *New York Herald*, December 22, 1867.
[2] *Congressional Globe*, July 10, 1867.        [3] Noel, *Congressional Globe*, July 20, 1867.
[4] Chase to Greeley, Warden, 669–70.        [5] Welles, III, 151–52.        [6] *Ibid.*, III, 157.

door turning others away,[1] and Johnson, cheered by the crowd, attended the *Schutzenfest* of the *Schutzen Verein,* and, trying his hand at shooting, hit the bull's-eye three times running.[2] 'The New York Herald'[3] was denouncing Stanton's unprecedented insubordination, and Greeley, puzzled, was comparing him to 'the Man in the Iron Mask or the veiled Prophet of Khorassan.'[4]

Meanwhile, Johnson, warned by Welles that 'Grant is going over' to the Radicals,[5] had a satisfactory interview with the latter and announced his appointment to the War Department,[6] and Grant, puffing a black cigar, completely calm, sauntered lazily to Stanton's office, where the encounter was polite, and the change was effected.[7] Instantly, the Radicals began baying in a chorus. 'To-day Grant is the staff that holds up the traitor President,' wrote Phillips in 'The Anti-Slavery Standard.'[8] 'This is our St. Michael whose resistless sword was to mow down the Satan of the fallen hosts,' he wrote again. 'He does not even know how to draw it.'[9] Theodore Tilton raged in 'The Independent,' and Greeley could not restrain his fury.

With the removal of Sheridan, the winds rose and howled. Thad Stevens, fighting physical collapse at Lancaster, denounced the Senate for striking out the provision in the Military Bill that would have saved Sheridan. All due, he said, to the Senate's preposterous scruples about the Constitution when Congress was acting 'outside' the Constitution, 'else our whole work of reconstruction were usurpation.'[10] The 'New York World,' commenting, paid tribute to the 'logical consistency' and 'the courage of this frank avowal.'[11] And as the storm abated, Greeley wrote: 'The President means war. War be it, then, and God speed the right.'[12]

Immediately the disciplining of Grant began. After dangling the prize of the Presidency before his eyes for months, the revolutionists turned upon him with disconcerting fury; and this was to continue through the summer and fall. The 'New York Tribune' began demanding a candidate who embodied Republican princi-

---

[1] *New York Herald,* August 7, 1867.        [2] *New York World,* August 9, 1867.
[3] August 8, 1867.        [4] *New York Tribune,* August 9, 1867.        [5] Welles, iii, 152–56.
[6] *Ibid.,* iii, 167.        [7] *New York Herald,* August 13, 1867.
[8] Quoted, *New York World,* August 22, 1867.        [9] *Ibid.,* September 7, 1867.
[10] Letter to Samuel Schock, Columbus, Pennsylvania, *New York World,* August 28, 1867.
[11] August 28, 1867.        [12] *New York Tribune,* August 28, 1867.

ples, avowed them, and was ready to stand or fall by them.[1] Soon
it was denying that Grant was 'a great man or even a great General.'[2] Veering slightly, two days later, it thought he might be
'a good Republican,' but it could not stand his backers.[3] And then
it lunged at him again: 'We have no relish for getting Presidents
out of a grab bag; it is better to be beaten than to be betrayed.'[4]
Out in Ohio, Ben Wade was striking at Grant, too. His political
views were unknown. 'As quick as I'd talk politics, he'd talk
horses,' he complained. 'In these times a man may be all right on
horses and all wrong on politics.'[5]

Meanwhile, rumors were afloat that Ben Butler had detectives
on Grant's trail, and there was a mild sensation in Washington.
When Grant sent for the detective, he denied it, but it was true,
as we shall see.[6] It was all very confusing and distressing to the
simple-minded Grant — especially with Montgomery Blair preparing an article for the 'New York World' urging his nomination
by the Democrats.[7]

This press abuse Grant was sharing with Mrs. Lincoln, who,
mentally unaccountable, had announced the sale of her wardrobe
in a New York auction room in a letter to 'The World.' The
'Albany Journal' was sure she had 'dishonored herself, her country and her husband.' The 'Pittsburgh Commercial' knew she
had been imposed on by designing Democrats. 'That dreadful woman!' exclaimed the 'Springfield Republican.'[8] The 'New
York World' protested against the abuse, but 'The Herald' was
sharper in its rebuke. 'The manner in which some Republican
editors are assailing Mrs. Lincoln . . . is disgraceful. The community of the Five Points would have as much decency and more
gratitude. . . . If they have no sense of propriety and decency, the
people have.'[9]

## XII

And in the midst of it all, the campaign and elections. The
Democrats swept California, and reduced the normal Republican
majority in Maine, in September. Put upon their mettle, the

[1] July 20, 1867.        [2] Ibid., November 6, 1867.        [3] Ibid., November 8, 1867.
[4] Ibid., November 13, 1867.        [5] New York Tribune, November 9, 1867.
[6] New York Herald, July 29, 1867.        [7] Welles, III, 184.
[8] Quoted, New York World, October 7, 1867.        [9] October 10, 1867.

Radicals resorted to the 'bloody shirt,' waving it hysterically from every hilltop; no one with more zest than Rutherford B. Hayes, running for Governor in Ohio, and side-stepping the issue of negro suffrage in that State. Not unmindful was he of Ben Wade's experiment in asking an audience if it would permit the negro to vote, without eliciting a single 'yes.' [1] General Sheridan, soldier out of work, was summoned to political duty, and was traversing the country making political speeches, and dancing with the girls. Sumner, lecturing in the West, was preaching more centralization in government. Did not great empires come from the extinction of petty States, he asked. Even Henry Wilson protested that 'the States are something yet,' and Parke Godwin, of the 'New York Evening Post,' refused to meet the orator after the lecture and hurried to his office to write a vigorous attack on the doctrine. [2]

In truth, the revolutionists were having their worries. The 'Chicago Tribune' was still hammering the tariff as destructive of agriculture, in devastating editorials. [3] Worse still — word flashed over the country from Lancaster that Thad Stevens, stricken with 'dropsy of the chest,' was thought to be dying. [4]

Then the elections. Democratic gains were made everywhere. New York, New Jersey carried; Pennsylvania — even Philadelphia — swept; Ohio close, and negro suffrage defeated. 'God bless Ohio,' wired Johnson. 'She has done well and done it in time.' And 'Bleeding Kansas' — she, too, voted down negro suffrage; and Minnesota! Even Thad Stevens's home town was carried by the Democrats, who made a gain of a thousand in his home county. The stricken old man looked out upon the wreckage, set his jaw, and cried, 'Impeach now.'

In Washington, cannon boomed, crowds marched, and a procession with three bands moved to the White House, where Johnson, thoroughly happy, responded. 'The people sometimes may be misled by the lying spirit in the mouths of their prophets,' he said, 'but never perverted; and in the end they are always right.' [5] Most of all, perhaps, Jay Cooke, with all his irons in the fire, was deeply distressed. 'The sad lessons of the war are for-

[1] New York Herald, September 19, 1867.
[2] Pierce, IV, 335.
[3] Quoted, New York World, September 15, 1867.
[4] Ibid., September 24, 1867.
[5] New York World, November 14, 1867.

gotten,' he wrote gloomily to Henry. 'Well, God reigneth.' [1] But Henry, less prone to prayer, replied that the Radical Republicans were responsible for the defeat. 'Their policy,' he wrote, 'was one of bitterness, hate, and wild agrarianism, without a single Christian principle to give it consistency except the sole idea of universal suffrage.' [2]

[1] Oberholtzer, *Cooke*, ii, 27.          [2] *Ibid.*, ii, 23.

# CHAPTER IX

## THE GREAT AMERICAN FARCE

### I

WHEN Congress met for the November session, Thad Stevens, strikingly pale and pitifully emaciated, fairly tottered to his seat.[1] It was evident that only an iron will kept him alive — that, and a grim determination to destroy Andrew Johnson. The Boutwell articles of impeachment had been contemptuously voted down, when the Senate sat in sullen silence listening to Johnson's explanation of the suspension of Stanton, setting forth an appalling record of treachery. This was a direct challenge to the Senate. Unawed by the rumblings, Johnson went his way unconcerned, and at the New Year's reception, more than ordinarily brilliant, it was observed of him that 'there was no trace of care on his brow,' as he moved about kissing little girls who were presented.[2] Grant was present, and almost gay, and later that day his own reception was a crush. Out on Capitol Hill, men with set jaws faithfully wended their way to the home of Stevens because 'anxious to inaugurate the new year thus.'[3] Within a week, Johnson, accepting a cane cut from the Charter Oak, wryly thanked the donors for bringing it to his support 'in these hours of trial.'[4] The next night he entered the hall where the devotees of Andrew Jackson were at dinner to listen to a letter from Franklin Pierce denouncing 'theories outside the Constitution,' to receive an ovation, and make a brief response.[5] At that very hour the House was planning a measure to deprive the Supreme Court of power to pass adversely on the constitutionality of a law without a two-thirds vote.[6]

If Johnson's brow was clear, it was because he thought he could force a court decision on the constitutionality of the Tenure-of-Office Act, through an understanding with Grant; though all the while Grant was secretly hostile.[7] There was, however, a distinct

---

[1] *New York World*, November 22, 1867.  [2] *New York Herald*, January 2, 1868.
[3] *Ibid.*    [4] *Ibid.*, January 8, 1868.    [5] *New York World*, January 9, 1868.
[6] *Ibid.*, January 14, 1868.
[7] Welles, III, 157; *ibid.*, 196, 231; Grant's Letters to a Friend, 52; *ibid.*, 55.

understanding between the two men as to the President's purpose.
This was that Grant should hold on to the office and force Stanton,
if reinstated by Congress, to go to court; or, should Grant shrink
from the responsibility, to notify the President, who could name a
successor who would assume it.

The Senate acted for Stanton; and the next morning Grant appeared in Cabinet to announce that with the notice of the Senate's
action he had locked the doors of his office, and turned the keys
over to the Adjutant-General, from whom Stanton received them
and resumed possession. Utterly astounded, Johnson demanded
an explanation, and Grant rambled off in a vague and wholly un-
convincing reply. 'But that, you know, was not our understanding,' protested the President; whereupon Grant, after more excuses, retired in some confusion.[1]

Smarting under the sharp criticism of the friendly press for a
slovenly management which failed to force Stanton into court,
Johnson publicly disclosed the agreement which had been broken.[2]
That very night, the Radicals pressed *en masse* to Grant's reception, causing such congestion that at one time it was impossible to
enter the house.[3] Grant was no longer 'going over' — he had gone.

With Johnson's statement, the press took up the quarrel, the
'New York World' denouncing Grant's action as unbecoming an
officer and gentleman.[4] 'A piece of turpitude that surprised even
some of the Radicals who were not in on the secret,' it added.[5]
The 'New York Herald' urged Johnson to fight.[6] It was easy for
Horace Greeley to understand Johnson's misapprehension —
Johnson had done the talking, and Grant had puffed silently at his
cigar; and silence had not given consent.[7]

But Grant was writhing under the charge of treachery, and unhappily he was drawn into a correspondence from which he did not
emerge with laurels.

II

Johnson had said that on the Saturday preceding the Senate's
action there was a distinct understanding with Grant that another

---

[1] Welles. iii, 259–61.			[2] *New York World,* January 16, 1868.
[3] *Ibid.,* January 16, 1868.			[4] January 16, 1868.			[5] January 17, 1868.
[6] January 16, 1868.			[7] *New York Tribune,* January 16, 1868.

conference on Monday would determine the latter's course. Grant's failure to call on Monday had given currency to uncomplimentary explanations of his action; and, his pride hurt, and fearing the effect on his prestige, he wrote the first of the letters bluntly denying he had agreed to call on Monday.[1] Johnson, no mean master in polemics, replied with the reminder that when Grant did call, he had excused himself in the presence of the Cabinet, on the ground that he had not expected the Senate to act so soon.[2] In his response, evidently worried, Grant expressed surprise that Cabinet members had corroborated Johnson; and then, at the instance of General Rawlins,[3] he added an unpardonable slur on his superior officer to the effect that his 'honor as a soldier and integrity as a man have been so violently assailed' he was convinced 'this whole matter' was 'an attempt to involve [him] in a resistance of the law.'[4] The reply of Johnson was a devastating submission of the signed statements of each Cabinet member, in complete verification of the President's version of the understanding reached in Cabinet.[5]

Throughout, Johnson's letters had been dignified and direct; those of Grant were not such as to delight his friends. He had clearly been left in 'a very equivocal position'[6] and the 'New York World' summed up in the comment that Johnson's 'last letter is a document which General Grant's reputation can ill afford to have pass into history.'[7] Even the wiser of the Radicals shared the opinion. A correspondent found Stevens at home, leaning back in an easy-chair alone, and 'looking almost entirely exhausted.' 'What the devil do I care about the question of veracity between Johnson and Grant?' he asked. 'Both may call each other liars if they want to; perhaps they both do lie a little, or, let us say, equivocate, though the President does seem to have the weight of evidence on his side. . . . If they want to settle the question between them, let them go out in any back yard and settle it.'[8]

Thus Grant, like Stanton, appeared thereafter, in the open, as a virulent enemy of Andrew Johnson.

[1] Letter of January 28, 1868.
[2] Letter of January 31, 1868.
[3] Badeau, 114.
[4] Letter of February 3, 1868.
[5] Letter of February 10, 1868.
[6] Professor Dunning, 127.
[7] February 12, 1868.
[8] *New York World*, February 14, 1868.

The position of Johnson had now become intolerable. Stanton had been a spy upon him from the beginning. It was a life habit. He was moulded by nature for conspiracy, if not treachery, albeit he had rendered Herculean service in the War Office under Lincoln. Even the latter found him trying, insolent, and domineering, and among the members of Lincoln's Cabinet he had no friends. To Grant he had been obnoxious because of his 'natural disposition to assume all power and control in all matters that he had anything to do with,'[1] and because 'he cared nothing for the feelings of others.'[2] Powerful as he may have been as a minister of war, it was Grant's opinion that 'the enemy would not have been in danger if Mr. Stanton had been in the field.'[3] Before the war, he had posed as an ultra-Democrat, and in the Cabinet of Buchanan his sycophancy was such that the worldly-wise old man in the Presidency wrote of him to his niece that 'he was always on my side and flattered me *ad nauseam.*'[4] One of his associates thought him 'in perfect accord with the Administration.'[5] And yet, such was his passion for double-dealing, that at the very moment his associates were convinced of his loyalty, he was establishing a secret connection with Seward, and communicating with him daily through an agent. That Stanton appreciated the nature of his treachery is evident in the pains he took to conceal it.[6] Flattering Buchanan, he was stealing at one o'clock in the morning to Charles Sumner's home with weird tales of dangers he was hiding from his chief.[7] Still posing as a Democrat, we have it on the authority of Henry Wilson that he had 'put himself in communication with the Republicans . . . and kept them well informed of what was going on in the councils of the Administration.'[8]

Then Buchanan retired to Wheatland, and Lincoln entered the White House. Presto, change! He who had spied for the Republicans now spied for Buchanan, and he was soon writing letters for the eyes of the old man at Wheatland abusing Lincoln. Again he was flattering the man he had been deceiving.[9] Entering Lincoln's

Cabinet, he maintained his relations with the Radicals who were his new chief's enemies — these relations too intimate immediately after the assassination to admit of any other conclusion. We have noted repeatedly his treacherous course toward Johnson. Stanton was impossible. No self-respecting President could, or would, have tolerated him longer.

IV

When notice of Stanton's removal reached the Senate, there was pandemonium. Conkling was speaking when the news arrived, and Zack Chandler, examining the papers at the President's desk, hastened to Sumner with the intelligence. Soon a crowd of Senators were grouped about the desk; soon a number of Radicals were rumbling over the rough street to the War Department, where they found Stanton reading a telegram from Sumner in one word — 'Stick.' Soon Stanton was writing Fessenden of imaginary threats, and of the necessity of immediate Senate action. This came forthwith — a declaration that the removal was illegal. The senatorial bodyguard, having stiffened Stanton's resistance, hastened to Grant, for was he not the head of the army? Thad Stevens was in a fret and fury.[1] Soon the hotel lobbies were crowded, and Pennsylvania Avenue was thronged like Broadway during a great procession, and the 'tramping of many feet sounded already like the tramp of an army.'

That night, strongly guarded, Stanton took up his long vigil in his office, and the gasconading General Thomas, named as his temporary successor, indulging in irresponsible boasting, so little understood the nature of the crisis that notice of the Senate's action was served upon him at a masquerade ball at Marini's. Johnson, dining the diplomats while the Senate deliberated, seemed 'excessively preoccupied' and looked 'fagged and discouraged.'[2]

Morning found the streets pulsating with excited people, with wild rumors of civil war throbbing in the air. Hundreds breakfasted early to hurry to the Capitol, and the earliest street cars were packed. The day was gloomy, snow swirling through the

[1] *New York Herald, New York World,* Gorham, II, 439.
[2] Bigelow, *Retrospections,* II, 155.

bare boughs of the trees. Down the avenue one mass of humanity slushed through the soft melting snow. Men and women filled the galleries, congested the corridors, pushed into the press section, and the floor was opened to women, who appeared as at an opera in their finery and gayety. It was a drama.

A rustling, and then a hush. Thad Stevens, black, bitter, conscious of the drama, entered and took his seat, and then, in a desert-like stillness, rose, 'haggard and trembling,' to offer impeachment resolutions. At length his day of jubilee! His enemy had played into his hands. The previous day, when the House was seething with excitement, the old warrior, ghastly pale, had moved about from group to group, leaning heavily on the arm of Bingham. 'Didn't I tell you so?' he kept saying. 'If you don't kill the beast, it will kill you.'[1] And now all was ready for the killing, and to him had been accorded the ecstasy of dealing the first blow. Colfax stilled the galleries, and, in low tones, Stevens offered his resolution. He then sat glumly listening to Brooks's impassioned protest and tribute to Johnson as 'one of the most illustrious of the lovers of liberty.' Then to Bingham, in a bitter partisan harangue; then to Farnsworth, calling the President 'this ungrateful, despicable, besotted, traitorous man'; and so on until adjournment at seven.[2]

That night all faces turned toward the brilliantly lighted dome. The globes within the building cast a pale, eerie light on the Capitol grounds. A conglomerate mass, unable to reach the galleries, stood stubbornly in the corridors.[3] And oratory! 'Bloody channels of Robespierre . . . the unassailable virtue' of Stanton '. . . Johnson and . . . his St. Arnaud' — this from 'Pig Iron' Kelley. The brilliant Beck of Kentucky made the one speech that can be read to-day without astonishment. It was Washington's Birthday, and Holman of Indiana asked the reading of the Farewell Address, and the clerk began. Bang! went Colfax's gavel — the Farewell Address was out of order. 'I suppose,' said Holman, 'the Constitution would scarcely be in order and I shall not ask to have it read.' Then, fearing the outside reaction, the Radicals relented, the Address was read, the speeches droned on.[4] Agreeing to vote

[1] Clemenceau, 153.    [2] *Congressional Globe*, February 22, 1868.
[3] *New York World*, February 23, 1868.    [4] *Congressional Globe*, February 23, 1868.

on Monday, the House adjourned at ten o'clock, and the politicians hastened to conferences, bar-rooms, gambling-dens, and hotels, while spectators streamed along the avenue talking in loud tones.

Sunday was no day of rest — the hotels jammed, buzzing, humming; messengers hurrying with telegrams, Stanton barricaded still and sleeping on a sofa, bellicose statesmen, like Chandler and Logan, on guard in the basement of the War Department. The comical Thomas, arrested, had been speedily released, since otherwise he could get to court and test the constitutionality of the Tenure-of-Office Act.

Monday dawned dark and stormy, with snow falling, streets sloppy, but every habitation poured forth its inmates for the show. The avenue was one slow-moving mass from building to building. A portion of the House was in shadow, for it was the low illumination of twilight that struggled through the ground-glass ceilings. Conspicuous in the galleries, gay with colors, sat Kate Chase Sprague.[1] In a chair at the Speaker's desk half reclined Stevens, and there he sat through seven hours of debate, listening solemnly.

At length his great hour came, and Stevens rose feebly, tottered forward a little, leaning heavily on his cane, and thus he stood in silence like an actor. All the Radicals had risen with him, and gathered about him, for his voice was weak. A correspondent noted that 'a sensation passed through the crowd.' A ghastly face — that of a man at close grips with death. Momentarily a light would flash across his countenance, and then die away to torpor, for he was very tired. The lips moved sometimes when there was no sound, and at length he turned his speech over for the clerk to read.[2] Yet there had been eloquence in the quivering of that sallow face, and in 'the fire of his implacable spirit gleaming from sunken eyes with a half smile of triumph.' [3]

An event fraught with dire possibilities, he thought, in conclusion. Strike down the 'great political malefactor' and thus 'perpetuate the happiness and good government of the human race.' No mere party triumph, but something 'to endure in its consequences until the whole continent shall be filled with a free

[1] New York World, February 25, 1868.
[2] New York Herald, New York World, February 25, 1868.
[3] New York World, ibid.

and untrammeled people, or shall be a nest of shrinking, cowardly slaves.'[1]

The roll was called — a strictly party vote — and Colfax named a committee to prepare articles of impeachment. But it had been a day of wild alarms, for it was whispered that armed men were marching on the Capital from Maryland to sustain the President. And that night the great crowds at the White House reception found Johnson looking 'wonderfully like a man whose mind was at ease and whose conscience did not torture him.'[2]

The next day, messengers at the Senate door announced the House Committee, the galleries swayed forward, and Stevens, relinquishing the arm of an associate, dramatically cast his hat on the floor, passed his cane to the doorkeeper, and, with an air, unfolded a paper.[3] The Senate was informed — the Senate many of whose members had worked zealously on the floor of the House for the impeachment in which they were to sit as judges.

Meanwhile, the committee preparing the articles worked feverishly, Stevens and Bingham irritable and quarreling heartily. 'Both are profane,' wrote Julian, one of the members, 'but Stevens is especially so.'[4] There was jealousy and acrimony in choosing the chairman of the managers, the choice falling on Bingham, who had threatened to withdraw if defeated.[5] Stevens was passed over because of his condition, though Ben Butler insisted it was 'on account of being so erratic.'[6]

The managers presented eleven articles, nine revolving around the removal of Stanton, the tenth concerning Johnson's speeches, and the eleventh, conceived by the cunning Stevens as a catch-all, and thus explained to the House: 'If my article is inserted, what chance has Andrew Johnson to escape? . . . Unfortunate man, thus surrounded, hampered, tangled in the meshes of his own wickedness — unfortunate, unhappy man, behold your doom.'[7]

V

But the politicians were on edge, and when some nitroglycerine mysteriously disappeared from New York, the event was awe-

---

[1] *Congressional Globe*, February 24, 1868.
[2] *New York Herald*, February 26, 1868; *New York World*, February 25, 1868.
[3] *New York World*, February 26, 1868.       [4] MS. Diary, March 1, 1868.
[5] Boutwell, II, 119.                          [6] *Butler's Book*, 927.
[7] *Congressional Globe*, March 2, 1868.

somely announced by Colfax, and additional guards were stationed about the Capitol.[1] Stanton, still barricaded, summoned more soldiers for his protection.

And yet the public was quite calm. A mass meeting at Cooper Union, New York, had protested against the proceedings, to the amusement of Greeley. 'They know very well,' he wrote, 'that Wall Street and Fifth Avenue are not with them.'[2] General Sherman, in St. Louis, found that 'the people generally manifest little interest in the game going on,'[3] and warned his brother, the Senator, that the Republicans 'should act as judges and not as partisans' since 'those who are closest to the law in this crisis are the best patriots.'[4] The everlasting clamor about 'law'! Somehow the enthusiastic acclaim hoped for was not manifest.

More serious was the discovery that the substitution of Ben Wade for Johnson gave no thrills outside a limited circle.[5] Even so, Wade and his cronies were arranging a Cabinet before the impeachment trial began,[6] and the heir apparent, when not engaged in conferences, sat in his simple apartment on Four and a Half Street in an armchair before an open fire, in a dressing-gown, awaiting the call to power.[7]

## VI

And Johnson, calm and dignified, pursued the even tenor of his way. One night at a reception of Chief Justice Chase, the guests were startled by the master of ceremonies announcing — 'The President of the United States'; and Johnson, with his daughters, entered, smiling, to receive a cordial greeting from the host. The tongues of the gossips began to wag. Shameful effrontery! And could Chase now be trusted to preside at the trial? 'The Nation' waxed facetious with the complaint that no one knew what Justice Field said at Mr. Black's party, and that 'a patriotic attendant at table, properly instructed by General Butler, could certainly, if he kept his ears open, pick up a good deal of interesting matter, and

[1] Welles, III, 297; New York Herald, February 28, 1868.
[2] New York Tribune, February 29, 1868.
[3] Sherman, Recollections, I, 423.          [4] Sherman, Letters, 313.
[5] Life of Garfield, I, 425; Bigelow, Retrospections, IV, 156; The Nation, February 27, 1868; New York World, March 17, 1868.
[6] Julian, MS. Diary, March 8, 1868.          [7] New York Herald, March 13, 1868.

perhaps . . . some startling facts about the political opinions of the monsters who now sit on the Bench of the Supreme Court.' [1] Little did Godkin know that even then detectives were on the trail of Senators, and would soon be watching the home of the Chief Justice from dark doorways.

Meanwhile, Johnson, engaged in the selection of his lawyers, was having a revolting experience. He had turned naturally to Jeremiah S. Black, a distinguished lawyer, who had assisted in the preparation of some veto messages, although Senator Hendricks had advised against the choice.[2] Scarcely had he been selected when he was mysteriously dropped; and enemies of the President circulated the story that Black's discoveries had been such that his patriotism had revolted against undertaking the defense of such a monster. Johnson's silence was all the more puzzling. This is what had happened:

For some time Black had represented clients with a million-dollar claim to the island of Alta Vela, the property of San Domingo, and his request that a man-of-war be sent had been rejected on the very grounds on which Black had refused a similar request when Secretary of State. Having become one of Johnson's counsel, he had placed in the President's hands an opinion favorable to his demand, signed by Butler, Logan, Stevens, and Bingham — four of the managers in the impeachment. With this, Black renewed his importunities and was again refused. Enraged at the failure of his scheme, he announced that since Johnson had refused the way to an acquittal, he could no longer act as counsel. Johnson had risen indignantly, and, looking Black in the eye, had said: 'You try to force me to do a dishonorable act, contrary to the law as I see it, and against my conscience, and rather than do your bidding I'll suffer my right arm torn from the socket. Yes, quit . . . Just one word more: I regard you as a damn villain, and get out of my office, or, damn you, I'll kick you out.'

Black stood not on the order of his going, but went at once; and then, relenting the next day, wrote Johnson offering to continue. 'Tell General Black he is out of the case and will stay out,' was the curt reply. The President's silence under the misrepresentations of the incident by the Radicals was due to positive instructions

[1] March 19, 1868.          [2] Welles, III, 304.

from his Attorney-General and counsel to keep a padlock on his lips.[1] From that hour on during the remainder of the trial, Johnson maintained a most dogged silence. It was not an easy rôle for him to play.

## VII

In the mean while the hotels and boarding-houses were overflowing with visitors eager for the spectacle in the Senate. The demand for tickets drove Senators to distraction, and the false report that Senator Anthony had charge of the distribution necessitated the stationing of police about his doors.[2] The life of Thad Stevens was flickering low. He was found 'ghastly and feeble,' sitting in a rocking-chair by a little writing-table in the simple brick house on B Street, but the excitement of the anticipated triumph brought 'a very slight hectic flush to his cheeks.' His blue eyes, deeply sunken, were of the brightness of a consumptive, and there was little vitality in his handclasp. During the session a carriage had conveyed him to the entrance of the House wing, where two husky negro boys carried him in a chair to his room — the 'Thad Stevens room,' as the Appropriation Committee room adjoining the House lobby was called. A little after three, he was taken back to his house, bearing his suffering like a Spartan, and with no fear of death.[3] Even in the valley of the shadows his sense of humor was keen. Turning a solemn face to the robust young negroes who bore him, he asked, 'What am I to do when you boys are dead?' Thus through the buzzing corridors he was borne in his chair at the head of the procession as the House moved to the Senate for the trial — a ghastly face, grim and slightly flushed, looming above the spectators and his associates. On the opening day he wore a sable suit and a black wig, and once or twice a sardonic smile played faintly over his features. For the most part he sat half reclining, his brows knit, his color that of a corpse, his lips twitching, and a supernatural expression in his bright eyes. Members gathered about him, but the old smile of amiability was gone that day.[4] He sat with the managers of the House.

[1] Welles, III, 311.        [2] *Congressional Globe*, March 12, 1868.
[3] *New York World*, March 7, 1868.
[4] *New York Herald*, March 14, 1868.

There, too, sat Ben Butler — robust, belligerent, bristling, pompous, his bald head with its thin fringe of hair glistening, his squint eyes half concealed by the pointed lids — sat sniffing nervously like a racer awaiting the signal, spasmodically puffing out his cheeks. The low-turned collar revealed a Danton-like throat.[1] These two, Stevens and Butler, dominated the group.

At the counsel table of the President was the imposing figure of Benjamin R. Curtis, seasoned on the United States Supreme Bench, and now, though close to sixty, in the fullness of his powers. Beside him, pale and frail, but handsome beyond most men, and tense in the determination to save a friend as well as client, was Stanbery. There, too, sat William S. Grosbeck, of Cincinnati, soon to have his laurels. Evarts had not yet arrived.

And presiding, the impressive figure of Chief Justice Chase, imposing with his great height and proportionate weight, huge head, massive brow, thick lips, and blue-gray eyes. One of the most notable figures in American history, he was to preside with dignity and decorum.

The articles are read; the defense asks time to prepare answers; the managers simulate indignation, Butler puffing his cheeks and calling the President a 'criminal'; the Senate retires to deliberate on the request for forty days and returns to grant ten.[2] A dull enough beginning, and yet the next morning the negro servant accustomed to enter Stevens's room and receive a hearty 'Good-morning' was startled to find the old man looking at him intently, unable to recognize him.[3] The flame was fast flickering to the socket.

## VIII

And the next day, when the Impeachment Committee assembled at Brady's for a group photograph, they found Stevens too ill to attend. 'I doubt whether he can live another week,' wrote Julian.[4] And yet, such was the tenacity with which he clung to life, that only three days later he had himself carried to the House to make a fervent appeal for manhood suffrage. A lyrical speech it was, steeped in poetry, a rhapsody. He spoke seated, his voice

[1] Dewitt, 208.        [2] Official Report, March 13, 1868.
[3] New York Herald, March 16, 1868.        [4] MS. Diary, March 15, 1868.

scarcely audible. 'Most of us,' he whispered, 'are separated from the dread tribunal . . . by the narrowest isthmus that ever divided time from eternity.' [1] And they carried him back to his rocking-chair by the little writing-table to husband his strength for the trial. With telegrams of anxious inquiry pouring in about his health, the 'New York Tribune' announced that 'it is better this week than it has been in a long time.' [2] And that was the week Julian did not expect him to survive.

Into the White House, letters were pouring upon Johnson — offers of enlistment for the new civil war many expected. Over the wires from Washington flashed idle gossip, malicious slanders, in an attempt to arouse the torpid country. Senator Grimes warned a correspondent that these stories were 'generally lies sent from here by the most worthless and irresponsible creatures on the face of the earth.' [3] And yet the country was stubbornly calm, the masses having no fears and little interest, and John Sherman was almost shocked because the proceedings had had 'so little effect on prices and business.' [4] The General, his brother, had warned him that 'the trial is one that will be closely and sternly criticized by all the civilized world' — and that was shocking, too.[5] Stanton, still barricaded, was sleeping on a sofa, having his meals brought in, while a guard surrounded him.[6] Meanwhile, Johnson, unguarded, was driving through the streets, and meeting his Cabinet in his library because in the Cabinet room his lawyers were bending over papers spread out on a table, preparing his defense.

## IX

On the morning of the resumption of the trial, Johnson, bare-headed, accompanied his lawyers to the portico, assured them of his confidence in their zeal, and, turning, reëntered the mansion.[7] That day the answer of the defense was read, and the real opening of the trial set for a week later; and two days thereafter, undaunted, with flag still flying, his head unbowed, Johnson sent a sizzling veto of a bill intended to curtail the power of the Supreme

[1] *Congressional Globe*, March 18, 1868.   [2] March 18, 1868.
[3] *Life of Grimes*, 336.   [4] *Letters*, 315; Sherman *Recollections*, I, 425.
[5] *Letters*, 315; Sherman, *Recollections*, I, 424.
[6] Welles, III, 309.   [7] Crook, 125.

Court.[1] The following day Hendricks spoke powerfully in support of the veto, declaring the Constitution contemplated that legislation should pass the test of the court. 'Marshall thought so; Taney thought so; I cite the lights of the law.' And Stewart of Nevada made the all-sufficient answer: 'The Supreme Court must receive the law from the law-making power.' The roll was called, and only nine Democrats voted to sustain the veto.[2] Courage it took, in the midst of the trial thus to rebuke the judges, and at that moment not a member of the Cabinet hoped for an acquittal.[3]

In the mean time, Ben Butler, with a corps of stenographers, and notes made the previous summer on English State trials, was feverishly at work on his opening speech, sleeping but nine hours in three days.[4] To prevent a premature publication, he had it printed in disconnected parts while an agent stood at the elbow of the printer to distribute the type immediately.[5]

The day arrived. Haggard, sepulchral, Stevens was carried to the Senate, and Butler entered to suffer a momentary attack of stage fright. He had worked himself into the notion that he was to play an immortal part. Not unnoticed by him was the ladies' gallery, 'resplendent with bright beautiful women in the most gorgeous apparel.'[6] Able, cunning, endowed richly in demagogic tricks, he tried to speak the language of restraint, and read from printed slips, though with ease and little damage to his elocution. Denying that the Senate sat in a judicial capacity, with a view to converting the hearing into a political lynching party, he entered upon an extravagant amplification of the articles. The young Georges Clemenceau, writing for the Paris 'Temps,' thought the orator possibly right 'in clipping his wings,' but regretted he had 'shaved them so close.'[7] The press was not impressed, and 'The Nation' thought 'his invective . . . like the commingled screeching of a hundred circular saws and the rumbling of one gun carriage on a bad pavement.'[8] Butler was exultant, and the Radicals generally were pleased.

The week required to present the managers' evidence found the chamber packed, the ladies' galleries festive with ribbons, colors,

[1] *Congressional Globe*, March 25, 1868.    [2] *Ibid.*, March 26, 1868.
[3] Welles, III, 324.    [4] *Butler's Book*, 928.    [5] *Ibid.*
[6] *Ibid.*, 929.    [7] Clemenceau, 173.    [8] April 2, 1868.

feathers. Boisterous crowds thronged the hotel lobbies at night, and saloons and gambling-houses thrived. A newspaper correspondent in Jay Cooke's employ sent him daily cipher telegrams on the proceedings.[1] The flame of Thad Stevens was flickering more feebly day by day, and Garfield saw that he was 'reeling in the shadow of death.' [2] He sat almost in a state of collapse, slowly sipping brandy to feed the failing flame, and occasionally he lunched on tea and crackers.[3] His skin was like dried parchment.

Immediately Chief Justice Chase found himself out of harmony with his new court. Did he rule evidence relevant? The Senate voted otherwise. Irrevelant? Usually by a party vote, he was overruled. There was neither rhyme nor reason anywhere; but Chase maintained his dignity by ruling for the record. The case against Johnson tottered on the first day, and was in a state of collapse before the defense began. The managers had shown that Johnson had removed Stanton and made some unhappy speeches at Cleveland and St. Louis.

When Curtis had completed his speech opening for the defense, the farce was over.[4] The day he spoke was damp and gloomy, the chamber filled with somber shadows, relieved only by the bright colors of the ribbons of the ladies.[5] Absolutely serene and confident, his impassive face betraying not the slightest anxiety, Curtis was the very symbol of dignity and urbanity, and he began in tones so low that they scarcely filled the chamber. Brushing aside the verbiage and sophistries, he showed there was nothing before the court other than the legality of the removal of Stanton. The constitutionality of the Tenure-of-Office Act aside, the question was whether it applied to the case of Stanton. It requires senatorial approval of a presidential dismissal of an officer named with the Senate's consent, when the officer was serving 'during the term of the President by whom he was appointed' — and Stanton had not been appointed by Johnson. The evasion that Johnson was merely filling out Lincoln's term was not impressive in the light of the debate when the law was passed. At any rate, it was a matter of construction involving no turpitude. Did Congress in-

---

[1] Oberholtzer, *Cooke*, II, 35.   [2] *Life of Garfield*, I, 424.
[3] *New York World*, April 4, 1868.   [4] *Butler's Book*, 930.
[5] *New York Herald*, April 11, 1868.

sist that the President could be forced, without recourse to the courts, to follow any law it might enact? Suppose it should enact a law forbidding the President to negotiate treaties? Thus, for three days, moving with relentless logic in the realms of history and law, he reduced the case against Johnson to an absurdity. 'Lucid and powerful, worthy in every way of the best days of forensic argumentation,' was the verdict of 'The Nation.' [1]

But Curtis had no illusions as to the attitude of Senators toward logic, and on the second day of his argument he wrote a friend that there were from twenty-two to twenty-five Senators determined to convict, and some hope that twelve or fifteen Republicans had 'not abandoned all sense of right and given themselves over to party at any cost.' [2]

The testimony of General Thomas, instead of revealing a desperate conspirator planning civil war, disclosed Johnson's purpose of getting the controversy into court. The personal conflict of Thomas and Stanton had been one of bantering over a bottle of liquor, with Stanton running his fingers playfully through Thomas's hair. 'Was that all the force exhibited that day?' he was asked. 'That was all.' Had Johnson ever instructed him to use force? 'He had not.' [3] It was a hard day for the managers, and even General Sherman was not permitted to relate his conversation with Johnson concerning Stanton's removal. Chase held it admissible; the Senate not. He was forbidden to answer the question whether Johnson had told him he sought to get the controversy into court. [4] Thereafter Ben Butler, in a towering rage, hung on like a bulldog, objecting to every question until reduced to writing and argued. At times his conduct was intolerable. On one occasion he launched upon a harangue which reveals the spirit of the trial. Every mail brought him accounts from the South of 'some murder or worse of a friend of the country. We want these things stopped!' he stormed. Union comrades were being 'laid in the cold grave by the assassin's hand' and 'threats of assassination were made every hour' against the managers. . . . Evarts rose with a contemptuous expression, which seemed to embrace the Senate itself. 'I have never heard such a harangue before in a court

[1] April 23, 1868.    [2] Life of Curtis, to Ticknor, i, 416.
[3] Official Report, April 10, 1868.    [4] Ibid., April 11 and 12, 1868.

of justice; but I cannot say that I may not hear it again in this court,' he said. Even the Senate seemed abashed, and immediately adjourned.[1] So the mockery of the trial went on. Chase was shocked at the shamelessness of the Senate in excluding evidence 'appropriate to enlighten the court as to the intent with which the act [of dismissing Stanton] was done.' [2]

In the mean time the defense, wishing to reassure some hesitating Senators that a worthy successor would be installed in the War Office, was negotiating with General John M. Schofield for permission to send in his nomination. The arguments had not begun when Evarts began the conferences in his room at the Willard. The throngs in the lobby had no inkling, but Grant was waiting for Schofield outside the door. Evarts reluctantly consented to Schofield's feeling Grant out, and the two soldiers discussed the proposal during a walk. Grant was disappointed, but if Johnson remained, Schofield would be satisfactory. The conference was resumed in Evarts's room, the pledge was given that the President thereafter would send military orders through the usual channels, and thus in the closing hours of the trial the country knew that, if Stanton went out, Schofield would go in.[3]

x

Outside the Senate Chamber there was wining and dining as usual, and the usual zest for entertainment. True, Charles Dickens's readings had been abandoned because of the impeachment, but the ailing novelist, dragging himself from his rooms to the ill-lighted and worse-ventilated Carroll Hall, where dogs barked and people coughed, and a drunken auditor mumbled audibly, was glad of an excuse. The bitterness of politics had disorganized, or reorganized, society, with the families of the two groups no longer on speaking terms.[4] But pleasure-seekers were not dependent on dinners and receptions. Anna Dickinson, of whom we shall hear more, was lecturing; Dr. Chapin, whom Julian thought 'the most eloquent man I ever heard,' was speaking; Maggie Mitchell was playing in favorite rôles; Fanny Kemble was giving dramatic readings to packed houses; and merry groups were wending their way

---

[1] Official Report, April 16, 1868.    [2] Schuckers, 577, to Gerrit Smith.
[3] *Life of Schofield*, his memorandum, 413–18.    [4] Welles, III, 278.

nightly to Dan Rice's Circus.[1] It was easy to forget the politicians, listening to Fanny Kemble in 'A Winter's Tale' and 'Othello,' and in sitting under the witchery of Ole Bull, who was also in town.[2] Joe Jefferson was delighting hundreds in 'Rip Van Winkle,' and Mrs. Daniels, the spiritualist, was talking at Harmonial Hall — 'very wordy.'[3] Spring had come early, and on lovely days the promenaders strolled under the budding trees as joyously as though no crisis confronted the nation.

Through all these days Johnson was calm and philosophical, happy in the fine loyalty of Mrs. Patterson, his daughter, and in that of the lovable Stanbery with his never-failing optimism. Addison's 'Cato' was often in the President's hands, and he amused himself tracing out the fate of the signers of the death warrant of Charles I.[4] Meticulously observant of routine duties, he did not even abandon his receptions, and at that given the night of the opening of the trial not a few of his enemies had the temerity to attend to 'see how Andy takes it.' They found him taking it standing, calm, unworried, unruffled.[5] It was at the time spiritualism was in vogue, and Johnson was both amused and annoyed by 'messages' sent 'from Lincoln' and others, Mrs. Colby being most determined in trying to make a convert by playing on his anxieties.[6]

Thus, reading, driving with his grandchildren, conferring with his lawyers, he went his way, making a profound impression by his dignity and faith on such men as Evarts and Curtis.

## XI

And now came the hectic days during the arguments of lawyers. Ben Wade was preparing to move into the White House. There was no longer any thought of his refusing to vote, and Greeley, shocked at the idea early, was now reconciled to any indecency. In truth, Wade was making his Cabinet, having offered Julian the portfolio of the Interior long before.[7] Sumner had solemnly accepted Wade's assurance that he had not spoken to a human being

[1] Julian, MS. Diary, March 31, 1868; *New York Tribune*, April 4, 1868.
[2] Julian, MS. Diary, April 5, 1868.            [3] *Ibid.*, April 24, May 3, 1868.
[4] Jones, *Life of Johnson*, 279.               [5] Crook, 126.
[6] *Ibid.*, 124.                                 [7] Julian, MS. Diary, March 8, 1868.

on appointments, which illuminates the veracity of Wade and the credulity of Sumner.[1] The day before the vote, Wade discussed the Cabinet with Grant, who listened silently, making no suggestions.[2] That very night the impeachers met in conference at the home of Senator Pomeroy and distributed loaves and fishes.[3] In this Cabinet-making it was impossible for Jay Cooke to keep his fingers out of the pie, and he was expecting George Opdyke to succeed McCulloch, and was hearing from W. E. Chandler, in the midst of the arguments, that 'we shall have Ben Wade in about a week.'[4] So complacent were the impeachers that the 'New York Herald'[5] was suggesting that they practice on a new plantation melody:

> 'Old Andy's gone, ha, ha!
> And Old Ben's come, ho, ho!
> It must be de kingdom am a-comin'
> In de year of jubilo.'

The speakers slowly went through their parts, a few brilliantly, most without sparkle. Clemenceau thought Boutwell's speech 'the longest, weakest, and dullest speech which has yet been made.'[6] Not until Grosbeck spoke did the galleries get a thrill. 'The Nation' thought his speech 'perhaps the most effective if not the ablest that has been made for the defense,'[7] and the 'New York Herald' pronounced it 'the most eloquent . . . heard in the Senate since the palmy days of oratory.'[8] Two days afterward, Washington was still ringing in praise of it.[9]

And then came Stevens, literally dragging himself from the edge of the grave. He had labored over this speech as over no other in his life, writing, printing, and revising it three times.[10] Just as the hour struck, the negro chair-bearers bore the old man to his seat. Steeling himself for a mighty effort, he rose with difficulty, and stood erect at the Secretary's desk, reading. Soon his failing strength forced him to sit down, and he continued for thirty minutes until his voice dwindled to a murmur, when he turned his

[1] Pierce, to Lieber, iv, 351.
[2] Badeau, 136.
[3] Schuckers, 559, note.
[4] Oberholtzer, *Cooke*, ii, 35.
[5] April 26, 1868.
[6] Clemenceau, 178.
[7] April 30, 1868.
[8] *New York Herald*, April 26, 1868.
[9] *Ibid.*, April 27, 1868.
[10] Welles, iii, 340.

manuscript over to Butler to finish. There he sat, silent with the rest, his eyes burning, a faint flush on his parchment face.[1] More moderate than could have been expected, the old hate flamed in the conclusion with his bitter description of Johnson as 'this off-spring of assassination,' and his warning to any Senator daring to vote for acquittal that 'dark would be the track of infamy which must mark his name and that of his posterity.' And then they carried the old man out, and took him home.

A dull interlude, with Williams of the managers, and then before a packed chamber William Maxwell Evarts began his four-day Ciceronian oration, moving like a giant trampling down the barbed-wired entanglements of prejudice and falsehood, at times a logician, always the forensic orator. His biting sarcasm, devastating wit, shamed and amused, and then, suddenly, a flash of eloquence that thrilled. Under his lash the managers writhed in silence, the audience sat in rapt attention, albeit Bancroft, the historian, old and depressed by the foul air, was seen to nod.

Came then Henry Stanbery, rising in a still chamber charged with sympathy and admiration. Then in his sixty-fifth year, he was a man of commanding presence and 'surpassing beauty of person,'[2] of whom it could be said that 'a more magnificent presence never graced a court or adorned a public rostrum.'[3] Seriously ill, and confined to his room, no one could dissuade him from the laborious preparation of his speech, and its delivery.[4] There was a hush, almost a shudder, when he began with an apology for his weakness and the consoling thought that 'a single pebble from the brook was enough in the sling of the young shepherd.'[5] Heard sympathetically, no one did more to shame the spirit of hate and prejudice, and when, in closing, he spoke feelingly of his personal relations with the President, he paid the perfect tribute, since it came welling up from an honest heart.

The defense had spoken its last word, and a day intervened before Bingham closed for the managers in a speech with 'rhetoric so rank and turgid that the argument has to be followed through it like a trail through a tropical jungle.'[6] Something had happened

[1] Official Report, April 27, 1868.    [2] Cox, 578.
[3] Ibid.          [4] Welles, III, 341.          [5] Official Report, May 1, 1868.
[6] The Nation, May 7, 1868.

too — something that made Julian describe the day as 'this day of gloom.' [1] Senator Fessenden had let it be known that he would not vote to impeach on the showing made by the evidence.

## XII

Then hysteria descended on Washington. Fessenden, clean and able, had been sickened by the scenes about him. A letter announcing his intention to respect his oath [2] had caused the conspirators to turn the thunderbolts of intimidation against him. A month before, he had sat in his room reading an amazing letter from General Neal Dow of Maine demanding that the Senate 'hang Johnson by the heels like a dead crow in a corn field to frighten all his tribe.' Outraged by the insult to his integrity, Fessenden had sent a stern rebuke. 'I wish you, my dear sir, and all my other friends, to know that I, not they, am sitting in judgment upon the President. I, not they, have solemnly sworn to do impartial justice. I, not they, am responsible to God and man for my action and its consequence.' [3] Early in May, with 'all imaginable abuse' heaped upon him, he had grown 'utterly weary and disgusted'; but he had not yet said he would vote to acquit, and the impeachers pursued him. [4] Even Justin S. Morrill, cognizant of the dishonorable nature of his request, was urging him to disregard the law and the evidence.

Utterly shameless now, the impeachers had summoned the forces of intimidation to the capital, and politicians were insolently canvassing the judges for votes against Johnson, as in a party caucus. [5] Moving in and out, a little worried, and seemingly misplaced, the stocky figure of General Grant — engaged in the canvass. At his room, too, this work went on; [6] and in Stanton's office, guarded by soldiers, while he slept on the sofa, senatorial conferences were held to devise means of lashing the doubtful into line — regardless of the law and the evidence. [7]

Meanwhile, detectives were dogging the footsteps of Senators, and spies in the social circles had their ears open for an unguarded word. [8] Because Senator Ross had a room in the home of Vinnie

---

[1] MS. Diary, May 5, 1868.          [2] Fessenden, II, 185.
[3] Ibid., II, 187.          [4] Ibid., II., 205.          [5] New York Herald, April 19, 1868.
[6] Ibid., May 9, 1868.          [7] Ibid.          [8] Dewitt, 517.

Ream, the sculptress, she was hounded in her studio in the Capitol basement by politicians demanding that she deliver the vote of Ross. Had not Congress given her a contract and a room in the Capitol? Listening in apprehensive silence, she went home in the evening in a state of nervous exhaustion.

Mingling with spies and whip-bearers were innumerable gamblers, changing their wagers day by day as the indications varied. On May 3, the odds were against Johnson,[1] and five days later the betting was even.[2] The day after Fessenden's views were known, the impeachers, more desperate, circulated the story that Senators were being bought, and that a huge slush fund for Johnson had appeared in the capital.[3]

Among Johnson's friends, hope rose, for Fessenden had heartened them, and in Administration circles it was hoped that Kate Chase Sprague would influence her husband, and that Miss Foote, daughter of the Commissioner of Patents, engaged to Senator Henderson, would have effect on him.[4] Every member of the Cabinet was now confident for the first time.[5]

It was under these conditions that all decency and decorum were thrown aside to stage a gallery demonstration for the close of Bingham's speech, intended to intimidate wavering judges.[6] A group of Southern carpetbaggers in one corner of the gallery directed the 'ovation.'[7] When Chase, enraged, threatened to clear the galleries, the offenders laughed, hissed, clapped; and when the order was given and the hisses increased, and Senator Grimes demanded arrests, Simon Cameron unctuously hoped that nothing would be done. Lyman Trumbull was sternly insistent. Mobbing a President was one thing; mobbing a court was quite another.[8]

### XIII

Then five days of utter madness — the town jammed with political vultures eager to shake the plum tree.[9] Among these, the money-bearers, prepared to buy Senators as swine. 'Tell the damn scoundrel,' said Ben Butler of a Senator, 'that if he wants

[1] New York Herald, May 4, 1868.          [2] Ibid., May 8, 1868.
[3] Ibid., May 6, 1868.          [4] Welles, III, 349.          [5] Ibid.
[6] Julian, MS. Diary, May 11, 1868.          [7] New York Herald, May 7, 1868.
[8] Congressional Globe, May 6, 1868.          [9] Ross, 151–52.

money there is a bushel of it to be had.' [1] One of the persecuted Senators wrote years later in cold blood that the conspirators were ready for assassination. [2]

But intimidation — that was the thing! The Grand Army of the Republic, then a political machine, was making flourishing demands, like the cadets of Gascony. The Methodist Episcopal Church, in General Conference in Chicago, was prevented from adopting a resolution for an hour of prayer for conviction only by the sanity and moral sense of an aged member, who reminded ministers of the sanctity of an oath. But Bishop Simpson, consummate Republican politician, rose smugly to the occasion with an amendment for an hour of prayer 'to save our Senators from error.' This rankly dishonest act, unanimously agreed upon, aroused the unutterable disgust of Senator Trumbull. Meanwhile, Johnson, in close touch with the trend of the trial through an agent, who learned of informal discussions at the Capitol every night from Reverdy Johnson, had met Grimes at the former's house and convinced him that, in the event of acquittal, he would do nothing not in conformity with the Constitution. That night Grimes went over, and through him others were satisfied.[3]

And now the fateful hour — the Senators discussing the evidence behind closed doors — great throngs about the Capitol — the Willard lobby packed with hysterical men, one pushing his way through waving five hundred dollars in bills and offering to bet that Johnson would be acquitted, and finding no takers. The streets filled, the talk that of sporting men at race track or prize ring. A correspondent, studying these faces, found 'hope, fear, love, hate, elation, depression.' [4]

Alarming enough the news that trickled out, and the hopes of the impeachers darkened as the afternoon passed. That night many looked ill at the Capitol. 'As I sat beside old Dr. Brisbane to-night,' wrote Julian, 'he said he felt as if he was sitting up with a sick friend who was expected to die.' [5] At the White House, corresponding elation, though Grosbeck's warning against an exulting outbreak was rigidly respected.[6] Besides, the illness of Senator

[1] Ross, 153.                    [2] Ibid.                      [3] Cox, 591–93.
[4] New York Herald, May 12, 1868.                     [5] MS. Diary, May 11, 1868.
[6] Welles, III, 351.

Howard gave the impeachers five days more, and there might be a change.

And now the terror stage. Big, husky politicians with glowering faces forced their way to little Miss Ream. Ross must vote to convict or——. Theodore Tilton was 'flying around from one Senator to another busy as a bee in favor of impeachment,' and Fessenden snubbed him.[1] The Cato from Maine was being deluged with insults himself, one man writing to ask his 'price'; and Philadelphia laboring men in mass meeting declaring his memory would be blackened if he did not convict the only President labor had ever had.[2] Trumbull was threatened with hanging from a lamp-post if he appeared in Chicago,[3] but the Illinois delegation in the House did not dare approach him with instructions how to vote. The Missouri delegation had the insolence to attempt to dictate Henderson's actions, and he was deluged with impudent telegrams from St. Louis. To one of these he hotly replied in a message phrased by 'Sunset' Cox: 'As I am an honest man I will obey my conscience and not your will. I shall vote "not guilty."'[4] That night Cox called at the White House and a 'festivity was improvised.'[5]

Meanwhile, work was found for Grant to do. He was sent to canvass Senator Frelinghuysen at his home, and to his influence is credited this one vote against Johnson.[6]

Both the West Virginia Senators, Willey and Van Winkle, were thought sure until the latter was seen talking with Trumbull and dining with Chase. It was dangerous for a conscientious man to talk with Trumbull. Van Winkle was lost. But there was hope for Willey, a pillar of the Methodist Church, and church influence was brought to bear upon him through 'Harlan, the Methodist elder and organ in the Senate,' at the behest of Bishop Simpson, 'the high priest of Methodism, and a sectarian politician of great shrewdness and ability' — or so the rumor ran.[7] All the while, too, the wires were humming in response to the appeal of the Union League Clubs for telegrams threatening annihilation to the wavering.[8]

[1] New York Herald, May 13, 1868.     [2] Fessenden, II, 208.
[3] Letter from Charles S. Spencer, President of the Republican Campaign Committee.
[4] Dewitt, 528; Cox, 524.     [5] Cox, 524.     [6] Badeau, 136; McCulloch, 398.
[7] Welles, III, 357; Dewitt, 533.     [8] Dewitt, 530.

And then, the climax. On the Saturday night before the vote on Monday, Chase gave a dinner attended by some of the wavering Senators, and a panic followed; spies in doorways took note of guests at the Chase home.[1] Sunday was a day of turmoil, the hotels a milling mass, bar-rooms crowded — maledictions, quarreling, betting, conferences in back rooms and at the home of Stevens. In the African Methodist Episcopal Church General Conference at Washington, the Reverend Sampson Jones fervently prayed that 'de Lord would stiffen wid de grace of fortitude de doubtful backbone ob de wavering Senators, and dat Andrew Johnson, de demented Moses of Tennessee, would be removed by de sanctimonious voice ob de Senate to whar de wicked cease from troublin' and de weary am at rest.'[2]

And so the day passed and the dawn of the great day came.

XIV

Early that morning a great mass moved like an army down the avenue, the conspirators rather confident. Theodore Tilton, their whip, had reported the prospects pleasing. Grimes was lost, but he was sick and might be unable to attend the Senate, and there was hope for Ross. For days Ross had been persecuted beyond precedent, his rooms crowded with threatening constituents, and his life had been microscopically examined for flaws. Spies had attended at his meals, and Sunday night General Dan Sickles, at the instance of Stanton, had camped all night at his lodgings awaiting his return, and driving Miss Ream to the verge of hysterics. Spies followed Ross Monday morning to his breakfast with Henderson, and that delectable purist and patriot, Pomeroy, his colleague, waited to pounce upon him when he entered the Senate Chamber. He had received a telegram from Kansas calling him a skunk. Could he stand that? — and the bullying of Pomeroy? As the latter approached him ten minutes before the vote, the burning eyes of Thad Stevens watched the drama closely.[3]

Cloudy and dull was the dawn, but through the morning the sun seemed trying to break through, and then the skies darkened again. The congested galleries amused themselves during the

[1] *New York Herald*, May 15, 1868.          [2] *Ibid.*, May 16, 1868.
[3] Dewitt, 541, 543–45.

wait looking down on the celebrities. At the managers' table, Logan, Stevens, and Sumner, the last two in earnest conversation. At times Stevens shook his head violently and his wig bobbed; at times he laughed sardonically.

In his seat sat Senator Howard, wrapped in a shawl, the stretcher that had borne him hence on the portico.[1] Soon the desperately ill Grimes was carried in on the arms of four men, his face pale and twisted with pain, and Fessenden sprang forward to grasp his hand and give him a 'glorified smile' the sick man never was to forget.[2]

And now, the roll-call. In the galleries, faces tense with anxiety; the faces of members pallid, some sick with fear. A death-like stillness with the calling of each name, and then a heavy breathing. When a doubtful Senator's name was called the spectators seemed to hold their breath, and then, with the vote, came a simultaneous vent.

Fessenden — 'Not guilty.'

That was expected.

Fowler — Grimes — Henderson — all known to be lost, and then ——

Ross — 'Not guilty.'

'Nearly all hope having fled, the last chance was with Van Winkle, and when he, too, voted to acquit, 'a long breathing of disappointment and despair.' The vote had been on Stevens's eleventh article, and, that failing, there was no hope for any other.[3]

Then, with adjournment, the excited throngs in the corridors looked upon an unforgettable spectacle.— Thad Stevens, carried by his negro boys, far above the crowd, his face black with rage and disappointment, waving his arms at friends and saying, 'The country is going to the devil.'[4]

The crowds hurried to the White House at a quickstep, to find the doors closed, and that afternoon, with the grounds thronged, Johnson did not show himself. He had received the news quietly — just a momentary filling of the eyes. That night, when sere-

---

[1] *New York Herald*, May 17, 1868.　　[2] *Life of Grimes*, 382.
[3] Julian, MS. Diary, May 17, 1868.
[4] Crook, 133–34.

naded by a band, he appeared at the window to thank the players.[1]

And then — depravity — the foul attempt to blacken the reputations of Republicans who had voted to acquit, with Ben Butler clawing among private telegrams, and private accounts at Jay Cooke's bank.[2] Even Greeley had the impudence to imply that men like Fessenden, Trumbull, and Henderson had been moved by dishonest motives.[3] Protesting against such indecency, 'The Nation' suggested that the impeachment trial 'ought to be dramatized, for it would certainly furnish material for a "side-splitting farce."'[4] The Butler investigation died with a squawk.

But the conspirators in their rage were not without their victory — little Vinnie Ream was deprived of her studio in the basement of the Capitol.

[1] *New York Herald*, May 17, 1868.   [2] Welles, III, 352.
[3] *New York Tribune*, May 14, 1868; May 18, and May 28, 1868.
[4] May 21, 1868.

# CHAPTER X

## CARPETBAGGERS AND A PROTEST

### I

IN the autumn of 1866, and through the winter and summer of 1867 strange men from the North were flocking into the black belt of the South, and mingling familiarly with the negroes, day and night. These were the emissaries of the Union League Clubs of Philadelphia and New York that have been unfairly denied their historic status in the consolidation of the negro vote. Organized in the dark days of the war to revive the failing spirit of the people, they had become bitterly partisan clubs with the conclusion of the struggle; and, the Union saved, they had turned with zest to the congenial task of working out the salvation of their party. This, they thought, depended on the domination of the South through the negro vote. Sagacious politicians, and men of material means, obsessed with ideas as extreme as those of Stevens and Sumner, they dispatched agents to turn the negroes against the Southern whites and organize them in secret clubs.

Left to themselves, the negroes would have turned for leadership to the native whites, who understood them best. This was the danger. Imperative, then, that they should be taught to hate — and teachers of hate were plentiful. Many of these were found among the agents of the Freedmen's Bureau, and these, paid by the Government, were devoting themselves assiduously to party organization on Government time. Over the plantations these agents wandered, seeking the negroes in their cabins, and halting them at their labors in the fields,[1] and the simple-minded freedmen were easy victims of their guile. One of the State Commissioners of the Bureau assembled a few blacks behind closed doors in a negro's hut, and in his official capacity informed them that the Government required their enrollment in political clubs.[2] Thus the Bureau agents did not scruple to employ coercion.

Orators were needed as well as organizers, for open agitation

[1] *Doc. Hist.*, ii, 639.      [2] Wallace, 42.

was as essential as quiet management, and soon the lowest types of the abandoned whites were being sent into the South to arouse the passions of the negroes with incendiary speeches. The Bureau agents summoned them to meetings in the fields at night. 'My friends,' the orator would say, 'you'll have your rights, won't you?' 'Yes!' shouted the eager freedmen. 'Shall I go back to Massachusetts and tell your brothers there that you are going to ride in the street cars with white ladies if you please?' 'Yes!' came the thundering response. 'That if you pay your money to go to the theater, you will sit where you please, in the best boxes if you like?' And the negroes would clap their hands and shout an affirmative reply.[1] In North Carolina, Holden, the former Governor, was exciting their cupidity with false hopes. The year before, the State had raised one hundred thousand bales of cotton. 'Whose labor made this cotton? Who got the money?'[2]

More vicious, however, were the imported agitators 'of the lowest character, destitute of principles,' such as 'Colonel' James Sinclair, the 'fighting parson,' a Uriah Heep of humility, mingling socially with the negroes, and promising them the division of the white man's acres among the blacks if they would vote the Republican ticket. One night [3] he urged the negroes to hate their former masters and treat them with insolence and contempt, and under the exhilaration of his harangue, a negro speaker said that within ten years the problem would be what the blacks would do with the Southern whites.[4] 'If my colored brother and myself touch elbows at the polls,' cried a carpetbagger in Louisiana, 'why should not his child and mine stand side by side in the public schools?'[5]

No imported emissary of hate and sedition surpassed the notorious James W. Hunnicutt of Virginia, a South Carolina scalawag, long a preacher, and later editor of a religious paper, who once owned slaves, voted for secession, and deserted the army to become a party leader and editor of the 'Richmond New Nation,' which exerted a dangerous influence over the negroes.[6] At the

[1] A Richmond meeting, Mrs. Leigh, 69–70.

[2] Worth to Ruffin, *Ruffin Papers*, 142; Worth, *Correspondence* (to Bedford Brown), II, 865.

[3] At Shoe Heel, North Carolina.          [4] Worth, from M. McRea, II, 952.

[5] J. R. G. Pitkin, Ficklen, 188.          [6] Eckenrode, 67.

moment the freedmen were refusing work, to meander about in threatening groups, and linger around the whiskey shops, it was Hunnicutt who advised them in a speech: 'There is corn and wheat and flour and bacon and turkeys and chickens and wood and coal in the State, and the colored people will have them before they will starve.'[1] The gaping audience liked the sentiment and cheered wildly. On another occasion Hunnicutt aroused enthusiasm with another characteristic sentiment: 'Yea, we would turn over Africa right into America if necessary, and those thick-lipped, flat-nosed, wooly-haired people that now swarm those sunny shores should be brought here as Irishmen from Ireland and in the same time be fitted [for suffrage] just as well.' What though the 'New York Herald'[2] denounced such sentiments as 'wicked and dangerous,' Hunnicutt was doing his work well.

Soon the imitative negroes rivaled the instructors from the North in abuse and in exaggerated demands, and one of them, speaking for the Union League at Chattanooga, advised his race to 'know the true thing in politics' from 'such men as Brownlow' and to 'teach your children . . . that they may grow up big-mouthed Radicals.'[3] When it was not yet certain that suffrage would be granted, Hunnicutt had shocked the staid people of a Northern city with the unclerical declaration that 'if the next Congress does not give us universal suffrage we will roll up our sleeves, pitch in, and have the damnedest revolution the world ever saw.'[4] And now that the revolution had come, the passions, cupidity, hates of the negroes were being aroused and constantly fed. Everywhere a new spirit of arrogance had been awakened. When an old plantation preacher told his race that the former masters were the blacks' best friends, a Radical paper noted that 'there was no little muttering in the crowd.'[5] Soon the whites, especially on remote plantations, were gravely apprehensive, and an English woman living in Georgia could see nothing but tragedy ahead with the governing forces 'exciting the negroes to every kind of insolent lawlessness.'[6] Then it was that the rioting began. At Norfolk,

[1] *New York World*, January 2, 1868.    [2] October 11, 1867.
[3] Thomas Kane, *McMinnville Enterprise*, a Radical paper, April 20, 1867.
[4] *New York World*, January 1, 1867.
[5] *McMinnville Enterprise*, April 6, 1867.    [6] Mrs. Leigh, 67.

when the negroes marched belligerently through the streets rattling firearms, the races clashed, with two fatalities on each side.[1] In Richmond, the blacks, determined to ride with the whites, rushed the street cars, and troops were necessary to restore order.[2] In New Orleans, where separate cars were provided, the negroes demanded the right to use the cars of the whites, who appealed to General Sheridan, without avail, and the blacks triumphed, and immediately demanded mixed schools and a division of the offices.[3]

It was under these conditions that the Union League was pushing the political organization of the freedmen, with the active aid of Bureau agents and a flock of ministers from the North, and Methodist pulpits were being converted into political rostrums. 'Old Methodist,' writing of the quarterly meeting, to the 'McMinnville Enterprise,' boasted that his church was as effective in making 'loyal men' as the secret societies. 'Show me a Northern Methodist,' he wrote, 'and I will show you a loyal citizen.' Then, he concluded, let all the negroes and Radicals join the flock of Wesley.[4]

## II

Soon the Northern demagogues were carrying their satchels into the paradise of the carpetbaggers, to accentuate the distrust and hatred of the races, and Welles was complaining that Senator Henry Wilson was 'stirring up the blacks, irritating and insulting the whites.'[5] But Wilson was the least offensive of the visitors, having been sent on a mission of conciliation to obliterate, if possible, the wretched impression made by the incendiary appeals of Hunnicutt. True, he appealed to the negroes to affiliate with the Republican Party, but he hoped also to gain the adherence of the old-line Whigs.[6] Unhappily the effect of his tour was to send others of less moderate views into the South, and soon 'Pig Iron' Kelley was fleeing in deadly fear from a howling Mobile mob that resented his brand of incendiarism. He had spoken in the loose, violent manner of the Northern Radical, inflaming both races and precipitating a riot he was afterward to trace to 'a recreant Northerner.'[7] Returning North, a bit embarrassed by the notoriety, he

[1] Eckenrode, 50.       [2] *Ibid.*, 72.       [3] Ficklen, 188.       [4] May 18, 1867.
[5] Welles, III, 87.     [6] Eckenrode, 70.    [7] *McMinnville Enterprise*, June 22, 1867.

had given glowing accounts of the superiority of negro genius and eloquence, for he had found among the blacks 'one of the most remarkable orators in the United States,' [1] and, in North Carolina, 'the ablest popular orator in the State,' and had met a negro shoemaker who 'had more sense than his master, though he was a Judge.' [2] This extravagance, republished by the carpetbag papers of the South, increased the growing arrogance of the blacks.

Meanwhile, day and night, Union League organizers were rumbling over the country roads drawing the negroes into secret clubs. There was personal persuasion in cotton fields, bar-rooms, and negro cabins, and such perfect fraternization that the two races drank whiskey from the same bottle, and the wives of some of the whites played the piano for the amusement of their black sisters. At every negro picnic, carpetbaggers mingled with the men and danced with the negro women. The time was short. An election was approaching. One July night in 1867, the fashionable Union League Club of New York, with the aristocratic John Jay in the chair, listened approvingly to a report from an organizer sent to Louisiana; and Mr. Jay announced that this was 'part of the Republican programme for the next presidential campaign.' The organizer [3] in ninety days had established one hundred and twenty clubs, embracing 'whites and blacks who mingled harmoniously together.' It was an inspiration. Why, asked one member of the Union League Club, should not a club be established in every township in the South? [4]

A master psychologist, familiar with the race, had devised the plan of organization. Night meetings, impressive, flamboyant ceremonies, solemn oaths, passwords, every possible appeal to the emotions and senses, with negroes on guard down the road to challenge prowlers, much marching and drilling — all mystery. And then incendiary speeches from Northern politicians promising the confiscation of the white man's land. Discipline, too — iron discipline. Intimidation, likewise — the death penalty for voting the Democratic ticket. Strangers arriving mysteriously in the night with warnings that the native whites were deadly enemies. Promises of arms, too — soon to be fulfilled. And the negroes

---

[1] L. S. Berry.          [2] *McMinnville Enterprise*, June 29, 1867.
[3] Thomas W. Conway.          [4] *New York World*, July 12, 1867.

moved as a race into the clubs. And woe to the negro who held back, or asked advice of an old master. This, they were taught, was treason to race, to party. Persuasion failing, recourse was had to the lash, and many a negro had welts on his back. One stubborn black man found a notice posted on his door: 'You mind me of the son of Esaw and who sold his birth Right for one mossel of meat, and so now you have sold your wife and children and yourself for a drink of Liquers and have come to be a Conservative bootlicker. Tom I would not give a damn for your back in a few days; you Conservative.'

Many were coerced through the agreement of negro women neither to marry nor associate with men who were not members.[1] Soon, nine tenths of the negroes were enrolled, oath-bound, impervious to reason, race-conscious, dreaming of domination. Soon, some of the Union or Loyal Leagues were refusing admission to whites, and others were quietly arming.[2]

A busy summer, that of 1867. Crassly ignorant or depraved organizers were exciting the passions of the blacks in Texas,[3] and in Alabama luring them with promises of social equality, and winning one doubtful Benedict with the promise of a divorce, which was kept.[4] Factions of the carpetbaggers worked at cross-purposes in Florida, competing in appealing mysteries and intimidations, with one group captivating the impressionable with initiations before a coffin and a skull, the leaders of the other rolling over the savage roads behind a mule team making personal contacts in the cabins.[5] In North Carolina, under the leadership of Holden, the Leagues soon numbered eighty thousand members, who would soon make him Governor again.[6] With some of the clubs converted into military companies drilling day and night in the highways,[7] and with the understanding that fully a fourth were armed with pistols and bowie-knives, the white men lived in constant fear.[8] Thus all over the South the consolidation of the blacks against the whites went on through the spring and summer.

[1] *Doc. Hist.*, ii, 23–27; Hamilton, 329–33.      [2] Eckenrode, 79.
[3] Ramsdell, 167.      [4] Fleming, 540.      [5] Wallace, 42–47.
[6] Hamilton, 336.      [7] *Ibid.*, 337.      [8] Worth, ii, 963.

## III

To strengthen the incendiary speeches, inflammatory pamphlets were sent broadcast, on the strange theory that the negroes could read. Radical papers were established to accentuate the rapidly developing race antipathies. The Union League Clubs sponsored and published thousands of pamphlets, and Forney, of the 'Washington Chronicle,' advertised in the carpetbag press urging a large circulation of his paper among the blacks.[1] One pamphlet, in the form of a catechism, set forth a favorite appeal:

Q. With what party should the colored man vote?
A. The Union Republican Party.
Q. What is the difference between Radicals and Republicans?
A. There is none.
Q. Is Mr. Sumner a Republican?
A. He is, and a Radical; so are Thad Stevens, Senator Wilson, Judge Kelley, Gen. Butler, Speaker Colfax, Chief Justice Chase, and all other men who believe in giving colored men their rights.
Q. Why cannot colored men support the Democratic Party?
A. Because that Party would disfranchise them, and if possible return them to slavery and certainly keep them in inferior positions before the law.
Q. Would the Democrats take away all the negro's rights?
A. They would.
Q. The colored men then should vote with the Republicans or Radical Party?
A. They should and shun the Democratic Party as they would the overseer's lash and the auction block.

Lest the negroes had heard of the strong Republican States of the North voting down negro suffrage, another section was added:

Q. What is the reason that several of the Northern States do not give negroes the right to vote?
A. Chiefly because they have, in the past, been controlled by the Democratic Party.

These questions and answers were read over and over again to the blacks and drilled into their memories.

## IV

Out upon all this the brooding eyes of a strange woman looked critically from her plantation house of 'Laurel Grove' on the west

[1] *McMinnville Enterprise*, November 16, 1867.

side of the St. Johns River, near the village of Orange Park, Florida. Occasionally she wrote her observations to her brother in the North. 'Corrupt politicians are already beginning to speculate on [the negroes] as possible capital for their schemes, and to fill their poor heads with all sorts of vagaries.' One day she wrote the Duchess of Argyll in praise of Johnson and in criticism of the Radicals. 'My brother Henry . . . takes the ground that it is unwise and impolitic to endeavor to force negro suffrage on the South at the point of the bayonet' — and so thought the writer.

The lady writing from 'Laurel Grove' was Harriet Beecher Stowe, author of 'Uncle Tom's Cabin,' who had taken up her residence in Florida in 1866.[1]

V

With most of the negroes now enlisted in clubs, and drilled to believe their freedom depended on Republican or Radical rule, the organization of the party went on apace. Long before, under the sway of Parson Brownlow, this had been effected in Tennessee, where Johnson's portrait in the House of Representatives had been removed to the Library, 'among the curiosities,' as a carpetbag paper phrased it.[2]

In Alabama, where there had been much fraternization of the races and talk of breaking bread at the same table,[3] a merger of the negro clubs and the Radical Party was arranged in Montgomery, where a joint committee from the Radical Convention and the clubs determined the personnel of the ticket.[4]

The first Republican Convention in South Carolina, overwhelmingly black, had but fifteen white members, eight of whom were carpetbag adventurers, and here a demand was made for representation of the negroes on the national ticket, with an agent of the National Committee looking on as an unofficial observer.[5]

In North Carolina the negroes, carpetbaggers, and scalawags had arranged in the spring for the conversion of the various organizations into a central machine. All the blacks were ordered to enroll in the Leagues or the 'Heroes of America,' and Holden emerged as leader with a battle-cry that carried a threat of con-

[1] *Life of Mrs. Stowe*, 395.        [2] *McMinnville Enterprise*, November 9, 1867.
[3] Fleming, 506.        [4] *Ibid.*        [5] Reynolds, 62.

fiscation and death to 'traitors.' Henry Wilson and 'Pig Iron'
Kelley were stumping the State, and, in the fall, the first party
convention, wildly Radical and predominantly black, was held at
Raleigh.

In Mississippi, the Radical Convention met at Jackson, with a
third of the delegates negroes, and most of the others Bureau
agents and carpetbaggers.

In Arkansas, the party organization was perfected under the
rigid discipline of the resourceful and unscrupulous Powell Clayton, with the negroes subordinated to a handful of Northern adventurers, and with the scalawags relegated, too.[1] This convention
denounced the granting of the franchise to any one who had served
in the Confederate army,[2] and refused to pledge itself against the
confiscation of property. Having arranged for the launching of a
party organ at Little Rock and papers in each district, the convention adjourned to witness the enormous mass meeting arranged
for the negroes in the State House grounds as a conciliatory gesture — for only three had sat in the convention.[3]

In Texas the convention found former Governor E. M. Pease on
the mourners' bench, having repented his original hostility to
immediate negro suffrage, and made his peace with Thad Stevens,
and he was restored to favor, made chairman, and promised the
place of Governor Throckmorton.[4] The bargain was carried out.
The negro organizations flooded military headquarters with false,
bizarre charges against the Governor,[5] and General Sheridan,
acting on orders from Radicals in Washington, speedily decapi-
tated Throckmorton, and Pease went in.[6] With carpetbaggers,
scalawags, Bureau agents, and negroes swarming the streets of
Austin in a festival of fraternity, the party in Texas entered the
arena with a bang.

In Louisiana, the Radicals had long been organized under the
leadership of the able, eloquent, but saturnine Thomas J. Durant,
with 57,300 negroes enrolled in ninety-four clubs, under the
strictest discipline.[7] General Longstreet had gone over to the Republicans, bag and baggage, on the theory that 'we are a conquered people' and 'the terms of the conqueror' were unescapable.

[1] Staples, 166.      [2] Ibid., 164.      [3] Ibid., 167.      [4] Ramsdell, I, 69.
[5] Ibid., 167.        [6] Ibid., 169.      [7] Ficklen, 186, note.

His letter was published with *éclat* by all the carpetbag papers of the South, and with his own people denouncing his desertion, he was soon importuning Lee for a blessing on his apostasy. 'I cannot think that the course pursued by the dominant party is best,' wrote Lee, from his retirement, where he was abstaining from political activity, 'and therefore cannot say so, or give it my approval.' [1] Denied Lee's blessing, Longstreet consoled himself with the surveyorship of customs, and the new party, booted and spurred, was ready to mount and ride.

In Virginia there was much groaning of spirit under the lash of the intolerable Hunnicutt, and conservative Republicans were turning hopefully to the brilliant John Minor Botts, a former Whig, and the 'New York Tribune' was urging the negroes to follow him.[2] The national leaders had been alarmed by the inflammatory speeches in a Hunnicutt convention in the spring, in which three fourths of the members were black. A year before, the party had been launched under Botts's leadership with a demand for the disfranchisement of all Confederates, but it had refused to recommend unqualified negro suffrage, and Hunnicutt had swept ahead. When his incendiary convention aroused the wrath of conservatives, who called another convention, the Union League Clubs of New York, Philadelphia, and Boston, fearing a disruption, hurried conciliators to Richmond to reconcile the factions. Thus fifty men sat down one day in the Governor's Mansion, with Henry Wilson representing the congressional end of the party, and John Jay, the Union League Clubs, and a compromise was proposed — a new convention at Richmond in the late summer. Botts hesitated. Richmond was the hotbed of radicalism, and Hunnicutt had no scruples, but Jay and Wilson insisted, and Botts reluctantly agreed.

The convention day arrived, the negroes on their toes, and with Hunnicutt's men jammed against the door of the African Church four hours before it was opened. With the opening of the doors, Hunnicutt's negroes rushed in and took possession, leaving Botts, his followers, and two thousand negroes outside. Within was Hunnicutt, raving and ranting. The excluded moved to Capital Square to organize under the leadership of Botts. Very well —

[1] *Recollections and Letters*, 268.          [2] Eckenrode, 69.

the two thousand negroes were on hand to elect a Hunnicutt man for chairman. Let Botts speak? 'No,' thundered the mob. Many were alarmed at the portent, the 'Richmond Enquirer' describing the scene as 'a seditious Radical carnival,' and many old-line Whigs passed sadly over to the Democrats, but Botts remained regular, a pitiful trailer to the Hunnicutt train.[1]

In Florida, the factions under Osborne, Saunders, and Stearns were disproving the theory that there is honor among thieves, but the party was in absolute control.

And in Georgia? There, with the negroes organized, the Republicans had found a leader in the most consummate of politicians, Joseph E. Brown, Confederate War Governor, whose spectacular rise from poverty and obscurity had made him a popular figure. That which his admirers called sagacity, his enemies denounced as trickery. Among the poor whites, he had an impressive following. Physically frail, his chest thin, his voice weak, his throat bad, the clearness of his enunciation and the smoothness of his tone gave him an eloquence having nothing to do with volume. Self-possessed, dignified, earnest, he inspired confidence and made friends strongly devoted to his fortunes. His extreme State Rights views during the war had made him a thorn in the side of Jefferson Davis, but he returned from his imprisonment in Washington completely metamorphosed, urging absolute surrender to the rabid policies of the conqueror. Why continue the fight? he asked. The Jeffersonian idea of the State was dead; State Rights were buried beyond hope of resurrection.[2] Soon he was responding to the toast 'Reconstruction — Let it proceed under the Sherman Bill without appealing to the Supreme Court, the arbiter of our civil rights and not of political issues.'[3] Such complete apostasy caused a sensation. When Robert Toombs was told of Brown's attitude, he denounced the story as a lie, and when verification reached him, took to his bed.[4] Soon Brown was rivaling Thad Stevens in his denunciations of the Northern Democracy, and eliciting rapturous applause from the Republican National Convention of 1868. Horace Greeley was delighted. 'Governor Brown deserves the thanks of all his neighbors,' he wrote. 'That this gentleman is by

---

[1] Eckenrode, 72–79.     [2] Life of Brown, 426–27; Thompson, 172–73.
[3] Thompson, 175–76.     [4] Stovall, 290.

no means lacking in intelligence is proved by the fact that he has found out the Democrats and avows that he wants nothing more to do with them.' [1] Thus the Republicans in Georgia, with the negroes thoroughly consolidated, entered the field, shouting for Joe Brown.

## VI

The action of Brown had this effect — it led Georgia first into the field aggressively against the reconstruction policy. Most of the Southern leaders, utterly depressed, were in retirement. Lee, eschewing politics, was spending the summer quietly at a Virginia watering place, and riding 'Traveller' over the surrounding hills. Lamar, teaching at Oxford, was in hopeless mood. Only the Southern press seemed articulate, and it was bitterly denouncing the Military Bill. 'It consigns three fourths of the Southern population to political Siberia,' said the 'New Orleans Crescent.' 'The people of the South, if wise and prudent, can live for a time under such damnable tyranny as this, but if they consent, they deserve it,' said the 'Louisville Journal.' 'There is no more American Union. It died with the Constitution which was the life of its body. Yancey is triumphant,' said the 'Mobile Advertiser and Register.' 'No nation has ever yet given itself up body and soul to vindictive legislation that it has not eventually been punished by God most terribly for its scarlet sins,' said the 'Richmond Times.' 'It is the funeral oration of the Republic,' thought the 'Richmond Examiner,' of the Johnson veto.[2]

And then, from Georgia, a voice reverberating over the South and throughout the North — the voice of Benjamin H. Hill. At Liberty Hall, Alexander H. Stephens sat in silent despair. Toombs was in exile. Howell Cobb was refusing the responsibility of advising, and Joe Brown was toasting the oppressors of his people and denouncing their supporters in the North. It was at this juncture that Ben Hill closeted himself with a copy of the Military Bill, after promising to address the people of Atlanta on July 10, 1867.

Through all the years of the 'bloody shirt,' Hill's name was to

[1] *New York Tribune*, May 20, 1867.
[2] Quoted, *New York World*, March 6, 9, 15, 1867.

be anathema to the ignorant and a byword and a hissing among the 'patriots.' His character and career deserve a better understanding, for he was an extraordinary man. Born of Irish-Welsh parentage, he had all the emotionalism that that implies. Held up to obloquy in the North as a disunionist, he had been a consistent champion of the Union in Legislature and Congress until the bugle called his people to the field. Fighting for the Union to the end, when he lost his battle, he cast his lot with his own people, and in the Confederate Senate, its youngest member, he was the spokesman of the Administration. His was the last speech for the Union; the last speech for the continuance of the war; and with the close of the struggle, he had retired to his estate at LaGrange to await events. Not one of his slaves deserted; not one betrayed. Taken at length, he was soon paroled, and for two years he devoted himself to his personal affairs.

In 1867, he was forty-four, and in the full fruition of his power. It was at this time in the great Corinthian-columned house, in the midst of beautiful grounds reached by granite walks from a massive iron gate, that a youth, Henry W. Grady, visited, and came to love, the master of LaGrange for his genial playfulness and affectionate nature.[1] Hill was a man of magnificent presence, six and a half feet in height and perfectly proportioned. His great head was covered with light brown hair, fine and straight, his complexion was clear, his forehead was high and broad, and his gray eyes dominated. Voorhees, who saw him about this time, was impressed by the 'intensity of his pale strong face and his firm determined features.'[2] In speech marvelously persuasive, he could be immeasurably bitter when occasion called. The brilliant Vest of Missouri compared him to Vergniaud;[3] the eloquent Voorhees thought some of his speeches 'as sublime as the words that fell from the lips of Paul on Mars Hill';[4] and John J. Ingalls was charmed by 'his diction, his confident and imperturbable self-control.'[5] He was a giant in mind, as in body.

## VII

Such the Tribune of the South who rose in a crowded hall, tense with excitement, with bayonets all about him, with the spies

[1] Hill, 91.      [2] Ibid., 145.      [3] Ibid., 136.      [4] Ibid., 71.      [5] Ibid., 135.

of the tyrannical General John Pope present to report his words to the Radicals in Washington. One who heard him thought his 'soul and intellect were both aflame,' and knew he 'lifted the people to their feet' and became 'a Greatheart to whom the new pilgrim turned' — this man who 'had set himself to the task of revolutionizing revolution.' [1] The hall was but dimly lighted when Hill stepped forth in full-dress suit, his face pale, his eyes burning, and defiantly swept with his glance the army officers in full-dress uniform in the front rows.

'Tinkers may work, quacks may prescribe, and demagogues may deceive, but I declare to you that there is no remedy for us . . . but in adhering to the Constitution'; and thus he threw this treason to the front rows. With a contemptuous thrust at the apostasy of Brown, he lunged at Thad Stevens, and hurried on. 'A great many Southerners,' he said, 'flippantly say the Constitution is dead. Then your rights and hopes for the future, and the hopes of your children are dead. . . . They say the Constitution does not apply to us? Then don't swear to support it. They say again that we are not in the Union — then why swear to support the Union of these States? What Union does that mean? When you took the oath, was it the Union of the Northern States alone that you swore to support?'

With a scornful look at the Bureau agents and carpetbaggers with the army officers, he went on. 'Oh, I pity the colored people who have never been taught what an oath is, or what the Constitution means. They are drawn up by a selfish conclave of traitors to inflict a death-blow on the Republic by swearing them into a falsehood. They are to begin their political life with perjury to accomplish treason. . . . They are neither legally nor morally responsible — it is you, educated, designing white men, who thus devote yourselves to the unholy work, who are the guilty parties. You prate about your loyalty. I look you in the eye and denounce you . . . morally and legally perjured traitors. . . . Ye hypocrites! Ye whited sepulchers! Ye mean in your hearts to deceive him, and buy up the negro vote for your own benefit.'

And then, to the Radicals: 'Go on confiscating; arrest without warrant or probable cause; destroy habeas corpus; deny trial by

[1] Joel Chandler Harris; Hill, 51.

jury; abrogate State Governments; defile your own race. . . . On, on with your work of ruin, ye hell-born rioters in sacred things — but remember that for all these things the people will call you to judgment. Ah, what an issue you have made for yourselves. Succeed, and you destroy the Constitution; fail, and you have covered the land with mourning. Succeed, and you bring ruin on yourselves and all the country; fail, and you bring infamy upon yourselves and all your followers. Succeed, and you are the perjured assassins of liberty; fail, and you are defeated, despised traitors forever. Ye aspire to be Radical Governors and judges. . . . I paint before you this day your destiny. You are but cowards and knaves, and the time will come when you will call upon the rocks and mountains to fall on you and the darkness to hide you from an outraged people.'

And then, to the negroes: 'They tell you they are your friends — it is false. They tell you they set you free — it is false. These vile creatures never went with the army except to steal spoons, jewelry, and gold watches. They are too low to be brave. They are dirty spawn, cast out from decent society, who come down here to seek to use you to further their own base purposes. . . . Improve yourselves; learn to read and write; be industrious; lay up your means; acquire homes; live in peace with your neighbors; drive off as you would a serpent the miserable dirty adventurers who come among you . . . and seek to foment among you hatred of the decent portion of the white race.'

And what should the people do about registration and the Convention? Register, run up the registration, and do not vote on the Constitution, thus defeating the scheme, which fails unless fifty per cent of the registered, vote for a Convention.[1]

As these bitter, burning words went sizzling over the South and fell like bombs in Northern cities, General Pope was writing Grant urging that the orator be banished from the State.

### VIII

But they were not through with Hill. Having dynamitized the people with his oratory, he sat down to the writing of the Federalist of Southern rights, his brilliant, powerful 'Notes on the Situa-

[1] Hill, 294–307.

tion,' which Henry Grady was to pronounce 'the profoundest and most eloquent political essays ever penned by an American.' [1] Beginning, artfully, in a minor strain, as one mourning over departed freedom,[2] he argued that the Military Bill led to 'the ultimate but complete change of all American government from the principle of consent to the rule of force' and to 'a war of races.' [3] Pouncing savagely on Stevens's admission that the Constitution was ignored, he denounced the hypocrisy of giving the semblance of consent 'by disfranchising intelligence, by military rule, by threats and . . . bribery.' Yes, 'the negro race, duped by emissaries and aided by deserters . . . is to give consent for the white race.' More: all the guarantees of liberty wrung through the centuries from the hands of despotism 'are abrogated and withdrawn from ten million people of all colors, sexes, and classes, who live in ten unheard and excluded States; and that, too, by men who do not live in these States . . . who never think of them but to hate . . . never enter them but to insult.' [4] Do they say the South cannot help herself? Then, why bother about consent? But the South can fight with the Constitution in her hands. 'Better to brook the courts' delay for ten years than accept anarchy and slavery for a century.' [5] Danger of confiscation? Admitted. 'Those who outlaw patriotism and intelligence would not scruple to rob.' And yet how absurd, proposing to confiscate the property of people when bread is sent them that they may live! 'The same train brings the bread to feed, the officer to oppress, the emissary to breed strife and to rob.' [6]

And the conquered, subject to the will of the conqueror? 'None but a very barbarous people, Northern radicals and Southern renegades, ever said so. A conquered people are subject to the terms of the conquest, made known and demanded before, or at the time the conquest is admitted, and to no other terms or will whatever; and none but a treacherous conqueror would demand more.' [7] Every demand in the Military Bill originated after the war; 'not one of them was demanded during the war or made a condition of surrender. There is not a respectable publicist or law-writer, ancient or modern, heathen or Christian, who can be quoted to sustain them.' [8]

[1] Hill, 51.  [2] No. 1.  [3] No. 2.  [4] No. 3.  [5] No. 4.
[6] No. 5.  [7] No. 6.  [8] No. 8.

And universal negro suffrage? 'Ignorance is more easily duped than intelligence, and . . . knaves have always been advocates of conferring power on fools; and so fools have generally thought knaves their best friends.' Yes, 'they go like the fattened ox with pretty ribbons streaming from their horns, frisking to the slaughter.' Do Radicals say they wish to elevate the black race? 'These Radical traitors and their Southern tools alone desire to degrade the white race.'

And the purpose? 'To secure these ten States to keep the Radical Party in power in the approaching presidential election, . . . to retain by force and fraud the power they are losing in the detection of their treason in the North.' Thus 'they annul the Constitution in the name of loyalty; exterminate the black race in the name of philanthropy; disfranchise the white race in the name of equality; pull down all the defenses of life and prosperity in the name of liberty, and with blasphemous hosannas to the Union, they are rushing all sections and all races into wild chaotic anarchy; and all, that traitors may hold the power they desecrate, and riot in the wreck of the prosperity they destroy.' [1]

And how combat it? First through the President, and then through the courts.[2] Yes, 'sue in damages for every injury; indict for every crime,' and 'be sure and include the thieving Treasury agents who were lately stealing your cotton.' No money for lawyers? 'Whenever you see me at court, understand I will aid you without fee or reward,' for 'the written Constitution is my client, and the preservation of its protection the only fee I ask.' [3] Then, for three numbers followed an excoriation of Brown, with logic that bites like acid.[4] And the concluding papers were appeals to Grant in whom the Military Bill then vested power.[5] 'There are many now who insist that General Grant is not really a great man,' he wrote. 'The question of his greatness will soon be settled. . . . If he has the wisdom to perceive, and the courage to perform his duty now, neither Cæsar nor Wellington nor Washington can be remembered longer or honored more.'

In these remarkable papers, Hill reached the height of the controversial discussions of the ten-year period. There was art in the eloquence, erudition in the references, truth in the assertions,

[1] No. 11.     [2] No. 12.     [3] No. 13.     [4] Nos. 15–17.     [5] Nos. 18–22.

power in the logic. But there was more significance in the militant note they sounded. The desponding raised themselves on their elbows to listen, and something of pride and the fighting spirit returned. All over the South men were reading them with renewed hope and determination; in the Radical circles there was gnashing of teeth. 'The Voice of the South uttering her protest,' says Henry Grady; and it was 'discussed on the streets of London and the Boulevards of Paris.'

Here was a man ready to give blow for blow, epithet for epithet. The stricken South was thrilled.[1]

## IX

In the mean time, under the autocracy of military masters, preparations were being made for registration, the calling of constitutional conventions, and the election of delegates. Many of the generals in control sought in every way to treat the people with respect, while others, like Pope, predicting the transfer of intelligence from whites to blacks within five years, and intoxicated with power, were busy in the decapitation of civil officials.[2] The University of Georgia was closed because of a student's speech, and the sheriffs were removed in numbers.[3] In Arkansas and Mississippi, the decent instincts of General Ord were overcome by political pressure, and with the closing of the courts the least semblance of liberty passed from Arkansas, with crime rampant.[4] In Louisiana and Texas, General Sheridan, reveling in his unpopularity, was replacing white city officials in New Orleans with negroes,[5] and, under the inspiration of an incendiary press and the Leagues, was permitting the Texas negroes to run amuck with guns and knives.[6] In Alabama, the military despotism was complete, with soldiers in posts at intervals of twenty and thirty miles, fraternizing with the negro mobs.[7] In Mississippi, with the courts open, forty-one men were tried by a military commission.[8] Everywhere military authorities were interfering with the freedom of the press, and in Vicksburg an editor who had criticized Radical policies was tried by a military tribunal. When, denied a writ of ha-

[1] Hill, 730–811.    [2] Avery, 371.    [3] Ibid., 372.
[4] Staples, 129, 135, 141, 143.    [5] Ficklen, 190.    [6] Ramsdell, 188.
[7] Doc. Hist., I, 443–44.    [8] Garner, 169–70.

beas corpus, he appealed to the Supreme Court, Congress hurriedly deprived that court of jurisdiction.[1]

Uglier still, these military autocrats were feeding the carpetbag press with public patronage, some restricting the publication of proclamations to Radical papers with meager circulations, and a carpetbag paper in Tennessee was announcing a forthcoming congressional enactment giving Government printing to party papers in the South. And why not? Had not Thad Stevens proposed that every American legation be supplied with Forney's paper at public cost? [2]

Under such conditions the people were registered and the vote on constitutional conventions cast. The negroes, under the drillmasters of the League, moved *en masse* to the polls, while multitudes of the whites, disgusted, and knowing themselves outnumbered, remained away. Thus the news flashed that the Conventions had carried, with great numbers of negro delegates elected who could neither read nor write, and with carpetbaggers in control. What though Stevens had lost the North, had not the South been won? — and the glad tidings gave infinite satisfaction to the intelligentsia in New York and Boston.

## X

Never more astonishing conventions, in personnel, in a civilized nation. Negroes and carpetbaggers dominated, property and intelligence excluded, and strangers in many cases represented districts they had never seen. In Alabama, an Ohioan, as temporary chairman, recognized a Pennsylvanian who nominated a New-Yorker for secretary, and the 'New York Herald' correspondent, glancing over the assembly, dubbed it 'The Black Crook.' [3] The irreverent described that in Arkansas as 'the bastard collection' or 'the menagerie.' [4]

Happily there was comedy to relieve the gloom. Thus, in Louisiana a reporter was excluded for calling the negro members 'colored,' and a North Carolina delegate of color demanded the publication of debates, since he wished to 'expatiate' to the convention and desired his words recorded 'in the archives of gravity.' [5] In

[1] Garner, 168.          [2] *McMinnville Enterprise*, February 16, 1867.
[3] Fleming, 517-19.          [4] Staples, 21.          [5] Hamilton, 258, note.

Florida, members with feet on desks and smoking heard from illiterate colleagues the 'pint ob orter' that 'de pages and mess'-gers' had failed 'to put some jinal [paper]' on the desks.[1] Sometimes in the Mississippi Convention, pistols and knives were as necessary as 'jinals,' and there were frequent fights, and in Virginia, arguments were not infrequently clinched with fists.[2] In Florida, legislation would be stayed to await the outcome of a pugilistic encounter while members puffed at their cigars and shouted encouragement to the combatants.[3] And everywhere, the delegates, having no taxes to pay and no stake in the State, were spending money with a lavish prodigality.

The first act of the president of the Florida Convention was to appoint a 'financial agent,' who hastened with an order for money to the State Treasurer, but the military commander intervened. Whereupon the Convention issued fifty thousand dollars in script, of which fifteen thousand dollars was immediately put out, and ten thousand dollars retained by the president. Pages were paid ten dollars a day, One delegate, living three hundred miles away, was given $690 in mileage; another, living in the convention town, received $630; and an emissary of the Radical National Committee (Saunders) drew $649.53, though his alleged home was but twenty miles distant. In Mississippi, the convention cost a quarter of a million, and four obscure Republican papers were paid $28,518.75 for publishing the proceedings.[4] In Arkansas, where each member was voted ten newspapers, the mileage graft was shameless, and the printing was let to a politician without competition at an astounding figure.

There was graft everywhere; for the constitution-makers of the day expected to be office-holders on the morrow, and all were in training.

Most of the constitutions were monstrosities, proscriptive, and frankly designed to serve the purposes of party. Incendiary talk marked the proceedings. While a Mobile delegate, supported by the carpetbaggers, clamored lustily for the legalization of intermarriage, the scalawags opposed; but as a rule the negroes showed more judgment and a keener appreciation of the realities than the

[1] Wallace, 56.  [2] Eckenrode, 97.  [3] Wallace, 54.
[4] Garner, 203.

white demagogues.[1] In some places, as in South Carolina, there was much wild talk of dividing the land among the freedmen.[2] Everywhere, except in Georgia, the conventions centered on the disfranchisement of large blocks of whites, and wrote this infamy into the fundamental law — for this was the real purpose of these conventions. In Louisiana, public conveyances were thrown open to both races — theaters, public schools, and the university as well — and the disfranchisements were sweeping. Again it was an intelligent negro who protested that his race asked no such proscriptions. The disfranchising scheme also encountered opposition from the scalawags of Arkansas, but these were powerless. The Virginia Constitution bristled with test oaths and disfranchisements, transferring power to the ignorant and proscribing intelligence, and even this was an improvement on the original plan, which had sent a chill through the politicians in Washington.[3] In Georgia, a reasonably conservative and sane document was framed because of the determining influence of Joe Brown.[4]

Ending their work to the satisfaction of the Washington Radicals, helping themselves to as much public plunder as was within reach, the conventions closed in jubilations, and in North Carolina there was a real thanksgiving, with the notorious General M. S. Littlefield, who was to get more than his share of the loot under the governments of 'loyal men,' singing 'John Brown's Body.'

These documents, framed by ignorance, malevolence, and partisanship, sounded the death-knell of civilization in the South.

## XI

Horrified by these fundamental laws, the conservatives everywhere hastily organized against their adoption. In some States they stayed away from the polls, since a majority of votes registered was required. In Georgia, they let the constitution go by default; in South Carolina, they issued an appeal to the people; in Florida, they knew themselves to be overwhelmed. In Mississippi, under the sagacious leadership of General J. Z. George, a Herculean fight was made in the open, with a utilization of both press and platform in every nook and corner, and with as many as sixteen

[1] Fleming, 522–23.          [2] Doc. Hist., I, 451.
[3] Eckenrode, 97; Stuart, 17.          [4] Thompson, 193; Avery, 377.

meetings a week in a country.[1] In Arkansas, the conservatives fought hard, denouncing the Radical leaders as bigamists and degenerates, intimate with the blacks.[2] There was no fighting chance in Louisiana and South Carolina, where the emissaries of the Union League had been moving familiarly in the negro cabins, the whiskey shops, and on the plantations. In Alabama, these agents warned the credulous negro that slavery for him was the alternative to adoption, and that the failure of the constitution would deprive their wives of the privilege of wearing hoopskirts. The day before the election, they were warned that the military commander would punish them if they failed to vote 'right.' Thus they were mobilized and marched to the towns the night before election — great droves of them armed with shotguns, muskets, and pistols and knives — and they terrorized the people by firing through the night.[3] Radical politicians, as overseers, marched with them to the polls, glowering upon the weaklings. A spectator described the scene for the 'New York Herald': 'The voter got his ticket from the captain, the captain had it from the colonel, and he from the general, and the general of course had it from the owners and managers in Washington of the grand scheme to secure political supremacy.'[4] The whites were denied access to the polls on the first day. Thus the negroes entered upon their freedom.

The result was ratification everywhere but in Mississippi, where it failed decisively, in Alabama, where the majority of the registered did not vote to ratify, and in Virginia, where the masterful management of Alexander H. H. Stuart, before the date was fixed for the election, secured a postponement and paved the way for a compromise on the basis of 'universal suffrage and universal amnesty.' In Georgia, it was the contention of Ben Hill that the constitution was lost by thirty thousand,[5] but no matter — it was declared adopted; and Alabama was admitted by Congress despite the failure of her poll, because the Radicals wanted her electoral vote in the election of 1868.

Immediately, the political parasites and looters, scalawags and scavengers, knaves and fools, took possession of the State Governments, and entered upon the pillaging of the stricken people.

[1] Garner, 213.     [2] Staples, 256.     [3] Fleming, 514–16.
[4] October 14, 1867.     [5] Bush Arbor speech, Hill, 308–19.

# CHAPTER XI

## A PASSING PHASE

### I

UNFORGIVING and relentless as was Thad Stevens, his manhood gagged at the punishment of Vinnie Ream — the petty persecution of a woman. On being ordered from the Capitol, she had appealed to Stevens's chivalry, not in vain. Without consulting his associates, he moved that her studio be restored to her, and, under the whip and spur of the previous question, he prevailed. 'Many of the Radicals were disgusted with Thad, but none of them attempted to cross swords with him,' said the correspondent of the 'New York Herald.' [1] But the flame was flickering feebly now, and at times he seemed to soften toward his foes. It was at this time that James Buchanan died. Citizens of the same town, they had ridden the circuit together years before, when Stevens still lived at Gettysburg. One afternoon, at York, they had gone out for a stroll together, and they returned bitter enemies. Just what occurred no one seemed to know. Politics widened the breach. When Buchanan, weary from the toils of State, returned to Lancaster in 1861, they had a common friend in Dr. Henry Carpenter, the physician of both; and both attended his second wedding in 1863. Stevens, who, strangely enough, was very sensitive, afterward complained to Carpenter that he had offered his hand to Buchanan, who had turned away. The physician, knowing the unfailing courtesy of the former President, assured the offended Stevens there was some mistake, and, speaking to Buchanan about it later, found he had seen no proffered hand. He, too, was old, too old to harbor animosities. 'Doctor,' he said, 'you drive about the country. Drive Mr. Stevens out past "Wheatland" and I'll be sitting at the spring and will come out and greet him.' Just then Stevens was unexpectedly recalled to Washington, and the meeting never took place; but Stevens knew of Buchanan's proposal. So runs one story [2] extant in Lancaster to-

[1] July 21, 1868.      [2] Told the writer by Judge Brown.

day. The daughter of Carpenter recalls that the two men met at the wedding and did shake hands.[1] When Buchanan's death was announced, the Senate instantly adjourned. In the House, such was the bitterness of the times a resolution of respect referring to the dead statesman's 'patriotic motives' was voted down, with sixty-nine not voting. It was observed that Stevens seemed embarrassed. He asked unanimous consent to offer a resolution on Buchanan's death, and was refused. Blaine made a similar request, with the same result. Then Stevens rose again. 'I trust,' he said, 'I will be allowed to offer the resolution.' The objection was renewed. Just what Stevens would have offered is not known; but he did not vote with those who tabled the first resolution.[2]

Once or twice the flame brightened, and with its old heat; as when he denounced the plan to pay the five-twenty bonds in gold, not stipulated in the bond. And his hate of Johnson was unrelenting. Toward the close of a speech on a new impeachment resolution, bitter and well phrased, his tone changed to one of sadness. 'My sands,' he said, 'are nearly run, and I can only see with the eyes of faith. I am fast descending the downhill of life, at the foot of which stands the open grave. But you, sir [the Speaker], are promised full length of days, and a brilliant career. If you and your compeers can fling away ambition and realize that every human being, however lowly or degraded by fortune, is your equal ... truth and righteousness will spread over the land and you will look down from the top of the Rocky Mountains upon an empire of one hundred million of happy people.'[3]

His last public utterance was in support of the Alaskan Purchase Treaty.

Adjournment found Stevens too feeble to return to Lancaster, but he stubbornly refused to take to his bed. Even his enemies respected certain robust traits of his character. 'Of Mr. Stevens I have never suffered myself to speak but with a certain respect,' wrote the correspondent of the 'New York World,' in an article on the old man's hatred of hypocrisy.[4] On August 2, he was too weak to leave his apartment, but it was not until a week later that he went to bed. For two days, declining all conversation, he lay with

---

[1] Her story to the author.
[2] *Congressional Globe*, June 3, 1868.
[3] *Ibid.*, July 7, 1868.
[4] July 25, 1868.

hands crossed and eyes closed as though in sleep.[1] When, on the afternoon of the last day, he discovered his physician changing his medicine, he said grimly, 'Well, this is a square fight.' With twilight came two colored Sisters of Charity, attached to the Providence Hospital he had been instrumental in founding, and then two colored ministers, who asked to pray with him. A little bored, but considerate, he admitted them, and prayers were said. Evarts and Sumner were among the evening callers, but it was the colored people who dominated the death chamber. There were Lydia Smith and the two Sisters, Loretta and Genevieve. As he was sinking rapidly, the doctor asked how he felt. 'Very mean, Doctor.'[2] Then Sister Loretta asked permission to baptize him in the Catholic faith. Lydia Smith was kneeling at the foot of the bed; the two Sisters were on their knees reading the prayers for the dying. And thus Thaddeus Stevens passed to eternity. At the moment, his hand was in that of Sister Loretta, his breast heaved, he pressed her hand, and thus the end came. A year before he had said that when sick, he would rather send a hundred miles to have her with him at the end than most ministers he knew.[3] That night a company of colored Zouaves stood guard by his dead body.[4] At noon the Butler Zouaves, followed by about fifty persons, mostly colored, accompanied his body to the Rotunda of the Capitol, where in a rosewood coffin he lay in state while throngs filed slowly by till midnight.[5] The next morning a hearse drawn by four white horses moved with the casket to the station through crowds of spectators of the pageant. Thus Thad Stevens left Washington forever.

As the train passed through Harrisburg, the bells tolled and the minute guns were fired; at Lancaster, he lay in state, again guarded by Zouaves. A procession of fifteen thousand people followed the casket to the simple old cemetery of the town. Baptized by a Catholic Sister, the burial service was read by a Lutheran minister, and the sermon was preached by an Episcopalian clergyman, though the only church for which he had a sentiment was the Baptist, the sect of his mother.[6]

[1] New York World, August 13, 1868.       [2] New York Herald, August 13, 1868.
[3] Ibid., August 14, 1868.                  [4] New York World, August 13, 1868.
[5] Ibid., August 14, 1868.                  [6] New York Herald, August 14, 1868.

In the will, Lydia Smith was given permission to occupy the house for five years and given an annuity of five hundred dollars for life, or five thousand dollars in a lump sum. The greater part of his fortune was left to a nephew on condition that he abstain from liquor for fifteen years — a condition that could not be met. In New York, Georges Clemenceau, the young Frenchman, mourned him sincerely.[1] A short time, and a monument marked the spot where he was sleeping with an epitaph of his own composition:

'I repose in this quiet and secluded spot, not from any natural preference for solitude, but, finding other cemeteries limited by charter rules as to race, I have chosen this that I might illustrate in my death the principles which I advocated through a long life, Equality of Man before his Creator.'

The faithful Lydia Smith lived some years, and, dying, was buried beside her husband in the Catholic Cemetery. And so the tale of Thad Stevens was told, and his movement passed to men less able, less sincere, and far more selfish.

II

Stevens had lived to see the nomination of Grant and Colfax by the Republicans. The nomination of Grant by one of the two parties had been assured for at least two years. The Republican politicians, deciding on his nomination, had assigned to John W. Forney the embarrassing task of establishing his Republicanism; and when the journalist, with the aid of Rawlins, submitted his five-column article launching the candidacy, Grant read it whimsically and expressed surprise to find himself so good a Republican. He had struggled with himself over the nomination. As General of the Army, he received twenty-five thousand dollars; if elected and re-elected, what would happen to him at the end of his second term?[2] Nor was it absolutely certain that the Radical group would have him. Until the quarrel with Johnson, not only was the tone of its press unfriendly — it was frequently scurrilous. Through 1867, Greeley in 'The Tribune' was cool to the suggestion.

Inspired by the fear that Grant was not a dyed-in-the-wool Radical, the pretense was that he drank too much. It is amazing

[1] Clemenceau, 226.        [2] Forney, I, 287–88.

to find how freely these extremists played with the topic. The story, previously referred to as a press rumor, that detectives were engaged to check up on his inebriety was true. In January, 1868, Ben Butler appeared at the home of Julian with 'a young friend of his who is a sort of political detective, and who is hunting up facts as to General Grant's drunkenness.'[1] Just a week before, two of Julian's friends had informed him that Grant had been seen in a befuddled state, but Julian had 'little hope that anything can arrest the popular madness which demands his nomination.'[2] Wendell Phillips was writing in 'The Anti-Slavery Standard' that 'rumors reach us from Washington . . . that General Grant has been seen unmistakably drunk in the streets of that city within a few weeks';[3] and Theodore Tilton was writing in 'The Independent' that 'occasionally a presidential candidate is seen fuddled in the street' and that 'one glass' of wine poured down the throat of the next President. . . may give this whole nation the delirium tremens.'[4]

But the Radicals were really not concerned with Grant's personal habits so much as with his political trend, and, after his break with Johnson, they easily became reconciled to his drinking, and we hear no more about it. Colfax had been aspiring, but he soon faded from the picture, and Godkin had dismissed a suggestion of George William Curtis's availability, with the observation that his political ideas 'all grow under glass and are feeble when exposed.'[5]

Thus the Convention met and nominated Grant; and, thanks to a Methodist Conference then in session in the city, Colfax was named for the second place.[6] Stevens and Julian had preferred Wade, who failed, and passed from the scene. The platform was a sweeping endorsement of reconstruction policies, and little more. Julian's plank on land plunder was rejected as an affront to the railroads, though he was convinced 'the people want . . . an end of thieving and corrupt monopolies' — a mistake to which idealists are prone.[7] On negro suffrage, the platform asserted that all

[1] MS. Diary, January 12, 1868.  [2] Ibid., January 5, 1868.
[3] Quoted, New York World, January 31, 1868.  [4] January 23, 1868.
[5] Ogden, I, 293.  [6] Life of Colfax, to Dr. Eddy, 322.
[7] Julian, MS. Diary, May 24, 1868.

negroes should be given the vote in the South through congressional action, but that 'the question of suffrage in all the loyal States properly belong to the people of those States.'

The feature of the Convention was the speech of Joe Brown, of Georgia, denouncing the Democrats, and declaring that 'the Hamiltonian and Websterian construction of the Constitution has been established by the sword,' and that he 'acquiesced in that.' This operation of the conscience and intellect through the guidance of the sword was wildly acclaimed.

The country now turned to the plans of the Democrats.

## III

The Democrats were embarrassed by the money question and threatened to divide on sectional lines. In 1867, there had been much hot discussion as to whether the five-twenty bonds had to be redeemed in coin or 'money.' The law made no stipulation as to coin, and Thad Stevens, in charge of the bill, had explained that the bonds could be redeemed in money. Disregarding the law, Jay Cooke, in charge of the sale, advertised that the redemption would be in coin; and a functionary of the Treasury, when asked, had said that, since all other bonds had been so redeemed, he supposed the same policy would be followed in the case of the five-twenties. When this assumption of Cooke's that he could supplement or change the law was bitterly challenged, he haughtily wrote that 'the pledge of my advertisements . . . was equivalent in equity and honor to any one of the loan laws.' [1] In other words, he insisted on the right 'in equity and honor' to misrepresent the law in his advertisements and thus commit the nation. These bonds had been sold to bankers at a discount of sixty and seventy per cent, and if paid in gold and silver the interest would be nearly trebled. Butler contended that this would be 'an enormous robbery of the people for the benefit of the bankers, without justice or reason.' [2] There was no possible misinterpretation of the law itself. Even John Sherman was momentarily shocked at Cooke's point of view. He had said the law made no provision for payment in gold; that 'soldiers and sailors who shed their blood and saved the Union were paid with greenbacks'; that pensions to their widows were

[1] Oberholtzer, *Cooke*, ii, 41.    [2] *Butler's Book*, 931.

thus paid; that all our people were forced by law to accept green-backs; and he could not understand why the money-lenders, who had taken the bonds at a cut-throat discount during the war, should be singled out from other creditors, and paid par in gold.[1] When Cooke wrote him in protest, Sherman stood his ground. 'I will neither violate the faith of the nation nor put upon the nation a burden not demanded by the loan or founded upon equity and justice,' he wrote. Legally he knew he was right. In equity, he asked if it was right that 'the holder of these bonds shall now refuse to receive the identical money in payment which he gave for the bonds.'[2] Whereupon Cooke had written sadly to his brother, he 'had no idea that Sherman was so fully committed to the miserable policy of repudiation.'[3]

In the House, Thad Stevens, who had personally managed the bond bill, protested bitterly against payment in gold as a swindle. The meaning of the law was clear. He had explained it a dozen times on the floor at the time, and the whole House had agreed what it meant. 'I will vote for no such swindle . . . no such speculation in favor of the large bondholders and the millionaires who took advantage of our folly in granting them coin payment in interest.'[4] Feeling was running high, for Welles's report had just shown that the rich were growing richer and the poor poorer. The nomination at the Democratic Convention was to turn largely upon this question.

## IV

The outstanding candidates were George H. Pendleton, Thomas A. Hendricks, Horatio Seymour, Andrew Johnson, and Chief Justice Chase. There never was the slightest possibility of the nomination of Johnson, though there would have been consistency in the award, and he had 'strong hopes of a nomination.'[5] More nearly possible would have been the nomination of Chase — who

---

[1] Interview with General A. B. Nettleton, Oberholtzer, *Cooke*, ii, 40, note.

[2] Oberholtzer, *Cooke*, ii, 42–43.          [3] *Ibid.*, ii, 43.

[4] Professor Woodburn, Stevens's biographer says (page 581): 'One may well doubt whether there was ever a more outrageous fleecing and robbery of a patriotic people than that perpetrated through the influence of capitalists and money lenders by the manipulation of government finance during and immediately following the American Civil War.'

[5] Welles, iii, 396.

fundamentally was a Jeffersonian — but for his views on negro suffrage. Able and experienced, he had delighted the Democrats by his course during the impeachment trial. No one ever had been more severely stung by the presidential bee, and this had been his undoing. Welles found, the previous winter, that Chase had strength 'among bankers, speculators, and a certain class of capitalists,' and some following 'among the Southern Radicals and negroes.' [1] When his prospects for the Republican nomination dimmed, and a spontaneous movement among Democrats manifested itself, he was immensely pleased — 'taken . . . entirely by surprise.' [2] He agreed to meet Samuel J. Tilden in conference,[3] and while something intervened, August Belmont, Democratic National Chairman, wrote him a long letter, 'private and confidential,' to which he replied with a definition of his attitude toward the Democracy. 'For more than a quarter of a century,' he wrote, 'I have been in my political views and sentiments a Democrat; and I still think that upon questions of finance, commerce, and administration generally the old Democratic principles afford the best guidance.' He affirmed his belief in universal suffrage, but added, as a coaxer, that he was against the proscription of Southern whites.[4] Two days later, he was writing Murat Halstead that he would 'not feel at liberty to decline' the proffered leadership of any party 'opposed to the present leadership.' He certainly had not committed himself to Grant's candidacy, as erroneously stated in Halstead's paper. As Mr. Webster once said, 'I will think of that; yes, sir, I will think of that.' [5]

Meanwhile the Democratic leaders were canvassing his prospects — especially those in New York. If the contest was to be made on military as opposed to civil government, he would be the ideal candidate.[6] On finance they thought him sound. In May, Tilden was informed that his nomination would mean an abundance of 'material aid,' and that his 'negro antecedents' could be got around 'by adopting a plank . . . conceding to each State the management of the franchise question.' [7] Less than a month later, Tilden was assured that Chase was 'out of the question' and

---

[1] Welles, III, 244.    [2] To Bryant, Schuckers, 588.    [3] Schuckers, 563.
[4] *Ibid.*, 584–86.    [5] Warden, 700.    [6] Seymour to Chase, Schuckers, 570–71.
[7] W. S. Hawlet to Tilden, *Tilden Letters*, I, 227.

'would be the weakest man we could have.' [1] Another wrote that
Chase had 'great defects.' [2]   Montgomery Blair thought that
'Chase has not the slightest influence with the only class of Republicans who are disposed to go with us, namely, the Lincoln
men.' [3]   And, to make the situation more confusing, another correspondent wrote urging Tilden to see Chase, since a conference
with men from 'practically every State' had convinced the writer
that he could win.[4]  Thus the swaying fortunes of the Chase candidacy up to the meeting of the Convention.

Meanwhile the rank and file were partial to the handsome, dashing Pendleton for the same reason that made him poison to the
New York intriguers — he was a greenbacker and unable to see
any reason for paying the five-twenty bonds in gold when it was
not so stipulated in the bond. The Eastern Democracy had determined to prevent his nomination, and it was hinted then that
the candidacy of Hendricks was used by New York to break
Pendleton's strength in the West.

Hendricks's candidacy required no explanation.  A sound partisan, able, popular, successful in contests before the people, he had
all the usual qualifications for the nomination. Welles thought he
would 'unite as many as any one.' [5]  Even the 'New York Tribune'
thought him 'able and plausible,' and less obnoxious than Pendleton because 'he has no Eastern prejudices.' [6]  Through all the preliminaries, New York flirted constantly with Hendricks, and the
letters of Tilden fail to reveal the strategy.  One of Tilden's correspondents wrote that 'in no case is it probable that Hendricks
can be nominated and for success he should not be.' [7]  But at the
same time one of the New York leaders was writing that 'the more
I consider the quest, the more I am inclined to favor Hendricks,'
since 'he would make a good candidate.' [8]  The availability of Seymour was constantly being discussed, with that wily politician
stoutly putting aside the crown.

The Convention met, listened to Seymour's powerful speech as
chairman, and settled down to a decision.  Pendleton's forces were
picturesque with ribbons and banners, but in the first days the

---

[1] S. E. Church, *Tilden Letters*, I, 228.     [2] A. Loomis, *ibid.*, I, 229.     [3] *Ibid.*, I, 232.
[4] Barlow, *ibid.*, I, 231.          [5] Welles, III, 394.          [6] July 17, 1868.
[7] Barlow, *Tilden Letters*, I, 216.      [8] Church, *ibid.*, I, 228.

Chase candidacy loomed large. The 'New York Herald' was supporting him, 'The World' was not unfriendly. The streets were noisy with festivities, with orators booming in hotel lobbies and on street corners. Not a few of these were of the silver-tongued tribe from the South, and the eloquent Vance, of North Carolina, was tickling 'The Tribune' with his sarcastic flings at the suffrage plank of the Republican platform. It published, with evident zest, the lines with which he amused the crowd in Union Square:

'To every Southern river shall Negro Suffrage come,
But not to fair New England, for that's too close to hum.' [1]

From the beginning, Chase's hopes ran high. He felt the prize within his grasp, and in his eagerness he wrote a friend on the ground that on suffrage 'I adhere to my old States' Rights doctrine.' Meanwhile, the balloting had begun, with Chase held back as a dark horse. New York gave her vote on the first ballot to Sanford E. Church and then swung to Hendricks. On that ballot, Pendleton led, with Andrew Johnson second. By the eighth ballot, Pendleton had reached the climax of his strength, with Hendricks second and but eighty votes behind. By the sixteenth ballot, Pendleton had lost the lead to Hancock by six votes, and by the twenty-first, with Hancock still in the lead, but losing, Hendricks was but four votes behind. Then the Pendleton leaders went through the form of forcing Seymour, and on the next ballot he was named. Thus the charge of Blaine that the New York leaders never had favored Hendricks.[2] But the day after the nomination, Tilden wrote: 'I had no agency in getting Governor Seymour into his present scrape.' [3] Rutherford B. Hayes wrote that day in his diary that Seymour was named because 'more decidedly against the Greenback theory of Pendleton than any one;' [4] and Ben Butler was certain the convention was dominated by August Belmont in the interest of the bondholders.[5]

Johnson received the news of the nomination without emotion, though clearly 'disturbed and disappointed,' [6] and Chase, pausing in a game of croquet to read the telegram, asked, 'How does Kate take it?' — and turned to his game again.

[1] *New York Tribune*, July 11, 1868.          [2] *Twenty Years*, II, 392.
[3] *Life of Tilden*, I, 211.          [4] *Life of Hayes*, I, 331.
[5] *New York Herald*, November 17, 1868.          [6] Welles, III, 398.

'The die is cast,' commented the 'New York Herald.' 'The Convention has decided that our next President shall be General Grant.' [1] It thought Chase might have won. Young Georges Clemenceau told the 'Paris Temps' that Hendricks would have polled the largest vote.[2]

### V

It was a weird campaign. The candidates were opposite. Seymour was a profound student of government and politics; Grant knew nothing of either. Seymour was a tireless politician; Grant had voted but once before 1864. Seymour was a polished orator; Grant was Orator Mum. Seymour had a long public record in civil service; Grant, none. In training and qualifications, there was no comparison.

The early part of the campaign was deadly dull, and 'The Nation' tried to explain the apathy over Grant's nomination on the ground that he avoided 'the whole of the theatrical apparatus commonly used to excite "enthusiasm."' [3] Seymour was busy with plans for organizing the young in clubs,[4] and Tilden was learning that thirty Washington correspondents could be bought for from three thousand to thirty-five hundred dollars a month through the campaign, since the Republicans conditioned payment on success at the polls.[5] Indeed, the campaign soon developed into a battle of money bags, with the heavier artillery with Grant. August Belmont, Tilden, and C. H. McCormick agreed to contribute ten thousand dollars each to Seymour, but, much to his discomfiture, Jay Cooke had been adopted as the angel of the Republicans. Close personal relations had been established between Grant and Henry Cooke, before whose bank the nominee often waited patiently in his carriage to drive the financier about town or out into the country; and early in 1867 the Grants had been regally entertained at Jay Cooke's castle near Philadelphia. The raid on Cooke began before the nomination, when he had been cajoled out of five thousand dollars for the spring election in New Hampshire by W. E. Chandler, the liaison officer between the politicians and the financier. Early in June, he was asking Jay's

[1] July 10, 1868.  [2] Clemenceau, 205.  [3] July 16, 1868.
[4] *Tilden Letters*, I, 242.  [5] R. W. Lathan, M.C., *Tilden Letters*, I, 240.

more approachable brother how much more than ten thousand dollars he could give, and promising immunity from further demands if the amount named were doubled. 'If you fix a large amount,' he added cunningly, 'we can get more than otherwise from M. O. Roberts and A. T. Stewart, etc.'[1] But as the campaign progressed, the demands increased, and Cooke found himself the quartermaster-general. Then came the demand for State funds, particularly heavy from Pennsylvania, where Simon Cameron was levying on the rich having governmental dealings, and building up the powerful machine which was to dominate the State for generations. Thus Chandler amassed an enormous fund for that day, sending as much as fifty thousand dollars to Indiana and forty thousand dollars to Pennsylvania.[2]

Meanwhile the press was fighting valiantly, and a young German cartoonist, Thomas Nast, in the employ of 'Harper's Weekly,' was doing such effective work that Grant afterward was to ascribe his election to 'the sword of Sheridan and the pencil of Thomas Nast.'[3] The Republicans were accusing Democrats of murdering negroes and 'loyal men,' and Democrats were retaliating by declaring Republicans committed to the social equality of the races.

## VI

In the midst of the campaign appeared the novel of Anna E. Dickinson, 'What Answer?' sympathetically telling the story of the marriage of a rich young white man with a colored woman, and the 'New York World' was in ecstasies. The novelist, beginning life as a factory worker, had educated herself, and lost her position because of her demonstrations against General McClellan. Instantly adopted by the Radicals, she had taken to the stump and scored a brilliant success in the Northern States. Sophomoric and extravagant, she was saved from absurdity by her sincerity, grace, and prettiness. Thus her novel was accepted by the Democrats as authoritative Republican doctrine. Not least among the crimes of the Radicals, thought the 'New York World,' was their spoiling of this 'nice little woman.' The scolding of Democrats, bristling in the novel, was ascribed to Republican politicians as 'a

[1] Oberholtzer, *Cooke*, II, 69.     [2] *Ibid.*, II, 71.     [3] Paine, *Nast*, 129.

good investment for the New England market.' And the book? 'Three hundred pages of a literary mess which can only be likened to a hash of Sylvanus Cobb with the editorials of "The Tribune."'[1] And such filth! 'In some countries such a book could not appear; in others, its authoress would only be laughed at as a dirty chatter-box.' And what treason to the Radicals, too, to make the heroine but three fourths black! Wendell Phillips should look after this straying sister. Some one should 'educate her up to the full glory of the wool head and the tar heel.'[2] The Republican press was chary in its praise, and retaliated by waving the 'bloody shirt' and filling its columns with 'outrage' stories from the South. The 'New York Tribune' was painting blood-curdling pictures of the savagery of the Southern whites. In Arkansas, 'the atrocious murder of thousands of good men, white and black,' with hundreds of unoffending blacks tied to trees, whipped unmercifully, and murdered. A reign of terror![3] William E. Chandler was writing from New Orleans that 'lawlessness and violence rule the city . . . with Republicans of prominence in hiding from assassins.'[4] Shocking tales, too, from Alabama and Texas. To dramatize the 'issue,' delegations of carpetbaggers hurried to Washington to importune Johnson for protection against the slaughter of 'loyal men,'[5] and even 'The Nation'[6] was waving the 'bloody shirt.' It was urging Grant's election to get rid of 'spiles' and 'claims.' No mere politician, he. 'Bred in a very different and very much better school.'[7]

And so the fight in the North waxed warmer, with much parading with banners and torches, with packed halls screaming approval of all manner of foolishness, with orators straining their voices above the traffic of street corners. In Philadelphia, a vast outpouring of soldiers, marching, marching all day long, with flags, garlands, inscriptions everywhere, at an enormous cost. And the next night in New York the counter demonstration, with forty thousand marchers, allegorical floats, featuring the goddess of liberty, draped and beautifully posed. Tammany had staged this spectacle, and the goddess was 'a powerfully built Irish girl, wearing her red cap with an audacious air, one hand resting on a pikestaff, while she held some broken chains in the other.' Georges Clemenceau had seen both demonstrations and was amazed.[1]

Thus, on a smaller scale, throughout the North.

## VII

And in the South? There, in anguish of spirit, the old-line Whigs were forced to go over to the despised Democrats, and some of these unwilling converts appeared on Democratic platforms with evident embarrassment and humiliation.[2] There was no measuring the bitterness toward the few old-line Democrats who went over to the negroes and the carpetbaggers.

Under Wade Hampton's generalship, a gesture of conciliation toward the reasoning element in the North met only with jeers. A brilliant son of Charles Francis Adams, a brother of Henry, with the traditional Adams indifference to popularity, had cast his lot with the Democracy of Massachusetts, to become its leader. An eloquent speaker, delightful conversationalist, John Quincy Adams II had attracted national attention by his sane views on reconstruction, and he was invited by Hampton to speak in South Carolina. 'What stronger reply could there be to the misrepresentations of the Radicals,' wrote Hampton, 'than to hear John Quincy Adams talk of Union and fraternal relations on the soil of South Carolina? Would it not be as the past speaking to the present?' Thus Adams was invited to 'a consultation upon the living principles of our free institutions,' since 'it is no longer a question of party, but of social life.'[3] Speaking in Charleston, with Hampton in the chair, Adams said that, after some days of intimate association with Hampton, it was safe to say that 'if he is a rebel, he is just such a rebel as I am and no more.'[4] The orator pronounced the Southern people as loyal as the Northern, and ascribed the trouble with the negroes to the work of the carpetbaggers.[5] The Adams speeches, soundest of their day, were published in the North without effect, albeit Greeley found in them 'evidence of ability and an aptitude for public affairs.'[6]

[1] Clemenceau, 249–51.          [2] Mrs. Smedes, 240.
[3] *New York Herald*, October 9, 1868.          [4] *Ibid.*, October 20, 1868.
[5] *Ibid.* October 19, 1868.          [6] *New York Tribune*, October 19, 1868.

The most aggressive fight of all was waged by the Democracy of Georgia, where high tide was reached in the Bush Arbor meeting in Atlanta. It was blistering hot, the air filled with stifling dust, but the uncomfortable plank seats were packed tight with men and women who sat five hours listening to the orators.[1] Ben Hill, summoned from his retreat at Indian Spring, weak from illness, and unprepared, was not expected by the twenty thousand people, who sprang to their feet on his arrival, in a five-minute demonstration. Pale as death, he rose, and plunged into one of the classic invectives of American oratory.

'There is not a single Southern man who advocates the acceptance of this reconstruction scheme who was not bought, and bought with a price by your enemies,' he began. The issue was whether there should be a restored Union of equal States or a new Union of unequal States. Grant stood for the latter; Seymour, for the former. The Supreme Court had made up its mind that the reconstruction measures were unconstitutional, but it was 'too cowardly to declare the decision.' Mincing no words, cutting and slashing, with sarcasm and invective, he held the twenty thousand literally spellbound, and closed with the admonition 'never to suffer a single native renegade who voted for the vassalage of these States and the disgrace of your children to darken your doors or to speak to any member of your family.'[2] As he concluded, the Old and New South sprang to its feet, the impetuous Toombs throwing his arms around the orator, while Henry Grady, then a boy, stood by the platform with burning eyes and flaming cheeks. Once more Ben Hill had dared the lightning, and dynamitized his party in Georgia.

In North Carolina, old-line Whigs put on the armor for Seymour, though Governor Worth would have preferred Andrew Johnson or John Quincy Adams.[3] Sentiment everywhere there seemed for Seymour, but Holden would name the poll-keepers, 'and his militia will, if possible, be used to overawe the timid.'[4] Men like Vance would have swept over the State, but they were too poor to pay traveling expenses.[5]

Thus, despite the army, Democrats of the South, with former

[1] Avery, 392.   [2] Hill, 308–19.   [3] Worth, to Baxter, ii, 1226.
[4] Ibid., to Montgomery Blair, ii, 1243.   [5] Ibid.

Whigs at their side for the first time, were in the field, and fighting.

It was soon evident, however, that nothing could stem the tide, and with Frank Blair's uncompromising letter against the acceptance of reconstruction, the Wise Men of the East among Democrats cringed and crawled, and cried *mea culpa* to the enemy, with Manton Marble's silly demand for Blair's removal from the ticket. Tilden sent an emissary to Johnson in an appeal for Administration support, and a satisfactory interview was granted. Seymour, persuasive and powerful, at length took the stump, while Grant sat in silence at Galena. When the October elections went badly, stupid Democrats again proposed to change the ticket and made their party ridiculous; and Grant won a signal triumph at the polls. Seymour had carried but four Northern States, but in Georgia, where his followers had not been too cowardly or too gentlemanly to fight, he won. Even with the victory, one impressive fact is found — with 5,716,082 votes cast, Grant had a popular majority of but 309,584.

But the Radicals now had their President.

### VIII

Meanwhile, Johnson, by no means deserted, observed his sixtieth birthday with an elaborate party for his grandchildren — perhaps the most beautiful of the sort the mansion has ever seen.[1] The Marine Band played, and Marini managed the dances and the grand promenade; and after dancing in their bright costumes in the East Room, the children marched into the State dining-room, where a long table was spread with all the delicacies. Johnson entered joyously into the festivity, and his invalid wife, for the second time during her tragic life in the White House, descended from her room to look upon the pretty scene. But the Grant children, who had been invited, were not there.[2]

When, three days later, great numbers pushed through the rain to the New Year's reception, the wife of one of the impeachers was disgusted because the plain people had crowded in — 'a fearful crowd from the streets, their feet muddy and clothing dripping

[1] Crook, 144.
[2] Welles, III, 483; Mrs. Logan, 240; *New York Herald*, December 30, 1868.

from the rain.' [1]  Quite early, a stern-visaged, bearded man was helped from his carriage by attendants, and the crippled Morton, who had voted for impeachment, warmly grasped Johnson's hand, and was cordially received. A little later, the crowd gasped its astonishment, as a bulky man with drooping eyelids hove in view and vigorously shook the hand of Johnson. Ben Butler, less embarrassed than the spectators, stood for five minutes in smiling conversation with the man he had called a 'criminal.' The news that he had attended flashed over the town, and at Evarts's reception it was wickedly suggested the meeting must have been pleasant. 'Yes, sir: a very pleasant and cordial meeting,' said Butler. 'My unpleasantness was political, not personal. I don't believe in carrying political disputes into social life.' [2]

Thereafter, until the end, Johnson's popularity seemed to increase, and he was overwhelmed with visitors.[3] He was methodically preparing for his departure, arranging his files and papers, calling in and paying bills. With steamship companies offering him transportation to any European port, he was longing for the quiet of the home in Greeneville.[4] His last reception, two days before he left, was most brilliant of all, with five thousand, including the charming Harriet Lane, mistress of the mansion during the Buchanan régime, in attendance. It was agreed that 'it exceeded any other . . . in brilliancy and the immensity of the throng.' [5]

The last night the mansion was closed to all but intimates at six o'clock, and Senator Hendricks, with others, called. Johnson, planning to be up late for tardy bills from Congress, was in perfect health, his energies undiminished.[6] He had refused two months before to ride in the carriage with Grant to the inauguration, and at length declined to attend the ceremonies, on the ground that he could not afford 'to witness the inauguration of a man whom he knew to be untruthful, faithless, and false.' [7] The morning of the 4th found him working quietly among his papers, surrounded by the Cabinet, and a few minutes before noon he rose, grasped the hand of each Secretary, descended to the portico, entered a car-

[1] Mrs. Logan, 238.                              [2] New York Herald, January 2, 1869.
[3] Ibid., February 27, 1869.                      [4] Crook, 145.
[5] New York World, New York Herald, March 3, 1869.
[6] New York World, March 4, 1869.                 [7] Welles, III, 500.

riage, and was driven to the home of his friend John F. Coyle, editor of 'The Intelligencer,' where he remained until his departure to Tennessee.[1]

His storm-rocked Administration was over.

## IX

Grant rode to the Capitol alone, and delivered his brief inaugural address, which Julian thought 'certainly nothing to brag on.' [2] It was observed that he bore himself with a frigid and repelling dignity — 'no geniality, no familiar jest, hardly a smile.' [3] His easy election had convinced him of his complete independence of the political forces with which he had been surrounded.[4]

Then, with the announcement of the Cabinet, the country gasped.

There had been some uneasiness because of his reticence, and his curt refusal to give Henry J. Raymond a line on his policy,[5] but Julian, in familiar conversation at Grant's home a week before, had found him communicative on the squandering of public lands and the Tenure-of-Office Act. 'Simple and natural as a child,' wrote Julian.[6] The speculation on the personnel of the Cabinet proved ludicrously wrong. The politicians, simulating confidence in his judgment, were trembling in their boots, and, when they approached him timidly with the suggestion that the leaders were curious about the Cabinet, Grant stopped puffing his cigar to say that Mrs. Grant shared that curiosity. William Cullen Bryant was almost pleased, delighted with Grant's 'frankness' on politics, and was sure he was going to end plundering and corruption, though the purging process would cost him 'one third of the Republican strength.' [7] Others were fearful that he lacked 'affirmative qualities' and doubted that much good could come from 'a military sort of government, the only kind he comprehends.' [8] Thus the gossip ran, and then, with the announcement of the Cabinet, a bomb fell with a mighty boom.

A commonplace Illinois Congressman, without a single qualification, for State Department; A. T. Stewart, the merchant prince,

---

[1] Welles, III, 436-42.    [2] MS. Diary, March 7, 1869.    [3] Badeau, 159.

[4] Ibid., 157.    [5] Ibid., 156    [6] MS. Diary, February 28, 1869.

[7] Godwin, II, 276.    [8] Bigelow, Retrospections, IV, 187.

with a distinct legal disqualification, for the Treasury; Borie, rich,
but unknown to politics or public men, for the Navy — these
startled the politicians. No objections were heard to Rawlins for
the War Department; there was universal praise for Cox, for the
Interior, able, clean, tested — a delightful conversationalist, too;
and while some mystery attached to the choice of Hoar for Attorney-General, he was a distinguished jurist of fine stock and
flawless character. But how had Grant assembled such an aggregation of incongruities? Smug-minded reformers who had rejoiced
over Grant's snubbing of the advice of practical politicians, began
to be less cocksure of their wisdom. Stewart — why, no one really
knew his politics, but every one, save the President, knew that because of his engagement in trade and commerce, and his connection with public lands and securities, his appointment was illegal.
Borie — no one knew him outside of Philadelphia, where he was
known for his wealth and social standing, and it is said that one
Senator had never heard his name before its announcement to the
Senate.[1] No one had greater cause for astonishment than Borie
himself. Calling on Grant the day before the inauguration, he was
asked facetiously, apropos of Grant's statement that a Pennsylvanian would be appointed, if he had called 'to learn the name of
the man from Philadelphia.' He laughingly disclaimed any such
thought, and read of his appointment on the train *en route* home.[2]
'Who in the world is Borie?' asked the 'New York Herald.'
'Where does he come from? What's his business. Borie! Borie!
That's a queer nomination.'[3] As for Washburne as Secretary of
State, it was to laugh.

The reaction of the press reflected the general amazement. If,
as said, Rawlins had warned Grant against raising a rival to the
Cabinet, he was safe,[4] but he was not safe from ridicule. 'The
World' thought that in deviating from the beaten path, Grant had
'deviated into absolute oddity' in making 'such a Cabinet as no
politician would have advised.'[5] 'A little obscure,' the 'Springfield Republican' thought the selections. 'A strange medley of
obscure men, chosen without rhyme or reason,' thought the 'Albany Argus.' The 'Boston Post' was positive the country would

[1] McCulloch, 350.          [2] Badeau, 163.          [3] March 6, 1869.
[4] Badeau, 164.             [5] March 6, 1869.

'not become excited over the cast.' 'The Nation' was sure the
selections 'did disappoint his [Grant's] friends and admirers, and
probably his friends and admirers rather than his enemies.' But
the 'New Haven Palladium' rejoiced that 'the reign of the politicians has passed,' and the 'Philadelphia Enquirer' reassured the
worried with the strange reflection that Grant 'is the possessor of
those analytical powers which enable men to judge character
with close and correct appreciation.' [1] Julian, a friendly critic,
was forced to record that 'when the Cabinet was announced, the
disappointment was deep and universal among Republicans,' and
that 'every one thinks that Grant has made a serious blunder'; 'if
he had consulted politicians . . . more, it would have been better.' [2]
Young Henry Adams, then in Washington, was to remember years
later that 'Grant's nominations had the singular effect of making
the hearer ashamed, not so much of Grant, as of himself,' and to
conclude that 'a great soldier might be a baby politician.' [3] Soon
the impression became fixed that in two instances the appointments had been inspired by Grant's deep reverence for money.
Stewart and Borie were rich, and it appeared that the former had
made considerable gifts to Grant, without an ulterior motive, and
the latter had entertained him handsomely at his home. Bigness
always appealed to the bluff soldier — big fortunes particularly.
It was a weakness born of his days of poverty.

It was on the confirmation of Stewart that Grant was most determined, and he was not disconcerted by the reminder that the
law forbade. The law? Then change the law! One day Carl
Schurz found Grant writing. 'I am only writing a Message to the
Senate,' he said, and it was the Message asking Congress to set the
law aside. But Congress declined, and Stewart made way for
Boutwell, the impeacher, and in a short while Borie retired and
George M. Robeson, a New Jersey lawyer, not of the first order,
became head of the Navy. Washburne was speedily transferred to
the French mission, and Hamilton Fish was made Secretary of
State — an excellent choice. He had made a good record as a Whig
in Congress, and his natural conservatism had held him to the old
party till the last. Cultured, wealthy, and socially fitted, he was

---

[1] Press comments quoted in *New York World*, March 6, 1869.
[2] MS. Diary, March 7, 1869.          [3] Henry Adams, 263.

invaluable not only as an official, but as a social mentor of the Grants.

But the apprehensions of party leaders did not pass with the final organization of the Cabinet, for it was evident that Grant's unfamiliarity with government and reluctance to consult would get him into endless trouble. Both Hoar and Fish were embarrassed by appointments urged upon them. The former, asked to make a soldier Chief Justice of a territory because he had lost a leg, managed to hint that 'mere absence of legs is not a sufficient qualification for a judicial position,' and Grant laughingly abandoned the idea.[1] One day the Senate Foreign Relations Committee was considering the nomination of a Minister to Belgium. 'Can any member give us any information concerning Mr. Jones?' Sumner asked gravely. It had been whispered that he was interested in horses. 'Well,' replied Morton, 'Mr. Jones is about the most elegant gentleman that ever presided over a livery stable.' The nomination was not confirmed.[2] The 'New York Herald,' commenting, said the Senators were disgusted.[3]

More disturbing to reformers was the disposition to appoint the 'lame ducks' of Congress, 'turned out by constituents for excellent reasons,'[4] and when the disreputable Ashley, the impeacher, was made Governor of Montana, 'The Nation,' shocked, denounced the confirmation by one vote as 'a scandal' — all the more scandalous since Charles Sumner voted to confirm.[5] The more facetious 'New York World' explained that Ashley was 'neither the cousin of General Grant, nor the aunt of Mr. Casey, for to him President Grant had truly been "a little less than kin and more than kind."'[6] Indeed, there were grumblings about nepotism within a month of the inauguration; within two months the 'Chicago Tribune' was saying that the Administration's moral power 'has been frittered away by small absurdities,' and that 'there never was an administration with more good intentions at heart and less aptitude for carrying them into effect.'[7] Thus the Administration opened with the Opposition jeering, and its friends apologetic. It was not an auspicious start.

[1] *Memoir of Hoar*, 175.     [2] Schurz, 309–10.     [3] April 16, 1869.
[4] *The Nation*, April 15, 1869.     [5] *Ibid.*, April 6, 1869.
[6] April 6, 1869.     [7] Quoted, *The Nation*, May 6, 1869.

X

Meanwhile, with the Opposition press quoting from Johnson's letter refusing the New York gift of an equipage and horses, Johnson had gone home. Greeted cordially at Baltimore, he had said he would rather be a free citizen than be inaugurated President 'over the ruins of the Constitution,' and 'rather be a free man than be President, and be a slave.' [1] Facing his old neighbors at Greeneville, he spoke feelingly of his earlier years of poverty and struggle, and in conclusion he lifted his hands and quoted the words of Wolsey:

> 'An old man, broken with the storms of state,
> Is come to lay his weary bones among ye;
> Give him a little earth for charity!'

A little rest, and he was on his travels again, speaking in all the leading towns of Tennessee, the plain people massed about him enthusiastically everywhere. Was it mere curiosity? The old mountain friends had gone over to the Radicals, but Johnson's activities were watched with misgivings in the North.

[1] *New York World*, March 12, 1869.

# CHAPTER XII

## WASHINGTON: THE SOCIAL BACKGROUND

### I

NO one visiting Washington immediately after the war, or throughout the period with which we are concerned, would have carried away memories of physical beauty. The overgrown village of the fifties had not improved under the rough usage of the war, and while Henry Adams thought it 'unchanged,' with nothing that 'betrayed growth,' [1] he was probably thinking of the inner social circles, for the four-year struggle had left its marks. The streets were streaks of mud, and at the second Lincoln inauguration a diplomat's carriage had been mired to the hub on F Street, and curious crowds had amused themselves by watching the dignitary being carried, with all his gold lace, to safety in the arms of a servant. [2] The street was paved soon thereafter from the Treasury to Judiciary Square, and plans were on foot for the redemption of the avenue from the mud. This thoroughfare of the state processions had fallen into such disrepute that merchants had threatened to move elsewhere. [3] The curtailment of the army camps about only offered a better view of the ravages wrought. The surrounding forts, deserted now, were crumbling to decay, and the shed-like corrals for army horses and wagons were abandoned to the town toughs, who found them a convenient rendezvous. [4] Street cars, with jingling bells, had displaced the old rickety omnibuses of pre-war days, mingling their rumbling and clanging with the cries of negro venders of oysters, milk, and vegetables in the streets. [5] The influx of population due to war had not diminished, and, for a time, there was a dearth of houses and rooms, but quite soon all this was changed. There was a building boom, and the rich, finding the capital entertaining, began the construction of pretentious homes. By the early seventies there was an air of smartness to the town.

[1] *Education of Henry Adams*, 245.   [2] *New York Herald*, July 8, 1865.
[3] Nicolay, 388.   [4] *Ibid.*, 387–88.
[5] *New York World*, January 21, 1870.

Drawn by the spectacular struggles, all sorts of men and women poured into the capital, and the promenader found a stroll diverting, mingling with the laughing freedmen, listening to the noisy venders, laughing, as did Godkin, of 'The Nation,' at the provincials who flocked a little awesomely to the Capitol to feast their eyes on greatness. That which impressed Godkin most in the members of the House was 'the cleanness of their shirts,' and he was sure that 'we underrate their honesty and overrate their intelligence.'[1]

In front of the Willard, a long row of hacks with black drivers. Up and down the avenue, after it was paved, a great parade of fine equipages, for fashion had a weakness for such display. A favorite drive was out to the park of the Soldiers' Home, from which one could look down upon the town;[2] another to Rock Creek Park, 'as wild as the Rocky Mountains,' where 'here and there a negro log cabin alone disturbed the dogwood and the judas tree and the laurel.'[3] Ugly as was the sprawling town, there was charm enough in its environs, and Henry Adams thought that 'the Potomac and its tributaries squandered beauty.'[4] Beauty, however, was less sought than entertainment by the official sojourners and the tourists, and of this there was enough. The streets were studded thick with bar-rooms, for it was a day of heavy drinking, and there had been times when 'the whole House was drunk.'[5] Gambling was the prevailing vice, and he who would tempt fortune had not far to go. At the close of the war, more than a hundred gambling-houses flourished, but with the passing of the soldiers these rapidly diminished, and five years later there were but seventeen. The most exclusive of these, within a stone's throw of the Willard, catered only to the rich and prominent, and the stranger was turned away at the door. So thriving was the business of John Chamberlain with Senators and Congressmen that, in 1873, he acquired the former British Legation on Connecticut Avenue, at I and Seventeenth Streets, at a cost of one hundred and fifty thousand dollars. It was a handsome brick structure, with broad bay windows, mansard roof, turreted towers, and massive gables, separated from the street by trees and shrubs, flowers and English ivy, the latter climbing the portico. This, for several years, was the favorite

[1] Ogden, I, 311–12.   [2] *New York World*, June 13, 1871.
[3] Henry Adams, 268.   [4] *Ibid.*   [5] *Marse Henry*, II, 23.

lounging-place of many statesmen high in the councils of the state. Chamberlain served meals which piqued the taste of the epicure; and after a satisfying dinner, and a smoke in the luxuriously furnished lounging-room, the statesmen could go upstairs, where were many small rooms, and sit down at the black walnut tables for play. At midnight, every night, the players paused, for obsequious and discreet waiters appeared with a lunch and the compliments of the master. Many were shocked at this desecration of His Majesty's Legation, at this invasion of the most exclusive residential neighborhood, and there was much shaking of heads and quiet laughing, until at length John Sherman presented his resolution on the vice of gambling.[1] If the tourist cat could not look at the kings at Chamberlain's, he could, if willing to pay the price, see them all in the famous restaurant of John Welcher, sacred still to the memory of statesmen sleeping in the dust. This incomparable Boniface of foreign birth was a gentleman of imagination and taste. Dreaming over his bookkeeping in his winehouse in New York, and utterly ignorant of the business of running a restaurant, he betook himself to Washington in war days to try his fortune. On the avenue he opened a restaurant, and soon the rumors ran that nowhere could be found such rich old wines, such lovely, witty women, as in the walnut-paneled rooms at Welcher's. Soon every statesman and politician and lobbyist found his way to its cheer. The lobbyists made it their headquarters, close to the wine-cellars and the hearts of the Nation's lawmakers; and for ten years much of American history was made within the paneled walls. Here the lobbyist mellowed the hard heart of the Senator, the lover met his mistress, the friends of Chase plotted against Lincoln, the Radicals against Johnson, the Crédit Mobilier conspirators against the Treasury. Here the fascinating Blaine, more than ever ingratiating in the easy, graceful talk of the table, wined and dined his way to the Speakership and party leadership, and it was here that Forney and the others planned the nomination of Grant. When the host passed on, it was to be written of his place that 'there is not a measure noted for importance in the last ten years but can be traced to these rooms'; that 'when the table was spread and the gas lit, what was

[1] *New York World*, March 20, 1870; February 3, 1875; January 15, 1876.

said or done or sought or pursued was of no interest to John.' He
who furnished the rare wines, the epicurean dinners, the cozy atmosphere, the seclusion, the charm and beauty of Welcher's deserves to live in history, for he gave the setting for great events.[1]

And there, too, was the restaurant of Sam Ward, a veritable gentleman of the world, grand master in the management of a dinner,
a genius in cuisine, a connoisseur in wines, and a famous *raconteur*,
who exchanged confidences with Senators, and remained the soul
of discretion. He moved among his guests with the grace and
bonhomie of a private host, pausing in passing at a senatorial table
to tell a story, gallantly presenting a bouquet to a lady, pressing
some French candies on a child — the friend of every one down to
the negro on the hack outside his door. It was said of him that he
'would have made a capital companion for Sheridan or Tom
Moore.' [2]

Among the hotels, that of Wormley at H and Fifteenth Streets,
was most exclusive, favoring family patronage and entertaining
politicians like Colfax, statesmen like Caleb Cushing, and the
diplomatic set. The Marquis and Madame de Noailles, and Señor
and Madame Flores lived here and entertained.[3] But the Willard
was most imposing, the new Ebbitt was to have its day, and the
National, where Clay had died, still drew its full quota of public
men. For a time, nothing was more popular than the hotel hops,
managed by a select committee of the leaders of fashion,[4] and there
was much private entertaining in the hotels, too. It was at the
Willard, soon after Miss Foote became the wife of Senator John
B. Henderson, that she entertained elaborately at receptions on
the eve of her husband's farewell to senatorial life.[5]

This was the season that opened the era of extravagance which
was to have its tragedies. Senator Zack Chandler startled the
town, forgetful of the golden fifties, by the prodigality of his entertainments. His imposing house on H Street blazed with light from
top to bottom many times that winter, and guests went away to
gossip long over the music and the flowers and the elaborate table
'looking like a miniature model of Pekin, with confectionery of all

[1] *Washington Capital*, April 4, 1875; quoted, *New York World*, April 7, 1875.
[2] Forney, I, 394.          [3] *New York World*, January 18, 1873.
[4] *New York Herald*, July 8, 1865.          [5] *Ibid.*, January 29, 1869.

kinds and colors framed into temples, towers, minarets, and pagodas.'[1] It was a merry season for the daughter of the household, and soon, 'unspoiled' by the adulation, she was the bride of young Eugene Hale, of Maine, described at the wedding as 'pale like one who has worked too hard.'[2] Another year, and Washington was really gay again, with 'diamonds in every hotel parlor, equipages on the Georgetown Road, capitalists in the Senate, state dinners unsurpassed among officials.' The old families that had attended Mrs. Gwin's balls in the pre-war days still held aloof, but never had toilettes been more sumptuous than those seen at the receptions of the ladies of the Cabinet,[3] and at the White House 'young men in hemstitched shirt-fronts gazed inquisitively at promenaders with undergraduate freedom.'[4] There was indubitably a change in the tone of official society. The *habitués* of the modest brick houses on I and J and K Streets, with their plate glass windows and shining doorsteps, donned their pink and blue dresses and pale gloves and sedately went to Grant's receptions as of old,[5] but there was more of the mob spirit in society, and this prevailed. True a few, like Kate Chase Sprague, were coldly to shut the door and become more exclusive, but few could afford such independence. Before the period was over, the mob, pushing into private houses to satisfy its curiosity, was to rush the Butler mansion on Capitol Hill, the home of a rich Senator, to stare, quite frankly, at the hostess, 'weary and heavy laden with precious stones,' dig their feet into the rich nap of rugs and carpets, and finger the furniture and upholstery.[6] Social functions lost something of their distinction, and receptions became 'an epidemic,' great throngs moving from one to another.[7] The social demands on modest official salaries were severely felt and there was much complaining. 'Ten pairs of lavender kid gloves makes quite an item'; 'a coach in livery, at five dollars a night and ten dollars on reception nights, cuts in'; 'one dinner at Welcher's takes all the money left.'[8] What with gambling, drinking, dining

[1] *New York Herald*, Febuary 2, 1869.
[2] *New York World*, December 23, 1871.
[3] *Ibid.*, January 16, 1870.
[4] *Ibid.*, January 14, 1870.
[5] *Ibid.*, January 16, 1870.
[6] *Indianapolis News*; quoted, *New York World*, March 24, 1876.
[7] *New York Herald*, February 14, 1870.
[8] *New York World*, March 23, 1873.

at Welcher's, driving, entertaining, dressing, the budget of many
a household failed to show a balance.

## II

Men of real distinction walked the avenue without attracting
notice and were overlooked by the hostesses. One, too picturesque
to escape attention, was frequently met on the street, tall, vigorous, portly, with bright eyes and florid complexion, swinging along
like an athlete, and looking like Santa Claus, with his flowing
beard. 'There goes Walt Whitman,' a young lady is heard saying
to her companion. She turns curiously. 'And is THAT the author
of "Leaves of Grass"?' she says. 'I might have known it,' [1] for
'Leaves of Grass' made him quite impossible, socially, and Harlan, Johnson's Secretary of the Interior, and a high priest of his
church, had sanctimoniously made it the pretext for dismissing
the poet from his department. Now a clerk in the office of the
Attorney-General, he, of necessity, lives cheaply, merely 'roost-
ing,' as he said, in a tiny room of a lodging-house and eating in the
cheaper restaurants. By day and night he may be seen striding
along on long rambles which take him into the country, and from
his little nook of an office, with pictures of Tennyson and John
Burroughs over his desk, he can look out over the river to the Virginia hills, and upon the unfinished Washington Monument. [2]
Later, his department moved from the Treasury to the Freedmen's Bank Building, where he was given a side room commanding
a view of brick walls. [3] Ignored by the hostesses and the politicians,
he had a friend holding a clerkship at the Treasury, and frequently
John Burroughs would stride out into the woods with the poet. No
one cared for the naturalist, either, and the cronies were left alone.
It was about the time that a breezy Westerner lingered awhile in
the rooms of Senator Stewart at Fourteenth and F Streets, to terrorize the landlady with his carelessness with matches and tobacco
and to find infinite amusement in the Vanity Fair that had no interest in Mark Twain. [4] Julia Ward Howe would run in and out
of the town, to be courted by the old Abolitionists and Radicals,
and Gail Hamilton, plain, short, plump, with curls of light hair

[1] *New York World*, January 21, 1870.
[2] *Ibid.*, April 1, 1871.
[3] *Ibid.*, December 24, 1871.
[4] Stewart, *Reminiscences*, 219.

clustering around her head, was invited to dinners because of her intimacy with the Blaines, but there was little literary atmosphere in the Washington of those times.[1] In a prosy little cottage in Georgetown, by the canal, dwelt a short-sighted, absent-minded little woman writing reams for Bonner's 'Ledger,' but the stories of Mrs. Southworth have no association with literature.[2] Anna Dickinson, who wrote and lectured, was socially acceptable in political circles, for had she not thundered on the stump? [3] Those with an artistic urge found their way occasionally to the studio of Vinnie Ream, to see her 'Miriam,' but she had lost caste with the politicians during the impeachment.[4]

Ever and anon, the politicians had a literary evening with John W. Forney in his apartments at 'The Mills House' on Capitol Hill, and, let it be recorded as part payment for his sins, the poets and painters were invited, and he had a real salon. There one might meet Thad Stevens and Grant; Prentice, of the 'Louisville Courier-Journal'; and Joseph Medill, of the 'Chicago Tribune'; Elliott, the portrait painter; and Brady, the photographer of the war; and see Edwin Forrest and hear him recite. For there were recitations, vocal and instrumental music, and good conversation, and there were memories hovering about the rooms, for Lincoln had been a guest.[5] But, alas, the cynical smiled or sneered, and it was whispered about that these literary evenings were but real estate lobby parties, and that Grant should not countenance them by his presence.[6] Indeed, the cautious might well ponder on the motive behind some invitations, and a few did. When 'Boss' Shepherd invited the scrupulously honest Michael Kerr to one of his parties, the latter indignantly replied that he 'would as soon enter a house of prostitution.'

Even so, those of literary tastes were not wholly in a desert where no fountain was springing. Fortunate was he who was invited to the table of Sumner, to spend an evening among his books and pictures, and listen to his monologues; and there was good talk and lofty thinking in the simpler home of Carl Schurz. Then, Horatio King was giving his famous literary parties with his

[1] New York World, February 25, 1872.  [2] Ibid., January 30, 1872.
[3] Ibid., February 19, 1871.  [4] Ibid., October 20, 1872.
[5] Forney, i, 75.  [6] New York Herald, February 22, 1870.

daughter, where one might meet Henry Adams, and linger until the lights were turned out at midnight, without missing the dances.[1]

## III

The society of the period had its pathetic side — a few women, once the toasts of the town, a little *passée* now, were looking on a bit pensively, perhaps. Peering from the windows of a house on I Street near Twentieth, one might see a sweet-faced old lady, still handsome, in whose petticoats the Jackson Administration had become entangled, for Peggy O'Neal Eaton, home from her travels, was living there in seclusion.[2] At receptions and dinners, one was sure to encounter a strikingly interesting woman with gray hair, and be presented to the wife of Frémont, who had been the dashing Jessie Benton of the Bodisco wedding and the elopement.[3] One year a ' beautiful and fascinating' old lady, who had presided at the White House almost thirty years before, sat in the seat of honor at Grant's table, but Mrs. John Tyler had a lonely season, because wives of officials insisted she should call first on them.[4]

The old was passing, or had passed, and a new society had preempted the field. One day the old house where Sue Decatur played her harp, and Mrs. Livingston charmed the gravest men, and her daughter Cora was driven beneath the mistletoe by Van Buren, and Clay nursed his disappointment was reopened with a blaze of glory at a dinner costing one hundred and fifty dollars a plate. The salads were served in dishes of ice, and Roman punches in beautifully cut ice goblets. General Fitzgerald Beale, bringing his gold from California, with two dashing daughters, had taken the Decatur house, whence one of the girls sallied forth in colonial costume to the fascination of King Kalakaua, and another issued to delight all promenaders by strolling about with a Scotch staghound, the size of a small pony, the gift of a foreign nobleman. One was to become the wife of the last Ambassador of the Romanoffs, and the other of John R. McLean, and to remain a social leader for forty years.

[1] *New York World*, December 23, 1871.
[2] *Cincinnati Commercial*; quoted, *New York World*, September 20, 1868.
[3] *Ibid.*, January 15, 1871.
[4] *New York World*, quoted from *Louisville Courier-Journal*, April 26, 1874.

In 1868, Henry Adams thought 'Lafayette Square was society,' since 'within a few hundred yards . . . one found all one's acquaintances,' and 'beyond the Square the country began.' But that was Henry Adams's society, and the other was not so circumscribed. At that time the invasion of the rich and fashionable had not begun, and 'no literary or scientific man, no artist, no gentleman without office . . . had lived there.' Few in the social set had known the society of a great city, and 'the happy village was innocent of a club.' On bright spring mornings society fared forth to the Pennsylvania Station to see its friends depart. An easy society it was, simple, human, almost genial, able to find amusement 'without houses or carriages or jewels or toilettes, or pavements or shops.' Such the almost pastoral picture of the capital in the last year of Johnson's stormy administration.[1]

Another year, and the change began, with society divided into the 'exclusives' and the mob; the former composed of the old residential families and such of the new as 'met outside of politics.' The politicians invited by these were gentlemen of some real distinction. The mob embraced all who crashed the gates.[2] The politicians could not afford to be exclusive and had to smile on vulgarians and bores. 'Had a large dinner,' wrote Mrs. Blaine, 'mainly of odds and ends — I mean people to whom I owe a dinner. I was, with few exceptions, indifferent to the people.'[3] Society had spread far beyond the vision of Henry Adams. The day of splurge had dawned, there was much competition in toilettes, though, in the case of the gowns of Mrs. Blaine and Mrs. Boutwell, more than one had 'felt the deadly pressure of an iron,' and, with alterations, rendered service throughout a season.[4] Not a few of these shrank from the ceremonies of a winter.[5] Snobbery had swished upon the scene.

Thus, when a girl clerk in her teens, petite, dimpled, plump, with auburn hair worn in a single braid down her back, with rounded arms, superb bust, dark eyes, and the complexion of a healthy child, married Senator Christiancy, old enough to be her grandfather, the senatorial and official ladies determined to ignore her.

[1] *Education of Henry Adams*, 252–53, 256.
[2] *New York World*, December 15, 1869.
[3] *Letters*, i, 97.          [4] *Ibid.*, i, 81, 85.          [5] *Ibid.*, i, 70.

The kindly Mrs. Fish, taking Mrs. Logan with her, rebuked the snobbery by calling on the girl at her simple home on Indiana Avenue; [1] but society was to see little of her, and the gossips had it that her venerable husband was 'not anxious for her to fare forth in the scanty costumes of society.' [2]

But the fashionable world, moving at a hectic pace, had little time to ponder the problem of the auburn-haired beauty. The leaders found the days all too short. Noon found them making the rounds of calls, and they turned homeward only with the set of sun to change hastily from calling dress to evening toilette for dinner — and then the round of gaslight receptions and dances that often extended toward the dawn. [3] The end of the season left them haggard, and it was observed toward the close that 'those who once could dance all night pant after the first round.' [4] Driving madly on calls from house to house, dressing for Senate field days as for the opera, midday found them at elaborate luncheons — and such luncheons! 'Oysters on the shell . . . clear soup . . . sweetbreads and French peas . . . Roman punch . . . chicken cutlets . . . birds . . . chicken salad . . . ices, jelly, charlottes, candied preserves, cake, fruit, candy, tea, coffee, and four kinds of wines' — such a luncheon at Mrs. Creswell's. [5]

But it was when the gaslights were on that society took possession of the town, loiterers crowding the streets before the houses of the receptions — noise and commotion, horses stamping, doors slamming, drivers shouting until midnight. [6] Beautifully gowned women poured through the doors, laboriously fought their way to the dressing-room, squeezed themselves upstairs at a snail's pace, [7] where pretty unmarried girls were in the receiving line. Then the peacock promenade, the sixty-five-inch trains dragging the floor, [8] bright, flirtatious eyes peering over the enormous fans then in vogue. [9] And then the dancing, eating, drinking, and more flirting — monstrous flirting. For had not Mrs. Schurz on leaving one

[1] Mrs. Logan, 269–70.
[2] New York World, quoted from Indianapolis News, March 26, 1876.
[3] Mrs. Belknap; New York World, December 30, 1875.
[4] Ibid., February 19, 1871.          [5] Mrs. Blaine, Letters, I, 79.
[6] New York Herald, February 28, 1869.
[7] A reception at Mrs. Belknap's, ibid., February 21, 1870.
[8] New York World, January 14, 23, 1870.          [9] Ibid., March 1, 1873.

reception observed 'Monsieur Mori standing motionless, his arm
tight around a young lady's waist? Imagine it!' [1]

Society reporters were amazed at the extravagance in dress, the
jewelry, the increasing elegance of the equipages, the epicurean
dinners, the spirit of abandon, so out of keeping with so many
official salaries. Let us attend a composite reception and get a
closer view of the women who dominated these gay scenes when
there was so much suffering in the South. Let us make it a reception at Kate Chase Sprague's — none less.

### IV

This amazing woman, surpassed by none in history in the imperial sway she held over men's imaginations, suggested in her
career the brilliant daughter of Burr. She had been the mistress of
her father's household at an age when many girls still find amusement with their dolls. The public men she thus met at the table of
Chase had greatly stimulated her intellectual growth, and the atmosphere of politics had early become part of herself. While still
in her teens, she was one of the most astute politicians in Ohio.
The father, idolizing her from birth, had written in his diary the
night she came: 'The babe is pronounced pretty. I think it quite
otherwise.' [2] When she was four, he was praying with her after
correcting her.[3] At five, she was listening to the reading of the
Book of Job and seeming pleased — 'probably with the solemn
rhythm' — and the father was praying with her again.[4] At that
age she was reading poetry to her father along with the Bible.[5]
When Chase entered the Cabinet, she took the social scepter
from older hands, and at twenty-one she was the belle of the
town. Her extraordinary beauty, grace, charm, her brilliant repartee, made her the darling of the diplomatic corps, her suitors
were legion, her triumph complete.[6] Even as her father was writing that 'her good sense' would 'keep her aloof from politics,' [7]
she was deep in political intrigue, and Lincoln was paying homage
to her judgment. Ambitious, brilliant, her imagination pictured
her father President, and herself presiding at the White House.

[1] Mrs. Blaine, *Letters*, I, 90–91.    [2] Warden, 290.    [3] *Ibid.*, 301.
[4] *Ibid.*, 302.    [5] *Ibid.*, 302–33.    [6] Mrs. Logan, 300.
[7] Chase to Mrs. Bailey Warden, 581.

KATE CHASE SPRAGUE

That her marriage at twenty-four to Senator Sprague, whose fortune was great, was dictated by ambition for her father seems probable. At that time she was the most dashing young woman in the country, the most popular in official society since Dolly Madison. Her wedding had been a social event, her trousseau that of a princess, her guests the most notable in the land, and Lincoln had claimed the privilege of a kiss. In less than a year, she was the acknowledged arbiter of the most exclusive society.[1] Reveling in her millions, astonishing by her splendor, importing her gowns from Paris, she dazzled the drawing-rooms with her jewels, and in 1865 created a sensation by wearing a huge diamond on top of her bonnet.[2] And yet she dimmed the splendor of her raiment and outshone the brilliance of her jewels. The correspondent of the 'Chicago News' thought her the only woman with a vast number of gowns and jewels who rose superior to them all. 'Not a gown, not a chain, not an ornament ever attracted attention except in so much as it shared her beauty. . . . She had more the air of a great lady than any woman I ever saw. She could make all the Astors look like fishwomen beside her.'

And yet a shadow fell upon her marriage early, her husband's inebriety humiliating her at social functions, but without disturbing the perfect poise of this radiant creature in pink satin, point lace, and diamonds. If romance died, ambition did not falter. Her position was in no sense endangered. She had her house at Narragansett, with eighty rooms magnificently furnished, and filled with works of art; her father's beautiful place at 'Edgewood,' on an eminence near the capital, had its forty servants; and in town her drawing-room more nearly resembled that of Madame de Staël than any ever seen in Washington. Statesmen, jurists, politicians, artists, diplomats mingled there with the cleverest and most charming women. There fashion and politics fraternized, and even the flirtations were political. Ever and anon she would arrange a parlor lecture — as for Julia Ward Howe.[3] Her dinners were regal in magnificence.[4] She controlled her household and servants with an iron hand in velvet gloves, and her French cook was a dignitary in the minds of those who sat at her table. Sometimes, in warm

[1] *New York Herald*, July 8, 1865.          [2] *New York World*, February 20, 1870.
[3] Warden, 566.          [4] Mrs. Logan, 239.

weather, her dinners would be spread in the garden behind the
house, and the gossips were thrilled when at one of her dinners a
floral ornament costing a thousand dollars decorated the table,
and was contributed to Grant's second inaugural ball.[1] Wherever
this enchantress went, she dominated the scene and figured most
conspicuously in the descriptions of the event. Did Madame de
Catacazy give a dinner? Mrs. Sprague was there 'in pale blue
silk, with an overdress of pale pink silk, the two colors harmoniously blending to produce beautiful combinations. Her ornaments
were turquoises and diamonds. She wore a tiara of these stones.'[2]
Did she attend a dancing party at Mrs. Fish's? She was there
'wearing a rose pink silk with train and silvery flounce brocaded;
her ornaments pearls and diamonds, and two sprays of these jewels
were fastened in her hair.'[3] Always she was the center of the picture. Men hovered about her and, while there was no gossip, except in the case of Roscoe Conkling, she was courted as much as
married woman as when maid. The birth of her first baby was a
national event, every woman in the country reading descriptions
of the layette; and when the child began to talk, its amusing sayings were passed from mouth to mouth.

And yet, always the grand lady, she was a little aloof, haughty,
frankly bored by commonplace people. She may at times have
been the Marie Antoinette of the Little Trianon, but she was always imperial. When Grant appeared in Washington to be lionized after his military triumphs, and society was obsequious, she
laid down the law on precedence and the General called on her
father first. There was magic as well as majesty in her pointed
finger.[4]

Such was the fascinating lady we are about to meet.

## V

The house is crowded, and as we note members of the Cabinet,
candidates for President, Senators and diplomats, and foremost
journalists, such as Ben: Perley Poore and Donn Piatt, it seems a
mobilization of all that is distinguished in our public life. The
diplomatic corps — not one is missing. The Senate? It seems to

---

[1] *New York World*, March 5, 1873.          [2] *Ibid.*, March 20, 1870.
[3] *Ibid.*, April 23, 1871.          [4] Badeau, 173.

have adjourned, *en masse*, to her drawing-room. Numberless wax candles with the gaslights make as much brilliancy as possible. On stands and tables, the most gorgeous flowers. Somewhere music. And there, standing beside her father, Kate Chase Sprague, 'dressed magnificently and yet so perfectly that the dress seems rather part of herself than an outside ornament.' Her hair is arranged with the usual simplicity, but across the front she wears a bandeau of turquoises and diamonds, and back of it feathers and flowers.[1] Her form is beautifully symmetrical, just plump enough for her height, the lines of bust and waist perfect, her hands and feet noticeably small. Her face is oval, and the texture of her skin smooth and firm. Her forehead is low and wide, and slender arched eyebrows set off the eyes, difficult to describe because of something mysteriously subtle and hidden among the thick dark drooping lashes, and 'they have always the look as if they had been crying hard without the redness — the most fetching eyes on earth.' There is a slight saucy tilt to the nose, and the lips are very red and full, with fascinating tints at the corners. The hair, richly golden. The form and features of the most devastating and provocative of women. Perhaps the most expressive feature is the deep brown eyes that seem brooding in the shade of the veiling lashes. Her magnetism pervades the room. Maybe it is the mind behind the beauty that makes her stand out so regally among all the pretty women about her. 'When she is talking to you, you feel that you are the very person she wanted to meet,' thought Hugh McCulloch, and that was a secret of her popularity. She draws out the most reticent like strong wine; even the dull shine momentarily under her mysterious gaze. After all, it is not the mere physical beauty that makes her 'the enchantress,' but the distinctive intellectual charm of her manner, the proud poise of her exquisite head.

We pass on into the library for punch, or up to the little room on the second floor for coffee. After a while, we shall file out into the grounds for supper in a pavilion, floored and covered with linen damask.[2] Meanwhile, we have time to gossip a bit about other interesting women who socially reflected the political spirit of the times.

---

[1] Description of one of Mrs. Sprague's receptions, *New York World*, April 28, 1872.
[2] *New York World*, April 28, 1872.

VI

Now, there, surrounded by men, evidently is a woman of fascinating qualities — Mrs. 'Puss' Belknap, wife of the auburn-whiskered Secretary of War. Romantic enough the story of how she came to be here. She had succeeded to the place of her dead sister, whose memory is still sweet to many about us. This sister was tall, slender, graceful, intellectually bright, with rare conversational charm, a lovely brunette with brilliant color and dark eyes. She had been a belle of the Kentucky bluegrass, and had enjoyed a gay girlhood here and on the Rhine.[1] She had, on becoming a lady of the Cabinet, leased the old Rogers house on Lafayette Square, where she had literally taken the town by assault. Her receptions were crowded, and it was said that 'it is enough to enliven any one to see her face — she appears so thoroughly to enjoy herself and to be on such good terms with all the world.' [2] The city rang in praise of her that first season, which was to be her last; correspondents had rhapsodized about her charm and beauty, and she burned the candle at both ends. The cordiality of her manner won the hearts of all.[3] The season had left her fagged, and it was noted that June at West Point at the Commencement, where she danced with gay abandon, that in repose her face seemed sad. In truth, as we shall learn later, her ambition had led her astray, and there was a burden on her heart.[4] Six months later, Hamilton Fish, General Horace Porter, and General Sherman were among those who carried her casket into Saint John's. Her meteoric career was over.[5]

It was through her that the present Mrs. Belknap, coquetting over her fan here at Mrs. Sprague's to-night, was drawn to Washington. On her sister's death, she had remained to care for her orphan baby, and to preside over the *ménage* of her brother-in-law, and had become a familiar figure at dances and receptions. Before she was married, to be widowed soon, she had been a dashing Kentucky belle, lively, prettier than her sister, and kind-hearted. When the war came, she became a partisan of the Union, making a silk flag herself and presenting it to Colonel Landrum's regiment. [6]

[1] *New York World*, February 20, 1870.     [2] *Ibid.*, March 6, 1870.
[3] *Ibid.*, February 10, 1870.     [4] *Ibid.*, June 15, 1870.
[5] *New York Herald*, December 30, 1870.
[6] *Quincy Whig, Louisville Commercial*; quoted, *New York Herald*, March 19, 1876.

Gossip had not missed this shining mark, nor spared her quite, but when the rumor spread of her engagement to the handsome Belknap, the Mrs. Grundys were frowned down.[1] None too eager to be caged, she had postponed her wedding for a year and gone to Europe, and Washington had lamented the loss of 'her beautiful face and witty conversation.'[2] Even the Parisian journey was to be rolled under the tongues of the scandalmongers and two men of political distinction were to be mentioned without justification.[3] But with a gay group she had learned the giddy spendthrift ways of Paris, and enjoyed the luxury, fashionable profligacy, and personal display; learned, too, from the courting something of her powers of fascination. One who had seen her in her widow's cap, and later in the delicate hues of the rainbow, striking an attitude in the Blue Room of the White House, was amazed that 'women have so many natures.'[4]

Home she had come to marry, but not to settle down. Belknap took a house in the fashionable West End, filled it with the rare and costly furniture she had collected in Paris, and installed a French cook, and her fêtes, dinners, and receptions were soon the talk of the town. With her Parisian costumes, her parasols with solid coral handles, and the forty pairs of shoes with which she shod the daintiest foot in Washington,[5] she is now rivaling the magnificence of Mrs. Sprague, and contesting her position as the arbiter of fashion. Her wardrobe is opulent from the loosest négligée to the most elaborate ball gown, and it is said that when Worth received the order for her trousseau 'he retired to a cave and fasted for seven days.'[6] As she rides by in a carriage rivaling that of Mrs. Fish, her bright face beaming, pedestrians pause to prolong the pleasure. Clara Morris is to remember her as 'the most beautiful woman I ever saw in Washington or anywhere . . . perfect.'

Note the Worth costume she wears, as she holds court now among her admirers. The petticoat of alternate stripes of white satin bordered with a heavy garland of ivy leaves, and green satin embroidered with gold wheat ears, the train of green satin bordered

[1] New York World, March 8, 1876.                [2] Ibid., December 8, 1872.
[3] George H. Pendleton and H. Clymer; ibid., March 9, March 25, 1876.
[4] Mary Clemmer, in Cincinnati Commercial; quoted, New York World, March 13, 1876.
[5] Ibid., March 13, 1876.                [6] New York World, March 28, 1875.

with a heavy garland of ivy and wheat. Ivy leaves, too, in her glossy black hair, and sparkling eyes to match the emeralds she wears. If tragedy stalks her even as she smiles, it is not to crush her.[1] How her eyes flash above the feathers of her fan! These men will linger long about her carriage door to fold her white cloak about her white arms and shoulders.

And now, observe the lady she displaced in the admiration of the men, walking by with fewer attendants — the tall, shapely, handsome, brilliant brunette, with the fresh complexion and the graceful carriage, vivaciously trying her repartee on her companions. Time was when that agreeable voice and ingratiating manner and keen intelligence promised her the scepter, but that was before the second Mrs. Belknap returned from Paris. She lives in some splendor in a great house on Rhode Island Avenue, where Saint Mark's is to stand, and men flock there to hear her talk. Later, some one, who probably had been snubbed by Mrs. Belknap, will describe Mrs. Williams, wife of the Attorney-General, as 'smart' and add, 'I do not know whether she will sell post-traderships or not, but if she does, she will not be caught.' [2] But she has the weakness of ambition, too, and, breezy Westerner though she is, she has aroused the deadly ire of Senators by announcing that, as a Cabinet lady, their wives must call first on her. Alas, the memory of that blunder is to send her to her bed one day when her husband's nomination for the Supreme Court will fail of confirmation.[3]

Enters now a woman to whom deference is paid less boisterously, and of whom it has been said that 'Mrs. Hamilton Fish, wife of the Secretary of State, deserves to be a leader of the *ton* by virtue of her carriage, if nothing more.' [4] Here is the happy woman who need not strive, for distinction is hers by nature. On her advice the lady of the White House leans. The style of her dress is regal enough, but in manner she has the simplicity, cordiality, and grace of high breeding — 'the most superb woman of her time.' [5] Hers is the practiced art that puts the timid at ease without inviting familiarity. To her home on Fifteenth Street, at the corner of I,

[1] *New York World*, March 28, 1875.   [2] *Ibid.*, December 10, 1876.
[3] *Ibid.*, December 17, 1871; Mrs. Logan, 272; Gail Hamilton, 244.
[4] *New York World*, January 23, 1870.   [5] Mrs. Logan, 268.

ladies and gentlemen of the stately old school find their way and linger in an atmosphere of literature and art.[1]

The tall, spare woman with light hair and a radiant complexion, so quietly dressed, with Mrs. Fish? That is Lady Thornton, wife of the British Minister, at whose table Grant, a little bored, despite the elegance of the dinner and the toilettes, had sat rolling bread crumbs into balls one evening.[2] And the pretty woman with the interesting face who speaks to Mrs. Fish? That is Madame la Marquise de Noailles, wife of the French Minister, noted for her cleverness and love of fun. 'Ah, madame,' said an admirer, 'if only I spoke your language, what graceful compliments I might pay you!' 'Tell them in your language,' she had replied with a roguish smile; 'I shall understand.'[3] And the beautiful woman with pretty arms and neck and the exquisite complexion, who now joins the group? It is Madame Potesdad, wife of the Spanish Secretary, a Miss Chapman, of Virginia, whose mother was a Randolph, and who has broken hearts in her time.[4] And note the young woman of exotic beauty who now joins the group about Mrs. Fish which comes and goes. A rounded, yet girlish, slender form, a perfect oval face, transparent skin of creamy whiteness, large, luminous dark eyes swimming with intelligence, soft brown hair, a perfect nose, and a rosebud of a mouth — such a picture! It is Madame Flores, the popular wife of the Minister from Ecuador, who is the son of the first President of the Republic. She lives on G Street, above the War Department, and her guests carry away the haunting memory of a beautiful singing voice. She passes on, and many curious eyes are furtively turned upon another woman approaching Mrs. Fish. You haven't heard? This, then, is the story: Madame García, for it is she, the wife of José Antonio García y Garcían, Peruvian Secretary, attending a reception at Mrs. Fish's and finding among the guests young Lopez, son of the tyrant, warmly received, had expressed astonishment to her hostess that such a cordial reception should be given the son of a tyrant. 'Madame,' Mrs. Fish had said, in her most stately manner, 'Mr. Lopez is a guest here.' Madame García had replied that

---

[1] *New York Herald*, May 31, 1869.
[2] *New York World*, April 18, 1869; Mrs. Blaine, *Letters*, I, 88; Mrs. Logan, 261.
[3] *New York World*, March 2, 1873.          [4] *Ibid.*, March 11, 1870.

if he remained, she would have to leave. Mrs. Fish had bowed stiffly, and the Peruvian lady, gathering her friends about her, had departed. It was whispered about that the lady's irritation was caused by meeting a woman who had made an unsatisfactory English translation of one of Madame's novels, and had been refused payment; that words had passed, and just then Lopez had loomed before her eyes.[1] Thus the curiosity behind the fans.

But there were other reasons, for Madame García was most clever and attractive, vivacious, musical, an accomplished linguist, and, besides, was the niece of Rosas, once dictator of Buenos Ayres. While living in Paris, she had written a novel in French, 'Love in the Pampas.' Not tall, yet weighing one hundred and sixty pounds, it was said of her that 'Venus had little to do with her, but Minerva very much.' But she is pretty, too, with her fine eyes and fair complexion, set off by her very dark hair, and her handsome white neck and shoulders.[2] At the grand ball for Prince Arthur, she had almost penetrated the defenses of Grant, 'restless, animated, brilliant as one of the metallic blue butterflies of Brazil, talking in her amusing, rapid fashion, tossing her diamond headset, upturning her arch, dark face to the President, who watched her, amused in his quiet, grave, scarce-smiling way.'[3] It was about this time that she had a full-length portrait taken for Mrs. Grant, at her request. Her parties and receptions at her home, at Fifteenth and H Streets, were brilliant, unique, enormously popular.[4] She had astonished Washington with a grand dinner served with thirty thousand dollars' worth of plate just received from Europe.[5]

But she lingers only a moment with Mrs. Fish, and is now lost in the crowd. Another has taken her place — evidently a famous beauty with an interesting story, Madame Catacazy, wife of the Russian Minister. Now long past the fresh bloom of youth, this statuesque, golden-haired woman, with superb neck and arms and melting eyes, is still beautiful and enticing. The society reporters rhapsodize about her with the rest. We hear much of 'the noble contour of her shoulders,' of her complexion 'delicately tinted as

[1] *New York Herald*, January 21, 1870.  [2] *New York World*, March 11, 1870.
[3] *Ibid.*, January 28, 1870.  [4] *Ibid.*, January 14, 1870.
[5] *Ibid.*, December 30, 1869.

the heart of the seashell,' of her gorgeous hair 'with massive braids shot through with a dead gold arrow,' of her features 'high-bred and queenly.' But mostly do we hear of her hair. 'The skein of pale yellow flossy silk sometimes hung up in manufacturers' cases to show how beautiful silk may be . . . may set one dreaming of this woman's hair.' [1] Mrs. Logan will remember her as 'magnificently dressed and crowned with that beautiful head of hair for which she was so generally admired.' [2] She dresses with perfect taste, with elegance, and always with the view to making the most of her charms — which are abundant. Men are fascinated; strangely enough, women share their admiration. They flock to her home on I Street, near Fourteenth, the furniture and decorations for which had been brought over from Paris. In the salon hangs a splendid portrait of the Czar Alexander, by a Russian painter.[3] Here there is gayety and high play and a courtly tone, though the colleagues of her 'short, ugly, scrubby' consort do complain that the Catacazys play against each other, she staking high, he low, and Madame's partner always losing.[4]

Indeed, there is much in this bewitching lady to make her interesting to the romantic. Married in girlhood against her will to a wealthy Italian Prince of the diplomatic service old enough to have been her grandfather, she went as the wife of an ambassador to Dom Pedro's court. There young Catacazy was Secretary of the Russian Legation. The lady and the Secretary fell in love, she disappeared, to be found a week later living in a cottage with her lover on the outskirts of the capital. When her lover was recalled, she went along, and in time, following a divorce or death, the lovers were married. The story was known to the women of Washington — but it was so long ago, and she was so charming, it was resolved to confine the story to the boudoirs.[5] Catacazy was old and ugly now, and she was blooming still, handsome and entrancing, and gossip still played with her reputation a little. When at length her husband was recalled, on the demand of Grant on purely diplomatic grounds, there was a disposition to ascribe the trouble to a Cabinet member's infatuation for Madame,[6] though

[1] *New York Herald*, February 21, 1870.        [2] Mrs. Logan, 261.
[3] *New York Herald*, January 12, 1870.        [4] Badeau, 374–76.
[5] *Ibid.*            [6] *Brooklyn Eagle*, and *New York World*, August 11, 1898.

Mrs. Blaine was sure the recall had nothing to do with the lady.[1] Happy she is to-night at Mrs. Sprague's, the center of admiring groups, but the drama of her life in Washington soon is to close. She is to remain to entertain the Grand Duke Alexis in a gorgeous manner, and the curtain is to fall upon this phase of her colorful life, with Madame, dressed in a pale lemon-colored silk tissue, or crêpe de Paris of very fine texture, standing at the door of the Legation, according to tradition, with a silver salver bearing a small loaf of black bread, to greet the Grand Duke with the words, 'I bring you bread and salt.' [2]

The guests are now moving to the garden for supper, but we have seen the most unusual women of this tragic era. We get a momentary glimpse of Mrs. Blaine, looking very well despite her dress feeling 'the deadly pressure of the iron,' and Mrs. John A. Logan, fragile, with a mobile face, a mass of turbulent black hair, and eyes of keen intelligence, and Blanche Butler Ames, charming in her youth and her Persian gown, and Mrs. Robeson, pretty and effervescent, and Mrs. Carl Schurz, a stately German matron, not agreeably impressed by the extravagance about her, and . . .

Thus, while the politicians were staking their reputations, and mobs were marching, and men were stealing in high places, there was festivity somewhere, and in the shadow of the Capitol. Some of these fine ladies will meet humiliation before our story is told.

[1] Mrs. Blaine, *Letters*, i, 50.          [2] *New York World*, November 23, 1871.

# CHAPTER XIII

## A SEASON OF SCANDAL

### I

THE first summer of his Presidency, Grant was to suffer an irreparable loss in the death of General John A. Rawlins, his Secretary of War, because no other living person was so warmly and wisely devoted to Grant personally. Impetuous, at times violent, uncompromising, and frequently domineering, he had been associated with the President throughout his military career in the capacity of friend and adviser. Wiser in many ways than his chief, he alone had dared to cross him, or to criticize. Time and again, in army days, he had remonstrated with him because of his drinking, and Grant never resented it. No one understood so thoroughly the strength and weakness of the great commander, or comprehended so completely his limitations. Others, convinced of his mistakes, were to be silenced by the grim reticence of the man with the black cigar; Rawlins never. Passionately he would protest, and Grant would listen, and be advised. Then, too, Rawlins was a better judge of men, and had he lived, the man he idolized, and yet did not idealize, would have been spared many of the associations that have so sadly marred the record of his Administration.[1] Sick on assuming office, Rawlins had gradually grown worse through the summer, and in the autumn he died, mourned by the Nation.

This was the first, perhaps the greatest, tragedy in the Grant Administration.

It was a season in which death was plucking busily at the leaders of men. The powerful, impressive, Cato-like Fessenden was no more. One night Henry J. Raymond was mysteriously carried to his home and left in the hall, where, in the morning, he was found dying. Gossip was busy with its curious tidbits about Rose Eytinge, the actress, who appears to have had no connection with

---

[1] 'How Judge Hoar Ceased to be Attorney-General,' by J. D. Cox, *Atlantic Monthly,* 1895.

his stroke.[1] Ruined politically by his support of Johnson, his death carried no political significance. Even less political importance attached to the passing of three greater men who had played more important rôles more than a generation before. Franklin Pierce died in October, and in November, Amos Kendall, very old and long forgotten, and Robert J. Walker, author of the famous tariff act that bears his name, passed away. One of the elder statesmen, Millard Fillmore, was writing articles that summer for 'The Western World,' on whether we were to have an empire, and Horace Greeley was commenting sneeringly that 'his voice can now excite no other interest than the mild curiosity aroused by any voice from the tomb.' [2]

Among the politicians much grumbling was heard against Hoar because of his contemptuous refusal to name improper men to office on a mere senatorial demand. A stern, unbending Puritan of high professional ideals was manifestly out of place, and an Attorney-General who dared respond to a Senate resolution instructing him to report on the status of certain cases with the curt comment that he was a subordinate of the Executive, and not a Senate clerk, was inevitably marked for slaughter. All through the summer and fall the clouds were darkening above him. Grant sat silently listening to the complaints and meditating a graceful way to rid himself of another adviser sadly needed.[3] Very soon he would be nominated for the Supreme Court and refused confirmation, and James Russell Lowell would be protesting against the withdrawal of the nomination, insisting that 'the responsibility lie with the knaves who hate you for your impregnability,' [4] and Godkin, of 'The Nation,' would be declaring that the secret of his offending was his refusal 'to degrade the Government by rendering dishonest opinions' and 'to degrade the public service by placing incompetent men in office.' [5] But the nomination was to be withdrawn, and Hoar was to linger in the Cabinet yet a while.

In the August mornings of that summer, people lingered longer than usual at the breakfast table over their papers containing columns of controversial matter concerning Harriet

[1] Bigelow, *Retrospections*, IV, 289.          [2] *New York Tribune*, June 29, 1869.
[3] *Memoir of Hoar*, 183.          [4] *Ibid.*, 193.          [5] December 30, 1869.

Beecher Stowe's amazingly frank volume defending Lady Byron, and describing her noble lord as a degraded wretch who had maintained incestuous relations with his sister. For the most part the criticisms were hostile, and the author's motives were roundly denounced — by no one more than by Theodore Tilton, of 'The Independent.' He carried his defense of his fellow poet and his denunciations of Mrs. Stowe to the platform; and at the Suffrage Convention at Newport the proceedings were enlivened by an animated debate on Mrs. Stowe's action, Tilton attacking, and Mrs. Stanton as vigorously defending. The irreverent 'New York World,' discussing the verbal battle, asked why 'was the absurd Tilton, who revolts the prime instincts of womanhood, invited to a woman's suffrage convention at all.' And so the jolly controversy simmered and boiled through the broiling August days.[1] Meanwhile, as the miasmic heat settled down on Washington like a hot, damp blanket, Grant had gone with his family to Long Branch, then the fashionable watering-place of the country. It was a place of much dancing and heavy drinking and billiard-playing, and, strangely enough, not so much given to bathing; albeit the ladies daily dressed with elaborate care to stand demurely, or flirtatiously, on the sands of the beach and look on discreetly. When a heavier wave than usual rose and broke on the beach, the timid screamed and were reassured and consoled by some strong man. Meandering over the beach, or through the lobbies, or on the piazzas of the hotels, were young men with note-books jotting down descriptions and comments on the celebrities among the men and beauties among the women, for the brightening of the press. The more sportive of the summer guests had their fast horses there; and, not to be outdone, Grant had his carriage horses, 'Egypt' and 'Cincinnati,' behind which he proudly drove along the neighboring roads.

And yet it was observed that first season, when he was living at the Stetson House, that he was not entirely happy. In the mornings he dressed in broadcloth and stood on the piazza bowing to smiling ladies who passed, and without lifting his hat. The glamour of the social life was a bit too glaring, and he was not the most self-possessed of the visitors. Dashing Phil Sheridan was

[1] *New York World,* August 19, 22, 24, 27, 1869.

there cutting quite a swath with his dancing, and even Grant was inveigled into the lancers at one big dance, to cut a sorry figure.[1] Just a little while before he had cut a sorrier figure when he had gone to the Boston Jubilee as the guest of Jim Fisk and Jay Gould, men deep in speculation, and one with a malodorous reputation.

Never two men so different in so many ways as these. Gould, slight, almost shy, soft-spoken, retiring, with all the domestic virtues and singularly free from the familiar vices of his sex; Fisk, flamboyant, vociferous, vicious in morals, gaudy in peacock feathers, given to a defiant flaunting of his faults — men of clashing temperaments with but one common instinct, that of acquisition. In the pursuit of gain, one was no more scrupulous than the other, and neither had any scruples at all. New York was buzzing with the stories of their management of the Erie Railroad, and their speculations on Wall Street. Rumor was bruiting it abroad that in official circles they gained their ends through bribery.

And yet, one June afternoon, Gould had called at the home of Abel E. Corbin, the brother-in-law of Grant, to escort the President to the steamer Providence, of the Fall River Line, gayly bedecked with fluttering flags, and with Fisk, the owner, gorgeous in the gold braid and brass buttons of an Admiral, at the gangway to welcome the distinguished guest. Dodsworth's Band had been engaged for the trip, and other distinguished gentlemen had been invited to keep Grant company. That night, at nine o'clock, the party had descended to the dining-room, where an epicurean feast had been spread, with an abundance of the choicest wines and liquors. There Grant had sat in silence mostly, chewing at his black cigar, as Gould and Fisk expatiated on the patriotic need of keeping up the price of gold, that the crops might be moved with profit. It was a drama in which Grant was playing a rôle without his knowledge.

From Boston, Gould, with other fish to fry, had hurried back to New York, but the dashing, gaudily bedecked Fisk lingered with the presidential party, moving with real gallantry through the ceremonies, overshadowing the modest, plain-bearded man he was attending; and so back to New York, where at night, in the

[1] *New York World*, July 19, 20, 23, 24, 28, 1869.

brilliant glare of the Fifth Avenue Theater, Grant, with his wife and daughter, sat in a proscenium box in familiar converse with the Corbins, Fisk, and Gould. And the spectators had looked on and marveled and spread the news of the intimacy of notorious speculators with the head of the Nation. Grant was on the stage that night — without suspecting it. And he was playing in a tragedy shot through with the elements of farce.

II

No one, perhaps, was shocked or greatly astonished, for it was a decade of none too much sensibility, when strong men with the instincts and daring of pirates and buccaneers were amassing fortunes by hook or crook, to the admiring applause of the multitude. Out in Ohio, young John D. Rockefeller, with vision and audacity amounting to genius, was laying the foundations of a mighty fortune through relentless and dubious methods; the coal industry was being built up through means as heartless; railroads were being constructed on graft, milked and wrecked; and even from the cathedral quiet of the castle of Jay Cooke, with its retinue of clerics hovering about, went forth strange messages concerning public men and governmental grants to the Northern Pacific. Though not then known, Oakes Ames had already been busy distributing alms to statesmen of distinction in the interest of the Crédit Mobilier. The North had gone money-mad, and glory be to him who had the gold, and no questions asked. Men with old-fashioned notions of morality, like Jonathan Worth, looked upon the scene following the election of 1868 with pessimism. 'Money has become the goddess of the country,' he wrote, 'and otherwise good men are almost compelled to worship at her shrine. 'The proof was manifest in the fact that legislators, State and National, 'are bribed by money or controlled by corrupt rings.' [1] The Capitol in Washington fairly teemed with lobbyists who were received on terms of familiarity by legislators and given the privilege of the floor.[2] Even the conservative William M. Evarts was impressed with 'the decline of public morality which presages revolution,' and Godkin, of 'The Nation,' was sure that in New York it had

[1] *To William Clark*, Worth, ii, 1259.
[2] Hoar, *Autobiography*, i, 307.

'confessedly never been so low.' [1] He was losing faith even in the
'loyal men' of the South, and was sure that 'at the bottom of all
these confiscation schemes there are rascals.' Boss Tweed was
busy at Albany with his bi-partisan corruptionists, and the charge
had been publicly made, without a libel suit, that Governor Fenton
had been bribed by Gould to sign the Erie Bill. There had been
a little wagging of tongues in Washington, whither Fenton had
been promoted by a grateful people to the Senate, but no one
suggested an investigation because 'too many Radicals in place
here are tarred by this or a similar stick.' [2] The Washington correspondent of the 'Cincinnati Enquirer' was commenting pointedly
on the number of statesmen building fine houses in the capital
and regretting that 'we have sunk so low in our political system
that the question of three-story brick and stone fronts must
enter largely into a discussion of the merits of public men.' [3]
Even the 'Chicago Tribune' was speaking bluntly. 'Why do we
say these things?' it asked. 'In the first place they are already
known — everybody is talking about them, in the streets, on
horse cars, in the railroad trains, in the clubrooms, around euchre
tables — everywhere except in the Executive Mansion.' [4] That
summer, the meticulously honest Julian, suffering physical tor-
ment, was dragging his ailing body through the Far-Western
country, and more than verifying his conviction that the public
domain was being stolen with impunity. Fraud everywhere!
'The saddest part is that the public officials, both State and
Federal, are in league with the capitalists in making the rich
richer, and the poor poorer.' [5] But Julian was beginning to lose
caste with the Radicals, and had made the fatal blunder of attacking the railroad lobby as corrupt the previous winter.[6] He was
already marked for slaughter. The clear-thinking Matthew Carpenter was convinced a year before that the new slavery power
was 'the combinations of capital, the consolidations of monopolies.' [7]

And meanwhile, the voice of Andrew Johnson was heard in the

---

[1] Godkin, to Norton, I, 301.      [2] New York World, March 27, 1869.
[3] Quoted, New York World, December 11, 1869.      [4] Ibid., April 30, 1869.
[5] MS. Diary, August 11, 1869.      [6] Congressional Globe, February 5, 1869.
[7] Speech at Madison on 'The Growth of Monopoly,' Life of Carpenter, 145.

land, hammering away at the moral standards of the time. It was annoying to hear that familiar voice crying from the balcony of the St. Cloud Hotel, in Nashville:

'I feel prouder in my retirement than imperial Cæsar with such a corrupt Congress at his heels, for ... when degeneracy and corruption seem to control Departments of Government; when "vice prevails and impious men bear sway, the post of honor is a private station." When I accepted the Presidency ... I accepted it as a high trust. ... I did not accept it as a donation, or as a grand gift establishment; I did not take it as a horn of plenty, with sugar plums to be handed out here and there. Thank God, I can stand before the people of my State and lift up both hands and say in the language of Samuel, "Whose ox have I taken, or whose ass have I taken? At whose hands have I received bribes and had my eyes blinded? If there be any, let him answer."'

And there was no answer.

It was soon afterward that the news flashed over Washington that Johnson was in town and at the Metropolitan, and that night a great crowd marched on him in a serenade, and when he appeared on the balcony the welkin rang. It was an unmannerly speech, perhaps, for he denounced Congress as 'tyrants standing with the heel of power on the necks of the freedmen, endeavoring to blot out the lines separating the States, and to wipe out the coördinate branches of the Government,' and he satirized Grant as 'the second Washington,' while the crowd laughed and cheered.[1]

The capital was still a lively place, fond of its cup and gossip and cards, and when a little scandal broke, it fairly rocked with glee. A young diplomat attached to one of the legations had taken the Radical philosophy of racial equality seriously, and had shocked the staid matrons of society by proudly escorting a beautiful mulatto to a party, and his chief, the Minister, was most abject in his apologies.[2]

And then there was Senator Sprague, husband of Kate Chase Sprague, the Mrs. Bingham of her time — he was both puzzling and amusing the country that spring and summer, too.

[1] *New York World,* July 2, 1869.
[2] *Ibid.,* October 23, 1869.

## III

Senator Sprague has been neglected by history, albeit he was an idol in war days as the dashing and efficient young War Governor of Rhode Island. Elected to the Senate, he had speedily fallen under the spell of Kate Chase's seductive beauty and suffered the eclipse that befalls men who mate with their superiors. Even so, his was the fortune that defrayed the cost of the elaborate entertainments and dinners given in the fine old house at Sixth and E Streets, where the Spragues lived with Chase — a roomy old house with wide hall and ample apartments richly, elegantly, tastefully furnished. Prone to dissipation, he seemed older than his age in 1869. With small head and features, his eyes were large and lustrous, and he wore his hair long with an affected carelessness.

In April, he had created a sensation in the Senate in a speech warning that money was becoming predominant in government and was threatening the economic liberties of the people. Attacking his colleague, Senator Anthony, as the tool of 'Brown and Ivers,' business rivals of the Spragues in Rhode Island, in attempting to destroy his credit, he charged corruption in the Senate, and baldly declared that Senators had taken employment with great corporations seeking government favor.[1] It took the Senate two weeks to prepare its defense; but two weeks later, numerous Senators attacked Sprague, who responded by reading thirty pages of commendatory letters into the 'Globe.'[2] The replies, read to-day in the light of what we now know, are flimsy enough; for, ignoring the major charges, the Senators, replying, seized on an incidental reflection on the military record of General Burnside and flayed Sprague on that alone.

On the afternoon of the night the workingmen of Washington serenaded him in approval of his philippic, Sprague sat in his library before the fireplace at a table with many wonderfully carved paper-knives and odd-looking inkwells, with books piled on top of Bohemian vases, and with an enormous pile of letters before him, talking with the correspondent of the 'New York Herald.' He was in jubilant mood — was going to New York to arrange for the printing of sixty thousand copies of his speech —

[1] *Congressional Globe*, April 8, 1869.      [2] *Ibid.*, April 22, 1869.

a million if required. 'Look there! there are my letters from every part of the Nation, from men of all parties and all conditions,' he exclaimed triumphantly. Would the correspondent look at them? Glancing at a few, the reporter concluded that, 'in spite of all that is said to the contrary, Sprague has touched the most vital chord in the popular heart.' His enemies had circulated the story that he was insane, but the reporter could see no indications, and, on entering the house, Chase, the picture of placid benevolence, was descending the stairs evidently unworried.[1] Indeed, that night, when the Senator denounced the 'money power' to a cheering multitude of workingmen, the Chief Justice stood beaming by his side.[2] Mysteriously embittered, Sprague persisted in frequent attacks on his associates. One day his wrath centered on Simon Cameron. 'I used to meet him a great deal some time ago,' said Sprague. 'He would take me down to his committee room and set out champagne and ask me to drink. Finally I said to him: "Cameron, you are a vicious old fellow. I am a young man and you are an old sinner, and you are always putting temptation in my way. Now, I don't intend coming to your room any more." Since that I have had little to do with Cameron.'[3]

In this gasconading escapade, a duel was narrowly averted. Under the lash of senatorial attacks, Sprague had described the North Carolina carpetbagger Senator Abbott as a 'puppy.' He had left the Senate that night late, and after his departure Abbott rose to begin a counter-attack, when Charles Sumner stopped him on a point of order. The morning following found the town rife with wild rumors. Abbott had threatened to horsewhip the husband of Kate Chase Sprague; the latter, heavily armed, had left the town that morning at dawn; Abbott could not be found. In truth, Sprague was found in his library busy with his secretaries, and, renouncing the idea of engaging in a street brawl, he announced his determination to continue his customary walks and his disposition to defend himself if assaulted.[4] The next night, Sumner and John Sherman, sipping their claret in Sumner's library, assumed the rôle of peacemakers, and the threatened

---

[1] *New York Herald*, April 16, 1869.  [2] *Ibid.*, April 14, 1869.
[3] *Ibid.*, April 24, 1869.  [4] *New York World*, April 24, 1869.

bloodshed was averted.[1] Somehow the explanation that Sprague was demented failed to satisfy Horace Greeley, who was sure he was planning to go over to the Democrats, despite his denunciation of both parties as 'rotten'; but a month later, when Sprague attacked free trade, the Man of the White Hat benignly beamed upon him again.[2]

Throughout the summer Sprague continued his mystifying attacks, and as late as July he was assailing the 'money power' at a Masonic picnic at Scituate, Rhode Island, as having supplanted the slave power, and charging Colfax's 'prosperity and happiness' talks to his subserviency to the plunderbund.[3] Thus he went his way sowing the wind, and in due time he was to reap the whirlwind in the withdrawal of credit, and the collapse of his business; but the incident reflects the tone and temper of the times. Right or wrong, the popular reaction was proof that he had voiced a general and growing distrust of the ruling forces, their purposes and integrity. And it was under these conditions that Black Friday cast a deep shadow on Wall Street, and, for a time, on the reputation of men in the highest stations.

IV

At the time Grant was the guest of Gould and Jim Fisk on the Providence, these speculators were engaged in a conspiracy to corner gold, and force merchants, compelled to have gold for the custom-house, to pay exorbitant rates. Even before the skeptical Fisk had been drawn in, Gould had made a confederate of Abel Corbin, also a speculator, and husband of Grant's sister. To assure themselves of foreknowledge of the intent of the Treasury, these two had succeeded in securing the appointment of General Daniel Butterfield, a prominent Union League politician, as Sub-Treasurer in New York. Soon the latter was compromised. It was not until Fisk was convinced that the conspiracy involved the White House that he entered; and thereafter, through spring, summer, and early autumn, these conspirators were buying gold at a premium and making headway. In August, the necessity of strengthening the impression among speculators that Grant had

---

[1] *New York World*, April 27, 1869.　　　[2] *New York Tribune*, May 20, 1869.
[3] *New York World*, July 9, 1869.

definitely decided against the sale of gold was manifest.  To these
ingenuous souls the method was easy.  Grant, passing through the
city, had seen Corbin; and immediately afterward Gould and
Corbin prepared an editorial captioned 'Grant's Financial Policy,'
and turned it over to the too credulous John Bigelow, of the 'New
York Times,' who published it, after some modification by the
financial editor, who was suspicious.  Even so, it served its purpose.

The fight now on, Gould bought heavily, handsomely providing
for Corbin and Butterfield, and Fisk, still dubious, was reassured
by the thought that there could be no possibility of loss, since
Corbin had a working arrangement with Grant and Butterfield.
When Corbin stoutly told the flamboyant gambler that his sister
was involved and Grant was in, Fisk was convinced.

In truth, Grant had instructed the Secretary of the Treasury
not to sell — partly because he had been impressed by Gould's
argument about the marketing of crops, and partly on the theory
that, with only the bulls and bears involved, the Government
should not interfere.  Conferring with Corbin in New York, when
about to return to Washington *via* western Pennsylvania, Grant
had left a note for Secretary Boutwell, due in the city the next
day, explaining the gold situation and suggesting again that it
would be wise to 'move on without change until the present struggle is over.' [1]  This was on September 12, and on the next night
Boutwell appeared at a dinner of the Union League Club.  On the
morning of the 15th, Horace Greeley published a leaded editorial charging a gold conspiracy and demanding that Boutwell
act.  'The Treasury has gold to sell — a good pile of it — and
it is the Secretary's duty to sell it when the market is highest,'
he wrote.  'If then the conspirators put up the price, let him
improve the opportunity to obtain such price for as many millions of that commodity as the market will take.  And to pre-
clude all pretense that he thereby makes money [greenbacks]
tight, let him buy bonds as fast as he sells gold, so as to leave
the money market wholly unaffected.' [2]

A little apprehensive now, the conspirators persuaded Corbin to
hasten an importunate letter to Grant, in his retreat near Pitts-

[1] Boutwell, II, 169.          [2] *New York Tribune*, September 15, 1869.

burgh, imploring him not to sell gold. The President then began
to see a great light. At his instance, Mrs. Grant wrote Mrs.
Corbin of his distress over Corbin's speculations, with the wish
that he get out at once. When Gould saw this message, he knew
the game was up, and he was thus able to save himself — but he
neglected to tell Fisk, who continued buying, while Gould was
secretly selling.

The scene in the Gold Room in Exchange Place on the 23d was
one of panic. Business men, with pale, drawn faces, were confront-
ing ruin. That day Greeley renewed his demand on Boutwell,
and that night Grant reached Washington and summoned his Secretary of the Treasury, but even then it was agreed to do nothing unless gold went higher. Meanwhile, ugly rumors affecting
the Administration were circulating in business circles, as Boutwell was informed by a trusted correspondent on the scene. 'Old
conservative merchants looked aghast,' he wrote, describing the
scene. 'Nobody was in their offices, and the agony depicted on
the faces of men who crowded the streets made one feel as if
Gettysburg had been lost and the rebels were marching down
Broadway.' [1] When morning brought no relief, Boutwell gave
orders to sell, and within a few minutes half of Wall Street was in
ruins. Gould and Fisk, protected by hired thugs, were barricaded
in their elegant offices against the vengeance of the threatening
mob, for many had been heard to say they proposed to blow out
Fisk's brains. Less culpable than Gould or Corbin, the brunt of
the abuse fell on him — his very flamboyancy made him a target.
And, besides, had not Lucille Western and another of Fisk's
women driven merrily through the financial section at the height
of the frenzy to witness their lover's triumph? [2]

v

It was in the aftermath that the prestige of Grant and the
Administration suffered most. 'The Tribune' paid a back-handed
compliment to Boutwell, and 'The Herald' bitterly attacked him
and the Administration for the 'superfluous parade of purity,' in
assuming that 'what was done in Wall Street was none of his

[1] Boutwell, ii, 169.
[2] New York World, September 26, 1869.

business.'[1] Then Corbin's sorry rôle became the sensation of the day — and the report that Mrs. Grant had profited, along with Butterfield. Fisk was furious. Had not Corbin told him in his own house that the Grants were in on the conspiracy? Half-crazed, he rushed to Corbin's home and upbraided him savagely, while the latter, holding a table between them, wrung his hands and wept. At length, overwhelmed with denunciation, and his life threatened, Fisk did an audacious thing — he summoned a reporter from 'The Herald' and made a clean breast, but charging that 'members of the President's family were in with us' — which was true of one — and insisting that 'the President himself was interested with us in the corner.' Four days before the interview, Corbin had written the 'New York Sun' that he did not associate with Fisk, and Grant would not, and Fisk had replied that he had 'visited [Corbin] on the very afternoon of the day he made these statements.'[2] A happy thought came to him as he faced the 'Herald' reporter, George Crouch. Would the reporter accompany Fisk in his carriage to the Corbin home? He would — and he sat in the carriage in front for the hour and a half Fisk remained within. This was on the 30th. Would Crouch make an affidavit to that effect? He would, and did. It was after this, and before the publication of the Fisk interview, that the same reporter called on Corbin, whom he found in bed.

'I swear to you that Fisk and Gould have never been in my house since Gould called last summer when the President was here. I have no connection with such men.'

'Then the statement that Fisk was here on the 30th was false?' asked the cunning reporter.

'False, every word. I will solemnly swear that Fisk was not in my house that day.'

There was no escape for Corbin — his culpability was unmistakably established. Was the rest of Fisk's story true? Three months later, James A. Garfield, approaching his task as chairman of the investigating committee of the House, was writing confidentially that the trail 'perhaps will lead us into the parlor of the President. I don't think it will touch him, but it may a member of

[1] *New York Tribune*, September 25; *New York Herald*, September 30, 1869.
[2] *New York World*, October 6, 1869.

his family.' [1] Long before that the 'New York World' had exonerated Grant, with the comment that 'the President compromised his independence by indiscreet acceptances of courtesies.' [2] 'The Nation' was less generous: 'One thing is certain — bankers here see traces of the operation of the hand of somebody in authority. Let us know who that person is.' [3] Butterfield was hopelessly compromised, and caught. He resigned, without disgrace, and his statue stands to-day on Riverside Drive looking everlastingly at Grant's Tomb. Gould appeared before the congressional committee, grave and soft-spoken, to insist that he speculated in the interest of the farmers' crops, and while no one believed it, he was let off lightly. Butterfield was given a love-tap, and Fisk, along with Corbin, was pronounced horrid.

The outcome was the ruin of numerous men, financially; the resignation of Butterfield; the resumption by Gould and Fisk of their activities in other lines; the general condemnation of Corbin, who continued on visiting terms with the brother-in-law he had wronged; and the general agreement that Grant had not sinned at all. And yet there were skeptics — even among fine young gentlemen like Henry Adams, who was to marvel, many years later, that one so cautious as Gould would have plunged so desperately on a gamble without some reason to believe that there would be no interference from Washington. He was sure that 'any criminal lawyer would have been bound to start an investigation by insisting that Gould had assurances from the White House or the Treasury, since none other would have satisfied him.' He was to recall that men like Secretaries Fish and Cox, lawyers like Evarts and Hoar, and publicists like Sumner were to remain mystified; that the congressional committee 'took a quantity of evidence which it dared not probe and refused to analyze.' Even at the time he was not alone in the feeling he recorded many years later in cold deliberation: 'That Grant should have fallen within six months into such a morass — or should have let Boutwell drop into it — rendered the outlook . . . mysterious or frankly opaque to a young man who had hitched his wagon . . . to the star of reform'; and that 'the worst scandals of the eighteenth century were relatively harmless by the side of this, which smirched

[1] *Life of Garfield*, i, 449.    [2] October 6, 1869.    [3] October 7, 1869.

executive, judiciary, banks, corporate system, professions, and people . . . in one dirty cesspool of vulgar corruption.' [1] To many such as Adams this episode weakened a fine faith in the Administration as rudely as the episode of the diamond necklace wrecked the reputation of Marie Antoinette — and perhaps with as little justice to the rulers who were the victims.

And that autumn the 'New York Evening Post' began its exposures of the corruption in the New York Custom-House.

### VI

That summer, however, Virginia contributed a silver lining to the cloud. We have seen that the Hunnicutts there had framed the Underwood Constitution, bristling with test oaths and designed to disfranchise the real leaders of the people, and empower the ignorant. Under the brilliant leadership of Alexander H. H. Stuart, the conservatives, organizing for resistance, and unfurling the banner of universal amnesty and universal suffrage, had marched on Washington in an appeal to the ruling powers. Few of the leaders were personally obnoxious to the Republicans. Stuart himself had been an uncompromising Whig; and enlisted with him was Gilbert C. Walker, an avowed Republican, a Northerner, but a resident of Norfolk, where he was a real figure in commerce and finance. A man of fine intelligence, imposing presence, and persuasive speech, he was ideally fitted to win the confidence of Republican leaders at the capital.[2] The Virginia committee sat daily at the National Hotel, and sent carefully chosen emissaries to the various congressional leaders; and later appeared before the committees of both houses. Grant, listening sympathetically to the Virginians, had agreed that the Underwood monstrosity meant negro domination. The outcome had been an agreement that the people should vote separately on all controversial clauses in the constitution. The conservatives — Democrats and moderate Republicans — had nominated Walker for Governor — a powerful merger. The absurdities and incendiarism of Hunnicutt had disgusted many Northern Republicans, and, with an avowed Republican nominee, these were hoping for the creation of a powerful white man's party in Virginia. In the midst of the

[1] *Education of Henry Adams*, 271–72.        [2] Stuart, 33–34, 47.

triumphant campaign progress of Walker, General Canby threw a bomb with the announcement that under the Reconstruction Acts he would exclude from the Legislature any one elected who was unable to take the ironclad oath. The people rose in wrath. Appeals were made to Grant, who peremptorily commanded Canby to rescind. The General complied, the election was held, the more obnoxious features of the constitution were voted out, and Walker was voted in. Thus through the sympathetic co-operation of Grant, Virginia was to escape the more appalling curses of reconstruction. Walker telegraphed Grant: 'I congratulate you upon the triumph of your policy in Virginia,' [1] and Northern Republicans were delighted with Walker's assurance that 'seven eighths of the men who voted the conservative ticket are as far removed from the old Northern Democracy . . . as they are from Radicalism.' For a moment it seemed that Grant would assist in creating a white Republican Party in the South and that darkness had fallen on the very dawn of the régime of the carpet-baggers and the blacks.[2]

But that illusion soon was dispelled. In Mississippi, where they were to vote again on the rejected constitution, and elect State officials, the Democrats, facing realities, proposed a merger with conservative Republicans on the basis of the acceptance of the Fifteenth Amendment, the guarantee of civil and political rights to the negroes, and a pledge to offer no partisan opposition to the Grant Administration. Seeking a leader, they turned to a Republican, a brother-in-law of Grant's, then living with the President in the White House.

Judge Louis Dent had lived in Mississippi before taking up his residence in the capital and had impressed the conservatives with his sound common sense and judgment. Importuned to take the gubernatorial nomination, he accepted in a letter from Washington,[3] and a hundred Democrats joined in a letter to the 'Jackson Clarion,' urging his support. Here was a gesture no less friendly than that in Virginia, but the Radicals had determined to take a stand. Within a week, Dent's recommendations for appointments were curtly rejected by Boutwell, with the blunt announcement that he had no respect for the kind of Republican Party led

[1] New York Herald, July 8, 1869.      [2] Ibid., July 14, 1869.      [3] Garner, 239.

by the Judge. The disillusioned Dent left the Treasury in a rage, and Boutwell complacently hurried to a Cabinet meeting, where he had no reason to expect rebuke.[1]

Followed then Grant's historic letter to Dent from Long Branch, repudiating the latter's candidacy and the conservative movement he represented — and with it the realization that the President's Virginia policy was a mere incident.[2] The astonished candidate sent a sizzling reply, savagely attacking the Radicals. 'To this class of men whom you foiled in their attempt to force upon the people of Mississippi the odious constitution rejected,' he wrote, 'you now give the hand of fellowship and spurn the other class, who, accepting the invitation of the Republican Party in good faith, came *en masse* to stand upon its platform and advocate its principles.'[3] The 'New York World' thought the reply 'justifies a doubt whether Judge Dent would not have been a better — it certainly makes it clear that he would have been a less deplorably bad President than his brother-in-law.'[4] The 'New York Herald' thought that, politically, 'it is Grant that is the brother-in-law,' and that Dent's letter 'puts the President's support of the extreme Radicals in a clear light as a mischievous step.'[5] It assuredly set Grant's feet in the path he was to follow for eight years as the militant champion of Radicalism at its worst.

Undaunted, Dent plunged with vigor into the campaign against J. L. Alcorn, a native Republican with large plantations, who had negroes with him on his ticket. The nominees met in joint debates, and Dent, constantly on the stump, discovered unsuspected powers of sarcasm, but it was of no avail. The solid negro vote went to the Radicals, and Alcorn was easily elected with an overwhelming Republican Legislature, containing forty former slaves, most of whom had to make their mark.[6]

Mississippi thus passed into the hands of the carpetbaggers and blacks, and a black United States Senator was sent to sit in the seat of Jefferson Davis.

In Tennessee, that summer, Andrew Johnson was waging a vigorous battle for the United States Senate, assailing Grant with

[1] *New York World*, July 15, 1869.    [2] Garner, 241.
[3] *Ibid.*, 242.    [4] August 16, 1869.
[5] *Ibid.*    [6] Garner, 246.

devastating sarcasm on his acceptance of valuable gifts, and mobs were being organized by Loyal Leagues to break up his meetings.[1]

One picture: On a platform in a grove at Maryville stands a familiar figure. The eyes are a little more sunken than when we first saw them, four years before, the hair a little grayer, the face a little whiter, the form a little less sturdy and erect. In the milling crowd are many flushed faces of men of the lower order prone to shove and jeer. For a while these watch the speaker, fascinated, and then they begin to groan and yell drunkenly. The old man on the stand speaks on undisturbed. The blear-eyed 'loyal men' pause to consider. Their anger rises. Again the grove rings with drunken yells, and the members of the Loyal League move toward the stand threateningly. The speaker proceeds unconcerned. He had encountered such gentlemen in the cultural centers of the North. Suddenly a supporter of the orator, noting the threatening advance of the drunkards, springs on his chair and reaches for his gun. He is struck — topples over. The man on the platform does not even pause. The 'loyal men,' awed by the indifference of Johnson, retire, and try to bribe a negro to pull him from the platform. Johnson continues, and finishes his speech.[2]

Thus, fighting his way always, Johnson canvassed the State and lost. Greeley was beside himself with joy. 'To be defeated by Cooper [Johnson's opponent] is like being rejected by a lady who prefers your valet,' he wrote.[3] What a man! said the editor, returning to his mutton. 'His verbs never agree with their nominatives or their hearers or anything else,' and, besides, he was 'dishonest.'[4] But Johnson had grown callous to the barbs of cultured blackguards, and after his defeat he smilingly gave a dinner at the Stacy House, in Nashville, for the members of the Legislature, and friend and foe broke bread with him. He had just begun to fight.

In the North, startled eyes were turned on Massachusetts, where John Quincy Adams II had accepted the Democratic gubernatorial nomination and was speaking the language of statesmanship, after the fashion of his family. His acceptance speech was more prophetic than acceptable to many, but none among the conservatives of either party but felt the force of his argument.

[1] *New York World*, June 7, 1869.    [2] *Ibid.*, August 8, 1869.
[3] *New York Tribune*, October 21, 1869.    [4] *Ibid.*, October 25, 1869.

Reconstruction had to be accepted — at least, then. Suffrage was settled. He turned his batteries on the extravagance in Washington and everywhere, on the tax system with its inequalities and injustice, on the tariff. The Democratic organ accepted the speech as 'clear and able.' A peculiarly attractive man — this forgotten orator and political leader. 'One of the best talkers in Boston society, and perhaps the most popular man in the State, though apt to be on the unpopular side,' wrote his brother Henry.[1] All through these dark days before us we shall occasionally catch a furtive glimpse of this brilliant figure, fighting against the current and destined to oblivion because 'apt to be on the unpopular side' in Massachusetts.

VII

The year ended like a melodrama. In December, Daniel McFarland walked into the office of the 'New York Tribune' and shot down Albert D. Richardson, a favorite journalist among the Radicals, said to have been living with the divorced wife of his assailant. Greeley himself was so shocked, he excused himself from attending an hilarious dinner being given a notorious character who had been appointed to a post abroad, where he speedily came to grief for attempting to put carpetbag theories into practice. Henry Ward Beecher hastened to the hot defense of the stricken man, denouncing the erstwhile husband as an adulterer, without justification. As Richardson lay dying, it was Beecher, not the minister of the stricken man, who married him to Mrs. McFarland — and New York and the country gasped at the audacity of the thing. Vice-President Colfax shared with Beecher the general abuse poured forth from the pulpits; for it was Colfax, a friend of Mrs. McFarland, who had advised her on her divorce under the amazingly lax divorce laws of Indiana, and had sponsored her socially in Indianapolis.[2] Beecher, cringing before the public reaction, made matters more messy in an attempt to exculpate himself, and, while Colfax fell somewhat from grace, it was observed that he was 'far too prudent to put out any defense of his unfortunate conduct.'[3] A private scandal

[1] *Education of Henry Adams*, 35.
[2] *New York World*, December 4, December 16, 1869.        [3] *Ibid.*, December 11, 1869.

— and yet it cast a shadow on the leaders of the forces of 'morality.'

The reformers, however, found a crumb of comfort before the year closed through the removal of the notorious Ashley, the impeacher, from the governorship of Montana. The 'New York Tribune' ascribed the brevity of his tenure to some grave suspicion in the mind of the President,' [1] but corruption does not appear to have been charged. Imbued with the Radical passion for racial equality, he found the people of Montana in revolt and his usefulness was over. 'The Nation' mournfully observed that this damaged him more than 'his corrupt partnership with Case,' and that the Case correspondence, known to every one, 'does not seem to have damaged him at all, or very little.' [2]

The people along with the politicians were still wallowing in corruption and enjoying the feel of the ooze.

[1] December 17, 1869.        [2] December 23, 1869.

# CHAPTER XIV

## WEIRD SCHEMES AND NEW LEADERS

### I

NEVER since the war had society been so gay or so brilliant as during the Washington winter of 1869–70. Never had women been more in the minds of men, and lights burned brightly in the homes of hostesses until the dawn came to put them out. It was the season of the triumph of the first Mrs. Belknap — a spectacular triumph. But triumphant women were not confined to social circles, for the capital swarmed with ladies of indifferent morality, representing perfectly respectable business organizations in pursuit of privilege. Attractive, fashionably dressed, and dashing were these women of the most daring lobby that had ever descended on a legislative body for the purposes of pelf. An alert correspondent observed that 'from the capital parlors to Georgetown, influences ramify and wires work which draw their power from a common battery.' The more audacious of these women of the lobby took pretentious houses as for a social campaign. These, the Grand Duchesses of the tribe, were good to look upon, clever conversationalists, altogether pleasing, and, while most were unmarried, their God-and-morality employers had conveniently provided them with husbands. Did the skeptical inquire as to their antecedents and credentials? Some one could always remember having met them in a distant city, where they were the models of the community. These had abundance on the board, wine and brandy, but it was the seductive charms of these ladies that lured statesmen to their parties. They subtly conveyed the impression that, tired of their prosy husbands, they were ready for a romantic interlude; and each observer was sure the lady's choice had fallen upon him. Flirt they certainly did, but it was just a flitting smile, the flicker of an eyelid, the faint suggestion of a blush. Was the lady 'prudishly quick to interpret anything as an insult?' All the more proof that she was of the aristocracy of her kind. And yet the cynical correspondent, studying her methods, noted that 'she will flare up at a mere glance of curiosity from a stranger, and pardon a kiss red-hot on the lips from a man who has a vote.'

Many of this tribe were found in boarding-houses and hotels frequented by statesmen. Demure at first, and with eyes cast down; and then — why not? since meetings were unavoidable in dining-rooms — a friendly nod of recognition. But nods were reserved for members with votes. The more sensitive of these were easily lured, and dinners, with wine flowing freely, followed. Again the correspondent observed that 'the lever of lust is used to pry up more legislators to the sticking point when money itself does not avail to seduce.' That there was no little blackmailing we may be sure. But, on the whole, the system was by no means crude or vulgar. Some of the women with most finesse had their coachmen, and even footmen, and 'always a pew in Dr. Newman's church.' Such elaborate plans for the entertainment of susceptible statesmen were made only when there was a big killing in prospect at the capital.[1]

It was the winter when tariff lobbyists descended in force, when railroads were planning more pillaging, when Congressmen were selling cadetships to West Point, and when Governor Bullock was trying to buy congressional intervention to protect him and his bandits in their stealing in Georgia. Men like Trumbull were saddened by the low moral tone of the time, and Fessenden and Grimes were corresponding pessimistically on the corruption of the day. 'Why, the war has corrupted everybody and everything,' Grimes had written in August. 'It is money that achieves success . . . nowadays. Thank God, my political career ended with the beginning of this corrupt political era.'[2] The career of Julian, impeccably honest, was darkening because he would not acquiesce in the moral debauch. 'The most frightful swindles are on foot and likely to go through,' he wrote in May, 'and the general wreck of the Republican Party through its espousal of these schemes is quite probable.'[3] A month later, he was sadly writing: 'I have never seen such lobbying before as we have had in the last few weeks and such crookedness and complicity among members.' He

---

[1] *New York World*, January 2, 1870.          [2] *Life of Grimes*, 377.
[3] MS. Diary, May 8, 1870.

was disgusted with Congressmen who talked one way while 'privately laboring for the other side for a consideration.' [1] This attitude had been viewed with stern disapproval, and he had been marked for slaughter. His bitter attack on the railroad lobby [2] had been the last straw. Julian was growing 'queer.' Soon Horace Greeley was to refuse him help for reëlection because he was 'not sound on the tariff.' [3] That year the old Abolitionist was rejected by his party and retired — no place for purists in the procession moving triumphantly on with the 'bloody shirt' for a flag.

The industrialists had marched *en masse* upon the capital — iron, coal, wool, steel, leather — in the making of the tariff act that year, and, with rumblings in the West, even Allison of Iowa grumbled that the rates were being fixed for private interests, and against the revenue. Greeley was a little disturbed, but not discouraged. 'A few leading journals have been carried over to the enemy' in the West, but 'the popular heart throbs responsive to Protection.' [4] A few notable Republicans met in Washington to launch a tariff reform movement, but it was really a blowing against the wind. While these intellectuals talked, men like Senator Sprague, who owned cotton mills, were quietly fixing the cotton yarn schedule which Allen G. Thurman was to describe as 'a perfect swindle.' [5] Godkin, with fine satire, in referring to the reform movement, said that, 'after the usual distribution of "British gold" from the Legation, the meeting separated.' [6]

The dominant wing of the party was not worried over the grumbling of the farmers. When the campaign approached, there would be much waving of the 'bloody shirt,' lurid talk of Democratic butchery of inoffensive negroes, and out from the groves would float the familiar refrain — 'Every man who poisoned the wells of Union soldiers was a Democrat; the man who shot down your father or your son was a Democrat; every one who ——' and it would suffice. Being practical politicians, they knew what the intellectuals did not suspect.

That winter the Democratic minority made its protest, but it was as futile as Don Quixote tilting at the windmills. No one really cared.

[1] MS. Diary, June 26, 1870.    [2] *Congressional Globe*, February 5, 1869.
[3] MS. Diary, March 27, 1870.    [4] *New York Tribune*, April 23, 1870.
[5] Thurman to J. S. Moore, *Thurman Papers*.    [6] *The Nation*, April 28, 1870.

## II

Grumbling, too, was heard about railroads looting through governmental action, but the sovereign people standing about the country stores were more interested in the latest 'outrages' in the South. Every one knew the railroad grants were steeped in corruption, and it was openly charged. 'All our railroad legislation is procured by corrupt practices and is formed in the interest of jobbery,' said the 'New York Herald,' without disturbing the serenity of Congress.[1] Greeley rebuked the New York Republican Club for petitioning against more grants to railroads,[2] but soon he was singing another tune and declaring that 'the sooner this land-grant business for railroads is stopped, the better.' [3] He had been shocked at the spectacle of the Senate wrangling 'for weary hours over a proposition to give a solid block of public lands fifty miles wide and two to three hundred miles long to comparatively useless railroad companies,' and was sure that 'a Senate that can do this can do anything.' [4] When twenty-five of the proposed grants made by the Senate failed in the House, he was delighted.[5] But nothing was permitted to interfere with the Northern Pacific grab of Jay Cooke — and thereon hangs a tale of the utter subserviency to the counting-room ambitions of this pious feeder of the campaign chest.

On assuming control of the Northern Pacific, it was characteristic of Cooke to call first of all for a history of the lobby that had backed Thad Stevens, author of the measure.[6] From that hour he had never calculated without the lobby, and he knew its cost. In 1870, when he was seeking another handsome subsidy, an ugly fight developed. Henry Cooke, in the Washington bank, worked like a Trojan with the aid of William E. Chandler of New Hampshire. Circulating on the floor of the House could be seen the picturesque Ignatius Donnelly, a former member, presumably representing the labor element in Duluth, but really on Jay Cooke's payroll. Night after night he drew the blinds and wrote lengthy reports to his employer. Mingling with members as lobbyists in disguise were governors of States, and money was

---

[1] April 19, 1870.     [2] *New York Tribune*, March 17, 1870.
[3] *Ibid.*, June 24, 1870.     [4] *Ibid.*     [5] *Ibid.*, July 15, 1870.
[6] Oberholtzer, *Cooke*, II, 147.

used freely. In the case of some obstreperous statesmen under
financial obligations to the house of Cooke, like Blaine, it was
Jay himself who delicately conveyed a reminder; and not a few
Congressmen found themselves discreetly remembered, and in
possession of stock.[1]

Even so, the fight waxed warm until, in March, Donnelly
reported that a land grant would have to be substituted for a
subsidy, and this was satisfactory. In the Senate, where the battle
was bitter, Allen G. Thurman, an intellectual giant, and new
Democratic leader, with Senator Harlan, Republican, were
causing distress in their opposition to bestowing an empire on
Cooke. But Cooke had the votes. 'We have been at work like
beavers,' wrote Henry to Jay, 'and have whipped the enemy on
every vote. . . . We let the other side do most of the talking and
we do the voting.' [2] The cunning Cameron, the trader, suggested
an amendment providing the exclusive use of American iron or
steel, and it was adopted. Cameron spoke Cooke's language.

But passage in the Senate did not end the fight, and under Jay
Cooke's instructions, Logan, Ben Butler, and Schenck of Ohio
were especially cultivated, though the latter was always obsequious as a butler to the banker. The attempt to bulldoze the measure through without debate raised a tempest among Democrats
and insurgents, and the plan was abandoned. Anxious days,
these, in the house of Cooke, even Ben Butler erratic in his voting
until Chandler of New Hampshire pointed out the possibility
of a retainer.[3] And so the fight was waged, and the heathen raged,
but Henry Cooke had his forces well in hand. 'Blaine is doing us
a great service,' he wrote his brother. That very day he had
considerately dropped in on Henry to explain that Jay had no
occasion for concern.[4] That was the day of the stormiest opposition. Thus the measure passed and Cooke got his 'empire' —
provided Grant did not veto the bill.

But the financier in Philadelphia, serene in the incense of his
clerics, was not in doubt. Had not Grant sent for members and
lobbied in the interest of the bill? Besides, Henry was not neglect-
ing the White House, nor the White House Henry. 'I have talked

[1] Oberholtzer, *Cooke*, II, 176.     [2] *Ibid.*, II, 178.
[3] *Ibid.*, II, 179.     [4] *Ibid.*, II, 179–80.

with the President about our bill,' wrote the latter to Jay a month before. 'He takes great interest in it, and there is no danger of his not signing it.'[1] Jay had sent a fishing-rod and creel to little Jesse Grant and received a note of thanks in a boyish hand, and had just invited the President and some friends on a fishing trip.[2]

Even so there was insurgency in the Cabinet, and a momentary uneasiness. On the morning the Cabinet was to meet, Grant sauntered into Henry Cooke's office, and by his conversation convinced the banker he was 'firm as a rock.'[3] Thus the victory was won, albeit George W. Childs, of the 'Philadelphia Public Ledger,' persisted in denouncing the whole thing as 'sublime effrontery,' until George Jones, of the 'New York Times,' graciously hurried to Philadelphia in a futile effort to silence his fellow journalist, and Cooke threatened to destroy 'The Public Ledger' by establishing a better paper. But all ended well, and the house of Cooke had never been stronger. It was soon offering Vice-President Colfax a job, and promising Schenck, then going as Minister to England, that he would be cared for on his return, and Colfax was recommending Ben Wade as legislative agent on the ground that 'no one stands higher with the President and Cabinet.[4]

This was the time, too, that less pretentious statesmen were replenishing their purses with the sale of cadetships, and there were some expulsions — including the delectable Whittemore of South Carolina, who was ardently defended in his morals by the philosophic Ben Butler. It is significant of the moral collapse of the times that these disclosures only added to the festivity of the Nation. Few were really shocked.

### III

The Senate that winter illustrated the passing of the régime of the idealists and the triumph of that of the practical politicians not greatly concerned with human rights, for blacks or whites. Fessenden was dead; Grimes was nursing his stricken body in Europe; Sumner, never a leader, was never less potent; and Trumbull, no longer powerful, was looking a little sadly upon the

[1] Oberholtzer, *Cooke*, II, 181.    [2] *Ibid.*
[3] *Ibid.*, II, 181–82; Henry to Jay.    [4] *Ibid.*, II, 230–32.

changing scene. The leadership of the dominant party had passed to a small group of able opportunists, of whom the most commanding figure was Oliver P. Morton. Upon his shoulders had fallen the mantle of Thad Stevens. Henceforth, he was to be the most forceful of the leaders, the most uncompromising on the plan to hold the South by hook or by crook.

Seen from the gallery, Morton was a striking figure, stricken by disease, as Stevens had been by age. His huge, well-proportioned body, with broad shoulders and powerful frame, made his physical infirmity all the more pitiful, for he had suffered a paralytic stroke. Two robust men bore him in a chair to his place in the Senate, and he usually spoke sitting. Medical science, here and in Europe, had failed to cure him, and he no longer looked forward to relief. His disease happily failed to dim the brightness of his intellect, or to weaken the force of his iron will. The spectator in the gallery, looking down upon this stricken giant, and noting his great body, the large well-shaped head with the high brow, the black piercing eyes matching hair and beard of the same color, would have known at once that here was no ordinary man. Had he entertained a moment's doubt, the instant Morton spoke the skepticism would have passed. In his oratory he was all clarity and force. Disdaining the ornamental, and probably without imagination, he spoke the plain language of the masses, going directly to the point to which his clear intellectual processes impelled him. He had no time for graceful gestures, and he was not the master that Stevens was in the use of wit, humor, or satire. Nothing of finesse shimmered on his blade. He wanted nothing on his sword but blood, and that he seldom failed to draw. In his more savage moments — and he was never gentle — he had no patience with a sword — he grasped a battle-axe. Given a cause of merit, his argument was devastating, and in support of the numerous causes we now know to have been unworthy, he was tremendous. A great giant, with flashing eyes and set jaws, smashing through the barbed-wire entanglements of logic and evidence, there was something in the spectacle to command respect. He was the symbol of audacity.

A political opponent, who thought that 'the small portion of his being in which disease had left vitality was set on vengeance,' described him not unhappily as the 'Couthon of his party.'[1] He himself, strangely enough, would have preferred to have been called the Vergniaud. In early manhood he had become enamoured of the brilliant leader of the Gironde while poring over the vivid pages of Lamartine. Not Mirabeau, who crushed all opposition, as Morton did; not Robespierre, who hated with an inveterate hate, as Morton hated; but Vergniaud, the polished orator of the conservative Republicans, the speaker of finesse, whom Morton resembled not at all, entranced him. It was Vergniaud's talk on immortality at the last supper of the doomed deputies that Morton treasured in his memory always.

It will be recalled that Stevens was sounding the keynote of Radicalism at Lancaster in the summer that Morton was bitterly and convincingly assailing everything that Radicalism meant at Richmond. Yet Morton was to wear Stevens's mantle. It is impossible to believe that Morton underwent a change of sentiment. He was an opportunist, a partisan, and when his party took its stand, he veered to meet it without a blush. It was this savage subserviency to party prejudices that made him the power he became.

As a politician, he was a rigid disciplinarian, autocratic, dictatorial, absolute. He exacted unquestioning obedience to his will, and woe to the Republican that crossed him. Julian had dared anticipate him in the radicalism of reconstruction — it wrecked him. Harrison had a pride of his own, and when Hayes wished to invite him into his Cabinet, it was Morton who turned thumbs down. He brooked no rivals.[2] Intensely practical, he was a genius in organization, and in every nook and corner of the State his followers slept upon their arms. His ambition was Napoleonic. He assumed the leadership of the Senate, won the complete confidence of Grant, who feared to cross him, and more than any other one man became the spokesman of the Administration.

Unlike so many of his associates, money did not tempt him. His ambition did not center on material things. Despite his infirmity, the nights found him hard at work in simple surroundings, and he would not tolerate pretensions. When his coachman put on livery,

---

[1] *Destruction and Reconstruction*, 260.

[2] Turpie, 221; *Life of Hayes*.

he ordered it off, and continued his journeys to the Capitol in a primitive vehicle. No touch of scandal stained his toga. 'There is temptation,' wrote a Southern leader, 'to dwell on Morton as one of the few Radical leaders who kept his hands clean of plunder.' [1] He died as poor as when he entered public life.[2] Living for years in the shadow of death, he apparently had no religion. In youth, the 'Evidences of Christianity' had shaken his faith, and he never recovered it. When he thought he was dying, he sent for a physician and a lawyer, but no minister. When a Quaker woman asked to talk with him about the state of his soul, he snappishly replied: 'That has been attended to.'

During the period we have now reached in our narrative, Morton lived at the Ebbitt House, and his rooms were the headquarters of the Southern carpetbaggers, and the negro politicians haunted his quarters. These all looked to him as their special champion, not without reason.

A monumental figure, not lovable, but awe-inspiring in its primitive strength.[3]

## IV

Quite the antithesis of Morton was another champion of Grant's policies, Roscoe Conkling. Morton was force; Conkling was beauty. Women in the galleries were fascinated by the handsome Adonis, six feet three in height, erect, graceful, a magnificent head on splendid shoulders, a flowing blond beard, and the mannerisms of an actor. Morton was primitive nature; Conkling was all art. Morton knew the minds and hearts of common men; Conkling would have concealed the fact as a matter of pride if he had known them. He was the orator of the Administration, the incomparable sophist, and he swayed audiences with his eloquence while charming them with his mere physical presence. Withal, he was as temperamental as a prima donna, nervous, arrogant. His egotism was sublime. Women were drawn to him, but his conceit protected him from the blandishments of most, though he succumbed notably to one of the most remarkable women of his generation; men admired his ability while resenting his arrogance. Dashing, deb-

---

[1] *Destruction and Reconstruction*, 260.      [2] Turpie, 225.
[3] I have made use of Foulke's excellent biography.

onair, scintillating, he was a true cavalier — the Aramis of the Three Musketeers of the President.

The third of the Musketeers lacked the intellectual qualities of Morton, and the polish of Conkling. But Zachariah Chandler was the master organizer of the three — he was the engineer. He symbolized more than any other the alliance of business and politics then being consummated as never before. Bluff, gruff, a little swaggering, he had no false sense of dignity, and among his friends was all affability. He was ready with a hearty laugh or a good story. Intensely practical, with the business man's idea that things worth having may be bought or bargained for, he was to establish the partnership of favor-seeking industries and politics on the frank basis of a trade — campaign contribution for the politicians, legislative and administrative favors for the contributors. While Morton threatened and Conkling argued, it was Chandler who moved affably about the floor and the cloak-rooms trading and bargaining for votes. He was as extreme in his partisanship as Morton, as bitter in his sectionalism as Stevens or Wade. Much of his party work was done quietly, but it was on a big scale, and not a little sinister, and the effect of his policy in party management still abides.

v

Opposing them, on the Democratic side, were two new men who had assumed the leadership. Hendricks had retired to Indiana, disgusted with the new atmosphere of the capital. With his departure the leadership passed to Allen G. Thurman, of Ohio, new to the Senate, who, in sheer intellect, character, and capacity, was the peer of the best and the superior of most of his colleagues on both sides of the chamber. Below the average height and heavy-set, with massive head and rugged features, with a rather shaggy beard and profuse locks of hair suggestive of a leonine nature, he looked the leader. His voice, though heavy, was pleasing. A little abrupt and brusque, he was inherently courteous and kindly, and in the heat of the debate maintained a cheerful good-humor. A gentleman of the old school, he made frequent visits to the Senate's snuffboxes, for he was an inveterate snuffer; this brought into view the red bandanna handkerchief he affected, and soon it became popularly associated with his fame.

Allen G. Thurman                    Thomas A. Hendricks

Thomas F. Bayard                    Daniel W. Voorhees

DEMOCRATIC LEADERS

His training had been of the best. In youth, he had sat in the inner circles of the Jacksonians in Washington, aroused the interest of Calhoun, and for years had been the trusted adviser of his uncle, William Allen, and of his party in matters of management and principles. A lawyer of erudition, a jurist of experience and distinction, few Senators cared to cross swords with him on legal or constitutional questions. 'When I speak of the law,' said Conkling, 'I turn to the Senator from Ohio as the Mussulman turns toward Mecca.' His method in debate was that of a great lawyer; his speeches were as the expositions of a great judge. He indulged in no frivolities, and took the floor only when he had something to say. In reasoning robust, his blows were titanic, and when occasion called, his sarcasm and satire were destructive. Fair in statement, honest in his conclusions, sincere in purpose, he commanded universal respect.

In political judgment, he was instinctively sound. On all the fundamentals of his party's faith he was safe. He not only had mastered the philosophy of the fathers; it was inherently his own. He believed in fighting the enemy cleanly — but he believed in fighting. In general culture, he was above the average in the Senate, an omnivorous reader, especially fond of the French masters, a lover of Molière and Racine, and in moments of social relaxation wont to quote pages of humorous passages from Balzac. A devotee of music and the drama, he was one of the most constant playgoers of the capital.

For the corruption and moral laxity of the times he had the utmost scorn, and he was repeatedly to stand forth against the organized forces of predatory wealth. His honesty was proverbial, and that made him loom large in his generation. He was of the race of giants — a reminder of the elder day.[1]

Of less heroic stature, and yet of commanding ability, in the first rank of statesmanship and leadership, was Thomas F. Bayard, of Delaware. More suave than Thurman, with a little less power in his punch, he was a seasoned statesman, a clever debater, a sagacious political manager. Where Thurman was the warrior, Bayard was the diplomat. Of pleasing presence, moder-

[1] *Historical and Biographical Cyclopedia of Ohio*; Blaine, *Twenty Years*, II, 442; *Thurman Papers*; *New York World*, December 20, 1869.

ate, urbane, dignified, he made an impressive figure on the floor. He never lost his balance or struck a blow beneath the belt. Socially a charming companion, fluent and interesting in conversation, his familiarity with the French language made him a favorite in diplomatic circles. Like Thurman, he was a book man, liking nothing better than a quiet evening in his library.

Hendricks, Thurman, and Bayard — these three led the minority through tragic years when constitutional barriers were being brushed aside, when courts were in contempt, and our institutions were being remoulded by the fingers of prejudice and fanaticism. With but a little band behind them, they managed, through the force of intellect and character, occasionally to give pause to the mad spirit of the times. This, not the mere wrangling of the majority, explains Grant's complaint that the dominant party was 'allowing the few Democrats to be the balance to fix amendments to every important measure.' [1] It was something that Grant could not understand.

## VI

This session witnessed the dramatic advent of another new Senator who illustrated the full flowering of the policy imposed upon the South. An artist would have found an interesting study in the faces of women peering down upon the floor in the first days of February. Some registered curiosity; others something of repulsion. For there, surrounded by admiring partisans, stood a black man — Hiram R. Revels, new Senator from Mississippi, elected to the seat of Jefferson Davis. A man of some education, not without some culture, modest and dignified in demeanor, he impressed a correspondent as a man 'able to take care of himself . . . who will not suffer himself to be browbeaten even by Sumner.' [2] On his arrival, he had been honored at a dinner at which both races had mingled about the board. There were some senators, the entire Mississippi delegation, Adelbert Ames, soon to marry the daughter of Ben Butler and now awaiting his admission to the Senate as the black man's colleague, and 'Pig Iron' Kelley, who had found the negroes in the South the intellectual superiors of the whites. The diners had lingered long at the board in merry conversation and

[1] *Grant's Letters to a Friend*, 66–67.    [2] *New York World*, January 31, 1870

perfect fraternity, and there was much lifting of eyebrows even among the political advocates of equality.[1] When Revels appeared in the Senate, he was lionized by the Radicals, Sumner the first to greet him with smiles and compliments, closely followed by Simon Cameron and the carpetbag Senators.[2]

That month John W. Forney gave his 'social equality party,' with the two races mingling as one. Grant dropped in, and members of the Cabinet, and chatted the evening away. The new Mississippi Senator was the center of attraction, and that venerable journalist, Major Poore, made a grave social error. Arriving late, he turned to a colored man seated at a table.

'Go and get me some wine, my good fellow,' he ordered.

'Sir, I think we have met before at Sumner's,' replied the negro with dignity. 'I believe I am addressing Major Poore, am I not? And the Major must remember that we dined together at Senator Sumner's.'

'Oh, I beg your pardon. So we did, sir. How are you, Professor?'

It was Professor Vashon. Under the new social dispensation, such social errors were almost unavoidable.[3]

Soon Revels made his maiden speech to galleries packed with both races, speaking in excellent taste, in language many Senators could not have matched in grace of diction; and Morton, who had sought vainly to secure for the negro the very seat once occupied by Davis, rose to compliment the speaker who 'so well vindicated the ability and intelligence of his race . . . and shows the country that in receiving him in exchange for Jefferson Davis, the Senate has lost nothing in intelligence.'[4]

Soon followed the ratification of the Fifteenth Amendment, and then, feverish activity among the Radicals. The Republican Club marched to the White House, and, responding to the serenade, Grant appeared at the door with Forney, to declare that 'no consummation since the Civil War affords me so much pleasure.'[5] Negro orators planned stumping tours in the North; and it was

---

[1] *New York Herald*, February 2, 1870.     [2] *Ibid.*, February 3, 1870.
[3] *Ibid.*, February 20, 1870.
[4] *Congressional Globe*, March 16, 1870; *New York Tribune*, March 17, 1870.
[5] *New York Herald*, April 2, 1870.

said the Union League Club would begin the organization of secret leagues in the Northern States for the purposes of the approaching campaign. To the politicians the Amendment meant the reclamation of some lost States — Delaware, Maryland, and New Jersey.[1]

Two months later, when the Union League held its conference at the Arlington, the reports were encouraging, the finances satisfactory, and the national secretary was instructed to proceed forthwith to the South.[2] The dominant party had never been more jubilant; the freedmen, never so enthusiastic over the prospects of real equality. And yet there was a fly in the ointment when Revels appointed a colored boy a cadet at West Point. 'A very foolish and cruel thing as far as the boy and his family is concerned, and a very injudicious thing as far as the colored race is concerned,' thought 'The Nation.' Of course, it said, the boy could not pass the examination. And all that came of it was a trip to West Point for the potential cadet, a breakfast at Couzzen's Hotel, 'with as much pomp and ceremony as any white cadet would have had shown him,' a courteous treatment by the authorities — and the dream was over.[3]

VII

United on negro suffrage, the dominant party was seriously disturbed when Grant dumped into the Senate hopper an amazing opéra-bouffe proposition — a treaty providing for the purchase of San Domingo for $1,500,000. Negotiated by General Orville E. Babcock, destined to much notoriety, signed by him as 'Aide-de-Camp to his Excellency Ulysses S. Grant,' there had been no consultation with the Secretary of State. Just how the President became involved remains a mystery. Obsessed with a craving for territory, it is probable that speculators and gamblers financially interested managed to divert him from the thought of Cuba to the black republic. Behind the screen the project had been brewing for two years. A friend of Senator Grimes had asked his advice about investing and had been dissuaded.[4] It was not until 1869 that Grant became interested, when a man-of-war was ordered to

---

[1] *New York Herald*, April 3, 1870.          [2] *Ibid.*, June 1, 1870.
[3] *The Nation*, June 9, 1870.          [4] Grimes to Rich, *Life of Grimes*, 379.

the ports of the Dominican Republic to ascertain the views of the people there of all parties regarding annexation and the sale or lease of the Bay of Samana, or of territory adjacent thereto. In July, General Babcock set forth on his diplomatic mission and a warship was instructed to give him the moral support of its guns. This may have been necessary to support the tottering régime of President Baez during negotiations, but not for his persuasion, for he was eager to sell his country. It was not information as to popular sentiment that the gay Babcock was after, but a sale; and he soon returned with the protocol of a treaty in which Grant was pledged to exert all his power to secure a ratification of any agreement made.

Shocked and disgusted by the proceedings behind his back, Secretary Fish wished to resign, but was dissuaded, and Babcock returned with an adequate naval force to continue and close negotiations, with the consent of the State Department. This was speedily accomplished; and, pending the ratification, warships were hurried to Dominican waters for the protection of the man who sought to sell his country. So precarious was his hold on power, that in February, 1870, Admiral Poor made a demonstration at the Haytian capital and served notice that any attack on Baez would be considered a declaration of war against the United States.

In his Message in December, Grant had painted an extravagant picture of the resources and value of San Domingo; and in early January, Charles Sumner, chairman of the Foreign Relations Committee, dining with Forney and Poore, the journalists, was interrupted by the sound of Grant's voice in his hall. Hastening to him, Sumner ushered the President into the dining-room. The guests rose to leave. Grant waved them to their seats. No objection to discussing foreign relations with the chairman of the Foreign Relations Committee in the presence of the press. Or, *was* Sumner chairman of the Judiciary Committee? Grant had thus addressed him — but no matter. He sought an offhand assurance of Sumner's active support for ratification. Dumbfounded, and yet forgiving something to Grant's simplicity in such matters, Sumner responded, 'Mr. President, I am an Administration man, and whatever you do will always find in me the most careful and candid consideration.'

Grant was delighted — Sumner was pledged! Had he not said he was an 'Administration man'? And could an 'Administration man' do other than obey orders like a subordinate in the army? Of course, Sumner, who took his duties seriously, had only pledged himself to 'careful and candid consideration,' but Grant wearied on long sentences. The next day, Babcock, military ambassador, called on Sumner with the treaty, and, when it reached the Senate, Sumner laid it before his committee. In the informal discussion he expressed no opinion. The others were unfriendly — all but Morton, who had Grant's idea of an 'Administration man.'

It was about this time that Senator Carl Schurz, calling at the White House, was casually solicited to support the treaty, and when the Senator, more amazed than Sumner, took his courage in both hands frankly to explain his objections, he observed that quite soon Grant's 'eyes wandered about the room' as though he were bored.[1]

The drama, which was to mean something to the Republican Party, was hurrying on. Sumner, hearing strange rumors that Baez was being sustained in power by the American Navy, hastened to the Navy Department to find he had not been misled, and that the treaty had been made under duress. That was enough for Sumner.

Meanwhile, with Sumner's committee failing to act, Grant, enraged at the delay, and holding the chairman responsible, began to threaten vengeance. 'The idea has got abroad,' wrote Forney to Sumner, 'that he has marked you out for sacrifice, and it excites much feeling.'[2]

At length, despite the President's active lobbying, the committee made an adverse report, and two days later, Grant appeared at the Capitol in belligerent mood. He appeared, said the 'New York World,'[3] 'somewhat in the style of Oliver Cromwell,' and, handing a messenger a list of Senators, said, 'Send these men to me immediately.' There was some excitement and no end of gossip. The fact, too, that New York speculators had moved on the Capitol, created an ugly atmosphere.[4] On March 24, Sumner opened the debate in secret session with a powerful attack on the treaty,

[1] Schurz, 307–09.    [2] Pierce, iv, 439.
[3] March 20, 1870.    [4] New York World, March 24, 1870.

and the next day Grant was at the Capitol again summoning Senators from the floor, 'taking them into committee rooms and out-of-the-way corners, buttonholing them to vote for the Grant-Baez Treaty.' [1]

The fight dragged on, increasing in bitterness, Morton cracking the party whip to no avail. Senator Wilson, supporting Grant for party solidarity, admitted that nine tenths of the people were against the treaty. When the Collector of the Port of New York attempted a popular demonstration for it at Cooper Union, it was a failure — the speculators on the platform all too conspicuous. In the Senate, Morton was fighting hard, a large collection of San Domingo products on his desk, for he was taking his colleagues to the mountain-top. A large block of salt from the mountains of Neibia proved most interesting to the statesmen, and they gathered about to taste it — 'including Revels,' said the 'New York Herald.' [2] But the opposition was thoroughly organized on a principle — the plans perfected in the library of Sumner's home by Sumner and Schurz.[3]

Two weeks before the vote, Secretary Fish appeared at Sumner's home one night and sought until midnight to swerve him from his purpose. 'Why not go to London?' asked Fish suddenly. 'I offer you the English mission; it is yours'; [4] or, 'How would you like to be Minister to England?' [5] None of the chroniclers of the incident describe it as an attempt to bribe, for Fish was above such methods. Badeau, never wholly reliable, offers the explanation that Fish found Sumner in tears, and assumed his condition due to his domestic or financial difficulties, and advised him, on adjournment, to go to Europe and forget his troubles. With Sumner's reply that he could not afford it, Fish impulsively blurted forth the offer. 'No, I cannot disturb Motley,' was the reply. 'No, I see you are right,' said Fish. 'You could not supplant Motley.' [6]

Even so, the day after the failure of the treaty, the blow fell on Sumner's friend — Motley was dismissed! With amusing simplicity, Senator Wilson protested to Grant that the dismissal would be interpreted in Massachusetts as a blow at Sumner.[7] And Sumner

[1] *New York World*, March 26, 1870.      [2] March 26, 1870.      [3] Schurz. 325.
[4] Pierce, IV, 443–44.      [5] Badeau, 216.      [6] Badeau, 216.
[7] Pierce, IV, 446.

wrote Longfellow: 'At last the blow has fallen on Motley. I am unhappy at the thought of the unhappiness in his house. . . . When I see you on the piazza, I will tell you the story of "Revenge."' [1]

While Sumner was sitting on the poet's piazza at Nahant telling him the story of 'Revenge,' Grant was trout-fishing with Simon Cameron in Pennsylvania. The Democratic organ said: 'Trout-fishing with an unscrupulous politician like Simon Cameron exhibits General Grant in a new light and Simon as a dexterous fisher of men. We do not know with what Simon baited his hook, but he has evidently caught a President.' [2]

And so he had, as we shall see later.

### VIII

Quite as trying to party solidarity was the case of Georgia. Here we must pause for a hasty survey of events in that State under the government of the carpetbaggers, protected by the sword. These had bestowed the governorship on Rufus Bullock, a large man of pleasant manners, and in less than two years his administration reeked with corruption. The genius of his merry group of marauders was H. I. Kimball, who craved no office, distributed places to his retainers with a blessing, and only asked the small boon of looting the Treasury. Nor was he parsimonious. Through him a seat in the Legislature could be made lucrative. The politicians bowed low before this dashing, affable, successful man with the Midas touch and with something of the generosity of Dives. The negro members chuckled at his approach, and sang a song in his praise:

> 'H. I. Kimball's on de flo',
> 'Tain't gwine ter rain no mo'.'

While building railroads with State money was his specialty, he was versatility itself. Thinking an opera house in course of construction wanton waste, he bought it, remodeled it, and sold it to Georgia as a State House at a handsome profit. The capital needed a fine hotel — enough; he built the Kimball House, and paid for it with the State bonds, over which, as semi-official financial agent of the Commonwealth, he had autocratic control, making no re-

[1] Pierce, IV, 448.          [2] New York World, June 20, 1870.

## "TIME WORKS WONDERS."

IAGO. (JEFF DAVIS.) "FOR THAT I DO SUSPECT THE LUSTY MOOR
HATH LEAP'D INTO MY SEAT : THE THOUGHT WHEREOF
DOTH LIKE A POISONOUS MINERAL GNAW MY INWARDS." — OTHELLO.

NAST'S CARTOON OF REVELS IN THE SENATE
About the colored Senator stand Henry Wilson, Oliver P. Morton
Carl Schurz, and Charles Sumner

ports. As railroad-builder — with State funds — he became a partner in the Tennessee Car Company, bought cars from himself, paid himself out of the Treasury, and overlooked the detail of delivery. And yet, a charming gentleman, kindly, affable, ready with loose change for the appeals of penury.

As railroad-builder, he was all romance. Money voted to roads on the completion of a stipulated number of miles was paid in great amounts without reference to the stipulation, and sometimes before a mile had been built.[1] In the classic case of the looting of the Brunswick and Albany, the rollicking marauders made merriest, allowing fraudulent claims for iron seized during the war, when it was the Confederacy and not the State that seized it, and when the Government had paid for it; allowing claims for carrying troops, when this was non-enforceable. The whole transaction was honeycombed with corruption.[2] Corrupt in building, the management of the State roads was crooked, and the thieving politicians in control plunged the State into debt three quarters of a million on a road that had regularly turned twenty-five thousand dollars a month into the Treasury before the war.[3]

And then the party press — it above all had to be nurtured, and public money poured into the coffers of forty-two papers for the publication of orders and proclamations. So easy was this steal that the leaders bought the 'Atlanta New Era' and bestowed patronage on themselves with gleeful prodigality.[4]

Unhappily the State Treasurer was not of the inner circle, and his report on the finances in January, 1869, tended to cast doubt on Bullock's integrity. The Legislature of 1870, strongly Republican, investigated.

'H. I. Kimball's on de flo',
'Tain't gwine ter rain no mo'.'

Naturally there was a whitewash, but suppose the Democrats should control the next Legislature! It was this fear that drove Bullock to Washington to disturb party solidarity.

Now, Georgia had been passing through many vicissitudes. The Legislature that had gone in with Bullock in 1868 was a cross

[1] Bainbridge, Cuthbert and Columbus Railroad; Thompson, 231; Cartersville and Van Wert Railroad; *ibid.*
[2] *Ibid.*, 230.    [3] *Ibid.*, 238–40.    [4] *Ibid.*, 227.

between a gambling-den and a colored camp-meeting. The overseer then, and for years afterward, was a glib, subtle Uriah Heep [1]
who manipulated the blacks. The scene sickened numerous Republicans, who joined with the Democrats in the expulsion of
twenty-five negro members of the House and two of the Senate.
Sumner moved — and the State was remanded to military rule,
with Bullock still in power. This was ideal. But Georgia's vote
was needed in the ratification of the Fifteenth Amendment, and
plans were made in Washington to have the Legislature recalled,
the expelled members reseated, and the State again taken under
military rule. Bullock and his associates were appalled. This
would mean an election in the fall of 1870; the Democrats might
win — and investigate. In December, Congress acted again on
Georgia, excluding from the Legislature all whites who had not
taken the disability oath, forbidding the exclusion of negroes,
granting Bullock the use of Federal soldiers to execute the law,
and providing that the State should be readmitted with the ratification of the Amendment.

Thus the Legislature was summoned in one of the most grotesque sessions of all time. To supervise the organization of the
House, Bullock found a Falstaff of from three to four hundred
pounds, a Western carpetbagger, A. L. Harris. One of the employees of the State roads, it was all in the day's work to this jolly
soul. Cool, amusing, witty, not oblivious to the absurdity of the
situation, he sat for days organizing the Legislature of a sovereign
State, jeering away all parliamentary rules under the protecting
shadow of Federal bayonets.[2] Thus the Legislature was organized,
Foster Blodgett, one of the Bullock Ring, was sent to the Senate,
and the next step would be the readmission of the State by Congress. We have now reached the drama of the present session.

### IX

That summer and autumn, Bullock and his associates were
closeted in many pow-wows. Anything but a Democratic Legislature, to investigate! At least, time was needed. Why not postpone the elections due that fall for two years on the ground that
there had been the intervention of a military government? Ben

---

[1] J. E. Bryant.                    [2] Avery, 427–28.

Butler undertook the task of convincing Congress. Bullock hastened to Washington with an abundance of State funds to do his
bit. Morton and Sumner espoused the cause of Bullock in the
Senate — and again the Republican majority split.

Bullock was no amateur lobbyist, for he had been there in the
early winter. Then he had taken expensive quarters at the Willard, entertained with the prodigality of a nabob, wined and dined
members of Congress, and charged the cost to Georgia. Daily he
had lolled in his carriage to the Capitol, strolling about House and
Senate, gorging himself and guests in the restaurants, entertaining
at elaborate dinners in the evening.[1] His sensibilities had been impervious to the scorn of members and the merriment of the press
gallery during the House debate, but in the Senate he had been
unable long to maintain his defiant pose, and he had wandered
possessively about the Chamber, finally finding a resting-place
at Morton's side. But he had triumphed then, and it was he who
carried the bill to Grant to sign — without reading.[2] That night
he had given a royal feast at the famous Café Française, where
every delicacy of the market was on the board, and wine flowed
freely — at the expense of Georgia.

And now he was back again, and Butler was fighting to prolong
his term and that of his minions in the Legislature for two years
more; back again, as a correspondent phrased it, 'to counteract
the influence of a delegation of respectable citizens of his State.'[3]

But the decency of Congress was rising in revolt against this
man's effrontery, and the oily manner of Ben Butler was without
effect. The forthright Beck of Kentucky was saying that in
Massachusetts such conspirators would be found hanging to every
tree in Boston Common,[4] and Bingham, openly charging that the
prolongation plan was to protect the pillagers in their plunder,
proposed to strike out this feature, and his amendment was
adopted by a good majority.

Desperate now, Bullock began to flood the press with tele-
graphic stories of 'outrages' in Georgia, and it was time. Trumbull, Edmunds, and Schurz had joined the indomitable Thurman
in the attack, and Trumbull was denouncing the scheme as 'worse

[1] Avery, 422.          [2] Ibid., 423.          [3] New York Herald, February 8, 1870.
[4] Congressional Globe, March 5, 1870.

than the Lecompton swindle.'[1] Sumner ascribed the opposition
to the 'venom' of rebels, and Morton waved the 'bloody shirt'
again. The Bingham amendment? Monstrous, thought Morton.
'In the interest of rebels' and desired by 'every unrepentent rebel
in the South.'

Meanwhile, press correspondents were informing their papers
that Bullock was resorting to 'the use of a female body in connection with the Georgia business,'[2] and in truth the desperate
exploiters were hesitating at nothing. The red-whiskered vulga-
rian had bought publicity in Forney's paper for $4459, and the ne-
gro delegation he had summoned to protest against the Bingham
amendment was living on the fat of the land — and Georgia paid
the bill.[3] And then, one day, Trumbull rose in a hushed silence
solemnly to refer to the rumors of corruption and ask an inquiry;
and the next day Zack Chandler, adopting the usual tactics of the
unscrupulous, proposed to extend the inquiry to determine if
'rebels' were using money for the amendment. The Judiciary
Committee found that corrupt and improper means had been employed by the Bullock leaders from Georgia,[4] but nothing was
done. The Bingham amendment was strengthened, however, and
the bill passed, and Bullock rushed back to Georgia to make his
last stand in the election of 1870.

x

Verily a year of sinister significance, this of 1870. The corruptionists and spoilsmen were still on the trail of Hoar. On the Senate's refusal to confirm his appointment to the Supreme Court, he
had tendered his resignation, which Grant had waved aside. Four
months had intervened. One June day a messenger entered Hoar's
office with a curt note from Grant, demanding his resignation, and
with no explanation. His dignity putting a curb on his indignation,
the fine old Puritan turned to his desk, wrote his resignation, and
hurried it to the press to make it irrevocable. That afternoon
Grant explained that the South was demanding a Cabinet post,
and that Hoar had pried into the qualifications of men recommended for judicial positions in the South — something intoler-

[1] *Congressional Globe*, March 14, 1870.        [2] *New York World*, March 18, 1870.
[3] Avery, 434.              [4] Report 175, 41st Cong., 2d Sess.

able.[1] And so the Massachusetts jurist and purist took his departure. Rawlins was gone — dead. Hoar had been thrust out. Only Cox remained to disturb the serenity of the spoilsmen, and he would linger but a little while.

That month the bill to pension Mrs. Lincoln was again shunted aside, and the 'New York Herald' thought it 'the most remarkable instance of petty malice ever evinced in any national legislature.' [2] Society was humming with the story of the suicide of the French Minister, and the chivalric reply of the German Minister, Baron Geroldt, to the question whether he would attend the funeral, 'I certainly will. After death, there is no war.' [3] Congress had passed an enforcement act to compel observance of the Fourteenth and Fifteenth Amendments and gone beyond its constitutional powers, and trenched still more on the rights of the States.[4] Centralization was moving triumphantly on. Congress had adjourned, and Grant had hurried to a cottage at Long Branch to escape the frivolities of the hotels.

But before he went, he had been in secret conference with the two Senators from North Carolina and learned that political prospects there were none too bright. The plan had been devised to terrorize the people into submission with a military force, under the pretense of protecting 'loyal men.' The Senators wanted uniforms and equipment, and the President was agreeable. He 'warmly approved' and would support the project 'with the full power of the Nation.' The visitors 'never knew him so talkative' or 'to talk so well.' Turning to his desk, 'with his own hand he wrote a page and a half letter to the acting Secretary of War, General Sherman, saying that, though the application was irregular, he would sign any paper to validate it.' The conspirators congratulated one another. 'Heaven seems to smile on us and our undertaking,' they thought.[5]

Let us journey to North Carolina and join the troops.

[1] Hoar, *Memoirs*, 209–11.  [2] June 18, 1870.
[3] *New York World*, July 23, 1870.
[4] Professor Burgess, 255; Dunning, 185.
[5] *Holden Papers*, W. J. Clark to Governor Holden, June 18, 1870.

# CHAPTER XV

## THE KLAN AND THE KIRK WAR

### I

PICTURESQUE enough was the march of the ragamuffins of Colonel Kirk through North Carolina, foreshadowed by the visit of that State's Senators to President Grant. To understand the pretext for the march, however, we must pause hastily to survey the Ku-Klux Klan, figuring luridly in the Northern press. The night before Christmas in 1865, six young men, who had seen service in the war, were seated about the stove in a law office in a small brick building in Pulaski, Tennessee. Penniless, with poor prospects, with poverty and depression all about, a pall of sadness rested on the little town that Christmas Eve. 'Boys,' said one of the young men,[1] 'let's start something to break the monotony and cheer up our mothers and girls. Let's start a club of some kind.' [2] It was agreed, and plans were made to be perfected at another meeting. This was held in the home of a leading citizen,[3] where many merry initiations were to be had that winter. In considering a name for the club, some one suggested 'Kuklio,' from the Greek word meaning a band or circle; another proposed adding 'Klan' because all the members were of Scotch-Irish descent; and a third offered Ku — Ku-Klux Klan.[4] Since the object was fun, why not costumes to deepen the mystery? Agreed — and the young men joyously raided the linen closet and brought forth stiff linen sheets and pillow-cases. It was a period of much masquerading and the costuming was a natural instinct. And why not ride horses? — and disguise these, as well, with sheets. Yes, and ride out into the black night and call at the houses of parents and sweethearts in a silent serenade?

Thus for the first time the Ku-Klux rode, and every one was merry for the moment — every one but the freedmen, who, being superstitious, thought they had seen ghosts from the near-by battle-

[1] Colonel John C. Lester.  [2] *Authentic History*, 6.
[3] Colonel Thomas Martin.  [4] *Authentic History*, 8.

fields. Many of these, who had been idling, hurried back contritely and subdued to their old masters' fields. At first the whites laughed over the fears of the blacks, and then, noting an improvement among them, with more industry and less petty pilfering, the serious possibilities of the society were envisaged. Within three months, the membership had outgrown its quarters, and an old house, half demolished by a cyclone, on the side of a hill at the edge of the town, was taken. The solitude, the ruins, the torn trunks of trees accentuated the weirdness of the scene at twilight. A fearsome awe fell upon the negroes. It was not the men they feared — but ghosts. Merrily the night riders pressed their advantage, parading the lonely roads at night.

From the intimidation of the negroes it was an easy step to the challenging of the carpetbaggers and agitators who were lustily instilling into the black men's minds a hatred and distrust of the native whites. Thus, more than once, when the simple blacks were gathered in groups about an agitator of the lowest type, the Klansmen, lighted by torches, would appear, silently to circle the crowd until the black men fled in terror. One night an aged negro, riding his mule past a meeting in an old church [1] grove where a carpetbagger was expounding the law of hate to the credulous blacks, overheard the discussion of a plan for the burning of certain houses. Hurrying home, he told his former master, a member of the Klan; and soon the spectral horsemen rode into the meeting and the audience fled.[2] Thus the society, formed for amusement, and found effective in controlling the negroes, soon developed into an agency to combat the Loyal Leagues formed under the inspiration of the Union League Clubs of the Northern cities.[3]

The original intent was to act for regulation and not for punishment,[4] and there was desperate need for regulation. The crusade of hate and social equality, and more, was playing havoc with a race naturally kindly and trustful. Throughout the war, when men were far away on the battle-fields, and the women were alone on far plantations with the slaves, hardly a woman was attacked. Then came the scum of Northern society, emissaries of the politicians, soldiers of fortune, and not a few degenerates, inflaming the

---

[1] 'Brick Church,' Giles County, Tennessee.
[2] *Authentic History*, 15–16.       [3] Leslie, 79.       [4] *Ibid.*, 90.

negroes' egotism, and soon the lustful assaults began. Rape is the foul daughter of Reconstruction. Robert Somers, an Englishman visiting the South, observed the work of 'agitators of the loosest type,' and noted the utterance of sentiments 'in all the circumstances anti-social and destructive,' and 'a real reign of terror . . . among the whites.'[1] An English woman living on a Georgia plantation saw an amazing change in the manner of her servants after the work of the Leagues began to have effect. They walked about with guns on their shoulders, spoke to their employers with studied familiarity, treated the women with disrespect, and worked when they pleased. Through 1869 this woman never slept without a loaded pistol under her pillow.[2] All over the South, white women armed themselves in self-defense.[3] Before the Klan appeared, and after the Loyal Leagues had spread their poison, no respectable white woman dared venture out in the black belt unprotected. 'We are in the hands of camp followers, horse-holders, cooks and bottle-washers and thieves,' testified a reputable citizen of Alabama.[4] The spectacle of negro police leading white girls to jail was not unusual in Montgomery.[5] Among the poor, the white women of the farms taking their produce to the markets traveled in large companies as a protection against rape.[6] In places the military and the Freedmen's Bureau offered no relief. Negroes who had criminally attacked white women, tried and sent to the penetentiary, were turned loose after a few days' incarceration.[7] It was not until the original Klan began to ride that white women felt some sense of security.

Controlled in the beginning by men of character and substance, the plan was to manage the freedmen by playing on their fears and superstitions. Novel schemes were often tried. Thus a night traveler, provided with a rubber sack, would stop at a negro's hut and ask for water. After 'drinking' three bucketfuls, to the consternation of the trembling black, the traveler would observe that he had traveled a thousand miles in twenty-four hours and 'that was the best water I have had since I was killed at the battle of Shiloh.' The negro, chattering, would take to his heels, and the

---

[1] Somers, 153.  [2] Mrs. Leigh, 131.  [3] Mrs. Smedes, 250.
[4] General J. H. Clanton.  [5] Doc. Hist., II, 269.  [6] Ibid., II, 333–34.
[7] Ibid., II, 342–44; testimony of General Forrest.

local paper would significantly announce that he was 'a radical negro.' Tales would be told of white men sailing through the midnight skies on white horses over neighboring towns. Could the bad negro escape? Not at all — these 'spirits always follow them and catch them and no living man hears from them again.' The leader of this spectral band was unthinkably terrible — 'ten feet high, his horse fifteen,' and he carried 'a lance and a shield like those of Goliath of the Philistines.' [1] Blood-curdling 'General Orders' would be published in newspapers.

Shrouded Brotherhood! Murdered Heroes!
Fling the bloody shirt that covers you to the four winds. . . . Strike with the red-hot spear. . . . The skies shall be blackened. A single Star shall look down upon horrible deeds. The night owl shall hoot a requiem over ghostly corpses . . . [2]

The negroes, clustered together in their cabins, recounted these awful stories and for a time grew humble, industrious, law-abiding.

In some sections the Klan was used to defeat the iniquitous cotton tax and the treasury thieves. Gins were built in the deep forests and Klansmen would haul the cotton there by night, hiding and guarding it.[3] The carpetbaggers were less pliable than the blacks, but where the Klan was strong, a notice to leave was often sufficient. One of these indulging in incendiary talk against his race was waited upon by members of the Klan, caught attempting to escape, given a stern lecture and warning, made to promise more carefully to guard his language, and let go.[4] Under the genuine organization there was little violence, but in sections that were bad the more offensive of the whites and blacks were first warned, then punished if the warning was unheeded.[5]

In the pioneer West, vigilance committees were formed for the protection of horses and cattle; in the South, the Klan was organized for the protection of women, property, civilization itself.

## II

With the success of the Klan in Tennessee, the organization of the society spread rapidly over the South. In the spring of 1867,

[1] *Doc. Hist.*, II, 365, from *Planters' Banner.*
[2] Published by Ryland Randolph in Alabama.
[3] *Authentic History*, 54.      [4] Fleming, 681.      [5] *Ibid.*, 678.

when Nashville was teeming with soldiers and officers, the first national gathering of the Klan was held in the Maxwell House without being suspected. General Forrest had been placed at the head, with the sanction of Lee, who strongly urged that the organization be kept a purely 'protective organization.' [1] This famous soldier, 'The Wizard of the Saddle,' had more than a touch of military genius, and he was a stern disciplinarian and, morally, a superior man. He neither drank nor swore, and he had been known to dismiss an officer under his command for immorality. In the midst of war, his tent, on Sundays, was converted into a church, and he had his chaplain pray before a battle. A brilliant tactician, he brought his genius to bear in the organization of the Klan forces. No one knew better how, through elusive tactics, by marching and countermarching, to deceive the eye as to the number of men in the saddle with features concealed.[2] His predominating trait was his reverence for women.

In the early phase only men of the highest order were in control. In Alabama, General James H. Clanton, an erstwhile Whig who had opposed secession but who had cast his lot with his own people when war came, was leader. A gallant soldier, a lawyer of distinction, an advocate of power, a man of commanding courage, it was his genius for organization and conciliation that solidified the people of Alabama and ultimately redeemed them from alien rule. On his death the mantle passed to General John T. Morgan, who later became one of the most distinguished of Senators and statesmen. In Mississippi, the head was General James Z. George, cavalry officer, able jurist, Senator and statesman, who organized and directed the ultimate redemption of his State. In Arkansas, General Albert Pike, poet and journalist, scholar and jurist, soldier and explorer, and a commanding figure in Masonry for half a century; in North Carolina, such men as Zeb Vance and William Laurence Saunders, silent, determined, effective;[3] in Texas, such as Roger Q. Mills, later a national figure in the House; in Georgia, General John B. Gordon, statesman, orator, military hero. Everywhere men of a high order, none of whom would have countenanced crime.

---

[1] *Authentic History*, 80–81.　　　[2] *Ibid.*, 97.　　　[3] *Southern Exposure*, 128–29.

## III

And yet it was inevitable that an organization with its masks and secrecy would appeal to a lawless element and ultimately suffer from the use of the rope and lash. With the Union League secret societies of blacks and carpetbaggers it was impossible to prevent the Klan from drifting into politics. Spurious organizations sprang up in far places, among men of the lower order bent on personal vengeance and violence. An eye for an eye and a tooth for a tooth became their motto. Ultimately cases were to be found where negroes, planning a personal chastisement of a fellow black, would don the white sheet and satiate their hate with whip or club. Soon the carpetbag politicians began bombarding the Northern press with stories of outrages. It was charged, and believed, that these occasionally organized bogus Klans to commit crime to the end that Federal bayonets could be had to sustain their rotten régimes in the stricken States. Cases there were, where men unable to give the password in the real Klan were stripped in Tennessee and found to be followers of Brownlow.[1] But it is indubitably true that the ignorant among the poor whites, who hated the negroes, crowded in, took possession in many places, and wrought deadly damage.

Thus, in the autumn of 1869, General Forrest issued a ringing denunciation of the lawless element. The order was being used, he said, to satisfy private vengeance, to break into jails, to interfere in family matters, to disarm harmless negroes having no thought of insurrectionary movements, and to whip both whites and blacks. The mask had become a curse; and an order for unmasking was issued.[2] But this availed not with the bogus Klans that had become virulent in sections inhabited by the poor whites.

Thus the outrages continued, furnishing a plausible pretext for the organization of State militias to serve the purpose of Radical politics. In Tennessee, an anti-Klan law was enacted that was stringent to the point of brutality and tyranny; and soon Brownlow's militia was scouring the State indulging in outrages of its own. In South Carolina, the odious Governor Scott was employing the militia to protect the 'good stealing.' In Washington, the politicians were planning supplementary legislation that would

---

[1] *Authentic History*, 109.     [2] *Ibid.*, 125–28.

violate all fundamental constitutional rights. In North Carolina, the plans were made to terrorize the State with Holden's militia. It was in furtherance of these plans that Senators Pool and Abbott had made their arrangements for equipment with President Grant.

IV

Governor W. W. Holden was one of the tragic figures of his day, his career twisted all awry by the war tornado. Called 'the Talleyrand of North Carolina politics,' he was essentially an opportunist, moved by an inordinate ambition, which aligned him with most parties and causes. A native of the State, with a distinguished record before the war, he personally was beyond the reach of corruption. Born in poverty, educated in a printing shop, he arrived in Raleigh one moonlight night in a coach heralded with trumpets, with just seven dollars to his name. Employed by a Whig newspaper, we see him first in youth, an ardent champion of the policies of Clay.[1] A fluent, witty, satirical writer, the Democrats, in search of an editor for 'The Standard,' turned to him, and, to the amazement of the Whigs, he accepted; nor was their astonishment abated by his stout assertion that he had always been a Democrat of the Jeffersonian school. He pronounced the Democrats 'the friends and supporters of equal rights . . . advocates of the many against the few.' More, they stood four square for the rights of the States.[2]

At the moment when the Whig aristocracy seemed hopelessly predominant, the militant tone of 'The Standard' aroused the Democracy to a will to victory. Never in his career had Holden seemed so effective and sincere. 'The fierce aristocratic pride of Southern society had been hard for him to surmount in his progress,'[3] and the aristocracy was with the Whigs. Holden was in his element, working out his natural resentment with the lash. It was he who drove the Democracy to free suffrage, and when, in the ensuing campaign, his party almost won, his leadership was conceded. By this time he had come under the influence of Calhoun, and he was opposed to congressional interference with slavery in the Territories.[4] Nine years before the war, he declared the right of secession 'an original, preëxisting, reserved sovereign right.'[5]

---

[1] Boyd, 43.          [2] *Ibid.*, 45.          [3] *Old Days at Chapel Hill*, 147.
[4] Boyd, 53–54.       [5] *Ibid.*, 55.

In 1858, his nomination for Governor was prevented by the aristocracy.[1] Through this decade he had been an ardent champion of the extreme Southern view. Suddenly, with his defeat, a strange silence fell upon him, finally to be broken by a declaration for the Union, and against secession. The Charleston and Baltimore Conventions found him against secession in the first, neutral in the second, though inclined to Douglas.[2] In the campaign, however, he voted for Breckinridge, as Johnson did, and for the same reason. With Lincoln's election he refused to acknowledge it a justification for secession; but when Lincoln called for troops, he opposed the plan of force. Two years more, and he was opposing the policies of the Confederate Government, and was urging peace, and Georgia troops were burning him in effigy and destroying his presses.

And then, the war over, in the month of Appomattox, Holden, facing the race problem, proposed colonization, insisting that 'the two races could not live in harmony together as free races.'[3] In October, he was describing himself as a member of the party 'of which Andrew Johnson is the head,' and immediately afterward he became the president of the Loyal League of North Carolina — fighting the policies of Johnson. Whig, Democrat, secessionist and unionist, sponsor of colonization and negro suffrage, Johnsonian and Radical, he had veered with the weather and thus far had escaped its inclemency. It was as an anti-Johnsonian Radical Republican, with the aid of the negroes, that he was elected Governor.

Personally, he had the appearance and manner of a gentleman. His was a good figure of average size. His abundant black hair was fine, not coarse or curly. His dark blue eyes, kindly and steady, were his dominating feature. Dark eyebrows, long nose, long upper lip clean-shaven, with the lower face covered with a closely trimmed beard — such the physical man. His voice, too weak for effective public speaking, was smooth and pleasing in conversation, in which he was entertaining. Among the poets he had his passions and prejudices. Shakespeare and Burns — these came first; and then Byron and Ossian; but he could not abide

[1] Boyd, 56.
[2] Ibid., 63.        [3] Holden, Memoirs, 35.

Tennyson. Fond of music, he liked to entertain his friends with a musical evening.[1]

Here was a man on whose overweening ambition for place and distinction a wretched period played to his undoing. Caught in the eddies and whirlpools of his times, he was as a straw bobbing crazily upon the waters. His happiest days were those before the war, when he was the idol of the masses of the Democracy. He was not made for revolutions. Sensitive, easily flattered, proud, and always resentful of the old aristocracy, he was to pass through the fiery furnace of corruption personally unscathed, and to live into old age — a dignified and patient old gentleman.[2] But he was neither keen enough nor strong enough to cope with the machinations of the party leaders about him.

## V

The evil genius of the Holden régime was John Pool, United States Senator. His colleague, Joseph C. Abbott, was a New Hampshire carpetbagger, mediocre, crafty, but not courageous. Inclined to gasconading, the warning that followed his inflammatory advice to negroes to arm themselves, made him the most docile of sword-rattlers.[3] Pool was of more sinister significance. He gambled on the tragedy of his own people to his own profit — a glutton for power. His brother, Solomon, was made president of the University, and the shadows fell deep on Chapel Hill. From his Senate seat Pool directed Holden in the distribution of patronage. His letters were those of the dictator — he did not recommend; he commanded. 'I find it of the utmost importance for Mr. Rollins to modify the law on distilling. Let no time be lost.' [4] 'I answer the enclosed letter by sending you a list of proposed offices for Clay, made up of our discreet friends. I made a special inquiry as to each.' [5] In Washington, he wormed his way into the confidence of the most rabid of the Radicals; through his affiliations there, he made a deep impression upon Holden, to whom he seemed the cornucopia of all good. 'I want to warn you about

---

[1] This description was furnished the author by Holden's daughter.
[2] *Old Days at Chapel Hill*, 150.          [3] Hamilton, 396.
[4] To Holden, August 27, 1868, Holden MSS.
[5] To Holden, September 12, 1868, Holden MSS.

Abbott,' wrote Deweese, the corrupt carpetbag Congressman. 'I am satisfied that Abbott is trying to lay the mine to beat you out of the senatorship. Pool . . . and myself have watched him and to-day they [Pool's crowd] thought I had better write you to be on the lookout.' [1]

The strength of Pool was in his domineering mastery, his revolutionary temerity. Constantly he inflamed the negroes. 'Did it ever occur to you gentlemen of property . . . to you, ye men, and especially ye women, who never received anything from these colored people but services, kindness, and protection — did it ever occur to you that these same people . . . will not be willing to sleep in the cold when your houses are denied them merely because they will not vote as you do?' wrote Pool in an address to the people in 1868. 'Did it ever occur to you that revenge which is sweet to you, may be sweet to them? Hear us . . . did it ever occur to you that if you kill their children with hunger, they will kill yours with fear?' [2] This reference to the white women was fashionable in the threats and jibes of the Pool machine. One day 'The Standard' — Holden's old paper — went too far. The women cold to the carpetbaggers and the scalawags? it asked. Patience! 'Our experience with female rebels is that with all their sins they have a vast amount of human nature, and only want to have it appreciated to be the most loving creatures imaginable.' By all means, then, cultivate the women. 'You are all good-looking and they know it, but with native modesty, like sweet New England girls, they like to be approached first. . . . Give them Shelley and Byron and you will have them in your arms if not in your party in less than a week.' [3] With the whites enraged and threatening, the publisher fled the city before nightfall.

Such audacity was having its effect — and there was enough in the record of the Radical régime to create uneasiness as the elections of 1870 approached.

## VI

It was a record of inefficiency and corruption, and the outstanding figure in the filth was the same General Littlefield, railroad builder and wrecker, whom we have encountered in Georgia. He

[1] March 27, 1869, Holden MSS.          [2] Hamilton, 365.          [3] *Ibid.*, 369.

had earned the privilege of looting by being the most conspicuous spokesman of the Radicals in the campaign of 1868. Thereafter, he owned the Legislature until the Democrats recovered power. There was much of rollicking munificence in his bribery. In the State House a bar was opened in a little room at the top of the stairs, and visitors to-day are shown the broken stone of the stairway due to the rough ascent of the whiskey barrels. There the mendacious and illiterate drank freely under the beaming countenance of Littlefield. All he asked was the control of the railroads, the manipulation of the bonds, the right to steal. The stealing in the railroads was positively bizarre.[1] When attempts were made by the minority in the Legislature to investigate the frauds, the cry that it was 'a stab at the Republican Party' was enough.[2] When finally a fraud commission was created, a gay scene followed one night, with the blithesome Littlefield as host. Inviting a great number of Republican members, he fed them on oysters washed down with liquor. Then followed speeches and much denunciation of the 'stabs,' and it was agreed to destroy the fraud commission on the morrow. That was in the spring of 1870. The trail was hot. The people were tired of the looting. The railroad swindlers were in close quarters threatened with indictments that spring when Holden made the arrangement with Grant for a little private army to deal with the Ku-Klux Klan.

Great was the Legislature in those days of Pool and Littlefield. One session adjourned amidst a memorable and inspiring scene, with two negroes presiding in turn, with members hurrying back and forth between the chamber and the whiskey barrel in the bar, with 'loyal' speeches, dancing on the floor, singing from the seats in maudlin tones. Occasionally there would be silence to hear an obscene story — then laughter, and more journeys to the barrel. Much could be, and was, forgiven these grotesque proceedings. If a law was passed to blackmail a foreign insurance company, were not the proceeds for the party campaign fund?[3] If thousands were squandered on the subsidization of newspapers, were they not 'loyal' newspapers? If unheard-of prices were paid in the furnishing of the State House, were not the purchases made of 'Union

[1] Hamilton treats of these extensively, at pages 427–51; Boyd, 114–15.
[2] Hamilton, 403.       [3] Ibid., 407.

men'? And did not 'loyal men' occupy the offices, feet on the tables and fingers in the pie? [1] Who dared complain of the $37,-718.83 spent in two years on stationery? — though the 'loyal' Secretary of State did sell a part and pocket the money. Wood purchased at twenty-five per cent above the market price? True — but was it not a boon to the carpetbagger patriots who had the wood for sale? [2] This brazen corruption went hand in hand with unspeakable ignorance in many of the appointed officials, and one of the magistrates insisted that a prisoner accused of murder be taken to the scene of the crime to see if the victim's blood would run.[3]

Under these conditions, the people were growing restive and an election was approaching. Here and there an outrage was committed by men in masks. To John Pool the path was plain — armed men must terrorize the people under the pretext of enforcing the law. A man of decision and action, he prepared a bill providing for the creation of an army to serve the purposes of politics, and, it is said, paid a Senator to sponsor it. Wrong in principle? Admitted, said the ruling party, but the conditions of the times demanded it. In private they said it was the only chance to save the party at the polls.[4]

## VII

And Holden hesitated — that was his weakness. Nature had not moulded him for desperate enterprises. In normal times, freed from his entanglements and advisers, he would have made a good executive. For months, however, pressure had been brought to bear upon him by interested partisans. His manuscript correspondence teems with these importunities for force. 'We are unable to administer the laws, and we feel that unless you can get our country under military rule we cannot protect our people,' wrote Senator Stephens, one of the most daring of the conspirators, who was to meet a violent death.[5] 'Have the peculiar provisions of the militia bill struck you in the same view as myself?' wrote another politician from Columbus.[6] 'It seems to me, when the Governor "in his discretion" declares a county to be in a state of

---

[1] Hamilton, 411.    [2] *Ibid.*, 412.    [3] *Ibid.*, 417.    [4] *Ibid.*, 403.
[5] Holden MSS., May 2, 1870.    [6] Judge Henry, January 31, 1870, Holden MSS.

insurrection, lawlessness, and disorder, that it at once suspends
the civil law and the right of voting and suffrage during the continuance of such proclamation. Is that so? and if so, might it not
be used with powerful effect in the approaching campaign?'

But there were conflicting currents that made Holden hesitate.
Another Republican wrote that agitators were urging negroes to
burn houses and barns and that some had been given to the flames.
'Two wrongs cannot make a right,' he wrote, 'and such advice to
negroes and bad white men will be ruinous to us unless put a stop
to instanter.' Holden had read this note and written on the back
that 'in this as in other cases resort must be had to the grand
jury.' [1] But John Pool knew that grand juries do not carry elections, and he had been consulted. 'I shall be with our friends at
Raleigh on the 7th as you request,' he wrote on June 2, 'unless
prevented by accident. It is important that action be taken.' [2]

### VIII

Thus, on the appointed day a group of politicians, in desperate
mood, sat behind closed doors in the Governor's office at Raleigh.
Pool was the master mind of the moment. Holden was uneasy.
He sat and listened. Pool had the plan — had brought it from
Washington — for forming two regiments of regular troops to be
employed in arresting disturbers of the party programme in the
State. He would have the men arrested, tried by the troops, and
certain counties put under military rule. Some of the conferees
drew back from the suggestion of military trials. Nonsense! said
Pool. Had not Powell Clayton done it with impunity in Arkansas?
However, it might be well to send a judicial officer with the troops
and try the accused by the soldiers only when that process failed.
And the writ of habeas corpus? Pool had thought about that, too
— had talked it over with President Grant, he said. Manifestly,
he thought, the writ should be answered, the bodies produced,
and, if discharged, the victim should be rearrested on a new
charge. That plan, said Pool, was favored by the President.

The personnel of the troops was a bit disturbing. Negroes would
be dangerous; the native whites unreliable. The troops would require aggressive leadership — a man of daring. There, for in-

[1] N. A. Ramsey, Haywood, May 4, 1870, Holden MSS.          [2] Holden MSS.

stance, said Pool, was his friend MacLindsay, with 'undoubted courage and capable of any desperate resolve.' Pleased with the thought, the Senator expanded. MacLindsay had been a sort of pirate, caught once, and saved only through Pool's influence. He could muster a hundred men in the community where he lived between fires during the war who were as desperate as himself. Now there was a man who would give Holden no trouble. If he arrested men and they resisted, he would kill them and they would be 'lost and never heard of again.' Holden, who had been seated, became excited and rose to walk the floor nervously. A moment of silence — and then one of the conferees declared hotly that such a course would forever damn the memory of Holden. Pool shifted quickly to the facetious mood. He had merely been joking! However, he had impressed the objector as 'meaning what he said until his project met with disfavor.'

A trying conference it was to Holden, who made more objections than suggestions. 'Governor,' said Pool impressively, 'you do not know how they are talking about you in Washington. The Republicans there say you are a failure, and Grant says you and Smith in Alabama were made Governors by the Republican Party under the Reconstruction Acts and that you are sitting still and permitting these Ku-Klux to take them away from you, or cause them to slip away from you.' And so they were criticizing him in Washington! — where his towering ambition might be thwarted. Really, he must pull himself together. Pool knew his man.[1]

Thus it came about that the command of the troops went to George W. Kirk, a dare-devil of thirty-three, residing in Tennessee, who had been notorious in the army as a man of brutality and desperate audacity.

Pool hurried back to Washington to launch the usual campaign of misrepresentation in the Northern press. Lacking finesse, and essentially brutal, he shamelessly informed the 'New York Tribune' that 'we intend to use the military in the election and must get these statements (of alleged outrages) disseminated through the North.'[2] Always there was fear of Holden's indecision, and

---

[1] Badger's testimony in Impeachment Trial of Holden; Holden, *Memoirs*, 187–99; Hamilton, 497–98.
[2] Hamilton, 503.

Pool had to stiffen him somehow. 'Our friends have been hoping to see you in Washington,' Pool wrote. 'The President would be glad to see you. I think it would be to your advantage to come.' [1] The Radicals of the North Carolina delegation had called on Grant and been assured of his sympathy with the movement, and Holden was warmly greeted at the White House. 'Let those men resist you, Governor,' said the President, 'and I will move with all my power against them.' [2] Grant had been imposed upon by Pool, but Holden returned to Raleigh in high feather.

## IX

His proclamation of martial law had unpleasant reactions in the North. The Democratic press ascribed lawlessness in North Carolina to its continued treatment as a conquered province. Imposed upon the people was 'a government not of their choice, administered by men in whom they have no confidence, and supported by Federal bayonets in lieu of the public opinion of free men.' No, concluded the 'New York World,' 'men do not grow grapes from thorns, nor figs from thistles. Rotten boroughs will return rotten members.' [3] This, considering the source, could be borne with equanimity, but, alas, there were Republicans in the State who wavered before this show of force. 'For God's sake, don't send troops here,' wrote one from Orange. 'The town is quiet and all works well. Avoid strife.' [4] From another: 'The Republicans do not want troops in this section, Governor. It will kill us in the next election. . . . We have no outrages of consequence here and I have not heard of any for two months.' [5] And then, the reverse: 'This is the only way to carry the State in the next election. . . . Will cause men to take a stand for you from fear.' [6]

Against the retention of Kirk in command, the protests were more earnest. 'Such men as Colonel Kirk do not do a political party any good. He is universally detested by the people as a military man. They fear and hate him,' wrote one correspondent. [7]

[1] Holden MSS., June 28, 1870.   [2] Holden, *Memoirs*, 187–99.
[3] June 9, 1870.   [4] From T. C. Evans, Holden MSS.
[5] From Albert H. Dowell, Asheville, Holden MSS.
[6] From W. F. Henderson, Salisbury, Holden MSS.
[7] From Dowell, Holden MSS.

From another community: 'He is very odious to a great many
citizens of this county. I hope you will at once revoke the commission.'[1] From still another: 'I ask you, if you do send troops to
this mountain county, not to have Kirk over them,' because in the
late war the county was overrun by 'the very worst of troops, or
men pretending to be such,' under his command.[2] General Erastus
B. Hampton added his protest: 'We look upon Colonel Kirk as a
man of bad character,' and his presence would drive political support away.[3] And then, again, the reverse. Thus, the President of
the Western North Carolina Railroad, hearing of petitions for the
removal of Kirk, was distressed. 'Don't do it,' he wrote. 'It was
the very best appointment that could have been made. ... The
Republicans who ask his dismissal should be marked. ... By the
Eternal God, I say, deluge the State in blood from one end to the
other rather than our people should suffer again the treatment of
the last six months.'[4]

It was all very confusing to Holden. But was not Pool standing
beside him? And had not Grant promised to stand behind him?
And could he afford to have the leaders criticizing him as a milksop in Washington? On with the dance!

## X

And so Kirk proceeded with his plans. He was a swaggering,
sword-rattling, violent type, noted for cruelty, and feared for outrages committed during the war.[5] His men were no more inspiring. When they appeared for the clothing Grant had ordered for
them, they were 'bad-looking and mighty ragged' and 'nearly all
barefoot.'[6] Of the lowest order of poor whites, with a sprinkling of
negroes, they were mostly morons at best. 'The most ignorant and
stupid creatures I ever talked with,' a witness was to testify later.[7]
'No intelligence among the privates as far as I could see,' said another.[8] 'They were uniformed like an army,' another added, 'but

[1] From W. N. Moore, Burnsville, Holden MSS.
[2] From David Proffit, Yancey County, Holden MSS.
[3] Holden MSS.          [4] J. J. Mott, Holden MSS.
[5] Holden Impeachment Trial, Isaac E. Reeves, I, 275; W. M. Cooke, I, 279; W. W.
Murdock, I, 280.
[6] Ibid., G. S. Rogers, I, 704.          [7] Ibid., Jesse Gant, I, 488.
[8] Ibid., J. S. Scott, I, 609.

their actions were more like a mob.'[1] Such were the six hundred
and seventy men who swaggered out of Morganton on one of the
most bizarre adventures in history. Four hundred were under age,
illiterate boys; two hundred were not even citizens of the State.[2]
Laughing, jeering, singing obscene songs, they lurched along the
highways and through the villages on a gay lark of utter irresponsi-
bility. As they swung along, an unregulated and awkward mob,
holding their guns haphazard, and shouting insults to citizens
they passed, a terror seized upon the people. But when they
struck camp, there was a touch of comedy. Men on guard amused
themselves by sticking their bayonets into the ground, and calling
to the officers that their time was up; then, cursing, squatted upon
the ground.[3] The privates cursed the officers of the day with gay
abandon,[4] and impressed beholders as 'a parcel of vagabonds' in
stolen clothing.[5] Sundays found them sitting about like tramps
upon the green, playing cards, cursing their luck, and insulting women on their way to church by undressing to wash in the open.[6]

But it was not all rollicking hilarity. As they swaggered along,
threatening to burn Salisbury, and bullying the people of Newton
with pointed pistols,[7] they were making arrests indiscriminately,
with the courts wide open, and gratifying sadistic impulses by tor-
turing prisoners. Refusing usually to give the reason for arrests,
Kirk's men seldom failed to hint of a court-martial and probable
execution. They simulated pity for the prisoners, since they would
'never see their homes again.'[8] One of these was approached by a
negro 'soldier' with a pointed pistol and the exclamation, 'God
damn him, let's hang him — that is the orders we have got.'[9]
When Kirk was served with a writ of habeas corpus from the Chief
Justice, he jauntily waved it aside with his sword. That kind of
business, he said, was 'played out'; and so it seemed, since the
Chief Justice ate humble pie.[10]

The climax of these outrages came with the attempt to force a
confession from a prisoner with nothing to confess. The vaga-

[1] Holden Impeachment Trial, Thomas H. Holt, I, 629.            [2] Hamilton, 504.
[3] Holden Impeachment Trial, A. C. McAllister, I, 587.
[4] Ibid., J. S. Scott, I, 609.            [5] Ibid., Jesse Gant, I, 488.
[3] Ibid., J. G. Moore, I, 646.            [7] Hamilton, 504.
[8] Holden Impeachment Trial, J. S. Scott, I, 605.
[9] Ibid., J. H. Albright, I, 715.            [10] Hamilton, 511.

bonds with guns crowded in upon him in the night. 'If you don't tell, I'll break your damn neck to-night,' he was told. After midnight, they returned with candles and ordered him out. 'Can I put on my shoes?' 'No, you will not have use for them long.' Four pistols were aimed at his breast. 'Now, will you confess?' Then, putting a rope around his neck, they drew him up until he lost consciousness. On recovering, he was again told to confess. Meeting dumb silence, the officer went into a rage. 'Then hang him on that limb till eight o'clock to-morrow morning and then cut him down and bury him under the tree on which you hang him.' But the officer changed his mind.[1]

Throughout this reign of terror, Holden was being savagely lashed daily by Josiah Turner, of the 'Raleigh Sentinel,' a journalist of much ability, with a gift for polemics, an instinctive sagacity in politics, ready, fluent, and calculating. He was bitterly denounced in the Holden press, his life was threatened, and his country home was showered with stones. In the midst of the terror, Turner defied his enemy. Holden was increasingly unhappy. The mock hanging was without his sanction or approval, and he was becoming restive under the vagaries of his anarchistic military agent, but he was on a tide he could not turn.[2] Then, too, the campaign was hot, and had to be considered. Kirk was not failing to inform him of the political conditions.[3] He had marched his ragamuffins into a Democratic meeting at Yanceyville, terrorized the crowd, arrested the leaders, and announced he was to meet resistance by shooting women and children.[4] Something had to be forgiven to such party zeal.

True the Democratic and independent press in the North was raging, the 'New York World' denouncing the march of the vagabonds as 'a disgrace to the nineteenth century'; but it did not hurt Holden for 'The World' to make Grant a partner. 'The President,' said 'The World,' 'is smoking the weed of ineptitude in the halls of indolence at Long Branch.'[5] It called upon him to corroborate or deny the Holden statement that he had authorized

---

[1] Holden Impeachment Trial, L. H. Murray, i, 660–63.
[2] *Ibid.*, i, 660.
[3] Kirk to Holden, Holden MSS.
[4] Holden Impeachment Trial, H. F. Brandon, i, 749, 764.          [5] July 22, 1870.

this making war upon a State.[1] 'The Nation' was shocked at this 'specially levied body of men, mostly black,' under the command of 'a wandering adventurer, trained to command by bushwhacking in Tennessee,' and concluded that the enterprise was 'an electioneering dodge.' [2] But the 'New York Tribune' was standing by, defending the venture as called for by the outrages of the Klan, acting for the Democrats. 'Governor Holden has taken measures that will effectually prevent the success of the game,' it said. 'Hence the wrath he has aroused, and the storm of slander.' [3]

XI

Then, in August, in righteous wrath, North Carolina went to the polls and the Democrats swept the Legislature, and, for the first time since reconstruction began, the Radicals were on the defensive. Holden realized, too late, what his action had done,[4] and in his fury he turned on Turner. While riding near Hillsboro, where his family lived, he was taken by Holden's troopers, and at midnight he was ridden into camp at Yanceyville amidst the shouts of Kirk's men and the negroes. For three days he was confined in the court-house. The weather was hot; the windows tightly closed. The 'soldiers' amused themselves by pouring water upon him as he slept, and he was forbidden to speak unless to order food or water. Drunken sentries found entertainment in pointing loaded guns at prisoners. That was Turner's purgatory; he was soon transferred to hell — thrown into an iron cage with a negro, condemned to execution on the morrow. The cell was filthy, swarming with vermin, and he was given stale water to drink. When his wife went to see him, the 'soldiers' threw stones at her and he was forbidden to approach the window.[5]

Thus the terror died in a spasm of rage when the Federal Court intervened, and Holden's protest to Washington brought instructions to yield. The jig was up — Grant had weakened on his promise, if it had ever been given. Kirk, arrested, was permitted to escape by a Radical sheriff, and in Washington he found protection and surcease from sorrow on the Capitol police force.[6] Less

---

[1] July 29, 1870.          [2] August 4, 1870.          [3] August 3, 1870.
[4] The Nation, December 24, 1870.
[5] Holden Impeachment Trial, Turner, I, 892–917.          [6] Hamilton, 533.

happy the fate of the pious preacher who had been his chaplain. The army disbanded near the scene of his desertion of wife and children to flee with another woman, and he was arrested for bigamy.[1]

And when the Legislature met, Holden was impeached.

### XII

The trial was political, though rules of evidence were better observed than in the case of Johnson. Some doubted the wisdom of impeachment and Zeb Vance, Democratic leader, took no part and expressed no opinion.[2] The evidence for the defense failed to connect politics with the outrages of masked men. Victims were paraded on the witness stand to tell their tales of terror and floggings, and a surprising number could conceive of no motive beyond their devotion to the Republican Party. But the cross-examination was devastating in uncovering other reasons. One victim had been insolent to the whites and had accumulated guns with which to kill Klansmen.[3] A white man had been found in bed with a negro woman.[4] Another had compromised a bastardy suit with a sister-in-law, and had abused an old man.[5] A white woman, never married, had seven children, one colored, which she admitted, while stoutly denying she ran a brothel.[6] Still another woman, unmarried and with children, denied she kept a loose house. 'I notice,' said the attorney for the managers, 'that you spit very much. Do you chew tobacco?' 'Yes, sir,' she replied, demurely.[7] Thus most of the assaults were on men and women who were not ornaments to their communities, and were not concerned with politics.

And so, with courts open, with absolute peace in most places and reasonable quiet in communities on which Kirk's men worked, this outrage had been perpetrated to serve the purposes of party politics. Even Horace Greeley had been aroused by an 'outrage' story given his correspondent by Governor Holden in a letter from Tourgée to Senator Abbott. When the author of the letter wrote

[1] *New York World*, October, II, 1870.        [2] *New York Herald*, December, 27, 1870.
[3] Holden Impeachment Trial, Donaldson Worth, II, 1215.
[4] *Ibid.*, Leonard Rippey, II, 1334.        [5] *Ibid.*, John Shatterlt, II, 1341.
[6] *Ibid.*, II, 1400.        [7] *Ibid.*, II, 1454.

Greeley that a cipher had been added to each figure he had given of the number of outrages, the editor demanded an explanation of the 'garbling.' [1] A few days later, Senator Abbott gave his version. He had shown Tourgée's letter to Senator Pool in Holden's presence in Washington, and the latter had requested a copy, which was furnished by a clerk who was 'a most trustworthy and honest man.' And now, said Greeley, 'perhaps the Governor will tell us who garbled it before he gave it to our correspondent.' [2] But the Governor was silent. He merely had followed the common practice of the times, of which Greeley had made full use.

Poor Holden was impeached and went to Washington, where Grant received him sympathetically.[3] Republican Presidents treated him kindly, but he soon passed from politics, to grow old gracefully and in grace; finding pleasure in his church, in acts of charity, and cherishing no resentments. He had wrecked his career on his ambition, but he had been no mercenary, and after all these years he is remembered kindly by the public, and his memory is cherished by the family to which he was tenderly devoted.

Thus the elections of 1870 had given a gleam of light to North Carolina and Georgia, with Democratic legislatures in each. Holden was impeached, and Bullock fled, but only a beginning had been made in the fight for redemption. Even so, the Radical politicians in Washington, ruminating the significance of these victories, determined that something more drastic still had to be done if the presidential election of 1872 was to be assured them.

And the plans were instantly on foot.

[1] *New York Tribune*, August 23, 1870.
[2] *Ibid.*, August 29, 1870.        [3] Holden, *Memoirs*, 168.

# CHAPTER XVI

## SUMNER'S BACK TO THE WALL

### I

BEFORE Congress again convened, the country was startled with the announcement that Secretary Cox had resigned from the Cabinet. Thoroughly honest, highly competent, and warmly devoted to reform, his unpopularity had been constantly deepening among the politicians and corruptionists. Petty explanations were on the tongues of the gossips. It was whispered about that Mrs. Cox had cut from a newspaper a letter attacking the assessment of clerks for party purposes, and sent it anonymously to Mrs. Grant, overlooking the monogram on the envelope, and that it had been returned 'with the compliments of Mrs. Grant.' [1] But the rupture required no such fantastic explanation. Cox had been anathema to the bosses — always in the way. It was common knowledge that he had been painfully in the way in the case of the notorious McGarrahan claim.

This claim on three square leagues of California land, rich in minerals, had been advanced years before by a disreputable party who contended that there had been a Mexican grant more than a quarter of a century before. This dubious pretense was not susceptible of documentary proof — the papers had been burned! More than one Attorney-General had rendered opinions hostile to the claim and there had been a succession of adverse decisions in the Federal courts. With marvelous vitality, the thing survived to reappear under the name of McGarrahan, representing a stock company, and under the aggressive sponsorship of Ben Butler, in Congress and out.

To Cox the claim was a transparent fraud, and he said so emphatically in Cabinet. Grant astounded him with the assertion that Congress had the right to determine. This was the beginning of the open rupture. In an age of corruption, Cox had set his face against it, and his doom was sealed. There was nothing else to do

[1] *New York Herald*, November 5, 1870.

— he resigned; and in his letter he made the reason clear. When the gossips began to make free with his reputation in undertones, he requested Grant to give the letters exchanged in the resignation to the press. Grant refused on the novel ground that they were confidential; and Cox forthwith summoned the press and gave them out. Thus the cat was out of the bag. 'There is a strong feeling against Cox among all the Senators with whom I have talked,' wrote Senator Morton. 'They say he has treated the President badly, and Chandler and others say very hard things.' [1] It was commonly understood that Chandler and Simon Cameron had been saying hard things to the President a long while. [2] With Cox out of the way, Congress was free to act on the McGarrahan claim, but it had been forced into a blighting light. The majority of the Judiciary Committee of the House reported against it; but Bingham of Ohio brought in a minority report and the business was threshed out openly in bitter debate. Garfield was impressed by the disciplined army of supporters that McGarrahan had upon the floor, and had no doubt 'many . . . were corrupt,' and observed that 'nearly all the worst class of carpetbaggers' voted with Bingham. [3] The claim went through by a small majority.

If Grant was interested, it was a costly victory. In the debate Beck of Kentucky had savagely charged that Cox had been driven from the Cabinet because of his hostility to the steal. The 'New York World' said the claim had passed because of 'Presidential influence in abetting a notorious fraud.' [4] The resignation of Cox was ascribed by Garfield to the 'surrender on the part of the President to the political vermin which infest the government.' [5] And, commenting on the rupture as due to Grant's refusal to support Cox in the prosecution of reforms, and denouncing 'the corruption and dishonesty of the great body of persons who carry on the government,' 'The Nation' thought the incident 'a pitiful story.' 'The wreck of General Grant's fame is a national misfortune,' it added. 'That fame was a national possession.' [6]

[1] To W. P. Fishback, Foulkes, ii, 145, note.
[2] *New York Herald*, November 11, 1870.
[3] Garfield to Cox, *Life of Garfield*, i, 463–65.
[4] November 15, 1870.          [5] Garfield to Cox, *Life of Garfield*, i, 462.
[6] October 20, November 17, 1870.

## II

Other events contributed to the uneasiness of the dominant group — the elections had gone wrong. New York and Indiana had been swept by the Democrats, and for the first time since reconstruction began, they had elected a Governor in Alabama, and a Lieutenant-Governor in Florida. In Congress the minority had lost the two thirds which had stood them in good stead. And, like an Old Man of the Sea on their backs, the San Domingo Treaty was still with them.

When Congress convened, it was greeted with a Message from Grant urging the annexation as though nothing had occurred before. It was evident that something had to be done to spare him humiliation, and the politicians agreed on a commission of inquiry, though even this met stubborn opposition and evoked plain speaking. The President, forced into lobbying again, had summoned Blaine, among others, to the White House. The Speaker, making clear his hostility to 'final acquisition,' agreed to support the resolution of inquiry.[1] Even so, it passed the House only after a prolonged night session, and when the agony was over, Colfax appeared at the White House door in the bitter cold of a winter morning to convey the news.[2] But no one was entirely happy. There were rankling wounds. Policy and not conviction had won the momentary victory. Garfield, like Blaine, found his 'sympathies . . . very strong with Sumner.'[3] Julian was writing in his diary that 'Grant has made a dreadful mistake about San Domingo and it will be hard work to save him in 1872.'[4] Three months later, riding in New York with Greeley, Julian was to hear him 'denounce the San Domingo business and to declare that Grant is done for and the Republican Party probably ditto.'[5] It would have been much easier to have ignored the President's unconventional diplomacy and to have taken the island and forgotten it. It was all Sumner's work, and the skies were darkening above him. During the preceding summer, when he was strolling with Hendricks through the historic parts of Boston, chatting with Longfellow on the piazza at Nahant, or lecturing, his enemies

[1] Gail Hamilton, 248.
[2] *New York World,* December 23, 1870
[3] *Life of Garfield,* i, 462.
[4] MS. Diary, January 8, 1871.
[5] *Ibid.,* April 2, 1871.

had been busy with Grant. The President had been told that Sumner had attacked him in his lectures, and the man of Appomattox had wrathfully declared that but for his office he would call his traducer to account. In truth, no such attack had been made, but Grant believed it.

Then came the San Domingo matter again; and, rising to oppose the San Domingo Commission Bill, Sumner had startled the Senate with his opening sentence — 'The resolution before the Senate commits Congress to a dance of blood.' Thence he plunged into one of the most bitter and eloquent philippics on the proceedings in San Domingo. Though he was said to have told Lieutenant-Governor Dunn of Louisiana that he feared personal violence from Babcock, Sumner never shone brighter in the vividness of a denunciation. General Babcock, 'aide-de-camp' to the President — he rolled the words like a sweet morsel on his tongue. Scoring and ridiculing the agreements between the 'aide-de-camp' and Baez, 'a political jockey,' he painted no flattering picture of Grant. He openly charged that Grant had planned the reframing of the Committee on Foreign Relations for the exclusion of Sumner from the chairmanship. 'Somebody told him this would not be convenient.' Then he proposed the dismissal of Schurz, 'and he was told that this could not be done without affecting the German vote.' Then the dismissal of Patterson, 'who unhappily was not German' — and thus he went on.

The Senators sat transfixed with wonder. 'I protest against this resolution as another stage in a drama of blood,' he said, in conclusion. 'I protest against it in the name of Justice, outraged by violence; in the name of humanity, insulted; in the name of the weak, trodden down; in the name of peace, imperiled; and in the name of the African race, whose first effort at independence is rudely assailed.' [1]

The champions of Grant withheld their fire until the night session, when all appeared for a concerted assault. Morton led off, amazed that any one dare assail one so unassailable as Grant. 'The general results of the Administration are grand, grand almost beyond precedent.' A dance of blood, indeed! Could blood dance? And who had told Sumner that Grant had attempted an interfer-

[1] *Congressional Globe,* December 21, 1870.

Roscoe Conkling

Oliver P. Morton

Zachariah Chandler

GRANT'S THREE MUSKETEERS

ence with the personnel of the Committee on Foreign Relations? Morton had never heard any such suggestion. Who was Sumner's informant? As the attack proceeded, Zack Chandler and Conkling wheeling into line, it was manifest that the anger was directed no more at Sumner than at the Senator on the caucus committee who had told. 'Will the Senator give the name of that Senator?' demanded Chandler, pounding the desk in front of Sumner with his fist.[1] 'I shall not,' Sumner replied firmly. Finally Thurman, speaking for the minority, sought to shame the Republicans for their attacks on a man who had fought their party's battles in the Senate when he had fought almost alone.[2]

That 'dance of blood' philippic had left deep scars, and Conkling threatened the orator with party discipline. Nothing satisfied Sumner's vanity more than the chairmanship of the committee, and of that they could deprive him. But of course they would not dare. Garrison, hearing such rumors, wrote that, if a servile compliancy with the President was to be the test of party fidelity, 'the sooner the party is dissolved, the better.'[3]

But Fate was playing pranks with Sumner in those darkening days. He had unwittingly offended Grant personally when the committee was considering the nomination of Cramer as Minister to Denmark. An exhorter in the West, before he went to Leipsic as consul, to have his face slapped in the street, Cramer's qualifications for diplomacy did not appeal to Sumner, who said so. It was only then that he learned that Cramer was the President's brother-in-law. Others, including Harlan, had shared Sumner's opinion until Cramer's identity was established, and then Harlan became his champion, impressively reading letters from ministers and bishops of the Methodist Church in his praise. Sumner could not change. Finally on motion of Zack Chandler, the nomination was taken out of the hands of the committee and confirmed. It was a dagger-thrust at Sumner — that had never happened before in the full decade of his chairmanship.[4] And the clouds grew darker.

Meanwhile, it was being whispered about the cloak-rooms that the British Foreign Office had informed our Minister that there

[1] New York Herald, December 22, 1870.          [2] Ibid.
[3] To Sumner, Pierce, IV, 461.          [4] New York Herald, Feburary 6, 1871.

could be no settlement of our differences with England as long as Sumner remained chairman of the committee; and that the Minister had informed Fish, who had told Grant; and that Grant had agreed Sumner should go.[1] The enemies were closing in.

### III

Charles Sumner was an extraordinary man; his career colorful; his character sometimes inexplicable. Never a real leader or manager of men, he was persistent as the crusader for causes; and one of the most impressive of orators. His eloquence, however, was in his polished rhetoric — he understood phrases better than psychology. Never from his earliest youth had he been quite as other men. As a boy, studious, reserved, disdainful of youthful pranks, he grew old before his time. He never rowed or fished; never danced or flirted; never cared for dogs or horses. No youth so insensible to the charms of women. 'It was in vain for the loveliest and liveliest girl to seek to absorb his attention.' [2] In early manhood he felt the urge for a home and wife and talked frankly with his friends about it, but there was no romance. At no time was he ever to know anything of feminine psychology. He admired beautiful women enormously as he grew older, but some fell short of his ideal, and others seemed too much above him. 'She is amiable and good and I doubt not possesses a judgment as fine as her character; but she does not seem endowed with the magical grace,' he wrote of one; and of another, 'I confess to a certain awe and sense of her superiority which makes me at times anxious to subside into my own inferiority.' [3] There was no perfect one who was not too perfect, and thus he was to lose the humanizing experience of domesticity.

Then, too, he had no sense of humor. When he attempted it, he was heavy; when he tried repartee, he stumbled; and he could not relish a joke. Oliver Wendell Holmes was oppressed with his lack of 'imagination, wit, or sense of humor'; and another friend was to say that 'if one told Charles Sumner the moon was made of green cheese, he would controvert the alleged fact in all sincerity.' [4] An omnivorous reader, a brooding thinker, a fluent talker, he was a

[1] *New York Herald*, March 13, 1871.     [2] W. W. Story, Pierce, I, 106.

[3] Pierce, II, 319, 320.          [4] *Ibid.*, I, 164.

favorite of older men, and his association with them did not tend to make him more exuberant. Never perhaps has a young American made a more favorable impression on British society than Sumner in his youth. England entranced him. He loved its country houses and countryside, its Parliament and London parlors, its statesmen and writers, and he lingered long on his first sojourn, welcomed everywhere. The coronation of Victoria found him present in court dress, the Garrick Club made him an honorary member, his feet were under the table at many of Rogers's breakfasts, the galleries of Parliament found him looking down upon Peel and Russell and listening delightedly to O'Connell's voice, 'rich in the extreme,' and to Sheil's 'splendid bursts.' From the front row he heard Carlyle lecture and thought him 'like an inspired boy.' [1] Macaulay, whom he met occasionally at dinners, amazed him with his conversation — 'rapid, brilliant, and powerful.' [2] But it was Brougham with whom he became most intimate, visiting him at Brougham Hall, where he was shocked at his host's profanity and surprised at his temperate use of wine.[3] Soon the eager youth was making a round of visits — to Wordsworth, in whose simple house he found more pleasure than 'in the emblazoned halls of Lord Brougham'; [4] to Carlyle, whose poverty impressed him; to Leigh Hunt, and to the poet Campbell in Chelsea, in 'an humble house with uncarpeted entry and stairs,' where the poet, then sixty, drank brandy instead of wine and swore like a trooper.[5]

That he was not a woman-hater is evident in the eagerness with which he sought the more famous of the sex. Lady Blessington, 'elegant and sparkling'; [6] Mary Shelley, 'an agreeable person with great cleverness'; [7] the Duchess of Sutherland, 'wonderfully beautiful'; and the Countess Guiccioli — all intrigued him. Before he left England, he had affected the English style of dress, from which he never was to depart, and had tried fox hunting with indifferent success.

France poured her riches into his mind, and he tarried long in the galleries and studios of Italy, where he acquired a critical appreciation of art, and passed on to Germany, where he had long talks with philosophers and historians.

[1] Pierce, I, 318.   [2] Ibid., I, 328.   [3] Ibid., I, 349.   [4] Ibid., I, 355.
[5] Ibid., II, 47.   [6] Ibid., II, 67.   [7] Ibid., II, 21.

I have dwelt at some length on this Continental journey because his familiarity with celebrities who had received him courteously on equal terms tended to feed his egotism and give him a sense of superiority which, too openly displayed, was not to contribute to his popularity. Some years were to intervene before the beginning of his political career, and he was to hold himself aloof from common men. A sense of humor would have saved him from his greatest vice, but he had it not. 'His egotism was such as to make it impossible for him to admit that he had an equal in either House of Congress.' [1] Nor was his egotism that of self-love only — that would have been passed over with an indulgent smile; his egotism was a flaming public proclamation of his superiority. 'He did not exhibit respect or deference for the opinions of others, even when the parties were on a plane of equality.' [2] 'Impatient of contradiction, his manner to those who differed with him was arrogant and offensive.' [3] Henry Adams thought him a 'pathological study,' and was sure at the time with which we are dealing that his mind 'had reached the calm of water which receives and reflects images without absorbing them; it contained nothing but itself.' [4] Like most egotists, always self-conscious, he had the manner of an actor, and impressed many as one enacting a rôle on the stage. 'He appeared to me an actor,' said one who knew him. 'There appeared in him but little of the simply natural,' [5] Another thought him 'an actor who played the martyr to the admiration of his friends.' [6] No one ever saw him off stage. Though not a fop, he dressed with meticulous care, with attention to every detail.[7]

No one would have more keenly resented the imputation that he was ruled by prejudices, and yet no one formed them quicker, with less investigation, and gave them freer reign.[8] An anonymous letter from the South was enough to convince him that the Southerners were amusing themselves by killing inoffensive negroes. Nor was he a constructive statesman. He was a theorist, an idealist, a crusader, advocate, but no creator. He had no patience with the details of legislation. His interest was in principles.

---

[1] Stewart, *Reminiscences*, 239.
[2] Boutwell, ii, 218.
[3] McCulloch, 234.
[4] *Education of Henry Adams*, 251-52.
[5] Warden, 808.
[6] Stewart, *Reminiscences*, 239.
[7] Forney, ii, 259.
[8] McCulloch, 234.

And in the furtherance of a principle he had no patience with legal obstacles. Indeed, he had an 'absolute disregard of constitutional restraints,' like most of his radical associates.[1] His hatred of slavery was sincere; his advocacy of negro suffrage and of equal civil rights was theoretical. He thought them sincere as well, but he loved the negro — at a distance. Sumner was the last man to share his bed with a black man; and McCulloch, no doubt, was right in the conclusion that 'his sympathies were for races — too lofty to descend to persons.' No member of the Senate could have been more fastidious in his social relatious.[2] He thought of himself as an American Cicero, and, indeed, his oratory was that of finished art. Here and there a touch of pedantry, an unnecessary allusion for the sake of the effect upon the groundlings, but there was much more than polished rhetoric, chaste diction, rounded periods in his finest speeches. He marshaled his material like a master, and in the preparation of these speeches, written out by his own hand, he was capable of prodigious labor. He liked to feel that after their utterance they were part of literature — like those of Cicero and Burke. The 'dance of blood' speech may have been too severe — it was oratory.

In appearance he was a model of manly beauty, and when he rose to speak he was imposing. Six feet four inches in height, vigorous and graceful in his movements, his voice far-reaching and melodious, he easily commanded the attention of an audience. And now he was old and breaking. He had fought many battles and bore more scars than those that Brooks's cane had inflicted. He had accomplished both good and harm — more harm than he imagined. He had reached the age where a certain veneration was due him from his party. Not usually given to the cherishing of resentments, he hugged few hates. In the midst of the war he had declared it improper to inscribe the names of victories over fellow Americans on regimental colors. Soon he was to propose a bill in harmony with this theory, and Massachusetts was to crucify him with a condemnatory resolution of its Legislature, and he was to suffer. A man of great ability, of good intentions, given to the making of great blunders, he is one of the most contradictory characters in our history.

[1] Hoar, *Autobiography*, I, 214.    [2] McCulloch, 234.

IV

Many reasons were to be given for the degradation of Sumner, but one was quite sufficient. He had crossed the President, and Grant hated him. It was said that at a dinner given to Englishmen in Washington, Sumner had met an observation on Grant's popularity with the comment that he would 'be impeached for high crimes and misdemeanors.' The next morning a Senator who had been present told Stewart, who summoned the chairman of the Republican caucus and suggested that Fish be invited to the Capitol to verify the story. The verification was forthcoming and a caucus was called.[1] The secret of the animosity was revealed by one Senator in his disclosures of the discussions of a caucus in which Sumner's position on San Domingo figured largely.[2] The night before the committee reported, Horace White, of the 'Chicago Tribune,' persuaded William B. Allison, then a member of the House, to accompany him to the home of Senator Howe, who was to submit it, and beg him for delay. Until midnight they labored in vain.[3] The caucus had one fixed purpose — to punish Sumner and to please Grant. Two methods were considered — one, to transfer Sumner to the chairmanship of a new committee; the other, to leave him where he was with the committee packed against him. A few, like John Sherman, favored the latter course, but the rebuke would not have seemed severe enough.[4] Not a few Senators were saddened by the decision forced upon them. Morton was hard as flint. The caucus would be binding. Here was the oldest man in service in the Senate, a party founder, the very soul of the reconstruction scheme, and better fitted by training for the post he held than any other, and he was to be sent to the Tarpeian Rock. But Morton was obdurate — Grant's will be done!

Thus the stage was set in the Senate for a sort of tragedy when Senator Howe submitted his report and Carl Schurz rose to inquire the reason for the change proposed. 'I would answer,' whispered Morton. 'I would not answer or say a word,' said Stewart. But Howe replied that Sumner, Fish, and Grant were socially not friendly.[5] 'The Nation' described Howe as appearing

---

[1] Stewart, *Reminiscences*, 247–48.        [2] *Tipton Globe*, March 10, 1871.
[3] White, *Trumbull*, 346.        [4] Sherman, *Recollections*, I, 472.        [5] *Ibid.*

'like a gentleman engaged in a dirty piece of work.' [1] The Democrats smiled at the reason given; and when, to the indignation of the caucus leaders, Tipton blurted out the truth, they laughed. Then followed the debate. Wilson of Massachusetts begged and threatened. Schurz smashed the claim that Sumner would not meet Fish or Grant officially and shamed the Senate for bowing to presidential dictation in its own affairs. Administration Senators solemnly declared that Grant knew nothing of the proposed action of the caucus. Trumbull, recalling the former status of Sumner in the anti-slavery fight, asked if men's positions in the Senate were to be determined by their response to dinner invitations. Thurman, speaking for the Democrats, announced that, since Republicans challenged the action of their caucus, the Democrats would vote. Bayard, from the Democratic side, solemnly proposed to change the name of the Committee on Foreign Relations to the Committee on Personal Relations. The roll was called — and Sumner's head dropped into the basket after Morton had cracked the party whip. The Democrats voted against the decapitation, and there was both irony and pathos in the action of the Republican carpetbag Senators from the South — they voted to a man against the Senator who more than any other had made it possible for them to vote at all! [2] Thrifty souls, they knew on which side their bread was buttered.

An artist would have been delighted with the expressions of Senators' faces during the roll-call. Henry Wilson's face was red with anger. 'Morton screwed around in his chair in a most uneasy mood.' Sherman nervously tore paper to pieces, and then rose to walk the floor. Trumbull smiled sardonically over his gold-rimmed eyeglasses as upon an amusing spectacle of human folly. It was dark outside, and the galleries were in a blaze of light. That night there was rejoicing at the White House, and Grant was reported to be 'in high glee.' [3] Simon Cameron, of all men, had been made chairman of the Committee on Foreign Relations — he had landed his man on that fishing excursion with Grant in Pennsylvania. The day of the idealists was dead; that of the materialists had been born.

[1] March 16, 1871.          [2] *Congressional Globe*, March 10, 1871.
[3] *New York World*, March 11, 1871.

Many thousands in the North were shocked, many hurt. 'The Republican Party is no longer a party of ideas and principles, but the personal property of President Grant held together "by the cohesive power of public plunder,"' said the Democratic organ.[1] Greeley, keeping a close rein on his indignation, thought the action 'a mistake.'[2] 'An act of the most stupendous folly,' wrote Garfield to a friend.[3] And the next day, as the rain splattered in Lafayette Square, Sumner sat at the window of his library looking out upon the dreary scene, reading an avalanche of letters and telegrams. Then came the election in New Hampshire — and New England spoke. The Democrats prevailed.

## V

But Sumner did not take his punishment meekly. Within two weeks he had offered a set of resolutions denouncing our action in San Domingo and the use of the American Navy to sustain Baez in power. He spoke on the resolution to an animated and excited chamber. The avenues leading to the Capitol, the corridors, lobbies, galleries, were packed, and, on motion, women were admitted to the lobbies and cloak-rooms. The greater part of the diplomatic corps were on the floor. The House adjourned, and Blaine, the Speaker, sat beside the Vice-President. More than two thousand people were within sight or hearing. As Sumner entered the chamber, the galleries burst into applause.[4] Sumner began with proof of the use of the navy to sustain the tottering power of the usurper; passed to a scathing characterization of him as 'an adventurer, conspirator, and trickster'; told of meeting him when he was in exile, at his own home, when Baez was seeking 'money and arms to aid him in the overthrow of the existing government'; and of his return to power through violence. Menaced again by the indignation of the people, he described the usurper's attempt to sell his country to England, France, or Spain. And then, said the orator, 'he was relieved by an answering voice from our Republic.' 'A young officer, inexperienced in life, ignorant of the world, untaught in the Spanish language, unversed in international law, knowing absolutely nothing of the intercourse

[1] *New York World*, March 10, 1871.      [2] *New York Tribune*, March 13, 1871.
[3] To T. J. McLain, *Life of Garfield*, I, 469.      [4] *New York Herald*, March 28, 1871.

between nations, and unconscious of the Constitution of his country, was selected by the President to answer the cry of the Grand Citizen.'

Conkling and Carpenter, who in the beginning had simulated contempt by scribbling at their desks, became more restive as the speaker proceeded, until finally their audible conversation called for a rebuke from the Vice-President.

Sumner was hurrying on with lurid stories of adventurers, speculators, corruptionists, with the recital of the incarceration of an American with the sanction of Babcock — a sorry tale and a true one. From the diplomatic pouch he had extracted letters and reports; and thence he launched upon a powerful application of international law and usage to the case. 'Thus stands the case.' And then he lunged at Grant. 'Presidential visits to the Capitol, with appeals to Senators, have been followed by assemblies at the Executive Mansion, also with appeals to Senators; and who can measure the pressure of all kinds by himself or agents, especially through the appointing power, all to secure the consummation of this scheme?'

Again loud talking on the floor — Edmunds was interrupting — and Sumner paused. Again the Vice-President had to intervene. With a stinging rebuke of the Ku-Klux methods of the Government in San Domingo and Hayti, Sumner sat down.

Morton, replying for the Administration, 'would not attempt to argue this question,' but confined himself to attacking Sumner's motives and praising Grant. Sumner 'could not strike a blow at him without striking a blow at the country . . . at the great party that elected him . . . and no man need tell me he is a friend of liberty . . . if he spends his time and talent for the purpose of putting the Government into the hands of the Democratic Party.' And that was that.[1] The answer of Sumner to his enemies had been made; and he had been unmade.

## VI

More disturbing to many was the effect on the dominant party. All about was evidence of disaffection. Sumner was on a rampage; the incisive logic and brilliant mind of Schurz was playing havoc

[1] *Congressional Globe*, March 27, 1871.

with party plans; Trumbull's sardonic smile was maddening. Everywhere rumblings about corruption. A disconcerting letter, purporting to be from Orville Grant to the President, concerning a proposal made to the President's brother to act as agent for the distillers, with the proposition that for twenty thousand dollars all papers touching on their guilt would be turned over to them, was going the rounds of the press.

And just at this juncture, George W. Julian, another of the old idealists, defeated for reëlection at the instance of the land-grabbers, made his farewell speech. He was the Charles Sumner of the West — an old Abolitionist, with extreme views on universal suffrage, but with an inveterate hate of jobbery and corruption. His farewell speech was an astounding piece of invective. 'Tariff laws for years past . . . framed in the interest of monopolists . . .' A tendency in legislation 'to render the many dependent on the few, and to divide society into classes. . . . Over two hundred million acres of public land given to railroads and other works of public improvement. . . .' The 'ownership of labor by capital necessarily involves the ownership of the laborer himself. . . . Readiness of the Government to espouse the cause of monopolists and corporations.' [1] More revolt! And the Julian speech was attracting attention, too. Within two weeks after its delivery, a new edition of one hundred thousand copies had been necessary, and a special edition of twenty thousand in German had been printed.[2]

The old leaders and idealists were slipping. Grimes was gone; Sumner was rebuked and resentful; Trumbull was disgusted and sarcastic; Schurz was in revolt; civil service and tariff reformers were meddling — and an election was approaching. Worse still, not a few were laughing, and a returning sense of humor might restore clear thinking and a sense of justice in dealing with the South. No time could be lost.

## VII

And none was lost.

On January 14, 1871, the executive committee of the Union League met in Washington with party leaders, including a negro Congressman from South Carolina, to plan the extension of its

[1] *Congressional Globe*, January 21, 1871.          [2] Julian, MS. Diary, February 6, 1871.

work in the South; then they marched to the White House to talk it over with Grant, who gave his unqualified approval to the plans. The negro Congressman declared these indispensable in the South.[1] Two days later, Senator Morton offered his resolution calling on the President for a report on 'outrages' in the subjugated States; the President responded immediately, and the plans were instantly adopted. Once more the air was filled with denunciations of the Southerners as murderers and traitors; again orators evoked the bitter memories of the war; the bloody shirt again was afloat; and soon Congress was grappling with a new measure to be known as the Ku-Klux Act. The bill was reported to the House on March 28. Meanwhile, the Union League executive committee was meeting in Philadelphia, with a flourish of trumpets and an unfurling of flags, to arrange to meet 'conditions' in North Carolina, Arkansas, Missouri, and Florida, and petitions were received from negroes asking protection from persecution because of their politics.[2] 'The New York Tribune' fairly screamed over the 'outrages.' The Republican mayor of Meridian, Mississippi, had been expelled. Outrageous! exclaimed 'The Tribune.' 'Mississippi is a strong Republican State; Meridian is a Republican city; and yet her Republican mayor is hunted out like a wolf.'[3] Putting all scruples aside, Greeley stormed over the turpitude of the South Carolinians in demanding that the unscrupulous Governor and his band of corruptionists return to their Northern homes.[4] Legislation and an investigation into 'Southern outrages' to serve a party purpose? Ridiculous, said Greeley; at the same time declaring that the 'five thousand victims of the Ku-Klux outrages in the South are Republicans.'[5]

Four days before the debate on the Ku-Klux measure opened in the House, Grant issued a proclamation describing conditions in South Carolina as frightful, declaring the inability of State officials to correct them, referring to the appeal of the delectable Scott for the use of the Federal army, and calling upon the wicked to disperse within twenty days.[6] The timing of these various incidents calculated to reawaken sectional hatreds was so perfect that

[1] *New York Herald*, January 15, 1871.          [2] *Ibid.*, February 13, 1871.
[3] March 17, 1871.          [4] *Ibid.*, March 21, 1871.
[5] *Ibid.*, March 22, 1871.          [6] *Messages and Papers*, IX, 4086.

Democrats charged the team work to the management of politicians.

Thus, after six weeks, emerged a measure more despotic than any known since the Sedition Law of the first Adams Administration which wrought the political revolution of 1800. It set aside the constitutional guarantees of the States as effectively as though they had never been written; turned over to the Federal courts those accused of assault, robbery, and murder; provided extraordinary means through which these courts and politicians could pack juries as effectively as in the days of Lord Clare in Ireland; authorized the President to declare martial law when he pleased and suspend the writ of habeas corpus when he wished.

The debate was spirited in both House and Senate, and yet, despite the tremendous importance of the measure, little interest was taken in the discussions. Time and again speakers complained of the absence of a quorum. After all, no one was seeking information. The caucus had decided. And yet it was a great debate led by some of the greatest constitutional lawyers the Senate has known — men like Lyman Trumbull, Allen G. Thurman, and Edmunds of Vermont. In the House, Beck of Kentucky and Voorhees of Indiana had thundered against 'tyranny,' to no avail. 'You tender General Grant the sword,' said Voorhees, 'and tell him to wield it upon his countrymen in any direction he chooses; strike whenever his passions, his hates, his ambitions, or his interests dictate, and upon such cause or provocation as to him alone may appear sufficient. Do you wish to establish lawless tyranny in this land? Here is its charter.' [1] Trumbull solemnly entered his protest, buttressed with constitutional arguments unanswered then or ever. To enter the States to punish individual offenders against their authority would be 'destructive at once of the State Governments.' [2] More complete and powerful was the masterful Thurman, throwing upon all the bizarre features of the measure the light of his learning. Suspend the writ of habeas corpus by executive decree? 'A monstrous thing to do.' And the effect of the whole? The destruction of the States and with them 'the liberties, the prosperity, and the happiness of the people.[3] That which

---

[1] *Congressional Globe*, Appendix, 42d Congress, 1st Sess., 180.
[2] *Ibid.*, April 11, 1871.  [3] *Ibid.*, Appendix, 42d Congress, 1st Sess., 216-24.

Thurman and Trumbull then said was afterwards echoed by the
Supreme Court, but Congress did not hearken. Great streams of
'outrage'-mongers had been testifying, for the edification of the
North, before a congressional committee, upon the savagery of the
South, and in justification of this amazing measure, and it was
no time to stumble on the Constitution. The purpose was to reawaken the old war hates and re-create the old war state of mind
in the interest of party solidarity. Did not Charles Sumner wheel
into line with his old-time partisan vigor? Thurman was amazed.
Only the other day Sumner had justly arraigned the President
'for usurping the war power against the black people ... of
Hayti,' but he was insensible 'when a bill proposes to confer upon
the President the power to make war on the white people of
America.' [1] Morton had manifested something of the fine audacity
of Thad Stevens when he protested against the termination of the
law until after the presidential election of 1872. 'Why,' he demanded, 'is not this law to be continued anyhow throughout the
next year? Why terminate it just before the arrival of that season
when the cause would most likely operate the strongest which produces these troubles?' [2] Passing flippantly over the grave constitutional questions involving the governmental structure, he concentrated his fire upon the Democrats. Their success in 1872
would mean the repudiation of the national debt. In the midst of
the debate he was serenaded by Indiana Republicans, and appeared on the balcony of the National Hotel, flanked on one side
by Grant and on the other by Colfax, the Marine Band in the
crowd.[3]

And so the measure passed and the reaction came. Greeley had
momentary tremors lest Congress shrink from the declaration of
martial law and the suspension of the writ of habeas corpus. Too
much timidity! [4] Garfield, too, had shuddered for an opposing
reason. To suspend the writ when there was neither rebellion nor
invasion would be 'a doctrine subversive of our government.' [5]
'The Nation' and the 'New York Evening Post' thought the whole
scheme 'a desperate attempt ... of political adventurers and cor-

[1] *Congressional Globe*, April 13, 1871.      [2] *Ibid.*, April 11, 1871.
[3] *New York Herald*, April 9, 1871.      [4] *New York Tribune*, April 6, 1871.
[5] To McLain, *Life of Garfield*, I, 489.

rupt speculators ... to prevent the restoration of peace and order,' [1] and denounced it as a violation of the 'entire spirit of the Constitution.' [2] The Democrats in Congress issued an address denouncing it as a menace to the liberties of the people and destructive of local self-government. 'Modeled on the sedition laws, so odious in history, they are at variance with all the sanctified theories of our institutions.' [3]

But the Klan investigations, partisan on both sides, and the debates, had opened the flood gates of hate again. What though men like John Quincy Adams II referred to the 'crowning and perfect infamy of the Ku-Klux Bill' [4] — was not this copperhead talk? The way to handle the South, cried Wendell Phillips at Steinway Hall, New York, was 'to march thirty million of men to the Gulf,' irrespective of men, women, and children, and 'hang a few Generals.' [5] But General Sherman in New Orleans thought all the clamor absurd. The outrages 'had been enormously exaggerated for political effect' — and the Radicals fumed and raged.[6] Ben Butler answered. Speaking to negroes in Boston, he hailed with joy the domination of the blacks in South Carolina. Any fair comparison of the races would show the negroes better fit to rule than the whites.[7]

## VIII

And it was these South Carolina whites who were first to feel the lash of the new law. Grant had been urged by some of the most infamous characters in that State to give it a touch of martial law.[8] There was need, as we shall soon see, for aid to the incomparably corrupt régime in that Commonwealth. The whites were ready for revolution. Many thought death preferable to such degradation and infamy. In the early autumn, Grant began issuing his series of proclamations on conditions in South Carolina, ending with a declaration of martial law and the suspension of the writ of habeas corpus in nine counties. These proclamations were clearly phrased to inflame the partisan spirit in the North and to intimidate the conservatives in Carolina.

[1] April 6, 1871.                        [2] April 20, 1871.
[3] New York World, April 22, 1871.            [4] Ibid., May 20, 1871.
[5] New York, Tribune, May 15, 1871.          [6] New York Herald, May 4, 1871.
[7] Ibid., May 9, 1871.                 [8] The Negro in South Carolina, 200.

Came then the reign of terror, with wholesale arrests, with business all but suspended, with every citizen at the mercy of a dishonest enemy with a private grudge. The trials were mockeries of justice, the United States Circuit Court at Columbia a shambles that would have shamed Jeffreys or Lord Clare. The juries were defiantly packed with partisans, and an astonishing number of Radical politicians became jurors. Thus a dastardly conspiracy was manipulated by officials of the Federal Government![1] In Charleston, the scenes were similar. As if by magic the Democrats and Conservatives seemed to disappear. The courts could find no one for jury service but negroes, carpetbaggers, and scalawags. Some of the accused were deservedly convicted; others were youths of little education who had joined the Klan for a lark without any real feeling of hostility to the blacks.

A correspondent of the 'New York Herald' on the ground sent in some disconcerting reports. At Spartanburg, under martial law, he found there had been no Klan activities for four months; that in numerous instances Radicals wishing to wreak their spite upon some neighbor had donned the paraphernalia of the Klan to put the blame upon it; that the Klan never had any thought of resisting the Federal Government; that there was no necessity for the suspension of the writ of habeas corpus; that the Government of the State, against which the agitation was bitter, was in the hands of infamous adventurers.[2] The correspondent showed that most of the cases in the courts were political in purpose. Thus, a woman, at Rutherfordton, was advertised in the party papers in the North as a victim of political persecution resulting in a visitation of the Klan. On the dismissal of the case against the accused because of the lack of evidence, the North, reading its family paper, was told there was no justice for 'loyalists' in South Carolina. 'The Herald' correspondent found it a queer case of 'political persecution.' The woman was a 'common strumpet' who had inveigled an old man into marrying her. The night of the wedding disguised men appeared and whipped her. Two or three of the band were sons of the old man; one was a Baptist deacon.[3] As the correspondent continued his investigations, he reported, 'the more

[1] Reynolds, 211.     [2] *Ibid.*, 196.
[3] *New York Herald*, May 24, 1871.

I am convinced that they [the whippings] are social in their nature. The Ku-Klux have spread dismay among the ranks of the immoral and the worthless, both white and black.'[1] He found that the most abandoned wretches, by pleading political persecution because of 'loyalty,' had been made heroes in the North over whom good women wept and strong men raged.[2] The fatalities among the Lowry gang of desperadoes helped to swell the list of 'outrages' for the Northern press; and the correspondent found that this degenerate family, with a mixture of white, black, and Indian blood, were Democrats — and members of the Union League![3]

Meantime, the courts were grinding away at the trials. Efforts to test the constitutionality of the Ku-Klux Law were thwarted. One case was dismissed by the Supreme Court on a technicality;[4] another was withdrawn; in another, the Court was equally divided; in still another the prosecution was abandoned while the case was pending, and dismissed.

While the people were being subjected to this tyranny and lawlessness of the courts, the notorious political gangsters were making more than political capital — everything was grist that went to their mill. So the Republican organ at Columbia published stenographic reports of the trials and the paper was paid handsomely out of the public Treasury. The Legislature ordered five thousand copies in pamphlet form, and the order was placed with a printing company of the régime, which charged $45,788 for the work, and had its claim allowed.

And this was the answer to the great constitutional arguments of Thurman and Trumbull.

## IX

It was this summer that Clement Vallandigham startled the country with his proposal that the Democrats accept as settled the issues of the war and the reconstruction as embodied in the three Amendments, and invite the coöperation of all the people in a common fight against the destructive policies of the Radicals and corruptionists. It was in large measure a restatement of the funda-

[1] *New York Herald*, 28, 1871.    [2] *Ibid.*, May 29, 1871.
[3] *Ibid.*, June 12, 1871.    [4] United States *vs.* Avery.

mental Democratic principles to which men like Chase and
Trumbull had subscribed before the slavery question became
acute. The reaction was surprising. To the dominant party it
was disturbing. 'You have rendered a great service to your country and party . . . God bless you for it,' wrote Chase to Vallandigham.[1] Julian commented in his diary: 'Interested in Vallandigham's "New Departure," which I hope will be accepted. Democracy . . . to be reorganized on the living issues of land and labor
reform, civil service reform, revenue reform. . . . The country
needs a thorough purification.'[2] The 'New York World' endorsed
it in a leader.[3] Even Theodore Tilton spoke kindly of it in 'The
Golden Age.'[4] Michael Kerr, in a letter to Jeremiah S. Black,
gave it his approval.[5] 'The Nation' thought it 'entitled to rank
as a political event of the first importance' which Radicals would
'contemplate with horror.'[6] A little later Vallandigham lay dying
in an Ohio court-room from a bullet wound accidentally self-
inflicted while handling a pistol used as evidence in a murder trial,
and the press was more than generous to the man who had once
been anathema. Even Greeley joined.[7]

Clearly it was no time to draw back from desperate enterprises
now. So the summer and autumn passed and winter came — a
year of tragedy, comedy, and farce. Let us journey to South
Carolina and to the South and observe the blessings of reconstruction under the Radical politicians and corruptionists.

[1] *Life of Vallandigham*, 446.          [2] MS. Diary, May 28, 1871.
[3] June 3, 1871.          [4] July 1, 1871.          [5] *Ibid.*, July 15, 1871.
[6] May 25, 1871.          [7] *New York Tribune*, June 20, 1871.

# CHAPTER XVII

## LAND AND YEAR OF JUBILEE

### I

TURNING South from Washington, we shall not pause in Virginia, where the skies are clearing somewhat, albeit Mrs. John A. Logan, looking in on the Legislature in Richmond found the spectacle 'repulsive,' [1] nor in North Carolina, which we have visited before, but hurry on to Columbia, South Carolina, where the policies of 'loyal men' are in full flower.

The little capital is in a sorry state of debilitation, pigs grunting in the unpaved streets, the blackened ruins of flame-gutted buildings here and there, and near the town the pillars of the portico of what had once been the baronial mansion of the Hamptons. The town is teeming with negroes, in from the plantations to enjoy their freedom, and a visit to their quarter reveals them living in one-room log cabins, with wooden shutters and mud chimneys, and lolling and strolling in the sunny streets, some clothed in gunny sacks, and not a few of the children stark naked.[2] In the fashionable section of the fallen society, which had impressed the cultivated LeConte as 'one of the most refined and cultivated' he had ever known,[3] the fine houses are strangely silent now, little merriment floating out of the open windows on the night. A new society has displaced it, and there is no merging of the two. The wives and daughters of the officers at the barracks are sternly frowned upon by the women of Columbia.[4] The new society, mixed in color, and composed largely of carpetbaggers, has gathered about the barracks, and this, known as the 'Gig Society,' parades the barracks grounds in its finery in the evening listening to the band, while politicians gather in groups in eager discussion of the latest swag.

Near by, we find the grounds of the university so recently presided over by the brilliant and eloquent Preston, but the buildings

[1] Mrs. Logan, 263.      [2] *The Negro in South Carolina*, 8–9.
[3] LeConte, 239.          [4] *Ibid.*, 237.

are now in desperate need of repair, and the grounds are tragically sad, like a deserted garden overrun by weeds. The Legislature of 1869, illiterate and corrupt, had seized upon the old institutions for reasons of pillage, and soon the trustees had been involved in charges of corruption.[1] A few poorly dressed, underpaid professors and a handful of students are all that are left of the once flourishing university.

Driving down the fine, wide street back of the State House, with its great spreading oaks, where the aristocracy had blossomed in the old days, we find the blinds of the houses drawn. Occasionally we pass a scion of the old families on his blooded horse, the last of his luxuries, but it is the speculator and carpetbagger, sweeping by a little insolently behind a dashing team, that compels our notice.[2] At length we reach the beautiful white marble State House surrounded by a rough wooden fence, the grounds littered with all kinds of filth.[3] Here let us enter and pay our respects to His Excellency Robert K. Scott of Ohio, by the grace of bayonets Governor of South Carolina.

## II

A fine figure of a man is he who greets us, tall and erect as an Indian, with a manner arrogantly self-assertive. We are impressed mostly by his shifty gray eyes, keen and penetrating, as they peer from beneath an overhanging brow. About his mouth are lines indicative of struggle, bitterness, or meanness, but he greets us with a breezy cordiality. A soldier of fortune, this carpetbag Governor, who had elbowed his way in the California gold rush, worked as a common miner and prospector, practiced medicine, won his shoulder straps by gallantry in the field, and, entering South Carolina with the Freedmen's Bureau, had cleverly applied his demagogy to negro credulity and won his way to the State House.[4] Congenial souls had accompanied him into office — Niles G. Parker of Massachusetts, in flight from criminal prosecution in his native State, in charge of the Treasury; Whittemore, purveyor of cadetships in Congress, and Frank Moses, Speaker of the House and Adjutant-General. In our meanderings we have

[1] Reynolds, 123.
[2] *New York Herald*, June 13, 1871.
[3] Pike, 10.
[4] *Representative Men*, 489–96.

heard much of Moses, member of a respected family, expelled from his college fraternity because of his low associations,[1] a fast liver, utterly unmoral, a gambler and libertine who had seized upon the opportunity to share in the plundering of his own people. The gossips have told us of his frequenting negro cabins, kissing negro babies, swirling through the dance with dusky maidens in his arms in negro dance-halls. He has none of Sumner's academic notions of social equality — he lives what Sumner preaches.[2] Gambling-dens, saloons, and brothels catering to both races, furnish him with his amusements. His manner of living has so enhanced his popularity that he is even now striding toward gubernatorial honors, and as we linger with Scott, he glides gracefully into the room and is presented. This degenerate bears the marks of his reckless and low living. His immaculate dress, the fluency and suavity of his conversation convey a momentary impression of gentility, but there is something in his heavy gray-brown mus-tache and shifty eye suggestive of his criminality and debauchery.[3] Degraded women were important factors in redeeming South Carolina to the 'loyal' cause.

Even Scott was not without his weakness, for had he not signed hundreds of thousands of dollars' worth of fraudulent convertible bonds in the room in the old St. James Hotel in New York under the persuasive influence of women and liquor? His reluctance had been overcome by the ringsters through the notorious Pauline Markham, of the burlesque stage, who had consented to seduce him for a percentage of the commission on the bonds. Saturated with wine and whiskey, he had signed and sealed while the delec-table charmer counted and piled the bonds.[4]

Enter now a third 'loyal' man, ironically known among the thieves as 'Honest' John Patterson, an alleged protégé of Simon Cameron, with a discolorful record in the Pennsylvania Legis-lature, who had been denounced by his brother-in-law as a 'swindler and cheat,' and had distinguished himself as pay-master in the army by stealing the money of the soldiers of an Ohio regi-ment. Thus had he qualified for the new statesmanship, and he is now looking forward to a seat in the United States Senate. 'Patterson will do what he says,' a friend explains, apropos of his

[1] Reynolds, 99.     [2] Pike, 45.     [3] Mitchell, 325.     [4] Ibid., 326.

sobriquet. 'If he promises to pay you, he'll do it; if he promises to steal for you, he will do it.' [1]

But it is time for us to leave — the three pillars of their party must confer.

### III

Before visiting the Legislature, we shall have time to sense the social atmosphere of the reconstruction régime in Columbia. One of its first acts had been to forbid discrimination between races in street cars, trains, and places of amusement. Governor Scott and his lady had thrown open their official entertainments to whites and blacks alike, and the races had mingled cordially at the mansion, to the delight of the educational director of the Freedmen's Bureau, who had reported enthusiastically to Washington.[2] There had been some defiance of the equality law in Charleston, which 'The Nation' thought natural, if not proper,[3] but Columbia was the political center and white men there bowed low over the hands of colored women, and found their way to the salon of a brown-skinned Madame Roland. Let us follow the fashion.

Once more we ride under the spreading oaks of the wide street near the State House, recalling the stories we have heard of the young women we are soon to meet. The Rollin sisters, Katherine, Euphrosyne, Marie Louise, and Charlotte, daughters of a Frenchman by a colored mother, were concededly pretty, their complexion that of a mixture of the white and the mulatto. Inordinately proud of their French blood, they preferred to be known as 'Mesdemoiselles'; and in their exuberant moments with white callers dwelt mournfully on the pre-war days when slaves danced attendance on their pleasures. Two of the sisters had attended a school in Boston with a niece of Wendell Phillips, and Louise had gone to a convent school in Philadelphia. Carpetbaggers and negro politicians spoke admiringly of their learning as well as their beauty. True, one of the sisters had married the coal-black head of the militia, but the ladies of the salon spoke of her as of one dead. They could not abide her husband because of his color. Many amazing tales we have heard of the Rollin sisters. The talk of the lobby, romanticists insisted they really directed the destiny

[1] Reynolds, 229.        [2] *Ibid.*, 121.        [3] January 27, 1870.

of the State through their relations with Scott and Moses; others declared their salon a mere clearing-house for the lobby. But here we are, at the house.

We draw up before a respectable white frame dwelling, to be met at the door by Marie Louise, the youngest, and conducted into a room and seated at an open window overlooking a garden in which a fountain is playing. A striking girl, with lustrous almond-shaped eyes, dimpled chin, and teeth white and shapely that flash in smiles. On a table, we observe Byron's poems, the books of Gail Hamilton, some of Miss Alcott's stories, a copy of the 'Atlantic Monthly.' . . . Almost immediately Charlotte Rollin enters, she of whom we have heard as the 'Madame de Tench of South Carolina,' reputed to possess uncanny power over the statesmen of the new régime. The same voluptuous figure and lustrous eyes, but more at ease than the younger sister. Do we speak French? she inquires musically. Ah, it is the language of poetry, she thinks. But the papers, the dreadful papers, how dare they publish such stories about her and her sisters? We venture to ask if the Rollin *ménage* really did determine the legislative policies of the State. Mademoiselle Charlotte smiles faintly, preferring to treat the suggestion as flattery. Then the lady bristles. What an outrage! — that report that she had written a letter to Frank Moses in the interest of a questionable claim. Of course she had done nothing of the sort. Moses might have forged one. And that absurd story that her sister Katherine was a major on the staff of Moses and got a salary. A joke, of course, perpetrated by Elliott [1] when in charge of the enrollment of militia, and by Moses, 'then our intimate friend.' The lady of the salon chuckles reminiscently. 'He used to write us a number of notes' — and she smiled. Pleased with the memories, she produces a letter from Moses informing her that he was getting her a salary as a clerk in his office as a personal compliment, and because of her sister's marriage to the negro militia chief. The lady grimaces at the mention of his name. Her family did not condescend to notice the brother-in-law, or Elliott — they were negroes; her people were French.

In glides Katherine, aged twenty-four, slender, graceful, her black silk rustling, her large black eyes shining, her long straight

---

[1] Later negro Congressman.

hair coiled behind. 'I just came from the reception at Governor
Scott's,' she says enthusiastically, 'and had a very pleasant time
there; he is a great friend of ours and we hope to see him President.
He is a noble man, indeed.' Whereupon the three ladies of the
salon draw their chairs in a semicircle about us, and forthwith we
are in the midst of a literary conversation. Did we like Byron?
'What a dear reckless fellow he was, to be sure!' exclaims Made-
moiselle Charlotte. 'I love Mrs. Browning above all the poets, and
I like Victor Hugo . . . but Whittier I adore . . .'[1]
But we must leave this literary atmosphere for the Legislature.

#### IV

We enter the House, where Moses, the Speaker, looks down
upon members mostly black or brown or mahogany, some of the
type seldom seen outside the Congo.[2] Some pompous in glossy,
threadbare black frock coats, some in the rough, soiled costumes
of the fields, others in stub jackets and rough woolen comforters
tight-fitting about the neck to conceal the lack of linen.[3] A cozy
atmosphere, too, with the members' feet upon their desks, their
faces hidden behind their soles. Chuckles, guffaws, the noisy
cracking of peanuts, and raucous voices disturb the parliamentary
dignity of the scene.

On one side a small group of whites, Democrats, representing the
shadow of the old régime, 'good-looking, substantial citizens . . .
men of weight and standing in the communities they represent,' sit
'grim and silent.'[4] Without influence here, they have even less in
Washington. Mingling with the negroes we see ferret-faced
carpetbaggers, eager for spoils; and, in the rear, 'Honest' John
Patterson, vulture-eyed, calculating the prices of members.
Two years hence he will reassure his kind with his classic statement that 'there are five years more of good stealing in South
Carolina.'[5]

Moses is hammering for order, members are shouting to one
another, ridiculing the man speaking, asking silly questions.
Ordered to their seats, the disturbers flop down with uproarious
laughter, their feet upon their desks. Then, like a jack-in-the-box,

[1] Interview by *New York Herald* correspondent, June 13, 1871.
[2] Pike, 15.          [3] *Ibid.*, 10.          [4] *Ibid.*, 13.          [5] Reynolds, 229.

up again. It is a lark, a camp-meeting. The oily carpetbaggers simulate a share in the hilarity, 'Honest' John smiles approvingly, the little group of native whites exchange melancholy glances.

And now a negro orator is speaking, fluently, with many-syllabled words, ludicrously misplaced, flowing mellifluously, and there is cheering, laughing. And then, silence, for the most able and eloquent of the negroes, of whom we have heard in the salon, is on his feet. Men listened to Robert Brown Elliott, idol of the negroes, who did much to inflame their ambition and cupidity with disturbing speeches on social equality. Even the carpet-baggers are obsequious. Moses had barely defeated him for the Speakership, but patience, he will yet preside. Meanwhile, his cunning and eloquence are being converted into money. His domination of the Railroad Committee had stood him in good stead, and rumor bruited it abroad that large bribes from the railroads had found their way into his rapacious pockets. An able man, educated in England, with morals as low as those of Moses, a power in the State.[1] But Elliott was an exception, for most of the negroes were illiterate, their intellectual level 'that of a bevy of fresh converts at a negro camp-meeting.'[2] Some laboriously had learned to sign their names; many made their mark. When 'The Nation' asserted that eighty per cent could neither read nor write, and Tilton, of 'The Independent,' and the 'Charleston Daily Republican' protested, 'The Nation' asked the latter to 'inform us plumply what number of members were . . . able to read a page of the "Pilgrim's Progress" decently or intelligently.'[3]

Meanwhile, amid the cracking of peanuts, the shouting, laughing, stamping, members are seen leaving and returning in a strange state of exaltation — they come and go in streams. Let us follow the trail to the room adjoining the office of the clerk of the Senate. We learn that it is open from eight in the morning till two or four the next morning, and now, as we push in, it is crowded. A bar-room! Solons are discussing politics over sparkling glasses of champagne, supplied by taxpayers. Here gallons of wine and whiskey are consumed daily. Members enter bleary-eyed in the early morning for an eye-opener or a nightcap —

[1] Reynolds, 286.        [2] Pike, 17.        [3] May 26, 1870.

some are too drunk to leave at 4 A.M. Champagne? Wine? Whiskey? Gin? Porter? Ale? — and the member orders to his taste. Does a special brand of liquor or fine cigars appeal especially? Boxes are ordered to the member's hotel or boarding-house.[1] 'One box of champagne, one box port wine, one box whiskey, one box brandy, one box sherry wine, three boxes cigars' — this the order for one negro member.[2] When the chairman of the Claims Committee found one box of wine delivered to his lodgings, he indignantly wrote: 'This is a mistake; the order calls for two boxes of wine. Please send the other.'[3] None but the finest brand of cigars was tolerated, and members, leaving, usually filled their pockets. Because of the visitors, lobbyists, State officials, enough liquor was consumed to have given each member a gallon daily, with no less than a dozen cigars.[4]

Since even 'good men and true' could not live on wine alone, the State was taxed to supply the refreshment-room with Westphalia hams, bacon, cheese, smoked beef, buffalo tongue, nuts, lemons, oranges, cherries, peaches — much of which found its way to hotels and boarding-houses and the homes of the mistresses.[5] 'The State has no right to be a State unless she can afford to take care of her statesmen,' said Senator C. P. Leslie.[6] Yes, and their wives and sweethearts, too. Thus much of the taxpayers' money went into tapestries, rugs, table linen, imported chignons, ladies' hoods, ribbons, hooks and eyes, extra long stockings, bustles, rich toilet sets; and white and dusky sirens found the Golden Age.[7]

A clubby crowd, too, these 'loyal men' of South Carolina; for when Speaker Moses and Whipper, a negro member who owned fast horses, arranged a race on a thousand-dollar bet, and Moses lost, did not the Legislature within three days vote a gratuity to the Speaker to cover his loss, 'for the dignity and ability with which he has presided'?[8]

Now that darkness has come, we must see the night life of Columbia. Bar-rooms and dance-halls are crowded with negroes, and a sprinkling of whites. In hotels and boarding-houses, sharp-faced men converse with legislators in low tones; in rooms behind

[1] *Fraud Report*, 9; *Doc. Hist.*, II, 60.  [2] James A. Bowley, *Fraud Report*, 10
[3] *Ibid.*  [4] *Ibid.*, 13.  [5] *Doc. Hist.*, II, 61–69.
[6] *Fraud Report*, 8.  [7] *Ibid.*  [8] Pike, 199.

locked doors, legislation is being determined. The open sesame
to legislative favor is the rattle of coin. Let us listen at the key-
hole of one of the locked rooms, where the lawyer of a mining
company is explaining to a negro member that he wants a charter
for a mine. It will be good for the State and help the people, he
explains. 'What is the thing worth?' asks the member. 'It has
not yet been tried, but we hope to make it profitable.' A burst of
incredulous laughter from the legislator. 'You are green; I mean
what are you willing to pay to get the thing through?' 'I am not
willing to pay anything,' replies the lawyer. 'You are legislating
for our people and we demand our rights.' The member explodes
with laughter, and the lawyer rises indignantly and makes for the
door.[1] Clearly the man was 'green,' as 'Honest' John Patterson
could have told him. 'How did you get your money?' asked
James Pike of a legislator. 'I stole it,' was the brazen reply. It
was safe to make such admissions in South Carolina with Federal
bayonets to sustain the system.

### V

Thus stealing was a virtue, with decent citizens submerged and
silenced. The only public opinion necessary to conciliate was that
of thieves. Robbers included men in politics and out. Public
officials made common cause against the Treasury. When one of
these was charged with stealing, he replied, 'Let them prove it.'[2]
'The Nation' was informing the North that South Carolina was
'almost completely at the mercy of white and black corruptionists.'[3]

To sustain the system a party press was required; the corruptionists created one, and then stole public funds to subsidize it.
These papers got public printing at outrageous rates, and then
collected more than was called for by the contracts. Thus the
'Charleston Republican' should have received $24,538.20 under
the rates, and received $60,982.14;[4] the 'Columbia Daily Record'
should have received $17,174.05, and was paid $59,987.64.[5]
Enough was squandered on the party press to have furnished each
voter with a bound volume of the laws.[6] When the 'Columbia

[1] Doc. Hist., II, 54–55.     [2] Pike, 28.          [3] May 12, 1870.
[4] Fraud Report, 241.         [5] Ibid., 242.        [6] Ibid., 248.

Union-Herald' found itself neglected, it blackmailed the Ring into including it in the loot.[1]

The corruption in State bonds, criminally issued and divided among official gangsters, mounted into the millions, but bribery and bond-looting was not enough for this avaricious horde, which had recourse to the pay certificate steals. With thirty-five attachés in the Senate, pay certificates were issued for three hundred and fifty. Senators demanded and received these 'for friends and party workers' in their counties, who had never pressed the sidewalks of Columbia.[2] When Moses, the Speaker, required more funds for his debauchery and made out a pay certificate for twenty-five hundred dollars, Lieutenant-Governor Ransier refused to approve unless included. A conference followed, and the five thousand dollars made out to 'John Gershon,' for 'room rent, fees, etc., for the Joint Investigating Committee in New York,' was divided between the presiding deities of the two houses.[3]

When bribery, illegal bonds, pay certificates did not suffice, the thieves bethought themselves of furnishing the State House. Within four years a people on the verge of bankruptcy was forced to pay out more than two hundred thousand dollars for the purpose. There was a $750 mirror to reflect the dissipated face of Moses, clocks for members in their private rooms at $480, and two hundred cuspidors at eight dollars each, for the use of one hundred and twenty-four members. The quarters of Moses at Mrs. Randall's rooming-house were elegantly furnished at the State's expense.[4] And yet, on the expulsion of the Radicals from power, there was less than eighteen thousand dollars in furniture to account for the two hundred thousand dollars spent; the rest was in the homes of the members and their mistresses.[5]

Meanwhile, the North knew precisely what was going on, and when the Charleston Board of Trade served notice that bonds issued by the criminals would be repudiated, 'The Nation,' commenting, said that 'any one who takes these bonds not only helps to sustain a pack of thieves ... but takes a thoroughly bad security.'[6] Even Horace Greeley, a bit disturbed, was accusing carpetbaggers of preying on the credulity of the negroes.[7]

[1] *Fraud Report,* 253–55.   [2] *Ibid.,* 418.   [3] *Ibid.,* 394.   [4] *Ibid.,* 14.   [5] *Ibid.*
[6] April 6, 1871.   [7] *New York Tribune,* July 19, 1871, August 14, 1871.

VI

And how did the corruptionists sustain themselves? The election of 1870 gives the answer. Because of the preponderance of negroes, South Carolina from the first had been the happy hunting ground of the Northern bandits. In 1870 there were 415,814 negroes to 289,667 whites. In Charleston there were 26,173 negroes; in Columbia, 5291.[1] These were not uniform in intelligence. Those on the coast and rivers were little above the intellectual level of the mules they drove. Even their jargon was unintelligible to the stranger. With abysmal ignorance and strong passions, they were easily organized and used by the Leagues and carpetbaggers.[2] In Charleston, negroes with mechanical skill had accumulated property, and this was true in a less degree in Columbia.[3] This more intelligent class sought to improve itself economically, and, in a meeting called for the purpose four years before, politics had not been mentioned.[4] It was not with these that the Radicals dealt. They soon found among the negroes men of cunning, cupidity, and some ability, with whom they affiliated for the control of the great mass of ignorance, and this mass dominated the State. The political power of Charleston was nullified through the merging of its vote with that of the swamp negroes within a radius of thirty miles. When Governor Scott entered his second campaign in 1870, his chief reliance was on the blacks. On these he could depend, for woe to the negro who, retaining respect for the native whites, dared give them political favor. Negroes supporting the Democrats were constantly assaulted.[5] When Stephen Riley, a former slave, joined the Democrats in 1868, he was repeatedly mobbed and beaten, and the Radicals chanted their contempt through the streets.

> 'Oh Riley, he am straight and tall,
> He hab no bone in de back,
> He bend and scrape to de white folks all,
> An' forget dat he am black.' [6]

But 1870 developed some disaffection under the leadership of Senator R. H. Cain, a Northern black, artful in mimicking the

[1] The Negro in South Carolina, 7.           [2] Pike, 263, 265.
[3] The Negro in South Carolina, 68.          [4] Pike, 35.
[5] Reynolds, 105.                            [6] New York Herald, May 11, 1871.

Southern negro. A preacher, he had made himself a power through the 'Missionary Record' he edited, and his vigorous personality, unbounded energy, and organizing capacity.[1] No one had appealed more shamelessly to the lowest passions of his race or made more incendiary attacks upon the whites. Usually corrupt, though destined to be a Bishop, he pretended to be shocked by the scandals of the Scott régime, albeit his real grievance was the subordination of the negro to the carpetbagger.[2] 'These long lank sharp-nosed gents may prepare for defeat,' he told his black audiences. 'The colored people have been sold often enough.'[3] To offset this flank attack, Scott had with him on the ticket as candidate for Lieutenant-Governor, A. J. Ransier, a negro with no prejudices against pillage.[4] Another advantage he had, too — James Lawrence Orr, a distinguished Carolinian, once Speaker of the National House of Representatives, and former Governor, went over to the Republicans in the vain hope that the corruptionists would reform themselves. He was to be rewarded with the mission to Russia, where he was to die, and the flag of the Union League Club of New York was to be lowered to half-mast when his remains reached New York.[5]

Even so the bitterness of a degraded people had become appalling — they were as a smouldering volcano. 'There is one recourse when all is lost — I mean the sword,' wrote Dr. Myron Baruch from Camden. 'What boots it to live under such a tyranny, such moral and physical oppression, when we can be much happier in the consciousness of dying for such a cause?'[6] The contempt for the scalawags had become cruel. Describing the deathbed of one of these, 'his couch not cheered by sympathizing friends or even loving relatives,' Dr. Baruch confessed to a feeling of sadness 'to see men made completely callous to the call of humanity by political differences.'[7]

## VII

But the carpetbaggers under Scott were not alarmed; the bayonet was master of the ballot. Preaching the virtues of the Winchester rifle in a speech in Washington, Scott returned home to

---

[1] *The Negro in South Carolina*, 114.          [2] Reynolds, 109.
[3] *The Negro in South Carolina*, 193.          [4] *Ibid.*, 195–96.
[5] *Ibid.*, 1867.          [6] Baruch MSS.          [7] *Ibid.*

turn the negro militia loose upon the State at the beginning of the campaign. More than seven thousand rifles were distributed among negro militiamen, and the only white company was driven to disbandment by having a negro officer put over it.[1] These armed negroes were stationed in communities where opposition was most feared; and the constabulary force of five hundred men was sent with Winchesters into doubtful counties, whence it reported regularly to Scott, not on lawlessness, but on the course of the campaign. Rough, swaggering bullies, with badges and bayonets, they promised to overawe the whites. The negro militia drilled constantly, parading the streets with fixed bayonets, forcing citizens from the highway. Not satisfied with these, Scott imported from New York a gang of gunmen under 'Colonel' James E. Kerrigan, and, later, he and some of his men were to testify they had been employed to defend Scott and to kill his enemies.[2] When even these did not satisfy, Scott called on Grant for Federal troops, and these soon appeared to reënforce the gunmen, the blustering constables, and the negro militia. The President assured Scott of all the military assistance required.

An amazing campaign, with Scott silent, depending on the guns. The negro nominee stumped the State with belligerent demands for social equality.[3] An appointee of the Governor exhorted the blacks to 'defend their rights' with the suggestion that 'matches are cheap.'[4] 'Taxes too high?' said Beverly Nash, negro, to an audience of thousands. 'I tell you they are not high enough.'[5] Colored men opposing Scott were beaten and divorced, for the women had been enlisted. The result was inevitable — Scott, reëlected by thirty thousand majority, plunged deeper than ever into pillage. It was after this that the railroad and furniture scandals reached their peak. Senator Robertson was reëlected to the Senate — the purchase price about forty thousand dollars.[6]

Such was South Carolina — let us hurry on to Louisiana.

## VIII

*En route* we may as well make a hurried trip to Tallahassee in Florida and visit a Legislature, now familiar, composed of swin-

[1] Reynolds, 136.　　[2] *Ibid.*, 152.　　[3] *Ibid.*, 143.　　[4] *Ibid.*, 145.
[5] Pike, 224.　　[6] Reynolds, 158.

dlers, stealing on mileage and dancing ostentatiously on auction blocks. Here again we meet the infamous Littlefield, busy with his railroad steals, and prodigal as need be with his bribery funds. He is interested in the Georgia Railroad and the Tallahassee Railroad, and legislation is required. No one knows better how to get it. The hotels and boarding-houses are filled with shabby strangers, the meanest of the carpetbaggers drinking champagne, and the poorest in possession of the finest of beaver hats. The lordly Littlefield, amiably accessible, keeps his carriage at the hotel door to facilitate responses to eager calls from members of the Legislature.[1] Nights find bright lights and abundant whiskey in hotel rooms, whence members, won by money, stagger joyously.[2] Having sold a United States Senatorship, these importunate statesmen are now blackmailing the purchasers with threats of exposure, and money is again forthcoming.[3] Negro members, suspecting a sliding scale of bribery to their disadvantage, have caucused and named a 'smelling committee' to investigate and exact justice.[4] Even the Northern Radicals are a little embarrassed by their leaders in Florida — M. L. Stearns, who as a Freedmen's Bureau agent, had made free with Government pork and flour, and Harrison Reed, the Governor, who was something of a hypocrite and everything of a scamp. These odious parasites had played, as elsewhere, on the credulity of the blacks for power. Nights found the carpetbaggers campaigning on plantations, kissing the babies, while the old black mammies fervently exclaimed, 'I will vote ebery day foh dat man,' for 'dat man is a good 'publican'; and the carpetbaggers would piously reply, 'Jesus Christ was a Republican.'[5] 'The worst imaginable spectacle that could afflict the eyes of anybody,' thought 'The Nation' in 1875.[6] That was the year William D. Bloxham, former slave-owner, who voluntarily had built the first negro school on his plantation, stepped forth to give cohesiveness and courage to the opposition and to revive the spirit of the native whites in a brilliant campaign of denunciation.[7]

Florida was putrid.

[1] Wallace, 102.   [2] *Ibid.*, 94.   [3] Senator Gilbert, Wallace, 97–99.
[4] *Ibid.*, 104.   [5] Wallace, 63.   [6] February 10, 1875.
[7] Wallace, 127.

Putrid, too, was Alabama, where we may pause a moment at Montgomery, and look in on its Legislature. We have heard of the scenes of the first sessions under reconstruction, with galleries, windows, and seats packed with negro spectators voting with the members with shouts and hysterical laughter, and with colored members sleeping in their chairs, eating peanuts, and, soaked with whiskey, quarreling, fighting, pursuing one another with murderous intent.[1] Well, conditions have not greatly changed. Less festivity, perhaps, more concentration on the main chance; for we are now shown a room set aside where the lobbyists can interview members in seclusion and distribute the bribe money.[2] In the Exchange Hotel we learn that the lobby maintains four rooms for entertainment and business.[3] The carpetbag members, all 'loyal men,' have their prices. Speaker Harrington boasts he had received seventeen hundred dollars for getting one bill through; a Senator had a fixed price of five hundred dollars for railroad bills; another exacted twice that sum; and a leader got thirty-five thousand dollars for the successful management of a railroad bond issue, most of it sticking to his hands.[4]

Alabama was saturated with corruption.

IX

And even worse was Louisiana. Here, even when thieves fell out, honest men failed to get their due. New Orleans, the reconstruction capital, is a city of charm, Canal Street with its imposing width and partly grass-grown dais in the center dominating all, the streets in the business section paved with large blocks. Close to the levee on Canal Street looms the Custom-House, important in our story, built of Maine granite, and presided over by Collector Casey, brother-in-law of the President, with a reputation none too good. Somehow through all its miseries the city has managed to preserve something of its Gallic gayety. Young blades still speed their racers over the famous Shell Road, 'straight as an arrow, hard as flint, and smooth as a backgammon board,'[5] pausing for a cocktail or a sherry cobbler in the shade of fragrant trees at the road-houses. The nights are lively with balls and

[1] Fleming, 783.          [2] Ibid.          [3] Ibid., 591–605.
[4] Ibid., 739–40.          [5] Somers, 193.

masquerades, and the gambling-houses are never deserted except on Sunday, when a pensive serenity descends upon the town.

Here in the capital sits Henry Clay Warmoth, ruling with a rod of iron. No ordinary person, this dashing young soldier of fortune who had drifted into town as blithesomely as a Gascon of the fourteenth century ever moved on Paris with his sword. Born in Illinois, he had just begun the practice of the law in Missouri, when the war swept him into the army, and at the close, in light-hearted mood, he moved on to New Orleans, where his commanding person, courtly manners, and genius for politics smoothed his path to political preferment. His enemies have said he was penniless when he reached the city; he himself insists he had enough, and had entered at once on a lucrative practice of his profession.[1] In the beginning it was all a lark — caucuses, conferences, were to his liking, and, besides, was not this the land of the plum tree? The negroes, attracted to the merry young blade, elected him to Congress before the State's Representatives were admitted, and he sallied forth to Washington to be cordially received by the Republican leaders and turned away. But it was ordained of destiny that he should have bigger fish to fry. When the Grand Army of the Republic was organized in Louisiana, he was made Grand Commander, and a few weeks later, at the age of twenty-six, he was elected Governor. His enemies soon were to comment significantly on his capacity to save one hundred thousand dollars a year on a salary of eight thousand dollars and to accumulate a million in four years.[2] But an English tourist, who found him 'a young man of spirit and ability,' observed that 'his wealth, if the wages of corruption, had been so deftly acquired that no one can lay his finger on the spot.'[3]

The Legislature we find sitting in Mechanics' Hall is typical of the others we have seen in the land of jubilee. Here, presiding over the House, we find a shrewd, unscrupulous, audacious youth of twenty-six, Carr of Maryland.[4] And such scenes! The lobbies teem with laughing negroes from the plantations, with whites of the pinch-faced, parasitic type; and negro women in red turbans peddle cakes and oranges to the very doors of the chambers.

[1] Warmoth, MS. Reminiscences.
[2] H. R. Report, 92–94, 42d Cong., 2d Sess.
[3] Somers, 228.
[4] Ibid., 24.

Within, some coal-black members, but most of lighter hue, though Lieutenant-Governor Dunn, presiding over the Senate, is a black.[1] The abysmally ignorant eschew debate, some of the coal-blacks speak incoherently. It is a monkey-house — with guffaws, disgusting interpolations, amendments offered that are too obscene to print, followed by shouts of glee.[2] Bad in the beginning, the travesty grows worse. The vulgarity of the speeches increases; members stagger from the basement bar to their seats. The Speaker in righteous mood sternly forbids the introduction of liquor on the floor.[3] A curious old planter stands in the galleries a moment looking down upon the scene, and with an exclamation, 'My God!' he turns and runs, as from a pestilence, into the street. Visitors from the North organize 'slumming expeditions' to the Legislature or go as to a zoo. A British member of Parliament, asking if there are any curiosities in the city, is taken forthwith to Mechanics' Hall.[4]

Corruption is inevitable, and members openly charged with bribery are not offended. 'I want to know how much the gentleman gets to support this bill,' demands one member of another, and it is not an insult.[5] Measures involving millions, many criminal, and having to do with railroads, canals, and levees, are passed without examination, and members vote vast sums into their pockets openly, defiantly. The mileage and *per diem* for members and clerks leap from a quarter of a million in 1869 to half a million the next year. Careless with the people's money? Preposterous. 'What we give to the community,' exclaims an outraged member — 'What we give to the community is without money and without price. It is so valuable that the price cannot be fixed — there is no standard.' 'I should like to know,' says another, 'if there is a good thing, in the name of God, why not let the representatives of the State of Louisiana have a hand in it.' [6] When the Appropriation Bill reduces the printing bill to a mere one hundred and forty thousand dollars a tearful plea that legislators 'open their hearts' and embrace more newspapers brings an amendment adding sixty thousand dollars.[7]

[1] Somers, 226–27.  [2] Lonn, 23.  [3] *Ibid.*, 25.
[4] *Ibid.*, 26.  [5] *Ibid.*, 28.  [6] Lonn, 30.
[7] *Ibid.*, 31.

For in Louisiana, too, the party press is heavily subsidized out of the Treasury. The Board of Printing Commissioners, dominated by the Governor, had been a godsend to Warmoth, who sent his agents to edit papers to which contracts were given, and, as fourth owner of the 'New Orleans Republican,' the chief beneficiary, he profited both politically and financially. Through his subsidized press he brought pressure to bear in favor of four measures intended to give him dictatorial power and prolong his reign. The Registration Bill made every parish registration official his minion, and gave them power to accept or reject votes without interference from the courts. Thus he could determine nominations. The Election Bill superseded sheriffs on election day with Warmoth's appointees, forbade the courts to interfere, and authorized him to deny certificates of election to successful candidates as he saw fit; and all this was climaxed by the creation of a returning board composed of members of the machine specified in the bill itself. The Constabulary Bill authorized Warmoth to name a chief constable in each parish who could name a deputy, and these were absolute. And the Militia Bill empowered him to organize and equip as many men as he wished and placed one hundred thousand dollars at his disposal for the purpose.[1]

These four revolutionary measures were the concentrated essence of Radicalism. The people in mass meeting protested violently, speakers denouncing the measures as designed for plunder and the perpetuation of pillage, and attacks on the legislators favoring them were greeted with cries of 'Kill them!' and 'Lynch them!' But behind the Legislature was Warmoth; behind him his militia and constables; and behind them Federal bayonets — and the laws went into operation.

X

But Warmoth had created a Frankenstein monster, and aroused the fiends of jealousy. His was a power worth fighting for, and in the Republican Convention of 1870 the struggle began. The Custom-House crowd, with the negro Lieutenant-Governor as its candidate, defeated Warmoth for the chairmanship, and almost

[1] In his MS. Reminiscences Warmoth says the Returning Board Law was 'a dangerous law' making possible the absolute control of elections.

defeated a resolution endorsing his administration.[1] Never, however, had Warmoth seemed stronger than when the Legislature met in January, 1871, with his Speaker packing the House committees with Warmoth men, and with his followers in the Senate depriving the Lieutenant-Governor of power and packing the committees there with minions of the Governor. But he had undergone a strange metamorphosis. He vetoed a gigantic swindling levee scheme in which members were financially interested. The House raged and overrode the veto in a tempestuous session, but in the Senate the steal was stopped, and the defeated corruptionists turned on Speaker Mortimer Carr for vengeance. Bargaining with Democrats to seat their contested members in return for votes to unseat Carr, the latter was forced out, and an enemy of Warmoth, not one whit better, became the commanding figure of the House. 'Thus,' said the 'New York Tribune,' 'by taking advantage of an outburst of virtuous indignation among a gang of thieves . . . was laid the foundation of . . . the first systematic organization in opposition to the power of Governor Warmoth.'[2]

The defeat of the senatorial ambitions of Collector Casey by the Warmoth forces intensified the feud,[3] and the Governor's new-found passion for reform poured in as many as thirty-nine vetoes, only five of which were overridden.[4] Thus Warmoth stopped steals — the veto of the Paving Bill alone saving the people a million and a half. Manifestly this man would not do.[5] When the session of 1871 cost $958,956.50, where the average cost before reconstruction had been one hundred thousand dollars, Warmoth denounced the squandering on extra mileage, on services never rendered, on publications in obscure newspapers, some of which did not exist, on elegant stationery, and on champagne.[6] It was civil war.

Speedily came the clash of the Republican factions as, fighting viciously, they lunged toward the Convention of August, 1871. Bribery and bludgeons now played their part, with hired ruffians smashing meetings with clubs. When Casey added five hundred

[1] Lonn, 74.          [2] December 1, 1871.

[3] Warmoth had agreed to support Casey if Grant, reputed to be interested, should ask him. MS. Reminiscences.

[4] Warmoth in his MS. Reminiscences says 'more than seventy.

[5] Lonn, 78.          [6] *Ibid.*, 86.

names to the payroll of the National Government, Warmoth added as many to the city payroll.[1] The morning of the convention found business suspended everywhere. Casey had called the convention for the Custom-House, Warmoth for the State House. Casey prevailed, with the energetic assistance of Gatling guns and Federal marshals, and Warmoth and his followers held a convention of their own. The Custom-House crowd read Warmoth out of the party, and Casey sent an explanatory message to Grant, his brother-in-law, at Long Branch.[2] A little later, the Warmoth delegation of whites and blacks reached Long Branch to make their explanation. The negroes were sparkling with diamond breastpins, as they pounded the pavement with their gold-headed canes, but Grant was visibly annoyed when they reached his cottage. Brusquely ordering an Associated Press reporter from the room, he received them coldly. He could not see what harm United States soldiers could do to a Republican convention and said so.[3] Standing by a piano, he listened impatiently to the reading of the petition, once banging the piano with his elbow. Once he stamped his foot, and the committee left convinced that Grant was committed to Casey. Consoling themselves with a feast at the Sans-Souci Beer Saloon, they hurried to New York — and the war was on. Soon Warmoth will be leading the Republican insurgents in the campaign of 1872.[4]

Meanwhile, the propertied citizens of Louisiana could see none of the humor of the situation. Under confiscatory taxation, numerous parishes were seeing tracts of the richest land going under the tax collector's hammer at a dollar an acre. In numerous instances buyers could not be found at that price because of the taxes. Real estate had declined twenty-five per cent in value.[5] It was costing half a million a year to collect six and a half million. Ruin everywhere — enforced by Federal marshals, backed, if need be, by Federal soldiers. The school system was a wreck.[6]

## XI

Let us turn away and visit Mississippi. Jackson, the capital, impressed an English traveler with its 'many private residences

[1] *New York Tribune*, December 1, 1871; Lonn, 97.   [2] Lonn, 96–104.
[3] Warmoth, MS. Reminiscences.   [4] *New York World*, September 6, 1871.
[5] Lonn, 84.   [6] *Ibid.*, 81–82.

denoting a large proportion of people of taste and culture.' [1]
Vicksburg and Natchez were in the shadows, and Meridian,
sprawling over sandy mounds, the ridges covered with yellow
pines, was growing rapidly because of the influx of negroes.[2]
Adelbert Ames, as Military Governor, had taken possession of the
State House and Executive Mansion in the fashion of Bombastes
Furioso, to rule supreme, and to pass on to the Senate to make
way for James L. Alcorn, a handsome, vain, imperious planter of
property, with forensic qualities of no mean order. But the Senate
soon claimed him, too, and soon he and Ames will be found in a
death struggle for Republican leadership. Though a native, there
is little that Alcorn can do — he has a Legislature, too. Nearly
forty former slaves, forced to make their mark, are enacting laws
in the spirit of a lark. These represent the wealthiest and most
aristocratic counties. The carpetbaggers lead; these simple souls
follow trustingly. A carpetbagger from New York, Dr. Franklin, sits in the Speaker's chair. The old governing element is
hopeless, though a few determined spirits like J. Z. George still
hope and plan. The gentle Lamar, depressed, is standing by the
gate of his cottage at Oxford in the twilight, looking sadly across
the solemn fields, watching his neighbors passing in the middle of
the road for safety.

Now let us cross over to Arkansas, the baronry of the most
astute and stern of the carpetbaggers, Powell Clayton, who has
just retired as Governor to enter the Senate, but whose work lives
after him. No cowardly mediocrity he, but a daring, resourceful,
unscrupulous man of vaulting ambition, with a touch of genius.
A brave soldier, even when he dismounted and laid the sword
aside he remained a cavalry dare-devil. The fighting had taken
him into Arkansas, and when the firing ceased he settled on a
plantation and remained. From that point of vantage, he cunningly studied the situation, and at the psychological moment
he grasped his opportunity. Gathering the negroes and carpetbaggers behind him, he seized on power. Coldly calculating, unsympathetic to suffering, autocratic, impatient of opposition or
restraint, he ruled for three years as an absolute monarch. The
argus-eyed Henry Watterson observed him critically. 'The dis-

[1] Somers, 248.      [2] *Ibid.*, 150.

tance between him and Washington, his friendliness to the
Government, the ease with which his acts could be concealed,
made him bold and careless. He knew his game. Clayton's
policy was extermination. Nothing could divert him. He is not
a milksop, but a man of genius and his field is fruitful.' [1] His was
the master mind that organized the Republican Party in Arkansas, that directed the framing of the constitution, making a despot
of the Governor; and he took the governorship. He waved his
wand, and a system emerged that destroyed civil liberty, and reduced overwhelming majorities to impotency.[2] This Clayton
system reserved the loaves and fishes for the carpetbaggers alone.
Adventurers from abroad, including the Governor and two
Senators, controlled the executive department, the courts, the
Treasury, the military power.[3] Nowhere such concentration of
power as in the hands of Clayton. He distributed printing
patronage to party papers, exacting as a consideration absolute
obedience to his will. In him was lodged the power to award
millions 'in aid of railroads, and he demanded that aid be given.[4]
His militia was so tied up with registration as to make it a
partisan army. In one campaign he set aside the registration in
eleven counties, ten with heavy Democratic majorities, on the
ground of 'interference with registration.' By the waving of his
wand, this cavalryman wiped out a Democratic majority of almost
three thousand.[5] When the people grumbled, he evoked the sword.
His militia was frankly an instrument of party, his followers
having demanded an instrument that 'would strike early and
strike hard.' The 'Daily Republican' boldly proclaimed that of
course the militia was to be armed to enforce the policies of the
party.[6] Immediately the negroes were enlisted and armed — with
the approval of Washington. The Republican Congressional
Executive Committee was sending assurance that Federal troops
were at Clayton's service whenever he declared martial law. The
Northern press was being fed with stories of 'outrages' in Arkansas. Soon the proclamation of martial law; soon two thousand

[1] *Louisville Courier-Journal*, January 25, 1869; quoted, *Doc. Hist.*, ii, 38–40.
[2] Staples, 278.
[3] *Arkansas Gazette*, December 22, 1869; quoted, *Doc. Hist.*, ii, 279.
[4] Clayton, 28–49.      [5] Staples, 287.
[6] April 20, 1868, quoted, Staples, 288.

undisciplined negroes were preying on the people of ten counties, stealing, arresting, imprisoning, executing, looting houses, and occasionally violating women. Clayton soon was sending the officers lists of men to be arrested, with the comment that many of them could be executed. 'It is absolutely necessary that some example be made,' he wrote.[1] So infamous did the brutality become that the 'Daily Republican' bitterly denounced the proceedings, but when he was disciplined by his removal from the Speakership of the House, and deprived of public printing, the editor made a hasty recantation with the inspiring statement that 'we'll make Arkansas Republican or a waste howling wilderness.'[2] This political army, mobilized for partisan war, cost the people $330,676.43.[3]

With a military autocrat as Governor, with terror spread by gun-men from the mountains, and armed negroes posing as militia, with no recourse to the ballot, the people, oppressed with unbearable taxation, have no recourse to the courts — for these too are packed with the tools of the system. Chief Justice John McClure, a notorious carpetbagger, is boasting of his guilt of bribery, editing the 'Daily Republican' from his chambers, and handling the slush funds for the debauchery of the Legislature.[4]

## XII

Our Southern survey is over. We have met and mingled with the loyal men, and observed the saturnalia of corruption everywhere. To understand the times, we must bear in mind that distinguished statesmen in Washington, honored with monuments to-day, were loudly defending the Scotts, the Moseses, Bullocks, Warmoths, Caseys, Ameses, and Claytons; that pious women in Northern villages, shamefully deceived, were praying for the success of these 'good men and true.' But some were growing weary of the sordid game, and Greeley, in the fall of 1871, was giving warning: 'Men and brethren, there is to be a general overhauling of pretensions, a sweeping-out of dark corners, a dragging to light of hidden iniquities the coming winter. If there be those who dread such an ordeal, they may wisely put an ocean between them and the scene of their misdoings without delay.'[5]

[1] Staples, 290; *Doc. Hist.*, II, 73.     [2] Staples, 302.     [3] *Ibid.*, 305.
[4] Staples, 365.     [5] *New York Tribune*, November 13, 1871.

# CHAPTER XVIII

## THE RADICAL RANKS BREAK

### I

CONGRESS met in December in an atmosphere heavily charged with cynicism and corruption. The lobby was more than ever open and insolent, that of the railroads, under the vigilant eye of Tom Scott, the most brazen and defiant of all. A correspondent suggested that Congress permanently adjourn with an explanatory placard on the door: 'The business of this establishment will be done hereafter in the office of the Pennsylvania Railroad.' Indeed, several of its attorneys were in Congress, and not a few press correspondents on its payroll. It was generally assumed that the Pacific Railroad had scored a triumph in the substitution of Williams, of Oregon, for Akerman as Attorney-General.[1]

Since the adjournment of Congress there had been colorful exposures of corruption in New York, the scandals involving the local Democratic organization in the case of Tweed, the National Republican organization in the case of Murphy and the Custom-House. Reformers had appeared in both parties to slay the dragon and the Democrats under Samuel J. Tilden and Charles O'Conor won. The Republican reformers went down before the Grant forces under the dynamic leadership of Conkling in the State Convention. Tweed was exposed and arrested, and of the two Democrats who led the fight against him, one was to be nominated as the straight-out Democratic candidate for President within a year, and the other was to be the presidential nominee of a united party in 1876.

The triumph over the Custom-House Ring was not so easy. The Collector had been a personal appointee of the President, who had not consulted either Senator from New York. Tom Murphy had won his way to Grant's affections by his familiarity with horses. Bad as he was, he found he had inherited a worse system, due again to Grant's inability to judge men.

[1] *New York World*, January 1, 1872.

Learning of Grant's intention to appoint Moses Grinnell as
Collector, a former member of Grant's staff, named Leet, with the
rank and pay of a colonel of the army, had solicited from the
President a letter of introduction to Grinnell. It was with the presentation of this letter that the latter first learned of his appointment; and when Leet confidently requested the 'general order'
business, Grinnell, assuming some connection between the letter
and the request, agreed. It seemed to be an order from the
President. When only a part of the business was assigned, Leet
threatened the new Collector with dismissal, and the whole was
given. The result was a wholesale looting of importers. They were
forced to send their goods to the Leet warehouses and pay a
month's storage, though the goods remained in the houses but a
day. Soon Leet and his associates were reaping a rich harvest, importers were bitterly complaining, and Chicago merchants importing from Europe were using the Montreal route to escape the
outrageous charges in New York. The New York merchants were
wroth over the destruction of the commerce of the city — and
nothing was done to stop it.[1] This is the system Murphy had
inherited.

In the summer of 1871, in the midst of the clamor of the merchants, Tom Murphy was Grant's veritable shadow at Long
Branch. 'If Grant goes to New York,' wrote a correspondent,
'Tom puts in an appearance *en route*. If the President goes out for
a walk, Tom accidentally meets him. If Grant wants to take a
peep at Monmouth Park Stables to look at the race-horses, Tom
decides to look at them also.'[2] That was the summer Murphy
opened a restaurant in the Custom-House in a room adjoining his
office, where 'Leet and Stocking scored their great victory over
Grinnell in securing the general order business,' and 'champagne
flowed like water.'[3]

With the election approaching, the grumbling increasing, and
merchants clamoring for an investigation, the Administration
was forced to part with Murphy, though with frank reluctance,
and Chester A. Arthur was appointed his successor in the latter
part of November. Grant, in accepting Murphy's resignation,

[1] *New York World,* August 30, 1871.      [2] *Ibid.,* June 6, 1871.
[3] *Ibid.,* July 27, 1871.

paid tribute to 'the efficiency, honesty, and zeal' with which he had 'administered the office,' and this shocked the sensitive. Even the appointment of Arthur, destined to the Presidency, was no reassurance to Greeley. 'The General,' he wrote, 'will be in the Custom-House a personal burlesque upon Civil Service Reform. He recently held a ten-thousand-dollar Tammany office from which he was only driven by the 'Tribune's' exposure; and he is a devoted servant of the Murphy clique; but he is not personally an objectionable man.' [1] The abandonment of Murphy failed to prevent a congressional investigation, but it was noted that Administration Senators viciously cross-examined witnesses giving damaging testimony — of which there was an abundance — and that Senator Howe, cross-examining one important witness, had Leet at his side to prompt him.[2]

Then, in the midst of the investigation the bizarre James Fisk died in his seraglio, for love of a tainted lady, and 'The Tribune' said 'his four-in-hand conveyed more spotted reputations than his own,' and 'his box at the Opera House was shunned as if infected by all who had any character to lose.' It was a back-hand slap at Grant, and 'The World' maliciously observed that he had been conveyed behind the 'four-in-hand' and had sat in the box 'without fear of infection.' [3]

Thus the embarrassments of the Administration multiplied. The Custom-House mess had left a frightful stench, and 'The Nation' turned on the President. For two years, it said, while the abuses continued and merchants were protesting, 'he gave no sign of displeasure, paid no attention to the complaints . . . and let Leet go on for nearly two years preying on the commerce of the port till a second congressional investigation, obtained with great difficulty, and the savage assaults of the press on the eve of an election made the change we have just witnessed imperatively necessary.' [4] Soon the corruptionists and their respectable partisan apologists were whimpering that 'the public is tired of these investigations,' and Godkin was surmising that 'the public, tired as it is, will endure as many more as may be necessary.' [5] Grant had developed a per-

[1] *New York Tribune*, November 21, 1871.
[2] *New York World*, January 5, 1872.    [3] January 9, 1872.
[4] March 14, 1872.    [5] *The Nation*, May 2, 1872.

secution complex, and Mrs. Blaine observed at dinner that he
'talked incessantly about himself' and felt 'dreadfully assailed.' [1]

The investigation trailed along in the slime, but nothing happened.

II

Then it was that Sumner offered his resolution for an investigation of the charge that American officials not only had violated the
law of neutrality in the Franco-Prussian War, by selling arms to
France, but had profited by the transaction. Nothing was to come
of this either — nothing but a deeper cleavage in the Republican
ranks through the bitter debate. The investigating committee was
packed, Schurz and Trumbull excluded, two carpetbaggers included, and but one Democrat selected. The brilliant debate was
as appallingly bitter as those of the factions in the death struggles
of the French Revolution. The dramatic climax was in Conkling's
eloquent defense, and Schurz's crushing reply. Ladies of fashion
occupied the seats of Senators as they spoke. These extraordinary
men were well balanced, and not dissimilar, both polished orators,
viper-tongued in verbal combat, striking in appearance, and both
with a bit of the peacock strut. Running through, and dominating,
the speeches was the political note — it was the opening skirmish
in the campaign of 1872. It was evident that the Administration
was worried by the possible effect of Schurz's disaffection on
the German vote.

'The Senator will take no offense, I hope, at my reading an ex-
tract from a German paper published in Chicago, the "Staats
Zeitung,"' said Conkling.

'Yes, sir,' replied Schurz, amidst laughter, 'and it is edited by
the collector of internal revenue there.'

When Conkling explained that he read the extracts to show how
the actions of the Senate affected the minds of the people, Schurz
corrected him: 'the minds of revenue collectors,' he said.[2]

Accused of endangering party prospects, Schurz replied with
spirit the next day. Danger to the party? 'It lies with the
sycophants who, by covering up every abuse . . . defending every

[1] To Walker Blaine, February 18, 1872, Letters, I, 90.
[2] Congressional Globe, 42d Congress, 2d Sess., Appendix, 58–66.

violation of the law . . . have produced . . . an atmosphere in which corruption can grow and thrive.' Conkling had said no one owned the Germans. 'No politician owns them,' said Schurz, 'no Senators do; not even the President of the United States; but least of all are the Germans of this country owned by that class of politicians who desperately cling to the skirt of power through whatever mire that skirt may be trailed' — and the galleries cheered.[1]

Schurz's closing defiance of the party whip was accepted by Morton as a challenge, and he wielded it as vigorously as Stevens at his best. When he said he was informed that the first break of Schurz with the President was over patronage, the German-American authorized him to tell his informant 'on my own authority, and on my own responsibility, that he lies.' Such was the savagery of the debate. Insisting that the arms sale was merely a hook on which to hang a political attack on the Administration, Morton closed with a furious assault on the Liberal Republicans.[2] But he was nonplussed when Trumbull entered the debate on the political side, attacking the Administration's hostility to investigations, and hotly denouncing the attempt to prevent disclosures in the Custom-House frauds by warning witnesses they 'would be prosecuted themselves as participants in the frauds they expose.'[3]

It was at this time that Morton, in a long personal letter, referred to the insurgents as 'soreheads,' and explained how the Administration took over the investigating committee. The whole thing was intended as a 'Smut Machine.' The press correspondents were 'from some cause unfriendly to the Administration.' The 'malcontents' had 'fired off their ammunition at a very early day and nobody has been hurt.' Indeed, 'Grant is stronger than ever.'[4] But a little later, Morton was compelled to report that 'the struggle is still going on,' with 'Sumner, Schurz, and Trumbull . . . doing all in their power to divide and distract the party.' Trumbull had 'surprised everybody by a speech . . . in which he gave his adherence to the Missouri movement.' He had 'displayed more feeling' than Morton 'ever before saw him manifest upon the floor.'[5]

---

[1] *Congressional Globe*, 42d Congress, 2d Sess., Appendix, 67–74.   [2] *Ibid.*, 74–82.
[3] *Ibid.*, 82–87.   [4] Morton MSS., to Simon Powell, December 19, 1871.
[5] *Ibid.*, February 26, 1872.

Even so, Trumbull's adhesion to the insurgent movement was not of recent origin. Two months before, he had written privately that only Grand Army members and office-holders were satisfied with Grant, whose 'indecent interference in Missouri and Louisiana, . . . disgusting nepotism, . . . indefensible course in regard to San Domingo, and recent complimentary letter to Collector Murphy have produced the conviction he is intellectually and morally unqualified for his present position.' [1]

Even among those certain to be regular there were grave misgivings on the reaction to Grant's renomination. Garfield confidentially admitted he looked 'forward with positive dread to the work that will be required . . . to defend him from the criticisms which will certainly be made upon his course.' Too bad, he thought, that the Administration should be run by 'a few Senators who represent a low level of American politics, such men as Cameron, Chandler, Morton, and Conkling.' [2]

Meanwhile, the spirit of insurgency was moving toward the Cincinnati Convention.

### III

The Liberal Republican movement, having its origin in the party divisions in Missouri over the removal of the political disabilities of those who had sympathized with the South during the war, was, in its broader aspects, a general revolt against privilege and corruption. It came as a protest against a system of taxation which tended to the monopolization of industry and to the advantage of one industry over another. A conference of Republican tariff reformers had met in Washington to discuss the possibilities of a union of the Republican revenue reformers with the Democrats to capture the House of Representatives. Learning of the call of the meeting, Blaine, the Speaker, hastened to Chicago to promise Horace White, of the 'Chicago Tribune,' two tariff reformers on the Ways and Means Committee, thus giving them a majority. He kept his word, and even urged reform himself, but to no avail. Even so, the tariff was not the only cause of discontent — the reformers wished to end the miserable misrule of the South, reform the civil service, purge the Government of corruption. It

[1] Horace White, 371.          [2] To Hall, Life of Garfield, I, 493.

was a major movement against the dominant party as organized and entrenched. In the early autumn of 1871, Schurz was urging Sumner to revolt, because his party was 'ruled by selfish interests' and it would be impossible to prevent Grant's renomination, since 'the men who surround him will stop at nothing.' As for himself, he would not support Grant, nor the Democrats. The way out was through a third party.[1] This thought had been behind all the heavy skirmishing in Congress. Thus came the Liberal Republican movement, built on the theory that the nomination of a candidate not obnoxious to the Democrats would secure their endorsement.

Under these conditions the most intelligent liberal sentiment of the country turned to Charles Francis Adams. A Democrat himself in early life, he had gone over to the Whigs on the slavery question in 1836. As our Minister to England during the war, he had brilliantly measured up to his obligations, and, returning to America in 1868, he had escaped entanglements with the early reconstruction policies. As the foremost American arbitrator of the Alabama claims, he had greatly extended his reputation in diplomacy. His background was perfect — one of culture, scholarship, statesmanship, and varied experience in the public service. No one of his day symbolized so completely the fine austerity of the early Republic. With an instinctive sense of right and wrong, he had the courage of his convictions. Never an intense partisan, he had been completely out of harmony with his party's policies from the close of the war. Indifferent to office, he had unhesitatingly responded to every call to public duty. On the tariff and civil service reform, on corruption and reconstruction, he was more in accord with the Democrats than any Republican of his day. His son has painted his portrait in a paragraph, disclosing a man 'singular for mental poise — absence of self-assertion or self-consciousness — the faculty of standing apart without seeming aware that he was alone — a balance of mind and temper that neither challenged nor avoided notice, nor admitted question of superiority or inferiority, of jealousy or personal motives, from any source, even from great pressure.'[2] The very absence of the conventionalities of a politician made him the ideal leader for the Opposition. 'It has always been obvious that Mr. Adams would be

[1] Schurz, *Reminiscences*, 338.      [2] *Education of Henry Adams*, 37.

among the best of Presidents,' wrote Manton Marble, of the 'New York World,' to Schurz, and he 'has been growing during the last few months into the best of candidates.' [1] August Belmont, Democratic National Chairman, had written in a similar vein.[2] In March the Democratic organ had said that 'no one would more surely restore to the [Presidency] the dignity it possessed in the better days of the Republic.' [3] When attacks were made upon Adams, it was 'The World' that went to his defense. An Eastern man? 'He has not merely a national but a European reputation [and] he no more belongs to Massachusetts than to Washington or Virginia.' Cold? 'This is but another way of saying that Mr. Adams is not a demagogue.' [4] When he wrote his super-independent letter declining to be 'negotiated for,' and the 'New York Times' described it as 'throwing a few sentences of bitter contempt into the faces of the scheming politicians,' the 'Boston Globe' interpreted it as a 'covert bid for the support of the Democratic Party'; the 'Springfield Republican' thought it would set all revolutionary blood tingling; [5] 'The World' hailed it as evidence of 'the elevation and moral robustness of the man.' [6] Thus one thing was evident — no man could be named so calculated to appeal to Democrats when victory rested with their rank and file. After Adams, the best appeal would have been made with Trumbull or Justice David Davis; because the first was fundamentally a Democrat, and, though tarred with reconstruction, had found his way to the mourners' bench, and the latter's decision in the Milligan case was a fine exposition of the Democratic position on the supremacy of the civil power.

The Convention met, and Schurz opened the proceedings with a powerful speech. But what a conglomerate mass of incongruities sat before him! 'Long-haired and spectacled doctrinaires from New England'; 'short-haired and stumpy emissaries from New York'; 'brisk Westerners'; and 'a few overdressed persons from New Orleans, brought up by Governor Warmoth' [7] — a convention composed of 'delegates without constituencies.' [8] The leaders,

[1] Horace White, 373.            [2] Ibid., 373; Schurz, Reminiscences, 344.
[3] New York World, March 14, 1872.            [4] April 24, 1872.
[5] Quoted, New York World, April 25, 1872.            [6] Ibid.
[7] Marse Henry, I, 242.
[8] Thurman MSS., Robert Chinselet to Thurman, May 7, 1872.

most of them amateurs in practical politics — Bowles, Halstead, Watterson, and White — undertook to manage the convention according to blue-prints. They resolved to confine the nomination to Adams or Trumbull, until Whitelaw Reid persuaded Watterson to include Greeley. Gliding among the delegates in the interest of the sage of Chappaquack was the debonair figure of Theodore Tilton. The stage was set just right — according to the theorists.[1] Judge Davis should be eliminated, said the gentlemen of the quill. Thus the pens of Watterson, Halstead, Bowles, and White moved feverishly one night, and the next day public opinion seemed unanimous, with editorials from widely separated cities pronouncing Davis's doom. The mimic politicians imitated the realists, mingling, meeting in their various rooms to drink and smoke. It was Watterson who first began to doubt the efficacy of their dreams. Colonel Alexander K. McClure had piqued their curiosity by his seeming cultivation of the group about the bottle, until, at length, Watterson blurted out, 'What in the devil do you want anyhow?' 'What?' snorted McClure. 'With those cranks? Nothing.'[2] A declaration of principles? What principles? There were as many principles as delegates, each of these clamoring for his own, each chattering incessantly — no one listening. That dinner 'over the Rhine' in the German quarter of Cincinnati was a burlesque. 'Coherence was a missing ingredient,' thought Watterson in his wiser years.[3]

And, alas, the elimination of Davis only brought Greeley to the fore. What though Schurz's speech had described Adams without naming him, some practical politicians, Frank Blair and Gratz Brown of Missouri, were speeding to Cincinnati. Julian was polishing his nominating speech for Adams; but speeches were dispensed with, and the balloting began.[4] Reid's and Tilton's activities had not been fruitless; Trumbull's supporters hung on too long; and the man with the Tall White Hat emerged the victor. The tariff reform plank was abandoned on demand of New York and Pennsylvania and a protectionist of the worst sort nominated.

That night Reid's love feast of jubilation was a study in expressions. There sat Horace White 'like an iceberg,' and Bowles

[1] *Marse Henry*, I, 243–44.        [2] *Ibid.*, I, 249–50.
[3] *Ibid.*, I, 251.                 [4] Julian, MS. Diary, May 7, 1872.

'diplomatic but ineffusive,' and Schurz 'like a death's-head at the board,' while Watterson and Halstead simulated joy in vain, and the celebration ended early and the reformers turned sadly homeward — 'reformers hoist by their own petard.' [1]

'We suppose,' said 'The Nation,' 'that a greater degree of incredulity and disappointment . . . has not been felt . . . since the news of the first battle of Bull Run.' [2] In the House, at Washington, Hoar ironically congratulated the Democrats on having a protectionist to follow.[3] Bryant, of the 'New York Evening Post,' thought it incredible that such a blunder could be made by men in their right senses, [4] and to Trumbull he predicted that an Administration of Greeley 'cannot be otherwise than shamefully corrupt' since 'his associations are of that sort.' [5] Trumbull replied that the nomination was 'a bombshell which seems likely to blow up both parties' — good riddance to bad rubbish.[6]

## IV

Tall, awkward, with big round face of infantile mildness, with spectacled blue eyes that gave him an owl-like appearance, with a fringe of white whiskers, a slouching movement, disheveled in clothing, his pockets bulging with papers, a common cotton umbrella in his hand — such was the physical Horace Greeley. His character was a medley of contradictions. Honest, emotional, dogmatic, cruel and humane, petulant, magnanimous, he reasoned frequently with his heart and confused his prejudices with principles. The most effective journalist of his age, he had his intellectual limitations, but there were no boundaries to his self-confidence. Erratic to a degree, it was not easy to calculate his conduct from his antecedents. No one could be more abusive when he willed. With all his brilliance in polemics, he was always a potential bull in a china shop.

His election depended on the united support of the Democrats of the rank and file, and a minute search of his record failed to find anything in common with the Democracy.

---

[1] *Marse Henry*, I, 257.     [2] May 9, 1872.
[3] *New York World*, May 4, 1872.
[4] To Dr. Powers, *Life of Bryant*, II, 323.
[5] Horace White, 386–87.     [6] *Ibid.*, 387.

V

Between the Cincinnati Convention and the Baltimore Convention of the Democrats, Sumner hurled another savage philippic at Grant from the Senate. Silent as to Greeley, it was inconceivable that the orator could support Grant after such an attack. Two months before, Whitelaw Reid had urged Sumner's adherence to the combination against the President.[1] Perhaps the answer came when Sumner rose in a sweltering Chamber to open war on Grant. On the floor to hear him were Belknap, Creswell, and Robinson, of the Cabinet. The speech was a protest against the consolidation of the power of a Cæsar and a bitter attack on gift-taking and nepotism. A dozen members of the family 'billeted upon the country,' he said; a military ring at the White House, military interferences in elections, San Domingo, interference in local politics, 'New York the scene and Thomas Murphy, the Presidential lieutenant.' Means well? 'That is not much. It was said of Louis the Quarreler that he meant well; nor is there a slate headstone in any village burial-ground that does not record as much of the humble lodgers beneath.'

As the ferocious assault proceeded, Morton, Conkling, and Carpenter conferred audibly in a group, occasionally moving to the cloak-rooms or lobby. Now and then, Conkling and Carpenter would station themselves near the orator to converse aloud. At times Sumner stopped in rebuke, glared at them savagely, until they would retire to their seats.

'I protest,' he concluded, 'against him as radically unfit for the presidential office, being essentially military in nature, without experience in civil life, without aptitude for civil duties, and without knowledge of republican institutions, all of which is perfectly apparent unless we are ready to assume that the matters and things set forth to-day are of no account — and then declare in further support of the candidate, boldly, that nepotism in a President is nothing, that violation of the Constitution and of law international and municipal is nothing . . . that all his presidential pretensions in their motley aggregation, being a new Cæsarism or personal government, are nothing. But if these are nothing, then is the Republican Party nothing; nor is there any safeguard for republican institutions.'[2]

[1] Pierce, IV, 51.          [2] *Congressional Globe*, May 31, 1872.

He sat down; no one answered.

The popular reaction was not good, many thinking the speech 'too heated, rancorous, and exaggerated.' [1] and Longfellow the poet found it 'a terrible speech,' though he thought 'the terror of it is in its truth.' He felt that 'the feeble attempts at reply must convince every one that no reply is possible.' [2]

## VI

Quite as sensational was the attack on Greeley's candidacy before the Baltimore Convention by a Democratic leader in the House. For months robust Democrats had been protesting against the proposed endorsement of Greeley, and the use of their party as a mere reserve 'to be brought up at the last moment to decide a contest between two wings of the Republican Party.' [3] And merge under Greeley of all men! The idea seemed grotesque. His own sense of humor had dismissed the possibility in a letter to a Virginia Democrat some months before. 'I am ferociously protectionist,' he had written; 'I am not the man you need.' [4] Scarcely more than a month before the Cincinnati Convention, he had been debating protection with Professor A. L. Perry before the Liberal Club at Williams College.[5] Even after the Cincinnati nomination 'The World' refused its allegiance. It would have supported Adams, but the Greeley nomination did not bind the Democracy. The general tone of the Democratic press was hostile. But unhappily for party solidarity, a portion of the Democracy was always fingering the white flag, eager to hoist it, and others were ravenous for the loaves and fishes. But Greeley! It seemed absurd to accept his leadership. One of Tilden's correspondents could 'even support Charles Sumner,' but could see no way to preserve his self-respect and vote for the man 'who is directly against us upon the great living issues.' [6]

But no open protest was heard until one day the most popular orator of the House, whose voice a woman had described as 'better than the Boston Jubilee,' [7] rose to throw an explosive into

[1] *The Nation*, June 13, 1872.                    [2] Pierce, IV, 528.
[3] *New York World*, December 8, 1871          [4] Seitz, 379.
[5] *New York World*, April 6, 1872.              [6] J. J. Taylor to Tilden, *Letters*, I, 306.
[7] *New York World*, March 24, 1872.

the camp of the amalgamationists. This striking man, with hair and beard partly red, always had an audience, and the room was jammed when Daniel Wolsey Voorhees, in an atmosphere of tense excitement, rose to make his protest. 'Am I expected to support Mr. Greeley because he has been a lifelong champion of doctrines I have always opposed?' he began; and then presented his bill of particulars — a devastating indictment of the 'Democracy' of the Liberal nominee. Even Grant had been less cruel to the South. 'Sir, he has simply executed the laws which the Cincinnati nominee asked this Congress to enact.' In behalf of three and a half million Democrats he entered his protest 'against any attempt to transfer them to a camp where they have nothing to gain and everything to lose.' Hastening home to Terre Haute, Voorhees continued his crusade, denouncing the journalist as 'the best embodiment of the principles of radicalism now living,' as 'an older and far abler Republican than Grant.'[1] 'The Nation,' unimpressed by Greeley, commented that 'Voorhees appears to have lost none of his courage,'[2] and that if the Democracy raised 'the old white hat' as its standard, the only thing for Republicans 'of our way of thinking to do is to choose the less of two evils and vote for General Grant.'[3] John Forsyth, the able editor of the 'Mobile Register,' was pleading with his party not to nominate Greeley and ditch its principles,[4] but it was a hopeless protest.

Thus the Baltimore Convention, a little surly, discouraged, bemuddled, set its jaw a bit stupidly and went through with the programme. Not, however, without a solemn protest from Bayard, one of its greatest leaders. Rising from a sick-bed, he entered the hall pale, emaciated, almost ghastly, his eyes abnormally bright with fever, his hair disheveled, and spoke with a persuasive eloquence. Sympathetically but silently they heard him — they were demoralized and paralyzed. The brilliant and impassioned M. P. O'Connor, of Charleston, replied in the oratorical triumph of an otherwise drab convention, as the delegates stood and cheered.[5] And thus the Democracy went over bag and baggage to the leadership of him who opposed all its principles.

[1] *New York World,* four columns, first page, May 26, 1872.
[2] May 30, 1872.          [3] June 13, 1872.
[4] June 20, 1872.          [5] O'Connor, 56–65.

## VII

General Sherman, observing events from the vantage-point of Paris, wrote his brother in laughing mood, 'Grant, who never was a Republican, is your candidate, and Greeley, who never was a Democrat, but quite the reverse, is the Democratic candidate.' [1] Others, observing the same thing, were less amused. Schurz was talking madly of calling another convention to nominate Adams and ask a Democratic endorsement, even writing Greeley of his plans. But the latter blithesomely replied with the assurance that he would sweep New York, New England, and the South and have a fighting chance in Pennsylvania.[2] And so the die-hards among the Liberals met in conference in New York to smooth the wrinkles of disaffection, Bryant sleeping in the chair, Schurz and Trumbull sourly accepting Greeley as a choice of evils, but leaving no doubt of their opinion of him as a reformer.' [3] Watterson wrote the candidate a sweet and clever letter to soothe the smart of Schurz's criticism.[4]

Among the Democrats there was a brave show of fidelity, though it limped on parade. Voorhees, who had burned his bridges, hastily built a pontoon and retreated, though it required all his eloquence to satisfy his constituents,[5] and 'The Nation' belabored him pitilessly for his reversal.[6] 'We have been singing Democratic hymns for forty years down here,' explained the brother of Zeb Vance, of North Carolina, 'and since the Baltimore Convention puts Greeley in our hymn book we'll sing it through if it kills us.' [7] After all, thought Governor Randolph, of New Jersey, Democrats supporting Greeley would 'be guilty of nothing more serious than "eccentricity."' [8] Democratic papers that had reared and snorted like war horses at first settled down as burden-bearers of 'The Tribune' as gracefully as possible. Lamar could find no enthusiasm in Mississippi over the man who had been 'the embodiment and concentration of all . . . Democrats are accustomed to regard as unsound.' [9] Charles O'Conor of New York

---

[1] Sherman, *Letters*, 337.  [2] Horace White, 391.
[3] *The Nation*, June 27, 1872; Horace White, 393.
[4] *Life of Reid*, I, 220.  [5] *New York Herald*, September 27, 1872.
[6] July 25, 1872.  [7] *The Nation*, July 4, 1872.
[8] *Ibid.*  [9] *Life of Lamar*, 170-72.

wrote Tilden that 'the tender-hearted Moloch whose lifelong mission of hate has filled the land with fratricidal slaughter of the white race,' could never have his vote; [1] and, late in the campaign, Horatio Seymour found it impossible to 'work [himself] into a heat' about the election because Greeley's abuse 'has been so gross.' [2]

Even so, the plan of the regular Democrats to unfurl their own flag in the Louisville Convention was sternly frowned upon, and denounced by Voorhees as 'countenanced by Morton and upheld by the money of the Administration Ring.' [3] In truth, Morton was jubilantly predicting to a correspondent that the Greeley movement would 'demoralize the Democracy much more than the Republicans.' [4] Thurman was appealing to Tilden to dissuade O'Conor from accepting the Louisville nomination, 'which is wholly in the interest of Grant.' [5] The 'regulars' met and nominated O'Conor with John Quincy Adams II, but it was an idle gesture.

Meanwhile, in the realignments, the Republicans were struggling with their problems, and Greeley had some accessions. Charles Sumner urged the negroes to support Greeley. He was an abolitionist, Grant voted for Buchanan; Greeley had long manifested friendship for the negroes, Grant never; Greeley wanted negro suffrage, Grant was opposed. Thus ran the letter. Instantly Sumner's old abolition comrades were deep in their ink-horns, and Garrison in a bitter reply was excoriating Greeley, shaming Sumner, and praising the 'illustrious administration of Grant.' [6] Wendell Phillips conceded that Grant had made blunders, but he had 'a Christian attitude toward the Indians,' and had done much for business and against the Ku-Klux Klan.' [7] Blaine, evoking sectional hates, charged Sumner with making an 'alliance with Southern secessionists in their effort to destroy the Republican Party,' and asked if he had forgotten Preston Brooks.[8] 'And what has Preston Brooks to do with the presidential election?'

[1] *Life of Tilden*, I, 218.  [2] Tilden, *Letters*, I, 311.
[3] *New York World*, September 2, 1872.
[4] Morton MSS., To Powell, May 10, 1872.
[5] Tilden, *Letters*, I, 311.  [6] *New York Herald*, August 6, 1872.
[7] *Ibid.*, August 17, 1872.  [8] Gail Hamilton, 271-72.

retorted Sumner, in a scornful reply. He had not missed Blaine among the Republicans joining in the support of Greeley until he 'reported absence.' [1]

Thus the bewildered negro, finding Greeley, Chase, and Sumner on one side, and Garrison and Phillips on the other, appealed to the gentle poet Whittier, who replied in a letter that could be read either way. It was not without agony of spirit that the partisans accommodated themselves to the abnormal conditions of the campaign.

## VIII

The effect upon the negro vote in the South was interesting alike to psychologists, sociologists, and politicians. The reaction in North Carolina, which voted in August, was soon felt. The Grant forces put the negro forward as never before, and James H. Harris, a negro demagogue, presided at the State Convention and demanded complete social equality 'on your cars, on your steamboats, and at the tables and in the parlors of your hotels.' This became the keynote, and the orator was sent on an inflammatory speaking tour, inciting hatred of negroes who aligned themselves with Greeley, the Abolitionist. [2] These were ostracized, deserted by their wives, hooted and assaulted when marching in Greeley processions, and driven from their homes at the instigation of carpetbaggers. [3] The Loyal Leagues were too powerful, as an organization of intimidation, to combat.

In South Carolina, the alliance of the Grant forces with negroes and carpetbaggers was complete and invincible. The negroes had dominated the State Convention, the correspondent of the 'New York Herald' finding but a sprinkling of white faces, and these bearing the imprint of depravity. The heat and odors of the room drove some of the more sensitive to the open air. Negro delegates were gorged on the choicest luxuries, washed down with the finest wines, and the debauchery continued through the night preceding the convention, corruptionists plying delegates with bribery money. Wanton women were to be had for the asking, and without cost. The unhappy Orr denounced the proceedings at the peril

[1] *New York Herald*, August 6, 1872.     [2] Hamilton, 583.
[3] *New York Herald*, July 18, 1872.

of his life, and when the negro leader Elliott, in the chair, drew his pistol, it was Whittemore, the purveyor of cadetships, who bade him return the pistol to the pocket. Frank Moses, the degenerate, bought the gubernatorial nomination, the victory acclaimed in a ten-minute demonstration, while a negro band played 'Hail to the Chief.' The disillusioned Orr passed from the hall, followed by jeers and hisses.[1] Clearly, the Greeley reformers had no chance here.

In Louisiana, Warmoth, who led for Greeley, had lost his grip, Longstreet was ostracized, the Custom-House gangsters under Casey were in the saddle, and Pinchback, the Lieutenant-Governor, a cunning negro, with some money and no character, who had begun life as a waiter on a Mississippi River boat, and was dreaming of the Senate and the Vice-Presidency, had been lured from Greeley by a trade.[2]

In Mississippi, an epochal candidacy — Lucius Q. C. Lamar had been enticed from his retirement, and was in the field as a candidate for Congress. Here and there, some ray of hope; and Texas was in the sunshine, having wrought her complete redemption the year before. In Tennessee, Andrew Johnson was attacking Grant with fierce invectives on the corruption and centralization of his régime, and for the acceptance of specified gifts.[3] His candidacy for Congressman-at-large was overshadowing the national contest as he traversed the State with his two opponents, entering the rooms of 'miserable little taverns' with as much dignity as in the White House.[4]

But North Carolina with her August election — politicians looked to her for the trend. Both parties hurried their heavy artillery to the battle — Boutwell, Senator Wilson, Secretary Delano, and Fred Douglass, for Grant; Carl Schurz and Colonel A. K. McClure, for Greeley. But the Democrats were cold to their nominee. Senator Pool had collected a big slush fund; the Administration was hectically busy with Ku-Klux indictments, and there were three thousand arrests just before the election. The Republican gubernatorial nominee, driven from the stump, was

[1] *New York Herald*, August 23, August 31, September 16, 1872.
[2] *New York World*, April 8, 1872.          [3] *Ibid.*, August 18, 1872.
[4] *New York Herald*, September 27, 1872.

relying on the negro vote, and blacks were imported to swell the number, nine hundred being sent from the capital of the Republic.[1]

An amazing campaign — meetings extending from morning till darkness; mails burdened with campaign literature from the North and transported in wagons from post-offices to headquarters.[2] And then, the election — and the news flashed that the Republicans had lost. After days of jubilation in the Greeley camp, the last 'returns' turned the tide. 'Radical frauds!' cried the friends of Greeley. But no matter — the election was lost. This had a depressing effect in the North — *Greeley had not drawn the blacks.*

## IX

The campaign continued with unabated fury in the North, the Greeleyites suffering nothing in comparison with their foe in the mastery of men at the guns. Schurz was firing with deadly precision in the West, Trumbull opened and maintained a raking bombardment on corruption and privilege, the brilliant O'Connor, of South Carolina, captivated Boston in a plea for sectional reconciliation that anticipated by many years that of Henry Grady,[3] and in New York a rising young orator, Chauncey M. Depew, was impassionedly denouncing Grantism with the assertion that 'the scum of society has been brought to the surface in the Government in the three years of Grant's Administration.'[4] With Hendricks and Julian leading the fighting in Indiana, Morton, in dire distress, was sending forth the Macedonian cry to Blaine.[5]

But Grant's Three Musketeers were at their best, according to their natures. Morton, evoking war hates, was solemnly charging that Greeley's election would mean the reënslavement of the blacks and the assumption of the Confederate debts.[6] Conkling, with less temerity, was pouring forth sonorous phrases in faultless elocution about Grant the soldier, not the statesman. 'While Senators that now hawk at him,' he said, 'were lolling on cushions, and eviscerating encyclopedias, books of quotations, and the

[1] Hamilton, 587–90.                    [2] *New York World*, July 27, 1872.
[3] O'Connor, 330–46.                    [4] *New York World*, September 12, 1872.
[5] Julian, MS. Diary, October 8, 1872; Gail Hamilton, 302.
[6] Julian, *Recollections*, 342.

classical dictionaries, the tanner of Galena swept rebellion from the valley of the Mississippi, and the father of waters goes unvexed to the seas.' Gifts? Why, England gave millions to Wellington, thousands to Cromwell, a stately mansion to Marlborough — why should Grant not take gifts from private citizens? [1]

But Zack Chandler was engaged in more important work, and doing it well. As Chairman of the Republican Congressional Committee, he had been perfecting a remarkable organization, raising money, spreading propaganda, feeding the press in the interest of uniformity, strengthening the hard-pressed carpet-baggers — doing it with mouse-like stealthiness. Beside him, the 'Bismarck of the campaign,' James M. Edmunds, tall, spare, plain, tireless, silent. It was he who proposed the searching of the 'Tribune' files for material damaging among Democrats; it was Chandler who advanced thirty thousand dollars for the purpose; it was Edmunds who directed the pens of three hundred writers.[2] The influence of this organization was felt in every township in the North, and in the counting-room of every favor-seeking industry. It was at this time that Chandler permanently married politics to business. With ineffable finesse, he worked on the fears of business men. 'Who knows what Greeley might do?' Again, and more than ever before, collectors found their way to the strong-boxes of Jay Cooke. At times the old man, in the midst of his ecclesiastics, writhed a bit, and cried out, calling W. E. Chandler 'Oliver Twist,' and Grant and the Cabinet laughed over the thrust. Before long, Cooke himself was passing the hat among the rich. Even Congressmen were begging at Cooke's door — Blaine especially clamorous. 'Blaine is so persistent . . . that I feel . . . he should be conciliated,' wrote Henry Cooke to his brother. 'He is a formidable power for good or evil, and he has a wide future before him. However unreasonable in his demands . . . my conviction is irresistible that he should in some manner be appeased.' [3]

Thus Cooke was a never-failing fount. The Secretary of the Navy demanded ten thousand dollars for his State of New Jersey, for had he not given Jay Cooke's house the naval account? 'If New Jersey went Democratic,' wrote a partner of Cooke, 'R.'s

[1] Conkling, 437.          [2] *Life of Chandler*, 314–15.
[3] Oberholtzer, *Cooke*, ii, 352–54.

influence would be at an end. . . . Of course this would probably result in a change of account.' [1]

The power of money in elections was beginning to alarm the old-fashioned, and there was some murmuring. A. H. H. Stuart of Virginia was writing in the 'Staunton Spectator' that 'capital has got possession of the Government,' to the detriment of agriculture and commerce, and 'is supplying the sinews of war for the Presidential contest.' [2] The State Chairman of the New York Liberal Republicans was asserting that the combined slush funds of all parties in previous presidential elections did not equal the sums being spent by Grant's followers in doubtful States.[3] 'No Crédit Mobilier has dexterously transferred millions to our pockets,' he said. This reference to the Crédit Mobilier was unhappily denounced by Colfax as 'a campaign lie.' The Whiskey Ring was raising campaign funds for Grant, though its activities were well covered. Money was with the President, and Wall Street was circularizing business men in his behalf.[4]

And never such personal abuse; the worst offender the cartoonist Thomas Nast, the genius of 'Harper's Weekly,' whose ridicule of Greeley and his friends exceeded the bounds of decency. The young German had visited Washington in the winter and had been beside himself with droll ecstasy over the flattery of the great. 'It certainly is funny the way the Senators are in a flutter about my being here,' he wrote his wife. 'Every one knows me, every one is glad to see me, from the President down. They are trying to keep me as long as they can.' [5] And Nast went back to New York to do his best, and it was brutal. Frequently the editor, George William Curtis, protested against the abuse of friends like Sumner, but Nast was defiant, and Fletcher Harper decided with him. When Curtis protested against a cartoon of Greeley shaking hands 'with the worst element of Irish Romish,' Harper wrote the cartoonist, 'If it is right to hit Pat, hit him hard.' [6] Even Mark Twain was delighted with these appeals to prejudice, thinking them in the interest 'of civilization and progress.' [7] That the cartoons were effective cannot be doubted; and Matt Morgan,

---

[1] Oberholtzer, *Cooke*, II, 357.    [2] Quoted, *New York World*, October 14, 1872.
[3] *Ibid.*, October 15, 1872.    [4] *Ibid.*, October 20, 1872.
[5] Paine, 221–26.    [6] *Ibid.*, 250.    [7] *Ibid.*, 263.

brought over from England by 'Leslie's Weekly,' was not quite able to match Nast in cruelty and savagery.

Even campaign songs were colored a dirty hue, those of the Republicans besmearing Greeley with 'free love and free farms and all that,' and the Liberals having Grant arm in arm with Tom Murphy, 'shouting the battle-cry of plunder.' [1]

x

With despair creeping upon him, the weary Old Man of the White Hat took to the stump, and his friends trembled. But not for long. He made a gallant figure, pitching his appeals on a lofty plane, expressing himself persuasively. Somehow the eccentricity and irritability were all gone. The country gasped its astonishment. The super-critical Watterson thought these speeches 'marvels of impromptu oratory'; [2] and the none too friendly Voorhees thought that 'for elevation of thought, propriety of sentiment, for broad philanthropy, and general benevolence,' they had 'no parallel in American history.' The 'New York World' described them as 'suffused with the healing spirit of magnanimous patriotism.' [3] But it was a sadly broken old man, bowed with sorrows and concern over a dying wife that gave way to lamentations when alone, and he hurried home to keep a sleepless vigil at her side until the end. When, election night, Grant sat with Jay Cooke rejoicing over the returns, something in the bosom of the old man of Park Row snapped. With mind and body broken, he sank rapidly, and in a few days he was dead. Sumner's request to utter a few words of tribute in the Senate was denied. But when the old man of 'The Tribune' lay in state in the City Hall, forty thousand passed the casket, and many that had ridiculed and abused him hastened with smug hypocrisy to bow at his bier.

When the Electoral College met, Greeley was dead, and most of his electors cast their votes for Hendricks, just elected Governor of Indiana. These Democrats, having browsed a while on poor rations in strange pastures, were glad to get back home.

[1] *The Nation*, October 10, 1872.      [2] *Marse Henry*, I, 262.
[3] September 22, 1872.

XI

Saddest of all, Greeley had accomplished nothing in the South, where the negroes had persecuted the few blacks who favored the old Abolitionist. Lamar was elected in Mississippi, which was something; but the degraded Moses had won in South Carolina, and it was predicted that he would 'in two years take the last of the sap out of the tree.' [1] The reform movement had not touched that unhappy State, and this year saw the elevation of 'Honest' John Patterson to the Senate. His election was a flaming scandal. Skilled in corruption, he had maintained a free house of entertainment over a saloon near the State House. The legislators were susceptible, because crassly ignorant. Many 'came fresh from the corn fields and the log cabins . . . clad in the homely garb of labor and anxious to change to fine clothes.' Soon it was known that the 'house of entertainment' exchanged money for votes for Patterson. Later, one legislator after another was to testify to the saturnalia of corruption in the rooms over Fine's saloon.[2] Arrested for bribery, and taken before a trial justice, Patterson's friends created a commotion during which he escaped. Taken again, and sent to jail for twelve hours for contempt, a complacent judge from another circuit issued a writ of habeas corpus. All this was common knowledge in Washington, where he was known as a protégé of Simon Cameron,[3] but he was seated in the Senate, soon to become more potent in the White House than the taxpayers of his State.

In Alabama quite as black a senatorial scandal resulted from the election of George E. Spencer, carpetbagger from Iowa, who bought his seat with money furnished by Zach Chandler's committee, and with Government funds, taken from the internal revenue offices of Mobile and Montgomery, and from the post-office of the former city. The collectors and postmaster were his appointees, and when he refused to reimburse them for the more than twenty thousand dollars taken, they were ruined.

[1] *New York World*, October 11, 1872.

[2] *Fraud Report*, Testimony of Senator Gaillard, 889; J. C. Tingman, 890; Jos. J. Gant, 890; R. B. Artson, 894; C. S. Minor, 894; W. L. Leggett, 895; J. J. Maxwell, 898; S. Randall, Jr., 904; Henty Riley, 914.

[3] *New York World*, December 12, 1872.

More than thirty members of the Legislature were given Federal jobs.

In Louisiana, where the Democrats had formed a coalition with the Warmoth faction, there was a shocking scandal involving a drunken Federal Judge; and a dual government, with Federal interference with bayonets, was the result. Of this, more later — for the confusion and chaos extended into 1875.

The election of 1872 was a sweeping triumph for reaction; and the South found itself in more dire straits than ever, as the corruptionists and carpetbaggers, triumphant, mounted and rode.

# CHAPTER XIX

## DEGRADATION AND DEPRESSION

### I

ALMOST immediately after the election, the political leaders who so gleefully and successfully had denounced the Crédit Mobilier charges involving their integrity as 'campaign lies' began to sing small. But Charles Sumner found himself paying the penalty of his insurgency when Congress met. Julian was shocked at his physical condition. Instead of remaining in Europe to recover completely through rest and fresh air, he had returned to his post and was keeping himself alive by 'taking drugs.' Ignored by the party he had helped to create, and humiliated in his committee assignments, he had just been denounced by the Legislature of Massachusetts because of the most generous act of his career. In the interest of 'national unity and good will among fellow citizens,' he had introduced a bill providing that 'the names of battles with fellow citizens shall not be continued in the Army Register, or placed on the regimental colors of the United States.' He set forth that 'it is contrary to the usages of civilized nations to perpetuate the memory of civil war.' Hale had presented a counter-bill in the House, which was passed by a party vote, leaving Sumner alone with the Democrats, and the lawmakers of Massachusetts had condemned Sumner's gesture of conciliation. It was this rebuke from his own people that hurt him most. 'I know I never deserved better of Massachusetts than now,' he wrote. 'It was our State which led in requiring all the safeguards of liberty and equality; I covet for her the other honor of leading in reconciliation.' [1] Nothing could have illustrated better the impracticality of Sumner the politician. His party's strategy at the moment called for a more flamboyant waving of the bloody shirt. 'I fear his continued hard work and his mental trouble will end his days prematurely as in the case of Greeley,' wrote Julian.[2] As Sumner sat in his library nursing his sorrows, Whittier the poet

[1] To W. P. Phillips, Pierce, IV, 552.          [2] MS. Diary, December 22, 1872.

launched a movement to rescind the offensive resolution of rebuke, and Wendell Phillips, strangely touched, was writing, 'I would despise a Southerner who would march under such a flag, despise yet more heartily a North that would ask him to do it.' [1] Soon Whittier was able to send Sumner reassuring news. 'The country is coming all right on thy flag resolution,' he wrote. 'The pitiful folly of our State Legislature is already repented of. Believe me, thee never stood higher with the best people of the State, of all parties, than now.' And he added a line that partly explains Sumner's unpopularity and isolation in a day of brazen corruption: 'Amidst the miserable muddle of the Crédit Mobilier, it is something to be proud of that the smell of fire has not been upon thy garments.' [2]

In time the resolution was rescinded, but the scar of the wound remained. And there were other wounds that still bled — especially that inflicted by his wife, and he was bitter. At this time he was reading in the press of her activities in Europe, where she was 'occupying her time . . . chiefly in doing good to others.' It was reported that 'more than one American family to whom dire disease has come in a foreign land has found a faithful and efficient nurse' in her, and that 'at one time she traveled from Florence to Vienna to nurse a family.' [3] But she had done no good to Sumner, and that spring he secured a divorce in Boston on the ground of desertion.[4] Desertion everywhere, by Massachusetts, by the Republican Party, by his wife. One night that spring, Wendell Phillips lingered with the lonely man till after midnight, and even then Sumner clung to him and would not let him go. When reminded that he was to take a footbath, he replied, 'Well, I will take it if you don't go.' And so, with Phillips looking on, the fallen idol bathed his feet, and the friend remained to solace him.[5] The shadows were closing in and deepening about the abandoned leader whose party deserted him to concentrate on a desperate effort to save the leaders caught in the net of the Crédit Mobilier.

[1] Pierce, IV, 554.
[2] Ibid., IV, 561.
[3] New York World, February 1, 1873.
[4] Ibid., May 10, 1873.
[5] Pierce, IV, 591.

## II

There had been scandal enough in the Government's relations to the Union Pacific Railroad, which had been loaded down with land and loans on terms of extraordinary liberality. The Crédit Mobilier was a corporation formed to take over the contract for the building of the road, and the stockholders of the two companies were identical. The stockholders then made a contract with themselves to build the road at a price that would exhaust the resources of the Union Pacific, including the proceeds of all the bonds, and the profits were then divided among the stockholders of the Crédit Mobilier. This meant that the railroad would be mortgaged to the full extent of its resources, and stripped of the endowment provided by the bounty of the Nation. Then came the quarrel between the thieves and litigation, and ultimately publicity for the fact that Oakes Ames had been given a quantity of stock to distribute among influential members of Congress as a precaution against an investigation. It was the plan that these statesmen should buy at par, but since a large dividend had been assigned the stock, and another dividend was soon due, it meant, in reality, a 'purchase' at a price far below par, and an assured profit. It was, in truth, intended as a bribe. It *was* a bribe.

Then came the investigation, and startling disclosures involving the Vice-President, the Vice-President-elect, the chairmen of the most important committees of the House, party leaders such as Patterson, Dawes, Boutwell, Garfield, 'Pig Iron' Kelley, Bingham, Allison, Wilson of Iowa, Scofield, and Brooks, the floor leader of the Democrats in the House. When the investigating committee began its labors, a spirit of gloom descended on the capital, and, as one distinguished leader after another was involved, the impression was painful. At first the Democrats seemed jubilant in spite of the involvement of Brooks, but so appalling were the revelations that this joy soon passed. Awed by the dreadful possibilities, and the significance of it all, real patriots trembled for the honor of the Nation.[1] The day that Oakes Ames drew his fatal memorandum from his pocket, with its shocking disclosures of the stupidity or turpitude of the leaders, it was remarked that the committee 'seemed to shrink from the depth of

[1] *The Nation*, January 30, 1873.

shame which disclosed itself.' [1] As the evidence appeared day after day, 'The Nation' surveyed the result. 'Its effect on congressional reputations may be briefly summed up in this way: total loss, one Senator; badly damaged and not serviceable for future political use, two Vice-Presidents and eight Congressmen.' [2] Caught red-handed, the strategists sought from the beginning to concentrate public contempt on Ames for tempting simple-minded statesmen who knew not what they did. Deserted by most, Ames, who was to tell the truth, was literally heartbroken, and we have a picture of him seated before the fire in the home of Blaine, 'silent and stunned into immobility,' his head bowed on his breast while the younger man sought means to solace and save him. [3]

But, alas, for Ames there was no escape. To save the party chiefs there had to be a victim thrown to the sharks; and by turning State's evidence he had committed the one crime which, throughout this period, seemed the most unpardonable. At first prone to defend himself, he soon noted with amazement and growing bitterness the plan of the prominent party leaders to turn upon him with well-simulated indignation as the wicked man who had played upon their impeccable purity and childlike credulity. Soon he determined to tell the truth, and his conduct thereafter was in striking contrast with the evasiveness and too apparent concealment of the others. His letter to H. S. McComb definitely fixed his purpose in the distribution of the stock. [4] By all accounts, he suggested no obligation when he transacted business with his colleagues. This was to be urged by the whitewash committee as proof of the innocence of the others; but no such conclusion was permitted in his case.

The extent of the implication of most was clear. Bingham of Ohio bought in the belief that the investment would bring large profits, and he had no apology to make. [5] Wilson of Iowa, admitting his purchase, solemnly insisted that he had no idea of the value of the stock. [6] Allison, notoriously a representative of the railroads, admitted having had possession and receiving dividends, and of having returned the stock under fire from motives of politi-

---

[1] *The Nation*, January 30, 1873.   [2] January 3, 1873.   [3] Gail Hamilton, 286.
[4] House Report 77, 42d Cong., 3d Sess., 4.   [5] *Ibid.*, 191, 195.
[6] *Ibid.*, 216.

cal expediency, not morality.[1] Dawes of Massachusetts, testifying that Ames had guaranteed him ten per cent on his stock, had pledged himself to buy it back if the purchaser wished to unload, conveyed the impression that there was nothing suspicious in such generosity in a business deal, and the committee pretended simplicity as amusing.

But politicians and historians have been embarrassed in explaining away the strange transaction with James A. Garfield and 'Pig Iron' Kelley. In the case of both not one penny had been paid for the stock. It had been held by the marvelously accommodating Ames until, with the proceeds of dividends, he was able to mark the debt canceled, and to deliver cash dividends to the two men. Kelley stoutly insisted that he could see nothing amiss in a member of the House voting on the Union Pacific measures getting Crédit Mobilier stock in this bizarre fashion. 'It was just like buying a flock of sheep,' he said.[2]

But Garfield was not so frank, insisting, contrary to the evidence, that he never owned stock or received a dividend.[3] The committee was to find that he had owned stock, did receive a dividend, and had perjured himself — and was therefore innocent.

The case of James Brooks differed, in that he was charged, not only with having owned stock, but with thus betraying the Government he represented as a director of the Union Pacific. He offered explanations quite as plausible as those of the others, but his were brushed aside.

### III

No one became so hopelessly enmeshed as Vice-President Colfax, who had politically capitalized his sanctimony, and had sweepingly denied the charge in the campaign in the fall. Ames testified that Colfax had got twenty shares and in June, 1868, had been paid twelve hundred dollars in cash dividends, a check for which had been given him on the Sergeant-at-Arms of the House.[4] Simulating utter astonishment, Colfax dumbfounded Ames by the audacity of his cross-examination. Did Ames really regard him as the owner of the stock? 'Certainly,' said Ames, 'you paid for it;

---

[1] House Report 77, 42d Cong., 3d Sess., 307.     [2] Ibid., 200.
[3] Ibid., 129.     [4] Ibid., 279.

it belongs to you; it has never been returned.'[1] Then the evidence in corroboration of Ames began to pour in. The Sergeant-at-Arms testified that there was a check for twelve hundred dollars bearing Colfax's initials;[2] and the cashier of his bank testified that at the time he had deposited twelve hundred dollars in United States and banknotes.[3] The Nation was stunned, and even Colfax's friends were momentarily silenced. For ten days he was silent, too, complacently leaving town to attend some religious meetings. 'The Nation,' losing all patience, sharply suggested that if the money deposited had been paid from some other sources 'the answer could be made in five minutes.'[4] Who paid him the twelve hundred dollars if Ames did not? Clearly a point worth considering; and ten days later, Colfax appeared again before the committee, having at length remembered the source of the money. It was a strange story — almost too strange, many thought. One day, it seems, he opened his mail at the breakfast table, and there, in a letter, was a thousand-dollar bill. It surprised him, he admitted. Indeed, he held it up to the family and explained that it was a gift from George F. Nesbitt, in New York, who was in the habit of sending him money for the campaign chest. This Nesbitt he scarcely knew — a printer who admired the Vice-President because he, too, had been a printer. About that time Colfax had borrowed two hundred dollars from a member of his family, who testified to that fact — after ten days. It all came back to him now — there was the twelve hundred dollars deposit! But how unfortunate that Nesbitt was dead and could not testify![5] Colfax smiled, and the lawyer he had employed sat triumphantly at his side. Ames listened grimly, smiling contemptuously, and then cross-examined. And so the philanthropist had sent money frequently? he asked. He had. Then why did this one donation make such a vivid impression on the entire family when none other had? Because it was a bill and not a check. Then the others had all been checks? They had. Could Colfax account for this one at this particular time having been sent in money? He could not. 'He must have been a very singular man,' commented Ames sarcastically. 'He was a very large-hearted one,' said Colfax. And the

[1] House Report 77, 42d Cong., 3d Sess., 383.    [2] *Ibid.*, 309.
[3] *Ibid.*, 341–42.        [4] February 6, 1873.        [5] House Report, 501–07.

committee listened without a smile.[1] But 'The Nation' thought it
'a most singular thing' that 'the whole matter should have been
entirely forgotten by Mr. Colfax when it was most necessary for
him to recollect it'; and even more significant that 'he refused to
put in his answer until Oakes Ames had come back and it had been
ascertained through cross-examination that he was not likely to
submit any previously unsuspected proof.'[2] Most of the Republican press rushed to the defense, however. 'All fuss and parade,'
growled the 'Boston Advertiser.' Who would hesitate on a question of veracity between Ames and men like Colfax, Garfield, and
Kelley? asked the 'Albany Journal.'[3] George William Curtis, the
purist, had begun by denouncing the committee, then had confessed a shock at the shiftiness of Colfax, and had ended with the
conclusion that, except in the case of the wicked Ames, and the
Democratic Brooks, nothing was wrong but the foolish attempt to
conceal perfectly innocent transactions.[4] This was the keynote for
the pure of heart among the partisans. It figures in the correspondence of Thomas Nast, who had raged in righteous wrath over
the turpitude of Tweed, but now kept a close rein on his virtue.
'The whole subject offers a rich theme for your pencil,' wrote a
friend, 'but I doubt the wisdom of availing yourself of it.'[5] But
he did make his contribution in the most comical of all his cartoons depicting Justice standing protectively before the statesmen
caught, and, with flashing eyes, pointing contemptuously at the
press, represented by Watterson, Reid, Bennett, Dana, and Manton, with the stern rebuke: 'Let him who has not betrayed the
trust of the people and is without stain cast the first stone.'[6]

Not for nothing had the leaders in Washington given Nast a
patronizing pat on the back.


IV

The Report was a partisan whitewash.

Blaine was properly exonerated, but almost all who had accepted of Ames's generous bounty, while acting indiscreetly, had

[1] House Report 77, 42d Cong., 3d Sess., 513-14.          [2] February 20, 1873.
[3] Quoted, New York World, February 8, 1873.
[4] Harper's Weekly, February 15, 1873.
[5] Chapman to Nast, Paine, 270.          [6] Harper's, March 15, 1873.

been perfectly innocent of an evil thought. The cases of Garfield and Kelley were difficult. It did seem 'they must have thought that there was something out of the ordinary course of business in the extraordinary dividends they were receiving as to render the investment itself suspicious' — ignoring the fact that there had been no 'investment.' Of course, if they had been 'aware of the enormous dividends upon this stock, and how they were to be earned, we could not thus acquit them.' It must be observed that, in concluding that Garfield did get stock and dividends the committee found him guilty of perjury, since he had sworn he had not — but nothing was made of it.[1] Having skated gingerly over thin ice in the case of the others, the committee turned its holy wrath on Ames, who had told the truth, and Brooks, recommending their expulsion with a Cato-like sternness.

The day the Report was read was bright and sunny and society went to the play *en masse*, the floors and galleries filled. Ames, excited for the first time, and despising not a few of his colleagues, sat, strangely enough, between the chaplains of the House and Senate; and Brooks, seriously ill, ghastly pale, his hands of bloodless hue, betrayed his mental and physical suffering. During the reading of the report, Ames smiled derisively, while Garfield, 'Pig Iron' Kelley, and Dawes sat 'smug and sanctimonious.' Brooks rose at the conclusion in a broken, bitter protest that he was innocent.

That night Ames, in an interview, offered a classic characterization of the findings: 'It's like the man in Massachusetts who committed adultery, and the jury brought in a verdict that he was guilty as the devil, but that the woman was as innocent as an angel. These fellows are like that woman.'[2]

## V

The Report was a whitewash — so recognized at the time. 'Hardly worth discussing,' said Godkin in 'The Nation.'[3] Whitelaw Reid, in the 'New York Tribune,' found in the case of Colfax 'another coat of whitewash,'[4] and ridiculed the findings. 'They found the prisoner on the highway rummaging the pockets of his

[1] Report, 129.
[2] *New York World*, February 19, 1873.
[3] February 27, 1873.
[4] February 25, 1873.

dead victim, tried him for murder in the first degree, and found him guilty — of breaking the peace.' [1]

The partisan nature of the Report was glaring. The Vice-President, Vice-President-elect, the Chairman of the Ways and Means Committee, the Appropriation Committee, the Judiciary Committee, the Naval Committee, the Banking and Currency Committee, and 'Pig Iron' Kelley, party leader, all exonerated; but Brooks, the lone Democrat, was tied tight to Ames, who had no political significance. More space was given to analyzing the infamy of Brooks than to all the Republican leaders combined, and the 'New York Tribune' commented on the strategy. Voorhees was reminded of a partisan melodrama. 'The Republicans were given minor rôles and allowed to slip off the stage unnoticed, but when Brooks came on the sheet thunder was sounded, the calcium lights were burned, and he was shown up in the most gorgeous colors as the chief villain of the plot.' [2]

Such brazen partisanship aroused the Democrats, for they had not defended Brooks, the 'New York World' had bitterly attacked him in January,[3] and the Democratic members of the committee had shown him no mercy. But the Report was a challenge much too smug. 'The Republican Party,' said 'The World,' 'has determined to punish Oakes Ames for exposing the venality of the Republican leaders, and James Brooks, the only Crédit Mobilier Congressman who was NOT bribed, because he is a Democrat.' [4] There were meditative citizens who could only wonder how a transaction between Ames and others could be perfectly innocent on the part of the others and reprehensible on the part of Ames, and why the perfidy of Brooks was so much blacker than of Colfax. It was suggested that the committee had sounded a warning 'to corrupt Congressmen against turning State's evidence' and 'against being Democrats.' [5] Describing Colfax as the Crédit Mobilier Pecksniff,' [6] the 'New York World' demanded his impeachment, and a resolution was offered in the House.

[1] February 28, 1873.
[2] New York Tribune, February 19, 1873.
[3] January 29, 1873.
[4] February 17, 1873.     [5] New York World, February 19, 1873.
[6] January 25, 26, February, 9, 1873.

VI

And yet there was much sympathy for Brooks, whose integrity had never before been questioned, who had refrained from voting on Union Pacific legislation or had voted against the road's wishes, and who was hastening to the tomb. The door of the committee room, opened three times to Colfax with an attorney, was sternly closed in Brooks's face when he sought a second hearing. Once or twice he had fainted in the corridor.

In the midst of the tragedy, the festivity and comedy of society continued, and between the submission of the Report and its consideration a magnificent ball was given at the home of Henry D. Cooke in Georgetown — on the night of the day the Report was read. It was the gayest, most brilliant of the season, and Kate Chase Sprague, with a band of her abundant hair bound round her head with a sprig of flowers at the side, was the belle as usual. There, too, were the Grants, and the attractive Mrs. Belknap, but most eyes were fixed on a less dashing woman, the wife of Brooks, whose 'sweet, kindly face' was 'bright and cheery' — the most tragic picture of the night.[1]

The debate on the Report opened on a crisp, cool day of sunshine, and the Capitol was crowded two hours before the galleries were opened. The scene was that of 'a stage view of the parquet of an Opera House,' because of the silks, ribbons, and furbelows blending in all colors. Ladies occupied chairs by members' seats and sat on documents piled high in the aisles, while in the rear men stood on sofas. In the Diplomatic Gallery, Mrs. Fish and Gail Hamilton sat with members of the legations, and, standing near the western door, in the midst of a fashionable group, Kate Chase Sprague looked down upon the scene. Opera-glasses constantly were turned on Ames. The dying Brooks, deathly pale, worked his way down the center aisle, sank into his seat, and buried his face in his hands.[2]

Dramatically, yet drearily, the debate dragged on through two days, with just two high spots. Ben Butler cynically defended Ames in a speech interspersed with witticisms that brought laughter. On the second day, Voorhees rose to make a plea for Brooks. The 'New York Tribune,' commenting on his marvelous voice,

[1] *New York World*, February 23, 1873.          [2] *Ibid.*, February 26, 1873.

thought that 'he could not have been more earnest and careful if Mr. Brooks had been his client before a jury.' [1] His was a sober, lawyer-like analysis of the evidence, with purple patches of moving pathos, touched at times with indignation when he compared the treatment of Brooks and Colfax. The galleries applauded when he concluded — the only applause of the debate.

A resolution to condemn all who had dealt with Ames was voted down, though eighty-two supported it; and resolutions 'absolutely condemning' Ames and Brooks were adopted. The attempt to impeach Colfax failed. In the Senate, action was taken in the case of Patterson. The drama was over.

### VII

Julian reached Washington after the curtain fell and was amazed at the evidence of suffering on the faces of 'the criminals,' and, like many others he was convinced that Ames was 'on the whole the best of the lot.' [2] He, at least, had not added perjury to bribery. In a few weeks Brooks was dead, and in a few days Ames followed; and men like Curtis, of 'Harper's Weekly,' set themselves to the task of rehabilitating Colfax, without much success. Brave efforts were made to laugh away the memory of the scandal. Senator Carpenter of Wisconsin from the platform was sneering at the investigations into 'private matters,' and complaining that they had 'diseased the public mind' and produced 'morbid public morality.' [3] But more prescient politicians were worried, and one of them, talking confidentially to the Washington correspondent of 'The Nation,' was not sure his party could survive what had happened, and knew it could not 'survive another such thing.' He was afraid that 'worse things are in store.' [4] And, indeed, about this time the Freedmen's Bank crash came, and the negroes were plucked by the 'patriots.'

### VIII

A hectic summer — with the Beecher scandal breaking and the Democratic 'World' vehemently defending the Republican preacher — and the Freedmen's Bank — and the lying in state at

---

[1] February 26, 1873.          [2] MS. Diary, March 16, 1873.
[3] Janesville Speech, *Life of Carpenter*, 467.          [4] March 13, 1873.

the City Hall of James L. Orr, the South Carolina Republican, while the Union League Club flag fluttered at half-mast. In politics, the Democrats swept Connecticut in April; and the same month the Supreme Court handed down decisions on the relations of the States to the Federal Government under the Reconstruction Amendments which gave no little comfort to the minority party. The skies were clearing for the Democrats if they could but unite — a possibility that seemed remote. That summer the 'New York World' made a gallant fight to rally the party against protection, protesting that 'the Pennsylvania influence has hamstrung it' and urging that the Democrats 'count on accessions from the West.' [1] Soon the Democratic papers were too busy hammering one another to concern themselves with the Republicans, who had a breathing spell. The Southern and most of the Western press fought with 'The World,' while that of Pennsylvania and a part of the papers of New England and New Jersey lined up with the opposition. The 'Cincinnati Enquirer' and the 'Cleveland Plain Dealer' went for protection.

A new wrinkle, soon to become commonplace, had been discovered in the way of propaganda. The Industrial League of Pennsylvania had been interrogating presidents of colleges as to the textbooks they used on political economy, and the 'Industrial Bulletin' had been publishing the replies. A Colorado college asked advice. One in Pennsylvania reported nothing in its library on economics beyond a volume of the speeches of 'Pig Iron' Kelley. Some mentioned certain books presenting the protection argument with the blunt suggestion that 'it would be to the interest of your industrial league to place such books in our library.' [2] Even higher education was soliciting a seduction.

## IX

And higher education might be needed, for there was a rising in the West just now, with infuriated farmers demanding railroad rate regulations and a reduction of the tariff. The domination of agriculture in government ended with the passing of the Jeffersonian Republic in 1860; and the rule of the industrialists and capitalists had come with the war. The now dominant party had formed

[1] April 22, 1873.        [2] *New York World*, July 7, 1873.

offensive and defensive alliances with these new groups, and felt as
certain of the farmers, however neglected, as of the negroes of the
South, for Radicansm had blossomed richest in the West. But the
farmers of the grain-growing States were now in real distress, their
homesteads falling under the hammer of the auctioneer, the banks
foreclosing on the mortgages. The railroads were exacting rates
for transportation that made it impossible to sell at a profit, and
the tariff had increased the price of everything the farmer had to
buy. Enraged at the conditions and the indifference of the Government, State and National; convinced that monopolies were in
the saddle and their horses fed at the public trough; certain that
the railroads owned legislators, executives, and courts, and not far
wrong, they suddenly rose, and organizations of revolutionary
militancy sprang up in all agricultural sections, North, South,
East, and West. While occasionally demanding tariff reform,
they centered their fire on the railroads — and it was time. Almost every State Legislature had its Crédit Mobilier; the roads
owned some of the governors, and many of the courts. Having
been built at public cost, they scoffed at the regulation of rates,
evoking Marshall's decision in the Dartmouth case to show that
regulation was none of the public's business. Public men everywhere were riding on free passes. It was the day when Money decided to rule, regardless of elections, and it was making a success
of the experiment.

Illinois pointed the way out in the spring of 1873. Three years
before, the new constitution had made it mandatory on the Legislature to enact laws prohibiting extortion and unjust rate discrimination; two years before, such laws had been enacted; that
spring, the Supreme Court set the law aside; and that very
month the challenge was accepted. The State Farmers' Association of Illinois was launched with a militant programme predicated on the pledge of the members to use their power at the polls
against their enemies and for their friends regardless of party
affiliations. When the Legislature met to make a law to meet the
objections of the Supreme Court, the farmers met in Springfield in
convention with the announcement that they were there 'for the
purpose of attending to our interest in the Legislature, and of
giving that body and the Governor to understand that we mean

business, and are no longer to be trifled with.'[1] Conservatives were shocked, legislators trembled in their boots, and responded with more radical regulatory laws than before.

But that was not enough — for this was a farmers' revolution. These embattled farmers, convinced by the action of the Supreme Court that the courts were in the hands of their enemies, marked these enemies for slaughter at the polls. The Chief Justice and one of his associates, then up for reëlection, were defeated, and hostile judges in seven or eight circuit court districts went down before the farmers' fire. The Eastern press protested loudly against the 'packing of the judiciary in the interest of a class,' and the farmers asked when the press had protested against the packing process for another class. Encouraged by the triumph, the farmers entered tickets in more than half the counties of the State in the fall, merging in numerous instances with the Democrats; and other Western States followed the example. Coalitions with the Democrats were made in Illinois, Iowa, Minnesota, and Wisconsin, and a working arrangement was perfected in other States. The whole Western country was on fire with a new spirit. The Fourth of July was taken over by the farmers for picnics and all-day rallies, and thousands listened to speeches and sang songs, and at every meeting listened to the fervent reading of a farmer's paraphrase of the Declaration of Independence, pulsating with specifications of outrages, throbbing with insurgency. No more railroad steals — tariff steals — salary-grab steals, they cried. The governmental regulation of railroads was demanded; equal banking privileges were asked; and the ending of land grabs for the railroads was insisted upon.

The result sent a chill to the hearts of the allied industrials and politicians. In Illinois, the farmers swept almost every county they contested, and had they made a State-wide fight and maintained their ratio, they would have carried the State by twenty-two thousand majority. In every other State the Republican majorities were enormously reduced; in Kansas a reformer was sent to the Senate; in California a coalition of Democrats and insurgents sent to the Senate an insurgent Republican[2] and an anti-monopoly Democrat.[3]

[1] Buck, 83.     [2] Governor Booth.     [3] John S. Hager.

This was something that called for the most prayerful medita-
tions of the dominant party; and, in the mean while, the panic had
struck, and amidst the crash of financial institutions intimately
identified with the party organization, the politicians were paralyzed with fear.  Henry Ward Beecher, always as much politician
as preacher, was moved almost to un-Christian wrath in a lecture
on the theme that it is good to get rich, sneering at the idea that
farmers were more honest than speculators.  Indeed, he said, they
were the easiest of the legislators to buy or seduce.[1]  'The Nation'
thought the farmers' 'denunciation of the railroad men as thieves
and swindlers when they want them to carry their grain for a
trifle . . . is at least immodest.'[2]  Better take a lesson from Jay
Cooke, and from John D. Rockefeller, who was then making a
profitable secret arrangement with the roads to carry his oil for
more than a trifle less than was being charged competitors.

## X

The panic came because there were too many who thought with
Beecher that it was good to get rich.  Just a little while before, Senator Morton had told the Republican State Convention in Ohio that
'the standard of public morals to-day is higher in this country than
it has ever been before.'[3]  Less than a month later 'The Nation'
was to explain that one of the causes of the panic was 'the closing
of the English markets to American railroad securities under the
influence of repeated cases of American rascality — such as the
Emma Mine, fathered by the American Minister, and General
Frémont's swindling Texas enterprise, and the default made by
several new roads in the payment of their coupons.'[4]  This, however, was but one of many contributing causes.  There had been an
abnormal and unhealthy absorption of circulating capital, with
railroads, docks, factories being built on a tremendous scale, with
too much capital invested in projects of ering no immediate or
early returns.  Railroads, wastefully and sometimes criminally
built, had been built greatly beyond the demand for their services
Overtrading, expansion of credits, rash investments, and un-

[1] Delivered October 20, 1873.
[2] October 23, 1873.
[3] *New York World*, August 27, 1873.                [4] September 25, 1873.

reasonable speculation on the part of those who thought it good to be rich, all enter into the explanation of the collapse.[1]

The crisis came to a head with the fall of the house of Cooke. There had been a wild day of deep anxiety on the New York Stock Exchange, and that night Grant arrived at 'Ogontz,' Jay Cooke's home in Philadelphia. The two men sat at breakfast the next day listening, over a private wire, to the disturbing news from the financial center. After breakfast the President was driven to the station by the banker; and that very day the New York branch of Cooke closed its doors, and Jay Cooke thereupon ordered the closing of the doors in Philadelphia. The Washington bank, in charge of Henry Cooke, closed, too.[2]

This tragedy did not descend without premonitions. Cooke's institutions were carrying the accounts of many politicians, and, two years before, the importunate Colfax had written the banker for a loan on which to carry his Northern Pacific assessments. Early in 1873, it had become necessary to call in loans, and there was some correspondence between Jay and Henry on the embarrassments of the necessity. Blaine had been given a loan on property that did not begin to cover it. 'Blaine will be a hard nut to crack,' wrote Henry.' . . . You will have to be very careful not to offend him. He is figuring for the Presidency. Has he paid his interest?'[3] With the announcement that the Cookes had closed, the excitement was intense, and that night great crowds of financiers milled about the corridors of the Fifth Avenue Hotel, the sidewalks in front crowded, the bar-rooms as well as lobbies packed. In Washington, great crowds surged about the First National Bank, where the political leaders had so long found generous accommodation and congenial company. Among the crowd were many depositors in ugly mood, and the police were hurried to the scene.[4] The next day it was even worse in New York, with the suspension of twenty more firms, and with pandemonium on the Stock Exchange. In a drenching rain crowds of haggard men tramped in the neighborhood of Wall and Broad Streets. 'The

[1] Burton, *Financial Crises*, 287–89; *The Nation*, September 25, 1873.
[2] Oberholtzer, *Cooke*, II, 421.
[3] *Ibid.*, II, 416.
[4] *New York World*, September 19, 1873.

nearer one got to the Stock Exchange, the more ghastly did the faces become.' [1]

Another day, and more failures, but thus far only the moneyed class had been hit. Salvini, the actor, played through all these dismal happenings to crowded houses.[2] And then, the next day, came the suspension of Henry Clews and Company. The collapse was complete. Grant, with Secretary Richardson, had hurried to New York for conferences with financiers and business men and was urged to issue part or all of the so-called reserve of $44,000,000 in greenbacks retired and canceled by McCulloch. Senator Morton was present and urged the issue of the whole amount. Grant refused, but decided to use the other surplus greenbacks in the Treasury to purchase bonds. The President and Richardson returned. Morton remained, constantly exchanging telegrams with Grant and the head of the Treasury. No one was more conspicuous in the lobbies of the Fifth Avenue Hotel, and not infrequently he was seen moving nervously in the throng on Wall Street. The collapse of Cooke and Clews, both built up to no little extent by party favor, and hitherto to a never-failing source of party sinews, was more than a national calamity — it was a party tragedy. It was being recalled that Cooke and Clews a year before had signed the circular letter to business men and bankers warning that the election of Greeley would disturb the 'unprecedented prosperity.' [3]

And then came other disclosures that seemed to an excited nation a little queer. It had developed that, with the Treasury itself across the street, Secretary of the Treasury Richardson had kept a balance of $287,782 in Government money with Henry Cooke, holding security for but $100,000 of that amount, though the law demanded that there be no deposit of Government money without the deposit of United States bonds or other security to cover it. Thus, said 'The Nation,' Richardson or the Administration had unlawfully lent $187,782 of Government money to a political friend.[4]

Then, with the appointment of a receiver, it was found that the bank contained but $67,000 in currency of all kinds, while the last

[1] New York World, September 20, 1873.    [2] Ibid., September 22, 1873.
[3] Ibid., October 6, 1873.    [4] October 9, 1873.

bank statement had shown it held $140,000 in greenbacks of the
$300,000 it was bound to hold as a reserve. The public clamor-
ously inquired what had become of the money. Charges were
openly made that influential depositors had been paid off before
the funds were turned over to the receiver, under the pretext that
they were special depositors.[1] It was said that Grant had withdrawn his $40,000 because of the precarious condition of the bank
at the very time the $187,782 of Government money was literally
loaned to the institution without legal security.[2] Why, asked the
critics, when the National Banking Law forbade a bank to advance more than one tenth of its capital, in this case $50,000, had
the Cooke bank been permitted to become debtor for thirteen
times the amount.[3] Under this bombardment, Richardson was
silent — but not indifferent. He managed to persuade Jay Cooke
and Company to deposit securities to the amount of $200,000, thus
making the Treasury safe. Whereupon 'The Nation' sharply
commented: 'Where Jay Cooke and Company got this money, no
one seems to know, as the firm are insolvent and making terms
with their creditors; and the creditors . . ., who find the Government treated as having a preferred claim, are naturally alarmed.
Altogether it is a very mysterious piece of business.' [4]

The case of Clews came in for criticism as severe. Some time before the naval account had been withdrawn from the Barings in
London and given to Henry Clews and Company; and soon this
was being denounced as 'a political job.' It was recalled that
Clews had appeared as a banker but nine or ten years before and
had been given the Government account as a reward for political
services. Instead of the banker's credit drawing the Government
balance, the balance was given to help the credit. At this time
John Swinton, the journalist, was telling John Bigelow that the
transfer from the Barings to Clews was managed by Orville Grant
in consideration of the cancellation of a debt owing to the American banker — and telling him on the authority of the manager
himself.[5] Certain it is that the politicians were profoundly moved
by the misfortune of Clews. 'I would not have had it happen for

[1] *The Nation*, October 16, 1873.
[2] *New York World*, October 13, 1873.
[3] *The Nation*, October 16, 1873.
[4] November 13, 1873.
[5] *Retrospections*, v, 131.

five thousand dollars,' said Tom Murphy. 'Henry's failure is the hardest blow the President has yet had,' said Senator Morton.[1] Out of it all one irresistible conclusion emerges — the laws had been laxly enforced or utterly ignored in the interest of great financiers who had been generous with campaign funds and easy on private creditors of political distinction.

Almost immediately the effect of the crash reached business generally, and factories not dealing in necessities found that the bottom had dropped out of their business. A few weeks, and the house of Sprague, manufacturers of Rhode Island, was a heap of ruins, and the daughter of Chase entered upon the lean years. No more would epicurean dinners be spread in the garden behind the Sprague house in Washington.

## XI

A dismal winter, one of several, turned its bitter blasts upon the unemployed. Men, women, and children were soon walking the streets in fruitless search of work, and the employment agencies of cities were jammed from morning until night. The placards displayed at a mass meeting at Cooper Union in December did not exaggerate:

10,000 homeless men and women in our streets.
7,500 lodged in the overcrowded 'charnel' station houses per week.
20,250 idle men from 11 trade unions, while only 5950 are employed.
182,000 skilled workmen belonging to trade organizations of the State idle.
110,000 idle of all classes in New York City.

And there were other placards having political significance:
Civil Rights have passed, now for the Rights of Work.
Freedom for Labor, Death for Monopolies.
Does Speculation or Labor produce wealth?
We demand suspension of Rent for three months.
When Workmen begin to think, Monopoly begins to tremble.[2]

Drawn to the capital by the failure of Cooke's bank, Andrew Johnson was serenaded one night at the Metropolitan Hotel. The request of the serenaders for the use of the Marine Band to honor

[1] *The Nation*, October 2, 1873.
[2] *New York World*, December 12, 1873.

a former President was refused, albeit a similar request had been granted just before to friends planning a dinner for Henry Cooke — which had to be abandoned now.[1] Without the band an immense crowd assembled to cheer Johnson. The grim warrior appeared upon the balcony.

'What kind of government have we now?' he asked.[2]

The answer came with the elections, with tremendous losses to the ruling party everywhere, and with a sweeping victory for the Opposition in New York.

## XII

But in Mississippi the Republicans made an advance in the election of General Adelbert Ames to the governorship. The two most conspicuous beneficiaries of Republican domination there were Ames and Alcorn, both having passed from gubernatorial honors to the Senate, where their rivalry became acute. Alcorn was a Mississippian, Ames a carpetbagger. Alcorn was a wealthy planter, Ames a soldier of fortune. Alcorn was a man of fine forensic ability, Ames was worse than mediocre on the platform. Alcorn was keen, Ames dull. The two had crossed swords on the Ku-Klux Bill, Ames supporting, Alcorn opposing it, and their bitter altercation led to the resignations of both, to test the temper of their party in a contest for the nomination for Governor. A few white Republicans aligned themselves with Alcorn, the Radicals went to Ames, and the Democrats, choosing between evils, made no nomination and lent support to Alcorn. Lamar defined the attitude of the Democrats when he wrote: 'I am for Alcorn. He has from the aggressive and combative qualities of his character, combined with the prominence of his position and his senatorial collisions with Ames, assumed the leadership of the conservatives of this State.' [3]

Alcorn immediately challenged Ames to joint debates, but the duller man declined on the ground that his opponent was not the nominee of a regular party. The attempt of Alcorn to get the negro vote by telling the colored people he had secured them the right to ride on cars with the whites alienated thousands of Demo-

[1] *New York World*, October 18, 1873.
[2] *Ibid.*, October 24, 1873.   [3] Letter to E. D. Clarke, *Life of Lamar*, 177.

crats for his support. Radicals, carpetbaggers, and negroes went in solid mass to Ames, who won overwhelmingly. On the ticket with him were three negroes — the Lieutenant-Governor, the Secretary of State, and the Superintendent of Public Instruction. All were elected, and Cordozo, thus placed in charge of the schools, was at the time under indictment for larceny in Brooklyn, New York, the indictment signed by Benjamin F. Tracy, District Attorney, and later to be a member of the Harrison Cabinet.[1]

Thus was notice served on Mississippi that the negroes would rule the State, and the worst element immediately demonstrated its ability to dominate the flabby Ames. The darkest days of Mississippi had dawned, and soon, driven to desperate resolves, we shall find her people in revolutionary mood making stern preparations for the elections of the next year. At the time Ames was thus imposed upon them by the organized ignorance of the State, the loyalty of the Mississippians was beyond all question. Voorhees, trying a lawsuit there, was writing home that, in the event of a war with Spain, 'the South will fight under the old flag in a way to command the admiration of the world.'[2]

The election of Ames, with all it meant, sounded the death-knell of the Republican Party in Mississippi. All over the North, thinking men were beginning to resent the policy of imposing ignorant and criminally corrupt governments on the Southern people. The scandalous contest over the Louisiana election of the previous year was still on, and many were shaking their heads in disapproval of the part played in Washington. It was the year Andrew D. White, visiting the South, was disgusted by what he saw and 'for the first time began to feel sympathy with the South,' after seeing personally how he had been deceived by partisan prejudice and dishonest propaganda.[3]

After all, the Republican victory in Mississippi was but the forerunner of redemption. So ended a memorable year.

[1] Garner, 293.        [2] To W. E. Niblack, *Life of Lamar*, 178.
[3] White, *Autobiography*, I, 176.

# CHAPTER XX

## THE SLIPPING SCEPTER

### I

THE year 1874 was not a happy one for the dominant party, and the gloss of Grant's military renown had been worn off in the harsh contacts of partisan politics. Even the most arrogant were a little dubious of the popularity of the Administration, and men like Bigelow were writing that it was impossible 'to give a good account of our government,' since 'Grant does not comprehend his position — neither its privileges nor responsibilities.' [1] The third-term gossip was being greeted with ugly hisses, and Bancroft, the historian, was saying that a third term 'would ... be a long stride toward changing our republic into a monarchy.' [2] Grant blundered again, in the nomination of a successor to Chief Justice Chase, by seeking without avail to force the superficial Williams, his Attorney-General, upon the Senate. Despite the almost universal protest of lawyers and public men, Grant stubbornly persisted in seeking his confirmation, and it was not until a third nomination had been made that the Senate gave consent. Bitter as the blow was to Grant, it was more bitter to Williams, and still more bitter to Mrs. Williams, consumed with pride and ambition, and within two months she was to take to her bed, crushed and heart-broken. [3] The appointment of Waite, while unexpected, met with no objections, but William Cullen Bryant could not forget 'what inconsiderate nominations the first two were,' and concluded that Grant lacked 'the discernment necessary for putting proper men in their proper places.' [4]

Very soon, however, the most popular act of Grant's two administrations promised for a moment the restoration of his earlier popularity. Hard times had seemingly come to stay, and there was prostration in business and suffering among the people. Finan-

---

[1] To Von Bursen, *Retrospections*, v, 143.     [2] To Bigelow, *Retrospections*, v, 167.

[3] *Missouri Republican*; quoted, *New York World*, April 28, 1874.

[4] To Miss Dewey, *Life of Bryant*, II, 339.

ciers were urging the resumption of specie payment, but the clamorous multitude was passionately demanding more paper money.
The politicians in Congress, cringing before the tide, went with it,
with much demagogic shouting, and it was assumed that Grant
would sign the inflation bill. The East, home of the financiers,
was for resumption, the West for expansion of the paper currency;
the South had more pressing perils to consider. 'Of course Grant
would sign.' Great, therefore, was the astonishment when he returned the measure with a vigorous veto. The East shouted its
approval and praise; the Republican West was sullen, but its
fidelity to the party was taken for granted. For a moment Grant's
veto overshadowed his blunders. 'I have seen nearly all the prominent bankers, bullion dealers, and brokers,' wrote the financial
editor of the 'New York Herald.' 'They unanimously applaud.' [1]
The final reaction was yet to be seen. There was no rejoicing
among the unemployed, and suffering among the masses threatened sinister possibilities. The silk workers of Paterson, New
Jersey, in mass meeting were demanding an immediate tariff reduction of twenty per cent.[2] The miners, in convention in Ohio,
and later at Wilkes-Barre, were calling on their fellows to organize
against the encroachments of organized wealth.[3] The jobless and
hungry, with communists and socialists, were marching and
countermarching in the streets of the larger cities; and, frightened
by the omen, the press was beginning to treat poverty and suffering as a crime to be handled with the mailed fist. The day the
marchers went back and forth from Union Square to Tompkins
Square, the entire police force of New York was kept on duty,
and the press announced that detectives were watching 'trade-
unionists and communists.' [4] When penniless heads of families,
threatened with eviction in mid-winter, demanded the suspension
of rents until the first of May, the 'New York World' declared
they were merely trying to rob their landlords and should be
handed over to the police.[5]

Infuriated by the callous indifference to their plight, the unemployed resorted to mass meetings, where defiant resolutions

[1] April 24, 1874.          [2] *New York World*, January 15, 1874.
[3] *Ibid.*, January 19, 1874.     [4] *Ibid.*, January 9, 1874.
[5] January 10, 1874.

were passed and speeches made. When a great throng gathered in New York, with a captain of the Union army in the chair, detectives were on hand to take down 'incendiary statements,' but arrests could scarcely be made because of resolutions protesting against 'the despotism of class rule,' and threatening the tools of monopolists in legislatures with punishment at the polls.[1] The New York Central Council of Labor fanned the fury with the assertion that 'the recent alarming development and aggression of aggregated wealth . . . will inevitably lead to the pauperization and degradation of the toiling masses.'[2] Under the provocation of such assertions, the police denounced all labor leaders as 'communists,' and charged that 'French radicals' were in control; and Labor replied that the charge was a lie and that the press was deliberately deceiving the people.[3] The result was an outrageous assault by the police on a peaceable meeting, where eight thousand jobless men were ordered to disperse, and did not stir. The police charged with clubs, beating down many who were weak from hunger.[4]

Such tactics played into the hands of a little group of communists and embittered thousands of law-abiding workers against the Government. For conditions could scarcely have been worse. A survey by the 'New York World' showed that thousands were living on from seventy cents to fourteen dollars a week; that clerks were receiving from five dollars to fourteen; that hundreds were existing on the refuse of the city, veritable scavengers. Some were found to be managing on thirty cents a day, and seeking station houses in which to sleep at night.[5] Occasionally groups, losing all control under the pangs of hunger, rushed the groceries, and the press described them as vagabonds — men who asked nothing better than a job. This condition, together with that of the embattled, organized farmers, was causing no little concern among the politicians at Washington. And to add to their discomfort it was at this time that an amazing book, 'A Prostrate State,' appeared, with graphic and relentlessly true descriptions of the barbarous government maintained in South Carolina through the

---

[1] *New York World*, January 11, 1874.
[2] *Ibid.*, January 12, 1874.     [3] *Ibid.*, January 13, 1874.
[4] *Ibid.*, January 14, 1874.     [5] *Ibid.*, January 21 and 22, 1874.

power of Federal bayonets. It was the 'Uncle Tom's Cabin' of the redemption of the South, and the author was James S. Pike, an Abolitionist, a Republican, an appointee of Lincoln as Minister to The Hague. Soon thoughtful men throughout the North were reading the truth which had been denied them. Democrats had declared it — but here was Republican authority!

Even so, the year had its light and amusing side. All through the summer, men and women were thrilling to the exotic story of Henry Ward Beecher and Theodore Tilton running in the press, and, strangely enough, the warmest defender of the 'Chaplain of the Radicals,' was the 'New York World.' The Frankfort, Kentucky, 'Yeoman' was asking why 'The World,' 'which claims to be a Democratic journal, is so ardent an admirer, advocate, and defender of the Radical apostle'; [1] and there was no answer.

That summer Charlie Ross, a child, mysteriously disappeared, to furnish a topic for the gossips for sixty years.

## II

And that spring Charles Sumner ceased from troubling. He was still anathema to the party he had helped to create. Even the negroes had gone over to Grant, with the politicians. He was alone, deserted by wife, by party, by his old associates — alone in the house on Lafayette Square, with his pictures and books. The antipathies he had created even curtailed his social life, and when asked to attend a dinner for Godkin, of 'The Nation,' he almost kicked the bearer of the invitation from the room. [2] There was ineffable loneliness in these closing days, and physical debility. He had been growing weaker day by day, when, one evening, the servants heard a fall, and found him in his chamber in great pain. Drugs were administered to alleviate the suffering, and two colored men were engaged as nurses. With the spreading of the news of his serious illness, crowds gathered before his house, all sorts and conditions of men, with the negroes predominating. These intercepted visitors emerging from the house, with anxious inquiries. A correspondent observed, however, 'that no one connected with the White House, nor any member of the Cabinet, gave any sign of interest.' [3] It was evident that his summons had

[1] Quoted, New York World, August 29, 1874.
[2] Letter by Godkin, Ogden, i, 311.     [3] New York World, March 12, 1874.

come. Former Attorney-General Hoar sat by his bedside holding
his hand. 'Judge, tell Emerson how much I love and revere him,'
murmured the dying man. 'He said of you once,' Hoar replied,
'that he never knew so white a soul.' To all who were admitted he
kept saying over and over again, 'You must take care of the Civil
Rights Bill' — his last thought. Just as Schurz entered the room,
the soul of Sumner broke from the clay, and Hoar, laying his hand
down gently, said, 'Well done, good and faithful servant! enter
thou into the joy of thy Lord!' [1]

And now, the White House was interested. Nellie Grant sent
violets.[2] The body was borne to the Capitol in a procession led
by a body of negroes, including Fred Douglass, and there in the
Rotunda it lay in state. An immense throng attended the funeral,
Grant and the Cabinet foremost, but the colored people outnumbered the others. Julian thought the services 'cold and hollow and
anything but a fit response to the popular feeling.' Some Scrip-
tural passages were read, some 'drawling prayers,' but there was
neither music nor a sermon. 'A grand opportunity lost,' wrote
Julian, 'of appealing to the sympathies of the multitude and impressing great moral and spiritual truths upon the minds of all.' [3]

Thus Sumner passed from the scene of his greatness to rest in
the quiet of Mount Auburn. Six weeks later, irreverent crowds
pushed into his home to a sale of his household effects. The
dining-room furniture familiar to so many of the great was
bought by Wormley, the negro hotel-keeper, with the view to
fitting up a Sumner Room.[4]

But Sumner's Civil Rights Bill failed of enactment that session.
All over the South the 'poor whites' were up in arms against it —
particularly in Tennessee, where the Radical mountaineers were
bitterest. The bill was thought destructive of the public schools,
and intended to force the two races to live together. In the Federal Cemetery at Knoxville, fifteen thousand mountaineers, meeting in protest, forbade the negroes to appear.[5] When the most
rabid of the Radicals, Parson Brownlow, now Senator, was denounced by a negro convention at Nashville for his opposition to

[1] Hoar, *Memoir*, 239; Pierce, IV, 598.   [2] *New York World*, March 14, 1874.
[3] MS. Diary, April 14, 1874.   [4] *New York World*, June 4, 1874.
[5] *Ibid.*, July 13, 1874.

the measure, he replied defiantly. These negroes, he said, were reversing the Dred Scot decision and holding that the white man had no rights the negro was bound to respect. Their conduct made for racial animosities that could only operate against the blacks. Their demands would be destructive of the public schools. Political reprisals? The Tennessee Republican Party could get along without the negro as well as the negro could get along without the party; and without the party there would have been no negro vote. Besides, 'twenty-five thousand white Republican voters of East Tennessee have resolved to get along without the colored voters sooner than submit to this sum of villainies and quintessence of abominations known as "the co-education of the races."' [1]

Thus 'party principles' were passing with the Stevenses and the Sumners. There was no deep grief for Sumner on the Republican side of the House; it was from the Democratic side and from a Southerner that the tribute came.

### III

When Lucius Q. C. Lamar, of Mississippi, rose to pay his memorable tribute, he faced an audience of more than ordinary distinction. The floor was full, the galleries thronged, the Diplomatic Gallery brilliant with colors; and intellect and fashion sat expectant, when the commanding figure of the bearded orator with the great gray eyes rose in the silence. It was a serious moment in Lamar's career. His friends had grave misgivings; his opponents, not unmindful of his fire-eating days, were cold and critical. No speaker ever undertook a more difficult task. In personal appearance he was impressive, his profile and features regular but massive, his abundant hair and pointed beard both brown, his eyebrows heavy. Practice with the sword and gloves had given him the solid powerful shoulders of a pugilist, though his hands and feet were slender and sensitive. Though an impassioned nature, his outer appearance was that of a dreamer; his manner always that of a cultivated gentleman. Unless intolerably provoked, he was gentle, and his heart was as tender as that of a young girl. His oratory was natural and at times inspired, and he

[1] *New York Herald*, May 18, 1874.

combined the qualities of a deeply analytical and philosophical mind with those of a master of exquisite English which clothed his arguments in beauty. Like Sargent S. Prentiss, he was at his best in extemporaneous speech. Such was the knight of Mississippi who rose to speak on Sumner, of Massachusetts. His voice was soft and musical, modulated to the solemnity of the occasion. Referring to the softening of Sumner in the later days he said:

'It has been the kindness of the sympathy which in these later days he has displayed toward the impoverished and suffering people of the Southern States that has unveiled to me the generous, tender heart which beat beneath the bosom of a zealot, and has forced me to yield to him the tribute of respect — I might even say of my admiration.'

The brilliant audience sat in rapt attention as the Southerner proceeded with a brilliant analysis of Sumner's character, without reflecting on his own people or yielding aught to the foe.

'The South, prostrated, exhausted, drained of her life blood, as well as of her material resources, yet still honorable and true, accepts the bitter award of the bloody arbitrament without reservation, resolutely determined to abide the result with chivalrous fidelity; yet, as if struck dumb by the magnitude of her reverses, she suffers on in silence. The North, exultant in her triumph, and elated by success, still cherishes, as we are assured, a heart full of magnanimous emotions toward her disarmed and discomfited antagonist; and yet, as if mastered by some mysterious spell, silencing her better impulses, her words and acts are the words and acts of suspicion and distrust. Would that the spirit of the illustrious dead whom we lament to-day could speak from the grave to both parties to this deplorable discord in tones which would reach each and every heart throughout this broad territory: "My countrymen, know one another and you will love one another."'

Blaine, motionless as a statue, with his face turned away, did not try to conceal the tears running down his cheeks, and on both sides of the House men wept openly. When Lamar closed, there was a deathlike silence, and then a burst of applause, as one Northerner said to another, 'My God, what a speech! It will ring through the country.'

And ring it did, party and section for the time forgotten in the universal praise. For a moment it seemed that a miracle had been wrought — but just for a moment. The exigencies of politics would soon unfurl the bloody shirt again, and Blaine himself would wave it, despite his tears.

IV

For the scandals of the Administration were accumulating, and even as Lamar spoke, the Foster Committee was just closing its investigation of the Sanborn contracts. Acting under a law authorizing the Secretary of the Treasury to employ no more than three men to assist officials in the discovery and collection of money due the Government, a contract had been awarded John D. Sanborn, of Massachusetts, then a special agent for the Treasury. The Secretary was to determine the conditions of the contract and to pay no compensation save for the money recovered. Having in his official capacity acquainted himself with the distillers, rectifiers, and purchasers of whiskey who had withheld taxes, Sanborn obtained a contract for collection in the case of thirty-nine. Finding the picking profitable, officials complacent, and his authorization from the Secretary of the Treasury sufficient to open the books of all the revenue offices to his inspection, Sanborn asked the Secretary to add to his contract the names of seven hundred and sixty persons charged with failing to pay taxes on legacies, successions, and incomes. They were added 'as a matter of routine.' Delighted with his easy conquest, he asked to have five hundred and ninety-two railroads added — and this was done. In a little more than a year he had collected $427,000, of which he received half.

The evidence disclosed that Sanborn had a political character, being a friend of Ben Butler, who had introduced him to the Commissioner of Internal Revenue, and that he had been a constant contributor to the campaign funds. When he was arrested in Brooklyn, it was Butler and W. E. Chandler, with whom we are familiar, who went on his bond. Summoned before the committee, the Secretary of the Treasury, William A. Richardson, disclosed an appalling ignorance. He was ignorant of the transactions in his office — no time to investigate. He had signed the instructions to supervisors and revenue collectors, placing them at the disposal of Sanborn without reading — had no recollection of it.[1] 'What,' asked the committee, 'you sign contracts without reading?' 'Oh, yes, sir.'[2] He had not answered the letter of the Commissioner protesting against the privileges of Sanborn, because he had never seen it. Had he inquired into the details of the railroad collections when he signed the order for the payment to Sanborn of forty-nine thousand dollars? Not at all — 'I signed in the regular course of business.'[3] The evidence of the other Treasury officials showed an ignorance or culpable indifference quite as amazing. With characteristic effrontery, Ben Butler, whose name had bobbed in and out of the testimony, appeared before the committee one day in a bulldozing mood, to receive shot for shot from Beck of Kentucky.[4]

There was but one thing to do. The committee found that the Secretary, the Assistant Secretary, and the Solicitor 'deserve severe condemnation for the manner in which they have permitted the law to be administered.' Thus Richardson's position became untenable — in the Treasury. When it was proposed to proceed against him in the House, Grant summoned the committee, with a plea to withhold action until he could find a successor — and another official position for the Secretary! Thus Richardson was transferred to the Court of Claims — and Bristow entered the Treasury to play havoc with the peace of the Administration.

v

Meanwhile, with Pike's book on the savagery of government in South Carolina sinking in on the consciousness of the North, an incident soon disclosed that no impression had been made on the President. For almost two years Frank Moses, a lecherous degenerate and corruptionist, had been in the gubernatorial chair at Columbia. The black sheep of a decent family, notoriously dishonest in the Legislature, he had been elevated to the executive office with the aid of the National Government and had entered into the land of milk and honey with an insatiate appetite. Almost immediately, this penniless adventurer had purchased a

[1] H. R. Report, 559, 43d Cong., 1st Sess., 88.
[2] Ibid., 89.           [3] Ibid., 92.            [4] Ibid., 176–77.

forty-thousand-dollar mansion, furnished it with elegance, maintained the grounds and buildings perfectly, and indulged himself in every luxury. Driving through the streets in an expensive equipage drawn by a span of the finest horses, he conveyed the impression of opulence. He was living at the rate of about forty thousand a year, and, while his debts had reached almost a quarter of a million, he was not without resources in the crimes he was committing.[1] A natural actor in the princely rôle, a correspondent described his domestic establishment as 'a well-trained *corps dramatique.*' In the presence of minister or bishop, he was all piety and humility and the good man was impressed with his sanctity and the charms of a pious household. When occasion called, he could 'preface a meal with a lengthy and unctuous grace and roll off a well-written family prayer.' Even the domestics enjoyed the comedy.[2] And yet this 'frowsy, hatchet-faced, pale young man of a debauched exterior, suggesting the celebrated Dick Swiveller,' with a big mustache and thin hair 'like a dried moss,' could be seen with negroes and low whites puffing cigarettes, and sitting down among the blacks with a hunchback billiard-player.[3] His was the golden age of stealing in South Carolina — he in the executive mansion, 'Honest' John Patterson in the Senate. Reeking with corruption, he and his followers in public station lived on the fat of the land, with fine wines and liquors, blooded horses and luxurious homes. Elliott, the negro Speaker of the House, dwelt in a white trellised cottage in the fashionable section, with his 'green vines, magnolias, mock orange, and long-thistled Carolina stem grass,' and 'a pretty, rose-tinted light mulatto.' This house was in his wife's name.[4] Scott, the former Governor, and Patterson, and the other pillagers, had homes in the capital, and a correspondent, surveying the sorry scene, described Columbia as 'an out-of-door penitentiary, where the members browse voluntarily, like the animals in the Zoölogical Garden.'[5]

And the taxpayers? They were ground to powder — their very civilization in peril. In Charleston alone, this year, two thousand pieces of real estate were forfeited for taxes, and in nineteen counties, 93,293 acres were sold, and 343,891 acres went to the

[1] Reynolds, 270.    [2] *New York World,* August 25, 1874.
[3] *New York Herald,* October 13, 1874.    [4] *Ibid.,* October 17, 1874.    [5] *Ibid.*

tax collector.[1] All attempts to reach Moses through the law were vain. Indicted for complicity with a county treasurer to rob the State, he defied arrest, and for three days three companies of negro militia guarded his house and office; and the courts declared him immune from arrest, and only liable to impeachment by the corrupt Legislature he controlled.[2] Under these shocking conditions, the taxpayers met in protest at Columbia and formulated an appeal to Congress. This set forth the exclusion of taxpayers from the Government, the constant increase in taxes until they consumed more than half the income from the property, and the fact that the exploiters boasted that the great body of the land would be taxed out of the possession of the owners. More: that public plunder was open and defiant, with the living standards of two governors only possible on stolen money.[3]

This was not news in the North. The 'New York Tribune,' 'Herald,' 'World,' 'Sun,' and 'Nation' had been drawing stronger indictments and describing Moses as a consummate thief. But there was no relief in Washington. A committee of the most reputable and distinguished citizens presented their petition to Congress, along with a copy of Pike's 'Prostrate State.' Nothing happened. The petition was flippantly laid on the table without discussion. The committee then turned to Grant.

Just before its arrival at the White House, the slouching figure of 'Honest' John Patterson sneaked into the Executive Office to prepare the President for the visitors and advise him. One of the speakers in the Taxpayers' Convention had severely reflected on Grant, and it was enough for Patterson. It served his petty purpose. Balancing himself with one foot on a chair, Grant listened impatiently to the spokesman, interrupting occasionally with tart reproaches, and then bursting into an extraordinary discussion of his personal grievance against one man in the convention. Even the 'New York Sun,' he said, had not been so villainous in its attacks. And perhaps the taxpayers had themselves to blame. Had they not refused to amalgamate with the carpetbaggers and the negroes — refused to affiliate with the Administration Party in South Carolina? Another speaker, resorting to manuscript lest under the provocation he lose his temper, tried to talk, only to

[1] Williams, *Columbia State*, August 8, 1927.    [2] Reynolds, 270.    [3] *Ibid.*, 250–53.

be interrupted. In sheer disgust the committee, of as high-minded men as South Carolina had produced, turned from the presidential presence.[1]

But again Grant had blundered. 'It is a new thing in our history, even after all these recent years of scandals in high places, for an American President to insult his fellow citizens coming before him on a lawful errand,' said the 'New York World.' [2] This, following on Pike's *exposé*, hastened the awakening of the North.

Nor was the bad impression brightened by the reply to the taxpayers by the Republican State Committee — a partisan tirade evading the issue. Among the signers were some disreputable characters, fourteen of the twenty-four being notorious bribe-takers. It was common knowledge. When the representatives of this group appeared before Grant, they were received with courtesy, and assured that their reply seemed satisfactory. The spokesman was a carpetbagger who had participated in the robbing of the Treasury, and afterward was to be convicted of forgery.[3]

Thus, with the appeal of the taxpayers worse than ignored, the conviction grew that the South would have to fight.

## VI

The character of the campaign being waged in the North accentuated the fact. With Lamar's speech forgotten, desperate politicians were waving the 'bloody shirt.' The embattled farmers were on the march; the unemployed of the cities were in an ugly mood; the small business man struggling against bankruptcy was rebellious now; and the masses were beginning to sicken at the multiplying scandals. The third-term aspirations of Grant were impressing stout Republicans as unendurable,[4] and this was to align Whitelaw Reid and 'The Tribune' behind the gubernatorial candidacy of Tilden in New York.[5] To arouse the dominant party to a fighting fury, Andrew Johnson was on a rampage again, waging a vigorous battle for the Senate in Tennessee, with the multitude reacting rapturously to his denunciations of the Administration.[6]

[1] Richard Lathers, *Reminiscences*, 321–24.     [2] April 13, 1874.     [3] Reynolds, 265.
[4] To Weed from Dix, Weed, *Memoirs*, II, 505.     [5] Cortissoz, I, 284.
[6] *New York Herald*, November 2, 1874.

Again the Nation rang with sectional assaults. A letter to the editors of Administration papers in Indiana was found and published: 'I desire to call your attention to the horrible scenes of violence and bloodshed transpiring throughout the South and suggest that you give them as great prominence as possible in your paper from this time until after the election.' Signed by Thomas J. Brady, State Chairman, it was charged that the author was Senator Morton, the powerful leader of the Administration forces.[1] Attorney-General Williams through his office was giving currency to such falsehoods. But the North had become skeptical at last, and for the first time since the beginning of the war the Democrats wiped out the Republican majority in the House of Representatives; and in the election of Tilden in New York, a commanding figure had been given to the leadership of his party.

## VII

The spirit of Alabama that year sent a chill to the heart of Administration leaders. With no more than four thousand whites in the Republican Party, the blacks met in high feather at Montgomery and demanded their choice of nominations in the negro counties, and a proportionate distribution of the plums in others. With the State Supreme Court deciding that intermarriages were legal, they noisily clamored from the platform for the Civil Rights Bill. The State was flooded with the Radical speeches of Morton and Boutwell in favor of mixed schools, and colored orators were parroting the words of Morton. The Union League Clubs, in a spurt of new life, again were promising a division of property, and campaign speakers were boasting that it would be taxed out of the possession of the owners. Negroes who could read were seriously perusing circulars, purporting to come from Grant, making continued freedom conditional on the support of the Republican Party. The colored preachers and women were declaring any other affiliation incompatible with eternal salvation, and colored Democrats were expelled from the churches. Children were withdrawn from schools having Democrats as teachers, and women pledged themselves to desert their husbands if they dared vote with the native whites.[2]

[1] *New York World*, October 14, 1874.  [2] Fleming, 772-76.

And the challenge was accepted. The taxpayers were ready to go up against guns or bayonets now.

The spirit of revolt in the South flamed in the bitter editorial of the 'Atlanta News'[1] demanding White Leagues in every city and hamlet, and organization for a tremendous struggle. 'We have submitted long enough to indignities, and it is time to meet brute force with brute force,' it said. Thus all the county conventions met and acted in belligerent mood. The race issue had been forced upon them. Very well, it would be met. The Civil Rights measure would not be tolerated, and all whites supporting the negro party, or the bill, would be relentlessly ostracized.[2]

And thus it was — ostracism, the most complete. Business relations were broken; the honesty and honor of the deserter denied; his children were considered tainted; and the presence of the deserters in public meetings, even at church, was enough to drive the others out.[3]

In convention, the Democrats nominated for Governor George S. Houston, a North Alabamian who had been a mild Unionist; the Republicans renominated Lewis — and the fight was on.

Moving with determination, but caution, the Democratic State Committee issued its rules of conduct. No one was to be injured; all causes for just complaint were to be avoided; personal conflicts were taboo, but, ran the orders, 'if forced upon us, act in that line of just self-defense which is recognized and provided for by the laws of the land.'[4]

Abundant cause there was for caution, for the 'outrage factories' were again at work, the North deluged with weird imaginings of infamies and slaughter. Hawley, of the 'Hartford Courant,' had solicited some choice morsels for his people from Charles Hays, a Congressman from Alabama — a former slave-owner who had been ostracized by his neighbors because of his cruelty to his slaves. The Connecticut editor wanted something from 'a gentleman of unimpeachable honor.' And the man of 'unimpeachable honor' set to work with a zest. Soon the country was shuddering over stories of brutal outrages in Alabama. The spirit of rebellion was still rampant. Everywhere were murders, riots, torturings — never so much before. For a moment the Hawley-Hays correspondence was a national sensation.

[1] *Doc. Hist.*, ii, 387.    [2] *Ibid.*, ii, 388.    [3] Fleming, 781.    [4] *Ibid.*, 786.

But, alas, the 'New York Tribune,' choosing 'a lifelong Republican' as its emissary, sent him to investigate and report — and the report was more sensational than the story. There were no murders, no torturings, no riots, no rebels, and the Hays story was a lie out of whole cloth. More: 'Hays knew that his statements were lies when he made them' — and he suffered for the sins of his Northern brethren who needed such stories at home.[1]

And yet there were outrages in Alabama on the other side. Taking advantage of the spring flood of the Alabama, Warrior, and Tombigbee Rivers, which had inundated a large section of the country, causing distress among the negroes, Congress had been asked for an appropriation for relief. Eighty thousand dollars was thus available for the purchase of bacon to be distributed under the supervision of the Republican politicians of the State. The flood was in the spring, the bacon money was soon available, but there had been no distribution, and the Democrats in Congress called for a report. An investigation showed that the bacon was being used, not so much in the flooded section as in communities where it would do the most good politically. The army captain sent to investigate seized 5348 pounds sent to dry territory eighty miles distant from the nearest flooded section, and 17,430 pounds in other communities untouched by the flood. Even so, there was enough left for bacon suppers in negro churches for all who pledged themselves to vote the Republican ticket. But the scandal broke, the supply was exhausted, and there was weeping and gnashing of teeth among hundreds of whites and blacks who had failed to get their quota.[2]

All this but intensified the campaign of the Democrats. With a perfect organization, they were abundantly supplied with money, for every white man contributed to his limit, and Northerners with Alabama investments increased the fund irrespective of politics. Tons of literature deluged the State, and since postmasters were not above the pilfering of the mails, messengers, wagons, and the express were used in getting the material to the voters. Every one who could took to the stump, and all but ten of the seventy-five lawyers of Montgomery were busy on the platform.

Through it all the Democrats measurably respected the in-

[1] Fleming, 787–88.    [2] H. R. Doc. 110, 43d Cong., 2d Sess., 10–11; Fleming, 763–65.

junction against physical conflicts. Here and there, they tore
opposition posters down, and egged on the more obnoxious incendiary speakers, and, seated on the front row at carpetbag
meetings, with guns on their laps, interrogated the speakers about
bacon. But Grant, thoroughly aroused by the threat of defeat,
preferred to believe Mr. Hays, the man of 'unimpeachable honor,'
and in September he had ordered Secretary Belknap to hold troops
in readiness to deal with the 'atrocities' in Alabama and South
Carolina. The Attorney-General began urging United States
Marshals to make arrests under the Enforcement Act; and in
October, the State was overrun with deputy marshals, agents of
the Department of Justice, and secret-service men, many of the
lowest order. With from ten to twenty-five deputy marshals in
each county, vouched for as 'good Republicans' by the State
Chairman, the making of wholesale arrests began. Federal
soldiers, with warrants from the United States Commissioner,
dragged citizens from political meetings and their homes, removed
them to distant parts with handcuffs on their wrists, and threw
them into jails. Among the victims of this policy was John T.
Morgan, who was afterward to win the admiration of the Nation
in the United States Senate.[1]

Whipped by such persecution into a frenzy of determination,
the people rose and marched, *en masse*, to the polls, defying the
attempts at intimidation, and, electing Houston and a Democratic
Legislature, swept the carpetbaggers and scalawags from power.

Alabama had joined Virginia, Georgia, Tennessee, and Texas,
and was free.

### VIII

And this year Arkansas joined the procession of the redeemed.

For six years that State had been a happy hunting ground for
the adventurers. Taking possession with $319,000 in the Treasury,
and the counties practically free from debt, they had run the
State into an indebtedness of $15,700,000, and most of the coun-
ties were in debt to the verge of bankruptcy. One looked in vain
for evidence of legitimate expenditure. No new public buildings
could be seen, and the old State House was in a state of dilapida-

---

[1] Fleming, 793–98; *New York World*, October 8, 1874.

tion. Nothing had been done for science or art, and the schools were all but closed, since the school funds had found their way into the pockets of the rulers. Little Rock, unpaved, presented a dreary prospect. Only in the new, or 'court' end, of the town, one found a number of pleasant new dwellings — built by the political hucksters who had handled the railroad bonds. It was through the State-aid bonds for the railroads that the carpetbaggers had enriched themselves — a process with which we are familiar, and on which Clayton had insisted in the beginning. There was still much laughing over the cleverness of a Speaker of the House who, persuading the people of one county to issue one hundred thousand dollars in bonds for a road of which he was president, hurried with them to New York, where he found a banker willing to give eighty per cent on the bonds, provided he could get a bank to guarantee payment of interest for five years. The Speaker had deposited thirty thousand dollars with a bank to guarantee the six per cent interest for five years, received the eighty thousand dollars and with fifty thousand dollars profit he hied himself to Colorado to enjoy his fortune.[1] Visitors to Little Rock were regaled with many a story as bizarre. Among these was the story of the creation of Faulkner County to provide more opportunities for the faithful, and the manning of the offices with carpetbaggers, who collected taxes, issued county script, sold offices, released prisoners for a price, prostituted the ballot, and gayly went on their travels.[2] Quite as profitable were the contracts for repairs for the benefit of the favored politicians. Thus a negro politician, employed to repair a hundred-dollar bridge, submitted a bill for nine hundred dollars; and with scrip worth ten cents on the dollar, he received nine thousand dollars in scrip for repairs on a hundred-dollar bridge — an obligation on the State.[3]

While lining their pockets, these gay exploiters lived in lordly fashion, and more champagne was consumed within the dilapidated State House than anywhere else in the country. No beverages less patrician were tolerated — champagne was free as water. Charles Nordhoff found that 'champagne and poker were the chief enjoyments of the thieves in office,' and they indulged themselves without stint, and openly without shame.[4]

[1] Nordhoff, 30.          [2] Ibid., 31.          [3] Ibid.          [4] Ibid., 32.

But the schism of the Republicans in 1872 foreshadowed the doom of the pillagers. A year before, Joseph Brooks, potent among the blacks, declared for 'universal suffrage, universal amnesty, and honest men in office.' Nominated for Governor by the Liberals, he entered the campaign with Democratic support, accorded in the Pickwickian sense. An exhorter with lusty lungs, pious pose, and severe demeanor, he plunged into the fight against Judge Baxter, the regular Republican nominee. The latter, with more ability and better control of his tongue, was a native, and was destined, later on, to earn some respect from the people. His was a nomination of expediency,[1] because of his nativity and former ownership of slaves. Many Democrats, despite Brooks's liberal battle-cry, thought Baxter the more promising of the nominees, and the campaign was sadly mixed, with some Democrats supporting Brooks half-heartedly, and others holding secret conferences with Baxter, traveling with Clayton, after the latter had retired, and exacting pledges.[2] These secret meetings, discovered late, were disturbing to the Clayton machine, but its fate was tied up with his election, and all the registration machinery was used frankly in his behalf. Under the leadership of Governor Hadley, the Union League rallied the negroes to his support, and on the face of the returns he was elected. Brooks contested the election before the Legislature, and lost; instituted *quo warranto* proceedings before the Supreme Court, which declined to act; and finally brought suit in a circuit court, which decided in his favor. With a copy of the judgment, he hurried to the State House and ousted Baxter — and thus began the Brooks-Baxter war. Grant intervened and forced Brooks out and Baxter in, and soon had occasion to regret it.

Through all his interferences in the affairs of Arkansas, Grant was inspired by Senators Clayton and Dorsey, both disreputable in history, and by Senator Morton, Administration leader in the Senate, moved by partisan motives. But again the machine guessed wrong. Soon Clayton and Dorsey were declaring war on Baxter, who was ascribing their animosity to his refusal to enter into a criminal conspiracy to control the election in their interest. He charged an attempt to bribe him with a Federal judgeship

[1] Clayton, 347.    [2] *Ibid.*

and as much money as he wished; and failing in the attempt, the two Senators revived the circuit court decision, now almost forgotten, as a pretext for setting up a rival government.[1]

Meanwhile, Baxter, interfering with the stealing, was acquiescing in the action of the Democratic Legislature in calling a new Constitutional Convention. This was serious, and a bitter campaign followed. The Democrats were first in the field, organized, determined, with the sympathy and support of Baxter, and under the leadership of Augustus H. Garland, an able lawyer of national renown since his successful argument against the test oath for lawyers in the Supreme Court. He had supported Bell and Everett in 1860; had been a Union member of the convention that adopted the ordinance of secession; had served in the Confederate Congress, and been elected to the United States Senate in 1867, and excluded. Firm, determined, perfectly poised, and rich in the qualities of leadership, his personal character was beyond reproach.

With the Democracy confident and jubilant, Baxter, now militantly with them, set aside a day in June for public thanksgiving for the deliverance of the State from the hands of public enemies. Prayers were uttered, sermons preached, the people poured into the churches, and the carpetbaggers, now alarmed, bethought themselves again of Federal bayonets. With but 8547 out of 80,259 votes cast against the convention, and the election of Garland concededly inevitable, Powell Clayton sat down that fall with Senator Morton at Hot Springs to find an excuse for Federal interference. And so the wires from Arkansas hummed again with stories of the savagery of the native whites, for the Northern press. Negroes were lured from labor to Clayton barbecues, and there were occasional brushes with the whites. Nordhoff, on the ground, warned that the North would be invited to shed tears over the occasional shooting of 'Union men,' who were, in truth, but notorious characters.[2] But the game had been played ragged — and Garland swept the State.

Instantly, the defeated gangsters, with their political allies in the North, turned to Congress for relief, in an attempt to influence the action of the congressional committee authorized in May

[1] Baxter's letter to *New York Herald*, April 29, 1874.          [2] Nordhoff, 33.

under the chairmanship of Judge Poland of Vermont. A parade of the looters passed in review before the committee — the corrupt Chief Justice McClure appearing a few days before General Sheridan, playing the Radical game from New Orleans, made his proposal to the President to declare great bodies of men in Louisiana and Arkansas 'bandits,' to be tried by military commissions. But neither cajoleries, importunities, nor threats of reprisal would budge Luke P. Poland, Republican, whose fidelity to duty wrecked his ambition for a Federal judgeship, and on February 6, 1875, he submitted a report against Federal interference in Arkansas.

And then it was, only two days after the submission of the report, that Grant played the trump card for the defeated. Clayton had offered a resolution calling on the President for a report on Arkansas. The President had been in conference with Clayton and Morton; and his Special Message in response to the resolution was part of a desperate game. *Ex-cathedra*-wise, he declared Brooks had been elected in 1872 and unlawfully deprived of office, and that the Constitution of 1874 was null and void and the election under it that fall not binding.[1] It was too much. The 'Springfield Republican' interpreted: 'The English of this Message is: Authorize me to make war upon the Government and people of Arkansas, in the interest of my third term'[2] — an interpretation to which Rhodes, the historian, agrees.[3] When Congress, sickened by the insolence of the suggestion, refused to act, a shameless attack was made on the integrity of Poland, which fell harmless at his feet. They could thwart his ambition; they could not rob him of his honor. And in due time his report was adopted, with the support of many leading Republicans, and all the Democrats.

Thus Arkansas, under Garland, joyously joined the free States, and the carpetbaggers stood not on the order of their going, but went at once, some consoled with petty Federal positions. It was at this time, with Sheridan's 'banditti' message before the people, that Charles Nordhoff wrote: 'Arkansas is, in March, 1875, as peaceable a State as New York, Massachusetts, or Ohio. I assert this on the authority of leading men of both parties.'[4]

Meanwhile, the struggle for redemption was on in Mississippi;

[1] *Messages and Papers*, x, 4273.  [2] Merriam, ii, 238.
[3] Rhodes, vii, 87.  [4] Nordhoff, 34.

and in Louisiana, Sheridan, rattling the sword, was spluttering epithets in an attempt to save the Radicals he served from the destruction they merited. Let us follow these events — dramatic as any in American history.

# CHAPTER XXI

## MILITARY SATRAPS AND REVOLUTION

### I

THE conditions in Louisiana growing out of the election of 1872 had directed national attention to Cromwellian methods, and a revolution. The conservatives had elected John McEnery Governor over William Pitt Kellogg, the Republican nominee, but an illegal returning board had given the victory to the defeated without the formality of canvassing the votes. The contest involved not only State officers and a Senator, but the Legislature. The legal De Feriet Board found the conservatives triumphant; whereupon Kellogg had wired Williams, the Attorney-General who prostituted his position to partisan ends, that the fate of the Republican Party was involved; and the drunken Federal Judge Durell, with the trembling fingers of inebriety, had written his midnight injunction against the legal returning board, and instructed United States Marshal Packard, Republican chairman and manager, to take possession of the State House and prevent any 'unlawful' assemblage there of the McEnery legislators. The next morning, the city vibrant in protest, the besotted judge declared the lawful board illegal and restrained it from canvassing the returns.

The despotism and audacity of the crime rocked the Nation. Imprecations against the drunken tyrant arose from all quarters and from both parties. 'Reprehensible and erroneous in point of law and wholly void for want of jurisdiction,' was the verdict of a congressional committee.[1] This committee, with a majority Republicans, found McEnery had a majority of almost ten thousand, and the conservatives a majority of thirty-nine in the House and eleven in the Senate.

Even so, the action of Durell, countenanced by the Attorney-General, resulted in a dual government, with one legislature electing a conservative to the Senate, and the Kellogg body choosing P. B. S. Pinchback, the mulatto. Thus the determination of

[1] Senate Report 91, 42d Cong., 3d Sess.

the issue had been transferred to Washington, where a series of major battles had been fought for more than two years. When Senator Carpenter, Republican, a brilliant lawyer, cut the ground from beneath Kellogg and his followers in a remarkable report, it seemed for a moment that the travesty in Louisiana would end. Thoughtful Republicans, nauseated by the action of the drunken Durell, were prone to hold for McEnery, or, with Carpenter, for a new election.

It was at this juncture that Senator Morton, resembling Stevens in his methods, established his claim to the absolute leadership of his party. Ignoring Carpenter's report and his unanswerable argument, Morton applied the whip to wavering partisans as remorselessly as had Stevens. Autocratic, dictatorial, direct, and almost brutal in his methods of management, he scrupled not to employ any weapon in a fight.

Thus nothing was done, and Louisiana was left to the mercy of the President. With a division of sentiment among his counselors, Grant hesitated, preferring to pass the responsibility to others. It was charged, on the responsibility of a reputable man, that he had prepared a message recognizing McEnery, when Morton, in glowering mood, forbade its transmission on the ground that it would cost the party eighty thousand votes.[1] This is given color by the assertion of Morton's biographer that Carpenter had influenced Grant until Morton drove to the White House in fighting trim and Grant had wilted before his fury.[2] The story is plausible enough, since Morton was by odds the stronger man. The result had been the presidential recognition of Kellogg, but the fight in the Senate over the seating of Pinchback had gone on.

II

Meanwhile, in Louisiana the domination of the Custom-House clique had become intolerable. With the people driven to distraction by taxation, the levying of taxes was in the hands of scamps and illiterates without property. Nordhoff, an old Abolitionist, visiting the Legislature, was startled — 'not because they were black, but because they were transparently ignorant and unfit.' [3]

[1] Dick Taylor, *The Nation*, May 20, 1873.
[2] Foulke, ii, 284–85.          [3] Nordhoff, 49.

The most vicious of the ruling element were prospering while the taxpayers suffered. Pass Christian, once the center of elegance and culture, with its fine residences along a beach of five miles' length, had been taken over by the negro politicians, and its social arbiter was now Caius Cæsar Antoine, Lieutenant-Governor by the grace of Grant's decree. Flamboyant, and abysmally ignorant, diminutive, with 'a head like a cocoanut . . . pure type of the Congo,' he was the leader of the Black League bent on the political ostracism of the carpetbaggers.[1] Under the rule of such men, the propertied class was being rapidly impoverished. Scarcely five in a hundred men were not on the verge of ruin. Houses had declined eighty per cent in value in four years. The distinguished citizen who wrote that 'we are all ruined here and to hold property is to be taxed to death by our African communists'[2] painted the picture with fidelity. The auctioneers and pawnbrokers of New Orleans were overworked, since elegant homes were being stripped piece by piece to buy necessities; families once comfortable were selling their beds to sleep on pallets on the floor, and bedsteads of rosewood and mahogany were going for from five to seven dollars. In the spring of 1874, planters were being denied the customary spring advances.[3] One overwrought man, who had seen piece after piece of the family property sold for taxation until only one remained, wrote the sheriff that this was the sole possession of his mother and sister and the day it was put on sale he would attend with his shotgun. 'Now I know the man,' wrote Nordhoff, 'and know him to be a peaceable, law-abiding citizen, one of the most important and most useful members of the community.'[4] In the parish of St. Landry alone within two years 821 plantations had gone for taxes,[5] and there had been 47,491 tax seizures by the sheriff in New Orleans. Parish papers were giving three and four pages to advertisements of tax sales.[6]

To divert attention in the North from these monstrous conditions, the press was fed on fabrications of 'outrages' on 'innocent blacks' and 'loyal men.' Every murder was given a politi-

---

[1] *New York World*, July 23, August 10, 1874.
[2] *Ibid.*, January 8, 1873.
[3] *New York Herald*, October 10, 1874.                    [4] Nordhoff, 59.
[5] *Ibid.*                      [6] *Ibid.*, 62.

cal motive and the victims were usually the negroes, slaughtered by the whites with impunity. Nordhoff investigated the criminal record of a parish controlled absolutely for five years by the Kellogg crowd, where there had been thirty-three murders, and found that thirty-one were of blacks by blacks, one of a white by a white, and one of a white by a negro because of the seduction of the black man's sister. Not one murderer had been hanged.[1] Overtaxed and underprotected, the whites in the black belt, imperiled by the incendiary talk of carpetbaggers, lived in a state of terror, and women were not safe on the highway.[2]

## III

Under these conditions the carpetbag régime determined to disarm the whites. Hunters returning from the hunt were dispossessed of their guns. Negro policemen arrested without cause, beating the victim without provocation, and there was no redress. Women were insulted and assaulted in all parts of New Orleans, and there was no protection. The black militia vied with the police, and the Black League, darling of Antoine, was never so insolent or defiant. In June, nearly every steamboat brought heavy shipments of arms for distribution among the negroes.[3]

Determined to capture the Legislature in the fall of 1874, the whites early began to enroll in the White League, and preparations were made for armed conflict in case of necessity.[4] The color line was drawn by the negroes in the plan to subordinate their white leaders, and Antoine's Black League was busy. The Democrats entered the campaign with an unequivocal declaration for white supremacy. Inevitable clashes occurred — all grist for the 'outrage' mill — and Grant, ordering troops to convenient points, made the customary gesture that had served political purposes well. The climax came when Federal officials began seizing guns consigned to citizens, and denying the native whites their constitutional right to bear arms. Indignation reached white heat — and the rising of the people came.

One September night, in expectation of another seizure, posters flamed, summoning the people to a meeting at Canal Street the

[1] Nordhoff, 49.      [2] Ibid.
[3] Lonn, 254.        [4] Ibid., 259.

next morning. Appealing to merchants to close their stores, 'The Bulletin' asked citizens to speak 'in tones loud enough to be heard the length and breadth of this land' and 'declare . . . that you are, and of right ought to be, and mean to be, free.' [1]

The morning found three thousand armed citizens at the Clay Monument. They were not a faction — they were the major part of the people in revolutionary mood. Nordhoff had found universal detestation of the rulers of the State, and the business men of New Orleans equal to the same class 'in New York, Philadelphia, and Boston.' It was these who had assembled in the open, with guns in their hands. These revolutionists moved with precision and formality. A committee was dispatched to Kellogg to demand his abdication, and was refused admission. The Lieutenant-Governor under McEnery immediately called upon all men between the ages of eighteen and forty-five to arm, assemble as a militia, and expel the usurper. There was a dramatic pause, with negro officials swarming to the State House and Custom-House for protection. Kellogg, in deadly fear, cringed in his office, heavily guarded by metropolitan police.

Thus passed the morning and early afternoon. At three o'clock a large body of armed men, marching in perfect order, began the erection of barricades of paving stones, horse-cars, and boxes. This was revolution. An hour later, General Longstreet with metropolitan police and artillery marched forth to battle, and, greeted by the familiar rebel yell as the revolutionists opened fire, he blanched. Ten minutes was enough — Longstreet's men broke ranks and fled to the protection of the Custom-House. Here, more barricades, another exchange of shots, and the captain of the metropolitan police fell wounded. Papers, still wet from the press, circulated through the excited crowd with a proclamation from Penn, the Lieutenant-Governor, assuring the negroes they had no cause for fear. The cars no longer ran. Night came, with pickets posted along Canal Street, and with the citizen's militia bivouacked in the streets. Thus passed the night.

The next morning, early, there was an unconditional surrender, with the revolutionists in possession of public buildings. Penn was formally inducted into office, and, in due form, all 'legally elected

[1] Lonn, 269.

in 1872' were sworn in. The barricades were speedily removed, business houses opened again, the citizen's militia marched triumphantly through the streets, the McEnery Legislature was summoned to assemble, perfect order was maintained, and Ogden, general of the victors, issued a statement:

'To that God who gave us the victory we commit with confidence and hope the spirits of our heroic dead; and, strong in the consciousness of right, record anew our holy purpose that Louisiana shall be free.'

Mass meetings applauded throughout the country, and it was generally agreed, by all but the radical press, that there had never been a better justification for evoking the right of revolution.

But the people had not won — not until Washington had spoken. The white-faced Kellogg appealed to Grant, who ordered the 'turbulent' people to 'disperse within five days.' They *had* dispersed within five hours after the victory. But that was not all — they were ordered to accept again the yoke of Kellogg, Packard, and Casey; and, to enforce the order, three men-of-war and Federal troops were hurried to New Orleans. Governor McEnery thereupon surrendered the public buildings under protest, and Kellogg emerged from his hiding to resume his station at the State House.

Grant had crushed the rising of the people.

## IV

These incidents only intensified the determination of the people to win the election. The Democrats proclaimed their policy — to employ no negroes who voted against them, to boycott merchants voting with the Opposition, to refuse advances to planters renting land to the Radicals, to publish the names of whites voting the negro ticket and to challenge the Radical speakers in their meetings. The Kellogg party, however, was not disturbed — not with the Federal Army and Government to lean upon. Packard, the Marshal and boss, began arresting citizens without cause, dragging Democratic leaders to New Orleans from distant parishes. Negroes were ordered from the fields to political meetings 'by order of General Butler,' and blacks were threatened with arrest and punishment if they voted the Democratic ticket.[1]  The Custom-House clique set up the cry of coercion early, and put in their plea for troops.

That year even Packard admitted that no more than five thousand whites voted the Republican ticket and that as many as five thousand negroes voted with the Democrats in a State where the whites had a majority.[2]  Packard was in the saddle, in shining armor — the man for the crisis.  He was a leader of courage and iron will, despotic in his sway, utterly without scruples.[3]  He was a master of organization — better still, he knew how to organize victory without majorities.  These, however, were sought, and soon great numbers of negroes from Mississippi, Tennessee, and Alabama were pouring into the upper parishes and being registered.  One parish proudly reported to Kellogg that the previous parity of the races had been overcome, the registration showing two hundred whites to twenty-three hundred negroes — mostly imported from Tennessee.  The correspondent of the 'New York Herald' estimated that as many as fifteen thousand had been brought in within the year.[4]

Efforts were made to bring on racial clashes, and when one occurred, Morton, in Washington, was delighted.  The army was ready — always ready.  But the manipulation of election machinery was the stoutest reed on which to lean.  After the election, an investigation disclosed fifty-two hundred false registrations in New Orleans alone, and a little later Nordhoff attended a court in an upper parish which adjourned for want of a jury because three fourths of the names drawn from the registration lists for jury duty were found to be fictitious.[5]

Election day found the Kellogg party amply protected, eleven companies of Federal soldiers in New Orleans and on the Red River, and a fleet of gunboats frowning from the stream upon a sovereign people.  The ballots cast, the determination of the result passed to a board packed for corruption, which did its dirty work in secret session, but it required two months of manipulation to count a Republican majority in the Legislature.  The delay was due to the hesitation at Washington to give assurances of support

[1] Lonn, 282.           [2] Nordhoff, 41.           [3] *Ibid.*, 63–64.
[4] October 11, 1874.    [5] Nordhoff, 43.

for the conspiracy.[1] The pledge made, the crime followed. Even in the North the press protested against the manifest dishonesty of the count. Bitterness was at white heat; the head of the canvassing board narrowly escaped assassination; and Warmoth, former governor, knocked down in the street, defended himself with a knife and killed his man. It was a clear case of self-defense.[2]

With two results announced, with two legislatures in prospect, and a conflict approaching, Grant sent General Sheridan on a secret mission to Louisiana. He carried authority to assume command in the South and act as he saw fit. A microscopic search of the army could not have discovered a single officer less fitted for the task or more provocative of the people of New Orleans.

## V

The special political functions of Sheridan are clearly indicated in the ignoring of Sherman, head of the army. 'Neither the President nor Secretary of War ever consulted me about Louisiana affairs,' wrote Sherman, who knew Louisiana well. 'Sheridan received his orders directly from the Secretary of War [Belknap] ... I have ... tried to save our army and officers from dirty work imposed upon them ... and may thereby have incurred the suspicion of the President.'[3] Washington knew of Sheridan's hate of the South and his relations with Radical politicians; knew, too, that he was anathema in New Orleans. Entering the breakfast-room of the hotel there, he was 'greeted by hisses and groans.' Pleased, rather than ruffled, he had astonished Hoar of Massachusetts with his idea of restoring peace. 'What you want to do, Mr. Hoar, is to suspend the what-do-you-call-it' — meaning the writ of habeas corpus.[4]

When it was learned that Sheridan was ordered to New Orleans, 'The Picayune' commented that 'if there is one man more responsible than another for the misfortunes of Louisiana, that man is General Phil Sheridan,' and the 'New Orleans Times' saltily observed that 'as a soother of political difficulties and corrector of political abuses ... he is anything but a success.'[5]

---

[1] Lonn, 288; *New York World*, December 26, 1874.
[2] *New York World*, December 28, 1874.     [3] *Letters*, 342.
[4] Hoar, *Autobiography*, I, 208.     [5] Quoted, *New York World*, December 29, 1874.

Events thereafter moved with the rapidity of a screen drama. The Democrats in the Legislature, catching their enemy napping, elected Wiltz, a strong man, Speaker, and organized the House. Within the chamber there was no confusion; in the corridors milled a tumultuous crowd. To clear the corridors, the Speaker summoned General De Trobriand, who appeared with soldiers and fixed bayonets, to announce his purpose to eject five members who had been seated. Thus did Charles I come to America. Wiltz declared he would yield to nothing but force. Clearly embarrassed by the 'dirty work' he was called upon to do, the General hoped this would not be required.

'I am thankful to you, General, for that,' said the Speaker. 'I recognize in you a gentleman and an officer, and while we submit to the United States Government, it is my duty to ask you to use force. Until then the five men refuse to leave the room.'

Thereupon the General ordered his soldiers to put the Radical Secretary in the chair — escorted there by Federal soldiers with bayonets. Wiltz rose to the occasion with the dignity of a Hampden, protesting against 'the invasion of our halls by soldiers of the United States with drawn bayonets and loaded muskets'; and concluded: 'I solemnly declare that Louisiana has ceased to be a sovereign State; that it is no longer a republican government; and I call on the representatives of the people to retire with me before this show of arms.' [1]

The Democrats withdrew, to organize a legislature elsewhere; soldiers guarded the State House with cannon; and Sheridan spurred himself into the picture with the clatter of a cavalryman. He sent his notorious telegram to Washington, reeking with partisanship, packed with misrepresentations of conditions, with the suggestion that, if Grant would proclaim the protesting people 'banditti,' 'no further action need be taken except that which would devolve upon me.'

No such shocking proposal, made with the rattle of a saber, and aimed at the liberties of a people, had ever been made by a responsible American official, civil or military.

[1] *New York World*, January 5, 1875.

## VI

With the Nation stunned, the reaction quickly came in passionate protests and unmeasured denunciation. Here was a propaganda telegram charging that twenty-five hundred people had been murdered in the State since 1868, and a plan to declare the most substantial people of two States bandits, to be dealt with by military commissions. 'Since blood must flow in defense of their liberties,' said a Southern paper, 'then let the streets of the Crescent City again be the scene of the conflict of patriots against the most infamous usurpation.' [1] The 'New Orleans Bulletin' pictured Grant 'grasping his sword to play the part of Cæsar.' [2] Business men from the North, East, West met at the St. Charles Hotel and wired Belknap a denunciation of the charges.[3] Clergymen of all sects and denominations signed a protest against the slander. The Board of Underwriters in resolutions denounced it as a lie.[4] The Cotton Exchange, the Merchants' Exchange Association, the Chamber of Commerce joined in the protest.[5]

The twenty-five hundred murders were figments of the fancy. Practically all political murders had antedated 1868, most murders had been of blacks by blacks 'instigated by whiskey and jealousy,' [6] and in the forty-one murders in the most unruly parish in seven years but three negroes had been killed by white men.[7]

The North, too, rose in protest, and conservative Republicans were dismayed. 'This is the darkest day for the Republican Party and its hopes I have seen since the war,' wrote Garfield in his diary.[8] 'To march a file of soldiers into the Representative Hall of a State . . . will not be tolerated by the American people,' he wrote a correspondent.[9] 'The most outrageous subversion of parliamentary government by military force ever attempted in this country,' said 'The Nation,' [10] savagely attacking the 'banditti' message. Comparing Sheridan's act to that of Claverhouse's dragoons, it declared that 'at no time in the present cen-

[1] Lonn, 302.                    [2] Ibid., 301.
[3] New York World, January 6, 1875.
[4] Ibid., January 7, 1875.        [5] Lonn, 302.
[6] Nordhoff, 55.                  [7] Ibid., 54.        [8] Life of Garfield, i, 519.
[9] Ibid., i, 520; to General McDowell.                 [10] January 7, 1875.

tury would a general in any country in Europe, except Russia, have dared to send such a dispatch to his government.' [1] Bowles, of the 'Springfield Republican,' excoriated Grant for sending soldiers 'on a revolutionary, treasonable errand.' [2] Mass meetings were hastily called at Faneuil Hall, Boston, and Pike's Opera House, Cincinnati, where resolutions denouncing government by bayonets were adopted.[3]

But the climax of protest was the meeting at Cooper Union, New York. Ten thousand outraged people clamored for admission before the doors were opened, and crowded in to the peril of life and limb. William Cullen Bryant, presiding, shaming Sheridan, thought he should have replied to the order so to act by saying that he would 'tear off his epaulets and break his sword and fling the fragments into the Potomac, sooner than go upon so impious an errand.' [4] More tremendous was the philippic of William M. Evarts, leader of the American Bar, and a foremost Republican, merciless in placing the responsibility directly upon Grant. 'I have observed,' he said, ' a growing disposition on the part of the depositories of political power to separate themselves more and more from the popular support of the party that gave them their authority.' [5]

Never had the public turned so ferociously upon Grant.

## VII

Meanwhile, a mighty struggle was on in the Senate. The fight was led brilliantly by Thurman, with Morton, more savage than usual, directing the defense, and forced to fight his fellow partisans. The galleries were tense when Thurman, in fighting mood, rose to offer a resolution calling upon Grant for a report on the strange proceedings. To Thurman it was an opportunity to impress the public with the threat to civil liberty; to Morton, a chance to revive war hates; to Conkling, assisting Morton, an occasion to display his cleverness in a desperate cause. No sooner had Thurman's resolution been read than Conkling suavely suggested adding to the call — 'if not incompatible with the public

---

[1] January 14, 1875.          [2] Merriam, II, 236.
[3] *New York World*, January 17, 1875.          [4] *Ibid.*, January 12, 1875.
[5] *Arguments and Speeches*, II, 574.

interest.' Thurman was thunderstruck. 'It is simply impossible to conceive of any injury to the public interest that can result from the President informing us what took place in New Orleans yesterday.' Then Morton offered his amendment, asking Grant for information 'in regard to the existence of armed organizations in . . . Louisiana hostile to the government of the State and intent on overcoming such government by force.' Utterly reckless in his statements, bent on diverting attention from the issue, Morton surpassed himself in the absurdity of his assertions. 'As many men murdered in Louisiana for political causes in the last six years as fall in many modern wars,' he said.[1]

When, a few days later, Grant's Message appeared, it was evident that Morton had inspired it. Utterly ignoring the solemn issue of the military outrage, the President plunged into charges as reckless as Morton's. Again Sheridan's twenty-five hundred murdered negroes marched in procession. 'The Nation' voiced the popular reaction in its demand for proof, and claimed the privilege of being 'somewhat incredulous about these appalling murders just before election.' [2] The debate dragged along, some, like Conkling, reasoning that Sheridan was really upholding the civil power; some, like Sherman, defending Sheridan's monstrous proposal on the ground that he was not a lawyer; while Morton was constantly interjecting charges of murder against Democrats. The feature of the debate was the masterful constitutional argument and philippic of Thurman, who denounced the Message. 'Nothing so full of errors of statement and of law, nothing so remarkable for omissions of material facts ever emanated from the Executive of the Republic,' he said.

In the end, Morton, standing lash in hand, held his restless majority to its party duty and Grant was voted an indorsement of his action. It was an historic day for the Senate, which formally went on record as finding nothing in the military invasion 'contrary to the spirit of Republican institutions,' and voted down Thurman's amendment to the effect that the Senate's action did not mean 'to approve the military interference of the United States troops in the organization of the Legislature of Louisiana.' By a vote of 32 to 24 it declared that it meant just that — nothing less.[3]

[1] Congressional Record, January 5, 1875.
[2] January 21, 1875.          [3] Congressional Record, March 23, 1874.

But it really meant nothing of the sort.  Pinchback, despite Morton's efforts, never was to be seated, and the Wheeler Compromise was to restore the Democrats expelled from the Louisiana House by bayonets, and thus give that body to their party, while continuing Kellogg in office until January, 1877, immune from impeachment.  This, together with the defeat of the Force Bill, was something of a triumph.

But to Louisianians it meant little.  The taxes continued to drive once prosperous business men to the verge of beggary,[1] and women, even in towns, could not venture on the streets without a pistol.[2]  And Nordhoff still saw negro legislators 'driving magnificent horses, seated in stylish equipages, and wearing diamond breastpins.'[3]

Louisiana was still in bondage, under the shadow of the sword.

That summer Morton lingered awhile in New Orleans with Simon Cameron and Tom Scott, with many visitors, mostly black, pouring in upon him, with Pinchback hovering about him like a shadow.[4]  He was actively campaigning for the Presidency.

## VIII

The events in Louisiana had their reactions in Mississippi, and immediately after sending his notorious messsage on bandits, Sheridan sent soldiers to Vicksburg to maintain the corrupt negro and carpetbag city government.

To grasp the significance of the Vicksburg drama we must have the background of the wreckage wrought by the alien rule of Governor Adelbert Ames.  Whatever may have been the intent of this deadly dull army officer, he lacked the courage or capacity to cope with the criminals around him.  His own election had drawn the color line; the blacks were more powerful than ever, and more exacting with the carpetbaggers.  They controlled the Legislature, one of the most grotesque bodies that ever assembled.  A mulatto was Speaker of the House, a darker man was Lieutenant-Governor, the negro Bruce had been sent to the Senate, a corrupt quadroon was in charge of the public schools, a black, more fool than knave, was Commissioner of Immigration.  The Lieutenant-Gov-

[1] Lonn, 345.        [2] Ibid., 346.        [3] Nordhoff, 43.
[4] New York World, June 30, 1875.

ernor was a merry soul who played high jinks with Ames when he
sought his native North for the hot season, dismissing Ames's
officials and appointing others, amusing himself with the personnel
of the judiciary, pardoning his friends out of the penitentiary —
six being pardoned before their trials.[1] He could be persuaded to
accept a monetary consideration for these favors.[2]

The people were breaking under the confiscatory taxes necessary
to maintain their rulers in the style to which they had become accustomed, and Ames's appeals for retrenchment fell on ears of
stone. He was arrogant, insolent, tyrannical toward the courts,
naming incompetents to the bench, and presuming to dictate
their decisions.[3]

Nowhere was the government such a farce as in Vicksburg,
ruled by incompetents and corruptionists levying destructive
taxes, and darker days loomed with the Republican nominations
for the city election. Scarcely a member of the board of supervisors could read or write, and the whites, paying ninety-nine per
cent of the taxes, had only three officers of their color in the
county. But the nominees for the election were even worse. For
mayor, a degraded white; for the eight aldermanic positions,
seven negroes; for the eight school trustees, six blacks.

The negroes were jubilant, increasingly threatening. Tramp,
tramp, marched the black militia through the streets, muskets
loaded, bayonets fixed. Night after night they drilled, with pickets
posted to search pedestrians for arms and demand their business
abroad. Talk there was of a slaughter of the whites in Vicksburg
on election day, too. The excitement of the negroes, drunk with
power, spread to the county, where they were organizing to march
on the city when called. The chancery clerk, a turbulent negro,
was challenging fate with his speeches: 'There are thousands of
Southern women . . . who would marry negroes to-day were they
not afraid,' he was saying, ' . . . for the white women now see that
the negro is the coming man, that they have control of the State
and city governments.'[4] When the whites accepted the issue and
nominated a strong ticket, the negro Lieutenant-Governor asked
Grant for troops, and Ames hurried back from his home in the

[1] Garner, 298.        [2] *Ibid.*, 299.        [3] Garner, 302–03.
[4] McNeilly, 297.

North to repeat the request. 'No harm can result, for troops are in many of our cities,' he wrote.[1] Belknap telegraphed Grant's refusal and the Democrats won a sweeping victory.

## IX

Encouraged with the triumph, they turned at once to the redemption of the county. With enormous taxes, mounting debts, and brazen stealing, the chancery clerk was refusing citizens access to his books; court clerks were blithesomely putting out fraudulent witness certificates and county warrants; and, with tax-collecting time at hand, it was found that the bond of Peter Crosby, sheriff and tax collector, was defective. When reluctantly ordered by the board, yielding to public pressure, to file a sufficient bond, he announced he would ignore the order. Meanwhile, the grand jury had found indictments against two officials, and that day the taxpayers acted. Ten taxpayers, led by a captain in the Union Army, were instructed, in mass meeting, to call on the officials at the court-house and demand their resignations.

The committee made its demands, met jeering refusals, and reported back; and the meeting resolved to assemble at the court-house at noon and demand the resignations. Marching in orderly procession, the taxpayers found the court-house deserted by all save Crosby, who resigned in writing. The Union soldier was put in temporary charge, guards were stationed about the jail, and the citizens dispersed until the morrow.

Meanwhile, Crosby had hastened to Jackson to be advised by Ames to summon a *posse comitatus* and demand his office; if this proved futile, Ames would send the militia to the scene. It was charged that Ames's Attorney-General had advised the summoning of the negroes of the county to Crosby's aid.[2] Accompanied by Ames's Adjutant-General, and an officer of Ames's staff, Crosby hurried home, and soon runners, bearing handbills urging the negroes to organize and arm and march on Vicksburg on Monday, were rushing over the county. On Sunday, negro ministers urged compliance from their pulpits. Ames, in the mean time, issued his proclamation denouncing the taxpayers as 'riot-

[1] McNeilly, 298.
[2] *Ibid.*, 309.

ous and disorderly persons' and flashed it over the country for political effect.

The news of the arming of the negroes to march upon the town reached Vicksburg on Sunday afternoon. Ames, ignoring the white militia, officered by a former Union soldier, had instructed the negro militia to coöperate with Crosby. Sleepless was that Sunday night, and by three o'clock Monday morning citizen soldiers had assembled to turn back the threatened inundation. The people were ordered to observe the laws and hold themselves in readiness.

At daybreak the watchman in the court-house tower saw a large black army moving on the town and sounded the alarm. The streets were filled with men, women, and children when a hundred mounted men rode out to meet the invaders. Halting his men, the commander rode forward to urge the negroes to turn back. When time was asked to consult Crosby, the request was granted. Meanwhile, not a move was made, not a shot fired. But the lust for battle in the negroes was too strong — they 'had come to fight.' A volley followed, a few fell dead, the rest fled.

From the south, another band was marching on the town, and, riding forth to meet them, the whites routed them easily, with some fatalities.

From down the Jackson road marched a larger crowd of negroes, who were met at the Pemberton Monument and scattered with a loss of twenty-five lives.

Thus the whites, of both political parties, including a hundred former Federal soldiers, prevailed. This was revolutionary; it was force; but it was necessary with the courts in possession of the tyrants and with no recourse from ruin in the law.

Throughout the crisis the people maintained their poise and common-sense. The representatives of Ames agreed with citizens that Crosby should resign and be given a safe-conduct from the town, and citizens battled to protect him. There was no feeling against the blacks. 'Grossly and criminally deceived,' was the verdict upon them by the 'Vicksburg Times.' [1] The negroes scattered to their homes, and absolute quiet was instantly restored. The Northern press justified the rising, and quoted Colo-

[1] McNeilly, 311.

nel Gordon Adams, Republican: 'My God! the whites have borne
and borne until forbearance ceased to be a virtue and almost became a crime.' [1]

At his wits' end now, Ames called the Legislature to his aid,
hoping for authorization to raise a military force to turn against
Vicksburg, but that body refused the responsibility and merely
petitioned Grant for troops. The President issued his proclamation, calling on the people, quietly going about their business, to
'disperse.' A successor to Crosby had been elected and installed.

And just then Sheridan's 'banditti' telegram flashed over the
wires.

And just then Sheridan telegraphed Ames that soldiers were on
their way to Vicksburg.

Crosby and the others were restored, and one of these, not being of the 'banditti,' was soon in jail for the commission of various
crimes.

x

Sheridan had blundered again — he had unified the whites and
intensified their determination to take possession of their government. They would fight in the fall to carry the Legislature, elect
members of Congress and a State Treasurer. They had been
dormant since Dent's failure in 1869. Now they were awake.

The Mississippi revolution began when the taxpayers met in
Jackson and planned taxpayers' leagues in every county, and
issued their call to arms. An impressive memorial was issued
comparing the tax levies with that of 1869. 'For the year 1871 it
was four times as great. For 1872 it was eight and a half times as
great. For the year 1873 it was twelve and a half times as great.
For the year 1874 it was fourteen times as great.' [2]

The situation had become desperate. At the tax-collectors'
sales the month the taxpayers met, half a million acres and four
fifths of the town of Greenville had been offered for sale for taxes,
because the people were striking against such waste. [3]

The cream of Mississippi manhood assembled in State Convention in August, listened to a dynamic, moving speech from

[1] *Cincinnati Commercial*, quoted, McNeilly, 323.
[2] McNeilly, 338-40.          [3] *Ibid.*, 344.

Lamar, conservative and constructive, and adopted a platform in conformity with the spirit of the speech. It was while five hundred of these substantial citizens were standing in the State House yard that the hatred of alien rule was dramatically disclosed. Ames emerged from the mansion, and, crossing to the executive offices, had to thread his way among them. Not a man spoke; not a nod of recognition was given.

That day General J. Z. George was made commander for the battle of the polls. Distinguished in the law, a genius in organization, cautious yet determined, courteous but uncompromising, tactful and courageous, he dedicated himself to the task. It was not a campaign he was to manage — it was a revolution. 'The contest is rather a revolution than a political campaign,' said the 'Aberdeen Examiner,' 'it is the rebellion, if you see fit to apply that term, of a downtrodden people against an absolutism imposed by their own hirelings, and by the grace of God we will cast it off.' [1] The negroes, no longer amenable to the carpetbaggers, raised the color line themselves. The Northern adventurers were alarmed. Had they created a Frankenstein monster? The Republican 'Columbus Press' complained bitterly of the disposition of the negroes to despoil the carpetbaggers. [2]

Then Ames, authorized to organize a negro militia, appointed, as brigadier-general, William Gray, a drunken and debauched negro senator and preacher, and the monstrousness of the act steeled the grim determination of the native whites. While floor leader of his party in the Senate, Gray was peculiarly loathsome, living in open adultery and preaching hatred of the whites. A dictator of his party, the carpetbaggers jumped when he cracked his whip — none quicker than Ames himself. When in a letter to Ames he threatened to slap his face, the utterly subservient Governor replied obsequiously with an expression of his esteem.[3] Exhilarated by his triumph, Gray was soon proclaiming from the platform that Ames was going to send him all the arms necessary for the election and that he would win if he had to kill every white man, woman, and child in the county, which was predominantly black.[4]

[1] *Doc. Hist.*, ii, 394.        [2] *Ibid.*, ii, 396.
[3] McNeilly, 379–80.        [4] *Ibid.*, 377.

Such was the spirit in which the negroes were being drilled and organized, and in lonely places they met at night to listen to harangues from white demagogues fanning racial hate, predicting reënslavement should the Democrats prevail, declaring that Grant wanted them to vote with the carpetbaggers.[1] Here was a menace greater than the Mississippians had yet confronted, and the effect was instantaneous. If there were to be armed bodies of men, the whites, too, would arm; if intimidation was to be used, they, too, would use it; if force was to be employed, they, too, would employ it; if the blacks under the inspiration of the carpetbaggers would march with arms, so, too, would the whites — and they would not yield. Soon Democratic clubs of a semi-military nature were formed in every county, with every able-bodied man and youth enlisting. That seething summer saw but little business done. Merchants abandoned their stores, lawyers their offices, planters their fields, and all gave themselves without stint or ceasing to the campaign. Under the fine organizing genius of George, a whole people was mobilized, prepared for every contingency, and the Democracy moved with banners and transparencies, amidst the firing of anvils and even of cannon. Barbecues by day, mammoth torchlight processions by night, intensified the will to victory.

A new psychology was employed in dealing with the negroes, against whom, in the mass, there was no feeling. The carpetbaggers held the government because of the blacks' support; this support was due to a loss of respect for the native whites; this loss had come from too much patience, which the simple freedmen had interpreted as fear — so ran the new psychology. The negroes' childlike faith in the carpetbagger must be destroyed. Their meetings must be invaded by the native whites facing the adventurers with denunciations as cowards and corruptionists imposing on the blacks. The experiment soon justified itself. Thus there was a singular lack of the old-time arrogance and confidence in the Republican State Convention that fall. Alarmed, a little awed, by the rising of a whole people, it sent a committee to Grant with a plea for troops.[2]

[1] Garner, 373–74.
[2] McNeilly, 382.

## XI

Never before since the days of Prentiss such meetings in Mississippi. Great masses moving from place to place with dash, daring, determination. Old men rising with trembling voices to pledge life, fortune, and sacred honor to the winning of the fight. Youths turning politicians, grandsires urging them to battle for constitutional liberty. 'What a marvelous uprising!' said one man to another. 'Uprising? It is no uprising; it is an insurrection.' Immense crowds moving in orderly procession with bands and banners, pausing on every hilltop to fire cannon. Prancing cavalry on the highways, all homes thrown open for the entertainment of visiting clubs, a people impoverishing themselves by hospitality. Women joyously cooking for multitudes everywhere.[1] The brilliant Lamar, literally inspired, rushing from meeting to meeting, arousing the wildest enthusiasm, without striking a demagogic note. Here the eloquent Gordon of Georgia thundering, there the able Barksdale, of the 'Jackson Clarion,' and, most dramatic of all, Cassius M. Clay, the old Kentucky Abolitionist, penetrating the black belt and calling on the negroes to stand by their own and reject the carpetbagger.[2] These enormous assemblies vibrant with emotion, these barbecues and basket meetings, these long processions of marching men with banners and music, this booming of cannon, put the fear of the Lord into the hearts of the enemy. There was just one hope — if rioting should begin and Grant should send troops.[3] No one understood the danger more than the Democrats.

## XII

With every one armed, even to many of the women, the iron discipline of George maintained order. Ames knew that his only hope was in bloody conflicts that would invite the intervention of Grant. When nothing happened, Ames hastened the organization of a negro militia — which was a bitter challenge. When the mere announcement of his purpose failed to incite the whites to slaughter, he sent a company of negro militia upon a march, without objective or occasion, through Hinds County. Here was a clear in-

---

[1] Smedes, 259-61.        [2] McNeilly, 421.        [3] Smedes, 262.

vitation to attack. But such was the rigid discipline of George that nothing happened.

Even so there were some armed conflicts that served the purposes of politics. In Yazoo City the carpetbag leader, a degenerate ex-Union soldier living with a mulatto woman, advertised a meeting where he would talk on the color line and welcome a reply. When a negro rose to answer, and was howled down, the whites demanded that he be permitted to reply. The crowd boiled with excitement, pistols were drawn, some shots fired, one man fell, and the carpetbag leader fled to Jackson for protection.

A few days later, a more serious conflict came at Clinton, where a Democratic judge was accorded the right to speak at a negro meeting. A quarrel of whites and blacks in the rear of the crowd — blows — shots — a general firing — a mad stampede. Half a dozen whites ran toward the town, a hundred negroes in hot pursuit. One was overtaken, killed, mutilated, stripped; another was shot farther on; a non-combatant white whose house was passed was murdered by the frenzied negroes in the presence of wife and children. Most of the whites were wounded, four negroes killed. Fearful of the reaction, the negroes hurriedly hitched up their mules and lashed them to the military post at Jackson. The town was put under martial law, a former Union soldier in command, and patrols were organized and picketed the roads. Whites of both parties speedily organized two military companies for defense — but nothing happened.[1]

Again the problem was beyond the solution of Ames's dull brain. His impulse was to put the Yazoo carpetbagger at the head of negro troops and send him back. Very well, said the 'Jackson Clarion,' that would justify any course the citizens of the town might adopt. Ames abandoned the idea.[2] Indeed, Ames's days were full of trouble, his nights of disturbing dreams. White men guarded the State House to prevent forcibly the distribution of arms and ammunition to the negro militia, and Ames was warned that the arming of the negroes would be the signal for his death.[3] All he could do was to phrase a proclamation for the inflaming of the North and call on Grant for troops. George protested vigorously to Edwards Pierrepont, the Attorney-General and a decent

[1] Garner, 375; McNeilly, 389.    [2] Garner, 375.    [3] McNeilly, 389.

man, and Ames was told he had the power to summon the Legislature. Until then, Grant refused to move.

That was the last straw. Utterly helpless, deserted by Washington, Ames accepted the request of George for a conference. The leaders sat down in the parlors of the Executive Mansion and agreed upon a peace pact. Ames was to dismiss the militia, turn the arms over to the Federal troops, and send no armed men to Yazoo City. George pledged himself to maintain peace and order — and kept the faith.[1]

A peaceful election, a Democratic landslide. Every candidate for Congress was elected, the Legislature carried, Lamar sent to the Senate he was to adorn. The day before the election, George sent telegrams everywhere demanding the maintenance of peace at all hazards. That many negroes were intimidated by the determination of the whites, there can be no doubt; and not a few actually voted with the Democrats. Senator Revels, the negro, so wrote Grant. 'A great portion of them have learned that they were being used as mere tools,' he wrote, 'and determined, by casting their ballots against these unprincipled adventurers, to overthrow them.'[2] As Grant sat pondering the explanation of Revels, he received a lengthy letter from the Republican Attorney-General of Mississippi putting the blame directly upon Ames.[3]

Ames's reign was drawing to an ignominious close.

## XIII

It was that summer that Charles Nordhoff, traveling in Mississippi, wrote of Ames, that 'his personal adherents are among the worst public thieves. . . . He has corrupted the courts, has protected criminals, and has played even with the lives of the blacks in a manner that, if this fall a good Legislature should be elected, ought to procure his impeachment and removal.'[4]

The result of the election announced, the 'Jackson Clarion' demanded Ames's impeachment. The fact that a negro Lieutenant-Governor would succeed was his one protection; but this man was notoriously corrupt and could be impeached on any one of a dozen charges. He was impeached for bribery. On Washington's

---

[1] Lowry, 403.   [2] Garner, 399.
[3] *New York World*, May 22, 1876.   [4] Nordhoff, 79.

Birthday, articles of impeachment were drawn against Ames. It was not unexpected. The day the articles were presented, Ben Butler, whose daughter had married Ames, sat in the House talking with Beck of Kentucky. The wily lawyer, canvassing the possibilities of conviction, expressed the utmost confidence, but he was clearly disturbed. He assured Beck that if the impeachment proceedings were dropped, Ames would immediately resign. That day Beck told Lamar of the conversation and he sent the word to Mississippi.[1] Thus negotiations were opened with the managers and an agreement reached. The proceedings were dropped; Ames resigned; and the reign of the Mississippi carpetbaggers was over.[2] Leaving an odorous and odious memory behind, Ames hurried back to his home in Minnesota. Time was to soften the hatred into a feeling of pity for a weakling; and he was to live to an extreme old age, to become the golf partner of John D. Rockefeller, Sr., in Florida.

Virginia, Georgia, Texas, Alabama, Tennessee, Arkansas, and now Mississippi, had broken their chains and resumed their sovereignty.

### XIV

In the midst of this fighting, Andrew Johnson had died. He had lived to witness his vindication and to stand in the Senate facing many who had voted to impeach him and denounce Grant's activities in Louisiana. He had lived a tragedy, and there was drama in his taking of the oath. It was a gala occasion for the galleries, and his desk was piled high with camellias, which he modestly had removed. Unobtrusively entering the chamber from the cloak-room, he took his seat. Hannibal Hamlin, who had bitterly assailed him, was also to take the oath, and there was drama in their meeting, too. Would there be a recognition or a rebuff? Meeting Hamlin before the Vice-President's desk, Johnson held forth his hand to him and to Wilson. The galleries cheered. As he turned to resume his seat, a page put a bouquet in his hand. The old fighter seemed annoyed, evidently doubting the propriety. To escape notice, he retired to the cloak-room, where he was surrounded by Senators. Among those on the floor witnessing his vin-

---

[1] Lamar, to General Wathal, 263.　　　　[2] Garner, 405–07.

dication was the disreputable Ashley, the impeacher — and that was drama, too.[1] Little changed Johnson seemed, a little older, a little grayer, somewhat thinner, with the lines in his face a little deeper. If anything, suffering and age had softened his features, giving them a delicacy they had not had before. Soon he summoned an old attaché of the White House to his rooms at the Willard to direct him to where, in his scrapbook, notices about Grant had been pasted. The fire of the warrior had not burned out.

Within three weeks a crowded chamber was listening to the attack. It was on Monday, and he had given notice the Saturday before. It was enough. There was always drama where Johnson moved. He spoke within the rules, but his was a stinging rebuke to both Grant and Sheridan, a ringing demand for the restoration of the supremacy of the civil over the military power in days of peace, and the old evocation of the Constitution. When he referred to the third term aspirations of Grant, and warned that the realization would mean 'farewell to the liberties of the country,' the galleries cheered. He would say to Grant as Cato said to the ambassador of Cæsar; 'Bid him disband his legions, and restore the commonwealth to liberty.' But the most biting feature was the most surprising, and the application was apparent. Describing, with something of the eloquence of Macaulay, the funeral of Queen Mary, consort of William of Orange, the gaudy trappings, the general grief, the procession of the peers and commons, he singled out the honors accorded in the parade to Sir John Trevor, the Speaker of the House. 'Thus was Sir John Trevor . . . publicly ennobled on the 5th of March, 1695. Within a week in the eyes of all England he was the lowest and most degraded among Englishmen. This is what had happened. We saw Trevor . . . leading the House after Queen Mary's coffin. What is it that only seven days later he had to do as Speaker? Standing in his high place, standing there before all the representatives of England, he had to read aloud words to this effect: "Resolved, That Sir John Trevor, Speaker of the House, for receiving a gratuity of one thousand guineas from the City of London, is guilty of a high crime."'

Thus Johnson dealt savage blows to the end.[2]

[1] *New York World*, March 6, 1875.        [2] *Congressional Record*, March 22, 1875.

Perhaps, with that attack, he was content. He was old and weary. With adjournment, he hurried home. The spring and summer found him in his library studying the currency question. In July, he visited the plantation of his daughter, and he had just concluded a chat with his granddaughter when he fell forward on the floor — his left side paralyzed. For a full day he lay quietly in his bed — his mind recurring to the scenes of his early struggles. Another day, and he was dead.

They took him back to the town of the little tailor shop, whither great crowds went on special trains to do him honor. They wrapped him in the flag for which he had fought so gallantly, and pillowed his head on his well-worn copy of the Constitution for which he had fought his greatest battles. All sorts and conditions of men filed by his casket in the court-house, and they then bore him to the hill, near by, that he had chosen for his grave. Among those present was a young reporter on his first assignment for the 'Louisville Courier-Journal,' Adolph Ochs, destined to a commanding position in American journalism. He was impressed with the deep feeling at the grave, with strong men weeping. The casket was lowered, the bugle sounded taps, and the most maligned of the Nation's greatest servants was left alone to his glory.

A summer of drama — Sheridan's sword, De Trobriand's troopers, Mississippi's revolution, the death of Johnson, the trial of Henry Ward Beecher. The old order was changing. No more would Theodore Tilton act as whipper-in for the Radicals — he hurried away to the cafés of Montmartre, never to return. And never again would Beecher feel in the mood to expatiate on the wickedness of political opponents.

# CHAPTER XXII

## THE FALLING OF ROTTEN FRUIT

### I

SO slowly moved events in the opening days of the Congress which met in December, 1875, that even Chamberlain was a bit tardy in opening his gambling-rooms. The Democrats, in possession of the House, were involved in a contest for the Speakership, which soon simmered down to Michael Kerr, of Indiana, and Samuel J. Randall, of Pennsylvania, and the preponderance of sentiment was with Kerr. He was like a steel engraving from the history of the early Republic, austere, passionately earnest, simple, impeccable in his integrity. His fine reserve in the contest set him apart,[1] and soon the 'New York World' declared for him as one who 'always regarded public station as a public trust.'[2] Bryant in the 'New York Evening Post' favored him, and 'The Nation' hailed his election as a pronouncement against privilege and corruption.[3]

Michael Kerr was not only a sound thinker, an assiduous worker in the public service, but a man of Cato-like inflexibility as to public morals. Even so, there was gentleness and tenderness in his nature that made men love him. 'The impression that he made was like that of a tall gray cliff, or a great oak tree, or any other noble work of God. In his grimness, his strength, his fidelity to convictions, his asceticism, there was much of the ideal Puritan about him,' wrote S. S. Cox.[4] His home in a comfortable old-fashioned brick house on a large sloping lawn in New Albany, with its library of well-used books and pictures of Jefferson and Jackson, was symbolical of the man. At the time of his election he was frail, for tuberculosis had already claimed him as a victim. He had the pallor and air of weariness of one who needed sleep and rest. 'As it is,' wrote a correspondent, 'he thinks too much. I doubt if in sleeping his mind rests.'[5]

[1] *New York World*, December 4, 1875
[2] *Ibid.*, December 1, 1875.
[3] December 9, 1875.
[4] *New York World*, August 20, 1876.
[5] *Ibid.*, November 15, 1875.

His innate decency and fairness, however, could not protect him from insults, and because in the assignment of committee chairmanships he gave proportionate representation to the South, he was attacked with positive indecency. Morton fairly frothed with simulated fury, and the cultured Curtis, of 'Harper's Weekly,' was shocked almost to tears. Nast in cartoons played meanly on the name Kerr, picturing the House presided over by 'a mongrel.' [1] Thus the bloody shirt was dragged out early to divert attention from the stealing by 'good men and true,' and never greater need for such diversion. For the House was shaking the tree, and rotten fruit was falling.

## II

The amnesty bill of Randall, removing disabilities from all under the Fourteenth Amendment, furnished the opportunity. Blaine, a candidate, embarrassed by the popularity of Morton and Grant, and conscious of the sagging prospects of his party, offered an amendment, excepting Jefferson Davis. This was intended to draw a defense from Southerners, since any other course would have been craven. Blaine prepared himself carefully to revive all the hatreds of the war. The galleries filled for the spectacle. With fine dramatic effect he stepped into the aisle, and set off his pyrotechnics — one of the most powerful appeals to passion and prejudice ever heard, with malicious bitterness in every word. The Republicans were delighted, and Blaine sat down triumphant. Perhaps the stealing could be covered, after all.[2]

From the point of view of party strategy it would have been as well for the Democrats to have treated the attack with silent contempt; but from the point of view of a Southerner, it would have been worse than base. As Blaine resumed his seat, Ben Hill of Georgia rose, but an adjournment shut him off for the day.

The Georgia orator had opposed secession, but had stood by his own blood and people, and silent he would not be. Returning home that evening saddened but determined, he was beset by Democrats urging caution or silence. He retired early to escape their importunities, and when morning found them on his step,

[1] Harper's Weekly, January 8 and February 5, 1876.
[2] New York World, January 11, 1876.

L. Q. C. Lamar

Zebulon B. Vance

Wade Hampton

Benjamin H. Hill

SOUTHERN LEADERS

he refused to see them. The honor of his people was involved and party considerations were subordinate. When he rose in the House, it was with a sense, and the appearance, of deep solemnity. The Senate was deserted, the House galleries were dense, and he launched into a speech which drew from Proctor Knott the exclamation, 'The man is a giant!' So excellent a judge of oratory as Henry Grady later was to pronounce the speech the best heard in twenty years and 'as sublime as the inspired words that fell from the lips of Paul at Mars Hill.' [1] Meeting Blaine at every point, countering charge with charge, he closed with a peroration of moving eloquence:

'Go on and pass your qualifying acts, trample upon the Constitution you have sworn to support; abnegate the pledges of your fathers; incite raids upon our people; and multiply your infidelities until they shall be like the stars of heaven and the sands of the seashore, without number; but know this: for all your iniquities the South will never again seek a remedy in the madness of another secession. We are here; we are in the house of our fathers; our brothers are our companions, and we are home to stay, thank God.'

In eloquence the honors were even; read after the interval of years, the reply of Hill is more impressive than the attack of Blaine. But Democrats, suffering from an inferiority complex, were afraid to meet blow with blow, and were frightened. The 'New York World,' shocked at Hill's reply, recorded the majority of Southern members as hostile to the tenor of the speech,[2] but in a few days it did tardy justice to the orator who refused to take blows lying down.[3]

But Blaine's speech, as an attempt to divert attention from scandals that struck the Cabinet and crept to the White House, met with the approval of his partisans. It was the one hope. The night of the day he spoke he was literally mobbed with praise at a reception at the home of Mrs. Fish. Mrs. Blaine was hugged. 'Oh, your glorious old Jim!' exclaimed the ladies.[4] Wendell Phillips, referring to the trend toward reconciliation eleven years after Appomattox, wrote hearty thanks for 'the check you have given to

[1] *Life of Hill*, 71.  
[2] *Ibid.*, January 13, 1876.  
[3] *Ibid.*, January 15, 1876.  
[4] Gail Hamilton, 378-79.

this ridiculous gush which threatens to wash away half the hall-marks of the war.' [1]  Charles Emory Smith sent assurances that 'Republicans are stirred and enkindled.' [2]  Others were not so sure.

But the momentary reaction among Republicans was maddening to Morton, also a candidate, who thought Blaine had invaded his own special territory, and, seizing on the Mississippi election, he rushed to the center aisle, crippled though he was, with the bloody shirt and waved it more aggressively if not so artistically. He made no such virile and handsome figure as Blaine when he grasped the banner.  Standing with difficulty, leaning on his crutch, he read his speech, replete with bitter phrases, and there was just a touch of pathos in the picture.  Disease was making inroads, and he seemed but a feeble echo of his former self.  A correspondent thought it a mistake to attempt the speech standing, since 'there was more grace in his action swaying from side to side in a movable chair.'  But the presidential convention was not remote and he stood to create a false impression of physical fitness.[3] The spirit within 'his enfeebled body seemed like a caged lion and visible always through the bars.' [4]  He knew the futility of his effort — the House was Democratic.  But Mississippi was a staff on which the bloody shirt could flutter in the campaign.

A few evenings later, the Pinchback clan gathered in Morton's rooms and plans were made to reopen the fight for the admission of the Kellogg 'Senator.'  It would furnish a pretext for reviving the war hates again; and so a few days later, Morton again held forth on Louisiana with tales of bloody outrages on 'loyal men.' But, alas, Pinchback had become a bore even to the patient correspondents, and that of the 'New York Tribune' was offering a marching air:

> 'Pinch, brothers, pinch with care,
> Pinch in the presence of the Senataire.'

### III

But all the gasconading of Blaine and Morton could not distract attention from a scandal that was shaking the Nation.  The induction of Benjamin H. Bristow into the office of Secretary of

[1] Gail Hamilton, 381.              [2] Ibid., 381.
[3] New York World, January 24, 1876.              [4] Ibid., January 25, 1876.

the Treasury had been an evil hour for the corruptionists. For
years the press had been charging corruption in the whiskey tax.
A ring had been formed with General John McDonald, supervisor
of internal revenue at St. Louis, as the leader, composed of internal revenue officers and distillers, with accomplices in Washington and the Treasury. These conspirators had been reaping a
golden harvest through the abatement of the whiskey tax. Bristow found a startling discrepancy between the amount of liquor
consumed and shipped and that on which taxes were paid. Mc-
Donald, notoriously unfit, had been appointed to his post over the
earnest protests of the two Republican Senators and all the Republican Congressmen from Missouri. The fight against him
found him serenity itself. 'They need not trouble themselves,' he
said. 'I know General Grant better than any of them, and I shall
be appointed.' [1] And he was right. In the early stages of the conspiracy, it was represented as a plan for raising campaign funds,
and this seems to have been thought legitimate. This pretense was
maintained through the life of the conspiracy, money from the
Whiskey Ring flowing freely into the campaign chest of 1872,[2]
with as much as thirty thousand dollars being sent to Indiana, on
the solicitation of Morton.[3]

Even so, the conspirators were primarily interested in feather-
ing their own nests. Boasting of their power in Washington, and
flaunting their money, they lived brazenly, far beyond the means
of an official salary in a petty position.[4] Certain it is that complaints sent to the Secretary and even to the President brought no
results; and when an 'investigation' was occasionally ordered, an
agent susceptible to a bribe was given the mission.[5] Warning was
also sent ahead by Avery, the chief clerk of the Treasury, who was
on a regular salary from the thieves.[6]

All went smoothly until January, 1874, when the unan-
nounced appearance of a Treasury agent in St. Louis caused so
much uneasiness that McDonald sent one of his associates to
Washington, where he was assured that nothing prejudicial would
be reported. That autumn, Grant, accompanied by Babcock,

---

[1] Statement of William Grosvenor, editor of the *Missouri Democrat*, McDonald, 39.
[2] *Ibid.*, 42.          [3] *Ibid.*, 51.
[4] *Ibid.*, statement of Grosvenor, 45.          [5] *Ibid.*, 44.          [6] *Ibid.*

visited the St. Louis Fair as McDonald's guest, stayed at the Lindell Hotel at his expense, and accepted a valuable team of horses. The ringsters provided the horses with a complete outfit — harness, blankets, a buggy whip costing twenty-five dollars, and gold breastplates with Grant's name engraved — and, chartering a special car, sent them on to Washington. Soon the President was driving his team about the city and its environs.[1] The appearance of the presidential party with McDonald in the presence of twenty-five thousand people caused some little stir.[2] That December, McDonald went to Washington personally to present Babcock with five thousand dollars as part of the swag, according to his story,[3] and certain it is that the Whiskey Ring did give the President's private secretary a twenty-four-hundred-dollar diamond shirt stud, and, on Babcock's complaint that it had a flaw, another and a more expensive one was given.[4]

In April, 1875, the clouds began to darken. Another Treasury agent mysteriously had appeared in St. Louis. There had been no warning. McDonald hurried to Washington, to find both Grant and Babcock out of town, and saw Bristow, who asked embarrassing questions. Going to Commissioner Douglass, the consternation grew with the discovery that Douglass knew nothing of an agent being sent. He was perceptibly embarrassed — even more so was McDonald. It was a good time to retire, and McDonald and some of his associates resigned.

A month later, Bristow seized distilleries, found abundant evidence, and McDonald and others were indicted; more indictments followed later. Babcock, lingering with Grant at Long Branch and in deadly fear of an informer, was assiduously cultivating the head of the ring.

Meanwhile, former Senator John B. Henderson, special prosecutor in the whiskey cases, was delving deep, learning much, and exhibiting a distressing indifference to results. Whispers were heard that much had been found involving Babcock; that Henderson would demand an indictment. More — that with the rumors of evidence implicating Babcock, the Attorney-General had advised the District Attorney to submit the evidence to him be-

[1] Rhodes, VII, 184; McDonald, 99.
[2] Ibid., statement of Grosvenor, 45.
[3] McDonald, 110.
[4] Rhodes, VII, 184.

fore determining his course and that Bristow had objected.[1] The President's ringing declaration, 'Let no guilty man escape,' no longer impressed press or public.

Then came the first sensation.

In the trial of the chief clerk of the Treasury, Henderson, prosecuting relentlessly, and thundering his closing argument to the jury, pointed unmistakably to the implication of Babcock. 'What right had Babcock to go to Douglas to induce him to withdraw his agents? . . . What right had the President to interfere with Commissioner Douglas . . . or with the Secretary of the Treasury? None — and Douglas showed a lamentable weakness of character when he listened to Babcock's dictates.'

The news flashed over the wires to Washington and instantly came the dismissal of Henderson. With characteristic courage he had stood by his speech and had no apology to make. This dismissal, at the moment it was understood Henderson was pressing for an indictment of Babcock, created an ugly impression. Press correspondents informed their readers that the real cause of the dismissal was the necessity of saving the President's secretary.[2] Among the conspirators there was jubilation — the removal of the leader meant the demoralization of the prosecution.[3] It was openly charged that Grant had tried to prevent the indictment of Babcock by destroying the force of the prosecution.[4] Meanwhile, behind the bars, McDonald in an interview was paying tribute to Babcock as 'one of the nicest little gentlemen you ever saw' who 'was a particular friend of mine.'[5]

IV

With an indictment inevitable, Babcock, involved in his civil capacity, demanded a military court of inquiry, since he was in the army. The motive was plain — he feared a civil court. Grant thought the civil process would yield to the military until his mind was disabused by the lawyers in the Cabinet. Even so, the request was granted. Again the press was puzzled. He asks a military court, as did Butterfield, said the 'New York Herald.' It added

---

[1] *New York Herald*, December 16, 1875.          [2] *Ibid.*, December, 13 1875.
[3] *Ibid.*, December 14, 1875.          [4] *New York World*, December 10, 1875.
[5] *Ibid.*, December 2, 1875.

that the questions involved 'affect the integrity of the supreme office of the land.' [1] It was said that just before the indictment was announced, a private message from Washington directed that the evidence be turned over to the court of inquiry, which would have deprived the District Attorney of the evidence before the grand jury.[2]

Babcock was hurrying to Chicago to the court of inquiry, when he was overtaken by the indictment, and the jig was up. Came then the maneuverings between the indictment and the trial. The lawyers for Babcock were convinced that he could not be convicted on the evidence. There was a haunting fear of an informer turning State's evidence and furnishing missing links in the chain. Less than two weeks before the trial, district attorneys engaged on the whiskey cases were astounded by instructions from the Attorney-General sharply shutting the door to immunity on any one turning State's evidence. The intent was clear — to close the mouths of possible informers. The careful guarding of these instructions from publicity, until a Chicago paper found and published them, made them seem all the more sinister. The House called for an explanation, and the Attorney-General answered with a quibble.

Meanwhile the press was complaining that the White House had become the headquarters of the Babcock defense.[3] The Washington correspondent of Whitelaw Reid's paper was saying that the President was in conferences with those who habitually referred to the prosecution as 'the conspiracy against Babcock.' [4] Then followed the President's deposition as a character witness, in which his memory seemed bad. From a private citizen it would have been utterly worthless; but the defense surrounded it with the glamour of Grant's name, and the successor of Henderson in the prosecution created another courtroom sensation by denouncing its use.[5] Babcock, who had clamored for a court of inquiry, restrained himself from taking the stand; the court instructed decisively for the defense, and Babcock was declared not guilty. Serenaded by a Government band and given a purse of ten thou-

---

[1] December 4, 1875.          [2] *New York Herald*, December 10, 1875.
[3] *New York Tribune*, February 23, 1876.          [4] *Ibid.*, February 22, 1876.
[5] *Ibid.*, February 21, 1876.

sand dollars by his admirers, he returned to Washington and resumed his work at the White House. Two days after the announcement that he had resigned [1] he jauntily appeared at the Capitol with a Message, to be received regally by Administration Senators, and 'even Morton dragged himself from his seat to welcome the returned prodigal.' [2] Another scandal breaking on the Administration made his position untenable, and he was given another and an obscure appointment and soon dropped from sight.

## V

The Emma Mine scandal involving the American Minister to Great Britain, R. C. Schenck, in a messy transaction was now nauseating the judicious on both sides of the water, and when an attempt was made to save him, the 'New York Tribune' observed sarcastically that 'General Grant always stands by a friend in trouble . . . though . . . involving the Government in disgrace.' [3] But there was no hope for Schenck. We have met him before, haunting the banking house of Henry Cooke, and sailing away on his mission with the assurance that on his return he would be provided for by the house of Cooke, but, alas, he was to resign under fire and return to find the house of Cooke in ruins. There was no shelter there.

And then, the public still busy with Babcock and puzzled about Schenck, scandal stalked into the Cabinet and laid its dirty hand on Secretary Belknap and the beautiful Mrs. Belknap, queen of the Administration social circle. Here was something to shake society with its incredible melodrama. A real estate agent with a personal grudge made serious charges and Clymer, chairman of the House Committee on Expenditures in the War Department, summoned him before the committee. He furnished a list of witnesses to call, including Caleb P. Marsh. Stark drama touched two members of the investigating committee, making it sheer tragedy. The wife of Blackburn of Kentucky had been a girlhood friend of Mrs. Belknap at Harrodsburg; and Clymer had been a roommate of Belknap at Princeton University. Never a more remarkable case of women dominating a play. Sixteen

[1] *New York World*, February 27, 1876.       [2] *Ibid.*, March 1, 1876.
[3] February 15, 1876.

years before, Mrs. Belknap had lived awhile in the same hotel in Cincinnati with the wife of Marsh. The intimate friendship had persisted until the year before. The two, both strikingly handsome, dashing, and gay, had gone to Europe together. Then came a quarrel; and when the scandal broke, Mrs. Marsh in vengeful mood demanded that her husband tell the truth.[1] He had slipped into Washington, however, to consult with the Belknaps and had spent the night at their home, and it was Mrs. Belknap who proposed that he perjure himself with a fantastic story of her concoction. He declined. He appeared before the committee. The pretty Mrs. Marsh, bewitchingly attractive, was along, and 'poor little Marsh trotted along by her side like one who knows he is in the midst of enemies, but feels that his protector is at hand.' It was she who embarrassed the committee most with her vamping, until Clymer blushed and looked out the window and Robbins was so confused that 'he got up and went for a drink.' [2]

This, then, the story: Almost six years before, the Belknaps, with Mrs. Bowers, the second Mrs. Belknap, spent the summer at Long Branch, where the Marshes were staying. Mrs. Belknap and Mrs. Bowers, on leaving, visited Mrs. Marsh in New York; and, the then wife of the Secretary of War becoming ill, the visit was prolonged. One day, in possible appreciation of his kindness, the first Mrs. Belknap proposed to Marsh that he apply for one of the lucrative post-traderships on the frontier. She would see that he got the place, and she coyly added that of course he would not forget her in the profits. Soon thereafter the arrangements were completed and Mrs. Belknap began receiving her remittances. In a few months she died, leaving a baby; and after the funeral, the sister, soon to become the second Mrs. Belknap, took Marsh to the nursery. Looking at the child in the cradle, he said: 'This child will have money coming to it before a great while.' 'Yes,' was the reply, 'the mother gave me the child and told me that money from you I should keep for it.' Thereafter the remittances were made to Belknap, with the understanding that it was to be transmitted to the second wife — in trust for the child. In truth, it was all squandered on luxuries to maintain the ambitious woman's commanding status in society. It was she who planned the

[1] *New York World*, March 25, 1876.    [2] *Ibid.*, April 3, 1876.

explanation for Marsh to give the committee. He was to testify that for years he had been a business agent for her, and that money sent to Belknap was her money sent on request. This he refused to do, though strongly tempted. 'Mrs. Belknap is a fascinating woman,' he said sadly to a reporter.[1] With the testimony of Marsh the committee was stunned.

## VI

The night the news flashed over the wire, W. E. Curtis, a newspaper correspondent, hurried in a hack to the Belknap home at 2022 G Street, where he found the accused man seething with rage and showing fight. He would face his accusers and force a retraction. In truth, this was but a pose, for he had already told Blackburn he would confess to anything if the investigation could be dropped and Mrs. Belknap protected. It was a painful appeal to the chivalric Kentuckian because of the girlhood relations of their wives, but he could make no promise.[2]

That night found Belknap sleepless. His one thought was the protection of the woman he idolized. Perhaps there was a way out — he would resign and prevent an impeachment. Early on the morrow, in dire distress, worn, haggard, with eyes bloodshot and swollen, he surprised Grant at the White House, as, hat in hand, he was about to leave for a studio. Just what occurred has been lost in the multiplicity of versions. According to one, Bristow had preceded the Secretary of War, and was in the midst of a recital of the charges when Belknap entered, accompanied by Chandler. The miserable man, almost incoherent, gave a rambling account of what had occurred and offered his resignation with a plea for its immediate acceptance. 'I understood,' Grant is reported to have told an Illinois Congressman, 'that he was expecting an investigation that he would avoid by resigning; that the facts, if exposed, would not damage him so much as his wife. He spoke of his dead wife, too. . . . So I wrote him a letter accepting the resignation.'[3] According to this report, Grant was so unnerved by the ordeal that he spent the whole of the afternoon with his son, walking on the river-bank in the rear of the White House, talking to relieve his mind.

[1] *New York World*, March 6, 1876.    [2] *New York Herald*, March 4, 1876.
[3] *Ibid.*, March 7, 1876.

Quite a different story is that of the 'New York Tribune,' which pictured him strolling down the avenue immediately after the scene and sitting to a portrait-painter for an hour and a half with such serenity that the artist suspected nothing of his distress.[1] However that may be, Grant's complicity in the attempt to shield the confessed corruptionist from impeachment was bitterly criticized at the Capitol and denounced in the press.[2]

The scandal brought consternation to the Capitol. In the Senate, the Republicans were dazed, gathering in groups, and Morton hastily left for the White House. Humorously enough, it was Simon Cameron who fumed the most and cursed the loudest. Conkling and Edmunds, flushed and furious, conferred with tight lips. When the false report spread that Belknap had shot himself, one Senator bitterly snorted, 'Oh, no, he hasn't shot himself, but he ought to.' The Democrats, if jubilant, restrained their joy. It was Senator Bayard who first voiced the generally accepted explanation of the scandal. 'I own my house in Delaware; I own my house here; I have no rent to pay; but I cannot afford to dress my wife as these Cabinet Ministers' wives are dressed.'[3]

More dramatic the scene in the House. In a deathlike stillness, Clymer, pale and wretched, rose to propose the impeachment of his Princeton chum. His voice trembled, and once or twice he choked with emotion and was compelled to pause. Quite as torn was Blackburn. The night before, clasping her baby in her arms, the beautiful 'Puss' Belknap had walked alone against the wind and rain to the Blackburn home to throw herself on her knees before him, pleading against an impeachment and taking the blame on herself.[4] It had not been easy, for the haughty lady had been prone to make the most of the advantage of her higher official position over the wife of the Kentuckian with whom she had played in childhood. The vision of that piteous face was before Blackburn as Clymer choked. Near by sat Blaine, pale and haggard, shaking his head. The election was so near.

'Mr. Speaker,' Clymer concluded tremulously, 'I would not if I could, and in my present condition I could not if I would, add anything to the facts just reported to the House.'

[1] March 3 and 4, 1876.          [2] New York Herald, March 3, 1876.
[3] New York World, March 3, 1876.          [4] Ibid., March 8, 1876.

The debate was brief. Hoar, of Massachusetts, fought for time, challenging the right to impeach after a resignation had been accepted. Blackburn, irritable from the memory of the night before, replied hotly: 'The action of the President in accepting the Secretary's resignation under the circumstances was unprecedented, and this is the first instance in the history of the country where any man claiming manhood and holding an exalted station has sought to shelter himself from legitimate investigation by interposing the dishonor of his wife.' The House stirred, uneasily — it was not the first time the sentiment had been heard. 'If the man who uttered the memorable sentence "Let no guilty man escape" holds it in his power to rob an American Congress of its right to inflict punishment or to pronounce censure on a publicly convicted criminal, where is the barrier to be found beneath whose shelter the liberties of the people can rest secure?' When a nervous applause greeted the attack, the opposition subsided, the vote was taken, and the articles of impeachment were unanimously agreed upon.

## VII

The immediate reaction was a wave of sympathy for the lovely lady admired by all. Her charm and fascination of manner, her radiant beauty, her cleverness, the elegance of her gowns, made the men merciful, and the women, who liked her for her graciousness and hospitality, forgot to envy her in their scorn of the husband accused of trying to hide behind her skirts. Her notable devotion to the child of her dead sister momentarily wiped out the disturbing memory of her pearls and diamonds, the magnificence of her gowns from Worth's. 'It is one of the pleasant features of this deplorable business,' wrote a correspondent, 'that her own sex with one accord commiserate Mrs. Belknap. While possessed of every charm of mind and person which would seem calculated to excite the envy and jealousy of the women, she has so conducted herself toward them as to win their admiration and esteem.' [1] The day after an impeachment was voted, every woman with a carriage was abroad crusading for the wife and gunning for the husband. Public sympathy was with her. Prostrated with fever, unable to

[1] *New York Herald*, March 3, 1876.

leave her bed, so changed in appearance that an old friend entering her chamber scarcely recognized her, she was an object of commiseration.[1] Belknap remained at home, receiving army officers and friends who called to divert him.

The storm had broken on Thursday; on Sunday wild rumors were afloat that the Belknaps planned flight. They were to go by river to Norfolk, thence to Boston, thence by the Cunard Line to Belgium, with which we had no extradition treaty. True or not, a warrant was sworn out, and the once proud couple tasted the dregs of humiliation. Arrested at his home, Belknap was permitted to remain there under guard. The curious pedestrian passing the house at night noticed only a lone policeman in front leaning against a tree. Low lights burned on the lower floor, but above they were brilliant and figures could be seen moving about the room. Next door lived another victim of the tragedy — Babcock had been forced to resign; but the lone policeman guarding Belknap was regaled with merry singing and piano music in the Babcock house.[2] That night Mrs. Belknap appeared at the door to beg the officer to come inside and watch there, but, finding other officers in the rear, she drove him out again. It was an unhappy evening.[3]

Within three days, Belknap was arraigned in police court and gave bond; the guards were removed; the pretty Mrs. Belknap recovered her erstwhile poise; company poured in upon her, to be received with the familiar smile and charm; and soon her carriage was seen rolling through the streets, the lady as beautiful as ever and as proud. A visitor found her lying on a blue satin sofa in an exquisite morning robe covered with the richest laces, and the wave of sympathy subsided.[4]

### VIII

But Belknap's troubles were not so soon over. His friends rallied around him, resorting to many devices, some questionable, to save him from impeachment. Scarcely had the House committee appeared at the bar of the Senate when the chairman and other

---

[1] *New York Herald*, March 5, 1876; *New York World*, March 6, 1876.
[2] *New York World*, March 7, 1876.      [3] *New York Tribune*, March 6, 1876.
[4] *Chicago Times;* quoted, *New York World*, March 11, 1876.

members of the committee were summoned by subpœna before the Supreme Court of the District and instructed to bring all books, papers, and evidence relating to the case. A bitter debate followed in the House. A clear attempt to intimidate witnesses and throttle the impeachment, declared one member. The fiery Blackburn used blunt speech. 'I do not like to charge,' he said, 'that it is the purpose of the Executive to intimidate witnesses, to throttle investigations, and to afford immunity from punishment to publicly convicted criminals. But I do say this: that this is the result, and unless this gag process is stopped, the country will believe, and I will believe, that such is the purpose.' Blaine attempted the hypocritical pose that his side of the House was interested in securing an indictment, and, striking a plumed-knight attitude, defied the Democrats to withhold the evidence. Lamar answered, denouncing the court's summons 'as an outrage on the privileges of this House.' Blaine, unhappy in a contest with Lamar on a legal question, and gently led into traps, had recourse to the bloody shirt, referring to 'another gentleman from Mississippi, Jeff Davis.' Lamar closed with the demand that the House 'see to it that its constitutional rights and its powers are respected,' and the committee was instructed to ignore the summons of the court.

But in the Senate the fight for Belknap was renewed on the question of jurisdiction after the resignation. A bitter debate dragged along through the month of May, Morton and Conkling denying jurisdiction, with Thurman and Bayard asserting it; but in the end the trial was ordered to proceed. The vote to proceed had disclosed the lack of the two thirds necessary to impeach. Sympathy was veering from Mrs. Belknap to her husband. He appeared at the trial in the spirit of a spectator at a comedy after a tasty dinner. Unconcerned and jovial, he laughed heartily at the thrusts of counsel,[1] and Julian thought him 'looking rosy and happy.'[2] Hoar of Massachusetts, one of the managers of the impeachment, closed his demand for conviction with an ugly indictment of the times: 'The Hallam or the Tacitus or the Sismondi or the Macaulay who writes the annals of our time will record them with an inexorable pen. And now when a high Cabinet officer . . . flees from the office before the charges of corruption, shall the

---

[1] *New York World*, July 12, 1876.     [2] MS. Diary, April 30, 1876.

historian add that the Senate treated the demand of the people for its judgment of condemnation as a farce, and laid down its high functions before the sophistries and jeers of the criminal lawyer?'

That is precisely what the Senate did. Politics played its part, with even Matt Carpenter, attorney for Belknap, stooping to remind the Republican Senate that, while Belknap was a 'Union man' and a Republican, the accusers were merely Democrats, and he waved the bloody shirt to the music of his eloquence. The vote was taken, thirty-five voting to convict and twenty-five to acquit — almost a party vote. Morton voted to convict, 'having,' according to 'The Nation,' 'an abounding sense of the folly of giving to his opponents in the coming Presidential election such a deadly weapon as the discharge of Belknap by his own party.' It thought 'all the proceedings [were] thoroughly bouffe' and hardly could have been made more so 'by music and a dance by all the company at the end.'[1] And so, rosy and jovial, Belknap stepped forth free and independent to practice law in the capital and maintain his pretty wife in Paris during the next twelve years. Appearing at the inauguration of Harrison in the dining-room of the Arlington, Mrs. Belknap resumed her magic sway over the imaginations of men, and that summer she was the sensation of Coney Island, then a fashionable resort. In a French bathing-suit of red and white, with bare arms and short skirt and silk stockings, she captivated the men on the sands and outraged their wives on the piazza of the Oriental Hotel, and figured again in the public prints. Once more she was installed in an establishment her husband could ill afford, but she was little at home, preferring to meander about to livelier places. Thus she was away when Belknap died in his office. He was carried to Saint John's for his funeral; distinguished men bore him to Arlington; Harrison ordered the War Department draped, to the disgust of the purists, who thought it 'an offense to public morality.'

Thus the Belknaps pass from history.

## IX

In the midst of the impeachment, Belknap was robbed of his first-page position in the press by a stirring drama in the House,

[1] *The Nation*, August 3, 1876.

where Blaine was fighting ferociously for his honor. Seven years before, while Speaker, he had entered into arrangements with Warren Fisher, Jr., of Boston, to interest himself personally, for a handsome consideration, in the sale of the bonds of the Little Rock and Fort Smith Railroad. A little while before, he had rendered a service to the road in one of its land-grant bills, and, while this was not improper, he unhappily reminded Fisher of it when discussing the arrangements for his personal participation in the bond sale. A satisfactory agreement being reached, in the fall of 1869 he sold to friends in Maine $125,000 of the first mortgage bonds, for which that money was received by Fisher, who made the delivery. The purchasers under the Blaine sale received as a bonus $125,000 preferred stock and the same amount in common stock. Had they been accorded the treatment of investors elsewhere, they would also have received $125,000 land-grant bonds — but this bonus went to Blaine as a commission. In addition, he was given $32,500 first mortgage bonds as brokerage. There were other transactions of a similar character, which, given publicity, would not have endeared the candidate to his friends or have received the applause of the public.

Then the Little Rock and Fort Smith bubble burst — the road was financially embarrassed, the bonds lost value, and Blaine's friends were resentful of their broker. Should they demand an investigation, there would be an *exposé* of the manner through which they had been taken in by their trusted friend. There was but one course open — take back the bonds, reimburse the purchasers.

But how to raise the money — that was the problem. Suddenly three railroad companies, including the Union Pacific, bought heavily of the Little Rock and Fort Smith bonds, despite their market standing, and it was whispered that the roads had thus served Blaine at a loss to themselves with the thought of equalizing matters through Blaine's influence on legislation in the House. Later, Tom Scott, of the Union Pacific, was to testify that he had owned the $75,000 in bonds that went to that road, but this Pennsylvania politician and notorious lobbyist for railroad legislation was not above suspicion.

Early in April, the newspapers flamed with astounding charges

against Blaine. There had been mutterings two months before
Blaine finally appeared in the House with a sweeping denial.[1] His
partisans were now jubilant. Their idol had spoken, and that was
that. Even 'The Nation' was satisfied that he had vindicated
himself.[2] But three days later, the melody of triumph was broken
by a discordant note. A Union Pacific director, curious about the
Little Rock and Fort Smith bonds held by the road, had proposed
an investigation, and the secretary of the board had begged him to
drop the matter, since Blaine was involved. Dumbfounded, the
director [3] took another director with him [4] to satisfy himself that he
had heard aright. Yes, they were told, an investigation would kill
Blaine. It was afterward, when the secretary was testifying before
a Republican congressional committee, that the director telegraphed the chairman suggesting certain questions, which were
not asked. A letter was then written the chairman — it was not
answered.[5]

With gossip growing louder, the Democratic House ordered an
investigation, and just when vindication seemed certain, despite
some distressing revelations, James Mulligan, of Boston, by common consent of contemporaries and historians, an honest man,
appeared before the committee with some startling evidence. He
had kept accounts for Fisher in the matter of the unfortunate
bonds, and had been informed by Elisha Atkins, a Union Pacific
director, that Blaine had given the $75,000 in bonds to Scott, who
had insisted that the Union Pacific take them at $64,000. Blaine
was listening intently. After all, it was not so bad. It was Mulligan against Scott. But suddenly Blaine stiffened, his countenance
fell, and he whispered to a Republican member of the committee
to move an adjournment. This is what he had heard — that
Mulligan was in possession of some of Blaine's letters to Fisher
which Blaine had thought had been returned to him.

That afternoon the capital buzzed and hummed, the Belknap
trial forgotten; and at the Riggs House, Blaine sat in conference
with Mulligan, Atkins, and Fisher. Blaine demanded the letters,
and they were refused. He begged for their return to save himself
from ruin and his wife and children from humiliation. Mulligan

was cold. Could Blaine see the letters? The request was granted, and he read them carefully more than once. When Mulligan returned to his own room, Blaine followed, and again securing the letters on the promise to return them, he kept them.

Another conference that day, this time with lawyers, who assured Blaine that the letters had no relevancy to the inquiry and need not be given to the committee. It demanded them, and was refused.

Meanwhile, the entire country was talking of nothing else; the National Convention was approaching with Blaine leading the field. The situation was desperate. Blaine, with fine audacity, playing for a mighty prize, was meditating action. There was turmoil and anxiety in the Blaine home. Mrs. Blaine was writing her son in Boston warning him against chastising Mulligan, since 'nothing could be worse for your father than notoriety of that kind.'[1] Anxious politicians with conflicting advice were passing in and out. 'Isn't the suspense hard to bear!' wrote Mrs. Blaine.[2]

It was the day after that a tremendous drama was staged in the House with Blaine the star performer. Rising in a tense House packed to suffocation, standing like a gladiator in the middle aisle, with flushed face and scornful mien, he declared the investigation aimed at him. It had been intimated among his friends that Morton, a rival candidate, had inspired the inquiry.[3] But it was not at Morton that Blaine aimed. Obsessed always with the value of the 'bloody shirt,' he charged his troubles to the exasperation of the Southerners. Had not two members of the investigating committee been in the rebel army? Passing to the inviolability of private letters, he reached the climax of one of the most historic speeches in history. 'I have defied the power of the House to compel me to produce these letters. ... But ... I am not afraid to show the letters. Thank God Almighty, I am not ashamed to show them. There they are' — and he held them above his head — 'There is the very original package. And with some sense of humiliation, with a mortification I do not pretend to conceal, with a sense of outrage I think any man in my position would feel, I invite the

[1] *Mrs. Blaine's Letters*, 135.          [2] *Ibid.*, to Manley, 136.
[3] *New York World*, June 6, 1876.

confidence of forty-four million of my countrymen while I read these letters from this desk!'

Did he read them? That he read part, and failed to read some is certain; that he read all in the letters he pretended to read is not known. He read as he pleased, interpolated as he would, but his friends were delighted. The very audacity of the act, the perfect drama of the delivery, was superb. And then, with the genius of a masterful stage director, he closed with the most dramatic, though meaningless, feature of all.

A none too reputable man in London, responding to the solicitation of Blaine's friends, had wired Proctor Knott, chairman of the committee, corroborating the sadly messed testimony of Tom Scott, and the telegram had not been presented. Turning to Knott, Blaine asked if he had received the telegram, and then announced the day and hour of its delivery. The House roared with hysterical applause, and Blaine sat down with the House throbbing with a marvelous ovation. Proctor Knott thought the exhibition 'One of the most consummate pieces of acting that ever occurred upon any stage on earth,' and Garfield had never seen such a scene in the House. But History has reversed the verdict as to the vindication. 'Blaine's defense was a master stroke,' says Rhodes the historian, 'but it was that of a criminal in the dock.' [1] The 'New York World' observed that 'Mr. Blaine's *coup de théâtre*, his audacity, and his desperation seem to make the country forget for a moment what is really due to truth, propriety, and good breeding.' [2] 'The Nation' thought 'it was an unseemly exhibition in which Ben Butler ought to have figured,' and that the 'audacity' and 'pluck' could be found 'in abundance among the faro bankers of this city.[3] But for the moment Blaine had triumphed — if he could only last until the convention, nine days off.

An ugly winter with a presidential campaign at hand — Babcock, Belknap, Blaine. If only the cry of 'stop thief' could be raised against a leader on the other side. A notorious person had been accusing Michael Kerr, the Speaker, of selling a cadetship outside his district. No one believed it, but Kerr was deeply stirred. In the midst of such corruption the public might believe anything. Seriously ill, in the last stages of consumption, he de-

[1] Rhodes, vii, 204.     [2] July 9, 1876.     [3] June 15, 1876.

manded an immediate investigation and his vindication was
complete. 'The Nation,' paying tribute to his integrity, and
scoring the investigation, predicted that the effect had been fatal
to his health and that he would not return to Washington when he
left in search of health.[1] Two months later, with S. S. Cox at his
side, this Mid-Western Puritan died at Rockbridge Alum Springs,
leaving the memory of a life without stain.

Meanwhile the National Conventions had met and nominated.

[1] June 15, 1875.

# CHAPTER XXIII

## THE YEAR OF THE CENTENNIAL

### I

THE Sunday following his great histrionic effort, Blaine fell senseless on the steps of his church, and the Cincinnati Convention was at hand. Every effort was made by his managers to reassure his friends, for he was easily the most popular of the candidates. Throughout the West, and in Pennsylvania, he had become a fetish with many thousands. No love was lost between Blaine and Grant, and the special champions of the latter were enemies of the former. Two of Grant's Three Musketeers were aspirants, but he was unable to help them much, and Bristow, another candidate, though a member of his Cabinet, Grant would have liked to serve with the tip of his boot. Conkling's candidacy was confined to New York, and Morton's extreme radicalism, together with his physical condition, operated against him. He was the favorite of the carpetbaggers and the negro leaders in the South, but the East disliked him for his money views, and reformers found him intolerable. These latter were loyal to Bristow, but, aside from being a man of courage and honesty, there was nothing in his character or career to arouse enthusiasm. The same was true of Rutherford B. Hayes, Governor of Ohio, whose candidacy was not taken seriously.

Thus, until the last moment all indications pointed to Blaine's triumph. Brilliant, strangely magnetic, eloquent, militant, sagacious, he was blessed with personality. He had the dash, virility, audacity, and spectacular qualities of popular leadership. There were warmth and seduction in his smile. He had been assiduous in the cultivation of the money groups, realizing that the party could not win forever with bayonets and the negro. Thus he supported the Grant régime without being of it — Conkling and Morton had seen to that. These were the idols of the Stalwarts and they dubbed Blaine the Halfbreed.

A month before the convention, Blaine seemed certain of victory. Feeling that 'his newly acquired wealth, and his connection with money interests depending on legislation' would damage him, Hayes could not see that he had been 'damaged by the investigations,' nor in any way to prevent his nomination.[1] As the convention approached, the Administration set found little to encourage its hope for the nomination of either Conkling or Morton. The superciliousness of the former had offended many leaders; the latter smacked too much of the old imperial sway of which the country was sickening. His enemies described him as 'a powerful man but a bad one.'[2] The rallying of the discredited Southern leaders to his standard was being described as 'the last stand of the carpetbaggers.'[3]

On one point all the leaders could agree — the necessity of defeating Bristow. Grant was hostile, as were Conkling and Morton. And so was Blaine. 'I have never been enthusiastic for the nomination,' wrote Mrs. Blaine in June. 'The interest I had is that it should not go to Bristow.'[4] Only one of the candidates had a kind word for him. 'I am not sure but that he would be the best candidate we could nominate,' wrote Hayes in his diary. 'I am sure I prefer him to any other man.'[5] There were points of resemblance in Hayes and Bristow. Both were rather dull, commonplace men, with a regard for honesty; and they had a common resentment — the bosses were against them.

With the crusading fervor of idolators, the Blaine followers swept upon the convention city, and a really marvelous orator, all the more effective because then comparatively unknown, sent them into a frenzy of enthusiasm with a militant nominating speech that could have been set to music. Robert G. Ingersoll, with magnificent presence and golden voice, and witchery in the use of words, unleashed the hounds of sectional hate to run down the memory of Mulligan. It was music superb, but not conclusive. Blaine led. Morton followed, Bristow trailed after Morton in the beginning. In the end, Hayes's very weakness won.

Conditions exacted the nomination of Samuel J. Tilden by the Democrats. The issue was corruption and reform, and he had

[1] Diary, *Life of Hayes*, I, 432–33.    [2] *New York World*, February 7, 1876.
[3] *Ibid.*, June 14, 1876.    [4] *Mrs. Blaine's Letters*, I, 136.
[5] *Life of Hayes*, I, 431.

fought corruption and wrought reforms. Able men were in the field against him, Hendricks, Thurman, Allen. The test of strength came in the election of a temporary chairman, and with the selection of Henry Watterson the triumph of Tilden was assured. The journalist sounded a ringing keynote on corruption; the Watterson denunciation was echoed in the platform; and Tilden was nominated with Hendricks.

In comparison, the Republican platform was colorless, and in places humorous, in view of the conditions. With Babcock, Schenck, Belknap hounding their party to the very sounding of the gavel, it was difficult seriously to read that the party rejoiced 'in the awakening of the conscience of the people'; or, in the light of the record, the affirmation of 'opposition to further grants of public lands to corporations and monopolies.' Each party denounced its opponent for cowardice in dealing with the resumption of specie payment, and both were right.

Thus the two tickets entered the field.

II

With the nominees both men of integrity, with similar views of inflation and resumption, there was a scurrying about among the Republican insurgents of 1872 to determine their allegiance. Lyman Trumbull went to Tilden along with Charles Francis Adams. Some, like Julian, hesitated. The tone of the Republican Convention had depressed him. 'Blaine with all his stock-jobbing record . . . was only defeated by a blunder of his friends,' he wrote in his diary.[1] He wanted to go with the Republicans, but the platform endorsement of Grant, 'a stupid blunder and a shameful piece of knavery and cowardice,' would have to be withdrawn.[2] At length he determined not 'to trifle with [his] conscience,' and he cast his lot with Tilden.

Carl Schurz shocked many of his former associates by going to Hayes. 'Shows himself weak, inconsistent, and vacillating,' wrote Julian.[3] From no one did Schurz receive such an excoriation as from Joseph Pulitzer, in a letter to 'The World':[4] 'Who, pray, is Mr. Hayes?' he asked his old comrade in arms. 'What great public service has he ever rendered, what eminent ability has he

[1] June 25, 1876.    [2] *Ibid.*, July 16, 1876.    [3] *Ibid.*, July 16, 1876.    [4] August 2, 1876.

ever shown, what reform ever accomplished, what independence of character displayed, what public or private virtues manifested, to merit the dazzling dignity of filling the place once ennobled by a Washington and a Jefferson? The answer came — Hayes has never stolen. Good God, has it come to this? . . . Four years of dull mediocrity in Congress, and five years of mediocre dullness in the gubernatorial chair stare us in the face, without a single act of reform, without a single thought or utterance of ability, without a single vote of independence to redeem the long record of obscurity — with nothing to justify it but pretended personal respectability. If Mr. Schurz will show but a solitary vote which Mr. Hayes ever declined to give for his party, or a single word of protest against any of the many wrongs committed by the party, I shall consider him right and myself wrong.'

But Schurz was unmoved, and soon he and Zack Chandler were equally zealous for Hayes and Reform. Godkin, of 'The Nation,' had been shocked when Chandler, the supreme spoilsman, was put in command as chairman. 'Just think of a Civil Service Reform party making Zack Chandler chairman of the Executive Committee!' he wrote. And yet, when Schurz wrote him a warm letter about Hayes, Godkin wrote: 'I suppose we must support him in "The Nation," but I confess I do it with great misgivings.' [1]

The choice was scarcely less difficult for William Cullen Bryant, of the 'New York Evening Post.' He thought no living man better fitted for the Presidency than Tilden,[2] and, comparing the candidates, thought 'Mr. Tilden the best, the most of a statesman, the soundest and most enlarged in opinions . . . and of the firmest character'; but like Schurz he could not abide Democrats.[3] Even after he had cast his lot with Hayes, he was pathetically insisting that 'Tilden is the abler and the more thoroughly a statesman.' [4]

But Charles Francis Adams took the Democratic gubernatorial nomination in Massachusetts, and Julian plunged vigorously into a speaking campaign with a speech at Indianapolis, so powerful that a million copies were circulated. Thus both escaped the embarrassments that pursued Schurz throughout because of the managerial tactics of Chandler, who was collecting a slush fund

[1] To Norton, Ogden, ii, 112–13.  [2] To Bigelow, *Life of Bryant*, ii, 376.
[3] To Derby, *ibid.*, ii, 377.  [4] To Miss Gibson, *ibid.*, ii, 379.

from Government employees through rank intimidation. Letters the most brazen, signed by him and Simon Cameron, that other crusader for Hayes and Reform, were found and published,[1] and Schurz, beside himself, protested to Hayes, who did not act. He never wrote to Chandler, never demanded his retirement, and accepted the fruits of his labors with Christian fortitude.

### III

There was no doubt of the superior ability and statesmanship of Tilden. He had trained himself for public life with the care of a member of the English aristocracy. In boyhood he had steeped himself in Jeffersonian philosophy, and in his father's home he had listened to the conversations of Van Buren and Silas Wright. As a youth he had heard Chancellor Kent read the final preface to his 'Commentaries.'[2] As a mere boy an article of his, aimed at the coalition of the Anti-Masons and the Whigs, had so impressed Van Buren that he had arranged for its publication over the signatures of leading Democrats; and the effect was such that Thurlow Weed had ascribed it to the pen of Van Buren himself.[3] Throughout the remainder of the life of the Wizard of Kinderhook, Tilden had sat at his knee as a disciple — a favorite pupil. He had written two powerful articles in support of Jackson's Nullification Proclamation[4] and luminous and forceful papers sustaining his war upon the moneyed aristocracy.[5] He had bitterly protested against a sectional party in the Convention of 1860, taking the floor twice against sectional divisions.[6] He believed the war unnecessary at the time, and to the end of his life.[7] But when the storm broke, he took his stand for the Union, and throughout the war was loyal, while asserting the right to criticize its direction. Thus he had opposed the policy of financing the struggle, favoring loans supplemented by taxes, with no non-interesting-bearing Treasury notes. He had the prescience to foresee the inflation of prices, the depreciation of Government securities, the impossible premium on gold.[8]

[1] New York World, September 27, 1876.  [2] Life of Tilden, I, 26.
[3] Ibid., I, 27.  [4] Ibid., I, 34.
[5] Ibid., I, 38–41.  [6] Ibid., I, 154.  [7] Ibid., I, 163.
[8] Ibid., I, 170–71.

Ten years before his nomination, he had enlisted in the fight against corruption, fought the Tweed Ring, and purged the party. As Governor he had fought the Canal Ring, and had made a profound impression by his philosophy of government incorporated in his messages and speeches.

Three years before, in resigning the State chairmanship he had issued a clarion call to his party, in an exposition of fundamental principles that established his status as an intellectual leader. He saw, as few men did, that the fight in reconstruction days was the same as that which Jefferson had waged against the Federalists. 'What the country now needs,' he said, 'is a revival of Jeffersonian democracy, with the principles of government and rules of administration, and . . . the high standards of official morality which were established by the political revolution of 1800. . . . The demoralizations of war — a spirit of gambling adventure, engendered by false systems of public finance; a grasping centralization, absorbing all functions from the local authorities; and assuming to control the industries of individuals by largesses to favored classes from the public Treasury of money wrung from the body of the people by taxation — were then, as now, characteristic of the period. The party that swayed the Government, though embracing many elevated characters, was dominated as an organization by the ideas of its master spirit, Alexander Hamilton. Himself personally pure, he nevertheless believed that our people must be governed, if not by force, at least by appeals to the selfish interests of classes, in all forms of corrupt influence. . . . As a means to the reaction of 1800, Jefferson organized the Democratic Party. He set up anew the broken foundations of governmental power. He stayed the advancing centralization. He restored the rights of the States and of the localities. He repressed the meddling of Government in the concerns of private business. . . . He refused to appoint relatives to office. He declined all presents. He refrained while in the public service from all enterprises to increase his private fortune. . . . The reformatory work of Mr. Jefferson in 1800 must now be repeated.' [1]

Such was the political character of Tilden. At the time of his nomination, he was in his sixty-second year, a tall, slender man

[1] *Life of Tilden*, I, 320–24.

of spare figure and with health more delicate than robust. Because of his frailty he had never married, and he lived in a fine old mansion in Gramercy Park among his books and pictures, following gracefully the even tenor of his way. 'A veritable Sir Roger de Coverley in his gallantries' toward young girls he loved to amuse and make happy, the home in Gramercy 'was as unchallenged as a bishopric,' and no breath of scandal ever reached him. He was most charming in his home with a few congenial friends, dining frugally and sipping his 'whiskey and water . . . with a pleased composure redolent of discursive talk, of which . . . he was a master.' Henry Watterson, who could appreciate such a personality, thought him 'a man of the world among men of letters, and a man of letters among men of the world.' [1] Perhaps no other Democratic leader has ever so closely resembled Jefferson in the quality of his philosophy and in his personal tastes.

A great lawyer, he was seldom seen in court; a brilliant political leader, he rarely appeared upon the platform. He was the lawyer of the closet and the leader of the conference room. Thus, notwithstanding his fame, an astonishingly few personally knew him. He had many admirers and few close friends, though to these he was deeply devoted. One of these was pained at his lack of personal popularity and thought that among men of remarkable powers he had never known one 'who attached people to him so little.' [2] And yet Julian, a Westerner, entertained at dinner in Gramercy Park, found him 'genial, familiar, and very instructive,' with 'nothing of the coldness that is attributed to him.' [3] In intellect, character, capacity, Tilden suffered nothing in comparison with any one who has ever held the Presidency.

## IV

Rutherford B. Hayes was concededly the intellectual inferior of Tilden. A man of average capacity, he was of the commonalty, destitute of dash or glitter. Physically handsome, he was kindly and gentle in manner and speech. Though of impressive appearance, and possessed of a well-modulated voice of great range, he was not an orator. He was neither philosopher nor thinker. His

---

[1] *Marse Henry*, I, 273–74.      [2] Bigelow, *Retrospections*, v, 291.
[3] MS. Diary, December 10, 1876.

very mediocrity gave him the presidential nomination — he invited no jealousies. His character was as unblemished as that of Tilden. In some ways puritanic, he was all conventionality. He had no petty vices. If Tilden sipped wine and whiskey and soda frugally, Hayes did not drink at all. Every Sunday found him in his pew, and he had some of the elements of piety. As incorruptible as Tilden, he lacked Tilden's courage to give battle to corrupt forces. Throughout the campaign the character of Tilden completely overshadowed that of Hayes. The former entered largely into the discussions of the speakers; there was nothing to be said of Hayes.

v

From the beginning all the advantage seemed with Tilden — business bad, unemployment general, the panic still taking its toll of poverty. The dismal procession of scandals in high places was the common topic of the breakfast tables. Babcock, Robeson, Belknap, Blaine, furnished the lurid background of the battle. The farmers were still on a rampage, and laborers were in a revolutionary mood. The consummate politician in his library in Gramercy Park had never been so active, leaders moving in a constant stream into his house. A great fear fell upon the dominant party. The mystery of Gramercy Park was appalling. A month after his nomination, Hayes sat in his grove at Fremont reading a disturbing warning from Whitelaw Reid that Tilden, 'the most sagacious political calculator I have ever seen,' was 'singularly confident.' [1] The sensitive souls under Zack Chandler, at headquarters, were sure it was bad taste for Tilden to maintain such close relations with his managers, and a former President of Yale was deeply grieved.[2] The corruptionists were quite as shocked with Tilden's activities, and turned on him with fang and claw. True, Hayes was in constant touch with his managers, conferring with such men as Morton and Blaine. The former, alarmed at the trend in Indiana, had hurried to Hayes with a gloomy story and the request for one hundred thousand dollars for the campaign there, and the candidate had not been shocked.[3] Soon Tilden was

---

[1] Cortissoz, i, 345.     [2] *Life of Hayes*, i, 469, note.
[3] Hayes diary, August 13, 1876; *Life*, i, 478–79.

being personally assailed with a malignity seldom seen in American politics. He was a corporation lawyer, a tax-dodger, a trickster, a double-dealer; and Weed's absurd story of the year before — 'He drinks, they say, dreadfully and neglects his business' — was being whispered about.[1]

Meanwhile, with Democratic speakers thundering denunciations of corruption and privilege to wildly enthusiastic multitudes, the managers of Hayes settled down to a definite plan of campaign. They dragged forth the bloody shirt, dyed a deeper red, and began spluttering epithets at the Democrats.

## VI

The one argumentative point their speakers urged was that, regardless of the financial views of Tilden, the nomination of Hendricks and the influence of the West would mean inflation and the indefinite postponement of resumption; but even this was limited in its appeal to industrial and financial centers. Manifestly there was but one course open — to revive sectional hatreds, refight the war, align the Democrats with 'rebels,' and arouse religious prejudice. The platform makers at St. Louis had warned against these two false issues. 'Harper's Weekly,' under the intellectual guidance of Curtis with the aid of Nast, had been picturing the Democrats as bartenders, thugs, and Papists for some time, and there was a revival now. The well-known views of Hayes made it a simple matter to conjure forth the 'menace' of the foreigners. He was unfortunately found to be on more than speaking terms with the American Alliance, and while he made a denial there was silence after General Franz Sigel declared from public platforms his personal knowledge of Hayes's membership.[2]

But the chief reliance was on the bloody shirt. Blaine had pointed the way in his amnesty speech the previous winter; had evoked it again in his own defense in the incident of the Mulligan letters; and Ingersoll had used it in his famous nominating speech. It had served its purpose well in former days — why not again? But measuring the need by the desperation of the situation, it was determined to surpass the malignity of previous campaigns. Soon the platforms rang with the most bizarre charges. Tilden's

---

[1] *Life of Tilden*, I, 285.          [2] *New York World*, October 9, 1876.

election would mean the recognition of immense claims of the South for damages sustained in the war. The Confederate soldiers would be pensioned. 'The main question,' said the 'Cincinnati Commercial,' 'is whether the voters of the North want to pay the bills of the Southern Confederacy.' All this was promptly met by Tilden with a letter of denial, and no one believed such statements but the ignorant — but the appeal was to ignorance.

To make the most of such appeals, a master pacemaker must be found — and thus Robert G. Ingersoll moved into the picture and to the head of the procession. An orator of tremendous force and charm, he had captivated the country by his nominating speech, and every one was eager to hear him. Soon he was on a triumphant tour, the outstanding and most popular Republican orator of the campaign, and smaller men were parroting his speeches. The Republican press was printing his astonishing assertions with approval, the ignorant were shouting their assent. The money question was shunted aside. 'A Bloody Shirt campaign and plenty of money and Indiana is safe; a financial campaign and no money and we are beaten,' wrote General J. Kirkpatrick from Indianapolis, to Hayes. This letter, found in the reading-room of the Grand Hotel, was published in the 'Indianapolis Sentinel' and throughout the country.[1]

To get the color of the campaign waged by the party in power let us follow Ingersoll about on his tumultuous tour.

Hear him in Bangor, Maine, attacking the Southern whites: 'The white Democrats . . . were as relentless as fiends. They killed simply to kill. They murdered these helpless people, thinking in some blind way that they were getting their revenge upon the people of the North.'

And Tilden? 'He never gave birth to an elevated noble sentiment in his life . . . a legal spider watching in a web of technicalities for victims . . . a compound of cunning and heartlessness . . . who believes in the Democratic doctrine of States' rights.' [2]

At Cooper Union, New York: 'Recollect that the men who starved our soldiers and shot them down are all for Tilden and Hendricks. All the hands dipped in Union blood were in the Democratic Party.'

[1] *New York World*, August 22, 1876.     [2] *Speeches*, Dresden edition.

And then on to Indianapolis, where he reached his grand crescendo:

'Every State that seceded from the Union was a Democratic State. Every ordinance of secession that was drawn was drawn by a Democrat. Every man that endeavored to tear the old flag from the heaven it enriches was a Democrat. Every man that tried to destroy the Nation was a Democrat . . . Every man that shot down Union soldiers was a Democrat. . . . The man that assassinated Abraham Lincoln was a Democrat. . . . Every man that raised bloodhounds to pursue human beings was a Democrat. Every man that clutched from shrinking, shuddering, crouching mothers babes from their breasts and sold them into slavery was a Democrat. . . . Every man that tried to spread smallpox and yellow fever in the North . . . was a Democrat. Soldiers, every scar you have on your heroic bodies was given you by a Democrat. Every scar, every arm that is missing, every limb that is gone is the souvenir of a Democrat. . . .' Yes, the question is, 'Shall the solid South, a unified South, unified by assassination and murder, a South solidified by the shotgun — shall the solid South with the aid of a divided North control this great and splendid country?'

And Tilden? 'Tilden says we are a nation of thieves and rascals' — referring to the Democratic excoriation of corruption among the politicians in power. 'If that is so, he ought to be President. But I denounce him as a calumniator of my country; a maligner of the Nation. . . . When Chicago burned, railroads were blocked with the charity of the American people. Thieves and rascals do not do so.'

Pausing in the midst of this abuse, the orator interspersed one of the most magnificent passages in all literature — 'The past rises before me like a dream . . .' [1]

Then on to Chicago: 'Every titled thief in Great Britain should like to see Tilden and Hendricks the next President and Vice-President of the United States. . . .' And here, with exquisite humor, he who was thus preaching hate, predicated on misrepresentations, went on: 'Every Democrat that is a Democrat is a Democrat because he hates something; every man that is a Re-

[1] *Speeches*, IX, 157–87.

publican is a Republican because he loves something. . . . I am proud that I belong to the Republican Party. . . . It is the first decent party that ever lived.' [1] Of corruption not a word; of the subordination of the civil to the military power, not a line; such was the strategy.

The Republican orators followed Ingersoll. The press did its bit. It took the words of Ingersoll, 'the brave Southern heroes who dipped their hands in Union blood are for Reform and Tilden,' put them into the mouth of Vance of North Carolina, and invited the fury of the North. Godkin, of 'The Nation,' calling attention to the fact that Vance had quoted the sentiment 'to repel it with scorn,' denounced the waving of the bloody shirt.[2]

Anticipating Ingersoll in Indianapolis, Voorhees protested against these methods. 'I understand the tactics of the enemy in this fight perfectly,' he said. 'They will denounce the people of the South — this is cheap. They are helpless, then abuse them; they are powerless, then malign them. They are not here to answer, then manufacture lies about them, misleading the people.' [3] Thus the corruption with which the public service reeked was ignored by the strategists of the dominant party, and only Mark Twain blundered into an admission of its existence in a political speech at Hartford in praise of General Hawley, the president of the Centennial Commission and a candidate for office, as having presented 'the most astounding performance of this decade . . . impossible perhaps in any other public official in the Nation.' He had 'taken in as high as $121,000 gate money at the Centennial in a single day and never stole a cent of it.' [4] The audience blushed as it laughed, and the humorist was finished on the stump.

Meanwhile, the Hayes strategists were more and more alarmed over the South. They had lost six of the Southern States, and in the others the native whites were in battle array as never before. In October, when the Democracy swept Indiana and West Virginia and cut the Republican majority in Ohio to a narrow margin, the realization grew that by hook or crook electoral votes had to be had in the South. That month Hayes wrote the National

---

[1] *Speeches*, IX, 191–223.        [2] September 7, 1876.
[3] *New York World*, August 18, 1876.
[4] *Ibid.*, October 3, 1876.

Committee that 'we must look after North and South Carolina, Florida, Mississippi, and Louisiana.' [1] In Mississippi there was not even a fighting chance. From Louisiana distressing news was trickling. The Democratic gubernatorial nominee was meeting a procession of unprecedented ovations, and 'it was a noticeable feature . . . that the negroes came arm in arm, side by side, with the white men, not merely out of curiosity, but bearing a banner blazoned with the names of Tilden and Hendricks.' [2]

In North Carolina the woods were on fire, ringing with the name of Vance.

## VII

The Kirk war had inflicted a deadly wound on the carpetbaggers. The Democrats had recaptured the Legislature, and now they were determined on the election of a governor. The night they placed the banner in the hand of Zebulon B. Vance, the idol of the people, an immense throng had stood in front of the National House in Raleigh, swaying, shouting, their bosoms heaving, their eyes glistening, listening to his acceptance of the leadership. His customary touch of humor was missing; he told no stories. He who had been War Governor spoke rather in tones of pathetic eloquence on the ruin wrought by the revolutionists, of the waste, corruption. With hand dramatically uplifted he exclaimed: 'Thank God, no dishonest dollar ever soiled these hands.' Every one knew it to be true. And so he went forth that night on a crusade that to him was holy, with the prayers and the cheers of the people.

His career had been romantic. Out in the hills of his boyhood he had learned his Scott, his Shakespeare, and his Bible, and his well-stored mind redeemed the crudity of his clothes and his home-made shoes when he appeared in college at Chapel Hill. The boy was father to the man. Joyous, witty, eloquent, tactful, he studied hard and remembered what he learned. At twenty-eight, and even then in Congress, the brilliant Corwin recognized him as a kindred spirit. Regardless of his youth, he plunged into debate, trying with wit and humor to calm the sectional storm then raging. Crusading against secession from the platform, his hand was raised in a fervent plea for the Union when word was brought that

[1] *Life of Hayes*, I, 485.    [2] *New York World*, October 24, 1876.

Lincoln had called for volunteers. He himself has told the story. 'When my hand came down from that impassioned gesticulation, it fell slowly and sadly by the side of a Secessionist. I immediately with altered voice and manner called upon the assembled multitude to volunteer, not to fight against, but for North Carolina.' [1]

Answering his own appeal, he raised a company for the South, the 'Rough and Ready Guards,' soon to be summoned from the field to the chief magistracy of the State. In this capacity he fed and clothed the soldiers as few did, maintained the supremacy of the civil power, compelled respect for the civil courts, and throughout the South the only spot where the writ of habeas corpus was never suspended was in North Carolina under Vance. Faithful to the end, he was made a prisoner; and so captivated were his captors with his personality that they let him ride ahead, taking his word he would not attempt escape. In the Old Capital Prison in Washington he lighted the gloomy precincts with his wit, and Tom Corwin, calling, declared that 'a man who can face extremities like this with cheerfulness and be the life of the prison cannot remain here if Tom Corwin can get him out.' [2] Within seven weeks he was back in North Carolina — still the idol of the great mass of the people. In the trying days that followed, he was irreproachable in his conduct, his spirit reflected in his address at the university at Chapel Hill: 'The noblest soldier now is he that with axe and plough pitches his tent against the waste places of his fire-blasted home, and swears that from its ruins shall arise another like unto it.' [3]

A fine figure of a man he was, more than six feet tall, with handsome features, steel-gray eyes that could twinkle merrily or flash with anger. His large, shapely head was covered with thick, glossy hair. His chest was full and heavy, his neck thick and short, his hands noticeably white and well formed. A boyhood fracture had left one leg slightly shorter than the other, a defect all but concealed by a high heel on one shoe. His personality was at once strong and endearing, magnetic to a degree. In a throng he was as a magnet among steel shavings. In social relations, gay, courtly, he admired women and loved the society of the cultured. He was a student, too, a lover of Scott and Dickens, none too busy in the

[1] Dowd, 441.        [2] *Ibid.*, 33.        [3] *Ibid.*, 404.

midst of war to read Motley's 'Dutch Republic.' Literally adored by the rough men of the mountains, he was a favorite in the drawing-rooms of the aristocratic Whigs.[1]

As an orator and debater, North Carolina has never had his equal, and it was the opinion of 'Sunset' Cox that he was 'the greatest stump speaker in America.' The essence of his eloquence was in his warmth and manifest sincerity. Capable of strong statements and destructive ridicule, he preferred the more generous, friendly manner, wit not too bitter, mimicry more humorous than hurtful. His extemporaneous campaign speeches, while argumentative and simple in diction, were often interspersed with brilliant imaginative flashes and some floridity. Always there was richness of thought and infinite variety of treatment. With an instinctive sense of dramatic values there was snap and dash in his delivery. In the mingling of pathos and humor he was a master. His prepared speeches were more literary in their phrasing, his notable tribute to the Jews in his lecture 'The Scattered Race' an example. His voice was soft, musical, of great flexibility, and in its higher notes clarion-like and thrilling.

Such the man who had put North Carolina on the march.

## VIII

The Republican nominee, Judge Thomas Settle, literally designated by Grant, was able, honest, gentlemanly, a worthy foeman. The two men who faced each other in debates have been compared by a contemporary: 'The two men . . . in the language of the countryside could be compared to a bull terrier and a game cock. Vance had the strong face and body and the savage desire to tear to pieces. Settle fought with a certain neatness, never condescending to frivolity.' [2] This means that Settle would have been at a disadvantage before a popular assembly were all things equal — and they were not. The two leaders set forth on their travels, courteous as two knights. After the fight was over, Settle was to testify that 'in all our heated campaign . . . Vance never quibbled or prevaricated.' [3]

Thus these were great debates, multitudes of frenzied men and

[1] *Old Days at Chapel Hill*, 101.   [2] *Southern Exposure*, 103.
[3] Dowd, 194.

women listening, sometimes hysterical in their enthusiasm for Vance, who had the advantage in crowds. His very presence was a thrill to his followers, and when he rose, the groves shook with the shout — 'Vance! Vance!' Speaking rapidly, every sentence the crack of a whip, he brought the people to their feet, and when he closed, they sought to carry him in their arms. More than once he had to plead for a hearing for Settle.[1] 'The mountains are afire for Vance,' said the correspondent of the 'Raleigh Sentinel.'[2] Settle blundered by making bitter partisan speeches, for that day was over for the Radicals of North Carolina. When Vance at Rutherfordton made a powerful attack on the Civil Rights Bill, Settle countered with a racial appeal to the negroes.

A typical scene, that at Bakersville. The mountain roads were a mass of animated humanity. The streets were swarming. Settle entered the town with an escort of eighty young men and boys, with flags, astride as many rat-tailed mules. The followers of Vance went out on the road to meet him in great numbers on horses and afoot, and marched in with greater pomp and dignity, escorting their hero to the boarding-house, where they gave three cheers. It was here that Vance began bombarding his opponent with questions:

'Was Holden's suspension of the habeas corpus legal?'
'Which of the Constitutional Amendments is good?'
'How did the South get out of the Union?'
'Were the Reconstruction Acts constitutional?'
'Can Congress confer the right of suffrage?'
'Was the Louisiana outrage constitutional?'
'Did Judge Settle approve of the Grant Administration?'[3]

The enthusiasm for Vance was irresistible. Old men on horseback rode fifty miles, over the rockiest and most dangerous roads, fording streams. Some rode across the Blue Ridge from South Carolina. Men tottering with age marched with the Tilden Clubs, impressive processions on dusty or muddy highways, dragging a cannon and firing it at frequent intervals. Soon Vance was matching the bitterness of Settle. 'If I owned a full-blooded Radical,' he said at one meeting, 'I would swap him for a dog and kill the dog.' It was on this occasion that he lashed the Grant Administration

[1] Dowd, 146.     [2] Ibid., 147.     [3] Ibid., 148.

for corruption. 'There has been so much corruption that the man in the moon has to hold his nose as he passes over the earth.' [1]

At times the bitterness of Settle met with clamor from the crowd, and up sprang Vance, indignant, to still the storm. He had a genius for turning glowering crowds into merry ones. Apologizing for his friends who had interrupted Settle, he said, apropos of the rain, that he knew they were 'wet inside and out.' [2]

And so the canvass went — great torchlight processions, with men and women marching through the woods, with women holding babes in their arms all day, with Vance moving like a conqueror, his carriage surrounded by escorts of mounted men, with girls on porches and in windows waving flags. Throughout he maintained his poise. When a mule broke loose and caused excitement, he calmed the fears that threatened a stampede with the laughing comment that it was 'one of the mules that went with the forty acres.' Sometimes he was bitter — as in his attack on the statement of Senator Pool that should Tilden be elected the North would not allow him to be inaugurated.[3] Hayes from Fremont, and Zack Chandler from Washington, were watching Vance's triumphant march with much uneasiness. They were even more startled with South Carolina, which was a seething caldron of revolt.

Let us visit the State of the palmetto and view the spectacle of a revolution.

[1] At Jonesborough; *ibid.*, 150.
[2] *Ibid.*, 152.        [3] *Ibid.*, 160.

# CHAPTER XXIV

## THE RED SHIRTS RIDE

### I

WITH Ingersoll and Morton appealing to sectional feelings in the North, strange scenes were being enacted in South Carolina. Day and night, men in flaming red shirts were dashing through the dust of country roads into villages, towns, and groves, singing, shouting, cheering — good-natured, and yet grim. The State had risen in revolt, and was moving to the polls.

It was not without a struggle that all the native whites had been mobilized and unified for the fight. After a career of intimate identification with the disreputable organization supporting the pillaging of Scott and Moses, Daniel H. Chamberlain, now elected Governor, had turned with dramatic ferocity upon his former confederates. A carpetbagger like the rest, he had distinguished himself at Yale and retained many of the qualities of New England culture. More scholar than politician, pallid, reserved, cold, a fringe of hair around his ears setting off his baldness, his features were good, and in dress, manners, and habits he resembled the cultivated New-Englander of tradition. There was a distinction in the literary quality of his speeches which was beyond the appreciation of his coarse and illiterate followers.[1] That he had many struggles with his conscience is probable. Craving the approval of cultured people, his sojourn in South Carolina had been one of heartache; the social ostracism of his beautiful wife and children had meant misery, and her very gallantry had made it harder to bear. Personally he was supersensitive to criticism. He would have seemed more at home in the drawing-room of Wade Hampton in pre-war days than he did in the mixed caucuses of degraded whites and blacks.[2] The passing of the years was to convert a 'diabolical fighter' into a 'very pathetic figure.'[3] When in his

---

[1] Williams, *Columbia State*, August 8, 1926.  [2] Bowen, 21.
[3] Williams, *Columbia State*, September 19, 1926.

inaugural address he dumbfounded the Carolinians with an enunciation of sound principles, he had waded through slime to power with the evident determination to be clean and decent.

Scarcely had he warmed his seat when his new pretensions were put to the test. The Legislature met in caucus to elect his campaign manager, an unworthy scamp, to a circuit judgeship, and he denounced and defeated the plan.[1] A negro militia, armed by Scott in Edgefield County, went on a rampage, and he compelled it to surrender its arms to the State.[2] Inflexible in his insistence on a rigid economy, he had used the veto freely on appropriation bills and had aroused the enthusiasm of the native whites. The 'Charleston News and Courier' became his champion. The press of the North was cheering, too. 'The Nation' was praising him for 'defending civilization against barbarism in its worst form.' Soon the social barriers against him were lowered. He was riding on the crest of the wave of personal popularity when in the autumn five thousand Charlestonians serenaded and cheered him wildly.

Meanwhile, his popularity was intensified by the bitter hostility of his own party, which reached its climax when the Legislature defiantly elected two of the most corrupt and depraved men in the State to circuit judgeships. Absent at the time, Chamberlain hurried home to denounce the action of his party associates as a 'horrible disaster — a disaster equally great to the State and to the Republican Party.' [3] When he refused to sign the commissions, he had every decent man in the State standing at salute. In the midst of the crisis thus created he thrilled the Nation with his message to the New England Society of Charleston: 'The civilization of the Puritan and the Cavalier, of the Roundhead and the Huguenot, is in peril. The grim Puritans never quailed under threat or blow. Let their sons now imitate their example.' [4] Strange language from a carpetbagger. It had the sinister swing of a 'copperhead' declaration. To the politicians of the Radical Party it resembled the 'rebel yell.' Instantly the 'National Republican' of Washington denounced him as a party traitor. It was rumored that Grant was displeased. Morton was quoted as saying

---

[1] *Chamberlain Administration*, 38–45.     [2] *Ibid.*, 68.     [3] *Ibid.*, 194–96.
[4] *History of the New England Society of Charleston*, 265–66.

that Chamberlain had 'already given up the State to the Opposition,' and that his action was 'a practical identification with the Democrats.'

With the Carolinians behind him cheering, Chamberlain challenged his critics sharply in letters given to the press. Nor did he spare the President. 'The character of F. J. Moses, Jr., is known to you and the world,' he wrote Grant, of one of the men elected to a circuit judgeship. 'He is as infamous a character as ever in any age disgraced and prostituted public position.' On Morton he turned with a savage protest. 'Now, sir, I have a word to say about what you are reputed to have said to the effect that you "already give up the State to the Opposition." The result rests very largely with you. You are influential, able; you hold a commanding position and you have a commanding voice in our party affairs. If South Carolina is to be given up to the Opposition, it is because you, and others whom you can influence, fail to help me and my friends "unload" . . . the infamy of these judicial elections. And here let me speak plainly. To cry "Democrat" at me at this time, is to support Moses and Whipper.' [1]

Driven to cover, Morton hastened to explain that his comment on Chamberlain's attitude had been made in 'casual private conversation' and 'seems to have been imperfectly understood.' [2] It had, in fact, been perfectly understood.

## II

It was this determination to maintain his position in his party that wrought Chamberlain's ruin. When 'Honest' John Patterson, the Senator, interested in the presidential candidacy of Morton, undertook to prevent the election of the Governor as a delegate to the Cincinnati Convention, Chamberlain accepted the challenge. His slight frame trembling, great beads of perspiration on his brow, he took the platform in the State Convention and his eloquence snatched victory from defeat. He sponsored the platform plank inviting the intervention of Federal bayonets in the elections in the South, and arm in arm with Patterson went to Cincinnati to vote fourteen times for Morton, after Bristow had withdrawn. The early summer found him speaking for Hayes in

[1] *Chamberlain Administration*, 229–34.    [2] *New York Herald*, February 27, 1876.

the North. He had made his peace with his party, and cast doubt on the sincerity of his conversion.

The ultra-conservatives, planning a fusion on Chamberlain for Governor, were a little embarrassed by this fresh flash of the old partisanship. They had hoped that the Republicans would refuse him a renomination, and it was their plan to support him, with a Democrat for Lieutenant-Governor to fight for a majority of fusionists in the Legislature, elect Chamberlain to the Senate, and thus secure control of both the executive and legislative branches of the Government. The 'Charleston News and Courier' was daily enumerating the good he had accomplished while preaching the futility of a straight Democratic ticket. It reflected the views of Charleston business and professional men, who, suffering most from taxes, had faith in Chamberlain's policy of retrenchment and reform.

Long before, however, a few strong men of iron will had determined on another course. Mississippi had pointed the way. The year of the Centennial was the time to strike. He who would be free must strike the blow. 'No compromise,' they warned. For eleven years Carolinians had been humble, and the time had come to fight, to name their own man, and elect him. The militant, resourceful leader of this movement was General Martin Witherspoon Gary.

### III

Picturesque, and in some ways resembling the sons of Gascony, he was described at the time by 'Pickaway,' the special correspondent of the 'Cincinnati Enquirer': 'General Gary is one of the oddest, finest, most original, gassy, genial, brilliant geniuses I ever encountered. He is an old bachelor of about forty, and yet his head is as bald as a billiard ball, and the fringe of hair about his ears is as white as snow. He looks like a man of eighty and acts like one of twenty. He is fiery, fearless, and one of the most fascinating talkers I ever heard. He has no secrets. He goes off in conversation like a skyrocket, and reaches a conclusion by bursting into showers of strange words and funny sayings. . . . He admires a beautiful woman, loves a horse-race, and keeps the best gamecock in the State.' This is only one side of 'The Bald Eagle of Edgefield,' as he was called. Five feet eleven in height, with an elegant, well-proportioned form, he bore himself with an air of distinction. His face was that of a thinker and doer combined. His classic features, mobile and full of expression, were lighted by the searching grayish-blue eyes of the natural fighter, and more than one man was to quail before his fiery glance. A member of the old aristocracy, he lived elegantly in the stately colonial mansion at Oakly Hall, which sat far back in an imposing park of oak trees near Edgefield.

Like the Gascons he resembled, he presented a different character to men from that he showed to women. With the former, he was commanding, with a touch of the arrogance of natural leadership. His temper was such that none but a brave man dare cross him. He had most of the vices of robust masculinity, but none to a damaging degree. Among women, he was all gentleness and gallantry, enjoying their society, especially if they were beautiful or intellectual. There was just the faint fragrance of romance in the traditions about him. At one time he sat for three years in his stately old home writing love letters to a Baltimore beauty, who rejected him in the end, but these letters reveal a tenderness, a gentleness, and sense of poetry that men seldom saw. For many years he was a close friend of Mattie Ould, a famous Virginia belle, but destiny ordained that he should dwell alone at Oakly Hall, and sally forth from among the oaks into many a bitter battle in the world of men.

In his profession, he was a powerful advocate; on the platform, he was fluent and forceful; in conference, he was daring and audacious. In politics, he was a robust partisan, and in organization, he had a genius for infinite detail. His prescience foresaw all contingencies, and he anticipated every crisis. His enthusiasm and confidence were contagious. His powerful passions and biting sarcasm sometimes made him difficult, and often brought him enemies. Quite early he had come to scorn the policy of petitioning Washington for redress. He was a hard-headed realist, and knew that only through the establishment of white supremacy could the State rid itself of its evils.

It was this powerful, ingenuous, two-fisted fighting man who stepped forth in 1875 to demand that the Democracy organize to the precincts, and place a straight-out ticket in the field the next year. In December, the Democratic State Central Committee, dormant for three years, issued an appeal for an intensive organization, with all Democrats enrolled in clubs. When a convention met in May to determine on policy, Gary assumed the leadership of the movement of '76. It was he who then and there, in a spirited battle with the conservatives and compromisers, brought the party out from nebulosity to reality and led it to the decision to put a straight-out ticket in the field. The nominating convention was set for August.

Through May and June, the Democratic controversy waxed warm, but all the while the organization of the clubs proceeded, and in the country the sentiment was strongly with the straight-outs. The aristocracy mostly favored fusion; the rank and file demanded independent action. With Gary and his associates, like General M. C. Butler, tireless and sleepless, with the enthusiasm rising, flaming, Chamberlain was embarrassing the fusionists by his reawakened partisanship; and then came the event that fixed his fate — the negro 'militiamen' ran amuck at Hamburg, and Chamberlain faced the supreme test.

IV

The little town of Hamburg, separated from Augusta by the river, had come to be completely dominated by the negroes, who held all the offices. A negro militia company, formed and armed during the Scott régime, had almost petered out when in 1876 it took on a new lease of life, recruiting up to eighty members. These were armed, and, under the captaincy of a lawless negro, they had long terrorized the community. The captain, whose obsession was hatred of the whites, accentuated the race feeling. White women were frequently crowded from the sidewalks, and white men were often arrested, fined, imprisoned on the most flimsy charges. The 'militia' was an undisciplined band of lawless men in possession of guns and ammunition. The crisis came when the 'militia,' drawn across the highway, refused for a time to break ranks to permit two white youths to drive through, and yielded finally after cursing and threatening them with punishment. The father of one of the young men had the captain arrested for obstructing the highway, and so outrageous was his conduct in court that the negro justice arrested him for contempt. Threats to lynch the young men at the trial drew a number of whites to Hamburg to protect them. General M. C. Butler, retained for the prosecution, sought to compromise the case. He proposed to abandon the prosecution if the captain would apologize; and followed the rejection of the proposition with another to stop proceedings if the undisciplined band would surrender their arms to some responsible person for shipment to the Adjutant-General. Again there was a refusal and much talk of battle. This soon developed, the 'militiamen' retiring to a brick building, whence they yelled defiance and shot from the windows. A young white man fell with a bullet through his head. This sealed the fate of the blacks. With a small cannon from Augusta turned against the building, the negroes attempted flight. They were captured, and five of the ringleaders were deliberately shot. It was a race war, having no connection with politics.

Chamberlain, at the crossroads, hesitated, and then sent a carpetbag Attorney-General to investigate. This official went directly to the first captain of the militia, a corrupt and provocative negro who had confessed taking bribes before Chamberlain honored him with a judicial appointment, and on information from this partisan source, based his conclusions. Abandoning now the rôle of defender of the civilization of the Roundhead and the Cavalier, Chamberlain prepared a lurid partisan story for propaganda purposes in the North and sent it to Senator Robertson, who gave it to the press. In a letter to Grant, prepared also as partisan propaganda, Chamberlain could conceive of no motive for the massacre beyond 'the fact that the militia company was composed of negroes . . . and members of the Republican Party,' and those who had demanded the disarming of the blacks 'were . . . white men and members of the Democratic Party.' He concluded with the usual appeal to the Federal Government to 'exert itself vigorously to repress violence . . . during the present political campaign.'[1] Clearly eager to meet expectations, Grant replied in a letter, plainly framed to serve the purposes of politics, denouncing the people of South Carolina, and disclosing the

[1] *Chamberlain Administration*, 321-25.

partisan animus in his reference to the Democratic victory in Mississippi as having been achieved by 'force and fraud such as would scarcely be credited to savages, much less to Christian people.' A strange and violent diatribe from the loftiest station in the land![1]

Chamberlain had returned to his associates and the practices of the days of Scott and Moses, and the straight-outs had won a victory.

V

The weeks intervening between the Hamburg riot and the nominating conventions found both parties feverishly at work perfecting plans, mobilizing men. Washington ordered Federal job-holders to rally to Chamberlain, whose party leadership was thus reëstablished. Among the Democratic straight-outs the work of organization went on apace, with the indomitable Gary seeking a candidate with an appeal. He turned to General Wade Hampton, who was to his people what Washington was to the colonies, and for much the same reason. He, too, was a planter with impressive estates and a hall of hospitality, honest, able, cautious, sincere. The war had played havoc with these estates; the hall of hospitality was in ruins; but the appeal of Hampton's name was no less potent. Between Gary and Hampton there had been an undercurrent of unfriendly feeling from the beginning of the war, but both were big enough to bury personal differences for a public cause. Meeting Hampton on the train one day, Gary broached the subject of the nomination, and though others had sought to dissuade him, Hampton yielded to the importunities of the irrepressible. Gary's straight-out policy had appealed to him, and he had written the Bald Eagle that 'the "News and Courier" must either be made to sustain our policy or quit the party which it is defeating and disgracing,' but that 'we must be gentle with our Charleston friends, appealing to them to go with us.'[2] Thus, long before the conventions, the choice lay between Chamberlain and Hampton.

---

[1] *Chamberlain Administration*, 325; *Doc. Hist.*, ii, 406.

[2] July 26, 1876. The original of this letter is in possession of the Honorable John Gary Evans, Spartanburg.

The former, campaigning far in advance of the nominations, was soon convinced that he was facing a bitter fight. The strategy of the Gary wing was to meet the Radicals on their own ground, answer them before their negro audiences, and denounce their rascality to their faces for the psychological effect upon their black followers. Chamberlain had encountered this at Edgefield, where he had been waited upon by Gary and Butler with punctilious formality with a request for a division of time. There was some evasion, but no escape. Great throngs of Democrats in the red shirts of the clubs were riding in the streets. When Gary appeared upon the platform, Chamberlain winced before his fierce gaze and paled. Butler, directing the movements of two thousand approaching red shirts, was on his way. The effect was seen in the mildness of the carpetbagger's speech, which was heard without interruption. But when, on concluding, Chamberlain turned to leave without hearing the reply, he was warned that red shirts would be sent to bring him back by force, and he resumed his seat, pale and angry. 'I spoke to him,' said Gary later, 'in rude and rough language in order that the rude and rough negro might understand it. This is what killed the spirit of the negro, to see the Governor of the State and the chosen leader of their party abused in such unmeasured terms. They would not stay to hear the speaking over, and left in great disgust.' Gary had denounced the rascality and thievery of the Radical régime and Chamberlain's associations to his face in the presence of his followers, and the spell was broken. There was no violence, no disturbance, only viper words in bitter debate.

The next meeting, at Abbeville, found Chamberlain distressed. Tired and worried, accompanied by a State official, he reached the town at night and retired to a private home on Magazine Hill, where a colored man, followed by fifty white Democrats, gave him a serenade. He excused himself from speaking until the morrow, but his less cautious companion essayed to talk. 'When articles of value are shipped,' he began, 'they should be marked ——'

'Agricultural implements,' shouted the whites, referring to the ruse for smuggling arms to the negroes.

It was a facetious interruption, but it denoted a defiant confidence in the Carolinians that boded no good. The next day he

again was forced to divide time and listen to plain speaking from
his foes, and he had seen something new at Radical meetings —
great processions of red-shirted, mounted men with flying banners
and prancing steeds.[1]

Before the Democratic Convention met, the straight-outs had
won their fight, the timid Carolina compromisers had been overwhelmed, but there still was timidity at Gramercy Park, where
Tilden was disclosing that weakness which was to be his undoing.
Learning of the forebodings at Gramercy Park over the prospective nomination of a distinguished Confederate soldier, Hampton
wrote Tilden of the pressure upon him and invited a frank expression. That letter was not even answered.[2] Thus Tilden ceased
to be a factor. The convention met, unanimously named Hampton,
and enthusiasm shook the hills.

The name of Hampton now was on every tongue, men, women,
and children wildly cheering him as the Messiah of their redemption, and that night Columbia gave itself over to a frenzy of delight, with military forces marching, the people parading with
torchlights, the entire city shaking with shouts of jubilation.[3]
The 'News and Courier' surrendered, and the name of Hampton
floated from its masthead.

## VI

Wade Hampton was symbolical of the finest flowering of pre-
war Southern chivalry and aristocracy. Patrician by birth, instinct, training, his manner was democratic. Born in the Charleston town house of his mother, his boyhood was passed among the
ancient oaks and rose gardens of Millwood, the baronial mansion
of the family, a short distance from Columbia. This stately house
with its impressive columns was the seat of a hospitality almost
mediæval in its magnificence. Guests were furnished with horses
and servants and left to their own devices, to mingle familiarly
with the family or to engage in the sport of riding, fishing, or
hunting. Great numbers of slaves, fat and contented, worked in
house and field, grinning in the sunshine and warmly attached to

[1] *Abbeville Press and Banner*, August 16, 23, 1876.
[2] Letter from Hampton to Manton Marble, September 19, 1876.
[3] Williams, *Columbia State*, September 12, 1926.

an indulgent master. In this atmosphere Wade Hampton grew to young manhood, devoted to all the sports, in which he excelled. In early boyhood he was a daring and graceful equestrian. Like the elder son of the English landed aristocracy, he had been educated to meet the traditional responsibilities of his class. After graduating at South Carolina College and studying law, he settled down to the management of plantations and the meeting of social duties. He entered the State Senate without political ambition and merely in response to tradition. There his speech against the reimportation of slaves had been described by Greeley as 'a masterpiece of logic, directed by the noblest sentiments of the Christian and patriot.' [1]

His largest agricultural interests before the war were in Mississippi, his last cotton crop before the struggle realizing a quarter of a million dollars. His life on the Mississippi plantation resembled that of a powerful baron of vast possessions in the days of feudalism. He had a patriarchal attitude toward the slaves, who reciprocated his friendliness. He personally supervised their accommodations and care. On chilly evenings, he was usually found in the library of the plantation house before a great log fire with his favorite books, but the house more closely resembled a vast hunting lodge, for he was a famous hunter. Large companies would attend his bear hunts. Though a capital shot, he liked nothing better than to pit his prowess and great physical strength against the black bears of the Mississippi swamps, going in on them when brought to bay with his hunting knife, and, though he carried the scars of more than one combat, he had the record of dispatching as many as eighty in this primitive manner.[2] Among his hunting companions, he alone could place a dead bear on his horse unaided.[3] Wealthy, cultured, physically powerful, successful in the cultivation of his acres, beloved by his slaves, untorn by ambition, idolized by friends, finding pleasure alike with rod, gun, horse, or book before a roaring fire, his was a happy life before the war.

When war came, he went with his own people. Nature had moulded him for leadership. Six feet in height, with deep chest, broad shoulders, narrow hips, and powerful legs, his was a superb

[1] Wells, 32.　　[2] Williams, *Columbia State*, September 19, 1926.　　[3] Wells, 14.

presence, and in the saddle he and his horse seemed one. His complexion, hair, and large bluish-gray eyes gave him the appearance of an old Saxon king. The call to arms naturally found him in the saddle at the head of the cavalry, where his genius for command, his quiet poise, dash, and daring, endeared him to Lee, and to his men, and to all his people. He had suffered uncomplainingly — a perfect Spartan. In one engagement he had seen one son fall; and, sending another son to his succor, had seen him fall, too, and had ridden back to kiss the dying youth and whisper in his ear — then back to the fight and to sleep on the ground that night in the rain, not knowing the fate of his children.[1]

The close of the war found his fortune gone, only the pillars of his home near Columbia standing, but no word of bitterness escaped him. Urging conciliation and peace, abstaining from politics, he faced hard times with courage, and with his former slaves, who clung to him, turned again to the cultivation of his acres. Thus his people found him in their need and he was summoned to lead a revolution. There was a strange magic in the name 'Hampton,' color in the picture it evoked about the reminiscent camp-fires of the men in faded gray.

### VII

With Hampton's nomination, the Republican factions drew together, and the night before their convention, Chamberlain, the reformer, sat in conference with 'Honest' John Patterson, in the reconciliation of their differences. The next day, in convention, Patterson proclaimed the perfect understanding reached, and revived the drooping spirits of the faithful with assurances from Washington.

'President Grant has his eye on South Carolina,' he said, 'and intends to take care of her, and I will warrant that Grant will bring the strong arm of the United States Government to support and keep the Republican Party in power. By the eternal gods, the Democrats shan't have any say at all in government.'

Following the nomination of Chamberlain, the understanding of the night before was revealed when Patterson rose to nominate

[1] Wells, 59.

the notoriously corrupt Elliott for Attorney-General. Chamberlain was to justify his surrender on the ground that Elliott possessed 'admitted ability' and had 'rendered political services to his party.' [1] Much later he was to admit to Garrison that he had blundered.

The plan of the Radicals was clear. Frantic appeals were telegraphed to Washington. The electoral vote for Hayes was in danger. Their own lives were in peril. The assistance of Federal troops would be required. Already Cameron, Secretary of War, had instructed the general commanding the army 'to hold all the available force under command' for the purposes of politics. The election machinery was entirely in their hands. The Attorney-General had announced that 'the marshals have absolute power over troops.' With the blacks in a majority, these could control and should be held in line. Many of them were tiring of the game; others were drifting toward Hampton. Negro Democratic clubs were being formed — and this should be stopped.

Thus the secret oath-bound Loyal Leagues began their work of terror and intimidation. The negro churches became Republican hustings. Negro Democrats were ostracized, and negro women pledged themselves against cohabitation with Hampton colored men. Threats were made against the lives of the deserters, and out of these, some days before Chamberlain's nomination, came the Charleston riot.

### VIII

Indeed, negro Democratic clubs were meeting in Charleston listening to plain speaking by Isaac Rivers, a huge black with an effective tongue. Attacks had been made upon these meetings, but nothing serious had happened. The whites had named a committee of seven to protect the Hampton negroes, and at one meeting these whites had formed a hollow square, placed the negro speakers in the center, and marched into King Street to meet the jeers and curses of the mob. The desperate Republican negro clubs, the Hunkydories and the Live Oaks, had waited for a meeting when few whites were present, and had surrounded the building, some with pistols, others with clubs, many with sling

[1] Reynolds, 367.

shots. As the meeting adjourned and the colored Democrats emerged, the mob with a Congo yell pressed forward. The few whites staked their lives in defense of the Hampton blacks, firing over the heads of the mob and gaining time until the police on foot and horseback swept upon the scene, charging with their clubs. The mob opened fire, the whites replied; but at Citadel Green, with the ammunition of the whites exhausted and policemen wounded, reënforcements for the mob poured out of Johnson Street, demanding blood. The fifteen whites, the negro Democrats in their midst, desperately struggled into the Citadel grounds and delivered the objects of the mob's fury over to the protection of Federal soldiers there.

Their work accomplished, the whites escaped as best they could, and the mob, divided into gangs, took possession of the streets, shouting, demanding blood, attacking whites, smashing store windows. Soon the guard-house was filled with wounded whites, and a physician worked all night, using his shirt for making bandages. The night was hideous with screams and yells. Reporters ordered to the scene were attacked and barely rescued by the police. The editor of 'The News and Courier,' on horseback, was forced to flee. The last street car drawn by horses was stopped, the driver beaten until saved by the police, and then he was followed to his home and his house was stoned.

Terror in every home. Then, as if by magic, the Carolina Rifle Battalion hurried at quick step from East Bay and Broad to Hibernian Hall, where they drew up in double rank facing City Hall Park — and there they stood for an hour and a half listening to the shooting in King Street. With the men pale and pleading for permission to get into action, Major Barker, the commander, passed up and down the line urging patience. Dry sobs from the men, fearing for their families, were heard, but the discipline was perfect. At midnight they were marched to the armory and their guns were stacked. Barker had determined to hold off if possible; to have turned his men upon the mob with rifles would have meant a heavy slaughter of the blacks, and political ammunition for Morton and Chandler in the North. The only person killed was white; many whites were beaten; a company with rifles had withheld its fire; and there was no 'outrage' story on the wires.

The next day rifle clubs were organized among the whites; four hundred men were assigned to guard the homes of the Democratic colored leaders; and that night the Light Dragoons began a three months' patrol of the streets.

This incident illustrates one feature of the strategy of the Democrats.[1] There was no Republican criticism of the mob.

## IX

And yet the Democratic campaign plan, patterned on that of Mississippi, was frankly revolutionary. The success of the tactics there had created an intense interest in South Carolina. One day Gary sat reading a letter to Major T. C. Barker, of Charleston, from General Samuel W. Ferguson, of Mississippi. It was a startling story of the redemption of a State. The Mississippians, hoping for assistance from the negroes, had determined to carry the election at all hazards. In the event of bloodshed the letter said, they had decided to 'kill every white Radical in the county.' No threats were to be made, but it was known as 'a fixed and settled thing.' The result had been that the white Radicals, anxious for a slaughter of the blacks to justify the summoning of Federal troops, were not 'ready to sacrifice themselves upon the altar of rascality.' Thus, 'instead of fomenting strife, they counseled peace.' The Democrats sent speakers to all Radical meetings and demanded a division of time, and the negro 'saw his leaders cower and finally retire from the contest.' He did not vote with the Democrats, but failed to vote, since 'he had no one on the spot to show him how the thing was done.' The success of the plan depended on the conservatives 'being in condition to make a fight if necessary,' and so they armed themselves. Then 'every man almost worked day and night for weeks.'

Gary and others, intrigued, sought further information, which came in a copy of the 'Mississippi Plan' thought to have been sent by General George.[2] With this as a basis, the plan of the South Carolina fight was formed. Every Democrat was to enlist in a club; every club was to be armed and under experienced captains; and all were to be instructed to hold themselves at all times, day

[1] Williams, *Columbia State*, November 7, 1926.
[2] Gary MSS., in the possession of John Gary Evans.

or night, subject to call. They were to attend all Radical meetings, going in numbers, and armed. At these Radical meetings they were to act, at first, with courtesy and assure the negroes they were in no danger; but when Radical speakers made false statements, there was to be an instant challenge to their faces as 'liars, thieves, and rascals,' trying to deceive the negroes. In appealing to the latter, no arguments were to be advanced, 'since they can only be influenced by their fears, superstitions, and cupidity.' No flattery or persuasion, but plain speaking on the grievances of the whites against the 'rascally leaders' of the Radicals, white and black. Warning was to be given that for murders, burnings, or frauds at the polls 'we will hold the leaders of the Radical Party personally responsible,' beginning with the whites, then the mulattoes, then the blacks. Public meetings were to be held frequently, and negro clubs formed. In all processions the white clubs were to wear red shirts and parade with banners. No idle threats were to be made, and violence was to be prevented.

With this as a basis, Gary perfected his plan.

x

Gary and Hampton held opposing views on the wisdom of cultivating the negro vote, but these were not permitted to clash. The former had no faith in the possibility of securing their political support, and his plan was frankly one of intimidation and to keep the negroes from the polls by persuasion or otherwise. Hampton, with the faith of an old master who had easily controlled his slaves, believed they could be reasoned into the support of the whites. There was no reason why each should not pursue his own course, since both agreed on the wisdom of simulating faith.

Thus the enrollment of negroes into Democratic clubs went on at a merry pace, the members being guaranteed protection against the intimidation of the Radicals and Leagues. The leaders of the blacks were ignored, but intensive work was done among the rank and file. Speakers harangued them on plantations, with a negro as chairman and the steps of the gin-house as a platform, and at all Democratic meetings a section near the platform was reserved for them.

Meanwhile, Hampton, speaking to them simply, kindly, frankly, without flattery, as though reasoning with them from the steps of his plantation house,[1] was appealing to their better natures. No one wished them back in slavery, he said; their labor as free men was more valuable. The interests of the two races dovetailed. 'The only way to bring about prosperity in this State is to bring the two races in friendly relations together.' And 'if there is a white man in this assembly . . . believes that when I am elected Governor, I will stand between him and the law, or grant to him any privileges and immunities that shall not be granted to the colored man, he is mistaken.' [2]

And so Hampton went his way and the militants went theirs, all uniting in the determination to prevent violence if possible. Hampton was the symbol of what was wanted; Gary was the grimly practical politician quietly superintending the machinery of the movement. Hampton's appeal was in his popularity and gentleness; Gary's power was in his organizing genius.

## XI

With Chamberlain nominated, he was soon in receipt of a challenge from A. C. Haskell, the able Democratic State Chairman, to meet Hampton in a series of joint debates. More than surfeited with the meetings at Abbeville and Edgefield, Chamberlain declined, in a long letter, intended as propaganda, on the ground that the State was an armed camp, with Democratic clubs marching on the meetings with guns. Hampton appealed to Chief Justice Moses, 'as a Republican and as Chief Justice,' to say whether his observations at the meetings were those of Chamberlain, and Moses replied that he had seen nothing of violence — just great bodies of men on horseback. The doughty carpetbagger had been driven from the stump.

It mattered little. From the mountains to the sea South Carolina was aflame for Hampton. Tirelessly he swept over the State, accompanied always by a colorful cavalcade, received with fervor everywhere, and nowhere making a mistake in utterance. Neither brilliant nor spectacular, he talked quietly, plainly, without fire or passion, seldom raising his voice, and never gesticulating. Never

[1] Williams, *Columbia State*, September 19, 1926.
[2] Speech at Abbeville, September 16, 1876; *Doc. Hist.*, ii, 411.

from him an expression that might not have been uttered in a drawing-room. Through all his talks ran a tone of nobility. 'Fear nothing so much as being in the wrong.' 'Let not a gust of passion destroy in a moment the edifice we have been so long and so laboriously constructing.' [1]

But there were fire and fervor enough in the meetings; for the entire State had taken to the saddle and was riding ceaselessly. The wretchedness of the roads, the lack of telephones or speedy means of locomotion, meant nothing with such organization and discipline. Day or night, through rain or shine, men clattered on horseback over the highways from house to house to inform the faithful when and where they were needed. The notice was enough. All else was dropped; within a few moments the man was in the saddle galloping to the meeting-place.[2] Day and night, wives, mothers, sweethearts, were plying their needles on the red shirts for their men, decorating the platforms in the groves with flowers and evergreens, draping them with bunting. The roads leading to a Democratic demonstration were congested with men on horses from distant places. From five hundred to five thousand mounted men moved like an army, their red shirts seen afar in the sunshine.

Thus word arrives of a meeting at a distance, mothers and wives pack hampers with food, the men don their uniforms of red, the women cheer them shrilly as they ride away. Swaying easily in their saddles, noisy and jolly, these armies ride into the night, pausing at times to rest and dance, and receive the applause of the villages and the countryside. Often they sing, always they shout. But discipline holds them within bounds. That was the order — 'no violence, no provocation.' Do they hear of a Radical down the road making inflammatory speeches to the negroes? A committee is assigned to wait upon him, and away it rides. Was the man guilty? Usually he confesses — usually he is ignorant. The red shirts give him a sound talking to, exact the promise to desist, and back they ride to their comrades — and away the army moves.[3]

---

[1] *Abbeville Press and Banner*, September 20, 1876.

[2] Williams, *Columbia State*, September 12, 1926.

[3] A participant's description of the ride to Anderson. *Abbeville Press and Banner*, September 6, 1876.

And now they reach the town of the demonstration, to merge with the red shirts entering on other roads, to be cheered lustily by women and children, to find even the homes elaborately decorated, for the women vie with one another, and the press describes the decorations of each house as it does the gowns at the opera. Banners of Tilden and Hendricks in cedar leaves. Pictures of Hampton — 'Savior of South Carolina'; of Tilden — 'Savior of America.' Sometimes men laugh or jeer before a picture displayed in the spirit of satire — 'Honest' John Patterson.[1] Then to the grove where the massed red shirts open a space for Hampton, with his red-shirted guard, young girls strewing flowers in his path, singing spirited songs.

Forty times Hampton spoke to great outdoor meetings without a blunder; only one speaker, under the influence of apple brandy, made a foolish statement and it escaped the notice of the enemy.[2]

Toward the close, the campaign was a throbbing thing, absorbing the business of the people, with women sewing, decorating, with men riding, children shouting 'Hampton! Hampton!' with the Democratic Committee asking a day of prayer in all the churches for the ending of the horrors of bad government, and with the places of worship crowded. The fiery Gary and the cautious Hampton were equally insistent on maintaining order, and there were few acts of violence. In Edgefield County, some red shirts, riding to a Hampton meeting, were ambushed, and one killed; but there was no retaliation. Not a Radical nor a negro hurt![3] Persistent warnings had borne fruit. Armed men maintained the peace.

To the Radicals this was sinister. The State was exuberantly for Hampton, and victory was in the air. Where were the troops? What of 'Honest' John Patterson's promise? And then came the Ellenton riots.

## XII

These had no more connection with politics than with philosophy. Two negroes had entered the home of a farmer, who was in

[1] The Abbeville Hampton meeting, *ibid.*, September 20, 1876.
[2] Williams, *Columbia State*, November 7, 1926.
[3] Wallace, MS. Life of Gary.

his fields, and had attacked his wife and child. One of the men taken, in the course of justice, implicated another, for whom a warrant was sworn out. Officers going forth to make the arrest found the accused with a company of armed negroes, who opened fire. The fire was returned, one negro was hurt, and the armed blacks took to the swamps and made threats to organize and arm for warfare. The community was sparsely settled by whites and their peril was real. About two hundred white men organized and armed for the defense, and a race war was on. The fighting continued for three days until the arrival of United States infantry, when the struggle ceased and the fighters dispersed. There had been casualties on both sides.

To Chamberlain and the Radicals it was an opportunity long sought, and Chamberlain issued a lurid proclamation, misrepresenting the casualties for the effect in the North and ordering the dispersal of the white rifle clubs. The negroes were not ordered to disband their armed organizations. Grant was called upon for troops, and promptly he responded with a proclamation describing the native whites as banded in lawless combinations, 'who ride up and down by day and night in arms, murdering some peaceable citizens,' and ordering them to 'disperse.' It was a strange distortion of the truth to be disseminated by the President of the country.[1]

So brazenly partisan was this amazing paper that the Hampton State Committee replied in an 'Address to the People.'

'We are not engaged in "unlawful and insurrectionary proceedings,"' it said. 'We cannot "disperse" because we are not gathered together. We cannot "retire peaceably to our abodes" because we are in our homes in peace, disturbed only by the political agitations created by the Governor and his minions. But we resignedly — and cheerfully, in the performance of our duty — suspend the exercise of our individual and private rights in order to prevent evil to the whole people.'

The demand was made that Chamberlain specify where lawlessness prevailed; the clergy and the judges of the Supreme Court denounced his charges; and bankers and capitalists, mostly from the North, assailed them as false. But the very day that Grant

[1] *Messages and Papers*, x, 4350.

issued his proclamation, the Secretary of War ordered all the available military forces of the Atlantic to report to General Ruger at Columbia, to meet resistance to the authority of the United States!

Then came the massacre at the village of Cainhoy — which was political.

This village, near Charleston, and reached by water, was the scene of a political meeting, and the Democrats chartered a boat and took a band. An agreement had been reached that guns were to be left at home, but the negroes, going early, had taken guns and concealed them in a thicket. Just how the shooting began remains a mystery. One story runs that a negro woman cried out that the guns had been taken; another that an altercation between a white and black in the rear of the crowd had precipitated the fight. At any rate, the negroes rushed from the meeting, grasped their guns, and opened fire. Six whites were killed, one negro — and it was heralded to the North as a massacre by the whites of inoffensive blacks because of their politics.[1] 'Honest' John Patterson was rejoiced. 'That Cainhoy massacre was a Godsend to us,' he said. 'We could not have carried Charleston County without it.'[2]

At last there was hope. Ellenton, Cainhoy — Grant's Proclamation — the Secretary of War's orders — if only there could be a little more shooting. Two days after the Cainhoy riot, a deliberate attempt was made to force another riot at Aiken, where Hampton spoke. In the midst of his meeting, a United States Marshal with a squad of troops boisterously swept upon it to arrest eleven prominent Democrats on the usual 'conspiracy' charge. The provocation was extreme. The Marshal and his troops could have been torn to pieces. Pale and grim, Hampton, who had been flagrantly insulted, urged the victims to accept arrest, and the attempt to involve Hampton in a 'massacre' failed.

Then came martial law, with Hampton telegraphing all his lieutenants: 'Urge our people to submit peaceably to martial law. I will see and consult with them.'[3] He had met Chamberlain's call for Federal troops with the assertion that the more sent the better, since soldiers of the regular army are 'brave and manly

---

[1] O'Connor, 135–36    [2] Wells, 136.    [3] Reynolds, 387.

men and their officers generally are gentlemen.' [1] And he had telegraphed General Ruger to send troops to Beaufort to protect the colored Democrats from intimidation.[2] In truth, the very audacity of the performances of Grant and Chamberlain had reacted badly in the North.

The 'New York Sun' was sure 'this attempt to overawe the vote of South Carolina by Grant's soldiers will react against the party in whose behalf it is made.' 'The Herald' concluded that Chamberlain had no real wish for order, and 'The World' that 'nothing . . . will be for one moment weighed in the balance by the men who rule this country to-day against the perpetuation of their power.' 'The Nation' protested against the Attorney-General's rules and regulations under which the troops were to be used. 'The marshals to whom he has committed the power of using soldiers as a posse are themselves political partisans . . . on whom usage has now imposed electioneering as one of their duties,' it said. 'In short, the soldiers . . . who are now making arrests for intimidation in South Carolina, and who are to preserve order at the polls on election day, are really an armed force in the service, and acting under the orders, of one of the parties to the political contest.' [3]

Even the hardened politicians were a little worried, and 'The Nation' compared them, naming Morton and Blaine, to 'a criminal haunted by remorse and flying from justice.' [4]

The Hampton-Gary leaders grimly held the passions and resentments of their people in check, but the old reliance on the soldiers intensified their determination to win. The closing Hampton rally at Charleston was hysterically enthusiastic, a picturesque procession of mounted red shirts clattering through the streets, with many negroes mounted on mules, with the handsome figures of Hampton and Gordon, of Georgia, in the front — marching through tumultuous throngs, with all the houses gay with flags and bunting, and with girls and gray-haired women waving from the windows. The people were thus moving with the troops, but these were sent scurrying all about, and before election day a company or more was stationed in every county seat. These were

[1] Williams, *Columbia State*, January 2, 1927.    [2] *Ibid.*, January 30, 1927.
[3] October 19, 1876.    [4] *Ibid.*

respected, but respect was exacted from them. Few slept at Charleston the night before the voting. Dawn had not broken when negroes with fife and drum, sent out by the Republican Committee, were passing from house to house, noisily summoning the negroes from their employers' homes.

The spirit of the Carolinians dramatically flared that day at Edgefield, the home of Gary, whither Grant had ordered General Ruger and some troops. In a conference, Ruger had agreed with Gary that the negroes and whites should vote at different polling-places to prevent collisions. Toward evening the mulatto county chairman, finding the colored voting-place crowded, determined to march twenty-five hundred to the polling-place of the whites at the court-house.

Gary heard, and stiffened. He had kept his word with Ruger, and Ruger should keep his. The grim 'Bald Eagle' ordered his men to pack the steps and porticoes of the court-house, and stationed sharpshooters on the roofs. Ruger, informed, hastened toward the court-house. Gary advanced to meet him. Ruger was in his uniform; Gary in a greatcoat and military boots.

'You must make your men give way and let these negroes to the ballot box,' said Ruger.

Gary's gray eyes flashed, and his voice vibrated with a desperate resolve:

'By God, sir, I will not do it. I will keep the compact I made with you this morning, that whites and blacks shall vote at different boxes, and if you think your bluecoats can make way for these negroes to vote again, try it.'

The whites yelled lustily, the negro politicians quailed, retired — and the crisis passed.[1]

Thus the day went by and the polls closed in the midst of excitement.

[1] Tillman's speech, in the Constitutional Convention, 1895.

# CHAPTER XXV

## THE CROWNING CRIME — AND RELEASE

### I

LATE on the night of the election, crowds in all the cities of the land were noisily celebrating the triumph of Tilden. No one doubted it. He had swept New York, Indiana, and the South. At the Republican headquarters, in the Fifth Avenue Hotel, hope was abandoned. The leaders there mournfully left early and sought their beds. Even the tenacious Zack Chandler, the chairman, retired to his room to sleep, leaving the headquarters deserted. The press of New York City, including 'The Tribune,' conceded the defeat of Hayes. At the office of the 'New York Times' the editorial council was going over the returns. It was no use. The figures were conclusive. And in the midst of the gloom an inquiry, which was to make history, reached 'The Times' from Senator Barnum of Connecticut, chairman of the financial committee of the Democratic organization, asking for the paper's figures on South Carolina, Florida, and Louisiana. And so the Democrats were not positive about these States? There was an inspiration. Pencils flew over paper — yes, these three States would give Hayes a majority of one in the Electoral College. Just what was required. And not one vote to spare. Strange things had been possible in the manipulation of election results in these three States during the last twelve years. Nothing was impossible now. In feverish haste the presses were stopped and 'The Times,' which practically had conceded defeat, claimed victory. No new returns had been received. No word from any of these States. Nothing, positively nothing, on which to predicate the new claim beyond the fact that a Democratic leader was not sure about them! Clearly they must be claimed by the Republicans and steps taken to sustain the claim.

Hurrying to the Republican headquarters, John C. Reid, of 'The Times,' found the rooms deserted — only the silent halls of the defeated. Zack Chandler must be found, apprised of the possibilities, set to work. In search of his room, Reid encountered W. E. Chandler, the 'Oliver Twist' of Jay Cooke, who had diverted many of the financier's dollars into the party chest. Into his too hospitable ears the journalist poured the story of Barnum's blunder. Could anything be clearer than the duty of the leaders? Chandler required no persuasion. Together, the two men hurried on to Zack Chandler's room. He was asleep, all hope abandoned. Kicking on the door, they aroused him and explained the situation. Heavy-eyed and weary, he told them to do what they pleased and let him alone. It was enough. The Yankee Chandler wanted nothing better than authority. Before the pavements of New York resounded with the footsteps of the sleeping people, telegrams were being flashed to 'good men and true' in the three States. No one knew better than Chandler the character of the men with whom he was communicating. The telegrams were imperative, and the recipients would know how to read between the lines. To Florida: 'Hayes defeated without Florida. Do not be cheated in returns.' To Louisiana: 'The presidential election depends on the vote of Louisiana, and the Democrats will try and wrest it from you. Watch, and hasten returns.' To South Carolina: 'Hayes is elected if we have carried South Carolina, Florida, and Louisiana. Can you hold your State?' There was not a carpet-bagger or corruptionist in these States who did not thoroughly understand just what was meant. Later that day, Zack Chandler, with not one new return, boldly announced Hayes had won the Presidency by one vote in the Electoral College — having carried South Carolina, Florida, and Louisiana! The party had its cue. 'The Times' claimed the election for its candidate. And the most daring conspiracy in American history was in motion.

II

With the amazing claim the country began to seethe with excitement. Conservative Republicans were incredulous, the Democrats were furious. Little fear was entertained by the conspirators as to South Carolina and Louisiana, where the men on whom they were depending were tried and true. But Florida was more doubtful. Not only were the powers of the Election Board there circumscribed, but the members were not so thoroughly trusted. Instant attention, then, for Florida! From Don Cameron, Secretary of War, flashed a telegram to the carpetbagger Stearns, the Governor, that 'a sufficient number of troops have been ordered to Tallahassee to give you the aid desired'; and Zack Chandler telegraphed the good tidings of great joy that W. E. Chandler was on his way to aid. The messages needed no interpreter. Instantly, local leaders over the State were telegraphed to hold every vote and that 'funds from Washington' would be available. Some of the local leaders, a little fearful of the fury of the people, asked military protection; Stearns ordered General Ruger to send troops, and Don Cameron instructed the General to obey. Soon Chandler was on the ground; the Second Assistant Postmaster-General appeared with a group of special agents of the Post-Office Department, and with money; and, following in their wake, detectives from the office of the Attorney-General. Checking accounts had been opened in a Philadelphia bank for Chandler, and the sunny skies of Florida never seemed brighter for political soldiers of fortune. Others, too, not so generally noticed, were on their way South, and one narrowly escaped rough treatment. When General Kilpatrick with a party stopped off at Warrenton, North Carolina, and began summoning Republican politicians to the Yarborough House, the mayor was hard put to it to hold back the fighting fury of the people, and the General hastily moved on.[1]

Meanwhile, the 'visiting statesmen' were on their way to New Orleans. Tilden had been warned early of the Chandler mission to Florida,[2] and the day after the election, Henry Watterson had telegraphed the man at Gramercy Park the suggestion that he, as Governor of New York, invite Hayes, as Governor of Ohio, to join with him in a committee to proceed to Louisiana to see justice done. The Western Union Telegraph Company, in those days a tool of the dominant party, dishonorably notified the Republicans of the message. It was not unusual. Telegrams to Tilden were not infrequently read at Republican headquarters before their transmission to Gramercy Park.[3] Thus, to save Hayes embarrassment, Grant hastily invited his 'visiting statesmen' to proceed to New Orleans. All his delegation was composed of Republicans of the

[1] *Southern Exposure*, 104.
[2] *Tilden Letters* (from Geo. W. Quackenbos), II, 487.     [3] Watterson, I, 296.

most bitterly partisan character. Garfield was asked to go, said Grant, because ' Governor Kellogg requests that reliable witnesses be sent to see that the canvass of the vote is a fair one.' [1] And so Garfield went, taking up his residence with a carpetbagger and joining with other reliable witnesses, including John Sherman, 'Pig Iron' Kelley, John A. Logan, Matt Quay, Lew Wallace, John A. Kasson, and Stanley Matthews. Whereupon Tilden selected representatives to watch the count. Three of these had wrecked their political careers through their devotion to principle and hostility to corruption — Lyman Trumbull, George W. Julian, and A. G. Curtin. Among the others were John M. Palmer, W. R. Morrison, Joseph E. McDonald, later a distinguished Senator of Catoesque integrity, Henry Watterson, former Senator Doolittle, and W. G. Sumner, the economist. There could be little doubt which group would make the stronger appeal to the confidence of the conservative and independent element of the country.

### III

Soon the St. Charles Hotel lobbies swarmed with national celebrities who were not a little amused, openly or secretly, at Grant's show of military strength. The city was perfectly quiet. Julian thought that 'sending troops was an insulting farce.' [2] The returns had given the Tilden electors a large majority ranging from six to eight thousand, and this could be overcome only by throwing out thousands of votes. The claim that there had been intimidation was based on the theory that there were 23,914 more negroes than whites, and that every negro had voted, and voted for Hayes. The latter clung ardently to the theory. But where did the 23,914 majority come from? asked the Tilden representatives. The census of 1870 had given the whites of voting age almost a thousand majority, and that of 1880 was to give the whites a majority almost identical. Some were prone to recall the scandals of false negro registration by the Kellogg clique in the campaign of 1874, when a congressional committee found no less than fifty-two hundred false registrations in New Orleans alone. Charles Nordhoff's book, 'The Cotton States in the Spring and Summer of

---

[1] *Life of Garfield*, i, 614.          [2] MS. Diary, December 10, 1876.

1875,' had been published within the year, and he, a supporter of Hayes, had told of witnessing the failure to secure a jury in a country parish because thirty-six of the forty-eight names drawn for the panel from the registration list had been found to be ficti-tious.[1]

This, however, furnished a pretext for lofty posing by pious statesmen of renown who were really depending confidently on the notoriously corrupt character of the Returning Board. It was not a Board with which they were unfamiliar. It was the same Board a Republican congressional committee had mercilessly de-nounced but a year before. The chairman was none other than James Madison Wells, Surveyor of the Port of New Orleans, and former Governor, whom Sheridan had described to Stanton nine years before as 'a political trickster and a dishonest man' whose conduct was 'as sinuous as the mark left in the dust by the move-ment of a snake.' Sheridan assured Grant that Wells 'has not a friend who is an honest man.' From that time on, according to Rhodes, the historian, he had 'done the dirty work of Louisiana politics and had steadily deteriorated in character.' Another mem-ber was Thomas C. Anderson, who literally stank of corruption, and the other two members were negroes without character or honesty. It would be impossible to conceive of a lower combi-nation of men with whom to determine the destiny of a nation.[2]

The law provided for a fifth member, a Democrat, but the Democrat had resigned long before and the four members stoutly refused to name a successor or to permit one to be appointed. Thus the Board was not only composed of members of one party, but there was not an honest man upon it. This had been conceded by all decent men in both parties during the two years preceding the election of 1876.

The Democratic 'visiting statesmen' invited the coöperation of the Republican visitors to secure 'an honest count and a true re-turn of the votes.' Nothing could have been farther from the thought of John Sherman and his associates. A true return and an honest count would have given Tilden a decisive majority. 'Counting the ballots as cast,' wrote a supporter to Hayes from New Orleans, 'would be in my judgment as great an infamy as

[1] Nordhoff, 43.    [2] Rhodes, VII, 231.

was ever perpetrated.'[1] To count Hayes in, and Tilden out, would require the throwing out of thousands of Democratic votes, and there was nothing to prevent it. The partisan Board of corruptionists had it in their power to disfranchise whole parishes on the pretext of intimidation. However, the pretext had to be as strongly buttressed with affidavits as possible, to meet public opinion and the test in Congress, and this was the work to which the 'visiting statesmen' named by Grant set themselves with a zest. Before finishing its work, the Board would disfranchise 13,214 Democrats; and do it in utter violation of the all-too-convenient law expressly framed for such purposes. This law provided that action could be taken only where affidavits were annexed to, and received with, the returns. In many instances the provision was disregarded, and a large part of the affidavits received with the returns related to previous elections.[2]

The process was all too simple. Five members of each visiting party were invited to attend the opening session of the Board. The returns from each parish were opened and the vote on presidential electors examined. Where there were no protests, these returns were sent to a room to be secretly tabulated by clerks every one of whom was a Republican, and five of whom were common criminals and under indictment for crimes.[3] Some were under indictment for murder. No Democrat was permitted to witness the tabulation.

Where affidavits charging intimidation and fraud accompanied the returns, testimony was taken on both sides; and it was in the active preparation of these affidavits that John Sherman and his associates were deeply concerned. These divided the parishes among them, and each man privately interviewed witnesses, and, where necessary, suggested changes in the testimony.

The activities of James A. Garfield will illustrate the work of the men Grant sent to see that the count was 'fair.' He was living at the home of a carpetbagger,[4] and there he remained for eighteen days. In an inner room of the office of Packard, Republican leader and candidate for Governor, he sat for days alone, undisturbed, shut off from prying eyes and ears, examining affidavits, noting

---

[1] *Life of Hayes*, I, 504, note.　　[2] Rhodes, VII, 232.
[3] *Ibid.*, Cowley.　　[4] *Life of Garfield*, I, 616.

weaknesses, sending for witnesses, whom he saw alone, suggesting changes through leading questions, preparing the case for the Board. Copies of all the affidavits were furnished by the Board to Garfield and his fellow partisans. It was he who examined Amy Mitchell, whose husband's death was being used to prove intimidation. Not content with her affidavit, he asked questions and the replies were added. There at the Custom-House she was drilled for her appearance before the Board. Later, she was to declare that her answers to all Garfield's questions were false, and that she said what she did because told to do so.[1] Because of these activities, Hendricks was to denounce Garfield's connection as 'one doubtful in character and worse than that of any other man now living.' Perhaps his work was not different from that of others, except for the fact that he was to serve on the Electoral Commission.

Thus, and by such were the affidavits made. Men like Sherman, Garfield, and Matthews pretended to be outraged by the 'revelations' — especially in the case of the prostitute, Eliza Pinkston. This appealing creature had been tried for the murder of a child and acquitted only because the chief witness was too young to understand the nature of an oath. Later the congressional committee that pried into the proceedings at New Orleans refrained from a full delineation of her character because 'too indecent to print.'

Meanwhile, as the evidence was being taken, there can be no doubt that the corrupt Board was seeking a buyer. Scarcely had Julian reached New Orleans when he concluded that 'the rascalities of the Board exceeded anything I had dreamed of.'[2] Wells was willing to sell to the Democrats if the price were high enough.[3] It was openly charged at the time that he sent an agent to Grant and Cameron to announce his price, with the threat to sell to the Democrats if the Republicans would not buy; and then on to New York City with the offer to sell to the Democratic National Chairman at a reduced figure.[4] Henry Watterson, the 'argus-eyed,' remembered years later that the air reeked with talk of corrup-

---

[1] Garfield in Louisiana, by Thomas A. Hendricks, September 6, 1880, based on the congressional investigation.

[2] MS. Diary, December 10, 1876.

[3] Manton Marble, 7–8; Bigelow, *Retrospections*, v, 299.          [4] Marble, 7.

tion. 'That the Returning Board was for sale and could be bought
was the universal impression,' he wrote.[1]

Through some strange magic in this air reeking with corruption, Grant's 'visiting statesmen' underwent a grotesque metamor-
phosis in their attitude toward the Board that all had agreed, but
a year before, were shamelessly corrupt. Garfield was dining with
them. 'Dined at Governor Kellogg's,' he wrote in his diary, 'with
J. Madison Wells and General Anderson of the Returning Board.
. . . Of our party Sherman, Hale, and Stoughton were with me.
My opinion of the Returning Board is far better than it was before
I came.'[2] But the change in John Sherman was most miraculous.
Writing Hayes of the Board, he said: 'I have carefully observed
them, and have formed a high opinion of Governor Wells and
Colonel Anderson. They are firm, judicious, and, as far as I can
judge, thoroughly honest and conscientious.'[3] Meanwhile, having
finished their labors in the interest of an 'honest election,' the
President's 'visiting statesmen' hurried away about the time the
Board went into secret session to reach a decision.

This was on December 2. The next day, three days before the
decision was announced, the United States Marshal was telegraphing Senator West in Washington that he had 'seen Wells,
who says, "Board will return Hayes sure. Have no fear."' And
on the fourth day, the Board threw out 13,250 Tilden votes and
gave the electoral vote to Hayes. In the mean time the 'visiting
statesmen' had stopped off at Fremont, to 'emphatically endorse'
the 'general fairness and honesty of the Board's conduct' and to
speak 'highly of Wells and Anderson, and frankly of the two
colored men.'[4] Reviewing the proceedings years later, Rhodes,
the historian, and a Republican, was to write: 'As a matter of fact,
Wells and his satellites in secret conclave determined the Presidency of the United States; but, before returning the vote of
Louisiana for Hayes, there is little doubt that he offered to give it
to Tilden for $200,000.'[5]

[1] *Marse Henry*, I, 298.
[2] *Life of Garfield*, I, 622.
[3] *Life of Hayes*, I, 502–03: Sherman, *Recollections*, I, 558.
[4] Hayes diary, *Life*, I, 506–07.
[5] Rhodes, VII, 233.

IV

Meanwhile, in Florida, W. E. Chandler, with 'funds from Washington' and a troop of agents of the Post-Office Department and the Department of Justice, was compelled to move with some circumspection and amidst embarrassments. There the Board, dominated by Samuel B. McLin, Secretary of State, had no judicial or discretionary powers under the law, and only ministerial power — the power of canvassing the returns as the country returning officers sent them, and declaring the result. There, too, were the soldiers to protect the Board in any villainy it might undertake, and soon Chandler had the invaluable assistance of distinguished Ohio politicians who were known to be intimate with Hayes — former Governor Edward F. Noyes and Stanley Matthews. When Chandler had the managers instruct the leaders in every county to 'save every vote,' it was with the hope that by hook or by crook the return of the county canvassers would show a small majority for Hayes. Under the law of Florida as interpreted by the Supreme Court in the case of Bloxham *vs.* State Canvassers he could then stand on the returns. But when the canvass was completed, and there was a small majority for Tilden, the situation was serious. Somehow the law had to be evaded, and technicalities' found on which to base a contest, to the end that Tilden votes might be thrown out, and in due time this was done. During the process the evidence is convincing that there was much talk of patronage, in which the good Mr. Noyes played a prominent part. And so it came about that Tilden voters were disfranchised, and the electoral vote was given to Hayes by the Board. It was done through trickery and the fabrication of affidavits, 228 of which were in the same handwriting. The story of the theft of Florida and Louisiana is told in the language of Rhodes: 'Had these been Northern States the dispute would have ceased forthwith. These two States would have been conceded to Tilden, and his election secured; but under the carpetbag-negro régime, the canvassing boards of Florida and Louisiana had the power to throw out votes on the ground of intimidation or fraud, and these boards were under the control of the Republicans.' [1]

In South Carolina the case was not so clear for Tilden. Re-

[1] Rhodes, VII, 229.

publicans of some note had supported Hampton for Governor while opposing Tilden, and there had been ample justification for the coolness of Democratic party workers toward the man of Gramercy Park, who had been cold to Hampton's nomination. That the Democrats had been approached with the offer of a trade was admitted by A. C. Haskell, the State Chairman, in reply to a letter by 'A Tilden Democrat' charging treachery, but the proposal had been rejected. The popularity of Hampton, with the desperate need to rid the State of its semi-savage government, unquestionably justifies the conclusion that Hampton polled more votes than Hayes; and many still insist that, though Hampton undoubtedly polled a larger vote, nevertheless Tilden did carry the State. It matters little, since South Carolina could have gone to Hayes and he still would have lost without both Florida and Louisiana.

Thus, when the time came to canvass the Electoral College, Tilden, with a popular majority of more than a quarter of a million, was defeated by one electoral vote if the actions of the returning Boards in Florida and Louisiana were permitted to stand. The Nation faced the most serious crisis in its history.

## V

Hayes was a man of almost uncanny foresight. As early as October, a month before the election, he was communing with himself on what he would do, or should do, in the event of a contested election threatening civil war, and he was hoping he would do his duty. 'It may lead to a conflict of arms,' he wrote in his diary.[1] There had been nothing of the sort before, and yet the man at Fremont was speculating on it before the votes were cast. The situation was threatening enough after the 'visiting statesmen' had concluded their work. No supporter of Tilden doubted his election, and thousands of thoughtful conservative supporters of Hayes had no doubt of their candidate's defeat. But desperate men had long been at the throttle, and these were as ready as ever to run down all opposition. That Grant and the army would be behind Hayes in a fight, there was evidence enough already. Hayes controlled the Senate, but the House was Democratic.

[1] *Life of Hayes*, I, 486.

This made the prospects of a peaceful settlement all the more doubtful. The rank and file of the Democrats had grown weary of Louisiana methods, and were ready for battle. Their nominee had won with a great popular majority, and it had been necessary to rob him of at least two States to give his opponent a bare majority of one in the Electoral College. It was too much. Henry Watterson, and many like him, thought self-respect and public honor called for armed resistance, if need be, to what they were convinced was an outrageous steal.[1] More cautious publicly, he urged that one hundred thousand Tilden men march on Washington unarmed, and Nast made merry over such an army. Already Grant had real soldiers there and gunboats in the Potomac. But the Democratic leaders, generally, were timid, and the closet lawyer sat in his library at Gramercy Park preparing worthless statistics on previous elections, and dreaming of a lawsuit. Soon his indecision and inability to rise to a crisis discouraged his followers. Julian, addressing a protest meeting in Indianapolis, found the rank and file on their toes prepared to fight rather than surrender to a fraud. But he observed that other speakers, even Voorhees, were cautious and responded 'in an offhand manner' in a speech 'tame and disappointing as the resolutions.'[2]

Very soon red-blooded men who had followed him zealously were almost contemptuous of Tilden. 'He was not formed in the same mould with the heroes,' wrote O'Connor of Charleston, to his daughter. 'The qualities he possesses . . . are not such as to regenerate a nation or save one.'[3] Many were making unfavorable comparisons with Wade Hampton, similarly situated as to the governorship of South Carolina, who had calmed his excited followers with the firm, dignified announcement: 'I have been elected, and I shall be Governor.' Watterson thought that had Tilden given his people any such declaration the result might have been different. Meanwhile, as the Democrats cringed at the mention of arms, the Republicans, having learned in the twelve-year revolution the power of audacity and effrontery, were responding in the House to the question of a cautious Democrat, as to whether they were ready for an armed conflict, with the shout, 'Yes.' Thus it

[1] Bigelow, *Retrospections*, v, 303–04.
[2] MS. Diary, January 21, 1877.                     [3] O'Connor, 148.

soon was evident that while the Republicans were ready to fight to make good the fraudulent action in the two States that barely turned the victory, the Democrats, backed by a quarter of a million popular majority and an electoral majority, on the returns, of thirty-seven, were not prepared to go so far. And so the Democrats timidly retreated as their foe advanced with much rattling of sabers. If it was a bluff — and it probably was — it served its purpose. In an appeal to force, many thousands of Republicans who believed Tilden honestly elected would have stood aloof. Even Roscoe Conkling seemed, in the beginning, a little outraged by what had occurred. Hayes was hearing from Sherman that Conkling, 'as the case stands,' would 'not vote that you have either Florida or Louisiana,'[1] and Tilden was hearing[2] that Conkling had asked if the Democrats intended 'to act upon the good boy principle of submission, or whether we mean to have it understood that Tilden has been elected and, by the Eternal, he shall be inaugurated.' But the tired old man of Gramercy Park was not impressed. He was studying precedents and the law.

Left in the dark or in doubt, and uninspired by a militant leadership, the Democrats in Congress were engaged in endless conferences with the Republicans, seeking a peaceable solution. They were prepared to fight the plan to give Ferris, the partisan President pro tem. of the Senate, the power to count the votes and declare the result. Some in the House were ready to refuse to meet with the Senate. Hayes and Tilden both properly rejected with contempt the plan to have them pitch a penny on the Presidency. And so matters drifted on and finally ended in the decision to stake the Presidency on the decision of a Commission with a majority of Republicans.

That was the surrender, and after that the end was as clear as the summer sun at noonday.

### VI

With the farcical proceedings before the Commission, with its interminable quibbling over technicalities, and its partisan refusal to hear evidence of fraud in the actions of the Returning Boards in Florida and Louisiana, we need not concern ourselves. That was

[1] *Life of Hayes*, i, 521.     [2] *Letters* (from J. Thomas Spriggs), ii, 491.

merely going through the form of declaring Hayes elected with a
decent regard for appearances. When the Commission gave Florida to Hayes, the contest was settled. No one doubted that
Louisiana would go likewise.

Meanwhile, the Republicans, encouraged by Hayes himself,
were busying themselves with Southerners in Congress and out,
in an attempt to divide the Democratic ranks, and in this way,
too, they were to succeed to the fullness of their hopes. While it
had been thought politically wise in the North to denounce slave-
owners of pre-war days as 'Democrats,' men like Hayes knew that
in some, if not most, of the Southern States, the old slave-holding
aristocrats had been Whigs, as, previously, their forbears had been
Federalists. These had been Federalists and Whigs because opposed to the fundamental principles and policies of Jefferson and
Jackson, and they had gone over to the Democrats after the war
from necessity and with reluctance. To Hayes it seemed reasonable that at heart these were more Republican than Democratic.
And to these he turned with hope, and not without encouragement
from Southerners, whatever their real politics may have been. He
had been informed that discreet friends of his were holding 'frequent conferences with the more conservative Democratic Senators from the South, especially those of Whig antecedents.'[1] Colonel A. J. Keller, of the 'Memphis Avalanche,' was especially active, and was being recommended to Hayes as 'just the man needed
to reach the Southern men.'[2] Garfield was writing Hayes that 'the
leading Southern Democrats in Congress, especially those who
were old Whigs, are saying that they have seen war enough and
don't care to follow the lead of their Northern associates.'[3] Indeed,
plans were afoot for a time to secure the services of Tom Scott, the
railroad president, noted, as we have seen, as a lobbyist, 'to exert
his persuasive powers with Southern members of Congress and
Southern business men to reconcile them to a Republican succession.'[4] Soon Kasson was writing Hayes that 'our security against
the subsequent election of Tilden by the House is to be found in
the division of sentiment in the Democracy led by Southern representatives.'[5] In the latter part of December, Hayes noted in his

[1] *Life of Hayes*, I, 520.          [2] *Ibid.*          [3] *Ibid.*, I, 530.
[4] *Ibid.*, I, 520.                   [5] *Ibid.*, I, 217, note.

diary that he had received a letter from Hampton presenting his 'views of duty in case of armed resistance by the Democrats.' [1] It was afterward to be admitted by Colonel A. C. Haskell, the State Chairman in South Carolina, in reply to the letter from 'A Tilden Democrat' charging a trade, that Judge Mackay, a Republican, had carried a letter to Fremont from Hampton, which merely explained conditions in the State. Even before the beginning of December, the editor of the 'New Orleans Times' had called on Hayes, who wrote in his diary that the journalist had brought him the views of Lamar, Hampton, 'and probably Gen. Gordon.' These views, as the editor expressed them, were that Hayes would be President and the South would make no trouble; that it wanted peace and the color line eliminated; and would 'not oppose an Administration which will favor an honest administration and honest officers in the South.' [2]

That there was desperate flirting with the Southerners, Tilden knew by the middle of December, if not before. Charles A. Dana had sent him a letter from his Washington correspondent, saying, 'There is undoubtedly danger of defection among the Southern Democrats,' and that 'the friends of Hayes are certainly bidding high in that direction.' [3] So far had the negotiations progressed by February 17, that Carl Schurz was writing Hayes on how far he should go toward satisfying the Southern hopes. 'Would it not seem worthy of consideration whether the appointment to a place in your Cabinet of some man of Confederate antecedents, and enjoying the confidence of that class, would not secure to your Southern policy great facilities?' he asked. 'If the right man can be found, he would be a living link between them and your Administration.' [4] It was in this letter that Schurz made his futile plea for the recognition of the deserted Bristow.

All the while, the meaningless chatter of the lawyers went on, with the Commission refusing the Democrats permission to offer proof of the lawlessness of the Boards in Florida and Louisiana, and in the end the mockery ceased, and the decision, known before an argument had been made, was rendered. The three States needed to elect Hayes by one vote were bodily transferred to his

[1] *Life of Hayes*, i, 516, note.    [2] *Ibid.*, i, 504-05.
[3] *Tilden Letters*, ii, 505.    [4] Hayes MSS., February 17, 1877.

column. For a moment there was talk of a filibuster in the House to prevent the declaration of an election until March 4, but Samuel J. Randall and Southern members frowned sternly upon the idea.[1] Indeed, at that time Senator Gordon and John Young Brown of Kentucky had discussed Hayes's Southern policy with Congressman Charles Foster of Ohio, and had an agreement in writing, signed by Foster and Stanley Matthews, of Ohio, one of the Republican counsel before the Commission, which read:

'Referring to the conversation had with you yesterday in which Governor Hayes's policy as to the status of certain Southern States was discussed, we desire to say that we can assure you in the strongest possible manner of our great desire to have him adopt such a policy as will give to the people of the States of South Carolina and Louisiana the right to control their own affairs in their own way, subject only to the Constitution of the United States and the laws made in pursuance thereof, and to say further that from an acquaintance with and knowledge of Governor Hayes and his views, we have the most complete confidence that such will be the policy of his Administration.' [2]

There was still some uneasiness about Louisiana, but one day, in William M. Evarts's room at Wormley's Hotel, there was a final conference and a distinct understanding. Henry Watterson had been invited to sit in by a member of the Louisiana delegation and by Garfield, and had been asked by General M. C. Butler to insist on equally favorable terms for South Carolina. There, in Evarts's room, sat Garfield, John Sherman, Stanley Matthews, and Evarts, and there all the details of the bargain were settled.[3]

Even then the die-hards still had hope. It was whispered loudly that Roscoe Conkling had organized a Republican bolt from the decision of the Commission and had secured the adhesion of enough Republican Senators to have reversed the decision in the case of Louisiana. If such a bolt was planned, it failed to materialize. Afterward it was to be rolled under the tongues of the gossips that Conkling was dissuaded by Kate Chase Sprague, who hated Tilden for preventing her father's nomination in 1868. This, however, was long afterward and her name does not appear in the con-

---

[1] *Life of Hayes*, i, 532.          [2] *Ibid.*, i, 533.
[3] Watterson, i, 309–11.

temporary gossip, and it is probable that she played no part at all.[1]

Thus the work of the Commission was ratified, according to one contemporary, because of 'Northern Democratic cowardice in November and Southern Democratic treachery in February'; though it may be doubted whether there would have been 'Southern treachery' had there been no 'Northern cowardice.'[2] 'Samuel Bowles, of the 'Springfield Republican,' put the rabid partisans of the two parties aside and found that the majority of thoughtful and conservative men believed Tilden was entitled to Louisiana, 'though rather wishing that he wasn't.'[3] After a careful study of contemporary evidence, Rhodes, the historian, and a Republican, was to declare years later that had the 'visiting statesmen' stayed at home both Louisiana and Florida would have gone to Tilden, and this was the opinion of Hugh McCulloch.[4] And on the day Hayes entered upon his Presidency, an old man in Gramercy Park sat reading a letter from Charles Francis Adams: 'It has been many years since I ceased to be a party man. . . . It is a source of gratification to me to think that I made the right choice in the late election. I could never have been reconciled to the elevation by the smallest aid of mine of a person, however respectable in private life, who must forever carry upon his brow the stamp of fraud, first triumphant in American history.'[5]

Scarcely a man, down to the most petty, connected with the transactions in Louisiana and Florida, failed to secure a Federal appointment. It is preferable to believe that with this distribution of the patronage among some of the most notoriously incompetent and corrupt, Hayes was not concerned. Much of it was passed out through John Sherman, as head of the Treasury. It is to the credit of Hayes that he did not find a place for Jay Cooke's 'Oliver Twist,' though earnestly urged to accord W. E. Chandler recognition. 'I beg you to remember him,' wrote Blaine in a pleading letter, 'not only for his own sake . . . but for the sake of the gratitude which so many of your best friends feel towards him.'[6] But Hayes was adamant, and soon Chandler was denouncing him as an ingrate.

---

[1] Hon. George Hoadley, in *New York Evening Post*; quoted, *Letters of Tilden*, ii, 511–13.
[2] Bigelow: *Retrospections*, v, 314.      [3] Letters to G. W. Smalley, Merriam, ii. 355
[4] *Men and Measures*, 420.      [5] *Tilden's Letters*, ii, 548.
[6] Hayes MSS., February 14, 1877.

Thus the crisis passed, with Hayes in the White House, but thoughtful men were shuddering over what might well have been. A desperate game had won once, but it would not be safe to try the methods of '76 again. The Nation had tired of the bludgeoning of the South; and Northern sentiment was turning against the manipulation of Southern elections through the methods used in Florida and Louisiana. It was disgusted, too, with this constant marching and countermarching of Federal soldiers about the polls: nauseated, as well, with the carpetbaggers and all their works. The hour for a change had come.

Nor was there further need for such desperate revolutionary methods, since the revolution had been entrenched. The party purpose avowed by Thaddeus Stevens had been served, and the dominant party no longer required the negro vote or the South. Power had passed, during the revolution, from the agriculturist to the industrialist and the financier, and these, more powerful than the politicians, had become the party's working allies. A degree of centralization not dreamed of in other days had been realized. State rights were to be denounced for forty years as the equivalent of treason. A new order had been established, built upon the ruins of the old. The Jeffersonian Republic that came in with the revolution of 1800 gave way to the Hamiltonian Republic brought in by the counter-revolution of 1865–76. The tables had been turned. The age-old fight would continue, the spirits of Jefferson and Hamilton leading as before, but the advantage, under the new order, had passed to the latter.

At any rate, the hour of the South's redemption from military despotism had struck. The bargain had been made — reduced to writing. And so Packard, the Republican gubernatorial nominee in Louisiana, who had received a thousand more votes than Hayes, according to the Returning Board, was turned out, and Nicholls, the Democrat, became Governor; Chamberlain in South Carolina was deprived of his bayonets and Wade Hampton went in; and in Florida the State courts made short shrift of Stearns, the carpetbagger, and Drew, the Democrat, entered upon his gubernatorial duties. In North Carolina, Vance had easily triumphed at the polls — and so the South was free again to rule herself.

## VIII

For the final scenes let us return to South Carolina, which had suffered most. It is New Year's Night in Columbia. Among the brighter of the carpetbaggers it was all too clear that 'Honest' John Patterson's promise of 'five years more of good stealing in South Carolina' would fall short. A company of United States soldiers in the State House was all that was keeping Chamberlain in possession there. Soon — too soon — Hampton would move in. Some of the public pillagers, in the spirit of the admonition to 'eat, drink, and be merry, for to-morrow we die,' proposed a farewell fling. Laughing would keep up courage.

And so New Year's Night found them assembled in Fine's Saloon, which had been so intimately associated with reconstruction; above which Patterson had held open house, and from which carpetbaggers and misguided negro legislators had so often staggered with bribery money in their pockets. There had been the glory, and there let the curtain fall. With the politicians were some army officers, for the army and its bayonets had long stood between the corruptionists and the wrath of the people. A few newspaper men were admitted, too. Some one had stolen the silken judicial robe of the negro Associate Justice of the Supreme Court Wright, whose elevation to the bench had been hailed joyously by 'Harper's Weekly.' Over the shoulders of a little hunchback gambler, 'Hunchy' Gaylord, a boon companion of Moses, the robe was thrown, and a court-room scene was improvised. The hunchback ascended to the top of a stepladder and called the court to order. A prime mimic, he had Wright's lisp, his ponderous air of unfathomable wisdom, and a smattering of mispronounced Latin law phrases.

Pounding for order among the clinking of glasses and loud laughter, he summoned culprits before him for trial and punishment. These were charged with all manner of offenses from attempting to steal the State House to maligning the character of the town's most notorious courtesan. Drinking, shouting, laughing, cursing, the burlesque continued throughout the night, and the dawn had come when the hunchback collapsed into a drunken stupor, and the 'court' adjourned.

In a corner of the room they laid him, wrapped in the silken robes of Justice Wright, and the others — carpetbaggers, army officers, and reporters — emerged from the farewell festival.[1]

A little later, Chamberlain, hoping against hope, was reading a disturbing letter from Stanley Matthews, one of the 'visiting statesmen,' who had sat in on the bargaining over the seating of Hayes. A courteous letter, but fatal. Did not Chamberlain think, in view of the dual governments of himself and Hampton, it would be well to withdraw the troops and see which government could stand without them? A monstrous proposition! And at the bottom of the letter a postscript, signed by William M. Evarts, now Secretary of State, endorsing the suggestion. It was a death warrant.

And thus, one sunny day, when the streets of the capital were thronged with men, women, and children, white and black, in festive mood over the visiting circus and its performing bears, a carriage left the State House bearing a white-faced, disillusioned man who had narrowly escaped greatness. As his carriage slowly made its way through the crowds and he looked straight ahead, no one seemed to see him. The crowd was busy with its peanuts and its anticipations of the bears and clowns. And thus Chamberlain rode from power to his political St. Helena.

And thus one day a company of United States soldiers filed out of the State House, led by a captain, and marched through the streets to the barracks, while a curious crowd watched the historic evacuation without a murmur. The reign of the carpetbagger was over. Wade Hampton moved into the gubernatorial chambers, and South Carolinians resumed the possession of their government and the direction of their destiny.

[1] Williams, *Columbia State*, March 13, 1927.

THE END

# MANUSCRIPTS, BOOKS, AND NEWSPAPERS
## CONSULTED AND CITED

## MANUSCRIPTS

BARUCH: MS. Letters of Dr. Simon Baruch. In possession of Bernard M. Baruch, New York.

DAUGHTERS OF THE CONFEDERACY: MS. Letters and Diaries. Collected for the author by the Daughters of the Confederacy.

GARY: MS. Biography of Martin W. Gary, by David Duncan Wallace. In possession of the Honorable John Gary Evans, Spartanburg, South Carolina.

HAYES: The Rutherford B. Hayes MSS. Fremont, Ohio.

HOLDEN: W. W. Holden MSS.; political and personal letters. North Carolina Historical Commission, Raleigh.

HOLDEN: Recollections of Gov. W. W. Holden, by his daughter. In author's possession.

JULIAN: Diary of George W. Julian, 1865–1877. In possession of Grace Julian Clarke, Indianapolis.

MORTON: MS. Letters of Oliver P. Morton. Henry County, Indiana, Historical Society.

THURMAN: The Allan G. Thurman Papers. Ohio Archæological and Historical Society.

WARMOTH: MS. Reminiscences of Gov. Henry Clay Warmoth. In his possession, New Orleans.


## BOOKS

ABBOTT, JOSIAH GARDNER. *See* Cowley.

ADAMS, HENRY: *Education of Henry Adams.* Boston, 1918.

ALLEN, WALTER: *Governor Chamberlain's Administration.* New York, 1888.

ARMES, W. D., editor: *The Autobiography of Joseph LeConte.* New York, 1903.

AVERY, I. W.: *History of Georgia.* New York, 1881.


BADEAU, ADAM: *Grant in Peace: A Personal Memoir.* Hartford, 1887.

BARNES, THURLOW WEED, editor: *Memoir of Thurlow Weed.* Two volumes, Boston, 1884.

BARNES, W. H.: *History of the Thirty-Ninth Congress of the United States.* New York, 1868.

BAYARD, THOMAS F. *See* Spencer.

BEALES, H. S. B.: *Letters of Mrs. James G. Blaine.* Two volumes, New York, 1908.

BELLOWS, HENRY W.: *Historical Sketch of the Union League Club.* New York, 1879.

BIGELOW, JOHN: *Letters and Literary Memorials of Samuel J. Tilden.* Two volumes, New York, 1908.

BIGELOW, JOHN: *Retrospections of an Active Life*. Five volumes, New York, 1909–13.

BIGELOW, JOHN: *Life of Samuel J. Tilden*. Two volumes, New York, 1895.

BLAINE, JAMES G.: *Twenty Years in Congress*. Two volumes, Norwich, 1884.

BLAIR, FRANK P. *See* Croly.

BOUTWELL, GEORGE S.: *Reminiscences of Sixty Years in Public Affairs*. Two volumes, New York, 1902.

BOWEN, HERBERT W.: *Recollections, Diplomatic and Undiplomatic*. New York, 1926.

BOWLES, SAMUEL. *See* Merriam.

BOYD, W. K.: *Governor W. W. Holden*. Trinity College Historical Papers, Durham, 1899.

BROWN, JOSEPH E. *See* Fielder.

BROWNLOW, W. P.: 'Defence and Vindication of Andrew Johnson,' *Taylor-Trotwood Magazine*, September, 1908.

BUCK, S. J.: *The Granger Movement*. Cambridge, 1913.

BURGESS, JOHN W.: *Reconstruction and the Constitution*. New York, 1902.

BURTON, THEODORE E.: *Financial Crises and Periods of Industrial and Financial Depression*. New York, 1909.

BUTLER, BENJAMIN F.: *Butler's Book*. Boston, 1892.

BRYANT, WILLIAM CULLEN. *See* Godwin.


CALLENDER, E. B.: *Thaddeus Stevens*. Boston, 1882.

CARPENTER, MATTHEW HALE. *See* Flower.

CHAMBERLAIN, ROSE S.: *Old Days at Chapel Hill*. London, 1926.

CHANDLER, ZACHARIAH: 'Life and Public Services,' *Detroit Post*, 1880.

CHASE, SALMON P. *See* Schuckers and Warden.

CHESTNUT, MARY BOYDEN: *A Diary from Dixie*. New York, 1905.

CLARKE, GRACE JULIAN: *George W. Julian*. Indiana Historical Collection, XI, Indianapolis, 1923.

CLAY, MRS.: *A Belle of the Fifties*. New York, 1905.

CLAYTON, POWELL: *The Aftermath of Civil War in Arkansas*. New York, 1915.

CLEMENCEAU, GEORGES: *History of American Reconstruction*. Letters to *Le Temps*. New York, 1928.

COLFAX, SCHUYLER. *See* Hollister.

CONKLING, A. R.: *Life and Letters of Roscoe Conkling*. New York, 1889.

COOKE, JAY. *See* Oberholtzer.

CORTISSOZ, ROYAL: *Life of Whitelaw Reid*. Two volumes, New York, 1921.

COULTER, E. MERTON: *Civil War and Readjustment in Kentucky*. Chapel Hill, 1926.

COWLEY, CHARLES: *Memoir of Josiah Gardner Abbott*. Boston, 1892.

COX, S. S.: *Three Decades of Federal Legislation*. Providence, 1888.

CROLY, DAVID G.: *Seymour and Blair: Their Lives and Services*. New York, 1868.

CROOK, WILLIAM H.: *Through Five Administrations*. New York, 1910.


DAVIS, S. L.: *Authentic History of the Ku-Klux Klan*. New York, 1924.

DAWSON, SARAH MORGAN: *A Confederate Girl's Diary*. Boston, 1913.

DEWITT, DAVID MILLER: *The Impeachment and Trial of Andrew Johnson*. New York, 1903.

DICKENS, CHARLES. *See* Forster.

DOWD, CLEMENT: *Life of Zebulon B. Vance*. Charlotte, 1897.

DUNNING, WILLIAM A.: *Reconstruction, Political and Economic*. New York, 1907.

ECKENRODE, H. J.: *A Political History of Virginia During Reconstruction*. Baltimore, 1904.

EVARTS, WILLIAM MAXWELL: *Arguments and Speeches*. Three volumes, New York, 1919.

FESSENDEN, FRANCIS: *Life and Public Services of William Pitt Fessenden*. Two volumes, Boston, 1907.

FICKLEN, JOHN ROSE: *History of Reconstruction in Louisiana*. Baltimore, 1910.

FIELDER, HERBERT: *Life, Times and Speeches of Joseph E. Brown*. Springfield, 1883.

FLEMING, WALTER F.: *Civil War and Reconstruction in Alabama*. New York, 1905.

FLEMING, WALTER F.: *Documentary History of Reconstruction*. Two volumes, Cleveland, 1906.

FLOWER, FRANK A.: *Edward McMasters Stanton*. Akron, 1905.

FLOWER, FRANK A.: *Life of Matthew Hale Carpenter*. Madison, 1884.

FORNEY, JOHN W.: *Anecdotes of Public Men*. Two volumes, New York, 1873.

FORSTER, JOHN: *Life of Charles Dickens*. Three volumes, Philadelphia, 1874.

FOULKE, WILLIAM DUDLEY. *Life of Oliver P. Morton*. Two volumes, Indianapolis, 1899.

FULLER, ROBERT H.: *Jubilee Jim: The Life of Colonel James Fisk*. New York, 1928.

GARFIELD, JAMES A. *See* Smith.

GARNER, JAMES W.: *Reconstruction in Mississippi*. New York, 1901.

GODKIN, EDWIN LAWRENCE. *See* Ogden.

GODWIN, PARKE: *Life of William Cullen Bryant*. Two volumes, New York, 1883.

GORHAM, GEORGE C.: *Life and Public Services of Edwin M. Stanton*. Two volumes, Boston, 1872.

GRANT, U. S.: *Personal Memoirs*. New York, 1885.

GREELEY, HORACE. *See* Seitz.

GRIMES, JAMES W. *See* Salter.

GUROSKI, ADAM: *Diary*. Three volumes, Boston, 1862-66.

HAMILTON, GAIL: *Biography of James G. Blaine*. Norwich, 1895.

HAMILTON, J. G. DE ROULHAC: *Reconstruction in North Carolina*. New York, 1914.

HAMILTON, J. G. DE ROULHAC, editor: *The Correspondence of Jonathan Worth*. Two volumes. Publications of the North Carolina Historical Commission, Raleigh, 1909.

HAMILTON, J. G. DE ROULHAC, editor: *The Papers of Thomas Ruffin.* Publications of the North Carolina Historical Commission, Raleigh, 1920.

HAMLIN, CHARLES EUGENE: *Life and Times of Hannibal Hamlin.* Two volumes, Boston, 1899.

HAYES, RUTHERFORD B. *See* Williams.

HENDRICKS, THOMAS A. *See* Holcombe.

HENSEL, W. U.: *Thaddeus Stevens as a Country Lawyer.* Pamphlet, no date.

HENSEL, W. U.: *The Christiana Riot and the Treason Trials of 1851.* Lancaster, 1911.

HILL, BENJAMIN H., JR.: *Senator Benjamin H. Hill: His Life, Speeches and Writings.* Atlanta, 1893.

HILL, BENJAMIN H. *See* Pearse.

HOAR, GEORGE F.: *Autobiography.* Two volumes, New York, 1903.

HOLCOMBE, JOHN W.: *Life of Thomas A. Hendricks.* Indianapolis, 1886.

HOLDEN, W. W.: *Memoirs of W. W. Holden.* John Lawson Monographs, Trinity College Historical Society, Durham, 1911.

HOLLISTER, C. J.: *Life of Schuyler Colfax.* New York, 1886.

HOLLOWAY, LAURA C.: *The Ladies of the White House.* Philadelphia, 1881.

HULL, GEORGE H.: *Industrial Depressions.* New York, 1926.

INGERSOLL, ROBERT G.: *Works.* Dresden edition.

JOHNSON, ANDREW. *See* Winston, Stryker, Jones, Dewitt, Moore.

JONES, JAMES S.: *Life of Andrew Johnson.* Greeneville, 1901.

JULIAN, GEORGE W.: *Speeches on Political Questions.* New York, 1872.

JULIAN, GEORGE W.: *Political Recollections.* Chicago, 1884. *See also* Clarke.

LAMAR, LUCIUS Q. C. *See* Mayes.

LATHERS, RICHARD. *See* Sanborn.

LEE, CAPTAIN R. E.: *Recollections and Letters of Robert E. Lee.* New York, 1926.

LEIGH, FRANCES BUTLER: *Ten Years on a Georgia Plantation.* London, 1883.

LESLIE, J. C. (and W. L. WILSON): *The Ku-Klux Klan.* New York, 1905.

LOGAN, MRS. JOHN A.: *Reminiscences of a Soldier's Wife.* New York, 1913.

LONN, ELLA: *Reconstruction in Louisiana After 1868.* New York, 1918.

LOWRY, ROBERT (and W. H. McCARDLE): *A History of Mississippi.* Jackson, 1891.

McCALL, SAMUEL: *Thaddeus Stevens.* Boston, 1899.

McCARTHY, CHARLES H.: *Lincoln's Plan of Reconstruction.* New York, 1901.

McCULLOCH, HUGH: *Men and Measures.* New York, 1888.

McDONALD, JOHN: *Secrets of the Whiskey Ring.* Chicago, 1880.

McNEILLY, J. S.: *Climax and Collapse of Reconstruction in Mississippi.* Vol. XII of the Publications of the Mississippi Historical Society.

McPHERSON, EDWARD: *A Political History of the United States During Reconstruction.* Washington, 1875.

MARBLE, MANTON: *A Secret Chapter of Political History.* Pamphlet, New York, no date.

MAVERICK, AUGUSTUS: *Henry J. Raymond.* Hartford, 1870.

MAYES, EDWARD: *Lucius Q. C. Lamar: His Life, Times and Speeches.* Nashville, 1896.

MERRIAM, GEORGE S.: *Life and Times of Samuel Bowles.* Two volumes, New York, 1885.
MITCHELL, EDWARD P.: *Memoirs of an Editor.* New York, 1924.
MOORE, FRANK: *Life and Speeches of Andrew Johnson.* Boston, 1865.
MORTON, OLIVER P. *See* Foulkes.

NAST, THOMAS. *See* Paine.
NEVINS, ALLAN: *Emergence of Modern America.* New York, 1927
NICOLAY, HELEN: *Our Capital on the Potomac.* New York, 1924.
NORDHOFF, CHARLES: *The Cotton States in the Spring and Summer of 1875.* New York, 1875.

OBERHOLTZER, E. P.: *Jay Cooke, Financier of the Civil War.* Two volumes, New York, 1907.
O'CONNOR, MARY D.: *Life and Letters of M. P. O'Connor.* New York, 1893.
OGDEN, ROLLO: *Life and Letters of Edwin Lawrence Godkin.* Two volumes, New York, 1907.

PAINE, ALBERT BIGELOW: *Thomas Nast: His Period and his Pictures.* New York, 1904.
PEARSE, HAYWOOD J.: *Benjamin H. Hill: Secession and Reconstruction.* Chicago, 1928.
PERRY, BENJAMIN F.: *Reminiscences of Public Men.* Philadelphia, 1883.
PIERCE, EDWARD L.: *Memoir and Letters of Charles Sumner.* Four volumes, Boston, 1877–93.
PIERCE, S.: *The Freedmen's Bureau.* Iowa City, 1904.
PIKE, JAMES: *The Prostrate State: South Carolina Under Negro Government.* New York, 1874.

RAMSDELL, WILLIAM: *Reconstruction in Texas.* New York, 1910.
RAWLINS, JOHN A. *See* Wilson.
REAGAN, JOHN H.: *Memoirs.* New York, 1906.
REID, WHITELAW: *After the War: A Southern Tour.* Cincinnati, 1866. *See* Cortissoz.
REYNOLDS, JOHN S.: *Reconstruction in South Carolina.* Columbia, 1905.
RIDDLE, A. G.: *Life of Benjamin F. Wade.* Cleveland, 1886.
ROSS, EDMUND G.: *History of the Impeachment of Andrew Johnson.* Santa Fé, 1896.
RUFFIN. *See* Hamilton.

SALTER, WILLIAM: *Life and Times of James W. Grimes.* New York, 1876.
SANBORN, ALVAN F., editor: *Reminiscences of Richard Lathers.* New York, 1907.
SCHOFIELD, JOHN M.: *Forty-Six Years in the Army.* New York, 1897.
SCHUCKERS, J. W.: *Life and Public Services of Salmon P. Chase.* New York, 1874.
SCHURZ, CARL: *Reminiscences.* Two volumes, New York, 1908.
SEITZ, DONN C.: *Horace Greeley.* Indianapolis, 1926.
SHERMAN, JOHN: *Recollections.* Two volumes, New York and Chicago, 1895.

SMEDES, SUSAN DABNEY: *Memoirs of a Southern Planter*. Baltimore, 1888.

SMITH, THEODORE CLARKE: *Life and Letters of James A. Garfield*. Two volumes, New Haven, 1925.

SOMERS, ROBERT: *The Southern States Since the War*. London, 1871.

SPENCER, EDWARD: *Public Life and Services of Thomas F. Bayard*. New York, 1880.

STAPLES, THOMAS S.: *Reconstruction in Arkansas*. New York, 1923.

STEVENS, THADDEUS. *See* Woodburn, McCall, Callender, and Hensel.

STEWART, WILLIAM M.: *Reminiscences*. New York, 1908.

STOREY, MOORFIELD (*and* E. W. EMERSON): *Ebenezer Rockwood Hoar*. Boston, 1911.

STOVALL, PLEASANT A.: *Life of Robert Toombs*. New York, 1892.

STOWE, CHARLES EDWARD: *Life of Harriet Beecher Stowe*. Boston, 1889.

STRYKER, L. P.: *Andrew Johnson: A Study in Courage*. New York, 1929.

STUART, A. H. H.: *A Narrative of Leading Incidents of the Organization of the First Popular Movement in Virginia*. Richmond, 1888.

SUMNER, CHARLES. *See* Pierce.

TARBELL, IDA M.: *History of the Standard Oil Company*. Two volumes, New York, 1904.

TAYLOR, A. H.: *The Negro in South Carolina During Reconstruction*. Washington, 1924.

TAYLOR, RICHARD: *Destruction and Reconstruction*. New York, 1879.

THOMPSON, C. M.: *Reconstruction in Georgia*. New York, 1915.

THOMPSON, HENRY T.: *Ousting the Carpetbagger from South Carolina*. Columbia, 1926.

THORNDIKE, RACHEL SHERMAN: *The Sherman Letters*. New York, 1894.

TRUMBULL, LYMAN. *See* White.

TURPIE, DAVID: *Sketches of My Own Times*. Indianapolis, 1903.

VALLANDIGHAM, J. L.: *A Life of Clement L. Vallandigham*. Baltimore, 1872.

WALLACE, JOHN: *Carpetbag Rule in Florida*. Jacksonville, 1888.

WARDEN, ROBERT B.: *Private Life and Public Services of Salmon P. Chase*. Cincinnati, 1874.

WATTERSON, HENRY: *Marse Henry: An Autobiography*. Two volumes, New York, 1919.

WAY, WILLIAM: *History of the New England Society of Charleston*. Charleston, 1920.

WELLES, GIDEON: *Diary*. Three volumes, Boston, 1911.

WELLS, EDWARD: *Hampton and Reconstruction*. Columbia, 1907.

WHITE, ANDREW D.: *Autobiography*. Two volumes, New York, 1905.

WHITE, HORACE: *The Life of Lyman Trumbull*. Boston, 1913.

WILLIAMS, ALFRED B. *See* Newspapers.

WILLIAMS, CHARLES R.: *Life of Rutherford B. Hayes*. Two volumes, Boston, 1914.

WILSON, JAMES GRANT: *General Grant's Letters to a Friend*. New York, 1897.

WILSON, JAMES HARRISON: *Life of John A. Rawlins*. New York, 1916.

WILSON, PETER MITCHELL: *Southern Exposure*. Chapel Hill, 1927.

WINSTON, ROBERT W.: *Andrew Johnson: Plebeian and Patriot.* New York, 1928.
WISE, JOHN S.: *Recollections of Thirteen Presidents.* New York, 1905.
WOODBURN, JAMES A.: *Life of Thaddeus Stevens.* Indianapolis, 1913.
WORTH. *See* Hamilton.

## PUBLIC DOCUMENTS

The numerous Congressional Reports and Investigations need not be enumerated here. They are each cited in full where referred to in the text. Aside from these:

*Congressional Globe* and *Congressional Record*, 1865–1877.
*Impeachment Trial of W. W. Holden.* Three volumes, Raleigh, 1871.
*Messages and Papers of the Presidents.*
*Official Report of the Impeachment Trial of Andrew Johnson.*
*Report of Joint Investigating Committee on Public Frauds, South Carolina, 1877–78.*
Third Annual Message of W. W. Holden with Appendix. Doc. I, Sess. 1870–71, North Carolina Legislature.

## NEWSPAPERS

*Abbeville Press and Banner* (South Carolina), 1876–77.
*The Columbia State*, August 8, 1926, to March 13, 1927, containing Alfred B. Williams's graphic reminiscences of the final fight for the redemption of South Carolina.
*Harper's Weekly.*
*The Independent.*
*Lancaster Intelligencer*, 1865–68.
*McMinnville* (Tenn.) *Enterprise* (Radical Southern paper), 1867.
*The Nation.*
*New York Herald.*
*New York Sun.*
*New York Times.*
*New York Tribune.*
*New York World.*

(The New York papers, especially *The World*, quoted extensively from newspapers of the West and South.)

# INDEX

Abbott, J. C., Sprague's attack, 271; character, 314, 315, 326

*Aberdeen Examiner*, on campaign of 1875, 453

Adams, C. F., on Johnson, 24; character, 377; Liberal Republican candidacy, 378, 379; support of Tilden, 484, 485; on contested election, 537

Adams, Gordon, on Vicksburg conflict, 452

Adams, Henry, on Johnson, 24; on Grant's Cabinet, 239; on Washington, 242, 243, 250; and King, 249; on Gold Conspiracy, 276; on brother's candidacy, 281; on Sumner, 334; on his father, 377

Adams, J. Q., II, Southern tour, 233; gubernatorial candidacy, 280; on Ku-Klux Act, 344; vice-presidential nomination, 385

Agriculturists, and development of industrialism, 117; Granger movement, 405–08

Akerman, A. T., displaced, 371

Alabama, Radical organization, 205; under military government, 215; under Radical rule, 362; election of 1872, 392; campaign of 1874, outrages question, 427–30; white recovery, 430

Albany, N.Y., Johnson at, 133

*Albany Argus*, on Grant's Cabinet, 238

*Albany Journal*, on Mrs. Lincoln, 168; on Crédit Mobilier, 400

Alcorn, J. L., as Radical leader, 279, 368; campaign of 1873, 413

Alexis, Grand Duke, in Washington, 262

Aliens, as issue in 1876, 490

Allen, William, and Thurman, 293; presidential candidacy, 484

Allison, W. B., and Sumner, 336; and Crédit Mobilier, 396, 397

American Alliance, in campaign of 1876, 490

Ames, Adelbert, and Revels, 294; as Radical leader, 368; campaign and election (1873), 413; and negro demands, 448, 449; and Vicksburg conflict, 449–52; campaign of 1875, 453–57; proposed impeachment, resignation, 457, 458

Ames, Blanche B., in Washington, 262

Ames, E. R., on Colfax's speech, 86

Ames, Oakes, Crédit Mobilier under cover, 267; scandal, 396–404; death, 404

Amnesty, bill (1876), speeches, 462–64

Anderson, T. C., Returning Board, 526

Anthony, H. B., Sprague's attack, 270

Anti-Masonic Party, Stevens, 68, 69

Antoine, C. C., as black leader, 438, 440

Arkansas, Radical organization, 206; under military government, 215; under Radical rule, Clayton, 368–70, 430, 431; Brooks-Baxter war, 432; election of 1874, white recovery, 433, 434

Army, occupation of South, character, 50–53

Arthur, C. A., appointment as Collector, 372

Ashley, J. M., on negro suffrage, 15; on Johnson's tour, 138; and Raymond, 149; impeachment resolution, 156, 157; and manufactured evidence, 157, 159, 165; character, 157; Governor of Montana, removed, 240, 282; and Johnson's return, 459

Atkins, Elisha, and Blaine scandal, 478

*Atlanta New Era*, Radical organ, 301

*Atlanta News*, and white revolt, 428

Auburn, N.Y., Johnson at, 134

Avery, W. O., Whiskey Ring, 465, 467

Babcock, O. E., Santo Domingo negotiations, 296, 297; Sumner on, 330, 338, 339; Whiskey Ring scandal, 465–69

Badeau, Adam, on Fish and Sumner, 299

Baez, Buenaventura, Babcock negotiations, 297; Sumner on, 338

Baird, Absalom, and New Orleans riot, 129

Bakhmeteff, George, wife, 249

Bancroft, George, Johnson's first message, 91; and Evarts's argument, 190; on third term, 415

Banks, N. P., and unseating of Voorhees, 107

Barker, T. G., and race conflict, 512

Barksdale, Ethelbert, in Mississippi campaign, 455

Barnum, W. H., and election returns, 522

Baruch, Myron, and resort to violence, 359

Battle flags, Sumner's bill, 394, 395

Baxter, Elisha, Brooks war, 432

Bayard, T. F., political character, 293; and Sumner affair, 337; on Greeley's candidacy, 383; and Belknap scandal, 472, 475

Beale, Fitzgerald, in Washington society, daughters, 249

Beck, J. B., and impeachment, 176; and Georgia, 303; on McGarrahan claim, 328; Ku-Klux debate, 342; and Sanborn contracts, 423; and Ames, 458

Beecher, H. W., Stevens on apostasy, 91; on Freedmen's Bureau veto, 103; letter to pro-Johnson convention, 126; recantation,